2007

STATE TAX

Handbook

CCH Editorial Staff Publication

Editorial Staff

Editors . . . . Timothy Bjur, J.D., Cathleen Calhoun, J.D., Julie Minor, J.D.,
Lisa Moore, M.A., Melissa O'Keefe, M.A., Corey Sapp, M.A.,
Jennifer J. Troyer, J.D., Paula Weglarz

Production . . . . Meghan Klick

This publication is designed to provide accurate and authoritative information in regard to the subject matter covered. It is sold with the understanding that the publisher is not engaged in rendering legal, accounting, or other professional service. If legal advice or other expert assistance is required, the services of a competent professional person should be sought.

ISBN 978-0-8080-1536-9

ISBN 0-8080-1536-2

4025 W. Peterson Ave.
Chicago, IL 60646-6085
1 800 248 3248
www.CCHGroup.com

Printed in the United States of America

Preface

The CCH *State Tax Handbook* provides readers an overview of the taxation scheme of each state and the District of Columbia, as well as multistate charts on income tax, sales and use taxes, property tax, and practice and procedure. The book is set out in five parts that together give an overall picture of the states' levies, bases and rates, principal payment and return dates, and other important tax information on major taxes.

In the first portion, the book details the taxing authorities for each jurisdiction, including addresses, phone numbers, and taxes governed by each office. Also included are uniform outlines of each jurisdiction's overall taxation system. The CCH STATE TAX GUIDEBOOK series should be consulted for additional details.

The second and third portions of the book are comprised of multistate charts relating to, respectively, income tax (personal and corporate) and sales and use tax. The charts cover discrete issues, for income tax, such as filing extensions and depreciation, and for sales and use, such as manufacturing exemptions and sales for resales.

The fourth portion of the book contains multistate charts addressing property tax issues, including personal property rendition filing requirements and administrative appeals.

Finally, the fifith portion features multistate charts concerning practice and procedure issues, such as electronic filing options and requirements and estimated taxes. Parts of this publication are compiled from the CCH STATE TAX GUIDE, MULTISTATE CORPORATE INCOME TAX GUIDE, MULTISTATE PROPERTY TAX GUIDE, and MULTISTATE SALES TAX GUIDE. All material in the *State Tax Handbook* is current as of October 31, 2006, unless otherwise noted.

October 2006

Table of Contents

Information by State

Income Taxes

INFORMATION BY STATE

The following pages contain general information regarding the taxes imposed in each state, as well as the relevant tax administration bodies. Topics include a state-by-state listing of taxing authorities and charts summarizing which taxes are imposed by each state, including information on rates and filing/payment dates.

Tax Authorities
State-by-State Listing of Tax Administration Bodies

All states have full-time appointive commissions or officials charged solely with the administration of the principal tax laws of the state. The State Tax Commission of Missouri, the Department of Revenue of Illinois and the Department of Taxation and Finance of New York are examples of such tax commissions. The states have assigned to such bodies all revenue functions formerly vested in elective department heads or ex-officio boards.

Taxes frequently administered by a board or official other than the principal tax administrative body include (1) corporation organization and qualification fees, which are usually administered by the Secretary of State, and (2) alcoholic beverage taxes, which are usually in whole or in part administered by a liquor control board.

The tax administration outline below lists the principal tax administrative body or bodies for each state along with the taxes they administer.

The listing for each state contains a general information phone number. The taxpayer assistance phone number is listed for states that have such a service; otherwise, the capitol switchboard number is noted.

Correspondence concerning state tax matters should be addressed to the director of the tax administrative body at the state capital for the state concerned. All such administrative bodies maintain offices in the state.

ALABAMA
State Capital—Montgomery
Department of Revenue (334) 242-1170
Office of Taxpayer Advocacy (334) 242-1055
Taxpayer Service Center (334) 242-2677
Web Site: www.ador.state.al.us
Department of Revenue
The Department administers and collects the following taxes:
Business privilege tax
Controlled substances tax
Corporation organization and qualification fees (with Secretary of State)
Estate tax
Fuel taxes
General income tax
License fees
Lubricating oils tax
Motor vehicle carrier fees (with Public Service Commission)
Motor vehicle registration
Pharmaceutical tax
Property taxes (with local officers)
Public utilities tax (license)
Sales tax
Severance tax
Tobacco stamp tax
Use tax
Utility gross receipts and use tax
Waste disposal tax
Secretary of State
Corporate organization and qualification fees
Alcoholic Beverage Control Board
Alcoholic beverage licenses and taxes
Department of Insurance
Insurance companies tax
Public Service Commission
Utility inspection fees
Department of Industrial Relations
Unemployment compensation tax
Local Taxing Officers
Chain store tax
Document filing tax (conveyances and mortgages)
License taxes (with Department of Revenue)
Property taxes (with Department of Revenue)
Medicaid Agency
The Medicaid agency administers the reimbursement of the hospital tax on disproportionate share hospitals and publicly owned hospitals.

ALASKA
State Capital—Juneau
Department of Revenue (907) 465-2300
Tax Division
Anchorage: (907) 269-6620
Juneau: (907) 465-2320
Web Site: www.tax.state.ak.us
Department of Revenue
The Tax Division of the Department of Revenue administers and collects the following taxes:
Alcoholic beverage tax (with Alcoholic Beverage Control Board)
Corporate net income tax
Dive fishery management assessment
Electronic cooperative

Estate tax
Fisheries business tax
Fishery resource landing tax
Mining license tax
Motor fuel tax
Oil and gas production taxes
Oil and gas properties tax
Salmon enhancement tax
Salmon marketing tax
Seafood marketing assessment
Telephone cooperative
Tobacco taxes

Department of Administration
The Division of Motor Vehicles of the Department of Administration administers and collects the following:
Motor carrier weight fees
Motor vehicle registration taxes

Department of Community and Economic Development
Biennial corporation tax (Division of Banking, Securities, and Corporations)
Corporate organization and entrance fees (Division of Banking, Securities, and Corporations)
Insurance companies tax (Division of Insurance)
License fees (Division of Occupational Licensing)

Department of Labor and Work Force Development
Unemployment compensation tax

Department of Environmental Conservation
Air contaminants emission fees

Attorney General

Local Taxing Officers
Gross receipts tax
Property taxes
Tax on casual sales of motor vehicles, trailers and semitrailers

ARIZONA

State Capital—Phoenix
Taxpayer Assistance (Corporate and Personal Income) (602) 255-3381
Taxpayer Ombudsman (602) 716-6024
Taxpayer Assistance (Transaction Privilege (Sales) and Withholding) (602) 255-2060
TDD (602) 542-4021
Web Site: www.revenue.state.az.us

Department of Revenue
The Department of Revenue administers and collects the following taxes and fees:
Alcoholic beverage tax
Cigarette, cigar, and tobacco products tax
Estate tax
Generation-skipping tax
Income tax
Jet fuel excise and use tax
Motor vehicle waste tire fees
Private car companies tax
Property tax (with local taxing officials)
Rental occupancy tax
Severance tax
Telecommunication service excise tax
Tobacco tax for health care
Transaction privilege (sales) tax
Use tax
Utility property tax
Water use tax

Corporation Commission
Corporate organization and qualification fees
Corporation annual registration fee

Department of Liquor Licenses and Control
Alcoholic beverage licenses

Department of Transportation
The Motor Vehicle Division administers:
Annual aircraft license tax
Motor carriers tax
Motor vehicle fuel tax
Motor vehicle registration fees
Underground storage tank tax
Use fuel tax
Vehicle license tax

State Treasurer
Insurance premiums tax (with Director of Insurance)

Department of Insurance
Insurance premiums tax (with State Treasurer)

Department of Water Resources
Water quality assurance fee

Department of Environmental Quality
Environmental fees

Department of Economic Security
Unemployment insurance tax

Local Taxing Officials
Property tax (with Department of Revenue)
Realty transfer fee

ARKANSAS

State Capital—Little Rock
Director of the Department of Finance and Administration (501) 682-2242
Taxpayer Assistance/General Information (501) 682-7751
Web Site: www.arkansas.gov/dfa

Department of Finance and Administration
The Department, through its Alcoholic Beverage Control Division, administers the alcoholic beverages tax.
The Department, through its Division of Revenue, administers the following taxes:
Amusement machine tax
Cigarette/tobacco tax
Estate tax
Gasoline tax
Gross receipts tax
Income tax
Motor vehicle registration fees
Realty transfer tax
Severance or production tax
Soft drink tax
Tobacco products tax
Use tax
Waste tire tax

Secretary of State
The Secretary of State administers and collects the corporate organization and qualification fees and the corporation franchise tax.

Public Service Commission
The Public Service Commission, with local taxing officials, administers the assessment and equalization of public utility and carrier property.

Assessment Coordination Department
The Assessment Coordination Department, with local taxing officials, administers the assessment and equalization of property.

Highway & Transportation Department
The State Highway Commission collects the motor carrier taxes.

Department of Insurance
The Department of Insurance administers and collects the insurance tax.

Department of Environmental Quality
The Department of Environmental Quality administers and collects the state's environmental fees.
Employment Security Department
The Employment Security Department administers and collects the unemployment insurance tax.
Attorney General
Local Taxing Officials
The local taxing officials administer and collect the general property tax.

CALIFORNIA

State Capital—Sacramento
State Board of Equalization/Tax Practitioner Hotline (800) 401-3661
(TDD) (800) 735-2929
(TDD assistance/voice) (800) 735-2922
Web Site: www.boe.ca.gov
Franchise Tax Board (800) 852-5711
Automated service (800) 338-0505 or (916) 845-6600
Tax Practitioner Hotline (916) 845-7057
TDD (800) 822-6268
Web Site: www.ftb.ca.gov
State Board of Equalization
Environmental fees
Excise taxes (alcoholic beverages, cigarettes, tire fee, emergency telephone users surcharge)
Fuel taxes
Property taxes
Sales and use taxes
Franchise Tax Board
The Franchise Tax Board, in the State and Consumer Services Agency, administers and collects the following taxes:
Bank and corporate franchise tax
Corporate income tax
Personal income tax
Public Utilities Commission
Motor carrier (household goods and passengers) fees
Propane surcharge
Business, Transportation and Housing Agency
The Department of Alcoholic Beverage Control administers and collects the intoxicating liquor license fees.
The Department of Motor Vehicles administers and collects the motor vehicle license and registration fees.
Conservation Department of the Resources Agency
Severance tax
Department of Housing and Community Development
Designates enterprise zones
Employment Development Department in the Health and Welfare Agency
Disability insurance training tax
Unemployment compensation tax
Withholding tax
State Controller
Estate tax and generation-skipping transfer tax
Property tax postponement
Gasoline tax refund
Department of Insurance
Insurance companies tax
Toxic Substances Control Department in the Environmental Protection Agency

Lubricating oil tax
Secretary of State
Corporate organization and qualification fees
Attorney General
Serves as legal counsel to state officers and to most state agencies, boards and commissions
Local Taxing Officers
General property tax (with State Board of Equalization)

COLORADO

State Capital—Denver
Taxpayer Assistance (303) 238-7378
Web Site: www.revenue.state.co.us
Department of Revenue
The Department of Revenue collects and enforces all taxes, imposts, fees and licenses including:
Alcoholic beverages taxes (Liquor Enforcement Division)
Cigarette and tobacco products taxes
Estate tax
Gaming tax
Gasoline tax
Income tax
Motor vehicle taxes
Property taxes (with Division of Property Taxation of the Department of Local Affairs and local officials)
Public utility regulatory fees (with Public Utilities Commission)
Sales tax
Severance tax
Use tax
Wage withholding
Department of Local Affairs
The Division of Property Taxation in the Department of Local Affairs has charge of the administration of the property tax laws of the state and the determination of the amount of taxes due thereunder, but it has no tax-collecting functions. It has powers of original assessment of public utilities and sees that all taxable property is uniformly assessed.
Secretary of State
The Secretary of State administers and collects (with the Department of Revenue) corporate organization and qualification fees.
Department of Natural Resources
The Oil and Gas Conservation Commission in the Department of Natural Resources administers the oil and gas conservation tax.
Department of Regulatory Agencies
The Public Utilities Commission collects and administers (with the Department of Revenue) the public utility fees and motor carrier taxes.
The Division of Insurance collects and administers the tax on insurance companies.
Department of Labor and Employment
The Department collects and administers the unemployment insurance tax.
Attorney General
Sets policy, oversees civil and criminal work and directs major litigation.
Local Taxing Officers
The local taxing officers collect and administer the following taxes:
Aircraft fees
General property tax (with Department of Revenue)
Motor vehicle fees
Realty transfer tax

CONNECTICUT

State Capital—Hartford

Taxpayer Services (800) 382-9463 (in-state)
Taxpayer Services (860) 297-5962 (out-of-state)
Web Site: http://www.ct.gov/drs/site/default.asp

Department of Revenue Services

The Commissioner of Revenue Services is the chief tax administration agent in Connecticut. The office administers and collects the following taxes:
Admissions tax
Cigarette tax
Corporate business tax, including additional tax on oil companies
Estate tax
Gift tax
Hazardous waste assessment
Insurance premiums tax
Liquor tax
Motor carrier fees
Motor carrier road tax
Motor fuels tax
Personal income tax
Petroleum products gross earnings tax
Regulated waste assessment fee
Sales tax
Succession and transfer taxes (with local officers)
Tobacco products tax
Use tax
Utility taxes

Office of Policy and Management

The Secretary of the Office of Policy and Management administers the property tax with local officers.

Secretary of State

The Secretary of State collects and administers the following taxes:
Annual report fee
Corporate organization and qualification fees
Foreign corporation fee

Department of Environmental Protection

Hazardous waste disposal taxes

Department of Motor Vehicles (Weathersfield)

The Commissioner of Motor Vehicles collects the motor vehicle registration fees.

Department of Public Health

The Department of Public Health, Division of Hospitals and Health Care, sets and collects the annual hospital assessment.

Department of Labor (Weathersfield)

The Department of Labor, Division of Unemployment Insurance, collects and administers the unemployment compensation tax.

Department of Transportation (Newington)

The Department of Transportation collects and administers the aircraft registration fees.

Local Taxing Officers

The local taxing officers (with the Secretary of the Office of Policy and Management) collect and administer the property tax, the succession and transfer tax, and the hazardous waste disposal facility tax.

Commission on Hospitals and Health Care

The Commission on Hospitals and Health Care imposes various assessments on hospitals.

DELAWARE

State Capital—Dover

Personal Income Taxpayer Assistance (302) 577-8200
Corporate Income Taxpayer Assistance (302) 577-8205
Division of Revenue and Taxpayer Assistance (302) 577-8200
Web Site: www.state.de.us/revenue/default.shtml

Department of Finance (Wilmington)

The Division of Revenue in the Department of Finance is the chief tax administrative agency in Delaware. It administers the following taxes:
Corporate income taxes
Estate tax
Gas, electric and steam companies' tax
Hotel occupancy tax
Manufacturer's and merchant's license tax
Personal income tax
Public utilities tax
Realty transfer tax (with county officials)
Tobacco products tax
Use tax on tangible personal property leases

Secretary of State

The Secretary of State collects and administers the corporate organization and qualification fees and the franchise tax.
The Bank Commissioner collects and administers the franchise (income) tax on banking organizations and building and loan associations.

Department of Natural Resources and Environmental Control

The Department of Natural Resources and Environmental Control sets and collects the annual operating permit fees from hazardous air pollutant sources and hazardous waste assessments from the treating and storing of hazardous solid waste.

Department of Transportation

The Department of Transportation, through the Motor Fuel Tax Administration, administers and collects the motor fuel tax, special fuel tax and motor carriers' fuel purchase tax.

Department of Public Safety

The Motor Vehicles Division administers and collects the motor vehicle fees.
The Alcoholic Beverage Control Commission administers the alcoholic beverage taxes.

Department of Insurance

The Insurance Commissioner administers and collects the insurance premiums tax.

Department of Labor (Newark)

The Department of Labor, Division of Unemployment Insurance, administers and collects the unemployment insurance tax.

Attorney General

Local Taxing Officers

The local taxing officers administer and collect the property tax and the realty transfer tax (with the Department of Finance).

DISTRICT OF COLUMBIA

Office of Tax and Revenue (202) 727-4829
Taxpayer Assistance (202) 727-4TAX
Web Site: http://cfo.dc.gov/otr/site
email: otr.ocfo@dc.gov

Department of Finance and Revenue

The Mayor, through the Director of the Department of Finance and Revenue, administers all laws pertaining to the following fees, taxes, and assessments:
Alcoholic beverages taxes
Cigarette tax
Corporate franchise tax
Deed recordation tax
Deed transfer tax
Economic interest tax
Estate tax
Health care provider assessment
Income tax
Insurance premiums tax
Motor vehicle excise tax
Motor vehicle fuel tax
Property tax
Public space rental
Public utility tax
Qualified high technology company tax
Sales tax
Toll telecommunications tax
Unincorporated business franchise tax
Use tax

Alcoholic Beverage Regulation Administration
The Alcoholic Beverage Regulation Administration, with the Office of the Mayor, administers the taxes on alcoholic beverages.

Insurance, Securities and Banking Regulation Department
The Administrator of the Insurance Administration administers and collects the insurance gross premiums tax.

Department of Employment Services
The Unemployment Compensation Board administers and collects the unemployment compensation tax.

FLORIDA

State Capital—Tallahassee
Department of Revenue (850) 488-6800; in Florida, (800) 352-3671.
Web Site: sun6.dms.state.fl.us/dor/

Department of Revenue
The Department of Revenue administers and collects the following taxes:
Communications services tax
Corporate income tax
Diesel fuel tax (with Department of Highway Safety and Motor Vehicles)
Documentary excise tax
Dry-cleaning facilities tax
Emergency excise tax
Estate tax
Gross receipts tax on utility (electricity or gas for light, heat, or power) and communications services
Insurance companies tax (with State Treasurer)
Intangible personal property and personal property tax (with local officers)
Motor fuel tax
Oil, gas and sulfur production taxes
Perchloroethylene tax
Petroleum pollutant taxes
Sales and use tax
Solid minerals tax
Unemployment compensation tax

Secretary of State
The Secretary of State administers and collects the corporate filing fees and the annual report filing fee.

Department of Business and Professional Regulation
The Division of Alcoholic Beverages and Tobacco issues licenses for the sale of alcoholic beverages and administers and collects the alcoholic beverage tax and the cigarette tax.
The Division of Pari-mutuel Wagering administers the various pari-mutuel racing taxes.

Department of Highway Safety and Motor Vehicles
The Division of Motor Vehicles under the Department of Highway Safety and Motor Vehicles administers and collects the motor vehicle registration fees and the aircraft registration fee.

Department of Agriculture and Consumer Services
The Commissioner of Agriculture (with the Department of Revenue) administers and collects the petroleum fuels inspection tax.

Public Service Commission
The Public Service Commission administers and collects the gross receipts tax on water and sewer utilities.

Department of Financial Services, Office of Insurance Regulation
The Department of Financial Services collects the tax on insurance companies (with the Department of Revenue).

Local Taxing Officers
Local taxing officers (with the Department of Revenue) administer and collect the general property tax.

GEORGIA

State Capital—Atlanta
Taxpayer Assistance (TIPS—Taxpayer Information Programs and Services) (404) 417-4477 or (877) 602-8477
Web Site: http://www.etax.dor.ga.gov/

Department of Revenue
The Commissioner of Revenue is the chief tax administrator in Georgia. Through the Department of Revenue, the Commissioner administers and collects the following taxes:
Alcoholic beverage taxes
Bank gross receipts tax
Corporate income
Corporate net worth tax
Estate tax
Gasoline tax
Individual income tax
General property tax (with local officers)
Motor carrier road tax
Motor vehicle ad valorem tax
Realty transfer tax
Sales and use taxes
Tobacco tax

Secretary of State
The Secretary of State administers and collects the following taxes:
Annual certificate registration fee
Corporate organization and qualification fees

Commissioner of Insurance
The Commissioner of Insurance administers the tax on insurance companies.

Department of Labor
The Commissioner of Labor administers and collects the unemployment insurance tax.

Department of Motor Vehicles and Safety
The Department of Motor Vehicle Safety administers and collects the motor vehicle registration fee.

Department of Natural Resources
The Environmental Protection Division of the Department of Natural Resources administers and collects the annual solid waste surcharge, the hazardous waste management fee, and the replacement tire fee.

Local Taxing Officers
The local taxing officers and the Commissioner of Revenue administer and collect the general property tax and the solid waste disposal facility tax.

HAWAII

State Capital—Honolulu
Department of Taxation (808) 587-4242
Taxpayer Assistance (800) 222-3229
Web Site: www.state.hi.us/tax/tax.html

Department of Taxation
The Director of Taxation appoints an assessor for each tax district to assist in the assessment of property taxes and appoints a tax collector for each district to assist with the collection of taxes under his supervision. These taxes are:
Banks and other financial corporations tax
Cigarette and tobacco taxes
Conveyance tax
Corporate income tax
Estate and transfer tax
Fuel tax
General excise tax
Generation-skipping transfer tax
Liquor tax
Personal income tax
Public service company tax
Transient accommodations tax
Use tax
Property taxes are administered by the county governments, except for the county of Kalawao, which is an uninhabitable island. County contacts are as follows:
County of Hawaii—East Hawaii: Aupuni Center, 101 Pauahi Street, Suite 4, Hilo, HI 96720, (808) 961-8201; West Hawaii: 75-5706 Kuakini Hwy, Suite 112, Kailua-Kona, HI 96740, (808) 327-3540; http://www.hawaii-county.com/
County and City of Honolulu—842 Bethel Street, Honolulu, HI 96813, (808) 527-5539, http://www.co.honolulu.hi.us/rpa/
County of Kauai—4444 Rice Street, Lihue, HI 96766, (808) 214-6222, http://www.kauai.gov/Default.aspx?tabid=178
County of Maui—70E Kaahumanu Avenue, Kahului, HI 96732, (808) 270-7297, http://www.mauipropertytax.com

Department of Commerce and Consumer Affairs
The Business Registration Division administers and enforces Hawaii laws relating to corporations, partnerships, securities, franchises, and the registration of trade names, trademarks, and service marks.
The Division of Insurance administers and collects the surplus lines tax.

Department of Budget and Finance
The Public Utilities Commission administers and collects the public utilities' regulatory fees.

Department of Labor and Industrial Relations
The Unemployment Insurance Division administers the unemployment insurance tax.

Department of Health

Motor vehicle tire surcharge (repealed 1/01/06)

Local Taxing Officials
The County Treasurer administers and collects the vehicle registration fees and taxes, and the property tax, with the Director of Taxation.

IDAHO

State Capital—Boise
Tax Commission (208) 334-7660 and (800) 972-7660
Web Site: http://tax.idaho.gov/contactus.htm

Department of Revenue and Taxation
The Department of Revenue and Taxation consists of the Idaho Tax Commission and a Board of Tax Appeals.

Tax Commission
The Chairman of the Idaho Tax Commission is the chief subordinate tax administrator in Idaho. The Commission administers and collects the following taxes:
Alcoholic beverage tax (with Idaho State Police)
Cigarette tax
Corporate franchise tax
Corporate income tax
Estate tax
Fuels tax
Hotel occupancy tax
Illegal drug tax
Individual income tax
License tax on electricity
Sales and use tax
Severance tax
Tobacco products tax
Wine excise tax

Secretary of State
The Secretary of State administers and collects the corporate organization and qualification fees and receives annual corporate reports.

Transportation Department
The transportation board administers the motor vehicle fees (with the county assessors) and motor carrier fees (with the Public Utilities Commission).

Public Utilities Commission
The Public Utilities Commission has jurisdiction over public utilities, including motor vehicle carriers (with Transportation Department).

Department of Insurance
The Director administers and collects the insurance companies tax.

Department of Environmental Quality
The Department administers the hazardous waste disposal fee.

Idaho State Police
The State Police, along with the State Liquor Dispensary and the Tax Commission, administers the alcoholic beverage tax.

Department of Labor
The Department administers and collects the unemployment insurance tax.

Attorney General

Local Taxing Officers
The local taxing officers administer and collect the following taxes:
Forest products tax
General property tax (with Chairman of the State Tax Commission)
Motor vehicle registration fees (with Transportation Department)

ILLINOIS

State Capital—Springfield

Department of Revenue (217) 782-3336
Customer Service/Taxpayer Information (800) 732-8866
Web Site: www.revenue.state.il.us/

Department of Revenue
The Department of Revenue is the chief tax administration agency in Illinois. It administers and collects the following taxes:
Alcoholic beverage tax (with Liquor Control Commission)
Cigarette tax and cigarette use tax
Environmental impact fee on receivers of fuel
Health care assessments
Hotel occupancy tax
Income tax
Invested capital tax
Motor fuel taxes
Property tax
Retailers' occupation (sales) and use taxes
Riverboat gambling taxes
Service occupation and service use taxes
Telecommunications excise tax
Tobacco products tax
Utilities taxes (with Commerce Commission)

Secretary of State
The Secretary of State administers and collects the corporate franchise tax, the corporate organization and qualification fees and the motor vehicles fees.

Director of Insurance
The Director administers and collects the net premium tax on insurance.

Department of Employment Security
The Department administers and collects the unemployment insurance tax.

Environmental Protection Agency
Air pollution fee
Hazardous waste disposal tax

Department of Nuclear Safety
Low-level radioactive waste management tax

Liquor Control Commission
The Commission issues state licenses.

Attorney General
Estate tax (with local officials)
Generation-skipping transfer tax (with local officials)

Department of Public Aid
The Illinois Department of Public Aid administers and collects the Illinois Hospital Provider Fund assessment.

Local Taxing Officers
The local taxing officers administer and collect the following taxes:
Estate tax and generation-skipping transfer tax (with Attorney General)
General property tax (with Department of Revenue)

INDIANA

State Capital—Indianapolis

Taxpayer Assistance (317) 232-2240 for personal income; (317) 233-4015 for sales tax; for corporate income (317) 615-2662
Taxpayer Advocate (317) 232-2345
Automated Refund Information (317) 233-4018
Web Site: www.in.gov/dor/

Department of Revenue

The Department of Revenue is the chief tax administration agency in Indiana. The Department employs a Commissioner of Revenue who administers through divisions the following taxes:
Adjusted gross income tax
Aircraft license excise tax
Alcoholic beverages tax (with Alcoholic Beverage Commission)
Cigarette tax
Estate tax
Financial institutions' franchise tax
Fuel taxes
Hazardous waste disposal tax
Inheritance tax
Motor carrier fees
Petroleum production tax
Sales and use tax
Solid waste management fees
Tobacco products tax
Utility receipts tax

Department of Local Government Finance
The Department of Local Government Finance has jurisdiction over the assessment procedure for ad valorem taxes and is the appeal agency on property tax rates, budgets of local taxing units and bond issues.

Secretary of State
The Secretary of State administers and collects the corporate organization and qualification fees and the annual corporation report.

State Auditor
The State Auditor, with the State Treasurer, administers and collects the vessels tax on all registered tonnage.

Alcohol and Tobacco Commission
The Commission administers the alcoholic beverages tax with the Department of Revenue.

Bureau of Motor Vehicles
The Bureau of Motor Vehicles administers and collects the motor vehicle tax and the motor vehicle and mobile home excise tax on all vehicles.

Utility Regulatory Commission
The Commission administers and collects the public utility assessment fee.

Department of Insurance
The Department administers and collects the insurance tax.

Department of Workforce Development
The Unemployment Insurance Board administers and collects the unemployment insurance tax.

Attorney General

Local Taxing Officers
The local taxing officers administer and collect the following taxes:
General property tax (with Department of Local Government Finance)
Public utility fee (with Utility Regulatory Commission)

IOWA

State Capital—Des Moines

Department of Revenue: (515) 281-8453
Taxpayer Assistance/General Information (515) 281-3114
Taxpayer Services (800) 367-3388 (from elsewhere in Iowa or Rock Island—Moline, or Omaha)
Web Site: www.state.ia.us/tax

Department of Revenue

The Department is the chief tax administration agency in Iowa. It administers and collects the following taxes:
Alcoholic beverage tax (with Department of Commerce)
Cigarette and tobacco tax
Controlled substances tax
Estate tax (with local officers)
Financial institutions franchise tax
Income tax
Inheritance—succession tax (with local officers)
Insurance companies tax (with the Department of Commerce)
Motor fuel and special fuel tax
Realty transfer tax
Sales and use tax
Sanitary landfill fee

Secretary of State

The Secretary of State administers and collects the following fees:
Annual report fee
Corporate organization and qualification fees
Franchise tax

Alcoholic Beverages Division

The Division (Des Moines), with the aid of the Department of Revenue, administers and collects the alcoholic beverage tax.

Insurance Division

The Division administers and collects the insurance gross premiums tax with the Department of Revenue (Des Moines).

Department of Commerce

The Utilities Board in the Utilities Division administers and collects the utilities taxes (Des Moines).

Department of Transportation

The Department of Transportation administers the interstate fuel use tax, motor carrier fees and aircraft registration.

Department of Employment Services

The Division of Labor Services administers and collects the unemployment insurance tax.

Racing and Gaming Commission

The Commission, in the Inspections and Appeals Department, along with the State Treasurer, administers and collects the excursion boat gambling tax and license fees.

Attorney General

Local Taxing Officers

The local taxing officers administer and collect the following taxes:
Credit unions tax
Estate tax (with Department of Revenue)
General property tax
Grain handlers tax
Inheritance-succession tax (with Department of Revenue)
Loan agencies tax
Motor vehicle fees
Public utilities tax (with Department of Revenue)

KANSAS

State Capital—Topeka
Taxpayer Assistance (785) 368-8222
TTY (785) 296-6461
Web Site: www.ksrevenue.org

Department of Revenue

The *Division of Taxation*, as part of the Department of Revenue, is the chief tax administration agency in Kansas. It administers and collects the following taxes:
Alcoholic beverage tax (with Division of Alcoholic Beverage Control)
Cigarette tax
Controlled substances tax
Document recording tax (with county registers of deeds)
Dry-cleaning taxes
Estate tax
Gasoline tax
Income tax
Liquefied petroleum gas tax
Liquid fuel carriers' fees
Private car companies tax
Sales and use tax
Severance tax
Tire excise tax
Tobacco products tax
Vehicle Rental Excise tax

The *Property Valuation Division* administers the general property tax with local officials.

The *Alcoholic Beverage Control Division* administers the alcoholic beverage tax (with Division of Taxation).

Secretary of State

The Secretary of State administers and collects the corporate franchise tax and the organization and qualification fees.

State Corporation Commission

The Commission administers and collects the following taxes:
Gas utility pipeline tax
Motor carrier tax
Oil and gas conservation tax

Insurance Department

The Commissioner of Insurance administers and collects the insurance tax.

Department of Human Resources

The Division of Employment Security administers and collects the unemployment insurance tax.

Department of Health and Environment

The Environment Division administers and collects the mined-land conservation and reclamation tax, hazardous waste fees and solid waste fees.

Attorney General

Local Taxing Officers

The local taxing officers administer and collect general property taxes, the mortgage registration tax and motor vehicle registration.

KENTUCKY

State Capital—Frankfort
Department of Revenue (502) 564-4581
Taxpayer Ombudsman (502) 564-7822
General Information/Taxpayer Assistance (502) 564-4581
Web Site: www.revenue.ky.gov

Department of Revenue

The *Department of Tax Compliance* administers and collects the following taxes:
Admissions tax
Alcoholic beverage tax (with Alcoholic Beverage Control Department)
Bank franchise tax
Cigarette tax
Coal severance tax

Corporation license tax
Estate and inheritance taxes
General income tax
Hazardous substances assessment
Health care taxes
Insurance premiums tax (with the Insurance Commissioner)
Intangibles tax
Motor fuels tax
Motor vehicle usage tax (with local officers)
Natural resource severance tax
Oil production tax
Public Service Commission annual maintenance assessment
Public service company property taxes
Racing taxes
Sales and use taxes
The *Department of Property Valuation* administers the property tax with local taxing officers.

Secretary of State
The Secretary of State administers and collects the corporation organization tax.

Department of Public Protection
The Alcoholic Beverage Control Department, with the Department of Revenue, administers and collects the alcoholic beverage taxes.
The Department of Insurance (with the Department of Revenue) administers and collects the insurance gross premiums tax.

Justice Cabinet
The Cabinet administers the charitable gaming fees.

Transportation Cabinet
The Cabinet has the responsibility for administering all laws relating to commercial vehicles, including the motor carrier fuel use tax and registration, taxation and safety provisions. It also administers motor vehicle registration provisions with local taxing officers.

Workforce Development Cabinet
The Workforce Development Cabinet administers and collects the unemployment insurance tax.

Attorney General

Local Taxing Officers
The local taxing officers administer and collect the following taxes:
General property tax (with Department of Property Valuation)
Motor vehicle usage tax (with Transportation Cabinet)

LOUISIANA
State Capital—Baton Rouge
Taxpayer Information (225) 219-2448
Web Site: www.rev.state.la.us/

Department of Revenue
The Secretary, Department of Revenue, is responsible for assessing, evaluating and collecting the consumer, producer and any other state taxes specifically assigned by law to the Department. The Department, through its offices of Tax Administration, administers and collects the following taxes:
Office of Tax Administration, Group II
Corporation income
Estate, gift, and inheritance taxes
Excise tax
Franchise tax
Misc. taxes, including alcoholic beverages, tobacco, transportation and communication utilities taxes

Personal income tax
Sales tax, including automobile rental excise tax
Severance taxes
Office of Alcohol and Tobacco Control
Certification and licensing of manufacturers, wholesalers, dealers, etc.
Office of Charitable Gaming
Issuing and renewing licenses for charitable games of chance (bingo, raffles)
Tax Commission
Administers, along with local assessors and officials, property tax
Taxpayer Services
Registers new businesses for all applicable taxes and provides general tax assistance and information.

Department of Public Safety
The *Office of Motor Vehicles* administers and collects the following taxes:
Drivers license
Motor vehicle registration and titling fees
Sales and use tax on motor vehicles and trailers (collects on behalf of the Dept. of Rev.)

Department of State
The Secretary of State administers and collects:
Corporate organization and qualification fees

Department of Insurance
The Commissioner of Insurance administers and collects:
Premium and surplus line taxes

Department of Labor
The Office of Employment Security administers and collects:
Unemployment insurance tax

Public Service Commission
The Public Service Commission administers and collects:
Motor carrier registration and violation fees
Utility initial application and registration fees (usually telecommunications and water companies)

Local Taxing Officers
The local taxing officers administer and collect the following taxes:
Chain store taxes
Occupational license taxes
Property taxes

MAINE
State Capital—Augusta
Maine Revenue Services (207) 287-2076
Web Site: www.maine.gov/revenue

Maine Revenue Services
The State Tax Assessor heads Maine Revenue Services in the Department of Administrative and Financial Services and is the chief tax administrator in Maine. His office administers and collects the following taxes:
Cigarette tax
Commercial forestry excise tax
Estate tax
Fuel taxes
Income tax
Insurance tax
Mining excise tax
Railroad companies tax
Realty transfer tax (with local registers of deeds)
Sales and use taxes
Telecommunications companies tax
Tobacco products tax

Tree growth tax

Secretary of State

The Secretary of State administers and collects the following taxes:

Corporate organization and qualification fees

Foreign corporation license fee

Motor vehicle registration fee

Department of Public Safety

The Bureau of Liquor Enforcement administers and collects the alcoholic beverage tax and fees.

Department of Labor

The Department of Labor administers the employment security law.

Department of Environmental Protection

The Department of Environmental Protection administers and collects the following fees:

Air emissions fees

Hazardous waste facility fee

Oil terminal facility fee

Solid waste disposal fees

Local Taxing Officers

The local taxing officers administer and collect the motor vehicle excise tax. Also, local governments collect state, county and local property taxes. Property in an unincorporated area may be assessed for state taxes by the State Tax Assessor and for county taxes by the County Commissioners.

MARYLAND

State Capital—Annapolis

Office of the Comptroller (410) 260-7801

Taxpayer Assistance (800) 638-2937

Web Site: www.marylandtaxes.com

Comptroller of the Treasury

The State Comptroller is the chief tax administrator in Maryland. The office administers and collects the following taxes and fees:

Admissions and amusement tax

Alcoholic beverage bulk sales taxes

Boxing and wrestling tax

Cigarette tax

Estate tax (with local officials)

Gasoline tax

Income tax

Inheritance tax (with local Register of Wills)

Motor carriers tax

Motor fuel taxes

Sales and use taxes

Tire recycling fee

Unclaimed property

Utility surcharges

Withholding tax

State Department of Assessments and Taxation (Baltimore)

The State Department of Assessments and Taxation is headed by the Director, under whose office the following taxes are administered:

Franchise taxes on financial institutions and public utility companies

Initial fees and taxes

Property taxes (with local officials)

Public utilities

Insurance Administration (Baltimore)

The Commissioner of Insurance administers and collects the insurance premiums tax.

Motor Vehicle Administration

The Motor Vehicle Administration administers and collects the motor vehicle titling excise tax and motor vehicle registration fees.

Department of the Environment

The Department of the Environment administers and collects various environmental fees.

Department of Labor, Licensing and Regulation (Baltimore)

The Division of Unemployment Insurance administers and collects the unemployment compensation (payroll) tax.

The Racing Commission administers and collects the pari-mutuel betting taxes.

Department of Natural Resources

Oyster and clam taxes

Vessel excise tax

Attorney General

Local Taxing Officers

The local taxing officers administer and collect the following taxes:

Estate tax (with State Comptroller)

Hotel rental tax

Inheritance tax (with State Comptroller)

State recordation tax (with Clerks of the Circuit Courts)

State transfer tax (with Clerks of the Circuit Courts)

MASSACHUSETTS

State Capital—Boston

Taxpayer Assistance (617) 887-6367 and (800) 392-6089

Commissioner's Office (617) 626-1500

Web Site: www.dor.state.ma.us

Department of Revenue

The Department of Revenue is the chief tax administration agency in Massachusetts. This office administers and collects the following taxes:

Alcoholic beverage tax (with Alcoholic Beverages Control Commission)

Cigarette tax

Controlled substances tax

Corporate excise (income) tax

Deeds excise tax

Estate tax

Financial institution excise

Gasoline tax

Insurance excise

Motor carrier fees

Motor fuels and special fuels tax

Motor vehicle excise tax (with local officers)

Personal income tax

Property tax (with local officers)

Room occupancy excise tax

Sales and use tax

Urban redevelopment excise

Secretary of the Commonwealth

The Secretary of the Commonwealth administers and collects the corporate organization and qualification fees.

Consumer Affairs and Business Regulation Office

The *Alcoholic Beverages Control Commission* has control over issuance of licenses and makes rules and regulations covering conduct of licensees in operating their businesses.

Executive Office of Environmental Affairs

The Department of Environmental Protection administers the hazardous waste transportation fee.

Labor and Workforce Development Department

The Division of Employment and Training administers and collects the unemployment insurance tax.

Public Safety Executive Office

The Registry of Motor Vehicles administers and collects the various motor vehicle fees.

Attorney General

Local Taxing Officers

The local taxing officers administer and collect the following taxes:

Motor vehicle excise tax (with Department of Revenue)

Property tax (with Department of Revenue)

MICHIGAN

State Capital—Lansing

Department of Treasury (517) 373-3200

TTY (517) 636-4999

Web Site: www.michigan.gov/treasury

Department of Treasury

The *Bureau of Revenue,* headed by the Revenue Commissioner, is the chief tax administration agency in Michigan. It administers and collects the following taxes:

Airport parking tax

Estate tax

Fuel taxes

Insurance companies (foreign) tax (with Office of Financial and Insurance Services)

Personal income tax

Realty transfer tax (additional state tax)

Sales and use tax

Severance tax

Single business tax

Tobacco products tax

The *State Board of Assessors* is responsible for the property tax assessment of certain state-assessed public utilities.

Secretary of State

The Secretary of State administers and collects the motor vehicle fees.

Department of Consumer and Industry Services

The *Bureau of Commercial Services* administers and collects the business corporation fees, the corporation annual report fee, and professional licensing fees.

The *Liquor Control Commission* issues licenses for and administers and collects the alcoholic beverage tax.

The *Public Service Commission* administers and collects the motor carriers fee on cars and trucks.

The *Office of Financial and Insurance Services* and the State Treasurer administer and collect the insurance companies tax.

The *Unemployment Agency* administers and collects the unemployment tax.

Department of Environmental Quality

The Department administers the following environmental fees:

Air quality fees

Emission fees for major emitting facilities

Local Taxing Officers

The local taxing officers administer and collect the following taxes:

City utility users tax

Convention and tourism marketing tax

Convention facility development tax

Forest lands tax

Local income taxes

Lodgings taxes

Property taxes

Realty transfer tax

MINNESOTA

State Capital—St. Paul

Department of Revenue (651) 296-3781

Taxpayer Assistance—see below

Taxpayer Rights Advocate (651) 556-6013

Web Site: www.taxes.state.mn.us

Department of Revenue

The Department of Revenue, headed by a Commissioner of Revenue, is the chief tax administration agency in Minnesota. It administers and collects the following taxes:

Alcoholic beverage taxes (with Department of Public Safety) (651) 297-1882

Cigarette tax (651) 297-1882

Corporate franchise tax (651) 297-7000

Deed tax (651) 556-4721

Estate tax (651) 296-3475

Franchise tax for nonprofit corporations (651) 297-5199

Fur clothing tax (651) 297-1772

Gaming taxes (651) 297-1772

Gasoline tax (651) 296-0889

General property tax (with local officers)

Income tax (651) 296-3781

Insurance taxes (651) 297-1772

Minerals taxes (218) 744-7420

MinnesotaCare tax (651) 282-5533

Net proceeds tax on mining companies (218) 744-7420

Petroleum taxes (651) 296-0889

Sales and use taxes (651) 296-6181

Tobacco products tax (651) 297-1882

Withholding tax (651) 282-9999

Secretary of State

The Secretary of State administers and collects the following taxes:

Corporate organization and qualification fees

Corporation annual report fees

Department of Public Safety

The Division of Alcohol and Gambling Enforcement issues licenses under alcoholic beverage taxes for alcoholic beverages sold in the state.

The Driver and Vehicle Services Division collects motor carrier registration and motor vehicle excise tax and fees.

Department of Transportation

The Commissioner administers and collects the motor carrier taxes and the aircraft tax on all airplanes.

Department of Employment and Economic Development

The Department administers and collects the unemployment insurance tax.

Department of Human Services

Health care provider surcharges

Local Taxing Officers

The local taxing officers administer and collect the following taxes:

General property tax (with Commissioner of Revenue)

Mortgage registry tax

Solid waste taxes

Taconite tax

Timber tax

Utilities earnings tax

MISSISSIPPI

State Capital—Jackson

State Tax Commission (601) 923-7000
Corporate Income Assistance (601) 923-7099
Personal Income Assistance (601) 923-7089
Web Site: www.mstc.state.ms.us

State Tax Commission
The State Tax Commission is the chief tax administration agency in Mississippi and administers and collects the following taxes:
Beer tax
Corporate franchise tax
Estate tax
Finance company privilege tax
Gas and oil severance tax
Gasoline, oil excise, compressed gas, petroleum, and lubricating oils taxes
General income tax
Insurance premium tax
License taxes
Motor carrier fees (with local officers)
Motor vehicle registration fees (with local officers)
Property taxes (with local officers)
Public utilities tax
Sales tax
Salt severance taxes
Timber or timber products tax
Title taxes
Tobacco tax
Use or compensating taxes
Waste taxes
Withholding taxes

Secretary of State
The Secretary of State administers and collects the corporate organization and qualification fees on both foreign and domestic corporations.

Department of Insurance
The Commissioner of Insurance and the State Treasurer administer and collect the insurance company tax.

State Gaming Commission
The State Gaming Commission administers the state's gaming taxes.

Department of Employment Security
The Department of Employment Security administers and collects the unemployment insurance tax.

Department of Environmental Quality
Waste disposal fees

Local Taxing Officers
The local taxing officers administer and collect the following taxes:
Banks and banking associations tax
Business licenses (revenue) tax
General property tax (with State Tax Commission)
Mineral documentary tax
Motor carrier fees (with State Tax Commission)
Motor vehicle registration fees (with State Tax Commission)

MISSOURI

State Capital—Jefferson City

Department of Revenue (573) 751-4450
Taxpayer Assistance/General Information (573) 751-3505
TDD (800) 735-2966
Web Site: dor.state.mo.us
E-mail: dormail@mail.dor.state.mo.us

State Tax Commission
The State Tax Commission administers and collects the following taxes:
Airline companies tax
General property tax (with local officers)

Department of Revenue
The *Division of Taxation and Collection* administers and collects the following taxes:
Alcoholic beverage tax (with Department of Public Safety)
Cigarette tax
Estate tax
Express companies tax
Financial institutions tax
Forest crop land tax (with Conservation Commission)
Freight line company tax (with State Tax Commission)
Fuel use tax
Gambling tax
Gasoline tax
Hazardous waste management fees and taxes
Income tax
Insurance companies tax (with Department of Insurance)
New tire fee
Sales and use tax
Tobacco products tax
The *Division of Motor Vehicles and Driver Licensing* administers and collects the following taxes:
Motor vehicle registration fee
Use tax on motor vehicles

Secretary of State
Corporate organization, qualification and annual registration fees, made payable to the Director of Revenue, are submitted to the Secretary of State with filing documents. The Secretary of State collects the corporate franchise tax.

Department of Economic Development
The Division of Motor Carrier and Railroad Safety in the Department of Economic Development administers the motor carrier tax.

State Treasury
The Board of Trustees of the Petroleum Storage Tank Insurance Fund assesses the Petroleum Transport Load Fee.

Department of Insurance
The Department of Insurance, with the Department of Revenue, administers and collects the insurance companies tax.

Department of Public Safety
The Division of Liquor Control, with the Department of Revenue, administers the alcoholic beverage tax.

Department of Agriculture
The Department sets the fuel inspection fee and is responsible for collecting the fee.

Department of Labor and Industrial Relations
The Division of Employment Security administers and collects the unemployment compensation tax in the state.

Department of Health
Soft drinks tax

Attorney General

Local Taxing Officers
The local taxing officers administer and collect the following taxes:
Boats and vessels (wharfage) tax
General property tax (with State Tax Commission)
Merchants' and manufacturers' license tax

MONTANA

State Capital—Helena
Department of Revenue
Customer Service Center (406) 444-6900
TDD (406) 444-2830
Web Site: http://mt.gov/revenue

Department of Revenue
The Department of Revenue is the chief tax administration agency in Montana. It administers and collects the following taxes:
Alcoholic beverage taxes
Cement tax
Cigarette tax
Coal severance tax
Corporate license (income) tax
Estate tax (with local officers)
General property tax
Lodgings tax
Metalliferous mines tax
Micaceous minerals tax
Mineral mining tax
Oil and natural gas production tax (with Board of Oil and Gas Conservation)
Personal income tax
Property tax (with local officials)
Public utilities tax
Tobacco products tax

Department of Transportation
The Department administers the various fuel taxes.

Secretary of State
The Secretary of State administers and collects the annual corporation report fee and the corporate organization and qualification fees.

Board of Oil and Gas Conservation
The Board (in the Natural Resources and Conservation Department) and the Department of Revenue administer and collect the oil and natural gas production tax.

Public Service Commission
The Commission administers and collects the motor carrier fees on the rate and gross operating revenue of motor carriers.

State Auditor
The Insurance Division administers and collects the insurance companies tax.

Department of Labor and Industry
The Department administers and collects the unemployment insurance tax.

Department of Environmental Quality
The Department administers and collects various waste management fees.

Attorney General

Local Taxing Officers
The local taxing officers administer and collect the following taxes:
Estate tax (with Department of Revenue)
General property tax (with Department of Revenue)
Motor vehicle registration fees and use taxes

NEBRASKA

State Capital—Lincoln
Department of Revenue (402) 471-5729
Taxpayer Assistance (800) 742-7474
Web Site: www.revenue.state.ne.us

Department of Revenue
The Department of Revenue is the chief tax administrative body in Nebraska. The *Tax Commissioner* is the chief executive officer of the Department who collects and administers the following taxes:
Bank franchise tax
Business income tax
Cigarette tax
Controlled substances tax
Documentary stamp tax (with county registrar of deeds)
Environmental fees
Estate tax (with State Treasurer)
Fuel taxes
Homestead exemption for property tax
Interstate motor vehicles tax
Litter tax
Lodging tax
Motor fuels tax
Oil, gas, and uranium severance taxes
Personal income tax
Railroad excise tax
Sales and use tax
Tire fee

Department of Property Assessment and Taxation
General property tax but not homestead exemption
The *Property Tax Administrator* administers and collects the public utility, air carrier, car line, railroad, and motor vehicle property taxes.

Tax Equalization and Review Commission
The Tax Equalization and Review Commission hears appeals regarding property tax valuations and exemptions and also reviews and equalizes property tax assessments.

Secretary of State
The Secretary of State administers and collects the corporate organization and qualification fee and the corporation franchise tax.

Liquor Control Commission
The Liquor Control Commission administers and collects the alcoholic beverage tax on all alcoholic beverages.

Department of Insurance
The Department of Insurance administers and collects the insurance premiums tax.

Department of Motor Vehicles
The Division of Motor Carrier Services administers and collects motor carrier fees and, with the county treasurers, administers and collects the motor vehicle taxes.

Department of Labor
The Division of Employment administers and collects the unemployment insurance tax in the state.

Department of Agriculture
The Department of Agriculture administers and collects a variety of taxes and fees on grain, seeds, and other agricultural products.

Attorney General

Local Taxing Officers
The local taxing officers administer and collect the following taxes:
Documentary stamp tax
General property tax
Grain brokers tax (with State Board of Equalization)
Inheritance and estate taxes
Motor vehicle registration fees

NEVADA

State Capital—Carson City

Department of Taxation (775) 684-2000
Web Site: http://tax.state.nv.us/

Department of Taxation
The Department of Taxation is the chief tax administration agency in Nevada. It administers and collects the following taxes:
Ad valorem property tax
Alcoholic beverage tax
Business privilege tax
Cigarette tax
Controlled substances tax
Estate tax
General property tax (with local officers)
Insurance premium tax
Lodging tax
Motor vehicle fuel tax
Net proceeds of minerals tax
Realty transfer tax
Sales and use tax
Short-term lessor fees
Tire surcharge fee

Secretary of State
The Secretary of State administers and collects the annual corporation report fees and the corporate organization and qualification fees.

Department of Motor Vehicles
The Department administers and collects the following fees and taxes:
Motor carrier license fees
Motor vehicle fuels tax
Motor vehicle registration fees
Special fuels tax

Commission on Mineral Resources
The Division of Minerals collects the oil and gas administrative fee.

Department of Employment, Training and Rehabilitation
The Employment Security Division administers and collects unemployment insurance tax from employers in the state.

Gaming Control Board
The Nevada Gaming Control Board and the Gaming Commission administer and collect the gambling taxes.

Attorney General
The Nevada Attorney General's office serves as legal counsel for state agencies in Nevada.

Local Taxing Officers
Local taxing officers administer and collect the following taxes:
General property tax
Utility fee

Commission of Economic Development
The Commission on Economic Development administers Nevada business tax abatement.

NEW HAMPSHIRE

State Capital—Concord

Department of Revenue Administration (603) 271-2191
Taxpayer Assistance (603) 271-2191
Web Site: www.state.nh.us/revenue

Department of Revenue Administration
The Department of Revenue Administration is the chief tax administration agency in New Hampshire. It administers and collects the following taxes:

Business enterprise tax
Business profits tax
Communications services tax
Electricity consumption tax
Estate tax
Gravel tax
Inheritance tax
Interest and dividend tax
Meals and rentals tax
Property tax
Real estate transfer tax
Refined petroleum products tax
Timber tax
Tobacco products tax
Utility property tax

Secretary of State
The Secretary of State administers and collects the annual corporation report fee and the corporate organization fees.

State Liquor Commission
The State Liquor Commission issues licenses for and collects the alcoholic beverage tax.

Department of Safety
The Department of Safety collects the fuel taxes, the oil spillage fee, and the automotive oil fee.
The Director of the Division of Motor Vehicles of the Department of Safety administers and collects motor vehicle registration fees.

Department of Transportation
The Aeronautics Division administers and collects the aircraft fees on airplanes in the state.

Department of Insurance
The Insurance Commissioner and the State Treasurer administer and collect the insurance premiums tax.

Department of Employment Security
The Unemployment Compensation Bureau administers and collects the unemployment insurance tax.

Department of Environmental Services
The Division of Waste Management administers and collects:
Hazardous waste cleanup fees
Out-of-state solid waste fees

Local Taxing Officers
The local taxing officers administer and collect the general property tax.

NEW JERSEY

State Capital—Trenton

Division of Taxation (609) 292-5185
Taxpayer Customer Service Center (609) 292-6400
Web Site: www.state.nj.us/treasury/taxation

Department of the Treasury
The Department of the Treasury, Division of Taxation, is the chief tax administration agency in New Jersey. It administers and collects the following taxes:
Alcoholic beverage taxes
Atlantic City luxury tax
Cape May County tourism sales tax
Cigarette tax
Corporation business tax
Cosmetic Medical procedures gross receipts tax
Domestic security fee
Emergency and 911 System fee
Gross income tax
HMO assessment
Insurance premiums tax

Landfill closure and contingency tax
Litter control fee
Local property tax
Medical malpractice fund attorney fee
Motor fuels tax
Motor vehicle tire fee
Municipal occupancy tax
Petroleum products gross receipts tax
Public community water system tax
Public utility taxes
Railroad franchise tax
Railroad property tax
Realty transfer fee
Sales and use tax
Solid waste services tax
Spill compensation and control tax
Tobacco products wholesale sales and use tax
Transfer inheritance and estate taxes

Division of Revenue
The Department of the Treasury's Division of Revenue administers and collects the corporate annual fee and the corporate organization and qualification fees.

Department of Law and Public Safety
The Alcoholic Beverage Control Division regulates and licenses the manufacture, distribution, sale and transportation of all alcoholic beverages and oversees the municipal licensing of retail sales.

Department of Banking and Insurance
The Commissioner administers the tax on insurance companies.

Department of Labor
The Commissioner administers and collects the unemployment and disability benefit tax.

Department of Transportation
The Motor Vehicle Services Division administers motor vehicle titling and registration.

Local Taxing Officers
The local taxing officers administer and collect the general property tax and the hazardous waste facilities tax.

NEW MEXICO

State Capital—Santa Fe
Department of Taxation and Revenue (505) 827-0700
Albuquerque Taxation and Revenue Department (505) 841-6200
Santa Fe Taxation and Revenue Department (505) 827-0951
Farmington Taxation and Revenue Department (505) 325-5049
Las Cruces Taxation and Revenue Department (505) 524-6225
Roswell Taxation and Revenue Department (505) 624-6065
Web Site: www.state.nm.us/tax

Taxation and Revenue Department
The Secretary of Taxation and Revenue is the chief tax administrator in New Mexico. The Department administers and collects the following taxes:
Alternative fuel tax
Cigarette tax
Compensating tax
Estate tax
Franchise tax
Gasoline tax
General property tax (with local officers)
Gross receipts taxes

Income taxes
Interstate telecommunications services tax
Liquor excise tax (with Regulation and Licensing Department)
Mining property tax (with local officers)
Motor vehicle taxes and fees
Natural gas processors tax
Oil and gas ad valorem production tax
Oil and gas conservation tax
Oil and gas emergency school tax
Oil and gas product equipment ad valorem tax
Oil and gas severance tax
Petroleum products loading fee
Resources excise tax
Severance tax
Solid waste assessment fee
Special fuels supplier tax
Tobacco products tax

Public Regulation Commission
The Commission administers the following:
Annual corporation report fee
Initial fees and taxes
Insurance gross premiums tax (with the Superintendent of Insurance)
Utilities taxes

Regulation and Licensing Department
The Director of the Alcohol and Gaming Division administers liquor licenses and collects the various liquor permit fees.

Department of Labor (Albuquerque)
The Employment Security Division administers and collects the unemployment compensation tax in the state.

Attorney General

Local Taxing Officers
The local taxing officers administer and collect the general property tax (with Property Tax Division).

NEW YORK

State Capital—Albany
Department of Taxation and Finance—Personal Income Tax Information Center (800) 225-5829
Business Tax Information Center (800) 972-1233
Web Site: www.tax.state.ny.us

Department of Taxation and Finance
The Department of Taxation and Finance is the chief tax administration agency in New York. It is divided into four Divisions: the Division of Taxation, the Division of the Treasury, the Division of the Lottery, and the Division of Tax Appeals. The Department of Taxation and Finance is headed by the Commissioner and is divided into administrative bureaus as follows:
The *Corporation Tax Bureau* administers and collects the following taxes:
Corporate organization and qualification fees of foreign corporations
Franchise tax—agricultural co-operative corporations
Franchise tax—business corporations, domestic and foreign; financial corporations, national banking associations
Franchise tax—gas, water, electric or steam companies
Franchise tax—insurance companies. Insurance companies' premium tax (with Superintendent of Insurance)
Franchise tax—real estate corporations

Franchise tax—transportation and transmission corporations

Tax on importation of gas services

Utility services tax

The *Income Tax Bureau* administers and collects the New York state and New York City personal income taxes and the New York City nonresident earnings tax (prior to its repeal).

The *Sales Tax Bureau* administers and collects the sales and use tax.

The *Miscellaneous Tax Bureau* administers and collects the following taxes:

Alcoholic beverage tax (with State Liquor Authority)

Cigarette tax

Estate tax

Fuel tax on carriers

Gift tax (prior to its repeal)

Hazardous waste assessments

Highway use tax

Motor carrier road tax

Motor fuel tax

Petroleum taxes

Racing taxes

State Board of Real Property Services

The State Board of Real Property Services and the local officers administer and collect the general property tax in the state.

Secretary of State

The Secretary of State administers and collects the corporate organization and qualification fees of domestic corporations.

State Liquor Authority (Albany)

The State Liquor Authority issues licenses for the sale of all alcoholic beverages.

Department of Motor Vehicles

The Commissioner of Motor Vehicles administers and collects the motor vehicle registration fee.

Department of Labor

The Unemployment Insurance Division administers and collects the unemployment insurance tax in the state.

Department of Insurance

The Superintendent of Insurance with the Corporation Tax Bureau administers and collects the taxes on all insurance firms.

Department of Environmental Conservation

The Department collects and administers the marine resource taxes.

Local Taxing Officers

The local taxing officers administer and collect the mortgage tax and, with the State Board of Real Property Services, the general property tax.

NORTH CAROLINA

State Capital—Raleigh

Department of Revenue (877) 252-3052

Tax practitioner (919) 754-2500

Web Site: www.dor.state.nc.us

Department of Revenue

The Secretary of Revenue administers and collects the following taxes:

Alcoholic beverages tax (with Department of Commerce)

Cigarette tax

Controlled substances tax

Corporation franchise tax

Dry cleaning tax

Estate tax

Freight car line company tax (with Commissioner of Insurance)

Fuel taxes

Gift tax

Inheritance tax

Insurance premiums taxes (except those collected by the Commissioner of Insurance)

License tax

Nonrecycled newsprint tax

Personal income tax

Piped natural gas excise tax

Primary forest product assessment (w/Dept. of Environment and Natural Resources)

Property tax (with local officials)

Public utilities tax

Realty transfer tax (with local officials)

Sales and use tax

Savings and loan association income and franchise taxes

Scrap tire disposal tax

White goods disposal tax

Secretary of State

The Secretary of State administers and collects corporate organization and qualification fees and the bank privilege tax.

Department of Environment and Natural Resources

The Division of Waste Management administers and collects the hazardous waste fees.

Department of Transportation

The Division of Motor Vehicles administers and collects the motor carrier fees and motor vehicle registration fees.

Department of Commerce

The *Alcoholic Beverage Control Commission*, with the Department of Revenue, administers the various alcoholic beverage taxes and licensing provisions. The *Employment Security Commission* administers and collects the unemployment insurance tax.

Department of Insurance

The Commissioner of Insurance administers and collects the surplus lines tax, the tax on risk retention groups not chartered in North Carolina, and the tax on persons procuring insurance directly from unlicensed insurers.

Attorney General

Local Taxing Officers

The local taxing officers levy and collect, with the Department of Revenue, the general property tax and the privilege tax on low-level radioactive and hazardous waste facilities.

NORTH DAKOTA

State Capital—Bismarck

Tax Commissioner (701) 328-2770; toll-free (800) 638-2901

TDD: (800) 366-6888

Fax: (701) 328-3700

Web Site: http://www.nd.gov/tax/

Tax Commissioner

The State Tax Commissioner administers and collects the following taxes:

Aircraft excise tax (with Aeronautics Commission)

Alcoholic beverages taxes

Coal conversion facilities privilege tax

Coal severance tax

Estate tax

Financial institutions tax

Fuel taxes

General income tax

General property tax (with local officers)
Oil and gas gross production tax
Oil extraction tax
Rural electric cooperatives tax (with local officers)
Sales and use taxes
Telecommunications gross receipts tax
Tobacco products tax

Secretary of State
The Secretary of State administers and collects the corporate organization and qualification fees and the corporation annual report fee.

Department of Transportation
The Department of Transportation administers and collects the motor vehicle registration fees.

Aeronautics Commission
The Aeronautics Commission collects the aircraft excise tax (with the State Tax Commissioner).

Insurance Department
The Commissioner of Insurance administers and collects the insurance premiums tax on all insurance firms.

Job Service
Job Service North Dakota administers and collects the unemployment insurance tax.

Local Taxing Officers
The local taxing officers administer and collect the following taxes:
General property tax (with State Tax Commissioner) and mobile home tax
Rural electric cooperatives tax (with State Tax Commissioner)

OHIO
State Capital—Columbus
Taxpayer Information—Individual (800) 282-1780
Taxpayer Information—Business (888) 405-4039
Web Site: www.tax.ohio.gov

Department of Taxation
The Tax Commissioner, as head of the Department of Taxation, administers the following taxes:
Alcoholic beverage tax (with Division of Liquor Control, Department of Commerce)
Cigarette and tobacco tax
Corporation franchise (income) tax
Dealers in intangibles tax
Estate tax (collected by local officers)
Gasoline tax
General property tax (with local officers)
Horse racing tax
Kilowatt-hour tax
Natural gas consumption tax
Personal income tax
Personal property of public utilities and interexchange telecommunications companies
Public utilities excise tax
Railroad property tax
Replacement tire fee
Resources severance tax
Sales and use tax
School district income tax

Secretary of State
The Secretary of State administers and collects the corporation organization and qualification fees.

State Treasurer
The State Treasurer collects all state taxes, except the personal income tax, horse racing wager tax, liquor gallonage tax, and motor transportation tax. These taxes are collected by the administering agencies.

Department of Public Safety
The Bureau of Motor Vehicles and local officers administer and collect the motor vehicles tax.

Public Utilities Commission
The Public Utilities Commission administers and collects the motor carriers tax.

Department of Commerce
The Division of Liquor Control in the Department of Commerce administers the alcoholic beverage taxes (with Tax Commissioner) and license provisions.

Department of Insurance
The Department of Insurance administers the insurance tax on all insurance firms.

Environmental Protection Agency
Air contaminants fees
Hazardous and other waste fees

Department of Job and Family Services
The Department administers the unemployment insurance tax and the health care taxes.

Attorney General
Oversees administrative, policy, public affairs, and legal and law enforcement activities.

Local Taxing Officers
The local taxing officers administer and collect the following taxes:
Estate tax (with Tax Commissioner)
General property tax (with Tax Commissioner)
Grain handling tax (with Tax Commissioner)
Lodging tax
Motor vehicles tax (with Registrar of Motor Vehicles)
Municipal income tax
Tangible personal property (with Tax Commissioner)

OKLAHOMA
State Capital—Oklahoma City
Tax Commission (405) 521-3160
Taxpayer Assistance (405) 521-3160
Web Site: www.oktax.state.ok.us

Tax Commission
The Tax Commission administers and collects the following taxes:
Additional estate tax
Admissions tax
Air quality control permit fees
Aircraft excise tax
Aircraft registration fees
Alcoholic beverage tax (with Alcoholic Beverage Laws Enforcement Commission)
Cigarette and tobacco products tax
Controlled dangerous substance tax
Estate tax
Franchise tax
Freight car tax
Fuel taxes
Games of chance tax
General income tax
General property tax of public utilities
Gross production tax (with local officers)
Motor carriers tax
Motor vehicle excise tax
Motor vehicle registration fees
Realty transfer tax
Sales and use taxes
Tourism promotion tax
Utility taxes

Secretary of State
The Secretary of State administers and collects the corporate organization and qualification fees.

Alcoholic Beverage Laws Enforcement Commission

The Commission administers the alcoholic beverage licensing provisions.

Department of Environmental Quality
The Department of Environmental Quality administers and collects various waste fees.

Department of Insurance
The Insurance Commissioner administers and collects the insurance gross premiums tax on all insurance firms.

Employment Security Commission
The Unemployment Insurance Division administers and collects the unemployment insurance tax.

Attorney General

Local Taxing Officers
The local taxing officers administer and collect the general property tax, together with the Tax Commissioner, and the real estate mortgage tax.

OREGON

State Capital—Salem
Department of Revenue and Tax Help Office (503) 378-4988 or (800) 356-4222 (Oregon only)
Web Site: egov.oregon.gov/DOR/

Department of Revenue
The Department of Revenue administers and collects the following taxes:
Corporation excise (income) tax
Dry-cleaner tax
Estate tax
Forest products severance tax
General property tax (with local officers)
Inheritance tax
Personal income tax
Property tax
Timber taxes
Tobacco tax
Transient lodging tax
Transit tax
Various waste collection fees

Secretary of State
The Secretary of State administers and collects the corporate organization and qualification fees and the corporation annual report and fee.

Department of Transportation
The Motor Carrier Transportation Division administers the following taxes:
Fuel use tax
Gasoline tax
Motor vehicle registration fees

Department of Consumer and Business Services
Insurance taxes

Liquor Control Commission (Portland)
The Liquor Control Commission issues licenses for and administers and collects a tax on all alcoholic beverages.

Public Utility Commission
The Public Utility Commissioner administers and collects the motor carrier fees and the public utilities tax.

Department of Employment
The Director administers and collects the unemployment insurance tax.

Department of Geology and Mineral Industries
The Department of Geology and Mineral Industries administers and collects the oil tax.

Attorney General (Portland)

Local Taxing Officers
General property tax (with Department of Revenue)

PENNSYLVANIA

State Capital—Harrisburg
Department of Revenue (717) 783-3682
Personal Tax Assistance (717) 787-8201
Business Tax Assistance (717) 787-1064
TDD (800) 447-3020
Web Site: www.revenue.state.pa.us

Department of Revenue
The Secretary of the Department of Revenue administers and collects the following taxes:
Alcoholic beverages tax (with Liquor Control Board)
Bank and trust company taxes
Capital stock tax (domestic corporations)
Cigarette tax
Corporate loans tax
Corporate net income tax
Estate tax
Foreign corporations franchise tax
Inheritance tax
Insurance gross premiums tax
Liquid fuels and fuels tax
Motor carriers road tax
Oil company franchise tax
Personal income tax
Public utilities tax
Realty transfer tax
Sales and use taxes
Utility taxes

Liquor Control Board
The Liquor Control Board, with the Department of Revenue, issues licenses for and administers and collects the tax on alcoholic beverages.

Department of Labor and Industry
The Bureau of Employer Tax Operations administers and collects the unemployment insurance tax.

Department of Transportation
The Department of Transportation administers motor vehicle registration provisions.

Local Taxing Officers
General property taxes
Intangibles taxes

RHODE ISLAND

State Capital—Providence
Division of Taxation (401) 222-3050
Taxpayer's Assistance (401) 222-1040
TDD (401) 222-6287
Web Site: www.tax.state.ri.us

Department of Administration
The Tax Administrator (Division of Taxation) administers and collects the following taxes:
Additional estate tax
Admissions tax
Alcoholic beverage tax
Bank deposits tax
Beverage containers tax
Business corporation tax
Cigarette tax and tobacco products tax
Controlled substances tax
Domestic corporations franchise tax
Estate tax
Gasoline tax
Hard-to-dispose materials tax
Health care provider assessments
Hotel taxes
Insurance companies tax (with Insurance Commissioner)
Local meals and beverage tax

Motor vehicle registration fees
Personal income tax
Public utilities tax
Realty transfer tax
Rental vehicle surcharge
Sales and use tax
Simulcast betting facility tax
Secretary of State
The Secretary of State administers and collects corporate organization and qualification fees and the annual corporation report fee.
General Treasurer
The General Treasurer administers and collects, with the Tax Administrator, the alcoholic beverages tax.
Department of Business Regulation
The Department issues manufacturer's and wholesaler's licenses.
The Insurance Division administers the insurance premiums taxes with the Department of Administration.
Public Utility Commission
The Public Utility Administrator administers permit and certificate requirements for common and contract carriers.
Department of Labor and Training
The Department administers the unemployment insurance tax.
Attorney General
Local Taxing Officers
The local taxing officers administer and collect the general property tax.

SOUTH CAROLINA

State Capital—Columbia
Department of Revenue (803) 898-5000
Income Tax Assistance (803) 898-5709
Taxpayers Advocate (803) 898-5444
TDD (803) 898-5656
Web Site: www.sctax.org
Department of Revenue
The Director of the Department of Revenue administers and collects the following taxes:
Admissions tax
Alcoholic beverage taxes
Bank tax
Chain store tax
Cigarette and tobacco tax
Corporation franchise tax
Corporation income tax
Electric power tax
Estate tax
Forest renewal tax
Health care tax
Low-level Radioactive waste tax
Marijuana and controlled substances tax
Motor carrier road tax
Motor fuels tax
Personal income tax
Property tax (with local officers)
Public utilities license tax
Recording fee
Sales and use taxes
Savings and loan association tax
Soft drinks tax
Solid waste excise tax
Secretary of State

The Secretary of State administers and collects the corporate organization and qualification fee and the foreign corporation annual report fee.
Department of Insurance
The Department of Insurance administers and collects the insurance companies tax.
Department of Health and Environmental Control
The Department of Health and Environmental Control administers and collects.
Hazardous waste taxes
Department of Public Safety
The Department of Public Safety administers the motor vehicle registration and licensing provisions and the motor vehicle property tax.
Employment Security Commission
The Unemployment Insurance Division administers and collects the unemployment compensation tax.
Aeronautics Commission
The Aeronautics Commission in the Department of Commerce administers and collects aircraft registration fees.
Public Service Commission
The Public Service Commission administers the motor carrier tax.
Local Taxing Officers
Recording fee (with Department of Revenue)
General property tax (with Department of Revenue)

SOUTH DAKOTA

State Capital—Pierre
Department of Revenue (605) 773-3311
Tax Assistance (800) 829-9188
Web Site: www.state.sd.us/drr2/revenue.html
Department of Revenue
The Secretary of Revenue administers and collects the following taxes:
Alcoholic beverage tax
Banks and financial corporation excise tax
Cigarette tax
Contractors' excise tax
Estate tax
Fuel excise tax
Gaming excise tax
Motor fuel tax
Motor vehicle fees (with county treasurers)
Oil and gas severance tax
Precious metals severance tax
Sales tax
Use tax
The Division of Insurance administers and collects the insurance gross premiums tax.
Secretary of State
The Secretary of State administers and collects the annual corporation report tax and the corporate organization and qualification fees.
Department of Labor (Aberdeen)
The Unemployment Insurance Division administers and collects the unemployment insurance tax.
Local Taxing Officers
The local taxing officers administer and collect the general property tax and motor vehicle fees.

TENNESSEE

State Capital—Nashville
Department of Revenue (800) 342-1003 (in-state only) or (615) 253-0600 (Nashville area and out of state)
Web Site: www.state.tn.us/revenue

Department of Revenue

The Commissioner of Revenue is the chief tax administrator in Tennessee. The Commissioner's office administers and collects the following taxes:

Alcoholic beverages tax (with the Alcoholic Beverage Commission)
Automotive oil sales fee
Bail bond tax
Business privilege tax (with Commissioner of Commerce and Insurance and local officials)
Cigarette and tobacco tax
Coal severance tax
Coin-operated amusement machine tax
Estate tax
Excise (income) tax
Franchise tax
Gasoline tax
Gift tax
Inheritance tax
Professional privilege tax
Public utilities tax
Retailers' sales and use tax
Soft drinks tax
Stocks and bonds income tax

Secretary of State

The Secretary of State administers and collects the corporation charter tax, the annual corporate filing fees, and the privilege tax on foreign corporations.

Comptroller of the Treasury

The Comptroller and local officers administer and collect the property tax on public utilities.

Department of Commerce and Insurance

The Commissioner of Commerce and Insurance administers and collects the insurance companies tax (Insurance Division) and, with the Department of Revenue, the business privilege tax.

Department of Environment and Conservation

Hazardous waste generator fee

Department of Transportation

The Department administers the railroad fees.

Department of Safety

The Department administers and collects the motor carrier fees.

Department of Labor and Workforce Development

The Commissioner administers and collects the unemployment compensation tax.

Attorney General

Local Taxing Officers

Business and occupation taxes
General property tax
Mortgage tax
Privileges taxes
Real estate transfer tax

TEXAS

State Capital—Austin

Comptroller of Public Accounts office (512) 463-4444
Tax Assistance (512) 463-4600; (800) 248-4093
TDD (512) 463-4621 (Austin); (800) 248-4099
Web Site: http://www.window.state.tx.us/taxes/

Comptroller of Public Accounts

The Comptroller of Public Accounts is the chief tax administrator in Texas. The office administers and collects the following taxes:

Alcoholic beverages tax
Beverage tax
Bingo tax
Boat sales tax
Carriers tax
Cement tax
Cigarette tax
Controlled substances tax
Dedicated reserve gas tax
Estate tax
Franchise tax
Gasoline tax
General property tax (with local officers)
Hospital assessments
Hotel occupancy tax
Inheritance tax
Insurance tax (with the Department of Insurance)
Lead-acid battery tax
Manufactured housing tax
Mixed beverage tax
Natural gas tax
Occupation tax
Oil production tax
Oil well service tax
Petroleum tax
Property tax on transportation business intangibles
Public utilities tax (with Public Service Commission)
Sales and use taxes
Severance beneficiary tax
Sulphur tax
Unclaimed property tax
Waste tire recycling fee

Secretary of State

The Secretary of State administers and collects the corporate organization and qualification fees.

Alcoholic Beverage Commission

The Alcoholic Beverage Commission, with the Comptroller and local officers, administers and collects the alcoholic beverage and bingo taxes.

Public Utility Commission

Utility tax (with Comptroller)

Department of Insurance

The Commissioner of Insurance administers the insurance tax with the Comptroller.

Natural Resources Conservation Commission

Hazardous waste fees
Solid waste fees

Railroad Commission

The Commission administers hazardous oil and gas waste generation fee provisions.

Workforce Commission

The Workforce Commission administers and collects the unemployment insurance tax.

Department of Transportation

The Department administers motor vehicle registration (with county officials) and motor carrier provisions.

Attorney General

Local Taxing Officers

The local taxing officers administer and collect the following taxes:

General property tax (with Comptroller of Public Accounts)
Motor vehicle registration (with Department of Transportation)
Motor vehicle sales or use tax (with the Comptroller)

UTAH

State Capital—Salt Lake City

Tax Commission (801) 297-2200
Web Site: tax.utah.gov/

Tax Commission

The Tax Commission is the chief tax administration agency in Utah. It administers and collects the following taxes:

Income Taxes

Corporation franchise tax

Corporation income tax

Homeowners associations tax

Individual income tax

Inheritance tax

"S" corporations tax

Unrelated business income tax

Withholding tax

Motor Vehicle Taxes and Fees

Automobile driver education fee

Motor vehicle business regulatory fees

Motor vehicle registration fee

Motor vehicle title and duplicate registration fees

96-hour in-transit temporary permits

Proportional registration fee

Temporary permit fee

Uniform fee on vehicles

Uninsured motorist identification fee

Sales and Use Taxes

Botanical, cultural and zoological tax

County option sales tax

Highway tax

Local option sales and use taxes

Mass transit tax

Municipal energy sales and use tax

Municipal transient room tax

Resort communities sales tax

Restaurant tax

Rural county health care facility tax

Short-term lease and rental tax on motor vehicles

State sales tax

State use tax

Tourism tax

Town option sales and use tax

Transient room tax

Fuel Taxes

Aviation fuel tax

International fuel tax agreement tax

Lubricating oil fee

Motor fuel tax

Special fuel tax

Property Tax

Farmland assessment tax

Privilege tax

Property tax

Uniform fee on vehicles

Miscellaneous Taxes

Beer tax

Cigarette tax and tobacco products tax

Emergency services telephone charge

Gross receipts tax

Illegal drug stamp act

Insurance premium tax

Mineral production withholding tax

Mining severance tax

Oil and gas conservation fee

Oil and gas severance tax

Radioactive waste tax

Self-insurers' tax

Waste tire recycling fee

Department of Alcoholic Beverage Control

The Department issues licenses for and administers and collects the tax on alcoholic beverages.

Department of Workforce Services

The Division of Workforce Information and Payment Services administers the unemployment compensation tax.

Insurance Department

Surplus lines premium tax

Department of Commerce

The Division of Corporations and Commercial Code administers the corporate organization and annual report fees.

Public Service Commission

The Public Service Commission administers the public utility regulation tax.

Local Taxing Officers

The local taxing officers and the Tax Commission administer and collect the general property tax.

VERMONT

State Capital—Montpelier

Department of Taxes (802) 828-2505

Taxpayer Services—Business (802) 828-5723

Taxpayer Services—Individual (802) 828-2865

Web Site: http://www.state.vt.us/tax/

Administration Agency

The *Department of Taxes* administers and collects the following taxes:

Alcoholic beverages tax (with Department of Liquor Control)

Cable tax (with Department of Public Service)

Cigarette and tobacco products tax

Corporate income tax

Electric energy tax

Estate tax

Express companies tax (with Department of Public Service & Public Service Board)

Fuels other than motor vehicle

Hazardous air contaminant tax

Hazardous waste tax (with Secretary of Environmental Conservation)

Insurance companies tax

Meals and room tax

Personal income tax

Property taxes (Waterbury) (with local officials)

Realty transfer tax (with town clerk)

Sales and use tax

Telephone tax

Waste management facilities tax

Secretary of State

The Secretary of State administers and collects the corporate organization and qualification fee.

Department of Liquor Control

The Department of Liquor Control issues licenses for and administers and collects the tax on alcoholic beverages (with Department of Taxes).

Transportation Agency

The Motor Vehicles Department administers and collects the fuel taxes, the vehicle sales and use tax, and the motor vehicle registration fees (with Department of Taxes).

Department of Employment and Training Administration

The Department administers and collects the unemployment compensation tax.

Human Services Agency (Waterbury)

Department of Prevention, Assistance, Transition, and Health Access administers the hospital and nursing home taxes (with Department of Taxes).

Attorney General

VIRGINIA

State Capital—Richmond

Taxpayer (Businesses) Information (804) 367-8037
Taxpayer (Individuals) Information (804) 367-8031
Web Site: http://www.tax.virginia.gov/

Department of Taxation
The Commissioner of the Department of Taxation, in the Finance Secretariat, administers and collects the following taxes:
Aircraft sales and use tax
Bank franchise tax (with local officers)
Cigarette tax
Corporate income tax
Deed and mortgage recording taxes (with local officers)
Estate tax
Forest products tax
Intangibles tax (with local officers)
Personal income tax (with local officers)
Pipeline company property tax (except companies whose operations and facilities are wholly within Virginia)
Railway company property tax
Sales and use tax
Soft drink excise tax
Watercraft sales and use tax

State Corporation Commission
The State Corporation Commission administers and collects the following taxes, including the assessment of physical properties of utilities, which are taxed at the local level:
Annual corporation registration fee
Corporate organization and qualification fees
Insurance premiums tax
Pipeline company property tax (companies whose operations and facilities are wholly within the state)
Public utility taxes (local) (with local officers)
Public utility taxes (state)

Department of Motor Vehicles
The Department (in the Transportation Secretariat) administers and collects the following taxes:
Carriers' road (fuel) tax
Fuel taxes
Motor carrier fees
Motor vehicle registration and license fees
Motor vehicle sales and use tax
Oil company excise tax
Tax on fuels other than motor fuel

Department of Aviation
The Department of Aviation (in the Transportation Secretariat) administers the aviation license fees.

Department of Alcoholic Beverage Control
The Department of Alcoholic Beverage Control (in the Public Safety Secretariat) administers and collects alcoholic beverage license taxes and the state tax on alcoholic beverages (except the beer tax, which is collected by the Alcoholic Beverage Control Commission).

Employment Commission
The Employment Commission (in the Commerce and Trade Secretariat) administers and collects the unemployment compensation tax.

Department of Professional and Occupational Regulation
The Department (in the Commerce and Trade Secretariat) administers and collects the tax on promoters.

Attorney General

Local Taxing Officers
Bank share tax (with Department of Taxation)
Deed and mortgage recording taxes (with Department of Taxation)
Intangibles tax (with Department of Taxation)
Personal income tax (with Department of Taxation)
Property tax
Public utility taxes (local) (with State Corporation Commission)

WASHINGTON

State Capital—Olympia

Taxpayer Information and Education (800) 647-7706
Tax Express Information System (800) 334-8969
Web Site: dor.wa.gov

Department of Revenue
The Director administers and collects the following taxes:
Business and occupation tax
Cigarette tax
Estate tax
Food fish and shellfish tax
Hazardous waste taxes
Litter tax
Property taxes (with local officers)
Public utility tax
Retail sales tax and use tax
Telephone program taxes
Timber excise tax
Tobacco products tax

Secretary of State
The Secretary of State administers and collects the corporate organization and qualification fees and the corporation franchise tax.

State Liquor Control Board
The State Liquor Control Board issues alcoholic beverage licenses for and administers and collects the tax on alcoholic beverages.

Department of Licensing
The Department of Licensing administers and collects the following taxes:
Aircraft fuel tax
Cigarette dealer permits
Motor fuel taxes
Motor vehicle fees (with local officers)

Department of Health
The Department administers and collects the uranium and thorium milling tax.

State Treasurer
The State Treasurer administers and collects the following taxes:
Estate tax (with Department of Revenue)
Insurance companies premiums tax (with Insurance Commissioner)

Department of Transportation
The Department administers and collects the motor vehicle carrier fees and the aircraft excise tax.

Office of Insurance
The Insurance Commissioner and the State Treasurer administer and collect the insurance companies premiums tax.

Department of Employment Security
The Commissioner administers and collects the unemployment compensation tax.

Attorney General
Local Taxing Officers
Admissions tax
Gambling tax
Motor vehicle fees (with Department of Licensing)

Property taxes (with Department of Revenue)
Real estate sales tax

WEST VIRGINIA
State Capital—Charleston
State Tax Department
Taxpayer Services Division (304) 558-3333 and
(800) 982-8297
Web Site: http://www.state.wv.us/taxdiv/
Department of Revenue
The State Tax Department, which is part of the
Department of Revenue, administers and collects
the following taxes:
Alcoholic beverage taxes and licenses
Beer barrel tax and license fees
Bingo license
Business and occupation tax
Business franchise tax
Business registration tax
Charitable raffle license
Consumers sales and service tax
Corporate license tax and attorney-in-fact fee
Corporate net income tax
Estate tax
Gasoline and special fuel excise tax
Health care provider taxes
Insurance taxes and fees
International fuel tax agreement
Motor carrier provisions
Motor carrier road tax
Personal income tax
Property tax
Property transfer tax
Racing taxes and fees
Raffle board wholesalers and distributors fees
Severance and business privilege tax
Severance tax
Soft drinks tax
Solid waste assessment fee
Sparklers and novelties registration
Special reclamation tax
Special two-cent tax
Telecommunications tax
Tobacco products excise tax (cigarette tax)
Use tax
Wine liter tax
Secretary of State
The Secretary of State administers and collects the
corporate organization and qualification fees, the
initial license tax and the tax on corporations holding
land.
Department of Transportation
The Division of Motor Vehicles of the Department of
Transportation administers and collects the following
taxes:
Identification markers under the motor carrier road
tax
Motor carrier fees (with the Public Service
Commission) and motor vehicle registration fees
Motor vehicle privilege tax
Public Service Commission
The Public Service Commission and the Division of
Motor Vehicles administer and collect the motor
carrier fees.
Insurance Commission
The Insurance Commission administers and collects
the taxes on insurance companies.
Bureau of Employment Programs

The Employment Programs Bureau administers the
unemployment compensation tax.
Department of Environmental Protection
The Office of Environmental Remediation
administers various solid and hazardous waste fees.
Attorney General
Local Taxing Officers
Business license fees
General property tax (with the State Tax
Department)

WISCONSIN
State Capital—Madison
Department of Revenue (608) 266-2772
Web Site: www.dor.state.wi.us
Department of Revenue
The Department of Revenue administers and
collects the following taxes:
Alcoholic beverages taxes
Cigarette tax
Controlled substances tax
Estate tax
Fuel taxes
General income tax
Metallic minerals occupation tax
Public utilities property tax
Public utilities tax
Realty transfer tax
Recycling surcharge
Sales and use taxes
Telephone company tax
Department of Financial Institutions
The Department administers and collects the annual
corporation report fee and the corporate
organization and qualification fees.
State Treasurer
The State Treasurer administers unclaimed property
and escheat laws.
Department of Natural Resources
Environmental and forestry taxes and fees
Public Service Commission
The Public Service Commission makes
assessments on mobile home park operators and for
stray voltage research, the air quality improvement
program, and telephone relay service to cover the
Commission's related expenses.
Department of Transportation
The Department of Transportation administers and
collects the motor vehicle fees.
Commissioner of Insurance
The Commissioner of Insurance administers and
collects the insurance tax.
Department of Workforce Development
The Unemployment Insurance Division administers
and collects the unemployment compensation tax.
Department of Administration, Division of Gaming
Bingo tax
Racing taxes
Local Taxing Officers
General property tax
Grain tax
Vessels tax

WYOMING
State Capital—Cheyenne
Department of Revenue (307) 777-7961
Web Site: revenue.state.wy.us
Department of Revenue

The Department administers and collects the following taxes:

Cigarette tax

Estate tax

Property tax (ad valorem)

Public utilities assessment

Sales and use tax

Severance tax

The *Liquor Division* issues licenses for and administers and collects the tax on alcoholic beverages.

Department of Transportation

Motor carrier fees

Motor fuel taxes

Motor vehicle registration fees (with County Treasurers)

Secretary of State

The Secretary of State administers and collects the corporate organization and qualification fees and the corporation franchise (license) tax.

Department of Employment (Casper)

The Employment Tax Division administers and collects the unemployment insurance and workers' compensation taxes.

Department of Insurance

The Department of Insurance administers the gross premiums tax and miscellaneous insurance fees.

Oil and Gas Conservation Commission (Casper)

The Oil and Gas Conservation Commission administers the oil and gas conservation charge.

Attorney General

Local Taxing Officers

General property tax

Motor vehicle registration fees

TAXES BY STATE

Alabama

Tax System.—A general property tax for state and local purposes in Alabama is imposed upon real and personal property at uniform rates in the taxing districts where such property is located. The property tax is supplemented by (1) state taxes on franchises, incomes, privileges and occupations, (2) county taxes on privileges and occupations and (3) municipal licenses and inspection fees. An outline of the Alabama tax system follows:

Tax	Basis—Rates	Due Dates
Corporate organization and qualification fees.	Domestic—fee for filing articles of incorporation, $40 state fee plus $35 for Probate Judge.	Domestic—at time of incorporation or increase of capital stock.
	Foreign—Application fee for certificate of authority to transact business in state, $175.	Foreign—at time of qualification or increase of capital employed in the state.
	Annual report—$10.	Annual report—between January 1 and March 15.
Business privilege tax.	Business privilege tax imposed on Alabama net worth: taxable income of the taxpayer is less than $1, $0.25 per $1,000; taxable income of the taxpayer is at least $1 but less than $200,000, $1.00 per $1,000; taxable income of the taxpayer is at least $200,000 but less than $500,000, $1.25 per $1,000; taxable income of the taxpayer is at least $500,000 but less than $2.5 million, $1.50 per $1,000; taxable income of the taxpayer is at least $2.5 million, $1.75 per $1,000.	Returns are generally due within 2½ months after the beginning of its tax year. Financial institutions—tax returns are due by March 15 of a group's tax year. A limited liability entity must file a return within 3½ months after the start of its tax year, and a disregarded entity is required to file a return when its owner is required to file a return. An initial business privilege tax return is due not later than 30 days after the date it comes into existence or begins doing business in Alabama, whichever comes first.
	Minimum tax—$100.	
	Maximum tax for corporations and limited liability entities other than financial institutions, insurance companies subject to insurance premiums tax, electing family limited liability entities, and certain nonprofit corporations—$15,000. Maximum tax for financial institutions and for insurance companies subject to insurance premiums tax—$3 million. Maximum tax for electing family limited liability entities—$500. Maximum tax for certain nonprofit corporations—$100.	
	Short taxable years—Taxpayers having an Alabama taxable year of less than 12 months are subject to a prorated business privilege tax, with a minimum tax of $100.	

Tax	Basis—Rates	Due Dates
General income tax.	Individuals: married filing jointly, 2% of first $1,000 of taxable income, 4% of next $5,000, and 5% of excess over $6,000; all others, 2% of first $500 of taxable income, 4% of next $2,500, and 5% of excess over $3,000. General withholding required.	Individuals—reports and payments due April 15 or the 15th day of the 4th month following the close of the fiscal year. Declarations and payments of estimated tax from larger taxpayers are due April 15, June 15, September 15, and January 15.
	Corporations: 6.5% of taxable net income.	Corporations—reports and payments due March 15 or the 15th day of the 3rd month following the close of the fiscal year. Declarations and payments of estimated tax from larger taxpayers are due April 15, June 15, September 15, and December 15.
	Financial institutions: 6.5% of taxable net income. Certain multistate businesses with gross sales volumes not over $100,000: 0.25% of gross sales receipts.	Financial institutions—reports and payments due April 15.
General property tax (state tax only).	State rate 0.65% annually.	Returns and payments—individuals and corporations, January 1. Public utilities, March 1.
Occupancy taxes.	Occupancy tax—5% in mountain lakes areas (Blount, Cherokee, Colbert, Cullman, DeKalb, Etowah, Franklin, Jackson, Lauderdale, Lawrence, Limestone, Madison, Marion, Marshall, Morgan and Winston counties); 4% in all other counties on renting or furnishing of a room, lodging or accommodations.	Reports and payments—20th of each month for preceding month.
Alcoholic beverages tax.	Excise—5¢ per 12 fluid ozs. or fraction thereof of malt or brewed beverages, plus statewide local tax of 1.625¢ per 4 fluid ozs. or fraction thereof of beer; spirituous or vinous liquors, 10% of selling price plus additional 46% tax; table wine, 45¢ per liter.	Reports and payments—Malt beverage excise: last day of the following month; beer and table wine excise: 15th day of following month; manufacturers and importers, 20th of each month; spirituous or vinous liquors: at time of purchase.
Gasoline, diesel fuel, lubricating oils taxes.	Gasoline—16¢ per gallon. Diesel fuel—19¢ per gallon. Rates for fuel used to propel aircraft are subject to annual adjustment.	Reports and payments—20th of each month except warehouses, carriers, and transfer companies, 15th of each month.
	Lubricating oils—6¢ per gallon, with certain exceptions. Wholesale dealers in illuminating, lubricating or fuel oils, 0.5% of gross sales for the preceding year.	Lubricating oils—returns and payments, 20th of each month except carriers, warehouses, and transfer companies, 15th of each month. Wholesale dealers must pay within 2 weeks from the beginning of the fiscal year.

Tax	Basis—Rates	Due Dates
	Motor carrier fuel tax—same as gasoline and diesel fuel taxes.	Motor carrier fuel tax—last day of January, April, July and October.
	Inspection fees—gasoline, 2¢ per gal.; lubricating oil, 15¢ per gal.; kerosene, 1¢ per gal.; diesel fuel, 2¢ per gal. except jet, maritime, locomotive, farm tractor and wood treatment fuel, 1/40¢ per gal.	Inspection fees—payment and certificate, 20th of each month.
Severance tax.	Iron ore—3¢ per ton mined. Coal severance—13.5¢ per ton. Coal and lignite severance—additional 20¢ per ton.	Iron ore and coal severance—20th of each month.
	Oil and gas—8%[1, 2] (plus 2% conservation tax) of gross value at point of production of oil or gas; 4%[2] for incremental oil or gas production resulting from a qualified enhanced recovery project; 4%[2] for wells producing 25 barrels or less of oil per day or producing 200,000 cubic feet or less of gas per day; 6%[1, 2] for oil or gas produced offshore at depths greater than 18,000 feet below mean sea level; and 6%[2] (for a 5-year period) for oil and gas produced from onshore discovery wells, from onshore development wells on which drilling began within 4 years of the completion date of the discovery well and producing from a depth of 6,000 feet or more, and onshore development wells on which drilling began within 2 years of the completion date of the discovery well and producing from a depth less than 6,000 feet.	Oil and gas—15th day of the 2nd month following month of production.
	Statewide severance tax equal to 10¢ per ton on certain severed products imposed by various counties. Some counties impose a higher rate.	Statewide severance tax returns—20th day of month following month of production.
	Forest products—pine lumber, 50¢ per 1,000 feet board measure, 75¢ per 1,000 feet log scale, or 10¢ per ton; hardwood and others, 30¢ per 1,000 feet board measure, 50¢ per 1,000 feet log scale, or 6.5¢ per ton; pulpwood and others, 25¢ per standard cord or 10¢ per ton; pulpwood chips, 25¢ per 190 cubic feet or 10¢ per ton; crossties, 1.5¢ per piece or 15¢ per ton; switch ties, 2.5¢ per piece or 17¢ per ton; turpentine, 15¢ per barrel; mine ties and coal mine props, 12.5¢ per 100 pieces or 15¢ per ton; piling and poles, $1.875 per 1,000 board feet or 20.5¢ per ton; pine ore mine props, 75¢ per 1,000 feet log scale; or hardwood ore mine props, 50¢ per 1,000 feet log scale. Additional privilege tax on processors and manufacturers using timber—50% of the severance tax.	Forest products—within 30 days after end of each calendar quarter.
Chain store tax.	Graduated from $1 for one store, either retail or wholesale, to $112.50 for each store in excess of 20 in the state.	Application of license renewal and payment due on October 31.
Tobacco stamp and use tax.	Cigarettes—42.5¢ per pack of 20.	Reports—20th of each month; use tax, 10th of each month.
	Cigars—4¢ on each 10 little cigars or fraction weighing 3 lbs. or less per 1,000; others, from $3.00 per 1,000 to $40.50 per 1,000, depending on retail price.	Payment—wholesalers and retailers, by affixing stamps immediately upon receipt of merchandise; users, with report.

Tax	Basis—Rates	Due Dates
	Smoking tobacco—4¢ to 21¢ on packages weighing up to 4 ozs. plus 6¢ per oz. over 4.	
	Chewing tobacco—1.5¢ per oz.	
Document filing tax; mineral documentary tax.	Document—Conveyances—50¢ for each $500 of property conveyed; mortgages—15¢ for each $100 of indebtedness.	Payment—at time of recording.
	Mineral documentary—Lease of 10 yrs. or less, 5¢ per acre; 11 to 20 yrs., 10¢; more than 20 yrs., 15¢.	
Sales and use tax; rental tax.	Sales—mining and manufacturing machinery and farm equipment, 1.5%; food sold through vending machines, 3%; casual sales of motor vehicles, motorboats, and trailers, 2%; all other retail sales and selected services, 4% of gross proceeds of sales of tangible personal property and gross receipts of amusement businesses. Rentals and leases of tangible personal property are taxed at 4% of gross proceeds, except the tax is 1.5% on vehicle and trailer rentals and 2% on linen and garment rentals. Street and highway contracts are taxed at 5% of gross receipts from public road, highway, and bridge contracts.	Reports and payments—sales, rentals or leases, 20th of each month; 20th day of the month following each calendar quarter for taxpayers owing not more than $200 per month (annually, if total tax does not exceed $10 per month). Taxpayers whose average state sales tax liability was $1,000 or more must make estimated payments on or before the 20th day of each month.
	Use—same as sales tax rates. Basis is sales price of tangible personal property used, consumed, or stored in Alabama.	Reports and payments—use, 20th day of each month.
Public utilities taxes.	Electric or hydroelectric utilities, 2.2% per $1 of gross receipts. Hydroelectric sellers and manufacturers, $2/5$ mill per kilowatt hour.	Returns and payments—hydroelectric sellers and manufacturers, September 25; others, October 1, except electric or hydroelectric utilities and miscellaneous utilities, 1st day of October, January, April and July.
	Express, 2.5% of gross receipts; alternative tax, flat fee based on intrastate miles of transit line used.	
	Freight lines, 3.5% of 30% of value of cars within state for the previous 12 months.	
	All utilities, except electric, telephone, telegraph, railroad, sleeping car and express companies, 2.2% per $1 of gross receipts.	
	Gross receipts and use tax—electric, domestic water and natural gas companies, from 4% if monthly gross receipts or sales price respecting a person is not over $40,000 to $2,200 plus 2% of the excess amount if such receipts or sales price exceeds $60,000 per month; telegraph and telephone companies, 6%.	Reports and payments—gross receipts tax—20th of each month. Estimated payments due on 20th of current month if preceding year's average monthly liability was $1,000 or more. Use tax—20th of each month liability occurs.
	Telecommunication services and providers, 6%.	Reports and payments—same as the gross receipts and use tax.

Tax	Basis—Rates	Due Dates
Insurance companies tax.	Foreign life insurers are taxed at 2.3%. Domestic life insurers are taxed at 2.3%. Individual life insurance policies in a face amount greater than $5,000 and up to $25,000, excluding group policies, 1%. Individual life insurance policies in a face amount of $5,000 or less, excluding group policies, 0.5%. For health insurance, and accident and health insurance for which a separate premium is charged, 1.6%. Health care benefits provided by an employer-sponsored plan for groups with fewer than 50 insured participants, 0.5%. Property and multi-peril insurance written in fire protection Classes 9 and 10 and mobile homes, mobile homeowners, homeowners and low-value dwelling policies in a face amount of $40,000 or less, 1%. Medical liability insurance, 1.6%. Surplus lines, 6%. Unauthorized foreign insurer, 4%. Foreign companies subject to retaliatory taxes.	Reports—March 1. Payments May 15, August 15, November 15, and March 1.
Estate tax; generation-skipping transfer tax.	As a result of the federal tax changes enacted in 2001, Alabama estate tax returns, affidavits of estate tax, and estate tax waivers are no longer required to be filed for estates of decedents who died after December 31, 2004.	
	Generation-skipping transfer—Tax imposed to absorb federal generation-skipping transfer tax credit.	Payment—Within 9 months after death.

[1] The rate is reduced by 2% for any well for which the initial permit issued by the Oil and Gas Board is dated on or after July 1, 1988, except for replacement wells if the permit for the original well was dated before July 1, 1988.

[2] The applicable rate is reduced by 50% for a 5-year period from the date production begins for any well for which the initial permit issued by the Oil and Gas Board is dated on or after July 1, 1996, and before July 1, 1999, except for replacement wells if the permit for the original well was dated before July 1, 1996. Thereafter, the tax rates in footnote 1 apply.

Alaska

Tax System.—The Alaska tax system is based primarily on income and license taxes. A direct tax on corporate income is the main revenue producer for the state, while many of the license fees are measured by income. Municipalities and boroughs are the only localities authorized to levy taxes on real and personal property. The personal income tax was repealed on January 1, 1979. The state levies no general property tax. Although Alaska does not impose a statewide sales and use tax, some boroughs and municipalities impose local sales and use taxes. An outline of the tax system follows:

Tax	Basis—Rates	Due Dates
Corporate organization and qualification fees.	Articles of incorporation or application for certificate of authority $150.00; articles of amendment, merger or consolidation, or an amendment of certificate of authority $25.00; filing certificate of election $10.00; filing articles of dissolution or certificate of dissolution $15.00; registration of corporate name $25.00; renewal of corporate name $25.00.	At the time of filing.
Biennial corporation fee and biennial report.	Biennial corporation fee—domestic corporations, $100; foreign corporations, $200.	Corporation fee—January 1. Biennial report—January 1.
General income tax.	Corporations—Taxable income of less than $10,000, 1%; $10,000 to $20,000, $100 plus 2% of the taxable income over $10,000; $20,000 to $30,000, $300 plus 3% of the taxable income over $20,000; $30,000 to $40,000, $600 plus 4% of the taxable income over $30,000; $40,000 to $50,000, $1,000 plus 5% of the taxable income over $40,000; $50,000 to $60,000, $1,500 plus 6% of the taxable income over $50,000; $60,000 to $70,000, $2,100 plus 7% of the taxable income over $60,000; $70,000 to $80,000, $2,800 plus 8% of the taxable income over $70,000; $80,000 to $90,000, $3,600 plus 9% of the taxable income over $80,000; $90,000 or more, $4,500 plus 9.4% of the taxable income over $90,000. A 4.5% alternative tax rate on capital gains; an alternative minimum tax equal to 18% of the taxpayer's federal alternative minimum tax; the personal holding company tax rate is 12.6% of apportioned income; and the accumulated earnings tax rate is 4.95% of the first $100,000 and 6.93% of the excess. Alternative minimum tax imposed.	Reports—within 30 days after the federal return is filed; payments—when federal tax is paid.
Mining license tax.	Net income of taxpayer reported to federal government and royalties from Alaska mining property at following rates: Over $40,000 to $50,000, $1,200 plus 3% of the excess over $40,000, $50,001 to $100,000, $1,500 plus 5% of excess over $50,000; $100,001 or over, $4,000 plus 7% of excess over $100,000.	Reports and payments—April 30 or first day of 5th month following close of fiscal year.
Property tax.	Property is assessed at full and true value. Rates fixed locally to meet budget, maximum of 3% for cities and 2% for second class cities.	Fixed locally.

Tax	Basis—Rates	Due Dates
Oil and gas properties taxes.	Property used or committed for use in exploration, production and pipeline transportation of unrefined oil or gas, 20 mills of full and true value. Municipal taxes may be levied on such property.	Returns—may be required. Payment—June 30.
Alcoholic beverages tax.	Excise—Malt beverages, $1.07 per gal.; wine and liquor, $2.50 per gal. if 21% alcohol or less; and $12.80 per gal. if more than 21% alcohol; cider, $1.07 per gal. if 0.5%-7% alcohol by volume; beer, $0.35 per gal. on first 60,000 barrels per year with qualifications.	Excise—last day of month.
Motor fuel oil tax.	8¢ per gal. of motor fuel transferred or consumed in Alaska. Aviation gasoline, 4.7¢ per gallon; aviation fuel other than gasoline, 3.2¢ per gallon; fuel for watercraft, 5¢ per gallon.	Reports and payment—last day of month for preceding month.
Oil and gas production tax.	Oil—22.5% of net value of oil ("production tax value") and includes a progressivity factor, under which the tax rate increases by 0.25% for each dollar the production tax value rises above $40 per barrel.	Reports and payments— annually, by March 31.
	Gas—22.5% of net value of gas, expressed in barrels ("production tax value"), and includes a progressivity factor, under which the tax rate increases by 0.25% for each dollar the production tax value rises above $40 per barrel.	
Fisheries taxes.	Fishery business taxes—Salmon canned at a shore-based cannery, 4.5%; other salmon and all other fisheries resources processed by a shore-based fisheries business, 3%;	Report and payment— before April 1.
	Fisheries resources processed by floating fisheries business, 5%;	
	Developing commercial fish species shore-based fisheries business, 1%;	
	Developing commercial fish species floating fisheries business, 3%.	
	Dive fishery management assessment—based on location, 1% to 7% of the value of fishery resources taken in dive gear.	Payment—Depending on business, due last day of month following end of calendar quarter or April 1 after close of calendar year.
	Fishery resource landing tax—For a developing commercial fish species, 1% of the value of the fishery resource at the place of landing.	Report and payment— before April 1.
	For a fish species other than a developing species, 3% of value of fishery resource at place of landing.	
	Salmon enhancement tax—based on the location of purchase or export, 1% to 30%.	Report—March 1. Payment—last day of next month.
	Seafood marketing assessment—For processors who purchase more than $50,000 of seafood products annually, 0.5% of the value paid to fishermen.	Report and payment— before April 1.

Tax	Basis—Rates	Due Dates
Cigarette and tobacco products taxes.	Effective July 1, 2006, $1.80 per pack of 20 cigarettes. Effective July 1, 2007, $2 per pack of 20. Cigarettes manufactured by a nonparticipating manufacturer, 10.25¢ per cigarette ($2.05 per pack of 20). Cigarettes manufactured by a nonparticipating manufacturer, 9.25¢ per cigarette ($1.85 per pack of 20). Tobacco products, other than cigarettes, 75% of the wholesale sales price.	Reports and payments— Last day of each month.
Insurance companies tax.	Domestic and foreign companies, 2.7% up to $100,000; $1/10$ of 1% in excess of $100,000; hospital and medical service corporations, 6% of gross premiums less claims paid; title insurers, 1%; wet marine and transportation contracts, 0.75%; nonadmitted and independently procured insurance, 3%, except 0.75% on marine contracts. Foreign companies subject to retaliatory taxes.	Reports—Before March 2; unauthorized insurance, within 30 days after procuring insurance. Payment—On or before March 1.
Vehicle rental tax.	Passenger vehicle tax—10% of the total fees and costs for the lease or rental of passenger vehicles. Recreational vehicle tax— 3% of the total fees and costs for the lease or rental of recreational vehicles.	Return and payment—April 30, July 31, October 31, and January 31
Tire fees.	Tire fee—$2.50 per tire on sales of new tires for motor vehicles designed for use on a highway. Studded tires—$5 per tire for tires studded with metal studs or spikes sold or installed on a motor vehicle designed for use on a highway.	Return and payment—April 30, July 30, October 30, January 30.
Estate tax.	Basic federal estate tax credit for state death taxes reduced proportionately on account of property outside state.	Return and payment— within 15 months after death.

Arizona

Tax System.—The revenue system of Arizona is based on a general property tax at uniform rates in the taxing district in which the property is located. The property tax is supplemented by taxes on income, occupations, and privileges. An outline of the Arizona tax system follows:

Tax	Basis—Rates	Due Dates
Corporate organization, qualification, and annual registration fees.	Domestic—filing articles of incorporation, $50. Additional $35 may be imposed for expedited service.	Domestic—fee paid at time of incorporation.
	Foreign—filing application to transact business, $150. Additional $35 may be imposed for expedited service.	Foreign—fee paid at time of qualification.
	Annual report, $45.	Initial date determined by Commission. Same date for future years.
General income tax.	Individuals—2006 rates: For married taxpayers filing jointly and heads of households: $0 to $20,000, 2.73%; $20,001 to $50,000, 3.04%; $50,001 to $100,000, 3.55%; $100,001 to $300,000, 4.48%; over $300,000, 4.79%. For single filers and married filing separately: $0 to $10,000, 2.73%; $10,001 to $25,000, 3.04%; $25,001 to $50,000, 3.55%; $50,001 to $150,000, 4.48%; $150,001 and over, 4.79%. 2007 and thereafter: For married taxpayers filing jointly and heads of households: $0 to $20,000, 2.59%; $20,001 to $50,000, 2.88%; $50,001 to $100,000, 3.36%; $100,001 to $300,000, 4.24%; over $300,000, 4.54%. For single filers and married filing separately: $0 to $10,000, 2.59%; $10,001 to $25,000, 2.88%; $25,001 to $50,000, 3.36%; $50,001 to $150,000, 4.24%; $150,001 and over, 4.54%.	Returns—April 15 or 15th day of 4th month after close of income year.
	Withholding required.	Payment—corporations, tax due by the 15th day of 4th month after close of income year; corporations having a tax liability in excess of credits that is at least $1,000 must make estimated payments at the same time such payments are due for federal purposes. Individuals, with return.
	Corporations and financial institutions—6.968%. Minimum tax: $50.	

Tax	Basis—Rates	Due Dates
General property tax and private car companies tax.	Property tax—sum of state, county and municipal rates fixed to meet budget. If not statutorily prescribed, measured by market value of real and personal property; property is divided into 9 classes and assessed at from 1% to 25%, depending upon classification. For 2006 through 2008 tax years, the state equalization assistance rate is zero. Beginning in the 2009 tax year, the rate will be $0.4358.	Property tax—Annual Statements—general business report statement, April 1 (except property leased or rented from inventory must be filed with the county assessor not later than the 10th day of each month for the previous month's activity); railroads and telecommunication companies, April 1. Payment—50% on October 1, the remaining 50% is due on March 1.
	Private car companies tax—equal to average rate of levy for all purposes in the several taxing districts of the state for the current year. Full cash value of property used in interstate and intrastate business.	Private car companies tax—Report—April 1. Payment—November 1.
	Lease excise tax on government property—based on space and use and ranging from 50¢ to $1.75 per sq. ft. Tax rates reduced by 20% every 10 years.	Report and payment—Dec. 1.
Rental occupancy tax (repealed eff. 11/1/2006).	Rental occupancy tax—3% on preexisting leases.	Reports and payments—on or before last day of month for rents received preceding month.
Alcoholic beverage tax.	Excise—sold at wholesale: spirituous liquor, $3 per gal.; vinous liquor to and including 24% alcohol, 84¢ per gal.; over 24% alcohol, 25¢ per 8 ozs.; malt liquor and hard cider, 16¢ per gal.	Reports and payments—Excise—20th day of month after tax accrues.
Motor vehicle fuel tax, use fuel tax.	Motor vehicle fuel—18¢ per gallon of motor fuel imported, manufactured, processed or possessed. Aviation fuel distributors pay an additional 5¢ per gallon tax.	Gasoline and aviation fuel—Reports and payment—on or before 27th day of each month for preceding month.
	Use fuel tax—26¢ per gallon, except no use tax on alternative fuels and 18¢ per gallon on vehicles exempt from gross weight fees. Alternatively, single-trip permits may be obtained for amounts ranging from $16 to $780.	Use fuel—collected and remitted by suppliers as advance payments and added to the price of use fuel and to be recovered from the consumer; tax imposed when fuel is imported into state or is removed from terminal or bulk plant for delivery within state.
	Jet fuel excise and use tax—3.05¢ per gallon for the first 10 million gallons; amounts over 10 million gallons are not subject to tax.	Jet fuel taxes—Reports and payments—same as sales tax.
	Underground storage tank tax—1¢ per gallon of regulated substance placed in a tank.	Returns and payments—March 31.
Severance tax.	Mining—2.5% of net severance base; Timbering (repealed 10/31/2006)—$2.13 per 1,000 board feet for products cut from ponderosa pine; $1.51 per 1,000 board feet for products cut from all other timber.	Returns and payments—same as provided under transaction privilege (sales) tax.

Tax	Basis—Rates	Due Dates
Cigarette, cigar, and tobacco products tax.	Cigarettes—$1.18 per pack of 20.	Reports—cigarette distributors, within 48 hours after receipt of unstamped merchandise. Distributors of cigars and tobacco products other than cigarettes, 20th day of month following accrual.
	Cigars—26.3¢ on each 20 small cigars, or fraction thereof, weighing 3 lbs. or less per 1,000; other cigars, 13¢ on each 3 retailing for 5¢ each or less and 13¢ on each retailing for more than 5¢.	
	Smoking tobacco, snuff, etc.—13.3¢ per oz.	
	Plug tobacco—3.3¢ per oz.	Payment—cigarettes, by purchase of stamps, payment for which may be made by the 20th day of each month by qualified distributors. Cigars and other tobacco products, with return.
Realty transfer fee.	$2 per deed or contract required to be recorded.	Payment—prior to recording the deed or contract.
Transaction privilege (sales) tax and use tax.	Transaction privilege (sales) tax rate: 5.6% of gross income on retail sales, motor carriers, public utilities, telephone and telegraph, railroads and aircraft, oil and gas pipelines, private car lines, newspapers and periodicals, printing, contracting, retailing, restaurants, amusements, personal property rentals; 3.125% of gross income on mining; 5.5% of gross income on transient lodgings.	Returns and payment—20th day of each month. Quarterly or annual tax payments are authorized for certain small taxpayers. A taxpayer with liability of $1 million or more in the preceding year or such anticipated liability in the current year must make an annual estimated payment of 50% of total liability for May or for the first 15 days of June, to be paid on June 20.
	Use tax—same rate as sales tax for the same type of transaction or business activity on sales price of tangible personal property purchased from a retailer.	
Utilities tax.	Toll roads, ferries and bridges—2% of gross receipts.	Reports and payments— quarterly.
Telecommunication service excise tax.	Telecommunication service excise tax— Beginning July 1, 2001, through June 30, 2006, the tax is 37¢ per month for each activated wire and wireless service account; for fiscal years beginning July 1, 2006, though June 30, 2007, the tax is 28¢; and for fiscal years beginning July 2007, the rate is 20¢ per month. A tax to finance telecommunications for the hearing-impaired is imposed at the rate of 1.1% of gross receipts.	Reports and payments— monthly. Large taxpayers ($100,000 or more) must report and pay estimated tax for the first 15 days of each month on or before the 25th day of the current month.
Water use tax.	Tax on water use—0.65¢ per 1,000 gallons of water.	Reports and payments— same as transaction privilege (sales) tax.

Tax	Basis—Rates	Due Dates
Insurance premiums tax.	2% of net premiums, except 2.2% for fire insurance premiums (except 0.66% for fire insurance premiums or property located in an unincorporated city or town that procures the services of a private fire company); 3% for surplus line brokers and industrial insureds contracting with unauthorized insurers; 2% for hospital and medical service corporations, prepaid dental plan organizations, health care service organizations, health care providers of Medicaid services, and prepaid legal insurance; 0.4312% of net premiums from insurance carried on or for vehicles.	Returns and payment—March 1. Insurers owing $2,000 or more for the preceding year must file a report on or before the 15th day of each month from March through August and pay 15% of the amount required to be paid during the preceding calendar year.
	Foreign companies subject to retaliatory taxes.	Surplus lines tax returns—semiannually March 1 and September 1; payment—March 1 or September 1, but not delinquent until 30 days thereafter.
		Health care providers of Medicaid services—four installments of estimated tax payments due by March 15, June 15, September 15, and December 15 of each year.
Estate tax; generation-skipping transfer tax.	Estate tax does not apply to decedents whose date of death is on or after January 1, 2006.	Returns and payment—at time federal return is filed.
	Generation-skipping transfer tax—Tax imposed to absorb federal generation-skipping transfer tax credit.	

Arkansas

Tax System.—The revenue system of Arkansas is based on a gross receipts tax, which is supplemented by (1) state taxes, part of the revenue from which in some cases is shared by local governments, on occupations, franchises and privileges, and (2) municipal license taxes and inspection fees that the General Assembly permits the local governments to exact. An outline of the Arkansas tax system follows:

Tax	Basis—Rates	Due Dates
Corporate organization and qualification fees.	$50 filing fee for articles of incorporation, $45 for online filing.	Domestic—at time of incorporation or increase of capital stock.
	$300 filing fee for application of foreign corporation to move domicile to Arkansas.	Foreign—at time of qualification or increase of capital stock employed.
	All foreign or domestic mutual corporations having no capital stock must pay $500 for the filing of articles of incorporation.	
Corporation franchise tax.	Mutual assessment corporations and nonstock corporations are subject to a flat tax of $300.	Reports and payments—May 1.
	Mortgage loan corporations—0.3% of the proportion of the par value of outstanding capital stock that its aggregate outstanding loans made in the state bear to the total aggregate outstanding loans made in all states. Minimum, $300. Legal reserve mutual insurance corporations—Assets of less than $100,000,000, $300. Assets of $100,000,000 or more, $400.	
	Insurance companies—Outstanding capital stock of less than $500,000, $300. Outstanding capital stock of more than $500,000, $400. Other corporations—0.3% of the corporation's outstanding capital stock that is apportioned to Arkansas. Minimum, $150.	

Tax	Basis—Rates	Due Dates
Income tax.	Individuals (for 2005): Less than $3,499 of net taxable income, the tax rate is 1%; at least $3,500, but not more than $6,999, the tax rate is 2.5% minus $52.49; at least $7,000, but not more than $10,499, the tax rate is 3.5% minus $122.48; at least $10,500, but not more than $17,499, the tax rate is 4.5% minus $227.47; at least $17,500, but not more than $29,199, the tax rate is 6.0% minus $489.96; and $29,200 and over, the tax rate is 7.0% minus $781.95.	Returns and payments— Personal income tax returns for the preceding calendar year are due on or before April 15. Corporate income tax returns for the preceding calendar year must be filed before March 15. A corporate income tax return for a fiscal year must be filed on or before the expiration of $2^{1}/_{2}$ months after the end of the period covered. Returns for cooperative associations for the preceding calendar year must be filed before September 16, or on or before the expiration of $8^{1}/_{2}$ months after the end of the period covered if the return is for a fiscal year. If corporation has federal extension, corporation has until federal extension date to file Arkansas returns. Declaration of estimated tax—Corporations or individuals expecting a tax liability of more than $1,000 must file a declaration on Form AR1100ESCT before the 16th day of the 4th month of the taxpayer's income year. The estimated tax may be paid in full at the time the declaration is filed or, if the estimated tax is greater than $1,000, the taxpayer may elect to pay it in four equal installments. Taxpayers must file the declaration and make the first or full estimated tax payment by the 15th day of the 4th month of the income year. Subsequent installment payments for corporate income taxpayers are due by the 15th day of the 6th, 9th, and 12th months of the income year. Subsequent payments for personal income taxpayers are due by the 15th day of the 6th and 9th months of the income year and the 15th day of the first month of the following year.

Tax	Basis—Rates	Due Dates
	Corporations—Graduated corporate tax rates are imposed at the following levels on net income not exceeding $100,000: $0 to $3,000—1%; $3,001 to $6,000—2%; $6,001 to $11,000—3%; and $11,001 to $25,000—5%. For net income of $25,001 through $100,000, the tax is $940 plus 6% of the excess over $25,000. For net income exceeding $100,000, the tax is $5,440 plus 6.5% of the excess over $100,000. Nonresidents and foreign corporations—same except that tax is imposed only on net income earned in Arkansas.	
General property tax.	Sum of county, municipal and school rates fixed to meet budgets. Measured by 20% of true or actual market value of real and tangible personal property. No state levy. Intercounty public transportation carriers—average of levies throughout state.	Returns—Real property, May 31; tangible personal property, April 10; utilities, March 1; motor carriers, March 31; private car companies, April 1. Payments—utilities and carriers: 25% 3rd Monday in April, 25% 2nd Monday in June, 50% October 10; others: October 10.
Tourism tax.	2% on the gross proceeds or gross receipts derived from the service of furnishing condominiums, townhouses, rental houses, guest rooms, suites, or other accommodations, and camp or trailer spaces (except federal campgrounds) by hotels, motels, lodging houses, tourist camps or courts, and any other provider of accommodations to transient guests, and the admission price to tourist attractions. The tax is also imposed on rentals of watercraft, boat motors and related motor equipment, life jackets and cushions, water skis, and oars or paddles by businesses engaged in the rental of watercraft.	Reports and payments—same as other gross receipts taxes.
Alcoholic beverages tax.	Excise—$2.50 per gallon of spirituous liquor; $1.00 per gallon of premixed spirituous liquor; 50¢ per gallon of light spirituous liquor; 75¢ per gallon of vinous liquor except native wines; 25¢ per gallon of light wine except native light wine; $7.50 per 32-gallon barrel of beer with an alcoholic content of 5% or less by weight; 20¢ per gallon of malt liquor. Additional taxes—5¢ per case of native wine, sparkling and still wines including light wines, liquor, cordials, liqueurs, premixed and light spirituous liquors, and specialties as having an alcoholic content of less than 21% by weight; 20¢ per case on liquor, cordials, liqueurs, premixed spirituous liquors, and specialties having an alcoholic content of 21% or more by weight.	Payment—The tax on malt liquors is due with the report. The 3% excise tax on retail receipts of liquor, cordials, liqueurs, specialties, and wine is due on or before the 20th day of each month. Licensed wholesale distributors and importers of spirituous liquors pay the excise tax on or before the 15th day of the month. The tax due on wines, including native wine, is due with the report.

Tax	Basis—Rates	Due Dates
	A consumer enforcement tax of 25¢ is levied upon each 32-gallon barrel of beer. The holder of a permit to sell or manufacture native brandy must pay a $1.00 tax per gallon sold. A privilege tax of 75¢ per gallon is imposed on native wines sold at the winery or in Arkansas, and a privilege tax of 25¢ per gallon is imposed on all light wine. An Arkansas winery importing fruits or vegetables grown outside the state for use in making wines is taxed at the rate of 75¢ per gallon on wines produced from those imported fruits and vegetables. An Arkansas winery is also taxed 75¢ per gallon on all wines imported into Arkansas for blending if the wines are sold in Arkansas. A special alcoholic beverage excise tax of 3% is levied upon all retail receipts or proceeds from the sale of liquor, cordials, liqueurs, specialties, sparkling and still wines, native wines, and beer sold for off-premise consumption. A supplemental tax of 10% is levied on alcoholic beverages (other than beer and wine) sold in hotels and restaurants, and private clubs (but not bed and breakfast private clubs) to members for the preparation and serving of mixed drinks and for the cooling and serving of beer and wine. An additional supplemental tax of 4% is levied on alcoholic beverages sold in private clubs to members for the preparation and serving of mixed drinks from the private stocks of the members for consumption only on the premises where served.	
		Reports—Wholesalers of malt liquors: on or before the 15th of the month following the month in which the wholesaler obtains delivery. Beer wholesalers: on or before the 15th day of the month following the month in which the wholesaler acquired possession of the beer. Licensed wholesale distributors and importers of spirituous liquors: on or before the 15th day of each month. Wholesalers and importers of wine: on or before the 15th day of the month following the month of delivery. Retailers of liquor and wine: on or before the 20th day of each month for the preceding month. Producers and manufacturers of native wine: monthly.
	A native brewer must pay a tax at the rate of $7.50 per barrel, and proportionately for larger and smaller gallonages per barrel, on all beer and malt beverages in quantities of up to 60,000 barrels per year and sold or offered for sale in the state.	

Tax	Basis—Rates	Due Dates
Fuel taxes.	21.5¢ per gallon of motor fuels sold or used, or purchased for sale or use in the state; 22.5¢ per gallon of distillate special fuel sold, used, or consumed in the state; 16.5¢ per gallon of liquefied gas. Special fuels: An additional fee not to exceed 0.2¢ per gallon may be imposed on motor fuel or special fuel depending on balance in Petroleum Storage Tank Trust Fund.	Reports and payments—20th day of the month following the reporting month for pipeline companies, water transportation companies, and common carriers transporting distillate special fuels within Arkansas, and persons, other than distributors, purchasing or acquiring motor fuel by pipeline, tank car, tank truck, or cargo lots who sell, use, or dispose of the motor fuel for delivery in the state. 25th day of the month following the reporting month for carriers transporting motor fuel, pipeline companies, water transportation companies, and common carriers transporting distillate special fuels within Arkansas, persons and terminals, other than distributors, purchasing or acquiring motor fuel by pipeline, tank car, tank truck, or cargo lots that sell, use, or dispose of the motor fuel for delivery in the state, distributors of motor fuels, suppliers of distillate special fuels, alternative fuels suppliers, and liquefied gas special fuels suppliers and dealers. Reports must be filed, even if no tax is due, until the taxpayer notifies the Director in writing that he or she is no longer liable for the reports. 25th day following each calendar quarter for liquefied gas special fuel interstate users and interstate users of alternative fuels. Last day of the month following each calendar quarter for interstate users of gasoline and interstate users of distillate special fuel.
	Alternative fuels tax—5¢ to 16.5¢ per equivalent gallon, depending on number of vehicles licensed in state to use such fuels.	

Tax	Basis—Rates	Due Dates
Severance or production tax; oil and gas conservation tax.	Severance—barite, bauxite, titanium ore, manganese and manganiferous ores, zinc ore, and cinnabar: 15¢ per ton;	Severance—reports and payment: within 25 days after end of month.
	coal, lignite and iron ore: 2¢ per ton (8¢ per ton additional tax on coal);	
	lead ore: the greater of 15¢ per ton or 10% of market value;	
	gypsum not used for, or sold for, manufacturing in Arkansas into ultimate consumers' goods, chemical grade limestone, silica sand and dimension stone: 1 1/2¢ per ton;	
	crushed stone including, but not limited to, chert, granite, slate, novaculite, limestone, construction sand, gravel, clay, chalk, shale and marl: 1¢ per ton (additional tax of 15¢ per ton on stone and crushed stone (including chert, granite, slate, novaculite, limestone but excluding limestone for agricultural purposes), construction sand, gravel, clay, chalk, shale, and marl);	
	natural gas: 0.3¢ per MCF produced;	
	oil: 5% of market value at time and point of severance (plus additional 25 mills per barrel and additional 2¢ per barrel) for wells producing more than 10 barrels per day; 4% for wells producing 10 or fewer barrels per day (plus an additional 25 mills per barrel and an additional 2¢ per barrel);	
	timber: pine, 17.8¢ per ton; all other, 12.5¢ per ton;	
	salt water yielding bromine and products used in bromine production, $2.45 (plus additional 30¢) per 1,000 barrels;	
	diamonds, fuller's earth, ochre, natural asphalt, native sulphur, salt, pearls, other precious stones, whetstone, novaculite, and all other natural resources except gypsum: 5% of fair market value at time of severance;	
	others: 5% of market value at time and point of severance.	
Tobacco products tax.	Cigarettes—$29.50 per 1,000 cigarettes (composed of $15.75 per 1,000 cigarettes (59.5¢ per pack of 20) plus additional taxes in the combined amount of $13.75). The tax may be lower for cities adjoining state lines.	Reports and payments—15th of each month.
	Tobacco products—32% of manufacturer's selling price (composed of 23% of manufacturer's selling price prior to any discounts or deals, plus additional taxes at the combined rate of 9%).	
	Cigarette papers—25¢ per package of approximately 32 sheets.	
Realty transfer tax.	$3.30 per $1,000 of actual consideration on transactions in excess of $100.	Payment—prior to recording, evidenced by tax stamps.

Tax	Basis—Rates	Due Dates
Gross receipts tax and use tax; utilities' compensating tax.	Gross receipts tax—6% of gross proceeds of retail sales of tangible personal property, utility services, telephone and telecommunications services, lodging, cleaning services, cable television services, printing services, photography and admission to places of amusement. Gross receipts tax in Texarkana is 7%.	Gross receipts—20th of each month; if average net sales for year are over $200,000 per month, 40% of monthly average is due by the 12th and 24th of each month, or 80% by the 24th of each month, with remaining 20% due with the regular report on the 20th day of the following month. If the average amount of tax due for the previous fiscal year does not exceed $100 per month, quarterly reports and payments are due on the 20th day of July, October, January and April. If the average amount of tax due for the previous fiscal year does not exceed $25 per month, annual reports and payments are due on January 20.
	Use tax—6% of tangible personal property purchased outside the state for storage, use, distribution or consumption in the state. Use tax in Texarkana is 7%.	Use—reports and payments: 20th of each month.
Nursing facilities quality assurance fee.	6% of the aggregate annual Arkansas gross receipts paid as compensation for services provided by the facilities to their residents.	Reports—due on the 10th day of each month listing the patient days for the preceding month. Payment for the previous month is due and payable by the 30th of each month.
Public utilities tax.	Not in excess of 0.4% of gross earnings of public utilities from properties in the state or gross revenues of rail carriers from operations in the state.	Reports—Public utilities and carriers, statements due March 31; payment due August 31.
	Natural gas pipeline (greater than 50 miles) transporters, owners, and operators—in proportion to the total pipeline safety program's cost that each transporter's, owner's, or operator's miles of natural gas pipeline in Arkansas, excluding service lines in distribution systems, bears to the total number of miles of pipeline in the state. Each natural gas transporter, owner, or operator of pipeline facilities of fewer than 50 miles must pay a fee equal to the product of 0.0015 multiplied by the total cost of operating the pipeline safety program for the assessment year.	Natural gas pipeline transporters, owners, and operators do not have to submit a certified statement of their gross earnings on or before March 31; instead, they must pay the annual assessment fee on or before June 30.

Tax	Basis—Rates	Due Dates
Insurance companies tax.	Foreign and domestic life and disability, 2.5% of net premiums; other insurers, except wet marine or foreign trade insurers, 2.5% of net premiums. Wet marine and foreign trade insurers, 0.75% of gross underwriting profits. Non-profit hospital and medical service corporations, 2.5% of gross receipts. Unauthorized insurers, 2%. Surplus line brokers, 4% of direct premiums written; health maintenance organizations, 2.5%. Legal insurers, 2.5% of gross premiums; Worker's Compensation, up to 3%.	Reports—Annual report of property and casualty insurers, May 1. HMOs subject to Arkansas insurance tax are required to file quarterly financial reports with the Arkansas Insurance Commissioner in addition to the annual financial report due March 1.
	Foreign companies are subject to retaliatory taxation if rates in home state are higher than those in Arkansas, except companies more than 15% of whose stock is owned by an Arkansas corporation.	Payments—Life and disability insurers, wet marine and foreign trade insurance, legal insurance premiums, health maintenance organizations, and workers' compensation carriers, made on a quarterly estimated basis and reconciled annually when the report is filed. Self-insurers tax on workers' compensation, April 1. Unauthorized insurers, within 30 days after the insurance was procured, continued, or renewed. Surplus lines brokers, within 60 days following the end of the month during which the insurance was procured. Hospital and medical service corporations, on or before March 1.
Estate tax.	Equal to maximum federal estate tax credit apportioned among states where property is located. Repealed for estates of decedents dying on or after January 1, 2005.	Payment—within 9 months after death.

California

Tax System.—The California revenue system is based on (1) state taxes on franchises, personal incomes, privileges and occupations and (2) municipal taxes and inspection fees that the legislature permits the local government to exact. An outline of the California tax system follows:

Tax	Basis—Rates	Due Dates
Corporate organization and qualification fees.	Domestic—$100 for filing articles of incorporation providing for shares; $30 for filing articles of incorporation not providing for shares. $100 for filing certificate of merger ($150 if merger involves corporations with one or more other types of business entities). Annual statement of information filing fee, $20.	Domestic—at time of incorporation or increase of capital stock. Report—due 90 days after filing original articles and annually thereafter.
	Foreign—the same fees applicable to domestic apply to foreign.	Foreign—at time of qualification and biennially thereafter.
Corporation franchise tax.	Corporations and LLCs electing to be treated as a corporation, 8.84% of net income derived from business transacted in California. S corporations, 1.5%. S corporation that is a bank or financial institution, 3.5%. Minimum, $800. No prepayment or minimum fee for corporations that qualify to do business after 1999 and for all corporations other than credit unions after 2000. A 6.65% alternative minimum tax is imposed.	Corporation franchise tax—15th day of 3rd month following income year; 15th day of 9th month following income year for agricultural cooperatives. Estimated payment due 15th day of 4th, 6th, 9th, and 12th months (due 15th day of 4th month if estimated tax does not exceed minimum tax).
Corporate income tax.	Direct tax on net income, derived from sources within the state, of corporations not taxable under Bank and Corporation Franchise Tax Act at same rate as franchise tax. Minimum, $800. A 6.65% alternative minimum tax is imposed.	Corporate income tax—15th day of 3rd month following income year; 15th day of 9th month following income year for agricultural cooperatives. Estimated payment due 15th day of 4th, 6th, 9th, and 12th months (due 15th day of 4th month if estimated tax does not exceed minimum tax).
Bank and financial corporations tax.	Equal to corporate franchise tax rate plus 2% (10.84%). Minimum, $800. An alternative minimum tax is imposed equal to the corporate rate plus 2%.	Bank and financial corporations tax—Returns and payments—15th day of 3rd month following income year. Estimated payment due 15th day of 4th, 6th, 9th, and 12th months (due 15th day of 4th month if estimated tax does not exceed minimum tax).

Tax	Basis—Rates	Due Dates
LLC tax.	$800 minimum franchise tax for an LLC classified as a partnership or as a "disregarded entity" doing business in California or that has articles of organization accepted or a certificate of registration issued by the Secretary of State. Fees are determined as follows: for income of $250,000 or more but less than $500,000, $900; $500,000 but less than $1,000,000, $2,500; $1,000,000 but less than $5,000,000, $6,000; $5,000,000 or more, $11,790.	LLC tax—15th day of 4th month after the beginning of the taxable year (fiscal year) or April 15 (calendar year).
Personal income tax.	**2006 rates:** For single taxpayers, married filing separately, and fiduciaries: $0 to $6,622, 1%; over $6,622 to $15,698, $66.22 plus 2% of the amount over $6,622; over $15,698 to $24,776, $247.74 plus 4% of the amount over $15,698; over $24,776 to $34,394, $610.86 plus 6% of the amount over $24,776; over $34,394 to $43,467, $1,187.94 plus 8% of the amount over $34,394; $43,467 and over, $1,913.78 plus 9.3% of the amount over $43,467. For married filing jointly and qualifying widow(er): $0 to $13,244, 1%; over $13,244 to $31,396, $132.44 plus 2% of the amount over $13,244; over $31,396 to $49,552, $495.48 plus 4% of the amount over $31,396; over $49,552 to $68,788, $1,221.72 plus 6% of the amount over $49,552; over $68,788 to $86,934, $2,375.88 plus 8% of the amount over $68,788; over $86,934, $3,827.56 plus 9.3% of the amount over $86,934. For heads of households: $0 to $13,251, 1%; over $13,251 to $31,397, $132.51 plus 2% of the amount over $13,251; over $31,397 to $40,473, $495.43 plus 4% of the amount over $31,397; over $40,473 to $50,090, $858.47 plus 6% of the amount over $40,473; over $50,090 to $59,166, $1,435.59 plus 8% of the amount over $50,090; over $59,166, $2,161.57 plus 9.3% of the amount over $59,166. Effective beginning with 2005 taxable year, additional 1% tax on income in excess of $1 million.	Returns and payment—April 15 following the close of the calendar year. Taxpayers with a fiscal year different from the calendar year, 15th day of 4th month after close of fiscal year. Partnerships—calendar year taxpayers, April 15 after close of calendar year. Fiscal year taxpayers, 15th day of 4th month after end of taxable year.
General property tax.	Rates fixed locally to meet budget. Property is assessed at 100% of full cash value. Intangible property is excluded from the value. The maximum amount of property tax on realty is limited to 1% of full cash value of the property (the 1975-76 assessed value of property is the base value, unless property is newly constructed or has changed ownership) plus taxes or assessments to pay interest and debt on acquisition or improvement of property approved by voters.	Returns—between January 1 and April 1. Payment—on secured personalty, Nov. 1; on unsecured personalty, January 1; on realty, $1/2$ by Nov. 1 and $1/2$ by Feb. 1.

Tax	Basis—Rates	Due Dates
Alcoholic beverage tax.	Excise—beer, $1.40 per gallon; still wines to 14% alcohol, 20¢ per gallon; over 14% alcohol, 20¢ per gallon; champagne and sparkling wines, 30¢ per gallon; sparkling hard cider, 20¢ per gallon; distilled spirits, 100 proof strength or less, $3.30 per gallon; above proof strength, $6.60 per gallon; nonliquid distilled spirits to 50% alcohol, 0.02¢ per ounce; over 50% alcohol, 0.04¢ per ounce.	Excise tax—Reports and payment—manufacturers, wine growers and importers, monthly by the 15th; common carriers, 1st day of 2nd month following each monthly period.
Fuel taxes.	Motor fuel tax—18¢ per gallon.	Returns and payment—25th day of following month.
	Diesel fuel—18¢ per gallon.	Returns and payment—last day of each month following the calendar month the tax liability accrues (quarterly for interstate truckers).
	Aircraft jet fuel—2¢ per gallon.	Same as motor fuels tax.
	Use fuel—18¢ per gallon; liquefied petroleum gas, 6¢ per gallon; compressed natural gas, 0.07¢ per 100 cubic feet of compressed natural gas used; liquid natural gas, 6¢ per gallon; ethanol or methanol containing not more than 15% gasoline or diesel fuel, $1/2$ the use fuel tax rate.	Reports and payments—last day of month following each calendar quarter.
	Annual flat rate tax—in lieu of taxes on liquefied petroleum gas, liquid natural gas or compressed natural gas, owners or operators of vehicles using such fuels exclusively in California may pay a tax ranging from $36 if vehicle unladen weight is 4,000 lbs. or less to $168 if 12,001 lbs. or over.	Annual flat rate—payment due annually.
	Lubricating oil—oil manufacturers pay 4¢ for each quart, or 16¢ for each gallon, of lubricating oil sold or transferred in, or imported into, California.	Reports and payment—due on or before the last day of the month following the end of each quarter.
Severance (oil and gas) tax.	5.38953 cents for the 2005-2006 fiscal year per barrel of oil produced or per 10,000 cubic feet of natural gas produced (rate determined annually based upon estimate of annual conservation costs).	Reports—monthly reports due on or before the last day of each month; annual reports due by March 1. Payment—assessments $10 but less than $500 due July 1 (delinquent after August 15); assessments $500 or more due July 1 ($1/2$ delinquent after August 15; remaining $1/2$ delinquent after February 1).

Tax	Basis—Rates	Due Dates
Timber yield tax.	2.9% of timber harvested.	Returns—filed the last day of the month following the quarter in which scaling occurs and for every quarter that the individual is registered as a timber owner, regardless of whether scaling occurs.
Cigarette and tobacco products tax.	Cigarette tax is 18.5 mills ($0.37 per pack of 20) plus an additional surtax of $0.50 per pack of 20, for a total tax rate of $0.87 per pack of 20. The rate of tax imposed on all tobacco products other than cigarettes is 46.76% of wholesale cost.	Reports, returns, payments—filed by the 25th day of each month. Payment is also due by the 25th day of each month. From 1/1/04 until 1/1/07, distributors electing twice-monthly remittance option—1st payment, 5th day of month; 2nd payment, 25th day of month. The return and report must be filed even if no distributions were made during the reporting period.
Sales and use taxes.	Sales—6.25% of gross receipts from retail sales of tangible personal property.	Returns and payments—quarterly by last day of month following each quarterly period. Prepayments required of taxpayers whose average monthly estimated measure of tax liability is $17,000 or more.
	Use—6.25% of sales price of tangible personal property purchased for storage, use or consumption.	Use tax due on or before 15th day of 4th month after tax year in which property becomes taxable.
Utility surcharges.	Effective January 1, 2005, the rate is $0.00022 per kilowatt-hour of electricity consumed in the state purchased from an electric utility. Intrastate telephone service surcharge—between 0.5% and 0.75% of gross receipts. For the period from November 1, 2005, through October 31, 2006, the emergency telephone user surcharge is 0.65%.	Returns and payments from electric utilities are due by the last day of the month following each calendar quarter; telephone service—on or before the last day of the 2nd month of each calendar quarter covering the preceding quarter.
Insurance companies tax.	General insurers—2.35% of gross premiums less reinsurance, return premiums and dividends; pension and profit-sharing plans, 0.5%.	Reports—April 1, except June 15 for ocean marine insurers and March 1 for surplus line brokers.
	Surplus line brokers—3% of gross premiums less 3% of return premiums.	

Tax	Basis—Rates	Due Dates
	Ocean marine—5%—underwriting profit apportioned to California on basis of gross premiums.	
	Foreign companies subject to retaliatory taxes.	
		Payment—with return April 1 except ocean marine insurers (June 15) and surplus line brokers (March 1). Quarterly prepayments due 4/1, 6/15, 9/15, and 12/15 from insurers whose annual tax for the preceding calendar year was $5,000 or more. Surplus line brokers whose annual tax for the preceding calendar year was $5,000 or more must make monthly installment payments on or before the 1st day of the 3rd calendar month following the month in which business was conducted.
Estate tax.	Estate tax equal to maximum credit for state death taxes under federal estate tax law attributable to property located in California. Estate tax credit has been repealed, effective for estates of decedents who die on or after January 1, 2005.	Estate tax—returns, on or before the date the federal estate tax return is due; payment, within 9 months of decedent's death. A California "Additional Estate Tax Return" is required to be filed whenever a federal "Additional Estate Tax Return" is required. The California "Additional Estate Tax Return" is due and the tax liability payable on or before 6 months from the date of disposition or cessation. The return must be filed even if no tax is ultimately due. Effective for estates of decedents who die on or after January 1, 2005, a return is no longer required to be filed.
Generation-skipping tax.	Tax equal to the amount allowed as a federal credit for state generation-skipping transfer taxes.	Returns are due and payable on or after January 1st, but not later than April 15th, of the year following the calendar year when the distributions were made or the terminations occurred.

Colorado

Tax System.—The revenue system of Colorado is based on a general property tax, assessed uniformly on all property for state, county, city and town, and district purposes. The property tax is supplemented by an income tax and by taxes on privileges and occupants. An outline of the Colorado tax system follows:

Tax	Basis—Rates	Due Dates
Corporate organization and qualification fees.	Domestic—filing articles of incorporation and filing a corporate report, fee set by the Secretary of State, online $25, paper $125.	Domestic—at time of incorporation or increase of capital stock.
	Foreign—filing application for authority to transact business and filing a corporate report, fee set by the Secretary of State, $125.	Foreign—at time of qualification or increase of capital stock.
Annual report.	Paper fee, domestic or foreign $100.	Report and payment—no later than the end of the second month following the mailing of the report form by the Secretary of State.
	E-filing, domestic or foreign $10.	
General income tax.	Individuals—4.63% of federal taxable income plus alternative minimum tax (excess of 3.47% of Colorado alternative minimum taxable income over flat state income tax rate).	Returns and payments—15th day of 4th month after end of income year. Estimated declaration of tax due on or before the 15th day of the 4th month of the tax year; estimated payments due on or before the 15th day of the 4th, 6th, 9th and 13th (12th for corporations) months of the tax year. Employers with annual withholding liabilities of more than $50,000 are required to pay through electronic funds transfer (EFT).
	Withholding required.	
	Corporations, banks, trust, finance, savings and loan companies and cooperatives—4.63%.	
	In lieu of the corporate income tax, a qualified taxpayer may pay an alternative tax of 0.5% of gross receipts if it is required to file a return, its only activity in Colorado is making sales, it has Colorado sales of less than $100,000, and it does not own or rent real estate in Colorado.	
General property tax.	Sum of state and local rates fixed to meet budget. Based on actual value of real property and tangible personal property. For 2006, residential realty is assessed at 7.96% of actual value. All other property is assessed at 29% of actual value.	Returns—Personal property, April 15; industries classified as utilities, by April 1.
		Payment—April 30; if $25 or more ¹/₂ last day of Feb. and ¹/₂ June 15.

Tax	Basis—Rates	Due Dates
Alcoholic beverage taxes.	Excise tax—malt beverages, 3.2% beer, hard cider, 8¢ per gallon; vinous liquors except hard cider, 7.33¢ per liter (plus additional surcharge of 5¢ per liter for the first 9,000 liters, 3¢ per liter for the next 36,000 liters, and 1¢ per liter for all additional amounts on Colorado wines); spirituous liquors, 60.26¢ per liter.	Reports—wholesalers and manufacturers, 20th of each month.
		Payment—with report.
	Tax on grapes—$10 per ton.	Payment—at the time of purchase or importation, whichever is later.
Gasoline and special fuel taxes.	Gasoline—22¢ per gallon of motor fuel sold, distributed or used (5¢ per gallon less for gasoline blended with denatured alcohol), except 6¢ per gallon on gasoline used in nonturbopropeller or nonjet engine aircraft and 4¢ per gallon on gasoline used in turbopropeller or jet engine aircraft (does not apply to air carriers).	Gasoline—reports and payments—25th of each month.
	Special fuel tax—20.5¢ per gallon.	Special fuel—25th day of each month.
Severance tax.	Metallic minerals—2.25% of income over $19 million. Molybdenum ore—first 625,000 tons produced by an individual in each quarter of a taxable year are not taxed, 5¢ per ton thereafter. Oil and gas—under $25,000 of gross income, 2%; $25,000 to $99,999, 3%; $100,000 to $299,999, 4%; $300,000 and over, 5%. Oil shale—4% of gross proceeds in excess of the greater of 15,000 tons per day or 10,000 barrels per day.	Returns and payment—molybdenum ore, 15th day of the month following each quarter; all others, 15th day of 4th month after end of year. Estimated payments due on the 15th day of April, June, September, and December if annual estimated tax is more than $1,000.
Coal severance tax.	54¢ per ton after first 300,000 tons produced each quarter (adjusted quarterly to changes in producers' price index). 50% credit for coal from underground mines; additional 50% credit for production of lignitic coal.	Reports and payments—15th day of 4th month following end of tax year.
Oil and gas conservation tax.	Not to exceed 1.5 mills on each dollar of the market value at the well plus a surcharge of not to exceed 0.2 mill per dollar of market value at the well; currently, 0.5 mills per dollar value.	Reports and payments—March 1, June 1, September 1, and December 1.
Cigarette tax; tobacco products tax.	4.2¢ per cigarette (84¢ per pack of 20).	Reports—10th of each month following the month of purchase.
		Payment—evidenced by affixing stamps.
	Tobacco products—40% of manufacturer's list price.	Reports and payments—20th day of month following each quarter. Payment must accompany return.
Realty conveyance tax.	1¢ per $100 of consideration in excess of $500.	Payment—prior to recording.

Tax	Basis—Rates	Due Dates
Sales and use tax.	2.9% of gross receipts from retail sale of personalty, telephone, telegraph, gas and electric services, meals furnished the public, cover charges and room rentals, or of sales price of personalty purchased for storage, use or consumption.	Reports and payments— sales tax, before 20th of each month; use tax, before 20th day of month following month in which cumulative tax due at end of month exceeds $300. If total tax due in a calendar year is less than $300, an annual return and payment are due before following January 20. If total tax due in a year is more than $75,000, all state and local taxes must be remitted to the Department of Revenue by electronic funds transfer (EFT). Taxpayers owing less than $75,000 may choose to remit by EFT.
Insurance companies tax.	For companies maintaining a home office or regional home office in the state, 1%. For companies not maintaining a home office or regional home office in Colorado, 2% of gross premiums less reinsurance premiums and, for companies other than life, returned premiums. Captive insurers, the greater of $5,000 or the sum of (a) 0.5% of the first $25 million, plus 0.25% of the next $50 million, plus 0.1% of each dollar thereafter of the direct premiums collected and (b) 0.25% of the first $20 million, plus 0.1% of each dollar thereafter of assumed reinsurance premiums. Unauthorized insurers, 2$1/4$%. Surplus line brokers, 3%. Foreign companies subject to retaliatory taxes.	Reports and payments— March 1. Insurers whose tax exceeded $5,000 for the preceding year pay an estimated tax on the last days of April, July and October and March 1.
Estate tax.	Colorado estate tax does not apply to decedents whose date of death is on or after January 1, 2005.	
Generation-skipping tax.	Tax equal to the amount allowed as a federal credit for state generation-skipping transfer taxes.	

Connecticut

Tax System.—Connecticut derives its revenue principally from a corporation franchise tax measured by net income, a personal income tax, gasoline taxes, and sales and use taxes and from taxes imposed on specified businesses and privileges. An outline of the Connecticut tax system follows:

Tax	Basis—Rates	Due Dates
Corporate organization and qualification fees; foreign corporation fee; annual report fee.	Corporate organization—franchise—domestic—first 10,000 shares, 1¢ per share; next 90,000 shares, $1/2$¢ per share; next 900,000 shares, $1/4$¢ per share; over 1,000,000 shares, $1/5$¢ per share; minimum, $150. Increases of shares, same. Foreign—$225 annual license fee. Certificate of incorporation—$50 for stock corporations, $10 for nonstock corporations.	Corporate organization—Domestic—franchise tax—payable at time of filing application for certificate. Foreign—fee payable at time of filing application for certificate and annually thereafter.
	Annual report—Domestic, $75. Foreign, $75 ($25 for domestic and foreign nonstock companies).	Annual report—due within 30 days of organizational meeting.
Corporation business tax.	The greater of 7.5% of net income of corporations, financial institutions, domestic insurers and passenger carriers, 3.1 mills per dollar of capital holdings, or the minimum tax of $250. (Maximum, $1 million). For state banks, trust companies, national banks, mutual savings banks, or savings and loan associations, tax is the greater of 7.5% or 4% of the interest or dividends on depositors' or discount holders' savings accounts for the preceding year.	Corporation business—by first day of the month next succeeding the due date of the corporation's corresponding federal income tax return for the income year. Payments of estimated tax due on or before the 15th day of the 3rd, 6th, 9th and 12th months of the income year.
	Surcharge—For the 2006 income year, a 20% surcharge is applicable to corporations with a tax liability that is greater than the $250 minimum tax. Corporations subject to the surcharge must calculate their surcharge amounts based on their tax liability before credits. The surcharge is repealed for 2007.	
	Additional tax on oil companies—5% of gross earnings.	Oil company tax—reports and payments—last day of January, April, July, and October.
Personal income tax.	For *unmarried individuals and married individuals filing separately,* 3% on the first $10,000 of Connecticut taxable income; Connecticut taxable income over $10,000, $300 plus 5% of the excess over $10,000. For *heads of households,* 3% of the first $16,000 of Connecticut taxable income; Connecticut taxable income over $16,000, $480 plus 5% of the excess over $16,000. For *married individuals filing jointly,* 3% of the first $20,000 of Connecticut taxable income; Connecticut taxable income over $20,000, $600 plus 5% of the excess over $20,000. For *trusts or estates,* 5% of Connecticut taxable income.	Reports and payments—on or before the 15th day of the 4th month after close of tax year. Payments of estimated tax due on or before the 15th days of the 4th, 6th, 9th, and 13th months of the tax years with fewer payments due if estimated filing requirements met later in the year. Farmers and fishermen must make one payment on or before the following January 15.

Tax	Basis—Rates	Due Dates
	A net minimum tax equal to the lesser of (a) 19% of adjusted federal tentative minimum tax, or (b) 5.5% of adjusted federal alternative minimum taxable income is imposed on individuals, including residents, trusts and estates, subject to the federal alternative minimum tax. Non- and part-year residents pay the same rate but multiplied by the ratio of the adjusted federal tentative minimum tax derived from sources within the state to the adjusted federal tentative minimum tax.	Reports and payments—on or before 15th day of 4th month after close of tax year. Estimated tax declaration and payment due 15th day of 4th, 6th, 9th, and 13th months of tax year.
Property tax.	All municipalities are required to assess property at uniform rate of 70% of true and actual value.	General property—Municipalities may require payment in a single payment or in equal semiannual or quarterly payments; single payment or first installment due July 1.
Admissions tax.	10% of admission charges to places of amusement, entertainment or recreation, and club or organizational dues. The rate of tax on admission charges to motion picture shows is 6%.	Reports and payments—due on or before last day of each month for preceding month.
Alcoholic beverages tax.	Excise—beer & cider, $6 per bbl.; liquor, $4.50 per wine gal.; liquor coolers, $2.05 per wine gal.; alcohol over 100 proof, $4.50 per proof gal.; wine to 21% alcohol, 60¢ per gal. (15¢ per gal. if produced by a person who produces not more than 55,000 gallons of wine during the calendar year); over 21% alcohol and sparkling wines, $1.50 per gal.	Excise—last day of each month.
Motor fuels tax; motor carrier road tax.	Motor fuels—25¢ per gal. of motor fuel sold, distributed or used. 25¢ per gal. of gasohol sold. Each gallon of diesel fuel, natural gas, or propane is taxed at 26¢ per gal.	Motor fuels—25th of each month.
	Motor carrier road tax—Amount of fuel used in operations within the state—same as motor fuels tax.	Motor carrier road tax—April 30, July 31, October 31, January 31 for preceding calendar quarter.
Cigarette tax; tobacco products tax.	$1.51 per pack of 20 cigarettes held for sale within the state or stored or used within the state.	Report—25th day of each month; unstamped cigarettes, within 24 hours of possession.
	20% of wholesale sales price of tobacco products.	Report and payment—25th day of each month.
	$0.40 per ounce of snuff.	

Tax	Basis—Rates	Due Dates
Real estate conveyance tax; farm and forest land conveyance tax; tax on sale or transfer of controlling interest.	Real estate conveyance tax—0.75% (0.5% base rate plus additional tax of 0.25%; after 6/1/07 additional tax is 0.11%) of the consideration paid for the interest in the real property conveyed, if the consideration conveyed exceeds $2,000. Nonresidential interests (except unimproved land), in lieu of the 0.5% base tax, 1%; residential property, 0.5% on the first $800,000, 1% on the remainder. Targeted investment communities and municipalities with certain manufacturing plants may impose an additional 0.25%. Property on which mortgage payments have been delinquent for at least six months and is conveyed to the financial institution or a subsidiary of the financial institution that holds the delinquent mortgage, 0.5%.	Payment—upon recording the deed or instrument.
	Farm and forest land conveyance tax—from 10% to 1% of sales price of farm, forest or open space land sold within 10 years of classification.	Payment—at time of transfer.
	Tax on sale or transfer of controlling interest in any entity that possesses an interest in real property if present true and actual value of the interest in real property so conveyed equals or exceeds $2,000—1.11% of present true and actual value of interest in real property conveyed along with the controlling interest in such entity.	Report and payment—on or before the last day of the month following the month of the sale or transfer.
Sales tax; use tax.	Sales—6% of gross receipts of retail sales of tangible personal property and enumerated services; hotel occupancy, 12%. Sales of repair or replacement parts exclusively for use in machinery used directly in a manufacturing or agricultural production process, exempt.	Sales and use tax reports and payments—If tax liability for 12 months preceding Sept. 30 less than $1,000, annual report and payment due before last day of month following tax year-end; if less than $4,000, quarterly return and payment due by last day of month following end of calendar quarter; all other taxpayers, monthly, by last day of month following month being reported. Use tax for non-business purchases, April 15.
	Use—6% of sale price of tangible personal property stored, accepted, consumed or used within the state and enumerated business services. Sales of repair or replacement parts exclusively for use in machinery used directly in a manufacturing or agricultural production process, exempt.	
	Computer and data processing services—1%.	
Public utilities (gross earnings) taxes.	Community antenna television systems and companies providing video programming by satellite, 5%; cable, telegraph, 4.5%; railroads, 2% to 3.5%; express, 2%; municipal utilities, 5%. Residential gas, electricity, 4%.	Returns and payments—railroads, July 1; others, April 1, except electric, gas, water and power companies, by the last days of January, April, July and October. Public service companies, telephone companies, certified telecommunications service providers, May 1.

Tax	Basis—Rates	Due Dates
Public utilities (sales) taxes.	Community antenna television systems, telecommunications service, 6%.	Returns and payments— same as sales and use tax provisions.
Insurance companies tax.	Domestic—1.75% of net direct insurance premiums; hospital and medical service corporations, 2% of net direct subscriber charges received; health care centers, 1.75% of net direct subscriber charges received.	Domestic, foreign, hospital and medical service corporations, nonprofit legal service corporations— returns and payments— March 1. Insureds involved with unauthorized insurers, 60 days after insurance procured, continued or renewed. Domestic and foreign insurers' declaration and payment of estimated tax due on or before the 15th day of the 3rd, 6th, 9th and 12th months of the income year (calendar year for foreign insurers), with fewer declarations due if estimated filing requirements are met later in the year.
	Foreign—1.75% of all net direct premiums received.	
	Unauthorized insurers, 4% of gross premiums.	
	Foreign companies subject to retaliatory taxes.	
Transfer tax.	Transfer tax—Applicable to estates of those dying on or after January 1, 2005, up to $2,000,000 exempt. Rates range from 5.085% of the amount from $2,000,000 but not over $2,100,000 to $1,082,800 plus 16% of the amount over $10,100,000.	Transfer tax—Payment— within 9 months after decedent's death.
Estate and gift tax.	Estate and gift tax—Up to $2,000,000 exempt. Rates range from 5.085% of the amount from $2,000,000 but not over $2,100,000 to $1,082,800 plus 16% of the amount over $10,100,000.	Estate and gift tax—Report and payment due April 15.
Generation-skipping transfer tax.	Tax equal to the amount allowed as a federal credit for state generation-skipping transfer taxes. Not applicable to transfers after December 31, 2004.	

Delaware

Tax System.—A general property tax is imposed locally in Delaware at uniform rates upon all real property within each taxing district. Personal property is not taxed. In addition, there are state taxes upon occupations, income, franchises and privileges and municipal license and inspection fees. An outline of the Delaware tax system follows:

Tax	Basis—Rates	Due Dates
Corporate organization and qualification fees.	Domestic par-value shares: up to 20,000 authorized shares, 2¢ per share; over 20,000 but not more than 200,000 shares, 1¢ per share; over 200,000 shares, $2/5$¢ per share. Each $100 unit of authorized capital stock with par value = 1 share. No-par shares: up to 20,000 shares, 1¢ per share; over 20,000 but not more than 2 million shares, $1/2$¢ per share; over 2 million shares, $2/5$¢ per share. Minimum—$15. Certificate of incorporation—filing fee $5, plus $20 municipal fee.	Domestic—upon filing the original certificate of incorporation or an amendment providing for an increase of capital stock.
	Foreign—$80.	Foreign—at time of filing for authorization.
Annual report fee.	Foreign corporation annual report fee—$60.	Annual report—June 30.
	Domestic corporation annual report fee—$25.	Annual report—March 1.
Franchise tax.	Up to and including 3,000 authorized shares, $35; 3,001—5,000, $62.50; 5,001—10,000, $112.50; over 10,000, $112.50 plus $62.50 per each additional 10,000 shares or fraction thereof. Alternative rate, $35 if assumed no-par capital is $300,000 or less; $62.50 if assumed no-par capital is $300,001—$500,000; $112.50 if assumed no-par capital is $500,001—$1 million; additional $62.50 for each $1 million of additional assumed no-par capital. For par-value shares, $250 for each $1 million, or fraction, in excess of $1 million of assumed par-value capital. Alternate rate, regulated investment companies, $250 per $1 million of average gross assets for tax year. 50% reduction for inactive corps. Maximum—$165,000 ($75,000 for regulated investment companies). Minimum—$35.	Annual return and payment—March 1. Corporations expecting $5,000 or more in tax for the current calendar year file tentative returns and pay 40% of the tax estimated to be due on June 1, 20% by September 1, 20% by December 1 of the current year, and the remainder on March 1 of the following year. Foreign corporations—June 30.
Corporation income tax.	Corporation income—8.7% of taxable income derived from Delaware, except for certain banking organizations, headquarters management corporations, and bank and trust companies.	Corporation income—tentative returns and final returns due April 1 of following year for calendar-year taxpayers; 1st day of 4th month following close of fiscal year for fiscal-year taxpayers.

Tax	Basis—Rates	Due Dates
Personal income tax.	Individuals—2.2% of taxable income between $2,001 and $5,000; 3.9% of taxable income between $5,001 and $10,000; 4.8% of taxable income between $10,001 and $20,000; 5.2% of taxable income between $20,001 and 25,000; 5.55% of taxable income between $25,001 and $60,000; and 5.95% of taxable income above $60,000. Withholding required.	Returns and payments—April 30 for calendar-year taxpayers; for fiscal-year taxpayers, due 30th day of 4th month following close of tax year. Declarations and payments of estimated taxes due with federal declarations (April 30, June 15, September 15, and January 15), unless the Director establishes other dates.
Banks and trust companies tax.	Banking organizations—1.7% to 8.7% of taxable income. Banks and trust companies (for tax years beginning after 2006)—0.5% to 7% of taxable income.	Banks and trust companies: March 1. Estimated tax returns, 40% by June 1, 20% by September 1, 20% by December 1, and balance by March 1 of the following year.
General property tax.	Fixed locally to meet budget. No state levy. Based on assessed value of real property for county, municipal, and school district purposes. In practice, property is valued at different ratios according to locality. Personal property exempt.	Returns and payment—various dates.
Lodging tax.	8% of rental for occupancies in a hotel, motel or tourist home.	Reports and payments—15th of the following month.
Alcoholic beverage tax.	Excise—beer, $4.85 per bbl.; cider, 16¢ per gallon; wine, 97¢ per gallon; spirits 25% alcohol or less, $3.64 per gallon; spirits more than 25% alcohol, $5.46 per gallon; 100 proof alcohol, $4.85 per gallon.	Excise—reports and payments: importers, last day of each month, except that the May report is due by June 15th.
Gasoline tax.	Gasoline—23¢ per gallon of motor fuel sold or used. Special fuels—22¢ per gallon sold, delivered or used. Motor carriers fuel purchase tax—same rates as above on fuel consumed in Delaware operations.	Reports and payments—25th of each month. Purchase tax—last day of April, July, October and January (annual reports and payments are authorized).
Cigarette tax; tobacco products tax.	Cigarettes—27.5 mills per cigarette (55¢ per package of 20); tobacco products—15% of wholesale sale price.	Reports—20th of each month. Payment—cigarettes, by purchase of stamps; tobacco products, 20th of following month.
Realty transfer tax.	2% on transfers of realty located in Delaware, provided value of property conveyed is more than $100, or 1.5% if the municipality or county has enacted a 1.5% local realty transfer tax. 1% on amounts exceeding $10,000 on contracts for improvements to realty.	Payment—by purchase of stamps.

Tax	Basis—Rates	Due Dates
Merchants and manufacturers tax; use tax on personal property leases.	Wholesalers generally, $75 plus 0.307% of gross receipts (less a $80,000 monthly deduction); food processors, $75 plus 0.154% of gross receipts (less a $80,000 monthly deduction); commercial feed dealers, $75 plus 0.077% of gross receipts (less a $80,000 monthly deduction); farm machinery, supplies, or materials retailers, $75 plus 0.077% of gross receipts (less a $80,000 monthly deduction).	
	Retailers generally, $75 license fee plus $25 per business location, plus 0.576% of receipts from goods sold or services rendered (less a $80,000 monthly deduction); transient retailers, $25 license fee plus 0.576% of gross receipts over $3,000; restaurant retailers, $75 license fee plus $25 per business location plus 0.499% of receipts from goods sold in Delaware (less a $80,000 monthly deduction); grocery supermarket retailers, $75 license fee plus $25 per branch plus 0.307% of first $2 million per month and 0.576% thereafter (less a $80,000 monthly deduction). If taxable gross receipts do not exceed $750,000 during the lookback period, a deduction of $240,000 is allowed on the aggregate gross receipts for each quarter.	Merchants, manufacturers, and contractors: Returns and payments—20th of each month for preceding month. If the taxpayer's gross receipts during the lookback period do not exceed the statutory threshold, the report and payment are due on the last day of the month following the close of the quarter.
	Wholesalers pay an additional 0.192% of gross receipts from sales of petroleum or petroleum products plus an additional 0.9% and 0.307% of such taxable gross receipts in excess of $80,000 except for sales of crude oil. Retailers pay an additional 0.9% on sales of petroleum or petroleum products except crude oil.	
	Contractors—$75 license fee plus 0.499% of aggregate gross receipts (less a $80,000 monthly deduction).	
	Manufacturers—$75 plus 0.144% of gross receipts (less a $1 million monthly deduction); automobile manufacturers, $75 plus 0.135% of gross receipts (less a $1 million monthly deduction).	
	Occupational licensees—$75 license fee plus $25 for each extra establishment, plus 0.307% of aggregate gross receipts (less a $80,000 monthly deduction).	Additional tax—20th day of each month.
	Use tax on personalty leases—1.536% of rent. Lessors—$75 license fee, plus $25 for each additional place of business in Delaware, plus 0.230% (0.288% for motor vehicles) of rental payments received, less a quarterly deduction of $240,000.	Use tax—returns quarterly.

Tax	Basis—Rates	Due Dates
Utilities taxes.	Gas, electric, and steam companies: $50 annual license fee plus 1 mill per $1 of gross receipts.	Gas, electric, steam—Report and payment 1st Monday in May each year.
	Distributors of electricity commodities or services to business locations used primarily for the manufacture of goods within Delaware or for food processing, agribusiness processing, or the hatching of chickens in conjunction with food processing or agribusiness processing within Delaware, 2% of gross receipts or tariff charges received.	
	Telegraph and telephone companies: Telegraph: longest wire, 60¢ per mile; next longest, 30¢; other, 20¢. Telephone: same plus 25¢ for each transmitter.	Telegraph and telephone—Reports—June 1; payment—June 15.
	Intrastate telephone service, 4.25% of sales price or tariff charge; intrastate electricity, telegraph and gas, 4.25% of gross receipts or tariff charges received; cable television, 2.125% of gross receipts or tariff charges received.	Intrastate telephone, telegraph, gas, electricity, and cable television—Payment, 20th of each month.
Insurance companies tax.	1.75% of gross premiums less dividends and return premiums. An additional 0.25% tax is levied on all insurers except wet marine and transportation insurers. Wet marine and transportation insurers—5%. Domestic insurers subject to annual privilege tax ranging between $10,000 if annual gross receipts are $1 million to $5 million and $95,000 if annual gross receipts are over $40 million. Captive insurance companies—0.2% on each $1 of direct premiums up to a maximum of $125,000 for the tax year, plus 0.1% on each $1 of assumed reinsurance premiums up to a maximum of $75,000 for the tax year. Company-owned or trust-owned life insurance policies covering key employees—ranging from 2% on the first $10 million of net premiums per case to 1% on net premiums of $100 million and over.	Returns and payment—returns due March 1, except wet marine and transportation insurers file June 1. 25% of estimated tax liability for current year due the 15th day of April, June, September and December of current tax year; balance due on March 1 of following year. Wet marine and transportation insurers must pay June 1.
Estate tax.	Tax is equal to the credit allowed under federal law for estate-type taxes paid to any state. (No federal estate tax is due for estates of decedents who died after December 31, 2004.)	Returns and payment—not applicable. Filing requirements eliminated for 2005 through 2010 if no federal estate tax return is due.

District of Columbia

Tax System.—The tax system of the District of Columbia differs from the system of all states in that, instead of a number of local taxing bodies with one central authority, there is but one taxing body engaged in the assessment, levy, and collection of taxes. In addition to the general property tax on all real and personal property in the District, there are taxes on corporate and personal income, sales and use taxes, taxes on banks, utilities, and insurance companies, a realty transfer tax, inheritance and estate taxes, and other excise taxes. An outline of the District tax system follows:

Tax	Basis—Rates	Due Dates
Corporate organization and qualification fees.	Domestic—Articles of incorporation, merger or consolidation, and dometication $150; articles of dissolution $75; application for reinstatement and issuance of certificate of reinstatement $250. Initial license fee: Up to 10,000 shares, 3¢ per share; 10,001 to 50,000 shares, 2¢ per share; 50,001 or more shares, 1¢ per share. Minimum fee, $35.	At time of incorporation.
Corporation report fee.	Two-year report—$750.	Domestic and foreign corporations—biannual reports due at the time the two-year report is filed.
General income tax; unincorporated business tax.	Individuals: First $10,000, 4% of taxable income; Over $10,000 but not over $40,000, $400 plus 6% of excess over $10,000; over $40,000, $2,200 plus 8.5% of excess over $40,000. Withholding required, except for U.S. legislative employees.	Returns—individuals, 15th day of 4th month after end of income year; corporations, 15th day of 3rd month after end of income year. Payments—in full when return is filed. Individual estimates of income not subject to withholding due April 15 and payments due April 15, June 15, September 15, and January 15. Estimated corporate income tax payments are due April 15, June 15, September 15, and December 15.
	Corporations, unincorporated businesses, and financial institutions (franchise tax): 9.975% (including a 5% surtax).	
Ballpark Fee.	For gross receipts of $5 million to $8 million, $5,500; for $8,000,001 to $12 million, $10,800; for gross receipts of $12,000,001 to $16 million, $14,000; and for gross receipts of $16,000,001 and up, $16,500	

Tax	Basis—Rates	Due Dates
General property tax.	The real property tax rates (including the special property tax rates) are (per $100 of assessed value); class 1; $0.92; class 2, $1.85; and class 3, $5. The personal property tax is $3.40 per $100 of assessed value, and the first $50,000 of taxable value is excluded from tax.	Returns—personal property, in July.
		Payments—realty taxes, March 31 and September 15. Personal property taxes, in July.
Alcoholic beverages tax.	Excise—beer, $2.79 per 31-gallon barrel; champagne, sparkling wine, and any wine artificially carbonated, 45¢ per gallon; wine containing 14% or less alcohol by volume, 30¢ per gallon; wine containing more than 14% alcohol by volume, 40¢ per gallon; spirits and all other alcoholic beverages or alcohol, $1.50 per gallon.	Common carrier licensees— information reports of alcoholic beverages, except beer and wine, due 10th day of each month.
		Reports and payments— 16th day of each month.
Motor fuels tax.	20¢ per gallon on motor fuels sold, used or otherwise disposed of by importers.	Reports and payments— 25th day of each month.
Motor vehicle excise tax.	Registration fee—6% of fair market value for vehicles weighing 3,499 lbs. or less; 7% of fair market value if weight is 3,500 lbs. to 4,999 lbs; 8% of fair market value if weight is 5,000 lbs. or more.	Fee—payable annually at registration anniversary date.
Cigarette tax.	5¢ per cigarette ($1 per pack of 20 cigarettes).	Reports by 25th day of each month; payments by purchase of stamps.
Deed transfer tax.	1.1% of consideration or fair market value. Minimum tax, $1.	Tax due when deed submitted for recording. Deed must be accompanied by a return.
Deed recordation tax	1.1% of consideration or fair market value	At the time of recording of deeds to real estate.
Sales and use taxes.	5.75% on all tangible property and selected services, alcoholic beverages sold in stores, food sold in vending machines; 8% on liquor sold for off-premises consumption; 10% on restaurant meals, liquor sold for consumption on the premises, and rental vehicles; 12% for parking motor vehicles in commercial lots; and 14.5% for transient accommodations.	Sales—Returns—monthly, 20th of each month; annually January 20. Payments—due at the time the return is filed.
		Use—Returns—monthly, 20th of each month; annually January 20. Payments—due at the time the return is filed.
Public utilities tax.	10% of gross receipts (residential) and 11% of gross receipts (non-residential).	Reports and payments— before the 21st day of each month for the preceding month.
	Electric companies—0.007 per kilowatt hour delivered to end-users in D.C.	Reports and payments— before the 21st day of each month for the preceding month.

Tax	Basis—Rates	Due Dates
Toll telecommunications tax.	11% of the monthly gross charges from the sale of toll telecommunications service that originates or terminates in D.C., and for which a charge is made to a service address located in D.C., regardless of where the charge is billed or paid.	Reports and payments—Return must be filed by the 20th day of each month. The tax must be paid before the 21st day of the succeeding calender month.
	For residential customers, 10% of the monthly gross charges from the sale of toll telecommunication service that originates or terminates in the District, and for which a charge is made to a service address located in the District, regardless of where the charge is billed or paid.	
Insurance companies tax.	1.7% on policy and membership fees and net premium receipts.	Reports—before March 1.
Estate tax.	Amount equal to credit allowable under federal estate tax laws, without adoption of the federal changes contained in the Economic Growth and Tax Relief Reconciliation Act of 2001 (P.L. 107-16).	Returns—10 months following decedent's death.
	Tax due is determined using the DC estate tax computation worksheet after computing the exempted amounts.	Payments—within 10 months after death.

Florida

Tax System.—The Florida tax system consists of the general property tax, sales and use taxes, corporate franchise (income) tax, estate tax, public utility taxes and other special taxes listed below. A constitutional amendment provides that no levy of *ad valorem* taxes upon real or personal property, except intangible property, may be made for state purposes, thus effecting a partial separation of state and local taxes. An outline of the Florida tax system follows:

Tax	Basis—Rates	Due Dates
Corporate organization and qualification fees.	Articles of incorporation—$35. Application for registered name—$87.50.	Fees due upon filing.
Annual report filing fee.	Domestic and foreign corporations authorized to do business in Florida, $61.25.	Reports and payments—due between January 1 and May 1.
Corporate franchise (income) tax.	Corporations, banks and savings associations— liable for the greater of the income tax or the alternative minimum tax ("AMT"). Income rate: 5.5% of federal taxable income apportioned to Florida with adjustments ($5,000 of net income exempt). AMT is 3.3%. Florida corporate income taxpayers are subject to an annual emergency excise tax on any depreciation deducted for assets placed in service after 1980 and before 1987. The emergency excise tax is imposed at the rate of 2.2% of a calculated amount of the deduction allowed for certain accelerated cost recovery system (ACRS) depreciation.	Reports and payments—April 1 for calendar-year taxpayers; 1st day of 4th month after close of tax year for fiscal-year taxpayers. Declarations and payments of estimated tax required if estimated tax over $2,500. Declaration due 1st day of 5th month of tax year; payments are due on the 1st day of the 5th, 7th, and 10th months of the taxable year, as well as the 1st day of the 1st month of the following taxable year.
General property tax; intangible personal property tax.	General property—rates fixed locally to meet budget. Assessed at full cash value of real and tangible personal property; no state levy on realty or tangible property.	Returns—tangible personal property, including railroad property, April 1. Payment—real property, due November 1; delinquent April 1. Installment payments allowed, due on last day of June, September, and December of current year and March of following year.
	Intangible personal property—The 2006 rate is 50¢ per $1,000 of property in excess of $250,000. (Repealed effective 1/1/07, except as it relates to qualifying government leasehold interests.)	Returns and payments—annual taxes, June 30.

Tax	Basis—Rates	Due Dates
Alcoholic beverages tax.	Wines, wine coolers, and other beverages with 0.5% or more, but less than 17.259% alcohol by volume—$2.25 (per gallon). Wines with 17.259% or more alcohol by volume—$3.00 (per gallon). Natural sparkling wines—$3.50 (per gallon). Ciders—$0.89 (per gallon). Other beverages with 17.259% or more, but less than 55.780% alcohol by volume—$6.50 (per gallon). Other beverages with more than 55.780% alcohol by volume—$9.53 (per gallon). Malt beverages—$0.48 (per gallon).	Reports and payments—manufacturers, distributors, brokers, sales agents, importers, vendors, and exporters, 10th of each month; railroad, steamship, bus, airplane companies, carriers, 15th of each month.
	Surcharge—the following surcharges are imposed on beverages sold at retail for consumption on licensed premises: 3.34¢ on each ounce of liquor and each 4 ounces of wine; 2¢ on each 12 ounces of cider; and 1.34¢ on each 12 ounces of beer.	Surcharge—Reports and payments—15th day of the month following the month in which the surcharges are imposed. The last report and payment of the surcharge due July 15, 2007.
Motor and diesel fuel taxes; petroleum taxes.	Motor fuel—The total motor fuel tax rate for 2006 is 14.9¢. Inspection fee, $1/8$¢ per gallon on gasoline, kerosene and #1 fuel oils sold in Florida.	Gasoline—Reports and payments—20th of each month. Reports of inspection fees, due to the Commissioner of Agriculture on or before the 25th of each month.
	Diesel fuel—The total diesel fuel tax rate for 2006 is 27.9¢. Alternative fuel users are subject to an annual decal fee in lieu of the excise tax. The amount of the decal fee is dependent on the class of the vehicle.	Diesel fuel—Reports and payments—20th of each month. Quarterly and semiannual reports and payments may be permitted.
	Use tax on diesel fuel for business purposes—6% of cost of diesel fuel consumed, used or stored by a trade or business.	Reports and payments—purchaser or ultimate consumer must pay tax directly to state.
	Special and motor fuel use—The rate of tax includes the minimum motor fuel tax and diesel fuel tax, and any pollutant tax imposed by the state. The tax is imposed on each gallon of diesel or motor fuel used for the propulsion of a commercial motor vehicle on a public state highway by a motor carrier.	Special and motor fuel use—Reports and payments—annual returns, July 1; semiannual returns, January 1 and July 1; quarterly returns, January 1, April 1, July 1, and October 1.
	Petroleum taxes—inland protection tax, not to exceed 80¢ per barrel of pollutants produced or imported (current rate is 80¢ per barrel). Coastal protection tax, not to exceed 10¢ per barrel of pollutants produced or imported (current rate is 2¢ per barrel). Water quality tax, rates vary depending on type of pollutant and fund balance.	Petroleum taxes—Reports and payments—20th of each month.
	Aviation fuel tax—6.9¢ per gallon.	Aviation fuel tax—same as gasoline tax provisions.

Tax	Basis—Rates	Due Dates
Oil, gas and sulfur production taxes; solid minerals tax.	Production—Oil, 8% of gross value (5% for small well oil and tertiary oil); escaped oil, 12.5% additional. Gas, through 6/30/07, 50.9¢ per MCF (rate set annually, based on gas fuels producer price index). Sulfur, through 6/30/07, $3.98 per ton (rate set annually based on sulfur producer price index).	Oil production tax—Reports and payments—25th day of the month following the month production occurred.
		Gas and sulfur production tax—Reports and payments—25th of 2nd month following end of each quarter. Declaration and payment of estimated tax due 25th day of each month.
	Solid minerals—8% of value of mineral severed. Heavy minerals—$2.93 per ton (rate adjusted annually by the change in the producer price index). Phosphate rock — $1.82 per ton (rate adjusted annually based on changes in the producer price index). Lake belt area limerock and sand (eff. for calendar year 2006)—7.1¢ per ton (suspended from 2007 to 2009).	Solid minerals tax—Reports and payments—April 1. Estimated tax payments due on 1st day of May, July, October, and January.
Cigarette and tobacco products taxes.	Cigarettes—Weighing not more than 3 lbs. per 1,000—16.95 mills each. Weighing more than 3 lbs. per 1,000 and not more than 6 in. long—33.9 mills each. Weighing more than 3 lbs. per 1,000 and more than 6 in. long—67.8 mills each.	Reports—wholesalers, jobbers, and agents, 10th of each month; railroads and Pullman company, 10th of each month.
		Payment—by means of cash paid for stamps to be affixed to cigarette packages. Payment due by the 10th of the month following the month in which the stamps were sold.
	Tobacco products—25% of wholesale price to distributors; 25% of cost price to consumers.	Reports and payments—10th of each month.
Documentary excise tax.	Bonds, debentures, certificates of indebtedness, promissory and nonnegotiable notes, assignments of salaries, wages or other compensation, 35¢ per $100 of face value. Instruments that convey an interest in realty, 70¢ per $100 of the consideration (60¢ per $100 in a county that imposes a surtax on documents). Promissory and nonnegotiable notes, assignments of salaries, wages or other compensation, 35¢ per $100 of value, not to exceed $2,450.	Payment—due at time of transfer or sale. For notes and wage assignments executed in connection with retail charge account services, tax paid quarterly.

Tax	Basis—Rates	Due Dates
Sales, use, rentals and admissions taxes.	6% of retail sales, rentals, admission charges, use, consumption, distribution or storage for use or consumption in Florida of tangible personal property and selected services. 4% on coin- operated amusement machine charges. 7% of charges for electrical power or energy.	Reports and payments—20th day of each month. Dealers who remitted $100 or less during the previous 4 calendar quarters report and pay annually; dealers who remitted at least $100 but less than $500, report and pay semiannually; dealers who remitted at least $500 but less than $1,000, report and pay quarterly; dealers who remitted between $1,000 and $12,000 report quarterly and pay monthly.
Utility taxes.	Electric or gas light, heat, and power—2.5% of gross receipts.	Reports and payments—light, heat, or power, last day of the month for the preceding month. Returns may be filed (1) on a quarterly basis if the tax remitted for the preceding 4 calendar quarters did not exceed $1,000; (2) on a semiannual basis if the tax remitted for the preceding 4 calendar quarters did not exceed $500; or (3) on an annual basis if the tax remitted for the preceding 4 calendar quarters did not exceed $100.
	Communications services tax is levied at a combined state and local tax rate. The general state rate is 9.17%. Local rates vary among local taxing jurisdictions. For residential service, the state rate is 2.37%. Direct-to-home satellite services are taxed at a state rate of 13.17%.	Reports and payments—same as for utility taxes.

Tax	Basis—Rates	Due Dates
Insurance companies tax.	Annuity policies—1%; wet marine and transportation insurance, 0.75%; surplus lines, 5%; mutual insurers, commercial self-insurance fund, medical malpractice self-insurance fund, 1.6%; all others, 1.75%. $2 surcharge on homeowner's, mobile homeowner's, tenant homeowner's, and condominium unit owner's policies; $4 surcharge on commercial fire, commercial multi-peril, and business owner's property insurance policies.	Payment—policies covering risks resident or to be performed in Florida and annuity policies and any surcharges due, April 15, June 15, October 15 and March 1; annual report— March 1. Surplus lines, last day of January, April, July and October. Other policies, March 1. Fire marshal assessment report, March 1.
	Fire marshal assessment—1% of gross premiums from fire insurance on property in Florida. Foreign companies, other than those with a regional home office in Florida, are subject to retaliatory provisions.	
Estate tax.	Amount equal to the credit allowable under the federal estate tax laws. (No federal estate tax is due for estates of decedents who died after December 31, 2004.)	Returns and payments— not applicable.
Generation-skipping transfer tax.	Amount equal to the federal generation-skipping transfer tax credit.	

Georgia

Tax System.—Georgia's principal sources of revenue are personal and corporate income taxes and sales and use taxes. The gasoline tax is also an important revenue source. Lesser, but significant, amounts are raised by the tax on tobacco, motor vehicle registration fees, the motor carriers tax, and taxes on alcoholic beverages and insurance companies. For counties and municipalities, the property tax remains the principal source of income. An outline of the Georgia tax system follows:

Tax	Basis—Rates	Due Dates
Corporate organization and qualification fees.	Domestic—articles of incorporation, $100. Foreign—certificate of authority to transact business, $225.	Domestic and foreign—fees due when filing articles or certificates.
Corporation franchise (license) tax; annual report fee.	Corporation franchise—graduated from $10 for $10,000 or less, based on net worth, including capital stock and paid in and earned surplus of domestic corporations, and on the proportion of issued capital stock and surplus employed in the state of foreign corporations, to $5,000 for over $22 million. Annual report (annual registration)—$30.	Corporation franchise—returns and payments—March 15 or the 15th day of 3rd month after beginning of tax period. Annual report—by April 1.
Corporate income tax.	Corporations—6% of federal taxable income, with adjustments. Financial institutions—0.25% of Georgia gross receipts.	Returns and payments—March 15 or the 15th day of 3rd month after close of fiscal year. Estimated tax payments—April 15, June 15, September 15, and January 15. Returns and payments—March 1.
Personal income tax.	Heads of households, married persons filing jointly—1% of 1st $1,000 of taxable net income; 2% of next $2,000; 3% of next $2,000; 4% of next $2,000; 5% of next $3,000; over $10,000, 6%. Single persons—1% of 1st $750; 2% of next $1,500; 3% of next $1,500; 4% of next $1,500; 5% of next $1,750; over $7,000, 6%. Married persons filing separately—1% of 1st $500; 2% of next $1,000; 3% of next $1,000; 4% of next $1,000; 5% of next $1,500; over $5,000, 6%. Nonresidents—income from Georgia sources. Withholding required.	Returns and payments—April 15 or the 15th day of 4th month after close of fiscal year. Estimated tax payments—different for annual, monthly, quarterly, and semi-weekly filers.
General property tax.	General property—state—1/4 mill on each dollar of the assessed value of real property and tangible personal property. Property is assessed at 40% of its fair market value for state and county taxes.	General property—returns—April 1; railroads, airlines, and public utilities, March 1. Payments—by December 20.

Tax	Basis—Rates	Due Dates
Alcoholic beverages tax.	Excise—malt beverages: $10 per 31 gallon bbl., 4.5¢ per 12 oz. container. Distilled spirits: 50¢ per liter excise tax, 50¢ per liter import tax. Alcohol: 70¢ per liter excise tax, 70¢ per liter import tax. Table wines: 11¢ per liter excise tax, 29¢ per liter import tax. Dessert wines: 27¢ per liter excise tax, 40¢ per liter import tax. Malt beverages or wines that contain less than 0.5% alcohol by volume are exempt.	Reports—malt beverages and wine—manufacturers, wineries, producers, shippers, wholesale dealers, importers, and brokers, 15th day of each month; distilled spirits wholesalers, 10th day of each month. Payments—with reports.
Gasoline tax.	Motor fuels—7.5¢ per gallon (1¢ per gallon on aviation gasoline), plus additional 3% or 4% "prepaid state tax" according to rates announced by the Department of Revenue twice a year.	Reports and payments—20th day of month for preceding calendar month.
	Motor carriers road tax—7.5¢ per gallon on fuel consumed in Georgia operations.	Motor carriers road tax—last day of month following the calendar quarter.
Tobacco tax.	Cigarettes—37¢ per pack of 20.	Reports—by the 10th day of each month.
	Cigars—23% of the wholesale cost price; little cigars, $2^{1}/_{2}$ mills on each item weighing 3 lbs. or less per 1,000.	Payments—by purchasing stamps or, for cigars and loose or smokeless tobacco, by alternative method of monthly reports.
	Loose or smokeless tobacco—10% of the wholesale cost price.	
Realty transfer tax.	$1 for the first $1,000 of value and 10¢ per additional $100 of value. Transfer for less than $100 exempt.	Payments—certification of payment issued by Superior Court clerks prior to recording.
Sales and use taxes.	Sales and use—4% of sales price.	Reports and payments—20th day of each month for preceding calendar month. If estimated tax liability for the month exceeds $,5,000, prepayments of not less than 50% of such tax are due by 20th day of the taxable period.

Tax	Basis—Rates	Due Dates
Insurance companies tax.	State taxes—2.25% of gross direct premiums on persons, property, or risks in Georgia, including annuity considerations, less return premiums; reduced to 1.25% if 25% of total assets are invested in Georgia and to 0.5% if 75% of total assets are invested in Georgia. 1% additional on fire insurance companies. Surplus line brokers and independently procured coverages, 4%.	Reports and payments—March 1. If the tax for the preceding year was $500 or more, the current year's tax is due March 20, June 20, September 20, and December 20 based on estimated quarterly premiums. Additional tax for fire insurance companies—by April 1. Additional tax for surplus line brokers—15th day of April, July, October, and January.
	Foreign companies subject to retaliatory taxes.	
Estate tax.	Amount equal to the maximum credit allowable under the federal estate tax (no longer imposed as of 12/31/04).	Returns and payments—not applicable.

Hawaii

Tax System.—The two main revenue producers for the state are the general net income tax and the general excise (gross income) tax. Real property is subject to tax at rates fixed to meet county budgets. An outline of the Hawaii tax system follows:

Tax	Basis—Rates	Due Dates
Corporate organization and qualification fees.	Domestic or foreign corporation—filing articles of incorporation or application for certificate of authority, $100 ($50 for nonprofit corporation).	Domestic—at time of incorporation or increase of capital stock. Foreign—at time of qualification.
Annual corporate reports and license fees.	Annual report—domestic or foreign corporation, $25.	Annual reports—March 31 if corporation's incorporation date is between January 1 and March 31; June 30 if incorporation date is between April 1 and June 30; September 30 if incorporation date is between July 1 and September 30; and December 31 if incorporation date is between September 1 and December 31.
General income tax.	The following rates apply for tax years beginning **after 2001 and before 2007**— *Married filing separately and single individuals:* $0 to $2,000, 1.40% of taxable income; $2,001 to $4,000, $28.00 plus 3.20% of excess over $2,000; $4,001 to $8,000, $92.00 plus 5.50% of excess over $4,000; $8,001 to $12,000, $312.00 plus 6.40% of excess over $8,000; $12,001 to $16,000, $568.00 plus 6.80% of excess over $12,000; $16,001 to $20,000, $840.00 plus 7.20% of excess over $16,000; $20,001 to $30,000, $1,128.00 plus 7.60% of excess over $20,000; $30,001 to $40,000, $1,888.00 plus 7.90% of excess over $30,000; over $40,000, $2,678 plus 8.25% of excess over $40,000. *Heads of households:* rates range between 1.4% of the first $3,000 of taxable income and 8.25% of taxable income over $60,000. *Married filing jointly and surviving spouse:* rates range between 1.4% of the first $4,000 of taxable income and 8.25% of taxable income over $80,000.	Returns and payments—20th day of 4th month following close of income year. Estimated tax—declaration, 20th day of the 4th month of the current year; payments, 20th day of the 4th, 6th, 9th, and 13th months of the year.

Tax	Basis—Rates	Due Dates
	The following rates apply for tax years beginning **after 2006**—*Married filing separately and single individuals:* $0 to $2,400, 1.40% of taxable income; $2,401 to $4,800, $34.00 plus 3.20% of excess over $2,400; $4,801 to $9,600, $110.00 plus 5.50% of excess over $4,800; $9,601 to $14,400, $374.00 plus 6.40% of excess over $9,600; $14,401 to $19,200, $682.00 plus 6.80% of excess over $14,400; $19,201 to $24,000, $1,008.00 plus 7.20% of excess over $19,200; $24,001 to $36,000, $1,354.00 plus 7.60% of excess over $24,000; $36,001 to $48,000, $2,266.00 plus 7.90% of excess over $36,000; over $48,000, $3,214.00 plus 8.25% of excess over $48,000. *Heads of households:* rates range between 1.4% of the first $3,600 of taxable income and 8.25% of taxable income over $72,000. *Married filing jointly and surviving spouse:* rates range between 1.4% of the first $4,800 of taxable income and 8.25% of taxable income over $96,000.	
	Corporations—first $25,000, 4.4%; next $75,000, 5.4% less $250; over $100,000, 6.4% less $1,250; plus 4% alternative rate on net capital gains.	
Bank franchise (income) tax.	Qualified taxpayers pay a tax of 7.92% of net income of banks and other financial institutions or an alternative tax (if less than the franchise tax) on financial institutions having a net capital gain equal to the sum of (1) the franchise tax computed on the taxable income reduced by the amount of the net capital gain plus (2) 4% of the net capital gain for the tax year.	Returns and payments—20th day of 4th month after tax year or payable in four equal installments on 20th day of 4th, 6th, 9th, and 12th months of year.
General property tax.	Rates set by county councils except that rates for Kalawao County are set by the state. Realty generally assessed at 100% of fair market value. Personal property is exempt.	Bills—mailed by July 20. Payments—installments due by August 20 and February 20.
Transient accommodations tax.	7.25% on gross rental income or gross proceeds from furnishing transient accommodations. Also imposed on fair market rental value of vacation time-share units.	Reports and payments—last day of following month; quarterly on last day of month following close of quarter if liability is $4,000 or less annually; semiannually on last day of month after close of semiannual period if liability is $2,000 or less annually.
Alcoholic beverages taxes.	Distilled spirits, $5.98 per wine gallon; sparkling wine, $2.12 per wine gallon; still wine, $1.38 per wine gallon; cooler beverages, $0.85 per wine gallon; beer other than draft beer, $0.93 per wine gallon; draft beer, $0.54 per wine gallon.	Reports and payments—last day of each month.

Tax	Basis—Rates	Due Dates
Fuel tax.	Aviation fuel, 1¢; diesel oil including state tax of 16¢ per gallon: Honolulu County 32.5¢, Maui County 32¢, Hawaii County 24.8¢, Kauai County 29¢; diesel oil (non-highway use), 1¢; LP gas (non-highway use), 1¢; LP gas (highway use), including state rate: Honolulu County 10.6¢, Kauai County 9.5¢, Hawaii County 8.1¢, Maui County 9.5¢; alternative fuels (including state tax): Honolulu County ethanol 4.8¢, methanol 3.7¢, biodiesel 12.3¢; Maui County ethanol 6.2¢, methanol 4.8¢, biodiesel 4.0¢; Hawaii County ethanol 3.7¢, methanol 2.9¢, biodiesel 6.2¢; Kauai County ethanol 4.3¢, methanol 3.3¢, biodiesel 4.0¢.	Reports and payments—last day of each month.
Environmental response tax.	5¢ per barrel of petroleum product sold by a distributor to any retailer dealer or end user, other than a refiner, of petroleum products.	Reports and payments—last day of each month.
Cigarette tax.	7¢ per cigarette ($1.40 per pack of 20). Effective September 30, 2006, 8¢ per cigarette ($1.60 per pack of 20); September 30, 2007, 9¢ per cigarette ($1.80 per pack of 20); September 30, 2008, 10¢ per cigarette ($2.00 per pack of 20); September 30, 2009, 11¢ per cigarette ($2.20 per pack of 20); September 30, 2010, 12¢ per cigarette ($2.40 per pack of 20); September 30, 2011, 13¢ per cigarette ($2.60 per pack of 20).	Reports—last day of each month. Payment—cigarette tax stamps purchased from Department of Taxation and affixed prior to distribution.
Tobacco products tax.	40% of wholesale price of all tobacco products.	Reports and payments—last day of each month.
Realty conveyance tax.	10¢ per $100 for properties with a value of less than $600,000, 20¢ per $100 for properties with a value of at least $600,000 but less than $1 million, and 30¢ per $100 for properties with a value of $1 million or greater. Sale of a condominium or single family residence for which the purchaser is ineligible for a homeowner's property tax exemption, rate is 15¢ per $100 for properties with a value of less than $600,000, 25¢ per $100 for properties with a value of at least $600,000 but less than $1 million, and 35¢ per $100 for properties with a value of $1 million or greater. Minimum tax, $1.	Payments—no later than 90 days after taxable transactions. Payments evidenced by seal.
General excise (gross income) tax; use tax.	Excise—0.15%, 0.5%, or 4% of the value of products, gross proceeds or gross income according to type of business. 4% is generally the retail rate. 0.5% is generally the wholesale/manufacturer rate. 0.15% is generally the insurance producer rate. On intermediary sales of services, the rate was 0.5% after 2005 (repealed, effective January 1, 2006).	Returns and payments—last day of each month; if annual liability does not exceed $4,000, quarterly on or before the last day of the month following the close of each quarter; or if annual liability does not exceed $2,000, July 31 and January 31. Annual report due 20th day of 4th month after end of tax year.
	Use—4% of purchase price or value of property for use or consumption, or, for resale at retail, 0.5%.	Returns and payments—same as under general excise tax.

Tax	Basis—Rates	Due Dates
Public service company tax.	Tax based on gross income for preceding calendar year. Rates are 5.35% for scheduled route passenger carriers on land; 0.5% for sales to another utility for resale; 4% for all other revenues. The rates for utilities selling telecommunications services to an interstate or foreign telecommunications provider for resale are 2.5% for 2006 and 0.5% after 2006. Airlines, motor carriers, common carriers by water, and contract carriers other than motor carriers are subject to the general excise tax instead of the public service company tax.	Reports—20th day of the 4th month following the close of the tax year.
		Payments—20th day of the 4th month following the close of the tax year or in four equal installments, by the 20th day of the 4th, 6th, 9th and 12th months following the close of the tax year. If estimated liability exceeds $100,000, due in equal installments by the 10th day of each month.
Insurance companies tax.	Authorized insurers, except life and ocean marine, 4.265%; life insurers, 2.75%; ocean marine insurers, .8775%; surplus lines brokers, 4.68%. Captive insurance companies, 0.25% on $0—$25 million of gross premiums; 0.15% on more than $25 million to $50 million of gross premiums; and 0.05% on more than $50 million of gross premiums.	Annual statements and payments—March 1. Quarterly statements and payments—last day of month following close of quarter. Payments—surplus line brokers, March 15.
Estate and transfer tax.	Repealed for decedents dying after 2004.	Reports and payments—not applicable.
Generation-skipping transfer tax.	Repealed for decedents dying after 2004.	Same as estate and transfer tax.

Idaho

Tax System.—The Idaho tax system is based on the general income tax on individuals and corporations, the gasoline and special fuel tax, and the sales and use taxes. A general property tax is imposed for local purposes, limited to 1% of market value, but the state property tax is suspended so long as the sales and use taxes are in effect. Other significant revenue producers are motor vehicle registration fees, alcoholic beverage taxes, cigarette taxes and the insurance gross premiums tax. An outline of the Idaho tax system follows:

Tax	Basis—Rates	Due Dates
Corporate organization and qualification fees.	Domestic—articles of incorporation if typed, $100, not typed or with attachments, $120; articles of amendment, or merger, $30. Foreign—certificate of authority if typed, $100, not typed or with attachments, $120; amended certificate of authority, $30.	At time of filing for incorporation or qualification.
General income tax.	Individuals—(Note: 2006 rates not available at time of print) 2005 Rates: Single, married filing separately: $1,159 or less—1.6% of taxable income; over $1,159 and less than $2,318—$18.54 plus 3.6% of taxable income over $1,159; over $2,318 and less than $3,477—$60.26 plus 4.1% of the amount over $2,318; over $3,477 and less than $4,636—$107.78 plus 5.1% of the amount over $3,477; over $4,636 and less than $5,794—$166.89 plus 6.1% of the amount over $4,636; over $5,794 and less than $8,692—$237.53 plus 7.1% of the amount over $5,794; over $8,692 and less than $23,178—$443.29 plus 7.4% of the amount over $8,692; $23,178 or more—$1,515.25 plus 7.8% of the amount over $23,178. Married filing jointly, head of household, qualifying widow(er): $2,318 or less—1.6% of taxable income; over $2,318 and less than $4,636—$37.09 plus 3.6% of the amount over $2,318; over $4,636 and less than $6,953—$120.54 plus 4.1% of the amount over $4,636; over $6,953 and less than $9,271—$212.54 plus 5.1% of the amount over $6,953; over $9,271 and less than $11,589—$333.76 plus 6.1% of the amount over $9,271; over $11,589 and less than $17,383—$475.16 plus 7.1% of the amount over $11,589; over $17,383 but less than $46,356—$886.53 plus 7.4% of the amount over $17,383; $46,356 or more—$3,030.53 plus 7.8% of the amount over $46,356. Additional $10 tax for all persons filing returns.	Returns—April 15 or 15th day of 4th month after close of income year.
	Banks and corporations—7.6% of taxable income. Minimum tax, $20. Corporations must pay an excise tax of $10 when returns are filed.	Payments—with return. Estimated income and franchise tax payments are due from corporations required to make federal estimated payments. Federal due dates apply.
	General withholding required.	

Tax	Basis—Rates	Due Dates
General property tax.	State, county and municipal—fixed within statutory limits to meet budget. The state property tax is not levied so long as the sales and use tax is in effect.	Returns—mines, May 1; public utilities, car and railroad companies, April 30. Payments—realty, December 20 and June 20; personalty, due on demand or, if no demand is made, December 20 and June 20.
Forest products tax.	Yield tax—3% of the stump value.	Reports—November 15 and May 15, by the county treasurer. Payment—By December 20 or June 20.
Alcoholic beverages tax.	Excise—beer, $4.65 per 31-gallon barrel sold for use in the state. A 2% surcharge, based on the current price per unit, is levied on alcoholic liquor and all other merchandise sold in the state dispensary. Wine, 45¢ per gallon.	Excise—Reports and payments—15th of each month.
Fuel taxes.	Gasoline and special fuel, 25¢ per gallon of fuel received or used to propel vehicles on the highways. Jet fuel, 4.5¢ per gallon; aviation gasoline, 5.5¢ per gallon. Petroleum transfer fee—1¢ per gallon (suspended as of 10/1/1999).	Gasoline—last day of each month. Special fuel—last day of each month for dealers. Special fuels permit holders operating IFTA licensed vehicles are required to supply the Commission with a copy of the IFTA report.
Severance tax.	1% of net value of royalties received or ores mined.	Reports and payment—15th day of 4th month following close of year.
	Oil and gas production tax—maximum 5 mills per barrel of oil or per 50,000 cubic feet of gas.	Oil and gas production tax—25th day of the next month following each quarter.
	Additional oil and gas production tax—2% of market value of oil and gas produced at site of production.	Additional oil and gas production tax—25th day of next month following each quarter.
Cigarette tax; tobacco products tax.	57¢ per 20 cigarettes.	Payment—by purchase of stamps. Reports and payments—20th of each month for the preceding month.
	Tobacco products other than cigarettes—40% of wholesale sales price.	Reports and payment—20th of each month. An estimated tax may be paid each month with quarterly reports required.
Sales and use tax.	Sales—Effective October 1, 2006, 6% (previously, 5%) of retail sales price of taxable property and selected services. Use—Effective October 1, 2006, 6% (previously, 5%) of value of property and selected services.	Sales and use—Returns and payment—on or before the 20th of the following month.

Tax	Basis—Rates	Due Dates
Utilities.	Electricity—¹/₂ mill per kilowatt hour of electricity and electrical energy generated, manufactured or produced in the state for sale, barter or exchange. Regulatory fees—not to exceed 1% on gross intrastate revenues of railroads and motor carriers other than those subject to the Public Utilities Commission which are exempt, and 0.3% on other utilities. Minimum, $50.	Electricity—last day of each month. Quarterly reports and payments may be allowed. Regulatory fees—Report—April 1. Payments—May 15 and November 15.
Insurance tax.	Calendar year 2006, 2.3%, CY 2007, 2.1%; CY 2008, 1.9%; CY 2009, 1.7%; CY 2010 and thereafter, 1.5%. Title insurance, 1.5%. Qualified companies with investments in the state, calendar year 2006, if investment is 20% or more, 1.42%; CY 2007, if investment is 15% or more, 1.44%; CY 2008, if investment is 10% or more, 1.46%; CY 2009, if investment is 5% or more, 1.48%. Surplus lines insurance, calendar year 2006, 2.75%; CY 2007 and thereafter, 1.5%, beginning with the effective date of the policy. Health maintenance organization or hospital and medical service corporations, 4¢ per subscriber's contract per month. Foreign companies subject to retaliatory taxes.	Reports and payments—March 1. Prepayments required from insurers owing $400 or more for the preceding calendar year, due on or before June 15, September 15 and December 15, with any balance due on or before March 1.
Estate tax.	Estate tax—Maximum credit allowed under federal law for state death taxes and generation-skipping taxes. (No federal estate tax is due for estates of decedents who died after 12/31/2004.)	Return and payment—not applicable.

Illinois

Tax System.—The Illinois revenue system was founded upon a general property tax at uniform rates upon all property within each taxing district. Since 1933, however, the tax has been entirely a local tax. The property tax has been supplemented by (1) state taxes, part of the revenue from which has been returned to the local governments, upon incomes, occupations, franchises and privileges and (2) municipal sales and license taxes and inspection fees that the legislature permits the local governments to exact. An outline of the Illinois tax system follows:

Tax	Basis—Rates	Due Dates
Corporate organization and qualification fees.	Domestic and foreign corporations—$150, plus applicable franchise tax. Annual report, $75, plus applicable franchise tax.	At time of filing for incorporation or qualification.
Corporation franchise tax.	Annual franchise tax—0.1% of paid-in capital for the 12-month period beginning on the first day of the anniversary month or the extended filing month of the corporation; minimum, $25; maximum, $2 million per year.	Reports—within 60 days preceding the first day of the anniversary month of the corporation or the extended filing month of the corporation.
	Initial franchise tax—0.15% of paid-in capital for the 12-month period beginning on the first day of the anniversary month in which the articles of incorporation are filed; minimum, $25; maximum, $2 million (plus $1/10$ of 1% of the basis) per year.	Payments—initial and additional taxes due at the time of filing articles, certificates or reports of changes; annual franchise tax due within 60 days prior to the first day of the anniversary month.
	Additional franchise tax—$1/12$ of 0.1% for each calendar month between the date of each increase in paid-in capital and its next anniversary month.	
Income tax.	Corporations—4.8% of federal taxable income with adjustments.	Returns and payments—15th day of 3rd month (4th month for individuals, estates and trusts) after the tax year. Estimated payments—15th day of April, June, September and December (Individuals, 15th day of April, June, September, and January). Exempt organization return due 15th day of 5th month following tax year.
	Individuals, estates and trusts—3% of federal adjusted gross income with modifications. Withholding required.	
	Additional personal property replacement tax: Corporations—2.5% of net income; subchapter S corporations, partnerships and trusts, 1.5% of net income.	

Tax	Basis—Rates	Due Dates
General property tax.	General property—levied to meet local budget needs. General property is assessed at $33^1/_3\%$ of fair cash value. Personal property is exempt.	General property—returns—realty, none required; railroads, on or before June 1. Payment—realty, equally on June 1 and September 1; Cook County (two installments), March 1 and August 1.
Hotel occupancy tax.	6% of 94% of the gross receipts from renting hotel or motel rooms for periods of less than 30 days.	Reports and payments—monthly; quarterly basis if average monthly liability does not exceed $200—30th of April, 31st of July, October and January; annual basis if average monthly liability does not exceed $50—31st of January.
Alcoholic beverages tax.	Alcoholic beverages—Per gallon—beer and cider with an alcohol content of 0.5% to 7%, 18.5¢; wine, 7% or less alcohol by volume, 73¢; alcohol and spirits, $4.50.	Reports and payments—15th day of each month.
Motor fuel tax.	19¢ per gallon on gasoline and special fuel, except diesel fuel is subject to an additional tax of 2.5¢ per gallon.	Reports and payments—Suppliers and distributors—20th day of each calendar month.
Motor fuel use tax.	Fuel used by commercial motor vehicles is subject to an additional use tax based on the average selling price of special fuel in the state. The rate is 6.25% of the average selling price of motor fuel purchased in IL.	Reports and payments—on or before the last day of the month following the quarter the return is filed.
	Fuel tax on receivers, 0.3¢ per gallon. [Repealed January 1, 2013.]	Returns and payments—20th of each month.
	Environmental fee on receivers, $60 per 7,500 gallons of fuel. [Repealed January 1, 2013].	Returns and payments—20th of each month.
Cigarette tax.	49 mills per cigarette (98¢ per pack of 20).	Reports—15th of each month. Manufacturers, 5th of each month.
		Payment—Distributors, by purchase of tax stamps; Manufacturers, 5th day of each month.
	Tobacco products tax—18% of wholesale price of tobacco products (other than cigarettes) sold or disposed of in state.	Return and payment—15th day of each month.

Tax	Basis—Rates	Due Dates
Retailers' occupation (sales) tax; use tax.	Sales tax—6.25% of gross receipts from retail sales of tangible personal property and selected services; 1% tax on qualifying food, drugs, medical appliances, and modifications to make a motor vehicle usable by a disabled person.	Reports—sales and use tax, 20th day of each month, or 20th day of the month following each quarter if average monthly liability does not exceed $200, or January 20 if average monthly liability does not exceed $50. Monthly reports from large taxpayers making quarter-monthly payments due 20th day of following month.
	Use tax—6.25% of selling price or fair market value; 1% tax on qualifying food, drugs, medical appliances, and modifications to make a motor vehicle usable by a disabled person.	
		Payment—with report; four times monthly if average monthly liability is $20,000 or more. Retailers of motor fuel must prepay 6¢ per gallon of motor fuel and 5¢ per gallon of gasohol to their distributors, suppliers or other resellers.
Service occupation and use tax.	Service occupation tax—6.25% of selling price of personalty, transferred by servicemen as an incident to "sales of service"; 1% on qualifying food, drugs, medical appliances, and modifications to make a motor vehicle usable by a disabled person.	Service taxes—returns and payment—20th day of each month or before 20th day of month following each quarter if average monthly liability does not exceed $200, or January 20 if average monthly liability does not exceed $50.
	Service use tax—6.25% of selling price of property transferred to the serviceman of property transferred as an incident to the sale of a service; 1% on qualifying food, drugs, medical appliances, and modifications to make a motor vehicle usable by a disabled person.	Payment—with report; 4 times monthly if average monthly liability is $20,000 or more.

Tax	Basis—Rates	Due Dates
Public utilities.	Gas, 2.4¢ per therm or 5% of gross receipts, whichever results in a lower tax. Gas use tax or gas revenue tax, 2.4¢ per therm or 5% of purchase price, whichever is lower.	Reports and payments— 15th of each month; quarterly or annual returns and payments may be authorized. Quarter-monthly payments are required of taxpayers whose average monthly tax liability is $10,000 or more, due on or before the 7th, 15th, 22nd, and last day of the month. Gas revenue tax—Reports and payments due on the 15th day of the third month following the close of the taxable period.
	Telecommunications excise tax, 7% of gross receipts.	Telecommunications (due dates)—monthly on or before the last day of the month following the month for which the return is filed; quarterly and annual returns may be authorized; quarter-monthly payments are required for taxpayers whose average monthly liability is $25,000 or more, due on the 7th, 15th, 22nd, and the last day of the month.
	Telecommunications infrastructure maintenance fee, 0.5% of gross charges.	Returns—on or before the 30th day of each month following the month for which the return is filed. Payments—due with the return.
	Some public utilities subject to Illinois Commerce Commission regulation pay an administrative services tax of 0.1% of gross revenue. Motor carriers of passengers, not to exceed 0.1%; rail carriers, 0.15% of gross intrastate revenues.	Return (estimate)—January 10; payments (estimate)— January, April, July and October. Reconciliation report and payment—March 31 of following year. Report and payment required for utilities that owe less than $10,000 annually, due on March 31 of the next year.
	Electricity excise tax: based on number of kilowatt-hours used or consumed monthly graduating from 0.330¢ for the first 2,000 hours to 0.202¢ for anything in excess of 20 million hours. Electricity excise tax on purchases from municipal utilities: 0.32¢ per kilowatt-hour or 5% of gross receipts, whichever results in a lower tax. Electric distribution tax: based on the number of kilowatt-hours distributed to a purchaser in Illinois. The rate escalates from 0.031¢ per kilowatt-hour for the first 500 million kilowatt-hours to 0.131¢ per kilowatt-hour in excess of 18 billion kilowatt-hours.	Report and payment— Electricity excise taxes— must be filed by the 15th of each month for the preceding calendar month; quarterly and annual filings may be authorized. Quarter-monthly payments may be required if monthly remittances average at least $10,000. Electric distribution fee—filed no later than the 15th day of the 3rd month following the close of the tax period. Estimated payments—15th day of 3rd, 6th, 9th, and 12th months of each tax period.

Tax	Basis—Rates	Due Dates
Insurance companies tax.	All companies doing any form of insurance business in Illinois must pay an annual privilege tax of 0.5% of the net premiums written in the state; except the rate is 0.4% for health maintenance organizations. Fire marshal's tax of 1%. Surplus line agents, 3.5%. Foreign companies subject to retaliatory taxes.	Report and payment—March 15. Surplus line agents—February 1 and August 1. Fire marshal tax—March 31. Estimated tax from larger taxpayers—15th of April, June, September and December.
Estate tax.	Estate tax—after 2005 and before 2010, an exclusion amount of $2,000,000 is allowed.	Return and payment—at the time required for filing the federal estate tax return.
Generation-skipping transfer tax.	Generation-skipping transfer tax—Not applicable to estates of decedents dying after 12/31/04.	Not applicable to estates of decedents dying after 12/31/04.

Indiana

Tax System.—The revenue system for the State of Indiana was founded primarily on a property tax, which continues to be the main revenue producer for local purposes, but the sales and adjusted gross income taxes are the major sources of state revenue. In addition, there are the inheritance, insurance company, and motor carrier taxes, the revenue from which accrues to the state. Income from motor vehicle registration fees, gasoline tax and liquor taxes is divided between the state and local tax bodies. An outline of the Indiana tax system follows:

Tax	Basis—Rates	Due Dates
Corporate organization and qualification fees; biennial corporation report.	Domestic corporations—articles of incorporation, $90; amendment of articles of incorporation, $30; articles of dissolution, $30.	When filing document with Secretary of State.
	Foreign corporations—application for certificate of authority, $90; statement of withdrawal, $30.	
	Biennial report—$30; electronic biennial report—$20.	Biennial report—due in same month that the corporation was incorporated or authorized to transact business.
Income tax.	Individuals—3.4% of adjusted gross income.	Individuals and corporations: Returns and payment—15th day of 4th month after close of taxable year.
	Corporations—8.5% of taxable income; 5% of adjusted gross income derived from sources in a qualified area with an inactive or closed military base.	Estimated reports and payments—Individuals, at the time provided under federal law. For calendar year corporations, 20th day of April, June, September and December. For all other corporate taxpayers, by the 20th day of the 4th, 6th, 9th, and 12th months of the tax year.
Utilities gross receipts tax.	1.4% on the gross receipts from providing utility services (including electrical energy; natural gas for heating, lighting, cooling, or power; water; steam; sewage; or telecommunications services).	Estimated returns and payments—for taxpayers with estimated tax liability greater than $1,000—due by the 20th day of the 4th, 6th, 9th, and 12th months of the tax year. For calendar year taxpayers, annual returns are due April 15 following the end of the tax year.
Utility services use tax.	Utility services use tax—Effective June 30, 2006, 1.4% of the gross compensation of utility services if utility receipts tax not paid.	Reports and payments—by 30 days after end of month in which the services were purchased.
Financial institutions.	Financial institutions tax—8.5% of apportioned income, computed by applying statutory formula to adjusted gross income and subtracting net operating loss and net capital loss deductions.	Financial institutions tax—Reports and payments—15th day of 4th month following the close of the tax year.

Tax	Basis—Rates	Due Dates
General property tax.	General property—Aggregate of state and local levies fixed annually to meet budget. Both real and personal property are assessed at true tax value.	General property—Returns May 15th. Payment—equally on May 10 and November 10 or only May 10 if under $25 and county council approves.
	Public utility—all utility property, real and personal, including rights, franchises, and privileges of communications, transportation, electricity, gas, steam, light, heat or power, and water distributing companies, is assessed at true tax value.	Public utility—railroad car companies report May 1; others March 1. Equal payments on May 10 and November 10; railroad car companies, December 31.
Commercial vessels tonnage tax.	3¢ per net ton of registered tonnage.	Returns and payment—July 1.
Alcoholic beverages tax.	Excise taxes—beer, 11.5¢ per gallon; liquor and wine (21% or more alcohol), $2.68 per gallon; wine (less than 21% alcohol), 47¢ per gallon; mixed beverages (15% or less alcohol), 47¢ per gallon; liquid malt or wort, 5¢ per gallon.	Reports and payment—20th of each month.
Gasoline and special fuel taxes; motor carrier fuel tax.	Gasoline—18¢ per gallon. Special fuel—16¢ per gallon. Inspection fees for petroleum products—50¢ per 50-gallon barrel.	Reports and payments— Gasoline—20th of each month; Special fuel—20th of each month.
	Motor carrier fuel tax—Carriers operating motor vehicles over Indiana highways pay a tax on fuel consumed in the state at the same rate at which special fuel is taxed (16¢ per gallon), plus an 11¢-per-gallon surcharge.	Motor carrier fuel tax— Reports and payments—by the last day of April, July, October and January.
Severance tax.	The value of all petroleum removed from the soil at the greater of 1% of the value of the petroleum, or 3¢ per 1,000 cubic feet of natural gas and 24¢ per barrel of oil.	Returns and payments— within 30 days after the last day of the month being reported.
Motor vehicle rental excise tax.	Rental excise tax—4% of gross retail income received from rental of passenger motor vehicles and trucks of 11,000 lbs. or less rented for less than 30 days.	Rental excise tax—same as sales and use tax.
Cigarette tax; tobacco products tax.	Cigarettes—3 lbs. per 1,000, $0.02775 per cigarette (55.5¢ per pack of 20); more than 3 lbs. per 1,000, $0.036881 per cigarette; more than 3 lbs. per 1,000 and more than 6 1/2 inches in length, $0.02775 per cigarette, counting each 2 3/4 inch or fraction as a separate cigarette.	Reports by distributors— sales to other distributors, 15th of each month; interstate sales, 10th of each month.
	Cigarette papers, etc.—50 papers or less, 0.5¢; 51 to 100, 1¢; more than 100, 0.5¢ for each 50 or fraction.	Payment—by purchase of stamps and affixing to individual packages.
	Tubes—1¢ for each 50 tubes or fraction.	
	Tobacco products tax—18% of wholesale price.	Reports and payments— before 15th of each month.
Sales and use tax.	Sales—6% of gross retail income.	Returns and payment— monthly within 30 days after close of the month (within 20 days if average monthly liability for prior year exceeded $1,000).
	Use—6% of sales price.	

Tax	Basis—Rates	Due Dates
Insurance (foreign companies) tax.	Foreign companies and domestic companies electing to pay the tax—1.3% of gross premiums less allowable deductions, including consideration for reinsurance, dividends paid or credited, premiums returned, and unearned premiums.	Reports—March 1. Payments—estimated tax due on or before the 15th days of April, June, September and December; balance of tax due with annual report.
	Fire companies—An additional 0.5% of gross premiums less returned premiums and consideration received from reinsurance.	Fire companies—payments—before March 2.
	Surplus lines brokers, 2.5%.	Surplus lines brokers—Financial statement—March 31; payments—February 1 and August 1.
Inheritance tax; estate tax; generation-skipping tax.	Inheritance tax—Class A—1% to 10% measured by fair market value of property transferred at death, or during lifetime in contemplation of death. Exempt—surviving spouse, fully exempt; any others, $100,000. Class B—7% to 15%; exempt—$500. Class C—10% to 20%; exempt—$100. Credit allowed for estate tax paid.	Inheritance tax—Returns—within 9 months after death to probate court. Payment—at time of transfer but no interest accrues until 12 months thereafter.
	Estate tax—amount by which federal credit exceeds inheritance taxes paid to all states including Indiana. Based on net estate, as defined by federal law, of resident and nonresident decedents.	Estate tax—within 12 months after death.
	Generation-skipping tax—tax equal to the federal credit.	Generation-skipping tax—Return and payment due 12 months after the date of death of the person whose death resulted in the generation-skipping transfer.

Iowa

Tax System.—The Iowa tax system was originally based primarily on a general property tax. The property tax has now been replaced as a source of state revenue (although property continues to be taxed at all other levels of government) by corporate and special income taxes, a sales tax and various occupational and license taxes. The legislature has delegated broad licensing powers to municipalities, but such powers are limited to specific authorizations. An outline of the Iowa tax system follows:

Tax	Basis—Rates	Due Dates
Corporate organization and filing fees.	Domestic—articles of incorporation, $50.	At the time of filing articles of incorporation.
	Foreign—certificate of authority, $100.	At the time of filing application for certificate of authority.
Biennial report.	Biennial report—$45.	Biennial report—Between January 1 and April 1 of even-numbered years.
General income tax.	Individuals—**2006 Rates:** First $1,300 of taxable income, 0.36%; over $1,300 to $2,600, 0.72%; over $2,600 to $5,200, 2.43%; over $5,200 to $11,700, 4.50%; over $11,700 to $19,500, 6.12%; over $19,500 to $26,000, 6.48%; over $26,000 to $39,000, 6.80%; over $39,000 to $58,500, 7.92%; and over $58,500, 8.98%; or an alternative minimum tax equal 6.7% of the taxpayer's minumum taxable income. Withholding required.	Returns and payment—last day of 4th month after end of tax year. Estimated payments—installments for calendar-year taxpayers on April 30, June 30, September 30, January 31; or installments for fiscal-year taxpayers on last day of 4th, 6th, and 9th months of current fiscal year and 1st month of the next fiscal year.
	Nonresidents—Same rates as above on income derived from Iowa.	
	Corporations—first $25,000 of net taxable income, 6%; $25,001 to $100,000, 8%; $100,001 to $250,000, 10%; over $250,000, 12% or the greater of the income or franchise tax or the state alternative minimum tax, which equals to 60% of the maximum Iowa corporate income tax rate (rounded to the nearest 0.1%) of the taxpayer's state alternative minimum taxable income.	Returns and payment—last day of 4th month after end of tax year. Estimated payments—installments for calendar-year taxpayers on April 30, June 30, September 30, December 31; or installments for fiscal-year taxpayers on last day of 4th, 6th, 9th, and 12th months of fiscal year.
	Financial institutions (franchise)—5% of taxable net income.	Returns and payments—last day of 4th month after end of tax year.
General property tax.	Rates fixed locally on an annual basis to meet budget needs. Property is generally assessed at 100% of market value; agricultural property is assessed according to productivity. Personal property is exempt.	Payments—in full before September 1, or in installments by September 1 and March 1.
Loan agencies and credit unions tax (moneys and credits tax).	Corporations engaged in business as loan agencies—5 mills per dollar of capital. Credit unions—5 mills per dollar times legal and special reserves in excess of $40,000.	Payment, same as general property. Report from loan agencies, March 1.

Tax	Basis—Rates	Due Dates
Public utilities property tax.	100% of actual value of: operating property of electric transmission lines outside towns and cities, telegraph and telephone companies, apportioned on mileage basis to various taxing districts; property of water works, gas works, pipelines, electric light and power, and street or electric railway companies.	Reports—May 1; railway and pipeline companies, April 1.
	$0.03 per $1,000 of assessed value of all operating property and other property that is primarily and directly used in the production, generation, transmission, or delivery of electricity or natural gas subject to a replacement tax or transfer replacement tax.	Payment—same as general property tax.
Grain handler's tax.	1/4 mill per bushel of grain handled.	Report—between January 1 and 60 days thereafter. Payment—same as general property tax.
Alcoholic beverage taxes.	Beer—19¢ per gallon; $5.89 per barrel of beer, prorated for lesser amounts. Wine—$1.75 per gallon or fraction.	Beer and wine—10th of each month.
Gasoline tax; special fuel tax.	Motor fuel—21¢ per gallon. Special fuel (diesel)—22.5¢ per gallon. Liquefied petroleum gas—20¢ per gallon. Aircraft fuel—8¢ per gallon for gasoline, 3¢ per gallon for special fuel. Ethanol-blended gasoline—19¢ per gallon (until 6/30/07). E-85 blended gasoline—17¢ per gallon. Compressed natural gas—16¢ per 100 c.ft.	Reports and payments—last day of each month; last day of the month following a quarter for interstate motor vehicle operators; importers must report and pay semimonthly, due on the last day of the month (for the first 15 days), and on the 15th of the following month (for the remainder).
Motor vehicle rental tax.	Automobile rental tax—5% of rental price.	Reports and payments—last days of April, July, October and January.
Cigarette and tobacco products tax.	Cigarettes and little cigars—18 mills per cigarette (36¢ per pack of 20) or per little cigar.	Payment—by purchase of stamps. Reports—10th of each month.
	Tobacco products—22% of wholesale price of tobacco products.	Tobacco products—20th of each month.
Realty transfer tax.	80¢ per $500 or fractional part in excess of $500 paid for the real property transferred.	Payment—when deed or other instrument conveying the property is presented for recording.

Tax	Basis—Rates	Due Dates
Sales tax; use (compensating) tax.	Sales tax—5% of gross receipts from sales of tangible personal property, utilities, admission to amusements, fairs and athletic events, operation of amusement devices and games of skill, sales of photography and printing services, vulcanizing, recapping and retreading services, service or warranty contracts, renting of sleeping quarters for 31 consecutive days or less, miscellaneous services, rents, royalties and copyright and license fees, prepaid telephone calling cards, and solid waste collection services.	Sales—last day of April, July, October and January. Monthly by the 20th if over $6,000 but not more than $60,000. Annually by January 31 if annual liability is less than $120. Deposits are required on the 25th of the month of collection and the 10th of the following month if semimonthly collections exceed $2,500.
	Use tax—5% of purchase price of tangible personal property for use within the state.	Use—last day of April, July, October, and January, except if monthly collections exceed $1,500, deposits are due on or before the 20th day of the month following the month of collection. Total quarterly amount due with quarterly report by the last day of the month following the end of the quarter. If annual use tax liability does not exceed $120, reports and payments due January 31.
Pipeline companies inspection fee.	Annual inspection fee—50¢ per mile of pipeline or fraction thereof for each inch of diameter of pipeline located in the state.	Pipeline companies—fee paid for calendar year in advance between January 1 and February 1.
Environmental protection charge.	Environmental protection charge—1¢ per gallon of petroleum products deposited in qualifying tanks.	Returns—by the last day of the month following the close of each quarter.

Tax	Basis—Rates	Due Dates
Electric and natural gas replacement taxes.	Electric replacement delivery tax—Equal to sum of the following: (1) the number of kilowatt hours of electricity delivered to consumers within each electric competitive service area during the tax year multiplied by electric replacement delivery tax rate in effect for each electric competitive service area and (2) the number of kilowatt hours of electricity delivered to consumers within each electric competitive service area during the tax year multiplied by the municipal electric transfer replacement tax rate for each electric competitive service area, if applicable. Natural gas replacement delivery tax—Equal to sum of the following: (1) the number of therms of natural gas delivered to consumers within each electric competitive service area during the tax year multiplied by the natural gas replacement delivery tax rate in effect for each electric competitive service area and (2) the number of therms of natural gas delivered to consumers within each electric competitive service area during the tax year multiplied by the municipal natural gas transfer replacement tax rate for each electric competitive service area, if applicable. Replacement tax is imposed on all natural gas delivered to or consumed by a new electric power generating plant for purposes of generating electricity within Iowa at the rate of 0.0111¢ per therm of natural gas. Replacement generation tax—$0.0006 per kilowatt hour of electricity generated on persons that generate electricity; $0.1847¢ per kilowatt hour on electricity generated by a hydroelectric generating power plant with a capacity of 100 megawatts or greater. Replacement transmission tax—Equal to sum of the following: $550 per pole mile not exceeding 100 kilovolts; $3,000 per pole mile greater than 100 kilovolts but not exceeding 150 kilovolts; $700 per pole mile greater than 150 kilovolts but not exceeding 300 kilovolts; and $7,000 per pole mile greater than 300 kilovolts.	Replacement taxes—Returns—March 31 of year following income. No return for any tax year if tax liability before credits is $300 or less. Payment—One-half of tax due by September 30, other half by succeeding March 31.

Tax	Basis—Rates	Due Dates
Insurance companies tax.	Life insurance companies and health service associations: 1% of adjusted gross premiums received in 2006 and thereafter. Insurers other than life insurance companies: 1.25% of adjusted gross premiums received in 2006 and 1% in 2007 and thereafter. Marine insurance underwriting profits: 6.5% of profits from insurance written in Iowa. Unauthorized insurers: 2% of gross premiums received.	Insurance premiums tax—Reports and payments—due March 1. Prepayment requirements for taxpayers with previous-year liability exceeding $1,000. Life insurance companies and health service associations, 50% of the prior year's tax, due June 1, and an additional percentage of the prior year's tax, due June 30 of each year. Insurers other than life insurance companies: 50% of the prior year's tax, due June 1, and an additional percentage of the prior year's tax, due June 30 of each year, 50% for 2006 and thereafter. Marine insurance underwriting profits: reports and payments due June 1.
	Foreign companies subject to retaliatory taxes.	
Inheritance tax; estate tax; generation-skipping transfer tax.	Inheritance—No tax imposed if the value if the estate is less than $25,000 after deducting liabilities. Class 1—Entire amount of property, interest in property, and income is exempt. Class includes surviving spouse, lineal descendants, and lineal ascendants. Class 2—5% to 10%. Exempt—none. Class 3—10% to 15%. Exempt—none. Class 4—10%. Exempt—none. Class 5—15%. Exempt—none.	Payment—on or before the last day of the ninth month after decedent's death.
	Generation-skipping transfer—Tax equal to the federal credit.	
	Estate tax—Amount by which federal credit exceeds inheritance taxes, based on value of entire estate, subject to federal estate tax, at market value.	Estate tax—Returns and payment—within nine months after date of death.

Kansas

Tax System.—The Kansas tax system was founded on a general property tax at uniform rates within each taxing district. The general property tax has been supplemented by taxes on incomes, sales, use, occupations and privileges. In the case of corporations, a franchise tax based on capital stock is also imposed. An outline of the Kansas tax system follows:

Tax	Basis—Rates	Due Dates
Corporate organization and qualification fees.	Domestic or foreign corporations: up to $100, nonprofit up to $20 application and recording fee.	When filing articles of incorporation of domestic corporation or qualification of foreign corporation.
Corporation franchise fee.	Nonprofit corporations $40 annual report fee. For-profit corporations $55.	At time of filing annual report.
Income tax.	Individuals—married individuals filing jointly, 3.5% of first $30,000 of Kansas taxable income, $1,050 plus 6.25% of next $30,000, and $2,925 plus 6.45% of excess over $60,000. The rate for single individuals and married individuals filing separately is 3.5% of the first $15,000; $525 plus 6.25% of excess over $15,000; and $1,462.50 plus 6.45% of the excess over $30,000.	Returns and payments—individuals and corporations—15th day of 4th month after end of income year. Domestic insurers, when federal income tax return is due.
	Nonresidents—same on income from sources in Kansas.	
	General withholding is required.	Payment of estimated tax is due on April 15, June 15, September 15, and January 15 (December 15 for corporations).
	Corporations: 4% on federal taxable income with modifications from business done in the state or derived from Kansas sources. A 3.35% surtax is imposed on taxable income in excess of $50,000.	Due dates—Corporate income-Annually, April 15 or the 15th day of the fourth month after end of income year.
Bank privilege (income) tax.	Banks: 2.25% on net income plus a 2.125% surtax on net income over $25,000. The tax on trust companies, savings and loan associations and development credit corporations is 2.25% plus a 2.25% surtax on net income over $25,000. These taxes are in lieu of taxes on stock or assets.	Financial institutions—returns and payment due 15th day of 4th month after end of federal tax year. Quarterly payments of estimated tax required.
General property tax.	Real and tangible personal property—Valued at fair market value, unless specifically classified at a lower percentage. 1 mill for educational institutions, and .5 mill for institutions that care for the disabled.	Tangible personal property—returns—March 15. General property—returns—railroads, motor carriers and public utilities, March 20. Oil and gas property statements, April 1. Payment—December 20 and June 20 (in full on December 20 if $10 or less).

Tax	Basis—Rates	Due Dates
Alcoholic beverage tax.	Excise—beer, 18¢ per gallon; wine and alcoholic beverages, 14% alcohol or less, 30¢ per gallon; over 14%, 75¢ per gallon; alcohol and spirits, $2.50 per gallon.	Liquor control tax—reports and payments, 15th day of each month.
	Enforcement—8% of gross receipts.	Enforcement—reports and payments, 25th day of each month.
	Clubs—10% of gross receipts.	Clubs—reports and payments, 25th day of each month.
Motor vehicle fuel and special fuel tax.	Motor vehicle—24¢ per gallon. Special fuel—26¢ per gallon. LP-gas—23¢ per gallon. Effective January 1, 2007, E85 fuel—17¢ per gallon.	Reports and payments—25th of each month.
	Additional 1¢ per gallon manufactured or imported, levied to fund storage tank release trust (tax may be suspended depending on fund balance).	Interstate motor fuel users—last day of January, April, July and October.
	Additional 1.5¢ per barrel petroleum products inspection fee levied on the manufacturer, importer, exporter or distributor for first possession of petroleum products.	
Severance tax.	Oil and gas, 8% of gross value; coal, $1 per ton.	Reports—oil and gas—on or before the last day of the month following the month of severance; coal—on or before the 20th day of the second month following the month of severance.
		Payments—on or before the 20th day of the second month following the month of severance.
	Conservation fee fund tax—Oil and gas-rates set by State Corporation Commission: Oil-54.7 mills per barrel; Gas-9.13 mills per 1, 000 cubic fee; Plugged well-.0325 cents per foot of well depth ($35 minimum)	Same as for oil and gas tax (above).
Cigarette and tobacco products tax.	Cigarette and tobacco products tax—79¢ per pack of 20 cigarettes; 99¢ per pack of 25 cigarettes	Cigarettes—report (wholesalers), 10th of each month. Payment, by purchase of stamps.
	Tobacco products—10% of wholesale sales price.	Tobacco products—reports and payments, 20th of each month.
Mortgage registration fee.	0.26% of the principal debt or obligation secured by real estate mortgage, or sales contract under which the vendee is entitled to possession.	At time of filing for record, or renewal or extension.

Tax	Basis—Rates	Due Dates
Sales tax; use (compensating) tax.	Sales tax—5.3% of gross receipts from retail sales, rendering certain services, serving drinks or meals, selling admissions, operating coin-operated devices renting hotel rooms, and renting property. Motor vehicle rental is subject to an additional 3.5% excise tax, imposed on gross receipts from rental or lease of motor vehicles for a period of 28 days or less.	Sales tax—Liability not over $80.00, annually-January 25; $80.01-$3,200, quarterly- 25th day of April, July, October, and January; $3,200.01-$32,000, monthly-25th day of each month; $32,000.01 and above-prepaid monthly.
	Use tax—5.3% of sales price of tangible personal property purchased for storage, use or consumption. This rate will decrease to 5% on July 1, 2006.	Use tax—same as sales tax.
Private car companies tax.	Private car companies—2.5% of gross earnings from use or operation of cars within state.	Private car companies—withheld by railroads—March 1.
Insurance companies tax.	Domestic companies, 2%; foreign companies, 2% of gross premiums or retaliatory tax, whichever is greater; captive insurers, 2%.	Reports—60 days after January 1; payment, when assessed. Estimated taxes due June 15 and December 15.
	Agents, 6% of gross premiums; individuals placing a policy with an unauthorized insurer, 6% of premium applicable to risk in Kansas.	Agents—report and payment due March 1. Policies placed with unauthorized insurers—report and payment due within 120 days after writing the risk.
	Fire insurance companies, 2% of all premiums on fire and lightning insurance covering Kansas risks the preceding year. Fire marshal tax, up to .80%.	Fire insurance companies tax—report and payment, April 1. Fire marshal—payment March 15.
	Professional and trade associations not subject to the Commissioner's jurisdiction, 1% of annual Kansas gross premiums.	Payment—May 1.
Estate tax	Estate—Effective for decedents dying after January 1, 2007, new graduated tax based on the value of an estate in excess of $1 million as follows: (1) for 2007, ranges from 3% on the value of estates in excess of $1 million through a maximum tax of $610,000 plus 10% of any estate value in excess of $10,000,000; (2) for 2008, range decreases to 1% on the value of estates in excess of $1 million through a maximum tax of $320,000 plus 7% of any amount in excess of $10,000,000; (3) for 2009, range further decreases to 0.5% of any estate with a value over $1 million through a maximum tax of $135,000 plus 3% of any excess over $10,000,000.	Estate—Return and payment—by date the federal return is due (generally within nine months of decedent's death).

Kentucky

Tax System.—A general property tax is imposed on real and tangible personal property at uniform rates in the taxing districts where such property is located. The property tax is supplemented by (1) state taxes on franchises, incomes, privileges and occupations and (2) municipal taxes and inspection fees. An outline of the Kentucky tax system follows:

Tax	Basis—Rates	Due Dates
Corporate organization and qualification fees.	Domestic—1¢ per share for 20,000 or less; 1/2¢ per share in excess of 20,000 up to 200,000; 1/5¢ per share in excess of 200,000. Minimum fee: $10. Annual domestic and foreign corporation report—$15. Foreign—certificate of authority, $90. Domestic—articles of incorporation, $40.	Domestic—payment at time of incorporation or increase of capital stock. Annual report—due by June 30. Foreign—payment at time of qualification.
Corporation license tax.	$2.10 per $1,000 of total capital employed in the business that is apportioned to Kentucky. Minimum, $30. License tax eliminated eff. for tax periods ending on or after 12/31/05.	Reports and payment—15th day of 4th month after end of fiscal year.
General income tax.	Individuals—2% of net income from up to $3,000; 3% of net income over $3,000 and up to $4,000; 4% of net income over $4,000 and up to $5,000; 5% of net income over $5,000 and up to $8,000; 5.8% of net income over $8,000 and up to $75,000; and 6% of net income over $75,000. Withholding required on all wages. Corporations—Taxpayers pay tax based on the greater of the taxable net income computation, the alternative minimum calculation, or the minimum tax. Tax measured by taxable net income is as follows: First $50,000, 4%; over $50,000 to $100,000, 5%; over $100,000, 7%. Effective 1/1/07, top rate reduced to 6%. For tax years beginning on or after 1/1/06 and before 1/1/07, with gross receipts or gross profits of $6 million or more, alternative minimum tax calculation is equal to the lesser of: 9 1/2¢ per $100 of the taxpayer's gross receipts; or 75¢ per $100 of gross profits. For taxpayers with gross receipts or gross profits over $3 million but less than $6 million, gross receipts or gross profits portion of alternative minimum tax may be reduced by $2,850, or $22,500 in the case of the gross profits computation, multiplied by a fraction, the numerator of which is $6 million less the amount of gross receipts or gross profits for the taxable year and the denominator of which is $3 million. Minimum tax, $175. Effective for taxable years beginning on or after January 1, 2007, every corporation, S corporation and limited liability PTE with over $3 million in gross receipts or gross profits from all sources must pay greater of an annual limited liability entity tax or $175.	Returns and payments—15th day of 4th month after end of income year. Declaration of personal income tax—April 15. Payment—estimated personal income taxes, 15th of 3rd, 6th, 9th, and 13th months thereafter.

Tax	Basis—Rates	Due Dates
	All corporations expecting tax to exceed $5,000 file declarations of estimated tax.	Declarations of corporate estimated tax—June 15 or 15th day of 6th month of the taxable year. Payments—with declaration, and on or before 15th days of 9th and 12th months of the taxable year.
Bank franchise tax.	1.1% of net capital; minimum $300.	Reports and payments—March 15.
General property tax; public service companies tax.	General property—Aggregate of state and local fixed annually to meet local budget requirements. State rate on real property, for 2006, 12.8¢ per $100; tobacco and unmanufactured agricultural products (not taxed locally), 1.5¢ per $100; freight car rolling stock for 2005, 71.12¢ per $100 (weighted aggregate state rate); money on hand, notes, bonds, accounts and other credits, 25¢ per $100; farm machinery, livestock and domestic fowl, 0.1¢ per $100; goods held for sale, raw materials and in-process materials, 5¢ per $100; manufacturing machinery, commercial radio, TV and telephonic equipment and pollution control equipment, 15¢ per $100; all other property, 45¢ per $100.	General property—real property returns between January 1 and March 1; intangible property returns between January 1 and May 15; utilities, April 30. Payment—September 15; public service companies, 30 days after notice.
	Intangibles (eff. 1/1/06, tax on intangibles is repealed)—Deposits in financial institutions, 0.001% of the amount of the deposit; broker's accounts receivable, 10¢ on $100; 1.5¢ per $100 on the following intangibles when a taxable situs outside Kentucky has not been acquired: (a) accounts receivable, notes, bonds, credits, etc.; (b) patents, trademarks, copyrights and licensing or royalty agreements; (c) notes, bonds, accounts receivable and intercompany accounts; and (d) tobacco base allotments; domestic insurers, 0.1¢ for each $100 of capital reserves and one of the following methods: method one requires 0.001¢ for each $100 of taxable capital and $1.50 for each $100 on premium receipts; or method two requires $1.50 for each $100 on premium receipts. Retirement plans, 0.1¢ per $100.	Intangibles—reports: May 15; banks, trust companies and real estate title insurance companies, February 1; Financial institutions, January 21; savings and loan associations and savings banks, during January; securities brokers, March 1; domestic life insurers, April 1; unmined coal, oil or gas reserves, April 15.
		Payment: Financial institutions, March 1; brokers, within 30 days of receipt of the bill; domestic life insurers, estimated payments are made in $1/3$ installments by June 1, October 1, and March 1 following.

Tax	Basis—Rates	Due Dates
Alcoholic beverages tax.	Excise—sale and distribution, beer $2.50 per barrel, wine 50¢ per gallon with a minimum tax of 4¢ on any container, spirits $1.92 per gallon; except 25¢ per gallon when placed in containers for sale at retail where the distilled spirits represent 6% or less of the total volume of the contents of the containers; wholesalers' distilled spirits per case tax, 5¢.	Excise tax—Reports and payments, on or before the 20th of each month.
	Gross receipts—wholesaler of distilled spirits and wine and distributors of beer, 11% of gross receipts.	Gross receipts tax—Reports and payments, on or before the 20th of each month.
Motor fuels tax; motor carrier fuel use tax; liquefied petroleum motor fuel tax.	Variable. Third quarter 2006, 18.3¢ on gas and 15.3¢ on special fuel, plus a petroleum environmental assurance fee of not to exceed 1.4¢ per gallon. Heavy equipment carriers are subject to a surtax of 2% on gasoline and 4.7% on special fuels. Liquefied petroleum gas motor fuels excise tax, 18.3¢ per gallon.	Reports and payments—25th day of each month, except last day of month following each quarter under the carrier gasoline use tax.
Oil production and severance taxes.	Oil production—4.5% of market value of crude petroleum produced.	Oil production reports and payment—20th of each month for the transporter.
	Coal severance—4.5% of gross value of coal severed and/or processed. Minimum tax, 50¢ per ton of severed coal. Tax limited to 50¢ per ton or 4% of the selling price per ton, whichever is less, on coal used for burning solid waste.	Coal severance—reports and payments, 20th of each month.
	Natural resources severance—4.5% of gross value of natural gas and other natural resources severed or processed. Tax limited to 12¢ per ton of clay and 14¢ per ton of limestone used to manufacture cement.	Natural resources severance—reports and payments, last day of each month.
Motor vehicle use tax.	6% of retail sales price or gross rental charge of U-Drive-Its, except 81% of such price for new trucks whose gross weight is over 10,000 lbs; minimum tax $6. $25 per month on dealers' loaner vehicles.	Payment—when owner titles a vehicle.
Cigarette tax.	3¢ plus a surtax of 27¢, for 30¢ per pack of 20 cigarettes, plus an enforcement fee set annually (currently 0.001¢ per package). Tax of 7.5% imposed on gross receipts of wholesalers of other tobacco products, including cigars and chewing tobacco. Tax of 9.5¢ per unit of 1.5 ounces imposed on wholesalers of snuff.	Reports—20th of each month. Payment—by purchase of stamps.
Realty transfer tax.	50¢ per $500 of value declared in the deed transferring title to realty.	Payment—collected by county clerk as prerequisite to recordation.

Tax	Basis—Rates	Due Dates
Sales and use tax.	6% of retail sales price of property and enumerated services sold. Property includes gas, electricity, water, and prepaid calling arrangements. Services include rental of transient accommodations, sales of admissions, sewer services, and communications services.	Reports and payments—20th of each month; if allowed by the Revenue Department, quarterly returns are due by the 20th day of the month following each quarter and annually are due by the 20th day of the 13th month. If average monthly liability exceeds $10,000, 25th day of the current month for period from 16th of preceding month through 15th of current month.
Transient room (lodging) tax.	1% of the rent on occupancy of any suite, room, or cabin charged by motels, hotels, inns, and other accommodation businesses, excluding campgrounds. Imposed in addition to 6% sales tax and any locally assessed transient room tax.	Payment—20th day of the following month.
Telecommunication services taxes.	3% on retail purchase of multichannel video programming services, such as cable service, satellite broadcast, and wireless cable service.	Payment—20th day of the following month.
	1.3% of gross revenues of telephone providers and 2.4% of gross revenues of cable, broadcast satellite, and wireless cable service providers.	Payment—20th day of the following month.
Insurance premiums tax.	$2 per $100 or retaliatory tax, whichever is greater. Fire insurers are subject to additional tax of 0.75%. Unauthorized insurers—2% of gross premiums. Surplus lines brokers—3% of premiums. Surcharge on domestic, foreign or alien insurers (other than life and health), $1.50 per $100 of premiums on Kentucky risks. Life insurance companies—one of two elective methods: method one requires 0.001¢ for each $100 of taxable capital and $1.50 for each $100 on premium receipts; method two requires $1.50 for each $100 on premium receipts.	Returns and payments—March 1, except surplus line brokers report and pay within 30 days of end of calendar quarter. Surcharge, 20th of each month.
		Payment of estimated tax—$^1/_3$ by June 1, October 1 and March 1 following.
Inheritance tax; estate tax.	Inheritance—Class A—Each beneficiary's total inheritable interest is exempt if the decedent dies after June 30, 1998.	Inheritance—returns and payment—at death, but no interest accrues for 18 months.
	Class B—4% to 16%; exemption, $1,000.	
	Class C—6% to 16%; exemption, $500.	
	Estate—Amount by which federal credit based on net estate as defined by federal law, and allocated to Kentucky, exceeds inheritance tax. Not applicable to estates of decedents dying after 12/31/04.	Estate—same as inheritance.

Louisiana

Tax System.—The tax system was founded upon a general property tax assessed by the several parish assessors, subject to review and approval of the parish boards of equalization and the State Tax Commission. Assessments are made uniformly according to value within each taxing district. The property tax is supplemented by other state taxes, the revenue from which in many instances is shared by the local governments. These include taxes on sales, use, severance, incomes, franchises, occupations and privileges. Municipal license taxes and inspection fees are also exacted within local jurisdictions for purposes of revenue or regulation. An outline of the Louisiana tax system follows:

Tax	Basis—Rates	Due Dates
Corporate organization and qualification fees.	Domestic and foreign—$60 for domestic corporations and $100 for foreign corporations. Annual report—$25.	Domestic—at time of incorporation. Foreign—at time of qualification. Annual report for foreign and domestic corporations due on or before the anniversary date of their qualification.
Corporation franchise tax.	Effective January 1, 2006, the franchise tax will be imposed on the tax base at a rate of $1.50 for each $1,000, or major fraction thereof, on the first $300,000 of taxable capital and $3 for each $1,000, or major fraction thereof, that exceeds $300,000 of taxable capital, with a minimum tax of $10 per year. The initial corporation franchise tax is $10.	Returns and payment—Initial return: An initial return covering the period beginning with the date the corporation first becomes liable for filing a return and ending with the next close of an accounting period must be filed on or before the 15th day of the 3rd month after the corporation first becomes liable. Payment due with return. Annual return: Louisiana franchise tax accrues on the 1st day of each accounting year, and the return for that period must be filed on or before the 15th day of the 4th month of that accounting year. Payment due with return.

Tax	Basis—Rates	Due Dates
Income tax.	Individuals—first $12,500 of taxable income—2%; next $12,500—4%; over $25,000—6%. The tax conforms to federal provisions and is determined by reference to appropriate tax tables based on Louisiana tax table income and whether the taxpayer is single, married filing separately, married filing jointly or a qualifying widow(er) or the head of a household (the tax may not exceed the above rates).	Returns and payment—May 15 for calendar year and 15th day of 5th month after close of income year for fiscal year. Estimated tax—declarations and payment due on 15th of April, June, September, and January for calendar year and 15th day of the 4th, 6th, 9th months of income year and 1st month following close of the fiscal year.
	Corporations—4% of first $25,000 of Louisiana taxable income; $1,000 plus 5% of next $25,000; $2,250 plus 6% of next $50,000; $5,250 plus 7% of next $100,000; $12,250 plus 8% of Louisiana taxable income in excess of $200,000.	Returns and payments—Due on or before the 15th day of the 4th month following the close of the accounting period (April 15 for a calendar year).
	Withholding required.	Returns and payments—Quarterly returns and payments due on the last day of the month following the close of the quarterly period (April 30, July 31, October 31, and January 31). Monthly returns and payments due on the last day of the month following the close of the monthly period. Semimonthly returns and payments due on the 15th day of the month for taxes withheld on wages paid during the period between the 16th day and the last day of the previous month or due on the last day of the month for taxes withheld on wages paid during the first 15 days of the same month.
General property tax.	Property is taxed at a rate equal to all lawful levies and is assessed at a percentage of fair market or use value.	Self-reporting forms to assessors by April 1 or 45 days after receipt, whichever is later. In Jefferson Parish, within 45 days after receipt. Payment by December 31 except for Orleans Parish, which is February 1.
Bank property.	Assessment fee—.015% of assessed property value from July 1, 2006, through June 30, 2008. Bank shares—15% of fair market value less 50% of assessed property value.	Bank condition statement—February 15 of following year.

Tax	Basis—Rates	Due Dates
Alcoholic beverages tax.	Excise—Beverages of low alcoholic content (beer), $10 per barrel containing not more than 31 gallons. Malt beverages, $10 per barrel. Liquor, 66¢ per liter. Sparkling wines, 42¢ per liter. Still wines per liter: 14% or less alcohol, 3¢; 14% to 24%, 6¢; over 24%, 42¢. Native wines per liter: 14% or less alcohol, 3¢; 14% to 24%, 6¢ (repealed, effective June 30, 2006).	Beverages of high alcoholic content (liquor and wine): Report filed and taxes paid on or before the 15th day of the month following the taxable month. Beverages of low alcoholic content (beer): Report filed and taxes paid within 20 days after the end of each calendar month.
Gasoline tax.	Gasoline and diesel fuel—16¢ per gallon, plus additional 4¢ per gallon, of gasoline or motor fuels (other than tractor fuel) used, sold, or consumed in state. Users of liquefied petroleum gas and compressed natural gas pay an annual flat rate or a variable rate, in lieu of the gallonage tax.	Reports and payments— Gasoline: Within 20 days after the end of each monthly period. Diesel fuel: For suppliers, returns and payments due monthly on or before the 20th of each month following the taxable month. For users, returns and payments due the 25th of the month after the close of each quarter. For liquefied petroleum gas or compressed natural gases, returns and payments due annually on July 31 for the year ended June 30.
	Inspection fee—$1/8$ of 1¢ per gallon.	
	Oil spill contingency fee—2¢ per barrel of crude oil (rate may be suspended or increased depending on fund balance and other factors).	Payment—quarterly, by the last day of the month following the calendar quarter in which the liability for the fee is incurred.

Tax	Basis—Rates	Due Dates
Severance tax.	**Minerals**—Sulphur, $1.03 per long ton of 2,240 lbs.; Salt, 6¢ per ton of 2,000 lbs.; Coal, 10¢ per ton of 2,000 lbs.; Ores, 10¢ per ton of 2,000 lbs.; Marble, 20¢ per ton of 2,000 lbs.; Stone, 3¢ per ton of 2,000 lbs.; Sand, 6¢ per ton of 2,000 lbs.; Shells, 6¢ per ton of 2,000 lbs.; Salt content in brine, when used in the manufacture of other products and not marketed as salt, 0.5¢ per ton of 2,000 lbs.; Lignite, 12¢ per ton of 2,000 lbs. An annual regulatory fee of 8¢ is imposed on all coal and lignite mined in Louisiana.	Reports and payments—Tax returns filed by the last day of the month following the taxable month except certain oil and gas severance tax returns, which are due the 25th day of the second month following the month to which the tax applies.
	Timber—Trees and timber, 2.25% of current stumpage value as determined by the Louisiana Forestry Commission. Pulpwood, 5% of current stumpage value as determined by the Louisiana Forestry Commission. Forest products grown on reforested lands, 6% of value. This tax is in lieu of all other taxes.	
	Gas—The tax rate for natural gas and equivalent gas volumes of natural gasoline, casinghead gasoline, and other natural gas liquids per 1,000 cu. ft. at a base pressure of 15.025 lbs. per sq. in. absolute and at 60 degrees Fahrenheit is adjusted annually on July 1 and may never be less than 7¢. Full rate, 37.3¢ per thousand cu. ft., effective July 1, 2006, to June 30, 2007 (25.2¢ per thousand cu. ft. prior to July 1, 2006). Incapable oil–well gas, 3¢ per thousand cu. ft. Incapable gas–well gas, 1.3¢ per thousand cu. ft. Contract rate, 7¢ per thousand cu. ft.	
	Oil (per barrel of 42 gals.)—Full rate oil/condensate, 12.5% of value. Incapable oil rate, 6.25% of value. Stripper oil rate, 3.125% of value (stripper oil is exempt as long as the average posted price for a 30-day period is less than $20 per barrel). Reclaimed oil, 3.125% of value. Approved mining and horizontal drilling projects, 3.125% of value (rate applies only to the working interest owner's share of production and reverts to the full rate of 12.5% of value when the cumulative value of hydrocarbon production is equal to 2⅓ times the total private investment in the project).	
	Oilfield site restoration fees—Fee per barrel on crude oil and condensate is 1.5¢ for full-rate wells; 0.75¢ for incapable wells; and 0.375¢ for stripper wells. The fee per thousand cu. ft. on full-rate natural gas and casing head gas production is 0.3¢; 0.12¢ for low-pressure oil wells; and 0.0525¢ for incapable gas wells. An annual fee of $10 is imposed on each nonproducing well in the state except temporary abandoned or saltwater disposal wells in stripper fields. Fee may be suspended depending on revenues.	Returns and payments—quarterly, on or before the 25th day of the second month following the quarter period.
Automobile rental tax.	Through June 30, 2012, 3% of gross proceeds from lease or rental of an automobile under a rental contract for 29 days or less.	Reports and payments—the 20th day of the month following the close of the reporting period.

Tax	Basis—Rates	Due Dates
Chain store tax.	$10 per store in parish or municipality for not more than 10 stores, wherever located, to $550 per store in parish or municipality for over 500 stores, wherever located.	Reports—February 1. Payment—February 1.
Tobacco tax.	Cigarettes—1.8¢ (includes additional tax of $4/20$ of 1¢) each (36¢ per pack).	Cigarettes and tobacco—reports—20th of each month. Payment—by purchase of stamps or use of metered stamping machines.
	Cigars—8% of invoice price if invoiced at $120 per 1,000 or less; 20% if invoiced at over $120 per 1,000.	
	Smoking tobacco—33% of invoice price.	
	Smokeless tobacco—20% of invoice price.	
Sales and use tax.	4% of retail sale, lease or rental, use, consumption, distribution or storage of tangible personal property, sales of services, including admissions and hotel accommodations. Additional 4% tax on mail order sales. Telecommunications and sales of prepaid telephone cards and prepaid telephone authorization numbers, 3%.	Reports and payments—20th of each month following the close of the calendar month or calendar quarter of the reporting period.
Transportation and communication utilities tax.	Public utilities—2% of gross receipts from intrastate business.	Public utilities—20th day of the month following the taxable period; except on or before 30 days after end of each quarter for motor freight lines with gross receipts for the previous fiscal year of not to exceed $5 million.
	Natural gas franchise—1% of the gross receipts from the operation of its franchise or charters in Louisiana.	Reports and payment—Every corporation, domestic or foreign, engaged in the business of transporting natural gas by pipeline in Louisiana must file a return. Returns and payments due quarterly on the last day of the month following the quarterly period and become delinquent after this date.
Telecommunications tax for the deaf.	Telecommunications—5¢ per month for each business and residence access line of every local exchange company.	Telecommunications—Reports and payment within 30 days of each calendar quarter.

Tax	Basis—Rates	Due Dates
Hazardous waste disposal tax.	$30 per dry-weight ton of hazardous waste both generated and disposed of at the same site in Louisiana; $40 per dry-weight ton of hazardous waste disposed of in Louisiana at a site other than the site where generated; and $100 per dry-weight ton of extremely hazardous waste disposed of in Louisiana. For hazardous wastes and extremely hazardous wastes generated outside of Louisiana and disposed of in Louisiana, the tax rate to be levied is the rate of tax or fee imposed on the disposal of such waste in the state where generated, but in no case shall the tax levied be less than the rate charged at the time of disposal for hazardous and extremely hazardous waste generated and disposed of in Louisiana.	Returns and payments— 20th day of the month following the taxable calendar quarter.
Insurance companies gross premiums tax.	Life, health and accident, and health maintenance organizations—premiums of $7,000 or less, $140; over $7,000, $140 plus $225 per each additional $10,000 over $7,000.	Report—March 1. Payment—15th day of the month following the end of each quarter, except that 4th quarter's tax is due March 1; surplus line brokers remit tax on or before the 1st day of March, June, September and December. Tax for support of municipal fire departments and additional tax on fire insurance premiums due within 60 days after end of calendar year. The tax for miscellaneous risks is paid on a quarterly basis.
	Fire, marine, transportation, casualty, surety, or other insurance—premiums of $6,000 or less, $185; over $6,000, $185 plus $300 per each additional $10,000 over $6,000.	
	Foreign and alien insurers (other than life) for support of municipal fire departments—2% of gross premiums on fire risks.	
	Fire marshal's tax—1.25% of gross premiums.	
	Insurers (other than life insurers)—additional 0.25% of annual premiums for insurance against loss or damage by fire on Louisiana property.	
	Unauthorized insurers—5%.	
	Surplus line brokers, same rate applicable to authorized foreign insurers.	
	Foreign companies are subject to retaliatary taxes.	

Tax	Basis—Rates	Due Dates
Inheritance tax; estate tax; gift tax.	Inheritance tax—not applicable to most deaths occurring after 2004.	Inheritance—report—not applicable to most deaths occurring after 2004.
	Estate tax—amount by which federal credit exceeds aggregate amount of death taxes paid to all states, including Louisiana, based on taxable estate as defined by federal law.	Estate tax—returns and payments—within 9 months after decedent's death or prior to filing federal return, whichever comes first.
	Gift tax—sum of gifts made by a donor in excess of the applicable annual exclusion and in excess of any portion of the specific exemption. Rates, 2% on taxable gifts up to $15,000; 3% on gifts over $15,000. Annual exclusion, $12,000 (adjusted for inflation). Specific lifetime exemption, $30,000.	Gift tax—returns and payments—April 15 of year following year in which gift was made.

Maine

Tax System.—Maine derives its revenue from taxes imposed on corporate and individual incomes and real and tangible personal property of residents, and from sales and use taxes, gasoline taxes, motor vehicle registration fees and the cigarette tax. An annual franchise tax on domestic corporations is imposed, and an annual license fee is required from foreign corporations. An outline of the Maine tax system follows:

Tax	Basis—Rates	Due Dates
Corporate organization and qualification fees.	Domestic—par value shares: graduated from $30 per $100,000 for $2,000,000 or less to $3,300 plus $70 per $1,000,000 in excess of $20,000,000. No-par value shares: graduated from 1¢ per share for 20,000 or less to $10,200 plus $\frac{1}{4}$¢ per share in excess of 2,000,000; minimum, $30. Same rates upon increase.	Domestic—at time of incorporation or increase of capital stock.
	Foreign—application for authority to do business, $250.	Foreign—at time of qualification or increase of capital stock.
Corporate annual report.	Domestic and foreign corporations must file an annual report. Domestic filing fee, $85; foreign filing fee, $150.	Annual report—determined by Secretary of State.
Corporate income tax.	Corporations—3.5% of the first $25,000 of Maine net income; $875 plus 7.93% of net income over $25,000; $4,840 plus 8.33% over $75,000; $19,418 plus 8.93% of net income over $250,000. Alternative minimum tax: 5.4% on all AMT income.	Returns and payments—due when federal tax is due; payments of estimated tax, 15th day of 4th, 6th, 9th and 13th (12th for corporations) months of fiscal year.
Franchise tax.	Financial institutions—1% of Maine net income for the tax year plus 39¢ per $1,000 of Maine assets.	Returns and payments—must be filed with the State Tax Assessor on or before the 15th day of the 3rd month following the end of the financial institution's fiscal year.
Personal income tax.	***For 2006 tax year:*** *Single individuals and married persons filing separately:* Less than $4,550, 2%; $4,550 to $9,100, $91 plus 4.5% of the excess over $4,550; $9,100 to $18,250, $296 plus 7% of the excess over $9,100; $18,250 or more, $937 plus 8.5% of the excess over $18,250. *Heads of households:* Less than $6,850, 2%; $6,850 to $13,650, $137 plus 4.5% of the excess over $6,850; $13,650 to $27,400, $443 plus 7% of the excess over $13,650; $27,400 or more, $1,406 plus 8.5% of the excess over $27,400. *Married filing jointly, surviving spouses:* Less than $9,150, 2%; $9,150 to $18,250, $183 plus 4.5% of the excess over $9,150; $18,250 to $36,550, $593 plus 7% of the excess over $18,250; $36,550 or more, $1,874 plus 8.5% of the excess over $36,550.	

Tax	Basis—Rates	Due Dates
General property tax.	General property—valuation of real and personal property based on 100% of current market value. Telecommunications companies—25 mills (2006, 24 mills; 2007, 23 mills; 2008, 22 mills; 2009, 21 mills; 2010 and later, 20 mills) multiplied by the just value of personal property.	General property—assessed as of April 1; due date determined by local jurisdiction.
	Unorganized Territory Tax—set by the State Tax Assessor.	Payment—by October 1.
	Tree growth tax—100% of value adjusted according to local assessment ratio.	Schedule—April 1 of first year.
Alcoholic beverages tax.	Excise—malt liquor: 25¢ per gallon; wine: 30¢ per gallon; sparkling wine either manufactured in or imported into Maine: $1 per gallon; hard cider: 25¢ per gallon either manufactured in or imported into Maine; low-alcohol spirits: $1 per gallon.	Excise—at time of purchase, or, for bonded manufacturers and wholesalers of malt liquor or wine, 10th of each month for preceding month.
	Additional taxes—malt beverages and hard cider: 10¢ per gallon; wine: 30¢ per gallon; sparkling wines and fortified wines: 24¢ per gallon; spirits: $1.25 per proof gallon; low-alcohol spirits products: 24¢ per gallon, plus 30¢ per gallon for product sold to a Maine wholesale licensee.	
Motor fuel taxes.	Gasoline—Effective July 1, 2006, 26.8¢ per gallon (previously, 25.9¢); diesel, 27.9¢ (previously, 27¢); internal combustion fuel bought or used to propel a jet or turbojet engine aircraft: $0.034 per gallon.	Gasoline tax—reports and payments—distributors, exporters, importers, reports due 21st of each month; wholesalers, last day of each month.
	Special fuel—Effective July 1, 2006, distillates, 23¢ per gallon; methanol, 15.2¢ per gallon; ethanol, 18.9¢ per gallon; non-exempt low-energy fuel, 21¢ per gallon; propane, 19.4¢ per gallon; compressed natural gas, 23.2¢ per standard cubic foot.	Special fuel tax reports and payments—suppliers and retailers, on or before the last day of each month; users, on or before the last day of January, April, July, and October (January 31 if annual tax is $100 or less).
	Ground Water Oil Clean-Up Fee—38¢ per barrel of gasoline; 19¢ per barrel of refined petroleum products and their by-products, other than gasoline, liquid asphalt and #6 fuel oil, including #2 fuel oil, kerosene, jet fuel, and diesel fuel; 4¢ per barrel of #6 fuel oil.	Payment—monthly.
	Petroleum Marketing Fund Fee—40¢ for each 10,000 gallons.	Payment—September 1.
Mining excise tax.	The tax on each mine site is the greater of (1) the value of facilities and equipment multiplied by 0.005; or (2) the gross proceeds multiplied by (a) if net proceeds are greater than zero, the greater of 0.009 or a number determined by subtracting from 0.045 the quotient obtained by dividing gross proceeds by net proceeds multiplied by 100, or (b) if net proceeds are equal to less than zero, 0.009.	Reports and payments—on or before date company's state income tax is due. Estimated tax payments due as under the income tax.

Tax	Basis—Rates	Due Dates
Motor vehicle excise tax; aircraft excise tax.	Motor vehicle excise tax—24 mills on each dollar of the maker's list price for the first or current year of model, 17.5 mills for the second year, 13.5 mills for the third year, 10 mills for the fourth year, 6.5 mills for the fifth year, and 4 mills for the sixth and succeeding years. The minimum tax is $5 for a motor vehicle other than a bicycle with a motor attached, $2.50 for a bicycle with a motor attached, $15 for a camper trailer other than a tent trailer, and $5 for a tent trailer. The excise tax on a stock race car is $5. Aircraft excise tax—9 mills on each dollar of the maker's average equipped price for the first or current year of model, 7 mills for the second year, 5 mills for the third year, 4 mills for the fourth year, and 3 mills for the fifth and succeeding years. The minimum tax is $10.	Payment—before property tax commitment dates to local collectors for vehicles (other than automobiles), aircraft owned in State on or before April 1; for those acquired after April 1, payment to local collectors at any time. A system of staggered payments has been adopted for automobiles and newly acquired motor trucks and truck tractors.
Cigarette and tobacco products tax.	100 mills per cigarette ($2.00 per 20 cigarettes). Tobacco products—78% of wholesale sales price of smokeless tobacco and 20% of wholesale sales price of all other smoking tobacco.	Payment—by affixing stamps. Tobacco products—reports and payments—last day of each month.
Realty transfer tax.	$2.20 per $500 or fraction of value of the property; grantor and grantee each liable for half.	Payment—the tax is paid by affixing stamps to the document.
Hospital tax operating revenues.	2.23% of net operating revenues.	Returns and payments—$1/2$ by Nov. 15, $1/2$ by May 15.
Sales and use tax.	Sales and use—10% on rentals of automobiles for less than one year (the general sales tax rate of 5% applies to automobile rentals of one year or more); 7% on liquor; 7% on rentals of rooms or shelter; 7% on the value of all food prepared by a retailer; 5% on all other tangible personal property and taxable services.	Reports and payments—15th of each month, less often for small taxpayers.
Railroad tax.	Rate determined by comparing the amount of gross transportation receipts with net railway operating income for prior calendar year. When net railway operating income does not exceed 10% of gross transportation receipts, the tax is 3.25% of the gross transportation receipts; if the proportion exceeds 10% but does not exceed 15%, the tax is 3.75%; if the proportion exceeds 15% but does not exceed 20%, the tax is 4.25%; if the proportion exceeds 20% but does not exceed 25%, the tax is 4.75%; and when the proportion exceeds 25%, the tax is 5.25%.	Reports—on or before April 15. Payments—15th day of June, September and December.

Tax	Basis—Rates	Due Dates
Insurance companies tax.	2% on domestic and foreign insurance companies; 1% on all gross direct premiums collected or contracted for on long-term care policies; 1% with respect to premiums written on qualified group disability policies unless the premium is written by a large domestic insurer (any insurer domiciled in Maine with assets in excess of $5 billion), in which case the rate is 2.55%. Fire insurance companies—additional 1.4% tax. Foreign companies subject to retaliatory taxes. Surplus line brokers—3% of gross direct premiums.	Reports and payments—last day of April, 25th day of June and last day of October. If tax is $500 or less, an annual return and payment due March 15 may be allowed. Annual reconciliation return due March 15. Additional tax on fire insurance companies paid on an estimated basis at the end of each calendar month.
Estate tax.	Maine has decoupled from federal estate tax law. There is no federal state death tax credit for estates of decedents dying after 2004. A *pro forma* federal state death tax credit will be used to calculate Maine estate tax.	Report and payment—within nine months of death.

Maryland

Tax System.—Maryland derives its revenue from taxes imposed on the income of individuals, estates and corporations, sales and use taxes and taxes imposed on specified businesses and privileges. Property taxes are levied by the local governments on real and tangible personal property and on certain intangible personal property for the benefit of the state and local governments. An outline of the Maryland tax system follows:

Tax	Basis—Rates	Due Dates
Corporate qualification fees and taxes.	Domestic—Articles of incorporation (stock, nonstock, close, professional, religious)—Organization and capitalization fee: $20 (no capital stock; savings and loan association; credit union; or aggregate par value of stock not over $100,000); $20 plus $1 per $5,000 or fraction thereof (aggregate par value of stock over $100,000); $200 plus $10 per $100,000 or fraction thereof (aggregate par value of stock over $1,000,000); $300 plus $15 per $500,000 or fraction thereof (aggregate par value of stock over $2,000,000); and $390 plus $20 per $1,000,000 or fraction thereof (aggregate par value of stock over $5,000,000). Additional recording fee, $100.	Domestic—at time of organization.
	Foreign—$100 qualification fee.	Foreign—at time of qualification.
Annual reports.	Domestic corporation, except a charitable or benevolent institution, nonstock corporation, savings and loan corporation, credit union, family farm, banking institution, $300 annual filing fee. Foreign corporation, except national banking association, savings and loan association, credit union, nonstock corporation, and charitable and benevolent institution, $300. Real estate investment trust, $300.	Reports and payment—April 15.
Income tax.	Individuals—2% of the first $1,000 of taxable net income; 3% of the second $1,000; 4% of the third $1,000; and 4.75% on Maryland taxable income over $3,000. Federal tax preference items are taxable if over $10,000 for an individual return; $20,000 for a joint return. General withholding required according to tables prepared by Comptroller. Nonresident contractors are subject to Maryland personal or corporate income tax withholding for contracts for $50,000 or more, at a rate of 3%, for contracts entered into on or after July 1, 2003.	Returns and payments—Individuals, 15th day of 4th month after end of income year; corporations, 15th day of 3rd month after end of tax year.
	Counties are authorized to impose local individual income taxes at a percentage of the Maryland tax rate.	

Tax	Basis—Rates	Due Dates
	Corporations—7% of net income allocable to the state.	Estimates of personal income tax due April 15; payments due April 15, June 15, September 15. Final payment due January 15 following or January 31 with final income tax return. Corporate and partnership estimated tax declarations and payments due by 15th day of 4th, 6th, 9th and 12th months of tax year.
	Partnerships and S corporations—6% of the sum of each nonresident partner's distributive share of a partnership's nonresident taxable income or the sum of each nonresident shareholder's pro rata share of an S corporation's nonresident taxable income.	
General property tax.	General property—aggregate of state and local rates fixed annually to meet budgets. Realty is assessed at 40% of its phased-in value. Farm and agricultural use land is assessed at 50% of its phased-in value. Personal property is assessed at its full cash value.	Reports (personal property)—corporations generally, April 15; distilled spirits, March 15.
		Payment—due July 1, delinquent October 1. Counties and cities allow semiannual payments, due July 1 and December 1.
Admissions tax.	Local admissions taxes are authorized at not over 10% of gross receipts. 5¢ to 15¢ per person for those admitted free or at reduced rates when other persons charged for admission.	Reports and payments—10th of each month.
Alcoholic beverages tax.	Excise—distilled spirits and other alcoholic beverages except wines and beer, $1.50 per gallon (39.63¢ per liter); and distilled spirits 100 proof or higher, an additional 1.5¢ per proof over 100 for each gallon (.3963¢ per liter); wines, 40¢ per gallon (10.57¢ per liter); beer, 9¢ per gallon (2.3778¢ per liter).	Excise—aircraft, steamboats and railroads (Class E, F, G licensees), 25th of each month; manufacturers and wholesalers, 10th of each month.
Gasoline tax.	Motor fuels—23.5¢ per gallon of gasoline, except 7¢ per gallon for aviation gasoline; and 24.25¢ per gallon for special fuel, except 7¢ per gallon for turbine fuel and 23.5¢ per gasoline-equivalent gallon of clean-burning fuel.	Reports and payments—last day of month for preceding month or postmarked not later than two days prior to the last day of each month.
	Motor carrier road tax—same as motor fuels rate for type of fuel used that is in effect when return period begins.	Reports and payments—last day of March, June, September, and December.
	Oil transfer license fees—4¢ per barrel of oil transferred in Maryland.	Reports and payments—quarterly.
Motor vehicle titling tax.	A 5% titling tax is imposed on the fair market value of each motor vehicle for which a certificate of title is made.	Titling tax—Upon issuance of the certificate of title.
Vessel titling tax.	5% of total purchase price or fair market value.	At time of registration.

Tax	Basis—Rates	Due Dates
Chain store tax.	Graduated from $5 for each of the first 5 retail stores to $150 for each store in excess of 20. (The fee is higher for stores in Cecil County or Baltimore City.) Traders' license fees—graduated from $15 for less than $1,000 of stock-in-trade to $800 for more than $750,000.	Payment—May 1.
Tobacco tax.	50¢ for each package of 10 or fewer cigarettes; $1 for each package of at least 11 and not more than 20 cigarettes; 5¢ for each cigarette in a package of more than 20 cigarettes.	Reports—wholesalers, 21st of month.
	Other tobacco products—15% of wholesale price.	Payment—by affixing stamps prior to sale.
State recordation tax.	Rate, which is set by 23 counties and Baltimore City, varies from $2.20 to $5 for each $500 of consideration. Ground rents, redemption sum plus any other consideration. Leases, capitalization at 10% of average annual rental plus any other consideration. Alternate method where rent is indeterminate.	Payment—when instrument recorded.
State transfer tax.	0.5% of consideration paid or to be paid for realty; 0.25% of consideration for sales of improved residential real property to first-time home buyers who occupy the property as a principal residence.	Payment—when instrument recorded.
Retail sales tax; use tax.	Retail sales—5% of purchases, except farm vehicles and equipment and manufacturing machinery and equipment, of tangible personal property and sales of certain services. Short-term vehicle rentals—23¢ for each multiple of $2; 8¢ for each $1 for a rental truck.	Reports and payments, retail sales—20th of each month. Also annual, semiannual, quarterly, and seasonal filing schedules.
	Use tax—5% on all purchases, except farm vehicles and equipment and manufacturing machinery and equipment, of personal property used, stored, or consumed in the state. Short-term vehicle rentals—23¢ for each multiple of $2; 8¢ for each $1 for a rental truck.	Reports and payments, use tax—same as sales tax.
Public service company franchise tax.	Gross receipts tax—telegraph, telephone, oil pipeline, electric or gas companies, 2% of gross receipts.	Reports and payments—March 15. Estimated tax—initial declaration and quarterly reports due by April 15, June 15, September 15 and December 15.
	Distribution tax on electric and natural gas utilities—.062¢ per kilowatt hour of electricity and .402¢ for each therm of natural gas delivered.	
Insurance companies tax.	2% of gross direct premiums; 2% on gross receipts received as a result of capitation payments made to a managed care organization, supplemental payments, and bonus payments, and subscription charges or other amounts paid to a health maintenance organization; 3% of gross premiums charged by unauthorized insurers.	Reports and payments—March 15; estimated tax—initial declaration and quarterly reports due by April 15, June 15, September 15 and December 15. Unauthorized insurers' tax payable before March 1.
	Foreign companies subject to retaliatory taxes.	

Tax	Basis—Rates	Due Dates
Inheritance tax; estate tax; generation-skipping transfer tax.	Inheritance—Class 1 (transfers to lineal descendants and/or siblings) is exempt. Class 2 (all others)—10%. No tax if transfer does not exceed $150.	Inheritance reports—3 months after appointment of personal representative or 3 months after date of death. Payment—at time of accounting for its distribution.
	Estate tax—amount by which federal credit (before reduction or repeal on or after January 1, 2001) exceeds inheritance tax, based on net estate as defined by federal law. Effective July 1, 2006, and applicable to decedents dying after December 2005, the amount of the federal credit used to calculate the Maryland estate tax is limited to 16% of the amount by which the decedent's taxable estate exceeds $1 million.	Estate tax—Returns and payment—9 months after date of death.
	Generation-skipping transfer—Tax imposed to absorb federal generation-skipping transfer tax credit.	Generation-skipping transfer—Returns and payment—same as federal.

Massachusetts

Tax System.—Massachusetts derives its revenue from taxes imposed on the income of individuals, estates and partnerships, from a corporation excise tax, measured by net income and tangible property or net worth, from sales and use taxes and from taxes imposed on specified businesses and privileges. General property taxes are levied by the local governments. An outline of the Massachusetts tax system follows:

Tax	Basis—Rates	Due Dates
Corporate organization and qualification fees.	Domestic—The minimum fee for filing the articles of organization, $275 for up to 275,000 shares and $100 for each additional 100,000 shares. The minimum, $250 if electronically filed. The minimum fee for filing the articles of amendment, $100 for up to 100,000 shares, and $100 for each additional 100,000 shares. The minimum fee for filing the articles of consolidation or merger, $250.	Domestic—fee paid at time of incorporation or increase of capital.
	Foreign—minimum fee for registering a foreign corporation, $400 or $375 if filed by fax; and fee for amending a foreign corporation registration, $100.	Foreign—fee paid at time of qualification or increase of capital.
Corporation annual report fee.	Annual report filing fee—$125 or $100 if filed electronically. The late fee is $25.	On or before the 15th day of the 3rd month following the close of the fiscal year.
Corporation excise (income) tax.	Corporations (excluding banks, etc.—see below)—Income portion, 9.5% of net income allocated to Massachusetts, including the 14% surtax; property portion, $2.60 per $1,000 of value of Massachusetts tangible property not taxed locally (or net worth allocated to Massachusetts for intangible property corporations), also including the 14% surtax. Each corporation subject to the corporate excise tax must pay a minimum tax of $456, including the 14% surtax.	Returns and payments—March 15 for calendar-year taxpayers, 15th day of 3rd month following close of tax year for fiscal-year taxpayers. Estimated tax payments due the 15th day of the 3rd, 6th, 9th and 12th months of the tax year, with fewer installments necessary if filing requirements are met later in the year.
Financial institutions excise (income) tax.	Financial institutions engaged in business in the commonwealth—10.5% of net income. The minimum tax is $456.	Returns and payments—March 15 for calendar-year taxpayers, 15th day of 3rd month following close of tax year for fiscal-year taxpayers. Estimated tax payments due the 15th day of the 3rd, 6th, 9th and 12th months of the tax year.
Utilities corporate franchise tax.	Public service (utility) corporation—entire net income of completely intrastate companies and allocated net income of interstate companies at the rate of 6.5%.	Returns and payment—15th day of 3rd month after close of tax year. Declaration of estimated tax provisions apply.

Tax	Basis—Rates	Due Dates
Personal income tax.	Income of residents and Massachusetts business income of nonresidents—Part A income (interest and dividends), 5.3%; short-term capital gains, 12%. Part B income (gross income not included in Part A or Part C gross income), 5.3%. Part C income (gains from the sale of capital assets held for 1 year or more), 5.3%. Taxpayers may elect to voluntarily pay tax at a rate of 5.85% on taxable income that otherwise would be taxed at 5.3%. This option is not available to short-term gains on collectibles.	Returns and payments—April 15 for calendar-year taxpayers or 15th day of the 4th month following the close of the fiscal taxable year for fiscal-year taxpayers.
		Declarations of estimated tax payments and returns due April 15, June 15, September 15 and January 15, including those for whom the expected estimated tax due on taxable income subject to withholding exceeds $400.
General property tax.	General property—fair cash value of real and personal property. Real property is classified according to use. Tax fixed locally to meet requirements. Total taxes assessed upon real property and personal property are limited to 2.5% of full and fair cash value.	Reports—at time required in assessors' notices. Tax due July 1, delinquent November 1. Preliminary payments may be required, generally on August 1 and November 1 (later dates may be approved by the Commissioner). Actual tax due February 1 and May 1.
Classified forest lands taxes.	Products tax—8% of stumpage value of forest products cut.	Products tax—Returns—May 1. Payment—October 1.
	Land tax—based on a value of not less than $10 per acre but at the rate applicable to Class III commercial property under the general property tax.	Land tax—Returns—same as general property. Payment—October 1.
Room occupancy tax.	Massachusetts imposes a room occupancy excise tax of 5.7% on rooms rented for $15 or more per day. Each Massachusetts city and town has the option of levying up to an additional 4%. In addition, a convention center financing fee of 2.75% is imposed on room occupancy in hotels, motels, or other lodging establishments in Boston, Cambridge, Chicopee, Springfield, West Springfield, and Worcester.	Returns and payment—20th of each month for previous month's rentals. Payment is due with return.
Alcoholic beverage tax.	Excise tax on manufacturers, wholesalers and importers—malt beverages, $3.30 per barrel. Other taxes per wine gallon as follows: cider, 3% to 6% alcohol, 3¢; still wine, 55¢; champagne and sparkling wines, 70¢; other beverages: 15% or less alcohol, $1.10; over 15% to 50% alcohol, $4.05; over 50% alcohol, $4.05 (per proof gallon).	Reports and payments (excise)—due within 20 days after the expiration of the period covered.
	Alcohol beverage gross receipts tax—0.5% of gross receipts.	Reports and payments (gross receipts)—April 15.

Tax	Basis—Rates	Due Dates
Gasoline tax.	Gasoline, other motor vehicle fuel, and diesel motor fuel sold, imported, exported, or used, 21¢ per gallon; special fuels (liquefied gases and propane) 22.9¢ per gallon for the fourth quarter of 2006 (21.9¢ per gallon for the third quarter of 2006); aviation fuel, 24.0¢ per gallon for the fourth quarter of 2006 (19.7¢ per gallon for the third quarter of 2006); certain localities tax aircraft (jet) fuel at a rate of 10.5¢ per gallon for the fourth quarter of 2006 (9.2¢ per gallon for the third quarter of 2006).	Reports and payments—20th day of January, April, July, and October for imported fuel. Distributors and unclassified exporters and importers, 20th day of each month.
Motor vehicle excise tax.	$25 per $1,000 of valuation of motor vehicles and trailers for the calendar year but not to exceed 50% of list price in the year preceding the designated year of manufacture, 90% of list price in the year of manufacture and scaled to 10% in the 5th and succeeding years.	Reports—none required. Payment—30 days from date of bill.
Cigarette tax.	75.5 mills per cigarette sold ($1.51 per pack of 20) plus any amount by which the federal excise tax on cigarettes is less than 8 mills per cigarette. Additional tax on cigars and smoking tobacco—30% of wholesale price. 90% of wholesale price of smokeless tobacco.	Reports—on or before the 20th of each month for previous month's sales. Payment—due with return; affixation of stamps.
Realty transfer tax.	$4.56 per $1,000 of sales price (includes 14% surtax). In Barnstable County, the rate is $3.42 per $1,000 (includes 14% surcharge).	Payment—by affixing stamps at time of execution.
Sales and use tax.	5% of gross receipts from retail sales or storage, use or consumption of taxable property.	Returns and payment—by 20th of each month. Reporting on a quarterly or other basis is allowed. Payment is due with the return.
Insurance taxes.	Domestic, 2% of taxable gross premiums plus 14% surtax. Foreign, 2% plus 14% surtax. Life insurance companies—0.25% of net value of policies until this tax equals or exceeds the premiums excise tax, after which the tax is based on premiums. Domestic life insurance companies—also a 14% net investment tax, which phases out after five years of contributions. Marine or fire and marine—5% of underwriting profit allocated to Massachusetts plus 14% surtax. Foreign companies are subject to retaliatory taxes, but the 14% surtax does not apply to retaliatory tax provisions.	Returns and payment—marine or fire and marine, May 15; all others March 15. Estimated tax payments due on the 15th day of the 3rd, 6th, 9th and 12th months of the tax year, with fewer installments necessary if filing requirements are met later in the year.

Tax	Basis—Rates	Due Dates
Estate tax.	Estate tax—The estate tax is assessed in an amount equal to the federal estate tax credit for state death taxes as computed under IRC Sec. 2011 as in effect on 12/31/00.	Estate returns and payments—within 9 months after date of death.
Generation-skipping transfer tax.	Generation-skipping transfer—tax imposed to absorb federal generation-skipping transfer tax credit.	Return and payment—same due date as federal return and payment.

Michigan

Tax System.—The state and all of its political subdivisions derive revenue from general property taxation. All property, except that specifically exempted, is subject to taxation according to a uniform rule. This is qualified by the provisions for specific taxes in lieu of the property tax. The property tax has been supplemented by taxes on personal income, sales, use, business and privileges. An outline of the Michigan tax system follows:

Tax	Basis—Rates	Due Dates
Corporate organization and qualification fees.	Domestic—$50 for 60,000 or fewer shares; $100 for 60,001 to one million shares; $300 for over one million to five million shares; $500 for over five million to 10 million shares; and over 10 million shares, $500 plus an additional $1,000 for each 10 million shares over the initial 10 million shares. Prior to 2006, $30 for each additional 20,000 shares.	Domestic—at time of incorporation or increase of capital stock.
	Foreign—$50 for 60,000 or fewer shares; $100 for 60,001 to one million shares; $300 for over one million to five million shares; $500 for over five million to 10 million shares; over 10 million shares, $500 plus an additional $1,000 for each 10 million shares. Prior to 2006, $30 for each additional 20,000 shares.	Foreign—at time of qualification. Increase in capital stock—reports and payment, May 15.
Corporation annual report.	Corporation annual report—$25 ($15, after September 30, 2007) filing fee plus the privilege fee.	Corporation annual report, privilege tax—May 15.
Single business tax.	1.9% in 2006 (if comprehensive annual report for the state reports an ending balance of at least $250 million) of federal taxable income, with adjustments, allocated or apportioned to Michigan. The first $45,000 of the adjusted tax base is exempt. The tax applies to individuals, corporations, financial institutions, estates, trusts and partnerships with business activity allocated or apportioned to Michigan. Insurance companies are subject to a surcharge of 1.26 times tax liability. The single business tax is scheduled to be repealed effective for tax years beginning after 2009.	Reports and payments—last day of 4th month after end of tax year. Estimated tax due last day of April, July, October, and January. Insurers—Must file an additional annual report by March 1.
Personal income tax.	Individuals, estates, and trusts—3.9% of taxable income.	Returns—calendar-year taxpayers, April 15; fiscal-year taxpayers, 15th day of 4th month after tax year. Estimated tax payments due 15th day of April, June, September and January. Balance of tax due April 15. Fiscal-year taxpayers may substitute the appropriate dates that correspond to the calendar-year dates.

Tax	Basis—Rates	Due Dates
General property tax.	General property—Property assessed at 50% of true cash value. Intangibles are exempt.	Personal property—returns—February 20. Assessment roll (real property)—first Monday in March. Payment—generally, February 14.
Public service corporations tax.	Equal to the average of property levies on commercial, industrial and utility property throughout the state for the preceding year based on true cash value of property.	Returns—Companies with gross receipts of over $1 million by March 31; $1 million or less, by March 15. Payment—July 31 and November 30, or all on July 1.
Low-grade iron ore properties tax.	0.55% of mine value per ton based on projected natural iron analysis of pellets or concentrated and/or agglomerated products prior to production times percent of construction completion; thereafter 1.1% (prior to 2007, 0.75%) of mine value per ton based on average natural iron analysis of shipments for that year of pellets and concentrated and/or agglomerated products times average annual production of preceding five years.	Payment—same as general property tax.
Forest lands tax.	Forest lands—private reserves stumpage tax—5%. Commercial forests—annual specific tax of $1.10 per acre.	Forest lands—private preserves—payment at time of cutting. Commercial reserves—same as general property tax.
Convention facility development tax.	3% of room charge in convention hotel if it has 81 to 160 rooms; 6% if more than 160 rooms. All other hotels, 1.5% if hotel has 81 to 160 rooms, 5% if more than 160 rooms.	Reports and payments—15th day of month following the month the tax accrued.
Alcoholic beverages tax.	Excise—beer, $6.30 per barrel; wine containing 16% or less alcohol, 13.5¢ per liter or 20¢ per liter if containing more than 16% alcohol; spirits and wine containing more than 21% alcohol, 12% for on-premises consumption or 13.85% for off-premises consumption; mixed spirit drink, 48¢ per liter.	Excise—Wine manufacturers, wholesalers, and out-of-state sellers of wine, report and payment due on 15th of each month. Brewers and out-of-state sellers of beer whose beer tax liability for the preceding calendar year has averaged (1) less than $50,000 per month, report and payment due on 15th day of each month; and (2) $50,000 or more per month, report and payment due by the 15th and the last day of each month. Sellers of wine for sacramental rites, quarterly reports on the 15th day of January, April, July and October.

Tax	Basis—Rates	Due Dates
Motor fuel tax.	Gasoline, 19¢ per gallon. Diesel fuel, 15¢ per gallon. LPG, 15¢ per gallon. Gasoline used in aircraft, 3¢ per gallon.	Reports and payments—20th of each month following reporting period. Motor fuel suppliers, monthly; LPG dealers, quarterly, on the 20th day of the month following close of reporting period.
	Effective September 1, 2006, a temporary 12¢ per gallon tax on gasoline that is least 70% ethanol and diesel that contains at least 5% biodiesel imposed in lieu of the 19¢ per gallon tax and the 15¢ per gallon tax currently imposed on gasoline and diesel, respectively.	
Motor carrier (diesel) fuel tax.	15¢ per gallon. Effective September 1, 2006, a temporary 12¢ per gallon tax on biodiesel imposed in lieu of the current 15¢ per gallon.	Reports and payments—last day of January, April, July, and October.
Oil and gas severance tax.	Severance—5% of gross cash market value of gas or 6.6% of gross cash market value of oil (4% of gross cash market value of stripper well crude oil and crude oil from marginal properties), plus a fee (computed annually) not to exceed 1% of the gross cash market value of all oil and gas produced in the state.	Report and payment—25th of each month.
Tobacco products tax.	$2 per pack of 20 cigarettes and 32% of the wholesale price of cigars, noncigarette smoking tobacco, and smokeless tobacco.	Reports and payments—20th of each month.
Realty transfer tax.	County tax—55¢ in counties of less than 2 million population and not more than 75¢ in a county with a population of 2 million or more for each $500 or fraction thereof of value of instrument.	No reports. Payment by affixing stamps.
	State tax—An additional state realty transfer tax is imposed at the rate of $3.75 for each $500, or fraction, of the total value of the property being transferred.	
Sales and use tax.	Sales—6% of gross proceeds from retail sales of tangible personal property, electricity, gas and steam. However, sales for residential use of electricity, natural or artificial gas, or home heating fuels are taxed at 4%.	Sales—reports and payments—20th of each month (1/2 due on 20th and 1/2 due on the last day of each month if required to file EFT payments). Refiners and pipeline and marine terminal operators must report and make prepayments on or before the 10th and 25th of each month.
	Use—6% of sales price of tangible personal property purchased for storage, use or consumption, including electricity, natural or artificial gas, steam, rental of rooms and lodgings, and intrastate telephone and telegraph service. However, consumption of electricity, natural gas, and home heating fuels for residential use is taxed at 4%.	Use—reports and payments—20th of each month (1/2 due on 20th and 1/2 on the last day of each month if required to file EFT payments).

Tax	Basis—Rates	Due Dates
Insurance companies tax.	Authorized insurance companies subject to single business tax plus a surcharge of 1.26 multiplied by the tax liability. The tax base is 25% of adjusted receipts. Foreign and alien insurers are subject to the greater of single business tax or retaliatory tax.	Returns—last day of the 4th month after the tax year. Annual report due by March 1. Retaliatory tax statement due March 1. Payments—quarterly, due on or before April 30, July 31, October 31, and January 31. For foreign and alien insurers, payments must be prepaid on the last day of April, July, October and January of the following year.
	Surplus lines insurers, 2% on premiums written plus a 0.5% regulatory fee. Insureds or self-insurers dealing with unauthorized insurers, 2% on premiums written plus a 0.5% regulatory fee. Unauthorized insurers, 2% of premiums written plus a 0.5% regulatory fee.	Reports—Surplus lines insurers, February 15 and August 15. Insurers and self-insurers dealing with unauthorized insurers, within 30 days after transaction. Payments—Surplus lines insurers and insureds dealing with unauthorized insurers, at the time of filing the report. Insurers and self-insurers dealing with unauthorized insurers, within 30 days after transaction.
Estate tax.	Resident decedents—the maximum allowable federal credit reduced for estate taxes paid to other states based on the proportion of tax paid on property in Michigan to taxes paid on property everywhere. Nonresident estate transfers are taxed based on the proportion of property in Michigan to property everywhere. Note: Michigan gives the personal representative the option to choose the IRC in effect on the decedent's date of death.	Estate—Returns and payments—same as for federal.
Generation-skipping transfer tax.	A tax is imposed on every generation-skipping transfer made by resident original transferors equal to the maximum allowable federal credit for generation-skipping transfer taxes paid to the states less such taxes paid to other states on a prorated basis. Nonresident original transferors are taxed on a prorated basis.	Generation-skipping transfer—Return, payment—same as for federal generation-skipping transfer tax.

Minnesota

Tax System.—The Minnesota tax system is founded on the general property tax. Money and credits are exempt. By far, the greater proportion of the property tax revenue is devoted to the support of municipal corporations and other local tax-levying bodies. Further revenue is derived from sales and use taxes, gasoline tax, motor vehicle taxes, cigarette and tobacco products taxes, liquor taxes, income taxes, insurance company taxes, estate tax, mining taxes, and several other miscellaneous taxes. Municipalities are given broad licensing power, but this power to license must be based on statutory enactment or charter provisions. An outline of the Minnesota tax system follows:

Tax	Basis—Rates	Due Dates
Corporate organization and qualification fees.	Domestic—$135 for articles of incorporation.	Domestic—at the time of incorporation.
	Foreign—$150 for initial license.	Foreign—at time of qualification.
Corporation annual report fee.	Foreign—$115.	Payments—December 31.
Income tax.	Corporations—9.8% of taxable income. An alternative minimum tax equal to the excess of 5.8% of Minnesota alternative minimum taxable income over the basic tax is imposed. Corporations are subject to an additional minimum tax ranging from $0 to $5,000 depending on the Minnesota property, payrolls, and sales or receipts, and the type of corporation or partnership.	Reports and payments—15th day of 4th month (3rd month for corporations) after end of income year.
	Banks—Same as corporations.	
	Individuals—Inflation adjusted brackets for tax year 2006: For married individuals filing joint returns and surviving spouses, 5.35% on the first $29,980, 7.05% if $29,980 to $119,100, 7.85% if over $119,100. For single individuals, 5.35% on the first $20,510, 7.05% if $20,510 to $67,360, 7.85% if over $67,360. For head of households, 5.35% on the first $25,250, 7.05% if $25,250 to $101,450, 7.85% if over $101,450. A 6.4% alternative minimum tax is imposed.	
	General withholding required.	Individual declarations of estimated tax--April 15, June 15, September 15, and January 15. Corporate estimated tax payments -- due 15th day of the 3rd, For 6th, 9th and 12th months of the taxable year.
General property tax; yield tax.	General property—all real and personal property valued according to numerous classes from varying percentages of its market value. Auxiliary forests—10¢ per acre.	General property—returns for utilities, March 31. Payments—May 15 and October 15 (or 21 days after postmark date on statement, whichever is later); Auxiliary forest—payments, May 31.
	Yield tax—40% of the market value at the time of cutting or removal of trees.	

Tax	Basis—Rates	Due Dates
Alcoholic beverage taxes.	Beer, 3.2% alcohol or less, per barrel of 31 gallons, $2.40; over 3.2% alcohol, $4.60; wines per gallon, 14% alcohol or less, 30¢ per gallon; more than 14% alcohol but not exceeding 21%, 95¢ per gallon; more than 21% alcohol but not exceeding 24%, $1.82 per gallon; over 24% alcohol, $3.52 per gallon; sparkling wines, $1.82 per gallon; cider 15¢ per gallon; liquors, $5.03 per gallon; low-alcohol dairy cocktails, 8¢ per gallon. Bottle tax, 1¢.	Reports and payments—18th day of each month.
Gasoline tax.	20¢ per gallon of gasoline and special use fuel used to propel motor vehicles on public highways (lower rates possible at service stations near the state line). Aircraft fuel, 5¢ per gallon; LPG, 15¢ per gallon; LNG, 12¢ per gallon; CNG, $1.739 per mcf or 20¢ per gasoline equivalent. Petroleum tank release cleanup fee, $20 per 1,000 gallons of petroleum products. Inspection fee, 85¢ for every 1,000 gallons of petroleum products sold or withdrawn from a terminal or refinery storage. Motor carriers fuel tax—20¢ on motor fuel consumed in Minnesota operations.	Reports and payments—23rd day of each month. Motor carriers' reports due last day of April, July, October, and January; payments required with reports.
Severance taxes.	Mining occupation tax—based on taxable income and imposed at same rates as income tax. Taconite, iron sulphides, and agglomerate taxes—the preceding year's tax rate ($2.137 per ton for 2004) plus an amount equal to the preceding year's tax rate multiplied by the percentage increase in the implicit price deflator from the fourth quarter of the second preceding year to the fourth quarter of the preceding year. Additional tax of 3¢ per gross ton of merchantable iron ore concentrate for each 1% that the iron content of the product exceeds 72% when dried at 212 degrees Fahrenheit. Direct reduced ore—different rate, lower yearly payments with 6-year phase-in. Net proceeds tax (applies to non-ferrous metals)—additional 2% of net proceeds from mining.	Mining occupation tax—reports and payments, May 1. Taconite, iron sulphides, and agglomerate taxes—reports, February 1; payments, February 24. Net proceeds tax—Reports and payments, May 1.
Motor vehicle excise tax.	Same rate (6.5%) as the sales tax applied to the purchase price of motor vehicles.	Payments—due at time of registration.

Tax	Basis—Rates	Due Dates
Cigarette and tobacco products taxes.	Cigarettes—Effective August 1, 2006, the total cigarette tax rate is $1.493 (48¢ excise tax plus 75¢ user fee plus 26.3¢ sales tax) per pack. Nonsettlement cigarettes—1.75¢ per cigarette.	Reports and payments—18th day of each month; sales tax paid by purchase of stamps. If fiscal year liability is $120,000 or more, 85% June liability for following year is due 2 business days before June 30, along with report and payment of actual May liability. Reconciliation report and payment due August 18.
	Tobacco products—35% of wholesale price.	
	Tobacco health user fee—75¢ per pack of cigarettes, 35% of cost of tobacco products (paid by distributors).	
	Cigarette sales tax—6.5% of the weighted average retail price (26.3¢ per pack as of August 1, 2006 (paid by distributors)) Prior to August 1, 2006, the rate was 25.5¢ per pack.	
Mortgage registry tax; real estate transfer tax.	Mortgage registry—0.0023% of amount of debt secured by real estate mortgage.	Payments—at time of registration or filing.
	Real estate transfer—$1.65 for $500 of consideration or less; 0.0033% when consideration exceeds $500.	
MinnesotaCare tax.	Hospitals, surgical centers, health care providers, and wholesale drug distributors—2% of gross revenues.	Hospitals and surgical centers—estimated tax payments due within 15 days of the end of the month. Others—quarterly estimated tax payments due April 15, July 15, October 15, and January 15.
Fur clothing tax.	6.5% of gross revenues from retail sales of clothing made from fur.	Returns and payments—quarterly by April 15, July 15, October 15, and January 15. Annual returns due March 15.
Sales and use taxes.	6.5% of gross receipts from, or the sales price of, retail sales, use, storage or consumption of tangible personal property. Intoxicating liquor and malt liquor, 9%. 6.2% on the lease or rental of a passenger automobile, a van or a pickup truck. Cigarette sales tax—see Cigarettes and tobacco products taxes above.	Reports and payments—20th day of each month for previous month. Accelerated EFT payments from taxpayers with annual tax liability of $120,000 or more are due on the 20th day of each month. EFT taxpayers must remit estimated June liability 2 business days before June 30; reconciliation payments due August 20. Quarterly and annual returns and payments allowed for small taxpayers. Annual use tax returns for businesses due February 5.

Tax	Basis—Rates	Due Dates
Insurance companies tax.	2% of gross direct premiums, less return premiums, received on all direct business written within the state. Town and farmers' mutual insurance companies—1%. Mutual property and casualty companies with assets of $5 million or less—1%. Mutual property and casualty companies with assets of $1.6 billion or less on December 31, 1989—1.875% on life insurance business and 1.26% on all other business. Fire companies also pay fire marshal tax of 0.5%. Surplus line insurers—3% of gross premiums. HMOs and nonprofit health service corporations pay a 1% tax. Foreign companies subject to retaliatory taxes.	Reports—March 1. Payments—estimated payments due March 15, June 15, September 15, and December 15; reconciliation payments due March 1. Surplus line insurers reports and payments—due February 15 and August 15. Firefighters' relief surcharge reports and payments—April 30, June 30, and November 30.
Life insurance tax.	1.875% of gross premiums, less return premiums, received on all direct business by insurers or agents; after 2006, 1.75%; after 2007, 1.625%; after 2008, 1.5%.	
Estate tax.	Tax equal to the federal credit for state death taxes allowed under 2000 federal estate tax law.	Returns and payments—within 9 months of death.

Mississippi

Tax System.—Mississippi imposes a general property tax for county, municipal, and district revenue, according to the rule of uniformity prescribed by the state Constitution. State taxes on privileges, excises, occupations, and income are imposed to supplement revenue from general property taxes. Municipalities and counties may not impose franchise taxes and may not tax any privilege that has been licensed for statewide purposes. An outline of the Mississippi tax system follows:

Tax	Basis—Rates	Due Dates
Corporate organization and qualification fees.	Domestic and foreign corporations—articles of incorporation, $50; articles of dissolution, $25; application for certificate of authority, $500; application for certificate of withdrawal, $25.	Payments—at time of incorporation or qualification, and when capital stock increases.
Corporation franchise tax.	$2.50 for every $1,000 or fraction thereof of the value of the capital used, invested, or employed by the organization.	Reports and payments—15th day of 3rd month following the close of the annual accounting period.
Annual corporate report.	Domestic and foreign corporations, $25.	Annual reports—due within 60 days of anniversary date of incorporation or authorization to transact business in the state.
General income tax.	Individuals, corporations—3% of first $5,000 of entire net income; 4% of next $5,000; 5% of amounts over $10,000.	Returns—15th day of 3rd month (4th month for individuals) after close of taxable year. Payments—Taxes are due with the annual return. Estimated income tax declarations and payments—due 15th day of 4th month; option to make payments on the 15th day of 4th, 6th, 9th, and 13th (12th in the case of corporations) months of income year.
General property tax.	General property—Taxable property is divided into 5 classes with assigned rates ranging from 10% to 30%. Rates are multiplied by local mill levy to determine tax.	General property lists—due April 1. Payments—due February 1. Payment may be authorized in 3 installments—50% on February 1; 25% on May 1; 25% on July 1.
	Banks—general property rates on adjusted net worth.	Bank reports—April 1; payments—December 1.
Alcoholic beverages tax.	Excise—42.68¢ per gal. on light wines and beer; $2.50[1] per gal. on distilled spirits; $11[1] per gal. on sparkling wine and champagne; 35¢[1] per gal. on wines and native wines. Privilege tax on native wine producers, $10 per 10,000 gallons produced per year.	Reports—15th day of each month; payments with reports.

Tax	Basis—Rates	Due Dates
Gasoline and fuel taxes.	Gasoline and blend stock—18¢ per gallon (14.4¢ per gallon as of the first day of the month following the date upon which the Mississippi Transportation Commission and the State Treasurer certify that specified financial conditions are satisfied concerning the Four-Lane Highway Program and the Gaming Counties Infrastructure Program. Aviation gasoline, 6.4¢ per gallon. Other motor fuels, 18¢ per gallon (14.75¢ per gallon beginning as of the first day of the month following the date upon which the Mississippi Transportation Commission and the State Treasurer certify that specified financial conditions are satisfied concerning the Four-Lane Highway Program and the Gaming Counties Infrastructure Program; special fuels other than undyed diesel fuel and special fuels used in aircraft, 5.75¢ per gallon; special fuels used in aircraft, 5.25¢ per gallon; undyed diesel fuel, 18¢ per gallon. Environmental protection fee, 0.4¢ per gallon if Groundwater Protection Trust Fund is between $6 million and $10 million.	Reports and payments—gasoline, ethanol, methanol, and special fuel distributors, 20th day of each month on fuels received the previous month.
	Tax on natural gas, locomotive fuel and compressed gas users—12¢ per 1,000 cubic feet upon any person using natural gas as a fuel in oil field or gas field production pumps in the state; 3¢ per 1,000 cubic feet upon any person using natural gas as a fuel in pipeline compressors or pumping stations or in engines or motors used for industrial purposes by a manufacturer or custom processor in this state; 0.75¢ per gallon upon any person using locomotive fuel in a railroad locomotive in this state; 2¢ per gallon upon any person using compressed gas as a fuel in oil field or gas field production pumps in this state; and 0.5¢ per gallon upon any person using compressed gas as a fuel in pipeline compressors or pumping stations or in engines or motors used for industrial purposes by a manufacturer or custom processor in this state.	

Tax	Basis—Rates	Due Dates
	Compressed gas tax—distributors of compressed gas (except compressed natural gas) for use in a motor vehicle, 17¢ per gallon (13.4¢ on the first day of the month immediately following the day upon which the Mississippi Transportation Commission and the State Treasurer certify that specified financial conditions are satisfied concerning the Four-Lane Highway Program and the Gaming Counties Infrastructure Program); distributors of compressed gas for all other uses, 0.25¢ per gallon. Annual privilege tax—$195 ($165 on the first day of the month immediately following the day upon which the Mississippi Transportation Commission and the State Treasurer certify that specified financial conditions are satisfied concerning the Four-Lane Highway Program and the Gaming Counties Infrastructure Program) for vehicles weighing 10,000 lbs. or less; 17¢ per gallon (13.4¢ per 100 cubic feet on the first day of the month immediately following the day upon which the Mississippi Transportation Commission and the State Treasurer certify that specified financial conditions are satisfied concerning the Four-Lane Highway Program and the Gaming Counties Infrastructure Program) of compressed gas used in vehicles weighing over 10,000 lbs.	
	Lubricating oils—2¢ per quart.	Reports and payments—lubricating oils, 20th day of each month.
Gas and oil severance taxes.	Gas—6% of value of natural gas produced and severed from soil or water, for sale, transport, storage, profit, or commercial use.	Reports and payments—25th day of each month.
	Oil—6% of value at the point of production, 3% if oil is produced by an enhanced oil recovery method in which carbon dioxide or other approved method is used. Additional 14% of gross value of escaped oil.	
	Additional maintenance charge—not to exceed 60 mills per barrel of oil or 6 mills on each 1,000 cu. ft. of gas.	
Salt severance tax.	3% of the value of the entire production of salt in the state.	Returns and payments—20th day of each month.

Tax	Basis—Rates	Due Dates
Timber or timber products tax.	Pine and soft woods used in manufacture of lumber and other products—$1 per 1,000 board feet (or 12¢ per ton).	Reports and payments— 15th day of each month; quarterly if tax does not exceed $3,600 per year.
	Hardwoods—75¢ per 1,000 board feet.	
	Lumber, including crossties—75¢ per 1,000 feet actual board measure.	
	Poles, piling, posts, staunchions, and other products not manufactured into lumber—$3.60 per 100 cubic feet.	
	For other timber products bought by the cubic foot—55¢ per 100 cubic feet for pine and other soft woods; 41¢ per 100 cubic feet for hard woods.	
	Pulpwood, except pine—22.5¢ per standard cord of 128 cubic feet; pine—30¢ per standard cord of 128 cubic feet.	
	Stumpwood, lightwood, or distillate—25¢ per ton.	
	Turpentine crude gum—30¢ per barrel of 400 pounds.	
	All others—75¢ per 1,000 feet board measure, or 37.5¢ per standard cord of 128 cubic feet.	
Tobacco tax.	Cigarettes—0.9¢ per cigarette (18¢ per pack of 20). Cigars, cheroots, stogies, snuff, chewing and smoking tobacco, and all other tobacco products other than cigarettes—15% of the manufacturer's list price.	Reports and payments— cigarettes, by purchase of stamps; other tobacco products, 15th day of each month. Interstate commerce—15th day of each month.
Mineral documentary tax.	3¢ per acre covered by conveyances or reservations of leasehold interests in nonproducing oil, gas, or other minerals for interests expiring 10 years or less from date of execution of instrument; 6¢ for terms between 10 and 20 years; 8¢ for terms exceeding 20 years. Minimum tax, $1.	Payments—by affixing stamps purchased at time of filing instruments.

Tax	Basis—Rates	Due Dates
Sales and use taxes.	Sales—on services and on most items of tangible personal property, tax imposed at rate of 7% of gross proceeds or value; various counties and cities impose, separately, convention and tourism taxes.	Reports and payments— filing frequencies of sales and use tax returns depend on the annual amount of taxes (for the preceding 12 months ended June) remitted: if the annual remittance is less than $300, annual returns will be filed; if the annual remittance is between $300 and $599, semiannual returns will be filed; if the annual remittance is between $600 and $3,599, quarterly returns will be filed; if the annual remittance is more than $3,599, monthly returns will be filed.
	Use—imposed at rates levied under sales tax on personal property acquired in any manner for use, storage or consumption within Mississippi on which sales or use tax has not been paid to another state at a rate equal to or greater than the applicable Mississippi rate.	
Public utilities tax.	Electric—$22.50 per mile of pole line; pipe line—from $15 to $125 (depending on diameter); telephone—4¢ per telephone in service at end of last calendar year or $25, whichever is greater; railroads—from $5 to $90 per mile.	Reports and payments— December 1.
Insurance companies tax.	Domestic and foreign—3% of gross premiums, less certain specified premiums. Fire insurance tax—1%. Foreign companies subject to retaliatory taxes.	Reports and payments— October 20, February 20, April 20, and June 15. Audited financial reports due June 1.
Estate tax.	Amount equal to the maximum state tax credit allowed under federal law.	Reports—advance returns due 60 days after death or qualification of legal representative; detailed returns and payments due 9 months after death.

[1] A total 27.5% markup is in effect.

Missouri

Tax System.—The state is divided into units, for property tax purposes, made up of counties, townships and cities of the first through fourth classes. The county is the principal unit for tax administration. The property tax is the aggregate of the levies in each of the governmental units in which the land lies. Major sources of state revenue are the sales and use taxes, the income taxes and the gasoline and fuel use taxes. An outline of the Missouri tax system follows:

Tax	Basis—Rates	Due Dates
Corporate organization and qualification fees.	Domestic—$3 for issuance of a certificate of incorporation and $50 for the first $30,000 or less; over $30,000, $50 plus $5 per $10,000 in excess of $30,000. No-par stock is assigned a value of $1 per share. Increases, $5 per $10,000 or less.	Domestic—at time of incorporation or increase of capital stock.
	Foreign—$150 for certificate of authority.	Foreign—at time of qualification or increase of capital stock.
Corporation franchise tax.	0.033% of domestic and foreign—proportion of par value of outstanding shares and surplus in excess of $1 million representing property and assets in Missouri. No-par stock valued at $5 per share or actual value, whichever is greater.	Report and payment—on or before the due date of the corporation's Missouri tax return.
Annual registration fee.	$40, plus an additional $5 fee for a technology trust fund if determined necessary by the Secretary of State (until 2010).	Report and payment—with franchise tax report.
Income tax.	Individuals—not over $1,000 of federal adjusted gross income with modifications, 1.5%; not over $2,000, $15 plus 2%; not over $3,000, $35 plus 2.5%; not over $4,000, $60 plus 3%; not over $5,000, $90 plus 3.5%; not over $6,000, $125 plus 4%; not over $7,000, $165 plus 4.5%; not over $8,000, $210 plus 5%; not over $9,000, $260 plus 5.5%; over $9,000, $315 plus 6%. Withholding required.	Returns and payments—calendar year: April 15; fiscal year: 15th day of 4th month after close of tax year. Financial institutions, April 15.
	Corporations and associations—6.25% of Missouri taxable income with adjustments.	
Financial institutions franchise tax.	Banks—the sum of the amount determined under the general corporation franchise tax, which is generally 0.05% of the par value of the taxpayer's outstanding shares and surplus employed in Missouri, and an amount equal to 7% of the taxpayer's net income, less the sum of the amount determined under the general corporation franchise tax and the credits for all state and local taxes allowable, provided the amount determined is not less than zero.	
	Credit institutions, credit unions, savings and loan associations, building and loan associations—7% of the net income less credits allowable for other state and local taxes.	

Tax	Basis—Rates	Due Dates
General property tax.	Personal property—Grain, 0.5%; livestock, 12%; farm machinery, 12%; historic motor vehicles and aircraft, 5%; poultry, 12%; pollution control and retooling equipment, 25%; all other personal property, 33^1/$_3$% of true value in money. Real property—19% of true value for residential property; 12% of true value for agricultural and horticultural property; and 32% of true value for utility, industrial, commercial, railroad, and all other real property. Aggregate of rates for state, county, municipality, road, bridge, school, and other district purposes.	General property returns—between January 1 and March 1; railroads and public utilities April 15. Payment—December 31.
Forest crop land tax.	Yield tax—6% of value of material cut.	Returns—Within 1 month after cutting, or if cutting continuously, at the end of each month.
Alcoholic beverages tax.	Excise—beer and malt liquor, $1.86 per bbl.; spirituous liquors, $2.00 per gallon; wines, 30¢ per gallon. Additional tax on wine of 6¢ per gallon for the Wine Marketing and Research Council. Additional fee of $6 per ton of grapes or 160 gallons of grape juice produced in the state.	Returns and payment—intoxicating liquor, 15th of each month. Manufacturers, out-of-state solicitors and wholesale dealers of nonintoxicating beer, 15th of each month.
Motor fuel tax.	Motor fuel—17¢ per gallon of fuel used to propel motor vehicles.	Motor fuel—Reports and payments—last day of the succeeding month.
	Aviation fuel use—9¢ per gallon of aviation fuel used in propelling aircraft with reciprocating engines.	Aviation fuel use—Reports and payments—last day of the succeeding month.
	Petroleum products surcharge—$60 per transport load (set by rule); imposition depends on the balance in the Petroleum Storage Tank Insurance Fund; if the fund's balance exceeds its liabilities by 10%, the surcharge reverts to $25 per transport load two months later. A petroleum inspection fee of 2.5¢ per 50-gallon barrel, also set by rule depending on the balance in the Petroleum Inspection Fund.	Petroleum products surcharge and petroleum inspection fee—Reports and payments—last day of each month for preceding month.
Cigarette tax.	8^1/$_2$ mills per cigarette (17¢ per pack of 20). The rate will drop to 13¢ per pack when the Legislature appropriates an amount equal to 25% of the net federal reimbursement allowance to the health initiative fund.	Report—20th of each month. Payment—by means of stamps.
Tobacco products tax.	10% of manufacturer's invoice price. The tax will expire when the Legislature appropriates an amount equal to 25% of the net federal reimbursement allowance to the health initiative fund.	Reports and payments—15th day of each month.

Tax	Basis—Rates	Due Dates
Sales and use tax.	4.225% (4.125%, eff. 11/8/08) of purchase price of tangible personal property and enumerated services. In lieu of regular use tax, a 4% special use tax is imposed on motor vehicles, trailers, boats, and outboard motors.	Sales and use tax—last day of January, April, July, October. If tax liability is less than $45 per calendar quarter, tax returns and payments are due January 31. If the tax due exceeds $500 for either the first or the second month of a calendar quarter, the tax is due by the 20th of the following month. Quarter-monthly payments due from large taxpayers.
Express company tax.	Express company—$2.50 per $100 of gross annual intrastate receipts. An additional annual assessment is levied by the Public Service Commission on public utilities up to a maximum amount of 0.25% of total gross revenue of all utilities subject to the Commission.	Express company—Returns and payments, April 1.
Insurance companies tax.	Domestic and foreign insurers, including risk retention and purchasing groups—2% of direct premiums less cancelled or returned premiums. Foreign companies subject to additional retaliatory taxes.	Returns—March 1.
		Payment—quarterly installments due on the first day of March, June, September, and December, with a fifth reconciling installment due on June 1. Foreign mutual insurance companies other than life or fire, May 1.
	Mutual insurance companies—1% of annual premiums or assessments over $1 million; 2% on annual premiums or assessments over $5 million.	
	Surplus lines brokers, 5% of net premiums. Insureds who procure insurance from surplus lines insurers, 5% of net premiums.	Annual statement—March 2. Payment—April 16.
Estate tax; generation-skipping transfer tax.	Basic federal estate tax credit for state death taxes reduced proportionately on account of property outside state. If the federal estate tax is repealed, no tax will be imposed on the transfer of a decedent's estate in Missouri as of the effective date of the federal estate tax repeal. Generation-skipping transfer—Tax imposed to absorb federal generation-skipping transfer tax credit.	Returns and payment—within 9 months of decedent's death.

Montana

Tax System.—The tax system of Montana is founded on a classified property tax levied at uniform rates, plus taxes on incomes, occupations, and privileges. A net income franchise tax is imposed on corporations. An outline of the Montana tax system follows:

Tax	Basis—Rates	Due Dates
Corporate organization and qualification fees.	Domestic—$70 for articles of incorporation. $20 for nonprofit articles of incorporation	Domestic—at time of incorporation.
	Foreign—$70 fee for certificate of authority. $20 fee for nonprofit certificate of authority.	Foreign—at time of qualification.
Annual report fee.	Domestic and foreign corporations—$15 for reports filed by April 15; $30 for reports filed after April 15.	Report and payment—between January 1 and April 15.
Corporation license (income) tax; corporation income tax; personal income tax.	Corporations and state and national banks and savings and loan associations—6.75% (7% for taxpayers electing water's-edge apportionment) of net income derived from Montana sources. Minimum tax, $50. S corporations exempt from corporation license tax unless special requirements met.	Corporation income—returns and payment—15th day of 5th month after close of income year. Payments of estimated tax (if income is $5,000 or more) are due on the 15th days of the 4th, 6th, 9th and 12th months of tax year.
	Nonresident taxpayers who do not rent or own real or personal property in Montana and whose in-state sales do not exceed $100,000 may elect to pay an alternative tax rate of .05% of gross receipts on Montana sales.	
	Personal income—**Rates for 2006 and thereafter:** $0 but less than $2,400, 1%; at least $2,400 but less than $4,300, 2% less $24; at least $4,300 but less than $6,500, 3% less $67; at least $6,500 but less than $8,800, 4% less $132; at least $8,800 but less than $11,300, 5% less $220; at least $11,300 but less than $14,500, 6% less $333; at least $14,500 and up, 6.9% less $464.	Personal income—returns and payment—15th day of 4th month after close of income year. Payments of estimated tax are due 15th days of the 4th, 6th, and 9th months of tax year and 1st month of following year.
General property tax.	Taxable property, real and personal, is divided into 14 classes for purposes of assessment and taxation. Property is assessed at 100% of market value, then reduced by a phase-in factor, and taxed at a percentage thereof. Aggregate of state, county, city and school rates fixed annually to meet state and local budgets.	Payment—Generally required in two equal installments due November 30 of relevant tax year and May 31 of the following year. In all cases, due date applies, or 30 days after notice postmark, whichever is later. Exception also for new industrial facilities.
Sales and use tax (limited).	4% lodging use tax, plus an additional 3% sales and use tax on accommodations and campgrounds; 4% sales and use tax on rental vehicles.	Reports and payments—last day of month after end of each calendar quarter.

Tax	Basis—Rates	Due Dates
Alcoholic beverages tax.	Excise—beer, over 20,000 barrels produced per year, $4.30 per 31-gallon barrel; less than 20,000 barrels produced per year, $1.30 per barrel for the first 5,000 barrels, $2.30 per barrel between 5,001 and 10,000 barrels, and $3.30 per barrel between 10,001 and 20,000 barrels.	Reports—beer, 15th of each month.
	Table wine—generally 27¢ per liter.	Payment—table wine, hard cider, 15th of each month; liquor, at time of sale and delivery in state; beer, end of each month.
	Cider—3.7¢ per liter.	
	Liquor—16% of retail selling price plus 10% license tax, except 13.8% of retail selling price plus 8.6% license tax for companies that manufacture, distill, rectify, bottle, or process and sell not more than 200,000 proof gallons of liquor nationwide in the preceding year.	
Fuel taxes.	Gasoline license tax—27¢ per gallon of motor fuel sold, distributed, received or used in Montana, except 4¢ per gallon for aviation gasoline.	Reports and payments—Gas: 25th of each month for the preceding calendar month.
	Special fuel use tax—27.75¢ per gallon of special fuel.	Special fuel users: last day of each month following a calendar quarter, or annually on January 31 if annual tax liability is $200 or less.
	Special fuel license tax—27.75¢ per gallon of special fuel distributed within state.	Reports and payments—25th day of each month for the preceding month.
	Petroleum Storage Tank Cleanup Fee—0.75¢ per gallon for gasoline, aviation gasoline, special fuel and heating oil distributed in the state (imposition depends on revenues).	Reports and payments—same as gasoline tax.
Compressed natural gas.	Compressed natural gas—7¢ per 120 cubic feet at 14.73 pounds per square inch absolute base pressure of compressed natural gas placed into the supply tank of a motor vehicle.	Reports and payments—25th of each month for the preceding calendar month.
Liquefied petroleum gas.	5.18¢ per gallon of liquefied petroleum gas placed into the supply tank of a motor vehicle.	Reports and payments—25th of each month for the preceding calendar month.
Oil and natural gas production tax.	In lieu of the resource indemnity and ground water assessment tax, natural gas and oil are taxed on the gross taxable value of production on the basis of type of well and type of production according to the following schedule for working and nonworking interest owners (the rates do not include the oil and gas privilege and license tax rate imposed on the market value of oil or natural gas produced).	Oil and natural gas production—Operators must report and pay the oil and natural gas production tax within 60 days after the end of each calendar quarter.

Tax	Basis—Rates	Due Dates

Natural Gas—(a)(i) first 12 months of qualifying production, working interest 0.76%, nonworking interest 15.06%, (ii) after 12 months (A) pre-1999 wells, working and nonworking interest 15.06%, (B) post-1999 wells, working interest 9.26%, nonworking interest 15.06%; (b) stripper natural gas pre-1999 wells, working interest 11.26%, nonworking interest 15.06%; (c) horizontally completed well production (i) first 18 months of qualifying production, working interest 0.76%, nonworking interest 15.06%, (ii) after 18 months, working interest 9.26%, nonworking interest 15.06%.

Oil—(a) primary recovery production (i) first 12 months of qualifying production, working interest 0.76%, nonworking interest 15.06%, (ii) after 12 months (A) pre-1999 wells, working interest 12.76%, nonworking interest 15.06%, (B) post-1999 wells, working interest 9.26%, nonworking interest 15.06%; (b) stripper oil production (i) first 1 through 10 barrels a day production, working interest 5.76%, nonworking interest 15.06%, (ii) more than 10 barrels a day production, working interest 9.26%, nonworking interest 15.06%; (c) stripper well exemption production, working interest 0.76%, nonworking interest 15.06%; (d) horizontally completed well production (i) first 18 months of qualifying production, working interest 0.76%, nonworking interest 15.06%, (ii) after 18 months (A) pre-1999 wells, working interest 12.76%, nonworking interest 15.06%, (B) post-1999 wells, working interest 9.26%, nonworking interest 15.06%; (e) incremental production (i) new or expanded secondary recovery production, working interest 8.76%, nonworking interest 15.06%, (ii) new or expanded tertiary production, working interest 6.06%, nonworking interest 15.06%; (f) horizontally recompleted well (i) first 18 months, working interest 5.76%, nonworking interest 15.06%, (ii) after 18 months (A) pre-1999 wells, working interest 12.76%, nonworking interest 15.06%, (B) post-1999 wells, working interest 9.26%, nonworking interest 15.06%. Certain reduced tax rates may apply during the first months of a primary recovery production, oil production from a horizontally completed well, or oil production from a horizontally recompleted well. Incremental production is subject to the tax rate on primary recovery production if the average price of oil for west Texas intermediate crude oil during a calendar quarter is $30 or greater. The stripper well exemption production rate is only in effect if the average price per barrel of oil for west Texas intermediate crude oil during a calendar quarter is less than $38 per a barrel. The stripper well bonus production rate is only in effect if the average price per barrel of oil for west Texas intermediate crude oil during a calendar quarter is equal or greater than $38 a barrel.

Tax	Basis—Rates	Due Dates
Oil and gas privilege & license tax.	$^{0.9}/_{10}$ of 1 % of market value of each barrel of crude petroleum or each 10,000 cubic feet of natural gas produced, saved and marketed or stored in Montana or exported.	Same as oil and gas production tax.
Coal severance tax.	Surface mining—10% of value for coal having a BTU rating per lb. of under 7,000 and 15% of value for coal having a BTU rating per lb. of 7,000 and over. Underground mining—rates are 3% of value on coal having a BTU rating per lb. of under 7,000 and 4% of value on coal having a BTU rating per lb. of 7,000 and over.	Reports and payments— within 30 days after end of each calendar quarter.
Cement tax.	22¢ per ton of cement and 5¢ per ton of gypsum products.	Reports and payments— within 30 days after each calendar quarter.
Metalliferous mines tax.	For concentrate shipped to a smelter, mill or reduction work, 1.81% if the gross value of the product is over $250,000. For gold, silver or platinum shipped to a refinery, 1.6% over $250,000.	Metalliferous mines—reports and payment—semiannually by August 15 for the reporting period ending June 30 and by March 31 for the reporting period ending December 31.
Micaceous minerals tax.	5¢ per ton of vermiculite, perlite, kerrite, maconite or hydrous silicates produced.	Reports and payment— within 30 days after each calendar quarter.
Mineral mining tax (resource indemnity and ground water assessment tax).	Mineral mining tax—$25 plus 0.5% of gross value of products extracted from Montana if production exceeds $5,000, except as noted below. $25 plus 4% of gross value of product in excess of $625 for talc extracted from Montana and $25 plus 0.4% of gross value of product in excess of $6,250 for coal extracted from Montana. $25 plus 2% of gross value of product in excess of $1,250 for vermiculite extracted from Montana. $25 plus 10% of the gross value of product in excess of $250 for limestone extracted from Montana. $25 per year plus 1% of the gross value of product in excess of $2,500 for industrial garnets and associated by-products extracted from Montana.	Reports and payments— March 31.
Bentonite production tax.	Gross yield in wet tons within boundaries of elementary school district. First 20,000 tons, exempt. 20,001 to 100,000 tons, $1.56 per ton. 100,001 to 250,000 tons, $1.50 per ton. 250,001 to 500,000 tons, $1.40 per ton. 500,001 to 1,000,000 tons, $1.25 per ton. 1,000,001 tons and more, $1.00 per ton. Royalties, 15% of the amount paid or apportioned in kind to the royalty owner.	Payments due semiannually; within 45 days after June 30 and December 31.
Motor carrier fees.	Motor carriers—as set by the Public Service Commission.	Motor carriers—at time of issuance of certificate and annually thereafter between October 1 and January 31.

Tax	Basis—Rates	Due Dates
Cigarette tax; tobacco products tax.	$1.70 per pack of 20 cigarettes or less sold or processed in the state ($2.125 per pack of 25). Tobacco products, except cigarettes, 50% of wholesale price. Moist snuff is taxed at 85¢ per ounce. Licensed wholesalers are entitled to a collection and administrative expense discount.	Cigarette tax—payment by affixing insignia. Tobacco products—payment prior to sale of product.
Public utilities tax.	Electric companies—$.002 per kilowatt hour of electricity generated, produced or manufactured. Electric distributors—$.00015 per kilowatt hour. Telephone—excise tax imposed at rate of 3.75% on sales of retail telecommunications services.	Electric—30th day after each calendar quarter; telephone companies, 60th day after each calendar quarter.
Insurance companies tax.	2.75% on all net premiums of authorized insurers; except 0.75% on gross underwriting profit from wet marine and transportation insurance. Foreign companies subject to retaliatory taxes. Fire insurance—2.5% on fire portion of companies' receipts of premiums.	Reports and payment—March 1. The Insurance Commissioner is authorized to require quarterly tax payments. Fire insurance—payment—during February or March.
Estate tax.	Amount equal to the maximum tax credit allowable for state death taxes against the federal estate tax imposed with respect to the portion of the decedent's estate having a taxable situs in Montana.	Estate—returns—at the time of filing federal return. Payment—within 18 months of death.
Generation-skipping transfer tax.	Tax equal to the federal credit.	

Nebraska

Tax System.—The major taxes comprising the tax system of Nebraska are corporate and individual income taxes, sales and use taxes, and gasoline and special fuel taxes. An initiative petition approved by the electorate at the 1966 general election amended the constitution to prohibit the state from levying a property tax. However, a locally imposed and collected general property tax on real and tangible personal property continues to be the most important source of local revenue. These taxes are supplemented by (1) state taxes on franchises, privileges or occupations, and (2) municipal taxes and inspection fees that the legislature authorizes the local governments to exact. An outline of the Nebraska tax system follows:

Tax	Basis—Rates	Due Dates
Corporate organization and qualification fees.	Domestic—articles of incorporation, $60 for $10,000 or less of authorized capital stock; $100 for more than $10,000 but not more than $25,000; $150 for more than $25,000 but not more than $50,000; $225 for more than $50,000 but not more than $75,000; $300 for more than $75,000 but not more than $100,000; and for over $100,000, $300 plus $3 per $1,000 in excess of $100,000.	Domestic—at time of incorporation or increase of capital stock.
	Foreign—Certificate of authority, $130. In lieu of procuring a certificate of authority, foreign corporations may file for domestication, in which case the fees are the same as those charged domestic corporations above.	Foreign—at time of qualification, domestication or increase of capital stock.
Corporation franchise tax.	Graduated from $26 for $10,000 or less based on domestic paid-up capital stock and foreign capital employed in Nebraska, to $23,990 for over $100 million. Foreign corporations pay double, but with a maximum tax of $30,000.	Reports and payments—April 15 of each even-numbered year.
Income tax.	Individuals—Rates for married couples filing jointly and qualified surviving spouses range between 2.56% of the first $4,000 of taxable income and $1,888.20 plus 6.84% of taxable income over $46,750. Rates for married couples filing separately range between 2.56% of the first $2,000 and $944.10 plus 6.84% of taxable income over $23,375. Rates for heads of household range between 2.56% of the first $3,800 and $1,381.62 plus 6.84% of taxable income over $35,000. Rates for single individuals range between 2.56% of the first $2,400 and $1,069.06 plus 6.84% of taxable income over $26,500. Additional tax rate schedule applies if adjusted gross income exceeds $142,700 ($71,350 if married filing separately). Additional (minimum) tax equal to 29.6% of total of federal alternative minimum tax plus federal tax on certain retirement distributions. Withholding required. Rates for fiduciary income (estates and trusts) range between 2.56% of the first $500 of taxable income and $697.78 plus 6.84% of taxable income over $15,150.	Returns and payments (including payments of estimated tax)—due on the federal return and payment dates.
	Corporations—5.58% of first $50,000 of taxable income and 7.81% of taxable income over $50,000.	

Tax	Basis—Rates	Due Dates
Financial institution franchise tax.	Lesser of $0.47 per $1,000 of average deposits or 3.81% of net income before taxes and extraordinary items.	Reports and payments—15th day of 3rd month after end of tax year (March 15 for calendar-year taxpayers).
General property tax.	General property—aggregate of local rates fixed annually to meet budget. Property is valued at its actual value.	General property—returns—tangible personal property, May 1; railroads, April 15. Payment—real, personal property, December 31 following date of levy; two installments (May 1 and September 1) to avoid delinquency; counties with a population of 100,000 or more, April 1 and August 1.
Car line companies.	Car line companies—state average property tax rate times value of each class of railcars.	Car line companies—Report—June 1. Payment—March 1 and July 1 of year following tax year.
Air carriers tax.	Air carriers—state average property tax rate times value of flight equipment based on ratio of arrivals and departures, revenue tons, and originating revenue.	Air carriers—Report—June 1. Payment—March 1 and July 1 of year following tax year.
Litter tax.	Annual litter fee—manufacturers and wholesalers whose annual gross proceeds exceed $100,000, $175 per $1 million of gross proceeds of products manufactured and sold in state or of wholesale sales; retailers of food and beverages for off-premises consumption whose annual gross proceeds exceed $100,000 annually, $175 per $1 million of gross proceeds.	Payments—October 1.
Lodging tax.	Lodging tax—state rate of 1% of total consideration. County rate may also apply.	Reports and payments—same as sales tax.
Alcoholic beverages tax.	Excise—beer, 31¢ per gallon. Wine produced in farm wineries, 6¢ per gallon. Wine, except wine produced in farm wineries, 95¢ per gallon. Alcohol and spirits, $3.75 per gallon.	Reports and payments—25th of each month for preceding month.
Motor vehicle and special fuel tax.	Motor vehicle fuel tax, diesel fuel tax, compressed fuel tax—12.5¢ fixed rate per gallon of motor fuel imported, manufactured, sold or used. Plus semiannually adjusted additional tax based on statewide average cost of fuel. Combined motor fuels total rate—27.1¢ (7/1/06 through 12/31/06); 26.1¢ (1/1/06 through 6/30/06). Gasoline used as a denaturant by ethanol producer, 2.5¢ per gallon.	Returns and payments—25th day after each reporting period.

Tax	Basis—Rates	Due Dates
	Alternative fuel tax—operators of alternative fuel-powered motor vehicles must obtain an annual alternative fuel user permit and pay a fee of $75.	Alternative fuel tax permit—within 30 days of becoming an alternative fuel user.
	Aviation gasoline, 5¢ per gallon; aviation jet fuel, 3¢ per gallon.	Aviation fuel—20th day of each month for preceding month.
	Petroleum release remedial action fee—0.9¢ per gallon of motor vehicle fuel and 0.3¢ per gallon of petroleum other than motor vehicle fuel. The fee is subject to adjustment or suspension depending on balance in cash fund.	Returns and payments—20th of each month for the preceding month.
Oil and gas severance tax.	3% of value of resources severed at time of severance, except 2% of value on oil produced from wells averaging 10 barrels per day or less for all producing days during the tax year.	Reports and payments—last day of each month for preceding month.
Oil and gas conservation tax.	3 mills per dollar (prior to 6/1/06, 4 mills per dollar), set by Oil and Gas Conservation Commission. Rate may not exceed 15 mills per dollar.	Reports and payments—last day of each month for preceding month.
Uranium tax.	2% of the value of the uranium produced each year in excess of $5 million gross value.	Reports and payments—last day of each month for preceding month.
Motor vehicle rental tax.	4.5% of rental contract amount for 31 days or less for motor vehicles with capacity of no more than 15 passengers.	Report and payment—February 15.
Cigarette tax; tobacco products tax.	64¢ per package containing not more than 20 cigarettes; over 20 cigarettes per package, 64¢ for the first 20 plus a proportional amount for each cigarette over 20.	Reports—10th day of each month for preceding month. Payment—by purchase of stamps prior to sale or delivery.
	Tobacco products tax—20% of purchase price of tobacco products paid by first owner or price at which first owner who made, manufactured or fabricated the tobacco product sells the items.	Reports and payments—10th day of each month for preceding month.
Documentary stamp tax.	$2.25 per $1,000 of value or fraction thereof.	Payment—affixation of stamps prior to recording.
Sales and use tax.	5.5% of gross receipts from retail sales of tangible personal property and certain services and upon the storage, use or other consumption in the state of tangible personal property. Local rate may also apply.	Reports and payments—25th day of each month for preceding month; quarterly and annual returns allowed for small taxpayers.
Railroad excise tax.	7.5¢ for each train mile operated in the state and $100 for each public grade crossing on the line.	Reports—March 1. Payments—quarterly.

Tax	Basis—Rates	Due Dates
Insurance companies tax.	1% of gross premiums, except 0.5% for group sickness and accident insurance, 5% for HMO managed care capitation payments, and 1% for property and casualty insurance, excluding individual sickness and accident insurance.	Payment—March 1; prepayments from insurers whose annual tax for the preceding tax year was $4,000 or more due the 15th of April, June and September.
	Fire—gross premiums and assessments received for foreign fire insurance less reinsurance and return premiums on all direct business received in the state, 0.75%; domestic mutual companies and assessment associations pay 0.375%.	Payment—March 1.
	Nonadmitted insurers—3% of direct writing premiums plus fire insurance tax.	Report and payment—February 15.
Inheritance tax; estate tax; generation-skipping transfer tax.	Inheritance—Class 1—1% of clear market value of property transferred at death, or during lifetime in contemplation of death. Exempt—surviving spouse, no tax; all others, $10,000.	Inheritance—reports—inventory within 3 months after appointment of legal representative.
	Class 2—under $60,000, 6%; over $60,000, 9%. Exempt—$2,000.	Payment—within 12 months of death of decedent.
	Class 3—6% to 18%. Exempt—$500.	
	Estate—Rates for estates range between $5,600 plus 6.4% of excess over $100,000 and $1,087,200 plus 16.8% of excess over $9 million. (Decoupled from federal tax.)	Estate—returns and payment—within 12 months after death.
	Generation-skipping transfer—16% of Nebraska taxable transfer. Maximum state tax credit allowed under federal law with certain reductions for transfer and inheritance taxes paid. (Decoupled from federal tax.)	Generation-skipping transfer—returns and payment—date of transfer.

Nevada

Tax System.—The Nevada tax system is based on a general sales and use tax law and payroll excise taxes. In addition, the legislature has levied a live entertainment tax, a property tax, and certain excise and license taxes. An outline of the Nevada tax system follows:

Tax	Basis—Rates	Due Dates
Corporate organization and qualification fees.	From $75 per $75,000 or less of authorized capital stock to $375 per $1,000,000 plus $275 per each additional $500,000. Maximum amount—$35,000.	Domestic and foreign—upon incorporation or qualification or increase of capital stock.
Annual corporation report fee.	$85 flat rate for domestic and foreign corporations; $165 for initial list of officers and directors.	Last day of the month in which anniversary of incorporation occurs.
Modified business tax on financial institutions.	2% of wages paid to employees.	On or before the last day of the month immediately following each calendar quarter for which the institution is required to pay an unemployment compensation contribution.
Modified business tax.	0.63% of wages paid to employees.	On or before the last day of the month immediately following each calendar quarter for which the business is required to pay an unemployment compensation contribution.
Bank branch excise tax.	Imposed on banks that maintain more than one branch office in Nevada at a rate of $1,750 for each additional branch office.	On or before the last day of the first month of each calendar quarter.
Live entertainment tax.	10% of the admission charge on admission to any facility providing live entertainment if the entertainment is provided at a facility with a maximum seating capacity of 200 up to 7,500. An additional 10% is imposed on the amounts paid for food, refreshments and merchandise purchased at the facility. If the maximum seating capacity of the facility is at least 7,500, the tax is imposed at the rate of 5%. The 5% rate for larger facilities is not applicable to food, refreshments and merchandise purchased at the facility.	On or before the 24th day of each month.
General property tax.	General property—35% of adjusted cash value of real and tangible personal property. Aggregate of state and local rates fixed to meet budget; not to exceed 5¢ per $1 of assessed valuation. 15.85¢ per $100 of assessed valuation of taxable property for 2005-2006 and 2006-2007 fiscal years plus 1.15¢ per $100 of assessed valuation for 2005-2006 and 2006-2007 fiscal years.	General property—Returns—July 31. Payment—by 3rd Monday of August or in 4 equal installments on 3rd Monday of August and 1st Monday of October, January and March.

Tax	Basis—Rates	Due Dates
Net proceeds of minerals tax.	Dependent on the ratio of the net proceeds to the gross proceeds of the operation as a whole: the rate is 2% for a net-to-gross percentage of less than 10%; 2.5% for a percentage of at least 10% but less than 18%; 3% for a percentage of at least 18% but less than 26%; 3.5% for a percentage of at least 26% but less than 34%; 4% for a percentage of at least 34% but less than 42%; 4.5% for a percentage of at least 42% but less than 50%; and 5% for a percentage of 50% or more and where annual net proceeds exceed $4 million.	Reports—February 16. Payment—May 10. Estimated report—April 1. Prepayments required from large geographically separate extraction operations on August 1 (for preceding 6 months) and on November 1 and the following February 16 (for preceding calendar quarter).
Gaming tax.	County licenses, from $10 to $50 per month; state licenses, from 3% to 6.25% of gross revenue per month; state licenses, minimum of $100, based on number of games operated.	Reports—as required. Payment—county licenses, quarterly in advance; state licenses, 24th day of the month following the month for which the fee is calculated; the additional state tax, due annually prior to December 31 for the ensuing calendar year.
Alcoholic beverage tax.	Excise—malt beverages, 16¢ per gal. Liquor, 0.5% through 14% alcohol, 70¢; more than 14% through 22% alcohol, $1.30; over 22% alcohol, $3.60 per gal.	Reports and payments—importers and manufacturers, by 20th of each month (0.5% discount if paid by 15th of month); out-of-state vendors, by 10th of each month.
Motor vehicle fuel tax; special fuel tax; inspection fee.	Gasoline and gasohol—24¢ per gallon. Additional county taxes—from 5¢ to 10¢ per gallon. Combined state/county rates vary from a minimum of 28¢ per gallon to a maximum of 33¢ per gallon depending upon the county. Diesel fuel—27¢ per gallon. Aviation fuel—2¢ per gallon; counties have an option, by ordinance, to impose an additional 1¢ to 9¢ per gallon tax.	Gasoline—Returns and payment—25th day of each month. Suppliers reports—last day of month.
	Special fuel—27¢ per gallon of fuel used in internal combustion engines to propel motor vehicles, except gasoline. Compressed natural gas, 21¢ per gallon. Liquefied petroleum gas, 22¢ per gallon. Water-phased hydro-carbon fuel, 19¢ per gallon.	Special fuel—Users' reports—last day of January, April, July and October; suppliers' reports—last day of each month. Payment—with report.
	Inspection fee—0.055¢ per gallon of motor vehicle fuel or lubricating oil shipped into or held for sale within the state.	Inspection fee—On or before the last day of each calendar month.
	Petroleum discharge fee—0.75¢ per gallon of motor vehicle fuel, diesel fuel of grade 1 or 2 and other heating oil refined or imported in Nevada. Imposition depends on the fund balance.	Petroleum fee—Payment due the last day of the month.
Oil and gas administrative fee.	20¢ per barrel of oil or per 50,000 cubic feet of natural gas, as appropriate.	Returns and payments—last day of month.
	Permit processing fee for oil wells—$200; geothermal wells—from $50 for domestic wells to $500 for industrial wells.	

Tax	Basis—Rates	Due Dates
Cigarette taxes.	Cigarettes—80¢ per pack of 20 cigarettes.	Reports—dealers, not later than 25 days after the end of each month.
	Tobacco products—30% of wholesale price.	Payment—at time of purchase of tax stamps, unless authorized to defer payment.
Realty transfer tax.	$1.95-$2.05 per $500 value or fraction in counties with less than 400,000 population; otherwise, $2.55 per $500 of value.	Payment—to be evidenced by county recorder.
Sales and use taxes.	2% of gross receipts from sales of tangible personal property or selected services or sales price of tangible personal property stored, used, or consumed plus 4.5% on sale or use of taxable property in any county.	Reports and payment—on or before last day of each month for the preceding month (quarterly for taxpayers having gross monthly sales of less than $10,000).
Utilities fees.	2% of net profits made in the operation of any public utility for which county franchise is granted.	Reports—first Monday of March. Payment—first Monday of July.
	Additional tax of not over 4.25 mills (3.5 mills for railroads) per dollar of gross operating revenue of intrastate utilities and general improvement districts. Minimum, $10.	Reports—April 15. Payment—July 1 or quarterly on first day of July, October, January, and April.
Insurance companies tax.	3.5% of gross premium income of preceding year covering property or risks in the state less dividends returned, return premiums and premiums received for reinsurance. The same rate applies to surplus lines brokers and independent procurers. 1.75% reduced rate for a Nevada domestic company maintaining a qualified home office in Nevada. The rate also applies to a foreign company establishing a qualified regional office.	Reports and payment—March 15 except unauthorized insurance, 30 days after procurement or renewal. Estimated payment—due quarterly on the last day of the last month of each calendar quarter. Surplus lines brokers owing more than $1,000 in a quarter must report and pay within 45 days after the end of the quarter.
	Foreign companies subject to retaliatory taxes.	
Estate tax; generation-skipping transfer tax.	Basic federal estate tax credit for state death taxes for residents and nonresident decedents.	Returns—on or before the date the federal estate tax return is due. Payment—within 9 months from the date of death.
	Generation-skipping transfer—Tax imposed to absorb federal generation-skipping transfer tax credit.	

New Hampshire

Tax System.—New Hampshire derives its revenue from the corporate profits tax, gasoline tax, vehicle registration fees and tobacco taxes, and from the taxation of banks, utilities and the income from intangibles, as well as from the general property tax. An outline of the New Hampshire tax system follows:

Tax	Basis—Rates	Due Dates
Corporate organization and qualification fees.	Domestic—Articles of incorporation, $50.	Domestic—at time of incorporation or increase of authorized shares.
	Foreign—Certificate of authority, $50.	Foreign—at time of qualification.
Annual corporation report.	$100 flat fee for all corporations.	Report—April 1.
Business profits tax.	8.5% of federal net income, before net operating loss and special deductions, adjusted by state additions and deductions. All business organizations whose gross business income from all sources before expenses exceeds $50,000 must file.	Returns and estimated tax declarations—March 15 or the 15th day of 3rd month after close of tax period. Taxpayers exempt from federal taxation, 15th day of 4th month following end of tax period. Payment—15th day of 4th, 6th, 9th, and 12th months.
Business enterprise tax.	0.75% of taxable enterprise value tax base of every business enterprise having gross business receipts in excess of $150,000 or an enterprise value tax base in excess of $75,000.	Reports and payments—March 15 or the 15th day of 3rd month for enterprises required to file a U.S. corporation return. 15th day of 4th month for all others.
Interest and dividends tax.	5% on interest from bonds, notes, money, debts, and savings deposits, and on dividends from shares in business or trusts paid to resident individuals.	Reports and payments—15th day of the 4th month. Estimated tax: 15th day of the 4th, 6th, 9th, and 12th months of the tax year (for calendar-year taxpayers, the final estimated payment is due January 15 of the following tax year).
Property tax.	Local property—fixed locally to meet budget.	General property—Reports—April 15; charitable organizations that are not exempt, June 1. Payments—December 1.
	State education property tax—The rate is set by the Commissioner of the Department of Revenue Administration at a level sufficient to generate revenue of $363 million when imposed on all persons and property subject to tax.	
Railroad tax.	Average state property rate. Railroad, express, freight and passenger car lines.	Reports—July 1. Payments—15 days after date of notice. Estimated tax—declaration, at time for filing annual return; payments, 15th day of April, June, September, and December.

Tax	Basis—Rates	Due Dates
Utility property tax.	$6.60 per $1,000 of the value of utility property.	Payments—four equal installments of estimated taxes paid on the 15th day of April, June, September, and December.
Forest yield tax.	Timber, 10% of stumpage value.	Reports—annually May 15; within 60 days after completion of operation. Payments—within 30 days after mailing of tax bill.
Meals and rentals tax.	Rentals: 8% of the rent for each occupancy for first 185 days or automobile for the first 180 days. Meals: 8% of the charge.	Returns and payments—on or before the 15th day of each month.
Medicaid enhancement tax.	6% of net patient services revenue for the hospital's fiscal year ending during the first full calendar year preceding the taxable period.	Reports—10th day of the month following expiration of the taxable period. Payments—15th day of the 3rd month.
Alcoholic beverages tax.	Excise—wholesale distributors, beverage manufacturers, and brew pubs, 30¢ per gallon. Domestic wine manufacturers, 5% of gross sales. Tax based on sale of beer and alcoholic beverages.	Excise—Returns and payments—10th day of each month.
Motor fuels tax.	Road toll tax on sale of fuels—18¢ per gallon.	Motor fuel—20th day of each month.
	Fuel use—18¢ per gallon.	Fuel use—last day of April, July, October, and January.
	Aviation fuel—4¢ per gallon of fuel sold to or used in the propulsion of aircraft, except 2¢ per gallon on the sale of aviation jet fuel and 0.5¢ per gallon for air carrier large aircraft.	Airways toll—20th day of each month.
Tobacco tax.	80¢ per pack of 20 cigarettes sold at retail. Smokeless tobacco products, 19% of the wholesale sales price as invoiced to the retailer.	Reports—cigarette wholesalers, by 30th day following regular reporting period. Smokeless tobacco wholesalers, monthly. Payments—by affixing stamps.
Realty transfer tax.	75¢ per $100 (to be paid both by seller and by purchaser) or fractional part of consideration or price paid for realty; minimum tax, $20.	Payments—by stamps affixed to document.
Electricity consumption tax.	$0.00055 per kilowatt hour.	Reports and payments—15th day of second month following taxable month or annually on February 15.
	Communications services tax—7% of gross charge.	Reports and payments—15th day of each month. Estimated reports and payments from large taxpayers, 15th day of current month. Small taxpayers may be authorized to report and pay quarterly.

Tax	Basis—Rates	Due Dates
Insurance premiums tax.	Authorized and formerly authorized insurers—2% of gross premiums less dividends returned or credited to policyholders (minimum, $200). Unauthorized marine insurance—2% of gross premiums. Effective 7/1/07, 1.75% of gross premiums; eff. 1/1/09, 1.5%; eff. 1/1/10, 1.25%; and eff. 1/1/11, 1%. Ocean marine companies—5% of taxable underwriting profit. Unauthorized insurance and independently procured insurance—4% of gross premiums.	Reports—authorized insurers, March 15; ocean marine companies, May 1; unauthorized insurers, within 60 days of procurement.
		Payments—ocean marine companies, within one month of receiving notice of amount. Unauthorized insurers, March 1. Through 2006, authorized insurers' estimated tax due March 15, June 15, September 15 and December 15. Beginning in 2007, the tax payments required on annual basis on or before March 15.
	Foreign insurance companies—2% of gross premiums less return premiums reported.	Returns and payments—during January.
Refined petroleum products tax.	Uniform rate of 0.1% of fair market value per barrel at refinery.	Returns—15th day following the end of taxable period. Payments—one-third of quarterly estimate is paid each month during the quarter.
Estate tax.	Estate—Repealed for decedents dying after 2004.	Returns and Payments—not applicable.

New Jersey

Tax System.—The New Jersey tax system is based on a real property tax at uniform rates within each taxing district. Business personal property is assessed by the Director of the Division of Taxation. The property tax has been supplemented by taxes on income, occupations, privileges and taxable sales and use. An outline of the New Jersey tax system follows:

Tax	Basis—Rates	Due Dates
Corporate organization and qualification fees.	Domestic—$125 incorporation fee.	Domestic—at time of incorporation or increase of capital stock.
	Foreign—certificate of authority, $125.	Foreign—at time the application is filed.
Corporation business tax; corporation income tax.	Corporation business (income) tax—9% of allocated net income. Corporations whose entire net income is $100,000 or less are taxed at 7.5%. Corporations with entire net income of $50,000 or less are taxed at 6.5%. S corporations tax rate is 0.67% for privilege periods ending on or after July 1, 2006, but on or before June 30, 2007; 0% for privilege periods ending on or after July 1, 2007 (1.33% for taxpayers with entire net income not subject to federal corporate income tax in excess of $100,000 for privilege periods ending on or after July 1, 2001, but on or before June 30, 2006). Investment companies are taxed at the regular rate on 40% of entire net income and 40% of entire net worth; pay minimum tax. Real estate investment trusts, 4% of entire net income and 15% of entire net worth. Regulated investment companies pay minimum tax. *Minimum tax:* For calendar year 2006 and thereafter, the minimum tax is based on gross receipts as follows: (1) gross receipts less than $100,000, $500; (2) gross receipts of $100,000 or more but less than $250,000, $750; (3) gross receipts $250,000 or more but less than $500,000, $1,000; (4) gross receipts of $500,000 or more but less than $1 million, $1,500; and (5) gross receipts of $1 million or more, $2,000. Prior to 2006, the minimum tax was $500. For privilege periods ending on or after July 1, 2006, and before July 1, 2009, a surtax of 4% is imposed on the liability remaining after any credits allowed, other than credits for installment payments, estimated payments made with filing extensions, or overpayments applied from prior privilege periods.	Reports and payments— 15th day of 4th month after close of taxable year. Installment payments of estimated tax due on or before the 15th day of the 4th, 6th, 9th, and 12th months of the current year.
Corporation annual report fee.	Corporation annual report fee—$50 flat rate for domestic and foreign.	Annual report—30 days before or after date designated for filing by Secretary of State.

Tax	Basis—Rates	Due Dates
Personal income taxes.	Personal income tax—Tax rates range from 1.4% of the first $20,000 of taxable income to 8.970% of taxable income over $500,000 for married individuals filing jointly, heads of households or surviving spouses, and from 1.4% of the first $20,000 of taxable income to 8.970% of taxable income over $500,000 for married individuals filing separately, other unmarried individuals and estates and trusts.	Returns and payment—15th day of 4th month after end of tax year. Estimated tax declarations due 15th day of April, June, September, and January in four equal installments.
General property tax.	General property—Aggregate of levies of all local levying bodies within whose jurisdiction the property lies. The taxable value of personal property of telephone, telegraph and messenger companies subject to local taxation is a percentage of true value corresponding to the average ratio of assessed to true value of real property in the taxing district.	Returns—none, except taxpayers subject to the tax on telephone, etc., companies file returns on or before September 1. Payment—quarterly installments on February 1, May 1, August 1, and November 1.
Railroad property tax.	Railroad property—Class II property, $4.75 per $100 of true value.	Railroad property—Reports—property schedule, March 1; payment—December 1.
Railroad franchise tax.	Railroad franchise—10% of net operating income allocated to New Jersey according to track mileage.	Railroad franchise—Reports—schedule of revenue, April 1. Payment—June 15.
Casino control tax.	Licenses—initial fee, not less than $200,000; renewal fee, not less than $100,000 for a one-year casino license, and $200,000 for a two-year casino license. Slot machines, $500 per machine. Tax—8% of gross revenues, plus an investment alternative tax of 2.5% of gross revenues.	Report and payment—March 15. Investment alternative tax due and payable on the last day of April following the end of the calendar year.
Alcoholic beverage tax.	Excise—beer, 12¢ per gal. Liquors, $4.40 per gal. Wines, vermouth, sparkling wines, 70¢ per gal. Cider, containing at least 3.2% but not more than 7% of alcohol by volume, 12¢ per gal.	Excise—Reports and payment—due 15th day following each 2-month period.
Gasoline (motor fuels) tax; fuel use tax.	General motor fuels tax rate and rate imposed on gasohol, 10.5¢ per gallon. Diesel, 13.5¢ per gallon; aviation fuel, 12.5¢ per gallon. Liquefied petroleum gas and liquefied or compressed natural gas sold or used to propel motor vehicles on public highways, 5.25¢ per gallon.	Reports and payment—distributors, 20th day of each month; blenders, within five days of receipt of fuel.
	Motor fuel use tax—Same as the motor fuel tax rate for fuel used in operations in the state.	Motor fuel use tax—Reports and payments—last day of Jan., April, July and Oct.
	Petroleum products gross receipts tax—Additional tax of 2.75% of gross receipts derived from the first sale of petroleum products on each company refining and/or distributing petroleum products in this state or importing petroleum products for use or consumption by it in this state (if consideration for all such deliveries made during a quarter exceeds $5,000).	Petroleum products gross receipts tax—25th day of the month following the end of the quarter.

Tax	Basis—Rates	Due Dates
Cigarette tax; tobacco products tax.	$2.575 per pack of 20, whether sold, possessed for sale, use, consumption or storage for use within the state (prior to July 15, 2006, $2.40 per pack of 20).	Reports—by 20th of each month.
		Payment—by stamps affixed to each package of cigarettes.
	Tobacco products tax—30% of wholesale sales or use of tobacco products other than cigarettes.	Reports and payments—20th day of each month.
	Effective August 1, 2006, moist snuff, $0.75 per oz. on the net weight (previously taxed at 30% of wholesale price).	
Realty transfer tax.	There are four realty transfer fees. There is a "basic fee," which consists of (1) a state portion at the rate of $1.25 for each $500 of consideration or fractional part thereof recited in the deed, and (2) a county portion at the rate of $0.50 for each $500 of consideration or fractional part thereof. There is an "additional fee" at the rate of $0.75 for each $500 of consideration or fractional part thereof recited in the deed in excess of $150,000. There is "general purpose fee," which is structured as follows: $0.90 for each $500 on the first $550,000 of the value recited in the deed of transfer; $1.40 on each $500 of the value between $550,000 and $850,000; $1.90 on each $500 of the value between $850,000 and $1,000,000; and $2.15 for each $500 of the value over $1,000,000. For each conveyance or transfer of property, the grantor will pay a "supplemental fee" of (1) $0.25 for each $500 of consideration or fractional part thereof not in excess of $150,000 recited in the deed; (2) $0.85 for each $500 of consideration or fractional part thereof in excess of $150,000 but not in excess of $200,000 recited in the deed; and (3) $1.40 for each $500 of consideration or fractional part thereof in excess of $200,000 recited in the deed, plus, for a transfer of title to real property upon which there is new construction, an additional $1 for each $500 of consideration or fractional part thereof not in excess of $150,000 recited in the deed.	Payment—prior to recordation.
	A 1% fee is imposed upon the grantee of a deed for the transfer of certain real property for more than $1 million under certain conditions.	Payment—at the time the deed is recorded.
Sales and use tax.	7% (prior to July 15, 2006, 6%) of taxable sales and uses, rentals, occupancies, admissions and selected services. Transitional rules apply for any taxable sale transactions that began before July 15, 2006, and are completed on or after July 15, 2006.	Returns and payment—20th day of April, July, October and January; if tax exceeds $500 for 1st or 2nd month of a quarter, due by the 20th of the following month.

Tax	Basis—Rates	Due Dates
Utilities—Excise tax on sewage and water corporations.	Excise on sewage and water corporations—5% of gross receipts; 2% if gross receipts are less than $50,000. Sewerage and water companies pay additional tax at the rate of 7.5% of gross receipts from New Jersey business for the preceding calendar year.	Reports—on gross receipts, February 1; on property, September 1. Payment—sewerage and water companies, 35%, 15 days after certification of apportionment, 35% on August 15, 30%, on November 15.
	Surtax—For sewerage and water companies, 0.625% of apportioned gross receipts taxes. If gross receipts are not more than $50,000, the tax is 0.25%; for businesses connected with lines or mains in the state, 0.9375%.	Surtax—prepayment of $1/2$ due by May 1.
Insurance companies tax.	All insurance companies (except marine)—2.1% of premiums less personal property taxes paid. Group accident and health insurance on residents, 1.05%.	Reports—domestic and foreign life insurance companies, March 15; marine companies, April 1; all others, March 1.
	Marine (state taxes)—5.25% of allocated underwriting profit.	Payment—marine companies, within 15 days after notice of amount of tax due; all others, March 1. Tax on insureds who procure or renew insurance with any unauthorized foreign or alien insurer, report and payment—30 days after such procurement or renewal. On March 1, stock, mutual and assessment insurance companies (domestic and foreign) prepay $1/2$ of the prior year's tax. Domestic and foreign companies prepay an additional $1/2$ of prior year's tax on or before each June 1. Surplus lines insurers, report and payment—due at the time of filing the quarterly report.
	Tax on insureds who procure or renew insurance with any unauthorized foreign or alien insurer—3% of gross premium. Surplus lines coverage—3% of taxable premium receipts.	
	Foreign companies subject to retaliatory taxes.	
Inheritance tax; estate tax.	Inheritance—Husband or wife—Exempt. Class A—Exempt. Class C—11% to 16%; exempt, $25,000. Class D—15% or 16%; exempt, $500.	Inheritance—returns and payment due within 8 months of death.
	Estate—For estates of decedents dying after December 31, 2001, New Jersey estate tax decoupled from federal estate tax. New Jersey tax computed pursuant to federal provisions in effect on December 31, 2001 or, upon election, pursuant to simplified system to be prescribed by Director of Division of Taxation.	Estate—Returns—within 30 days after filing federal return. Payment—within 9 months after death.

New Mexico

Tax System.—New Mexico imposes a general property tax and taxes on incomes, occupations and privileges. An annual franchise tax on domestic and foreign corporations is imposed. An outline of the New Mexico tax system follows:

Tax	Basis—Rates	Due Dates
Corporate organization and qualification fees.	Domestic corporations—$1 for each 1,000 shares of total authorized shares; minimum, $100; maximum, $1,000. Foreign corporations—$1 for each 1,000 shares of total authorized shares; minimum, $200; maximum, $1,000.	At the time of incorporation of domestic corporations or qualification of foreign corporations and increase of capital stock.
Corporate merger, consolidation, or exchange fees.	$1 for each 1,000 shares of the total amount of authorized or exchanged shares or $1 for each 1,000 shares that exceed the amount of shares prior to merger or consolidation; minimum, $200; maximum, $1,000.	Upon filing certificate of merger, consolidation, or exchange.
Franchise tax; corporation annual report filing fee.	Franchise tax—$50 per year, or prorated.	Return and payment—15th day of the 3rd month after end of tax year.
	Corporation biennial report—$25.	Corporate report—within 30 days after issuance of certificate of incorporation or authority; thereafter, on 15th day of 3rd month after end of tax year.
Income tax.	**For 2006: Individuals, estates, and trusts:** first $5,500, 1.7%; over $5,500 but not over $11,000, $93.50 plus 3.2% of excess over $5,500; over $11,000 but not over $16,000, $269.50 plus 4.7% of excess over $11,000; over $16,000, $504.50 plus 5.3% of excess over $16,000. **Heads of household, surviving spouses and married individuals filing joint returns:** first $8,000, 1.7%; over $8,000 but not over $16,000, $136 plus 3.2% of excess over $8,000; over $16,000 but not over $24,000, $392 plus 4.7% of excess over $16,000; over $24,000, $768 plus 5.3% of excess over $24,000. **Married individuals filing separate returns:** first $4,000, 1.7%; over $4,000 but not over $8,000, $68 plus 3.2% of excess over $4,000; over $8,000 but not over $12,000, $196 plus 4.7% of excess over $8,000; over $12,000, $384 plus 5.3% of excess over $12,000.	Returns and payments—individuals—15th day of 4th month after end of taxable year; corporations and financial institutions—15th day of the 3rd month after the end of taxable year. Estimated payments—individuals, 15th day of 6th, 9th, and 13th months of the income year and 4th month of following year; corporations, 15th day of 6th, 9th, and 12th months of the taxable year and 3rd month of following year.

Tax	Basis—Rates	Due Dates
	For 2007: Individuals, estates, and trusts: first $5,500, 1.7%; over $5,500 but not over $11,000, $93.50 plus 3.2% of excess over $5,500; over $11,000 but not over $16,000, $269.50 plus 4.7% of excess over $11,000; over $16,000, $504.50 plus 5.3% of excess over $16,000. **Heads of household, surviving spouses and married individuals filing joint returns:** first $8,000, 1.7%; over $8,000 but not over $16,000, $136 plus 3.2% of excess over $8,000; over $16,000 but not over $24,000, $392 plus 4.7% of excess over $16,000; over $24,000, $768 plus 5.3% of excess over $24,000. **Married individuals filing separate returns:** first $4,000, 1.7%; over $4,000 but not over $8,000, $68 plus 3.2% of excess over $4,000; over $8,000 but not over $12,000, $196 plus 4.7% of excess over $8,000; over $12,000, $384 plus 5.3% of excess over $12,000.	
	Nonresidents—same rates on income derived from business, employment and property in New Mexico.	
	Corporations—first $500,000, 4.8% of net income; over $500,000 but not over $1,000,000, $24,000 plus 6.4% of excess over $500,000; over $1,000,000, $56,000 plus 7.6% of excess over $1,000,000. Qualified taxpayers may pay alternative tax of 0.75% of gross receipts from New Mexico sales.	
	General withholding is required.	
General property tax.	General property—Aggregate of state and local rates fixed to meet budget. Property is assessed at 33^1/₃% of market value.	General property—returns—last day of February. Payment—November 10 and April 10, delinquent 30 days thereafter. Prepayments due July 10 and January 10, may be allowed if the tax due is $100 or more.
	Mining property—Assessment of mining property is based on production or market value depending on the mineral produced.	Mining property—Returns—last day of February; payment, 50% November 10 and 50% April 10.
Oil and gas production equipment tax.	Oil and gas production equipment tax—based on the taxable value of equipment at each production unit that is 27% of the value of the products of each such unit.	Payment—on or before each November 30.
Health facility daily bed tax.	Surcharge not to exceed either 6% of total annual gross receipts or $8.82 per day per occupied bed.	Payment by the 25th day of month following month in which surcharge is applied.
Alcoholic beverages tax.	Excise—beer, 41¢ per gallon; spirituous liquors, $1.60 per liter; wine, 45¢ per liter; wine produced by small wine growers, 10¢ per liter on first 80,000 liters and 20¢ per liter over 80,000 but less than 560,000; fortified wine, $1.50 per liter; beer produced by microbrewers, 8¢ per gallon; alcoholic cider, 41¢ per gallon.	Excise—Reports and payments—25th of each following month.

Tax	Basis—Rates	Due Dates
Gasoline tax; special fuel supplier tax; alternative fuel tax.	17¢ per gallon of gasoline and 21¢ per gallon of special fuel received or used.	Reports and payments—gasoline tax—on or before 25th of each following month. Special fuel suppliers—25th of the month following the month the fuel is received in the state; special fuel users—25th of the month following the last day of the calendar quarter in which the special fuel is used (annual report and payment for small users due January 25).
	Alternative fuel distributed in the state—12¢ per gallon. Users may pay annual flat tax rate (currently $60—$1,100) based on gross vehicle weight).	Alternative fuel tax—Distributors' reports and payments due on or before the 25th of each month.
	Petroleum products loading fee—$150 per load (8,000 gallons) of gasoline or special fuel. Rate reduced if revenues exceed specified amounts.	Reports and payments—on or before 25th day of each following month.
Severance tax.	Severance tax—gross value less rental and royalty payments and other deductions. Tax rates are: timber and nonmetallic minerals, 0.125%; potash, 2.5%; copper, 0.5%; gold and silver, 0.2%; lead, zinc, molybdenum, manganese, thorium, rare earth and other metals, 0.125%; surface coal, 57¢ per ton plus a per-ton indexed surtax; underground coal, 55¢ per ton plus a per-ton indexed surtax; uranium, 3.5%.	Severance tax reports and payments—25th of the month following the month in which the taxable event occurred.
Oil and gas severance tax.	Oil and gas severance—natural gas, 3.75% of the value of products. Natural gas from a new production natural gas well, 3.75% of the value of products. Oil, liquid hydrocarbon and carbon dioxide, 3.75% of taxable value. Oil and liquid hydrocarbons from qualified enhanced recovery project, 1.875% of taxable value, if annual average price of west Texas intermediate crude oil was less than $28 per barrel. Oil and gas from well workover projects in excess of production projection, 2.45% of taxable value if annual average price of west Texas intermediate crude oil was less than $24 per barrel. Natural gas removed from a stripper well property, 1.875% of taxable value, if the average annual taxable value of natural gas was $1.15 or less per thousand cubic feet; 2.8125% if the average annual taxable value was greater than $1.15 but not more than $1.35 per thousand cubic feet. Oil and liquid hydrocarbons removed from natural gas at or near wellhead from a stripper well property, $1.875% of taxable value, if the average annual taxable value of oil was $15.00 or less per barrel; 2.8125% if value was greater than $15.00 but not more than $18.00 per barrel.	Oil and gas severance tax—25th day of 2nd month following each calendar month.

Tax	Basis—Rates	Due Dates
Oil and gas conservation tax.	Oil and gas conservation—0.19% of taxable value of oil, natural gas, liquid hydrocarbons, coal, uranium, geothermal energy, and carbon dioxide if unencumbered balance is less than or equal to $500,000 (0.18% if certain fund criteria are met).	Oil and gas conservation tax—25th day of 2nd month.
Resources excise tax.	Resources excise tax—potash, 0.5%; molybdenum, 0.125%; all other taxable resources, 0.75%.	Resources excise tax—due by 25th of month following month in which sale, transportation out of state or consumption occurred.
	Resources excise tax (Processors' tax)—timber, 0.375%; potash and molybdenum, 0.125%; all other taxable resources, 0.75%.	Processors' tax—Reports and payments due on the 25th day of each month.
Oil and gas (ad valorem) production tax.	Oil and gas (ad valorem) production tax—assessed value of products severed and sold from each production unit.	Oil and gas production—25th day of 2nd month following the close of each calendar month.
Oil and gas privilege (emergency school) tax.	Oil and gas privilege tax (emergency school tax)—3.15% taxable value of oil and other liquid hydrocarbons removed from natural gas at or near the wellhead or of carbon dioxide; 4% of the taxable value of natural gas.	Oil and gas privilege—25th day of 2nd month following the close of each calendar month.
Natural gas processor's tax.	Natural gas processor's tax—Rate is determined by multiplying $.0065 per mmbtu by a fraction, the numerator of which is the annual average taxable value per mcf of natural gas produced in New Mexico during the previous calendar year and the denominator of which is $1.33 per mcf, and rounding to the nearest one hundredth of a cent per mmbtu.	Gas processors—Returns due within 25 days after close of calendar month. Payment accompanies return.
Leased vehicle gross receipts tax.	5% of gross receipts from leasing small passenger vehicles plus a $2 per day per vehicle surcharge.	Leased vehicles—25th day of each month.
Cigarette and tobacco products tax.	4.55¢ per cigarette (91¢ per pack of 20).	Payment—by purchase of stamps.
	25% of the product value of tobacco products.	Payment—on or before the 25th day of each month.
Gross receipts, governmental gross receipts and compensating tax.	Gross receipts—5% of gross receipts from sales of tangible personal property and services.	Gross receipts—Reports and payments due 25th of each month; semiannual or quarterly reports and payments allowed if liability is less than $200 per month.
	Compensating tax—5% of value at time of acquisition, conversion or introduction into state.	Compensating tax—Reports and payments due 25th of each month; semiannual or quarterly reports and payments allowed if liability is less than $200 per month.
Electric, gas, water, steam companies tax.	Utility inspection and supervision fee—0.506% of gross receipts from business transacted in the state for the preceding calendar year.	Electric, gas, etc.—Payment—payable on or before the last day of February.

Tax	Basis—Rates	Due Dates
Telephone and transmission companies, carriers tax.	Utility and carrier inspection fee—carriers, not more than 0.256% of gross receipts from business transacted in the state for the preceding calendar year; utilities, not more than 0.511% of gross receipts from business transacted in the state for the preceding calendar year.	Telephone, transmission, carriers—Payment—annually by January 20, or equal quarterly installments by 20th day of January, April, July, and October.
Pipeline companies tax.	Pipeline—gas, from $500 up, depending on horsepower; oil, from $500 up, based on miles of line.	Pipeline—payment due during July.
Railroad car companies tax.	Railroad company—1.5% of gross earnings from the use or operation of cars within the state.	Railroad company—railroads withholding tax due March 1.
Interstate telecommunications tax.	Interstate telecommunications—4.25% of interstate telecommunications gross receipts.	Interstate telecommunications—25th day of each month.
911 emergency surcharge and network and database surcharge.	Local exchange access lines—monthly 51¢ 911 emergency surcharge; 26¢ database surcharge.	Payment—25th day of month following month of imposition of surcharge.
Insurance companies tax.	3.003% of gross premiums collected in the state, less return premiums, dividends and amounts received for reinsurance.	Return—April 15 of following year. Payments—Estimated payments due on April 15, July 15, October 15, and January 15, with any adjustment due with the return.
	1% surtax on gross health insurance premiums and membership and policy fees received by the insurance company on hospital and medical expense incurred insurance or contracts; nonprofit health care service plan contracts, excluding dental or vision only contracts; and health maintenance organization subscriber contracts covering health risks within New Mexico during preceding calendar year, less return premiums, dividends, and amounts received for reinsurance.	
	Foreign companies subject to retaliatory taxes.	
Estate tax.	An estate tax is assessed in an amount equal to the state death tax credit allowable under the federal estate tax laws.	Return and payment—due on or before the due date for the federal return.

New York

Tax System.—New York has not adopted the system of segregation of revenues for state and local purposes. The law permits the levy of income, property, franchise, sales and use, gross receipts, inheritance and miscellaneous taxes. An outline of the New York tax system follows:

Tax	Basis—Rates	Due Dates
Corporate organization and qualification fees.	Domestic—par value shares of authorized capital stock, 0.05%; no par value shares, 5¢ per share. Minimum, $10. Certificate of incorporation, $125.	Domestic—at time of filing certificate of incorporation or increase in capital stock.
	Foreign—par value shares, 0.05% of face value of issued capital stock employed in state; no par value shares, 5¢ per share. Minimum, $10. Similar fees for increase in capital stock. Annual maintenance fee, $300. Application for authority, $225.	Foreign—with next franchise tax return after qualification and after increase in capital stock employed.
Franchise taxes: agricultural cooperative corporations; business corporations, domestic and foreign; unrelated business tax; financial corporations; and national banking associations.	Agricultural cooperatives—Greater of 1 mill per $1 of net value (not less than $5/share) or, if dividends of 6% or more are declared, 0.25 mill per 1% of dividend per dollar of par value of capital stock. Minimum, $10.	Agricultural cooperative corporations—returns and payments—by March 15.
	Business corporations—(A) principal tax; the greater of: (1) allocated entire net income, 7.5%; or (2) business or investment capital allocated to New York, 1. 78 mills per dollar (0.4 mill for cooperative housing corporations) (maximum tax, $350,000); or (3) 2.5% of minimum taxable income; or (4) minimum flat rate ($1,500 for a taxpayer with gross payroll of $6.25 million or more, $425 if gross payroll is more than $1 million but not more than $6.25 million, $325 if gross payroll is not more than $1 million but greater than $500,000, $225 if gross payroll is not more than $500,000 but greater than $250,000, and $100 if gross payroll is $250,000 or less. $800 if gross payroll is $1,000 or less with total receipts within and without this state of $1,000 or less and average value of gross assets is $1,000 or less (the minimum tax is prorated). (B) Additional tax on allocated subsidiary capital: 0.9 mill per $1. (C) Small business taxpayers: Entire net income base of $290,000 or less, 6.5%; over $290,000, but not exceeding $390,000, $18,850, plus 7.5% of the amount over $290,000, plus 7.25% of the amount over $350,000. (D) New York S corporations: S corporations are subject only to the fixed-dollar minimum tax. (E) Surcharge on business activity within the Metropolitan Commuter Transportation District of 17% of tax imposed for tax years ending before December 31, 2009.	Business corporations, domestic and foreign, including real estate and omnibus corporations: Report and payment (plus first estimated installment for current year, if preceding year's tax exceeded $1,000) due 2½ months after end of tax year.

Tax	Basis—Rates	Due Dates
		Estimated payments required for corporations that can reasonably expect tax in excess of $1,000, due in installments.
	Unrelated business income tax—9% or $250, whichever is greater, of unrelated business income of certain tax-exempt charitable organizations and trusts subject to the federal tax on unrelated business income.	Returns and payments—15th day of 5th month after close of taxable year.
	Banking corporations (applicable only to savings banks and savings and loan associations after 2005)—Greater of (a) 7.5% of allocated entire net income; (b) $250; or (c) larger of 3% of allocated alternative entire net income, or 0.1 mill on each dollar of allocated taxable assets (if net worth ratio is at least 4% but less than 5% of average total value of all assets and total assets are comprised of 33% or more of mortgages, 0.04 mill on each dollar of allocated taxable assets; if net worth ratio is less than 4% of average total value of all assets and total assets are comprised of 33% or more of mortgages, 0.02 mill on each dollar of allocated taxable assets). Metropolitan Commuter Transportation District surcharge: 17% of tax imposed for tax years ending before December 31, 2009.	Financial institutions—report and payment (plus first estimated installment for current year, if preceding year's tax exceeded $1,000) due 2$1/2$ months after end of tax year.
		Estimated payments required for financial institutions that can reasonably expect tax in excess of $1,000, due in installments.
Personal income tax.	For taxable years beginning after 2005: for married individuals and surviving spouses: Not over $16,000, 4%; over $16,000 but not over $22,000, $640 plus 4.5%; over $22,000 but not over $26,000, $910 plus 5.25%; over $26,000 but not over $40,000, $1,120 plus 5.9%; over $40,000, $1,946 plus 6.85%. For heads of households: Not over $11,000, 4%; over $11,000 but not over $15,000, $440 plus 4.5; over $15,000 but not over $17,000, $620 plus 5.25%; over $17,000 but not over $30,000, $725 plus 5.9%; over $30,000, $1,492 plus 6.85%. For unmarried individuals, married individuals filing separately, and estates and trusts: Not over $8,000, 4%; over $8,000 but not over $11,000, $320 plus 4.5%; over $11,000 but not over $13,000, $455 plus 5.25%; over $13,000 but not over $20,000, $560 plus 5.9%; over $20,000, $973 plus 6.85%.	Personal income tax—on or before April 15 for calendar-year taxpayers, 15th day of 4th month after end of tax year for fiscal-year taxpayers.
		Payments of estimated income tax due April 15, June 15, September 15 and January 15. For farmers single due date is January 15 of succeeding year.
	A supplemental tax (the tax table benefit recapture) is also computed for taxpayers with certain levels of income.	

Tax	Basis—Rates	Due Dates
	Minimum income tax on individuals, estates and trusts—6% of taxpayer's federal tax preference items, with modifications, in excess of $5,000 ($2,500 for married persons filing separately).	
General property tax. (Assessed and collected locally.)	Aggregate of all levies for local purposes fixed annually by each locality to meet budget. Based on full value of real property including special franchises. Equalization rate in each locality determined by State Board of Real Property Services. Personal property is exempt.	Returns—special franchises, 30 days after acquisition.
		Payment—generally by January 31 but payment date may vary according to locality.
Alcoholic beverage tax.	Excise—beer, 11¢ per gallon; cider, 3.79¢ per gallon; Still wines, artificially carbonated sparkling wines, and natural sparkling wines, 18.93¢ per gallon. Liquor containing more than 2% but less than 24% alcohol, 67¢ per liter; liquor containing not more than 2% alcohol by volume, 1¢ per liter; all other liquor, $1.70 per liter.	Excise—distributors and noncommercial importers, reports and payments—20th of each month.
Motor fuel tax; fuel use tax; petroleum business tax.	23.95¢ per gallon on motor fuel (includes 8¢ excise tax, 15.9¢ petroleum business tax, and petroleum testing fee of .05¢) and 22.15¢ per gallon on diesel motor fuel (includes 8¢ excise tax and 14.15¢ petroleum business tax).	Reports and payments—20th of each month. Larger taxpayers must make EFT payments or payments by certified check on or before the third business day following the 22nd day of each calendar month for that month.
	Effective 6/1/06 through 5/31/07, pre-paid sales tax per gallon of motor fuel is 14.75¢ in Region 1 and 14¢ in Region 2. Pre-paid sales tax per gallon of diesel motor fuel is 14.75¢ in Region 1 and 14¢ in Region 2.	
	Fuel use tax—carriers pay a tax whose rate is a composite of a fuel use component (equivalent to the motor fuel tax rate) and a sales tax component.	
	Petroleum business tax—*Petroleum businesses:* 15.9¢ per gallon for motor fuel; 14.15¢ per gallon for automotive-type diesel motor fuel; 14.9¢ per gallon for nonautomotive-type diesel motor fuel; 15.9¢ per gallon for aviation gasoline; and 6.3¢ per gallon for kero-jet fuel. (Rates are indexed annually and include any applicable surcharge.) *Tax on carriers:* same as the total petroleum business tax rate on motor fuel and automotive-type diesel fuel imported into New York in the fuel tanks of vehicular units.	Petroleum business tax—20th day of each month. Larger taxpayers must make EFT payments or payments by certified check on or before the third business day following the 22nd day of each calendar month for that month.
Cigarette tax; tobacco products tax.	Cigarettes—$1.50 per pack of 20 cigarettes sold or used within the state. If pack exceeds 20 cigarettes, an additional tax of 37.5¢ per 5 cigarettes (or fraction) is imposed.	Report—Sales tax, agents, 15th of each month. Use tax, within 24 hours.
		Payment—Sales tax, by means of stamps. Use tax, within 24 hours.
	Tobacco products—37% of wholesale price on all tobacco products (non-cigarette).	Report and payment—20th of each month; use tax, within 24 hours.

Tax	Basis—Rates	Due Dates
Stock transfer tax.	Stock transfer tax—2^1/2¢ per share on transfers of stock or certificates of interest in property or accumulations other than by sale. Sale or agreement to sell at less than $5 per share, 1^1/4¢ per share; sale at $5 or more per share but less than $10, 2^1/2¢; sale at $10 or more but less than $20, 3^3/4¢; sale at $20 or more per share, 5¢. Maximum tax on a single transaction, $350.	Stock transfer tax—daily by clearing corporations; weekly by registered dealers in securities; or by purchase of stamps.
Mortgage recording tax.	Mortgage recording tax—50¢ for each $100 or major fraction of debt secured by real estate mortgage, including sales contracts under which vendees are entitled to possession. Additional tax is 25¢ for each $100. Special additional tax is 25¢ for each $100. Rate in MCTD 30¢ per $100.	Mortgage recording tax—at time of recording instruments or making additional advances.
Realty transfer tax.	$2 per $500 of consideration or value of property conveyed; no tax if value is less than $500. Additional 1% tax on conveyance of residential realty for which the consideration is $1 million or more.	Report and payment—due 15th day after delivery of the instrument.
Sales and use tax.	4% of receipts from retail sales or the consideration given for the use of property or selected services. An additional 5% imposed on receipts from entertainment or information services provided by telephone, telegraph or interactive network services (if received exclusively in an aural manner). 5% imposed on passenger car rentals.	Reports and payment—due 20 days after last days of Feb., May, Aug., and Nov. if taxable receipts are less than $300,000. If such receipts are $300,000 or more for any quarter of the preceding four quarters, reports and payments are due within 20 days after each month. Larger taxpayers must make EFT payments or payments by certified check on or before the third business day following the 22nd day of each calendar month for that month.
Gross income tax on utility services; transportation and transmission corporations franchise tax.	Utility services gross income tax—2.5% on the gross income of telecommunications service providers. Other utilities subject to DPS supervision—2% on the portion of gross income derived from the transportation, transmission, or distribution of gas or electricity by conduits, mains, pipes, wires, lines, or similar means.	Utility services gross income tax—on or before March 15 for year ending December 31 preceding.
	Other utilities not subject to DPS supervision— no tax on gross operating income beginning January 1, 2005.	
	Transportation and transmission corporations franchise tax—1.5 mills per $1 of net value of capital stock allocated to New York; or 0.375 mills for each 1% of dividends provided that dividends paid in preceding calendar year amounted to 6% or more; or $75, whichever is greatest. Additional gross earnings tax: 0.375% of intrastate gross earnings.	Transportation and transmission corporations franchise and earnings taxes—on or before March 15.
	Telecommunication services tax—2.5% of gross receipts.	Telecommunication services—on or before March 15.

Tax	Basis—Rates	Due Dates
	MTA surcharge—17% of utility services gross income tax, telecommunication services tax, and transportation and transmission corporation franchise tax and additional franchise tax for business activity carried on within the Metropolitan Commuter Transportation District.	Utility estimated tax declarations, from companies whose tax is expected to exceed $1,000, due June 15; payments due March 15, June 15, September 15 and December 15.
Insurance companies tax.	Franchise (income) and premiums taxes—Beginning in 2003, net income component is eliminated, except for life insurance companies, and tax is imposed on premiums only at rate of 1.75% for accident and health insurance contracts, 2% for other non-life premiums. Life insurance companies subject to 1.5% premiums tax. A 17% Metropolitan Commuter Transportation District surcharge is imposed on insurance corporations and life insurance corporations with business activities in the District for tax years ending before December 31, 2009. Life insurance companies, additional franchise tax, 0.7% of gross direct premiums, less return premiums. Foreign and alien fire insurance companies, $2 per $100 of premiums. Foreign mutual fire insurance companies, 2%.	Franchise and premiums taxes: Returns and payments—15th day of 3rd month after end of tax year. Estimated tax declaration due June 15; estimated taxes due 15th of June, September and December. Foreign fire insurers' reports due March 1, foreign mutual fire insurers' annual return due February 15.
	Independently procured insurance—3.6% of the premiums paid, less returns thereon, on the purchase or renewal of a taxable insurance contract from an insurer not authorized to transact business in the state.	Independently procured insurance: Returns and payments—within 60 days of the end of the calendar quarter during which an independently procured insurance contract took effect or was renewed.
	Foreign companies subject to retaliatory taxes, unless organized or domiciled in a state or country that does not impose retaliatory taxes on New York insurers or provides for reciprocal exemptions.	
Estate tax.	Estate tax—The estate tax is assessed as an amount equal to the credit allowable under the federal estate tax law in effect on July 22, 1998. The New York estate tax law does not provide for the decreases in the federal credit resulting from 2001 federal legislation (EGTRRA). Thus, for a date of death after 2001, the New York estate tax liability will generally exceed the allowable federal credit for state death taxes. For decedents dying after 2004, the federal credit for state death taxes is eliminated and replaced with a deduction.	Returns and payments—within 9 months of decedent's death.
Generation-skipping transfer tax.	Generation-skipping transfer—Tax imposed to absorb federal generation-skipping transfer tax credit (determined under amendments enacted on or before July 22, 1998).	Reports and payment—on or before April 15.

North Carolina

Tax System.—North Carolina imposes a general property tax on all property for local purposes only. Intangible personal property is separately taxed. The state derives its revenue under the Revenue Act from personal and corporate income taxes, gasoline taxes, and sales and use taxes. The legislature has empowered counties, cities and towns to impose license taxes. An outline of the North Carolina tax system follows:

Tax	Basis—Rates	Due Dates
Corporate organization and qualification fees.	Domestic and foreign—fee for filing articles of incorporation, $125; for filing amended articles of incorporation, $50; for filing articles of merger or share exchange, $50; for filing application for certificate of authority, $250.	Domestic and foreign— at time of incorporation or qualification or increase of capital stock.
Corporation franchise tax.	Domestic and foreign—$1.50 per $1,000 (.15%) of whichever yields highest tax: (1) capital stock, surplus and undivided profits or alternative basis, (2) investments in North Carolina tangible property, or (3) 55% of the appraised tangible personal property plus all intangible property in the state. Minimum tax, $35. Annual report, $20.	Reports and payments— 15th day of 3rd month following the end of the income year.
Corporation income tax.	6.9% of the taxable income of all taxable corporations.	Returns and payments— 15th day of 3rd month after close of income year. Corporate or franchise returns of foreign corporations that file a federal return pursuant to IRC Sec. 6072(c), 15th day of 6th month following the close of income year. Estimated tax payments due (if tax liability $500 or more) by the 15th day of the 4th, 6th, 9th and 12th months of the tax year, depending on when filing requirements are first met.

Tax	Basis—Rates	Due Dates
Personal income tax.	**Rates for 2006 and 2007:** *Married filing jointly, or qualifying widow or widower:* 6% of first $21,250; $21,251 to $100,000, $1,275 plus 7% of excess over $21,250; $100,001 to $200,000, $6,787.50 plus 7.75% of amount over $100,000; amount over $200,000, $14,537.50 plus 8.25% of amount over $200,000 (2007, 8%). *Heads of households:* 6% of first $17,000; $17,001 to $80,000, $1,020 plus 7% of amount over $17,000; $80,001 to $160,000, $5,430 plus 7.75% of amount over $80,000; amount over $160,000, $11,630 plus 8.25% of amount over $160,000 (2007, 8%). *Single individuals:* 6% of first $12,750; $12,751 to $60,000, $765 plus 7% of amount over $12,750; $60,001 to $120,000, $4,072.50 plus 7.75% of amount over $60,000; amount over $120,000, $8,722.50 plus 8.25% of the amount over $120,000 (2007, 8%). *Married filing separately:* 6% of first $10,625; $10,626 to $50,000, $637.50 plus 7% of amount over $10,625; $50,001 to $100,000, $3,393.75 plus 7.75% of amount over $50,000; amount over $100,000, $7,268.75 plus 8.25% of amount over $100,000 (2007, 8%).	Returns and payments— April 15 for calendar-year returns; 15th day of 4th month after close of fiscal year for fiscal-year returns.
		Estimated tax— individual returns, on or before April 15; payment, 15th day of April, June, September and January.
	Nonresidents—same rates on income from property and business in North Carolina.	
General property tax.	General property tax—fixed by cities and counties to meet budget. Based on true cash value of real property and tangible personal property.	General property tax— reports: property is listed during January; railroads and public service corporations, March 31. Payment, September 1, payable without penalty until January 6.
Alcoholic beverages tax.	Excise—malt beverages, 53.177¢ per gallon; unfortified wine, 21¢ per liter; fortified wine, 24¢ per liter; liquor, 25% of retail price.	Reports—on or before the 15th of each month. Payment—tax payments are due with the return.
Fuel taxes.	Motor fuels excise, special fuels, and road tax—a flat rate of 17.5¢ per gallon plus a variable wholesale component equal to the greater of 7% of the average wholesale price of motor fuel during the preceding six-month base period or 3.5¢ per gallon. However, for July 1, 2006, through June 30, 2007, the variable wholesale component of the motor fuel excise tax rate may not exceed 12.4¢ per gallon. Current rates: 29.9¢ for 1/1/06 to 12/31/06.	Motor fuel—reports and payments: 22nd day of each month, with following exceptions: distributors report and pay by the last day of month for preceding quarter; occasional importers, 3rd day of each month; terminal operators, 45 days after end of calendar year.

Tax	Basis—Rates	Due Dates
		Road tax—Reports and payments due on or before the last day of January, April, July, and October for preceding quarter.
	Inspection fee—0.25¢ per gallon of kerosene, motor fuel and alternative fuel.	Reports and payments—informational returns of licensed suppliers of kerosene, 22nd of each month; informational returns of kerosene terminal operators, 25th of each month (eff. 1/1/07, 22nd of each month); inspection fee on motor fuel due when excise tax on motor fuel tax is payable (22nd of each month).
Primary forest product assessment.	50¢ per 1,000 board feet for softwood products measured in board feet; 40¢ per 1,000 board feet for hardwood and bald cypress products measured in board feet; 20¢ per cord for softwood products measured in cords; 12¢ per cord for hardwood and bald cypress products measured in cords.	Payment—last day of month following end of quarter.
Highway use tax.	3% of the retail value of a motor vehicle (maximum, $1,000 for a Class A or B commercial vehicle and $1,500 for all others).	Payment—semimonthly in the same manner in which semimonthly sales and use taxes are required to be paid.
Cigarette tax; tobacco products tax.	Eff. 7/1/06, 1.75¢ per cigarette (35¢ per pack of 20); from 9/1/05 through 6/30/06, 1.50¢ per cigarette (30¢ per pack of 20).	Reports and payments—20th of each month.
	Tobacco products—3% of cost price.	Reports and payments—20th of each month.
Realty transfer tax.	$1 per $500 or fractional part of the consideration or value of the interest or property conveyed.	Payment to the county where the realty is situated. Payment evidenced by tax stamps. Affixation of stamp not necessary; register of deeds may merely mark instrument to show tax was paid.

Tax	Basis—Rates	Due Dates
Sales tax; use tax.	Sales tax—4.5% of retail sales through 11/30/06; 4.25%, effective 12/1/06; 4%, effective 7/1/07; manufactured homes, 2% (maximum, $300); aircraft and boats, 3% (maximum, $1,500); food not otherwise exempt but exempt if bought with food stamps, exempt; electricity for farm or industry use (until 7/1/07), 2.83%; electricity measured by separate meter sold to manufacturing industries, 2.6%, eff. 7/1/07; horses or mules, semen for artificial insemination, agricultural fuel, commercial laundry fuel, farm machinery, telephone company central office equipment, commercial laundry and dry-cleaning machinery, broadcasting equipment, grain, feed, or soybean storage facilities, exempt; mill machinery and manufacturing fuel, mining and quarrying equipment, recycling facility purchases, 1% privilege tax effective January 1, 2006; certain research and development companies, 1% privilege tax effective July 1, 2007; toll or private telecommunications services, 4.5% (4.5% through 11/30/06, 4.25% effective 12/1/06, and 4% effective 7/1/07); sales of aircraft lubricants, aircraft repair parts, aircraft accessories, and aircraft simulators used for flight crew training to an interstate passenger air carrier for use at the carrier hub, exempt; sales of aircraft lubricants, aircraft repair parts, and aircraft accessories to an interstate air courier for use at the courier's hub, exempt; air courier purchases of materials handling equipment, racking systems, and related parts and accessories for use at a hub for the storage or handling and movement of tangible personal property at an airport or in a warehouse or distribution facility, exempt.	Returns and payments—payable quarterly, monthly, or semimonthly; effective 10/1/07, payable when return is due. Taxpayers consistently liable for less than $100 in taxes per month may file on quarterly basis by last day of the month following the end of the quarter. Taxpayers consistently liable for more than $100 but less than $10,000 per month must file a return and pay the tax due on a monthly basis by the 20th of each month; effective 10/1/07, taxpayers consistently liable for more than $100 a month must file a return and pay the tax due on a monthly basis by the 20th of each month. Taxpayers consistently liable for at least $10,000 per month must pay the tax twice monthly. First payment covering period from 1st to 15th is due 25th of the month; second payment covering period from 16th to end of month is due by 10th day of following month. Return covering both semimonthly periods is due by 20th day of following month; others, monthly. Effective October 1, 2007, taxpayers consistently liable for at least $10,000 a month, must make monthly prepayments; prepayment is due with the return (20th day of the following month).
	Use tax—same rate on sales price of tangible personal property or taxable services stored, used or consumed in the state.	

Tax	Basis—Rates	Due Dates
Public utilities tax; freight car line company tax.	Public utilities tax—the following percentages of gross intrastate receipts from these corporations: 3.22% for electric power; 6% for public sewerage; 4% for water companies. An excise tax is imposed on piped natural gas in lieu of a sales and use tax and a percentage gross receipts tax. The tax rate is based on monthly therm volumes of piped natural gas received by the end-user of the gas from $.003 to $.047 per therm.	Public utilities tax— electric power, gas, water, sewerage.— Reports—last day of January, April, July and October. Payment— water and public sewerage companies, with quarterly report; electric power and gas companies, last day of month for preceding month (May payment due by June 25).
	Freight car line company tax—3% of intrastate gross earnings. Tax is in lieu of all ad valorem taxes.	Freight car line company tax—tax withheld by railroad company using or leasing cars of freight car line company. Railroad company must remit tax withheld together with a report, annually, on or before March 1 for preceding calendar year.
Public utility regulatory fee.	Assessed at the greater of (1) a percentage rate of each public utility's NC revenues for each quarter or (2) $6.25 per quarter. The percentage rate to be used in calculating the fee is 0.12%.	Payment due to the North Carolina Utilities Commission on or before the 15th day of the second month following the end of each quarter.
Insurance companies tax.	All insurance contracts and Article 65 corporations, 1.9%; health maintenance organizations, 1.9% (prior to 2007, 1%); 1.33% additional for fire and lightning coverage. Rate on gross premiums (or equivalent in case of self-insurers), collected on contracts applicable to liabilities under the Workers' Compensation Act, 2.5%.	Reports and payments— March 15. Estimated (if $10,000 or more in business the prior year)—quarterly, three equal installments of *at least* $33\frac{1}{3}$% due April 15, June 15 and October 15 of tax year; if necessary, balance due by following March 15. Health maintenance organizations with estimated tax liability of $10,000 or more, eff. 1/1/07, two equal installments due before April 16, 2007, and June 16, 2007.
	Foreign companies subject to retaliatory taxes.	

Tax	Basis—Rates	Due Dates
Estate tax; generation-skipping transfer tax; gift tax.	Estate tax—North Carolina applies the maximum credit allowable under the federal estate tax. The tax is the amount of the state death tax credit that, as of December 31, 2001, would have been allowed under IRC Sec. 2011 against the federal taxable estate. The tax may not exceed the amount of federal estate tax due determined without taking into account the deduction for state death taxes allowed under IRC Sec. 2058 and the credits allowed under IRC Secs. 2011 through 2015.	Estate tax—follows federal estate tax.
	Generation-skipping transfer—Tax equal to federal credit.	
	Gift tax—Class A: 1% to 12% of aggregate sum of the net gifts made by the donor; exempt, $100,000. Class B: 4% to 16%; exempt, none. Class C: 8% to 17%; exempt, none.	Gift tax—Return—April 15 following year in which gift was made unless and extension is granted. Payment—with report; if extension granted, April 15.

North Dakota

Tax System.—The North Dakota revenue system is founded on a general property tax at uniform rates within each taxing district. The general property tax has been supplemented by taxes on incomes, occupations, and privileges. An outline of the North Dakota tax system follows:

Tax	Basis—Rates	Due Dates
Corporate organization and qualification fees.	Domestic—$50,000 or less of authorized shares, $50; $10 per additional $10,000, or fraction, of authorized shares over $50,000 ($12 if paid after shares are issued).	Domestic—at time of incorporation or increase of authorized shares.
	Foreign—initial license fee of $85, $40 fee for certificate of authority; $10 for change of registered agent plus same rates as domestic, based on total authorized shares, and proportioned according to business transacted in the state.	Foreign—at time of qualification or increase of authorized shares. Additional fee due before annual report can be filed.
Corporation annual report fee.	Domestic—$25 flat rate.	Domestic—August 1.
	Foreign—$25 flat rate.	Foreign—May 15.
General income tax.	Individuals, estates and trusts—**Optional method:** first $3,000, 2.67%; next $2,000, 4%; next $3,000, 5.33%; next $7,000, 6.67%; next $10,000, 8%; next $10,000, 9.33%; next $15,000, 10.67%; over $50,000, 12%. *Simplified method, 2006 indexed rate brackets: Single individuals:* first $30,650, 2.1%; $30,650 but not over $74,200, $643.65 plus 3.92% of amount over $30,650; $74,200 but not over $154,800, $2,350.81 plus 4.34% of amount over $74,200; $154,800 but not over $336,550, $5,848.85 plus 5.04% of amount over $154,800; and income over $336,550, $15,009.05 plus 5.54% of amount over $336,550. *Married filing jointly or widowed:* first $51,200, 2.1%; $51,200 but not over $123,700, $1,075.20 plus 3.92% of amount over $51,200; $123,700 but not over $188,450, $3,917.20 plus 4.34% of amount over $123,700; $188,450 but not over $336,550, $6,727.35 plus 5.04% of amount over $188,450; and income over $336,550, $14,191.59 plus 5.54% of amount over $336,550. *Married filing separately:* first $25,600, 2.1%; $25,600 but not over $61,850, $537.60 plus 3.92% of amount over $25,600; $61,850 but not over $94,225, $1,958.60 plus 4.34% of amount over $61,850; $94,225 but not over $168,275, $3,363.68 plus 5.04% of amount over $94,225; and income over $168,275, $7,095.80 plus 5.54% of amount over $168,275. *Head of household:* first $41,050, 2.1%; $41,050 but not over $106,000, $862.05 plus 3.92% of amount over $41,050; $106,000 but not over $171,650, $3,408.09 plus 4.34% of amount over $106,000; $171,650 but not over $336,550, $6,257.30 plus 5.04% of amount over $171,650; and income over $336,550, $14,568.26 plus 5.54% of amount over $336,550.	Returns—calendar, April 15; fiscal, 15th day of 4th month after close of income year. Cooperatives, 15th day of 9th month after close of tax year.

Tax	Basis—Rates	Due Dates
	Corporate rates—first $3,000, 2.6%; $3,001 but not over $8,000, $78 plus 4.1% of amount over $3,000; $8,001 but not over $20,000, $283 plus 5.6% of amount over $8,000; $20,001 but not over $30,000, $955 plus 6.4% of amount over $20,000; and over $30,000, $1,595 plus 7% of the amount over $30,000.	Payments—with returns. Individual and corporate estimated tax payments—4 equal installments on the 15th day of 4th, 6th, 9th, and 13th months of year.
	If a corporation elects to use the water's edge method to apportion its income, the corporation will be subject to an additional 3.5% surtax on its North Dakota taxable income.	
Financial institutions privilege (income) tax.	7% of federal taxable income with state adjustments. Minimum, $50.	Returns and payments—return and $2/7$ of tax due April 15; remainder of tax due January 15 of following year.
General property tax.	General property tax—aggregate of state, county and municipal rates fixed annually to meet budget. Property subject to tax based on value is assessed as follows: residential property, 9%; agricultural property, 10% of its agricultural value; commercial property, 10%; and centrally assessed property, 10% (except qualifying wind turbine electric generators, 3%).	Returns—railroads, February 15 and May 1; utilities, May 1. Payments—January 1, but may be paid without penalty as follows: realty, 50% on March 1, 50% on October 15; personalty, March 1.
Alcoholic beverages taxes.	Excise (per wine gallon)—beer in bulk containers, 8¢; beer in bottles and cans, 16¢; wine containing less than 17% alcohol, 50¢; wine containing 17% to 24% alcohol, 60¢; sparkling wine, $1; distilled spirits, $2.50; alcohol, $4.05.	Payments—due on 15th day of each month.
Gasoline tax; special fuel tax.	Gasoline tax—23¢ per gallon of motor fuel used and sold. Inspection fee, 0.025¢ per gallon.	Reports and payments—25th day of each month.
	Special fuels tax—21¢ per gallon; eff. 11/1/06, 23¢ per gallon.	
	Aviation fuel tax—8¢ per gallon. Additional 4% tax on fuel on which the aviation fuel tax is levied and refunded.	
	E85 fuel tax—1¢ per gallon.	
Oil and gas gross production tax; coal severance tax; oil extraction tax.	Oil gross production tax—5% of gross value at well. Gas gross production tax—rate determined annually by the State Tax Commissioner. Coal severance tax—37.5¢ per ton plus an additional 2¢ per ton. Oil extraction tax—6.5% of gross value at well of oil extracted, except 4% for wells drilled and completed after April 27, 1987, and not otherwise exempt and 4% for a qualifying secondary recovery project and a qualifying tertiary recovery project. However, if the average price of a barrel of crude oil for any consecutive 5-month period of any year is $35.50 or more, then the rate of the tax on all taxable wells is 6.5% until the average price is less than $35.50 for any consecutive 5-month period.	Gas gross production tax reports and payments—on or before the 15th day of the 2nd month following production. Oil gross production tax, coal severance tax, and oil extraction tax reports and payments—on or before the 25th day of each month succeeding the month of production.
Motor vehicle excise tax.	Motor vehicle excise tax—5% of purchase price.	Payments—upon registration.

Tax	Basis—Rates	Due Dates
Aircraft excise tax.	Aircraft excise tax—5% of purchase price. For aircraft and helicopters designed or modified for exclusive use as agricultural aircraft in the aerial application of agricultural chemicals, insecticides, fungicides, growth regulators, pesticides, dusts, fertilizer, and other agricultural material, 3% of purchase price.	Payments—upon registration.
Cigarette and tobacco products taxes.	Cigarette tax—2.2¢ per cigarette for cigarettes weighing not more than 3 lbs. per 1,000; 2.25¢ per cigarette for cigarettes weighing more than 3 lbs. per 1,000. Cigars and pipe tobacco tax—28% of wholesale price. Snuff tax—60¢ per ounce. Chewing tobacco tax—16¢ per ounce.	Cigarette and tobacco products taxes, reports and payments—15th day of each month for the preceding month.
Sales and use taxes.	Sales tax—5% of gross receipts from retail sales of tangible personal property, furnishing or service of communication services, steam not used for agricultural processing, tickets or admissions to places of amusement or entertainment or athletic events, periodicals, leasing or renting of hotel or motel rooms or tourist accommodations, coal used for heating buildings except for coal used in agricultural processing or sugar beet refining plants, prewritten computer software, and the leasing or renting of tangible personal property. 3% on mobile homes that are no longer in the possession of the person who bought it from the retailer and on which the sales tax has already been paid. Temporary additional 1% sales tax on retail sales, leases, and rentals of hotel, motel, and tourist court accommodations (but not bed and breakfast accommodations) for less than 30 consecutive days, effective January 1, 2006, through June 30, 2007.	Reports and payments—January 31, April 30, July 31, and October 31. If total taxable sales for the preceding year equal or exceed $333,000, monthly reports and payments are due on or before the last day of each month for the preceding month (June 22 of odd-numbered years for May collections).

Tax	Basis—Rates	Due Dates

Use tax—5% of sales price of tangible personal property or selected services, except items subject to the state retail sales tax, motor vehicles, tangible personal property currently subject to a special tax, railway cars and locomotives used in interstate commerce and property that becomes part of them, newsprint and ink used in the publication of a newspaper, tickets or admissions if the film is subject to the sales tax, certain agricultural products, receipts from leasing or renting manufactured homes for residential use rented for more than 30 consecutive days, certain religious materials, prosthetic devices, durable medical equipment, mobility-enhancing equipment, electricity, nonprofit voluntary health associations exempt under IRC Sec. 501(c)(3), sales of money, the sale of a mobile home that is no longer in the possession of the person who bought it from the retailer and on which the use tax has already been imposed, donation by a retailer of tangible personal property to an organization that is exempt under IRC Sec. 501(c)(3), air carrier transportation property subject to property tax, flight simulators or mechanical or electronic equipment for use with a flight simulator, initial sale of beneficiated coal, receipts from electronic games of chance licensed by the attorney general, and receipts from the sales of carbon dioxide used for enhanced recovery of oil or natural gas. 3% on the sale of new mobile homes. 2% on natural gas when the applicable sales tax has not been imposed. 7% for alcoholic beverages. 8¢ per ton for sand or gravel severed when it is not sold at retail as tangible personal property by the person severing the sand or gravel.

Tax	Basis—Rates	Due Dates
Rural electric cooperatives tax; cooperative electric generating plants tax; telecommunications carriers tax.	Rural electric cooperatives—during first 5 years of cooperative's existence, 1% of gross receipts; 2% thereafter. In lieu of all personal property taxes.	Rural electric cooperatives, telecommunications carriers—reports—May 1. Payments—January 1; for rural electric cooperatives, first installment delinquent after March 1, second installment delinquent after October 15.
	Telecommunications carriers—taxed on adjusted gross receipts in lieu of real and personal property taxes. Rate is 2.5% of adjusted gross receipts.	
	Cooperative electric generating plants—1% of gross receipts from plant operations during first two years; 2% thereafter. In lieu of all personal property taxes except on transmission lines.	Cooperative electric generating plants annual reports—April 1. Payments—June 15 following year in which tax was levied.

Tax	Basis—Rates	Due Dates
	Coal conversion facilities—4.1% of gross receipts; electrical generating plants—0.65 mill times 60% of the installed capacity of each unit times the number of hours in the taxable period plus 0.25 mill on each kilowatt hour of electricity produced for sale; coal gasification plants, the greater of 4.1% of gross receipts or 13.5¢ on each 1,000 cubic feet of synthetic natural gas produced for sale.	Coal conversion plants— reports and payments due on or before the 25th day of each month.
	Coal benefication plants—20¢ per 2,000 lbs. or 1.25% of gross receipts.	Coal benefication plants— reports and payments due on or before the 25th day of each month.
Insurance premiums tax.	Stock and mutual insurance company, nonprofit health service corporation, health maintenance organization, prepaid limited health service organization, and prepaid legal service organization doing business in the state—2% with respect to life insurance, 1.75% with respect to accident and sickness insurance and all other lines of insurance.	Reports and payments— March 1. Estimated reports and payments due quarterly.
	Foreign companies subject to retaliatory taxes.	
Estate tax.	Basic federal estate tax credit for state death taxes reduced proportionately on account of property outside state.	Payments—at death, but no interest charged if paid within 15 months after death.

Ohio

Tax System.—The revenue system of Ohio is founded upon a general property tax on real property and a classified property tax on tangible and intangible personal property. A corporate and personal income tax is also levied, as well as local income taxes. The taxes are supplemented by: (1) state taxes, part of the revenue of which is returned to the local governments, upon occupations, franchises and privileges; and (2) municipal licenses and inspection fees. An outline of the Ohio tax system follows:

Tax	Basis—Rates	Due Dates
Corporate organization and qualification fees.	Domestic—10¢ per share for the first 1,000 shares of authorized capital stock to 0.0025¢ per share in excess of 500,000 shares, provided no fee shall be less than $125 or greater than $100,000.	Domestic—at time of incorporation or increase of capital stock.
	Foreign—initial license fee of $125.	Foreign—at time of qualification.
Corporate franchise (income) tax.	5.1% of first $50,000 of taxable income and 8.5% on taxable income in excess of $50,000, or 4 mills times taxable net worth, whichever is greater. Financial institutions are taxed at 13 mills times taxable net worth. Minimum tax, $50. However, the minimum payment is $1,000 for corporations that have either (1) $5 million or more in worldwide gross receipts for the tax year, or (2) 300 or more employees worldwide at any time during the tax year. Beginning in the 2006 tax year, the corporation franchise (income) tax is being phased out. For the 2006 tax year, tax liability is multiplied by 80%. For the 2007 tax year, tax liability is multiplied by 60%. For the 2008 tax year, tax liability is multiplied by 40%. For the 2009 tax year, tax liability is multiplied by 20%. No tax is imposed for the 2010 tax year.	Returns and payment—due between January 1 and March 31 unless an estimated return and $1/3$ payment is made by January 31, in which case the annual return and payment is due March 31 unless a second estimated return and $1/3$ payment is made by March 31. This extends the due date for the annual return and remaining $1/3$ payment to May 31.
	All corporations, except financial institutions and family farm corporations, also subject to litter tax. Tier one—If franchise tax paid on net income basis, litter tax equal to .11% of first $50,000 of taxable income and to .22% of taxable income in excess of $50,000. If franchise tax paid on net worth basis, litter tax equal to .14 mill (.00014) times taxable net worth. Tier two—Applicable to manufacturers and sellers of "litter stream products." Payable in addition to franchise tax and tier one litter tax, this tax is assessed at the greater of .22% of taxable income in excess of $50,000, or .14 mill times taxable net worth. Amount of tier one or two litter tax charge may not exceed $5,000.	

Tax	Basis—Rates	Due Dates
Commercial activity tax.	Applicable to gross receipts received on or after July 1, 2005, for gross receipts greater than $150,000 and up to $1 million, a privilege tax of $150 is imposed. For amounts greater than $1 million, the tax is phased in over a five-year period: 2005: from July 1 through December 31, the rate is 0.26% multiplied by 23%; 2006: from January 1 through March 31, 0.26% multiplied by 23%; from April 1 through December 31, 0.26% multiplied by 40%; 2007: from January 1 through March 31, 0.26% multiplied by 40%; from April 1 through December 31, 0.26% multiplied by 60%; 2008: from January 1 through March 31, 0.26% multiplied by 60%; from April 1 through December 31, 0.26% multiplied by 80%; 2009: from January 1 through March 31, 0.26% multiplied by 80%; from April 1 through December 31, 0.26%; and 2010 and following years: the rate is 0.26%.	Returns—40 days after the end of each calendar quarter; for the semiannual tax period from July 1, 2005, to December 31, 2005, for purposes of making the first CAT payment, a tax return for both calendar year and calendar quarter taxpayers must be filed not later than February 10, 2006.
	Special provisions apply from July 1, 2005, to December 31, 2005. The tax imposed is a semiannual privilege tax measured for the semiannual period commencing July 1, 2005. The semiannual tax payment for all taxpayers for this semiannual period is $75 for the first $500,000 in taxable gross receipts during this semiannual period. In addition, a tax is imposed on all taxable gross receipts for this semiannual period in excess of $500,000. The tax equals the product of 0.06% (the result of rounding 23% of 0.26%) times the remaining amount of taxable gross receipts after subtracting $500,000 in taxable gross receipts.	Payments—Calendar years after 2006, $150 minimum tax due as part of the prior year's fourth quarter return; for calendar year 2006, the $150 minimum tax is due on May 10 for both calendar year and calendar quarter taxpayers.
Personal income tax.	For the 2006 tax year, individuals and estates: under $5,000, 0.681%; $5,000 to $10,000, $34.05 plus 1.361%; $10,000 to $15,000, $102.10 plus 2.722%; $15,000 to $20,000, $238.20 plus 3.403%; $20,000 to $40,000, $408.35 plus 4.083%; $40,000 to $80,000, $1,224.95 plus 4.764%; $80,000 to $100,000, $3,130.55 plus 5.444%; $100,000 to $200,000, $4,219.35 plus 6.32%; over $200,000, $10,539.35 plus 6.87%. General withholding required.	Returns and payments— April 15. Declaration of estimated tax due on or before 15th day of 4th month of tax year if estimated tax in excess of withholding will exceed $500; estimated payment due with declaration and on or before 15th day of 4th, 6th, 9th and 13th months.
	For the 2007 tax year, individuals and estates: under $5,000, 0.649%; $5,000 to $10,000, $32.45 plus 1.299%; $10,000 to $15,000, $97.40 plus 2.598%; $15,000 to $20,000, $227.30 plus 3.247%; $20,000 to $40,000, $389.65 plus 3.895%; $40,000 to $80,000, $1,168.65 plus 4.546%; $80,000 to $100,000, $2,987.05 plus 5.194%; $100,000 to $200,000, $4,025.85 plus 6.031%; over $200,000, $10,056.85 plus 6.555%. General withholding required.	

Tax	Basis—Rates	Due Dates
General property tax.	Real property—aggregate of local rates fixed to meet budget, but taxable value may not exceed 35% of true value. Tangible personal property—generally assessed at 25% of its true value, but natural gas, telephone or telegraph company's property first subject to tax after 1994 tax year assessed at 25% and its other property assessed at 88%, but beginning in tax year 2005, the percentage for all other taxable property is reduced to 67% of true value; for tax year 2006, the percentage is 46%, for tax year 2007, the percentage is 20% of true value, for tax year 2008, the percentage is 15% of true value, for tax year 2009, the percentage is 10% of true value, for tax year 2010, the percentage is 5% of true value, and for tax year 2011 and thereafter the percentage is 0% of true value; pipeline, waterworks, or heating company assessed at 88%; railroad, interexchange telecommunications, or water transportation company assessed at 25%; rural electric company's transmission and distribution property assessed at 50% and its other property assessed at 25%, electric company's transmission and distribution property assessed at 85% and electric company's taxable property assessed at 24%. Intangibles—shares in and capital employed by dealers in intangibles, 8 mills.	Payments—real property and utility taxes payable by December 31, if full payment. If in 2 installments, 1st half due by December 31; 2nd half due by June 20 of following year. Tangible personal property: 1st half due between February 15 and April 30; 2nd half by September 20.
Alcoholic beverage tax.	Excise—beer, $5.58 per barrel. Bottled beer, 0.14¢ per oz. in containers of 12 ozs. or less and 0.84¢ per 6 ozs. in containers of more than 12 ozs. Wines, per gal., 4% to 14% alcohol, 30¢; over 14% to 21% alcohol, 98¢; vermouth, $1.08; sparkling and carbonated wine and champagne, $1.48. Additional 2¢ per gal. tax levied on vermouth, sparkling and carbonated wine and champagne, and other wine. Bottled mixed drinks, $1.20 per gal. Liquor, $3.38 per gallon.	Reports and payments—beer: advance payment, 18th of current month; balance, 10th of following month. Wine and mixed beverages: 18th of each month for preceding month.
Motor fuel tax.	28¢ per gallon.	Reports and payments—last day of each month.
Resources severance tax.	Coal, 7¢ per ton (plus additional 1¢ per ton contingent tax and 1¢ per ton temporary tax); salt, 4¢ per ton; limestone and dolomite, 2¢ per ton; sand and gravel, 2¢ per ton; oil, 10¢ per barrel; natural gas, 2$^{1}/_{2}$¢ per 1,000 cubic feet; clay, sandstone, shale, gypsum or quartzite, 1¢ per ton.	Reports and payments—within 45 days after each calendar quarter. Feb. 14 for annual returns.
Cigarette and tobacco tax.	Cigarettes—6.25¢ per cigarette 1.25¢ per pack of 20, and $1.56 per pack of 25) sold, used, consumed or stored within the state. In Cuyahoga County, the tax is $1.295 per pack of 20 and $1.61875 per pack of 25.	Reports—wholesalers and retailers, January 31 and July 31. Users, 15th of each month. Payment—retailers and wholesalers must remit taxes due for tax stamps and meter impressions by electronic funds transfer. Users, with reports.
	Tobacco products—17% of wholesale price of tobacco products and snuff.	Reports and payments—last day of each month.

Tax	Basis—Rates	Due Dates
County realty transfer tax.	Realty transfer tax collected by the counties— 10¢ per $100 of value; additional tax of 30¢ per $100 of value may be levied.	Payment—at time of recording.
Sales tax; use tax.	Sales tax—Sales price of tangible personal property sold at retail, taxable services, rentals, lodgings, production and fabrication: 5.5%.	Report and payment—23rd day of each month.
	Use tax—Storing, using or consuming (including rentals and production) of tangible personal property or receiving the benefit of a service— same rate as retail sales tax.	Report and payment—23rd day of each month.
Public utilities tax.	Pipeline companies, 6.75%; all other public utilities, 4.75%. Minimum, $50. Electric and rural electric companies are not subject to the public utility tax, but are subject to the corporate franchise (income) tax. A kilowatt hour excise tax is imposed on electric distribution companies at the following rates per kilowatt hour of electricity distributed in a 30-day period by the company through a meter of an end-user: for the first 2,000 kilowatt hours, $0.00465; for the next 2,001 to 15,000 kilowatt hours, $0.00419; for 15,001 and higher kilowatt hours, $0.00363. Natural gas companies and combined electric and natural gas companies are subject to a natural gas company tax of 4^3/$_4$%. Natural gas distribution companies are subject to a natural gas consumption tax at the following rates per Mcf of natural gas distributed to an end user per month: for the first 100 Mcf's, $0.1593; for the next 101 to 2000 Mcf's, $0.0877, for 2001 and higher Mcf's, $0.0411.	Reports—Kilowatt hour excise tax returns—20th of each month for preceding month. Annual reports— railroads, September 1; express, telegraph companies, and all other public utilities subject to the public utility tax, August 1; natural gas companies and combined companies, within 45 days of the last day of March, June, September, and December; natural gas companies and combined companies with annual tax liability for preceding year of less than $325,000 may elect to file annual return within 45 days of December 31; estimated reports from taxpayers owing $1,000 or more due October 15; also on March 1 and June 1 if tax levied in prior year reached these levels. Natural gas consumption tax—quarterly returns due May 20, August 20, November 20, and February 20.

Payments—30 days after mailing notice of tax due; estimated payments from larger taxpayers (owing $1,000 or more) due October 15; also on March 1 and June 1 if tax levied in prior year reached these levels; natural gas companies and combined companies, within 45 days of the last day of March, June, September, and December; natural gas companies electing to file annual return, within 45 days of December 31. Natural gas consumption tax—quarterly payments due May 20, August 20, November 20, and February 20. |

Tax	Basis—Rates	Due Dates
Insurance tax.	An annual franchise tax is imposed on both domestic and foreign insurance companies at the rate of 1.4% of the gross amount of premiums received from policies covering risks in Ohio. A 1% rate also is imposed on the balance of the premiums received by a health insurance corporation operated by an insurance company. All premium calculations exclude Medicare and Medicaid payments.	Reports—Within 60 days after January 1. Foreign risk retention groups, annual statement, January 31; also, reports due 30 days after end of each quarter.
		Payments—domestic, 20 to 30 days after bill is mailed; foreign, partial payment equal to $1/2$ of previous year's tax due October 15, balance due June 15 when the annual reports are filed; foreign risk retention groups, January 31.
	The minimum tax for domestic and foreign insurance companies (health insurance corporations and non-health insurance corporations) is $250.	
	Additional fire marshal tax on fire insurance companies—0.75% of gross premiums.	
	Unauthorized and foreign risk retention groups—5% of gross premiums, fees, assessments, dues, etc., for subjects of insurance in Ohio.	Unauthorized—report and payment, January 31.
Estate tax.	Estate tax—from 2% to 7% of value of taxable estate. Credit—Lesser of $13,900 or the amount of the tax. Exemption—Marital deduction allowed in amount equal to net value of property passing from decedent to surviving spouse (if asset included in value of Ohio gross estate). Property transferred to a spouse is exempt.	Estate tax—Report and payment—9 months from death. No return is required if the value of the estate is $338,333 or less.
	Additional estate tax—Maximum allowable federal credit minus state death taxes actually paid (repealed for decedents dying on or after June 30, 2005).	Additional estate tax—estate law applicable.
Generation-skipping transfer tax.	Generation-skipping transfer—equal to federal credit (repealed for decedents dying on and after June 30, 2005).	

Oklahoma

Tax System.—The Oklahoma state and local revenue system consists of a locally administered general property tax, intangibles tax, and mortgage recording tax in lieu of general property taxes and state-administered taxes on minerals and oil and gas, also in lieu of general property taxes, plus state-administered taxes on franchises, incomes, gasoline, alcoholic beverages, sales, cigarettes and tobacco, motor vehicles, insurance companies, estates and gifts. An outline of the Oklahoma tax system follows:

Tax	Basis—Rates	Due Dates
Corporate organization and qualification fees.	Domestic—0.1% of authorized capital stock. Minimum, $50. Not for profit, $25.	Domestic—at time of incorporation or increase in capital stock.
	Foreign—0.1% of maximum amount of capital invested in the state. Minimum, $300. Not for profit, $300.	Foreign—at time of qualification.
	Shares without par value are valued at $50 each.	
Corporation franchise tax.	$1.25 per $1,000 or fraction thereof used, invested or employed in Oklahoma. Maximum, $20,000; minimum, $10.	Reports and payments—July 1 unless filed in conjunction with income tax return.
General income tax.	Married persons filing jointly, surviving spouse, heads of household, not deducting federal income taxes[1]—0.5% of 1st $2,000 of taxable income (federal taxable income with adjustments); 1% of next $3,000; 2% of next $2,500; 3% of next $2,300; 4% of next $2,400; 5% of next $2,800; 6% of next $6,000; remainder, 6.25% (5.65%, eff. 1/1/07; 5.55%, eff. 1/1/08). Single individuals, married persons filing separately, estates and trusts not deducting federal income taxes[1]—1st $1,000, 0.5%; next $1,500, 1%; next $1,250, 2%; next $1,150, 3%; next $1,300, 4%; next $1,500, 5%; next $2,300, 6%; remainder, 6.25% (5.65%, eff. 1/1/07; 5.55%, eff. 1/1/08).	Personal income returns and payment—15th day of 4th month after end of income year or April 15. Declarations of estimated tax—15th day of 4th month of tax year or April 15. Payment of estimated tax—15th day of the 4th, 6th, 9th, and 13th months of tax year.
	General withholding required.	
	Corporations—6% of Oklahoma taxable income, i.e., federal taxable income with adjustments.	Corporate income returns and payment—15th day of 3rd month after end of tax year or March 15. Declaration of estimated tax due on the 15th day of the 4th month of tax year with payments due on the 15th day of the 4th, 6th, 9th and 13th months of the tax year.
	Pass-through entities are required to withhold 5% of any Oklahoma-source income distribution made to a nonresident member of an entity.	
Bank excise (income) tax.	6% of federal taxable income.	Reports and payments—15th day of 3rd month.

Tax	Basis—Rates	Due Dates
General property taxes.	General property tax—aggregate of local rates fixed to meet budget. No state levy. Real property is taxed at not less than 11% or more than 13.5% of its fair cash value; tangible personal property is taxed at not less than 10% or more than 15% of its fair cash value.	General property tax—Returns—utilities, April 15; corporations and other personalty, March 15. Payment—before January 1 and before April 1.
Tourism promotion tax.	0.1% on accommodations, meals, private tourist attractions, vehicle rentals and tour bus tickets. (Repealed eff. 7/1/07)	Reports and payments—20th day of each month. Semiannual by January 20 and July 20 if total tax due in preceding calendar year is $600 or less.
Alcoholic beverages tax.	Excise tax—beer, $12.50 per barrel; distilled spirits, $1.47 per liter; light wine, 19¢ per liter; wine with more than 14% alcohol, 37¢ per liter; sparkling wine, 55¢ per liter; low-point beer, $11.25 per barrel.	Excise—beer tax—reports and payments—10th of month; liquor taxes—reports and payments, 10th of each month.
	Gross receipts tax—holders of mixed beverage, caterer or special event licenses, 13.5%.	Gross receipts tax reports due 20th of each month.
Motor fuel tax.	Motor fuel tax—16¢ per gal. for gasoline; 13¢ per gal. for diesel fuel; 0.08¢ per gal. for aircraft fuel; 2.08¢ per gal. for agricultural fuel.	Reports and payments—suppliers, 27th day of each month.
	Special fuel use tax—16¢ per gal.	Reports and payments—20th day of each month.
	Motor fuel/diesel fuel importer use tax—motor fuel, 16¢ per gal.; diesel fuel, 13¢ per gal.	Reports and payments—last day of April, July, October and January.
Severance taxes.	Minerals, oil and gas—asphalt and mineral ores, 0.75% of gross value. Oil and gas, 7%. Uranium, 5%. Oil recovered or from unknown sources, 12.5%. Additional tax on gross value of oil or gas produced in state, 0.095% (0.085%, eff. 7/1/11).	Reports—by 10th day following month. Payment—1st day of following month.
Motor vehicle rental tax.	Rental tax—6% of gross receipts from motor vehicle rentals of 90 days or less (tax is in lieu of excise tax).	Rental tax—15th day of each month.
Cigarette and tobacco products tax.	Cigarettes, $1.03 per pack of 20 cigarettes. Cigars, 3.6¢ per Class A cigar ; 11¢ per Class B cigar; 12¢ per Class C cigar. Smoking tobacco, 80% of factory list price; chewing tobacco, smokeless tobacco, and snuff, 60% of factory list price.	Reports—cigarettes, 10th of each month; tobacco products, 15th of each month. Payment—by purchase of stamps.
	Sales at tribal stores if the tribe or nation has not entered into a compact with Oklahoma, 75% of the state rate.	Reports and payment—same as above.
Real estate mortgage tax.	Rate per $100 of debt secured by and length of term of real estate mortgages and sales contracts: less than 2 years, 2¢; 2 to 3 years, 4¢; 3 to 4 years, 6¢; 4 to 5 years, 8¢; 5 years or more, 10¢. 10¢ on sums under $100.	Payment—at time of recording.
Realty transfer tax.	75¢ per $500 of value of deeds, etc., conveying realty when the consideration or value exceeds $100.	Payment evidenced by stamps purchased from county clerks.

Tax	Basis—Rates	Due Dates
Sales tax; use tax.	Sales tax—4.5% of gross receipts from sales or rental of tangible personal property, services, meals, advertising, public services and rooms, passenger transportation, auto parking and admissions.	Sales tax—Reports and payments—20th of each month; if tax for month does not exceed $50, 20th of January and July. Sales taxpayers owing an average of $2,500 or more in the previous fiscal year must participate in the Tax Commission's EFT and electronic data interchange program.
	Use tax—4.5% of sales price of tangible personal property purchased or brought into Oklahoma for storage, use, or consumption within the state, insofar as no sales tax was paid on such property.	Use tax—20th of each month.
Public utilities and freight car tax.	Rural electric cooperatives—2% of gross receipts.	Electric cooperatives—Reports and payments—20th of month.
	Freight car companies—4% of taxable gross revenue derived from use within state.	Freight line, equipment and mercantile companies—Reports, April 1. Payment—due after demand.
		Railroads withholding tax—Reports and payments—April 1.
Insurance companies tax.	2.25% of gross premiums less returned premiums. Foreign companies subject to retaliatory taxes. Fire companies, $5/16$ of 1%.	Report and payment—March 1. Estimates and payments of premium taxes are due April 1, June 15, September 15 and December 15.
	Surplus lines tax—6% of gross premiums.	Surplus line brokers—Report—April 1. Payment—last day of the month following each quarter.
	Unauthorized insurance—6% of annual premiums.	Unauthorized insurance—Report and payment—30 days after premiums are determined.
	Captive insurance companies—0.4% on the first $20 million; 0.3% on the next $20 million; 0.2% on the next $20 million; and 0.075% on each dollar thereafter.	Captive insurance companies—Report and payment—the first day of March.
Estate tax; additional estate tax.	Estate tax—Class 1 beneficiaries (lineal heirs)—$1/2$% to 10% of net estate at time of death; exemption, a total aggregate of $1 million for decedents dying in 2006 and 2007, $2 million for decedents dying in 2008, $3 million for decedents dying in 2009, tax repealed for decedents dying in 2010 and after. Class 2 beneficiaries (collateral heirs)—1% to 15% of net estate at time of death; no exemption. Note: Estates of all decedents dying on or after 1/1/07 will be taxed at Class 1 rates.	Estate tax—Report due 9 months after death (15 months with requested extension). Payment due 9 months after death.

[1] Optional tables are enacted for taxpayers who deduct federal income taxes.

Oregon

Tax System.—The state imposes an income tax, gasoline tax, cigarette tax, inheritance tax, insurance companies tax, alcoholic beverage tax and motor vehicle fees. There are numerous other taxes and fees of minor importance, and municipalities are given the broad power to "license, regulate and control any lawful business, trade, occupation, profession or calling." An outline of the Oregon tax system follows:

Tax	Basis—Rates	Due Dates
Corporate organization tax.	Domestic—filing articles of incorporation, $50.	Domestic—at time of incorporation.
	Foreign—application for authority to transact business in Oregon, $50.	Foreign—at time of qualification.
Corporation annual report.	Domestic—$50.	Reports—by the anniversary dates. Payment—at the time of filing articles of incorporation or certificate of authority and annually thereafter by the anniversary date.
	Foreign—$50.	
Corporation excise (income) tax.	Corporation excise tax—6.6% of taxable income ascribable to Oregon activities by corporations doing or authorized to do business in Oregon. Financial institutions are subject to the tax. Minimum tax, $10.	Corporation excise tax—Reports and payments—15th day of fourth month. Estimated tax payments (for liability of $500 or more) due 15th day of 4th, 6th, 9th and 12th months of tax year.
	Corporation income tax—6.6% of taxable income ascribable to Oregon activities of corporations not doing or authorized to do business in Oregon (foreign corporations). Qualified taxpayers with minimal Oregon sales may elect to pay alternative tax of 0.25% or 0.125% of gross sales in Oregon.	Corporation income tax—same as corporation excise tax above.
Personal income tax.	**20056 Rates:** Single and married persons filing separately, 5% on first $2,750; $2,750 to $6,850, $133 plus 7% of the excess over $2,750; over $6,850, $413 plus 9% of the excess over $6,850.	Returns—same as due date of corresponding federal return. Estimated tax declarations—April 15.
	For married persons filing jointly, heads of households and qualifying widow(er)s, the tax is twice the tax that would be imposed on single persons if taxable income was cut in half.	Payment with return. Estimated tax payments due in 4 or fewer equal installments on or before April 15, June 15, September 15 and January 15.

Tax	Basis—Rates	Due Dates
General property tax.	General property tax—aggregate of state and local rates fixed to meet budget. Tax based on real market value of real property and tangible personal property. All property assessed at 100% of its real market value.	Return—personal property, March 1; real property, when requested by county; public utilities, February 1, except Class 1 railroads, March 15. Payment—all taxes, November 15 or, if $40 or more, tax is payable in 3 equal installments due November 15, February 15 and May 15.
State lodging tax.	1% of consideration for sale, service or furnishing of transient lodging.	Reports and payments—last day of month following end of each calendar quarter.
Alcoholic beverages tax; winery tax.	Excise—malt beverages, cider, $2.60 per 31-gal. barrel. Wines containing 14% alcohol or under, 67¢ per gallon. Wine containing over 14% alcohol, 77¢ per gallon.	Reports and payment—manufacturers must submit a statement on the 20th of each month; payment due 20th of each month, or 20th of the month after withdrawal from federal bond.
	Winery tax—$25 per ton of vinifera grapes or imported vinifera or hybrid grape products for use in a licensed winery to make wine; for all other products used to make wine, $0.021 per gallon of wine made from those products.	Winery tax—Payments—December 31 of current year and June 30 of following year.
Motor fuel tax; fuel use tax.	Motor fuel tax—24¢ per gallon of motor fuel; aircraft fuel sold, distributed or used by a dealer, 9¢ per gallon; fuel for turbine engines, 1¢ per gallon.	Gasoline tax—Reports and payment—25th of each month.
	Fuel use tax—24¢ per gallon of motor fuel other than gasoline used in propelling motor vehicles on the highways.	Fuel use tax—Reports, by 20th of month; payment with report. Annual use fuel tax report and payment due January 20 if annual tax is less than $100; quarterly reports and payments due 20th day of April, July, October and January if monthly tax is less than $300.
Oil and gas gross production (privilege) tax.	6% of gross value at well on all oil and gas produced within the state.	Reports and payments—due on the 45th day following the preceding quarter.
Forest product taxes.	Privilege tax on harvesting timber—67¢ per 1,000 ft., board measure, of merchantable forest products harvested. Tax for payment of fire suppression benefits, 50¢ per 1,000 feet. First 25,000 ft., board measure, exempt. Forest products harvest tax—additional 75¢ per 1,000 ft., board measure, on forest products harvested on forest land. Tax to partially defray costs of Oregon Forest Practices Act on forest products harvested, 55¢ per 1,000 ft., board measure, but not to exceed 40% of total approved expenditures for 2006 and 2007.	Timber tax—Reports and payment—due by last day of January. Estimated tax returns and payments due quarterly if annual tax liability is expected to exceed $1,500.

Tax	Basis—Rates	Due Dates
Cigarette tax.	59 mills per cigarette ($1.18 per pack of 20).	Reports—20th of each month. Payment—by stamps. Unpaid taxes due quarterly. Distributors pay tax on quarterly basis.
	Tobacco products tax—65% of wholesale sales price, except tax imposed on cigars is limited to a maximum tax of 50¢ per cigar. Actual amount payable is 98.5% of total tax due.	Reports and payments—last day of January, April, July, and October.
Public utilities tax.	Telecommunications and public utilities—subject to annual fee not exceeding 0.25% of the utility's gross operating revenue in the preceding calendar year. Electric companies are subject to an annual fee not exceeding 0.18 of one mill ($0.00018) per kilowatt hour delivered in preceding calendar year (may be paid in lieu of public utility fee). Minimum fee in both cases, $10. Railroads—Class I railroads subject to annual fee not exceeding 0.35% of combined gross operating revenues of Class I railroads derived in Oregon. Electric cooperatives—lesser of (1) 4% of all gross revenues from use or operation of transmission and distribution lines (exclusive of revenues from leasing lines to governmental agencies), less the cost of power to the association, or (2) sum of (a) amount obtained by multiplying the real market value of the transmission and distribution lines for the current fiscal year by the maximum school tax rate allowable, plus (b) amount obtained by multiplying the market value of the transmission and distribution lines for current fiscal year by $10 per $1,000 of market value, plus (c) amount obtained by multiplying market value of transmission and distribution lines by tax rate for county for exempt bonded indebtedness.	Reports—public utilities, annually, April 1, except for electric cooperatives, Feb. 1, and railroads due with payment. Payments—generally, 15 days after date of notice mailed (mailed on or after March 1); electric cooperatives, July 1.
Insurance companies tax.	Surplus lines licensees—2% of gross premiums, less return premiums and dividends paid.	Reports—annual financial statement, March 1, except for wet marine and transportation insurers, June 15. Payments—wet marine and transportation insurance, June 15; surplus lines licensees, quarterly on 45th day following quarterly period; all other insurers, April 1.
	Foreign and alien insurers writing wet marine and transportation insurance—5% of underwriting profit.	
	Fire marshal tax—domestic and foreign—1% of gross premiums less return premiums and dividends.	Reports and payment—April 1.
	Foreign companies potentially subject to retaliatory taxes.	
Estate tax.	Maximum amount of state death tax credit allowable against federal estate tax.	Payment due when federal estate tax is payable.

Pennsylvania

Tax System.—The local governments in Pennsylvania are supported mainly by the ad valorem assessment and taxation of real estate; tangible personal property, for the most part, is not assessed. The counties secure further revenue from a tax on intangible personal property that has not been otherwise taxed by the state. There is no state tax levy on real property. Principal sources of state revenue are the sales and use taxes, corporate and personal income taxes, and gasoline taxes. The state levies a tax on the capital stock of domestic and foreign corporations, joint-stock associations, limited partnerships, and regulated investment companies, according to the value of such stock, and payment of this tax by the corporation exempts the shares of stock from taxation in the hands of the stockholders. The tax on corporate obligations issued by domestic corporations and foreign corporations, whose fiscal officer is within the jurisdiction of the state, is collected from the corporation, and this payment by the corporation exempts the security from taxation in the hands of the security holder. The corporation may, in turn, charge the security holder for this tax unless the obligation contains a covenant to the contrary. Public utilities are subject to gross receipts taxes, which are paid into the State Treasury. The state receives further revenue from taxes on bank shares, title and trust companies, and private bankers; taxes on the gross premiums of insurance companies; inheritance and estate taxes; liquor taxes; and cigarette taxes. An outline of the Pennsylvania tax system follows:

Tax	Basis—Rates	Due Dates
Corporate net income tax.	9.99% of taxable income as reported on federal returns, with certain additions and deductions, allocated to Pennsylvania.	Reports—April 15 for calendar-year taxpayers, or 30 days after federal returns are due for fiscal-year taxpayers. Estimated payments are due on the 15th day of the 3rd, 6th, 9th, and 12th months of the tax year.
Personal income tax.	3.07% of taxable compensation; net profits; net gains or income from disposition of property; net gains or income from rents, royalties, patents or copyrights; dividends; interest from non-exempt obligations; gambling and lottery winnings other than Pennsylvania state lottery prizes; and net gains or income derived from estates or trusts. Withholding required. Nonresidents taxed at same 3.07% rate on income derived from Pennsylvania sources.	Returns and payments—April 15 for calendar-year taxpayers, or 15th day of 4th month after end of tax year for fiscal-year taxpayers. Estimated tax declarations if income other than compensation subject to withholding exceeds $8,000—April 15; payment—15th day of April, June, September, and January.

Tax	Basis—Rates	Due Dates
Financial institutions taxes.	Financial institutions taxes—national and state banks and trust companies having capital stock, located in Pennsylvania and title insurance companies, 1.25% of the taxable amount of shares. Mutual thrift institutions, 11.5% of taxable net income. Private bankers, 1% of gross receipts.	Financial institutions taxes— all except private banks and mutual thrift institutions, March 15 for annual report and payment of tax balance for previous year. Private bankers, February 15. Mutual thrift institutions, annual report and payment of tax balance for previous year, April 15 or within 105 days after the close of their fiscal year; estimated tax payments due on 15th day of the 3rd, 6th, 9th, and 12th months of tax year.
General property tax; Intangibles tax; Corporate loans tax.	General property tax—fixed locally to meet budget. No state tax. Based on fair market value of real property. Personal property is exempt.	General property tax— payment date varies by county. Taxing districts may authorize installment payments.
	County intangibles tax—not to exceed 4 mills per $1 value of intangible personal property of resident individuals and corporations.	Intangibles tax—returns, varies among counties; payment, same as general property tax.
	Corporate loans tax—assessed on private corporations at rate of 4 mills per $1 nominal value of all scrip, bonds, certificates, and other evidences of indebtedness held by residents of Pennsylvania, on which interest is paid by a domestic private corporation or by a foreign private corporation doing business and having a resident treasurer in Pennsylvania.	Corporate loans tax— returns and payments—April 15 for calendar-year taxpayers and 105 days after the end of the preceding fiscal year for fiscal-year taxpayers. Corporation treasurer collects tax whenever interest is paid, withheld tax remitted annually with report.
Capital stock/ franchise tax.	Capital stock/franchise tax—2007 tax year, 3.89 mills; 2006 tax year, 4.89 mills. Regulated investment companies—the sum of (1) the net asset value of the regulated investment company divided by $1 million, rounded to the nearest multiple of $75, and multiplied by $75, plus (2) the result of multiplying the personal income tax rate by the apportioned undistributed personal income tax income of the regulated investment company.	Returns—April 15 for calendar-year taxpayers; within 30 days after federal corporate income tax return due for fiscal-year taxpayers. Estimated payments due on the 15th day of 3rd, 6th, 9th, and 12th months of tax year.
Public utility realty tax.	Millage rates on which utility realty is assessed are calculated on yearly basis by dividing total realty tax equivalent by total state taxable value of all utility realty located in Pennsylvania. Also subject to an additional tax of 7.6 mills.	Utility realty tax—Report and tentative payment due May 1. Notice of any changed assessment valuation or predetermined ratio given by August 1; any unpaid tax must be paid within 45 days of date of notification. Estimated tax due annually on or before April 15.

Tax	Basis—Rates	Due Dates
Hotel occupancy tax.	6% of the rent.	Same as sales and use tax due dates.
Alcoholic beverages tax.	Excise—malt beverages, $2.48 per bbl. sold or imported. Liquor sold by the Liquor Control Board, 18% of the net price of all liquors.	Excise—reports, malt beverage manufacturers, 15th day of each month; payment with return.
Motor carriers road tax.	12¢ per gallon, plus an additional 4.9¢ per gallon on diesel and kerosene.	Motor carriers road tax—reports and payments—last day of April, July, October, and January.
Liquid fuels taxes.	Liquid fuels and fuels tax—12¢ per gallon. Oil company franchise tax, 19.2¢ per gallon on liquid fuels (motor gasoline and gasohol) (combined rate, 31.2¢ per gallon); 26.1¢ per gallon on fuels (diesel and kerosene) (combined rate, 38.1¢ per gallon). For 2006 calendar year, aviation gasoline and other liquid fuels used in propeller-driven piston engine aircraft or aircraft engines, 5.3¢ per gallon; jet fuels used in turbine-propeller jets, turbojets and jet-driven aircraft and aircraft engines, 2.0¢. Rates on aviation gasoline and jet fuels subject to change on each January 1 based on fluctuation in producer price index for jet fuel.	Liquid fuels and fuels, alternative fuels, and oil company franchise reports and payment—20th day of each month, or first business day thereafter.
Cigarette tax.	Cigarette tax—6.75¢ per cigarette sold or possessed within state ($1.35 per pack of 20).	Cigarette tax—returns, 20th day of each month; payment, purchase of stamps.
Realty transfer tax.	Realty transfer tax—1% of actual consideration or price for property transferred by deed; if no consideration stated in document, 1% of property's actual monetary worth computed through use of assessed value adjusted to market value.	Payment—earlier of the time the document is presented for recording or within 30 days of acceptance by affixation of stamps.
Sales and use taxes.	6% of purchase price of tangible personal property, with exclusions, and certain services.	Reports and payments—20th day of April, July, October, and January, for preceding quarter; if tax for the third quarter of preceding year was $600 or more, monthly by the 20th day of following month; if annual tax liability does not exceed $75, August 20 and February 20. Use tax returns from purchasers—20th day of succeeding month.

Tax	Basis—Rates	Due Dates
Public utilities gross receipts tax.	44 mills per $1 (4.4%) on gross receipts from business of electric light, water power and hydroelectric corporations; 45 mills per $1 (4.5%) plus 5 mill surtax (5%) per $1 on gross receipts from business of transportation companies, telephone and telegraph companies (the gross receipts tax is not imposed on sales of natural gas). Electric distribution companies and electric generation suppliers: 44 mills per $1 (4.4%), plus or minus Revenue Neutral Reconciliation rate set by Secretary of Revenue annually. Combined rate, 5.9%.	Reports and payment—Annual report, estimated gross receipts tax, balance of tax due for the preceding year, March 15. Estimated taxes due March 15 of current year.
Insurance taxes.	Domestic, foreign, alien—2% of gross premiums; title insurance and trust companies—1.25% on each dollar of actual value of capital stock; surplus lines—3% on gross premiums, less premiums placed with unlicensed insurer other than risk retention groups; marine—5% of allocated underwriting profit; unauthorized insurers—2%.	Reports and payments—domestic, foreign, alien—Estimated taxes due March 15 of current year. Annual report and any remaining tax due by April 15 of following year. Title insurance companies—report and payments by March 15. Marine—annually, June 1. Surplus lines—annually January 31.
Inheritance tax; Estate tax.	Inheritance tax—Class A—4.5%, except that the transfer of property passing to or for the use of a surviving spouse is exempt; transfer of property from a child 21 years of age or younger to or for the use of a parent is not subject to the tax; 12% on transfer of property passing to or for the use of a sibling. Family exemption of $3,500 is specifically allowed as a deduction. Class B: 15%, no exemption.	Inheritance tax—returns, 9 months after death; payment, at death, but no interest accrues for 9 months; 5% discount if paid within 3 months of date of death.
	Estate tax—assessed to absorb difference between state inheritance tax and maximum credit of basic federal estate tax as allowed by the Internal Revenue Code as amended to June 1, 2001. Not applicable to estates of decedents dying after 12/31/04.	Estate tax—Not applicable to estates of decedents dying after 12/31/04.

Rhode Island

Tax System.—The revenue system of Rhode Island is primarily based upon a general property tax assessed uniformly according to value within the taxing district by the cities and towns. Real and personal property not otherwise taxed is subject to this tax. The general property tax is supplemented by various other state taxes on occupations, franchises and privileges, a portion of the revenue from which is returned to the local governments. An outline of the Rhode Island tax system follows:

Tax	Basis—Rates	Due Dates
Corporate organization and qualification fees.	Domestic and foreign—$1/5$ cent per share if the total number of new shares being authorized is 75 million or greater; $160 if the total number of new shares is less than 75 million. Certificate of incorporation, $70; foreign, certificate of authority to transact business, $150.	Domestic—at time of incorporation or increase in authorized shares. Foreign—at time of filing authority to transact business or increase in authorized shares.
Domestic corporation franchise tax.	Domestic corporation franchise tax—$2.50 per $10,000 authorized capital stock. Minimum, $500. Corporations not engaged in business in state during year—capital stock of $1 million or less, $500; $12.50 per additional $1 million or part. No-par stock valued at $100 per share. Domestic corporations subject to the business corporation tax pay only the amount by which the capital stock tax exceeds the business corporation tax.	Domestic corporation franchise tax—reports and payment, 15th day of 3rd month after close of taxable year. Declaration of estimated tax due 15th day of 3rd month of tax year; payments due with declaration and by 15th day of 6th month of tax year.
Annual corporation report fee.	Annual corporation report fee—$50 flat rate for domestic and foreign corporations.	Annual corporation report—due between January 1 and March 1.
Business corporation tax.	Business corporation tax—business corporations, 9% of net income; minimum tax, $500. Regulated investment companies, real estate investment trusts and personal holding companies, greater of 10¢ per $100 gross income or $100. Up to a 6% rate reduction is allowed for development of new jobs.	Business corporation tax reports and payments—business corporations: 15th day of 3rd month following close of taxable year.
Bank excise (income) tax.	State banks—9% of net income or $2.50 per $10,000 of authorized capital stock (whichever is higher); minimum, $100. National banks—9% of net income apportioned to the state; minimum, $100.	Banks—15th day of 3rd month after end of tax year. Declaration of estimated tax due 15th day of 3rd month of tax year; payments due with declaration and by 15th day of 6th month of tax year.

Tax	Basis—Rates	Due Dates
Personal income tax.	Ranges between 3.75% and 9.9% (25% of federal tax rates in effect prior to the enactment of EGTRRA) or, eff. 1/1/06, taxpayers may choose an alternate flat tax rate of 8% (7.5% for 2007). General withholding required.	Returns and payments—15th day of fourth month after end of tax year. Declaration of estimated tax due 15th day of 4th month of tax year (or when federal declaration is due); payments due 15th days of April, June, September and January.
General property tax.	General property tax—fixed by cities and towns to meet budget. Based on full and fair cash value of real and personal property.	General property tax—dates vary with each locality.
Admissions tax.	1¢ per 5¢ or fraction of admission charge at racing events where pari-mutuel betting is permitted.	Reports and payments—10th of following month.
Alcoholic beverages tax.	Excise—beer, $3 per 31-gal. bbl.; still wines, 60¢ per gal., except still wines made entirely from fruit grown in Rhode Island, 30¢ per gal.; sparkling wines, 75¢ per gal.; distilled liquor, $3.75 per gal., except distilled liquor that measures 30 proof or less, $1.10 per gal.; ethyl alcohol used for beverage purposes, $7.50 per gal. on beverages manufactured in the state for sale.	Excise—reports: manufacturers, 10th of each month (quarterly reporting may be authorized). Payment: 15 days after assessment.
Motor fuel tax.	Motor fuels—30¢ per gallon on all taxable motor fuels.	Motor fuels—reports and payment, 20th of each month.
	An environmental protection regulatory fee of 1¢ per gallon is imposed on owners or operators of underground storage tanks.	Environmental fee, quarterly.
Motor vehicle excise tax.	Excise tax, in lieu of property tax—same rate established for other property except manufacturer's machinery and equipment. (Phase-out subject to annual review.)	Excise tax payment—same schedule as property tax.
Rental vehicle surcharge.	Rental vehicle surcharge—6% of gross receipts from private passenger vehicle rentals for each of the first 30 consecutive days.	No later than February 15.
Cigarette and tobacco taxes.	Cigarette tax—123 mills on each cigarette ($2.46 per pack of 20) sold or held for sale within the state.	Reports—by 10th day of each month. Payment—by affixing stamps.
	Unstamped cigarettes—123 mills for each cigarette ($2.46 per pack of 20 cigarettes).	Storage or use—returns and payment within 24 hours of receipt.
	Tobacco products tax—40% of wholesale cost of smokeless tobacco, cigars, and pipe tobacco. Effective July 1, 2006, through June 30, 2008, tax on cigars capped at $0.50 per cigar and the tax on snuff is calculated by net weight. For snuff, the tax is $1.00 per ounce; any snuff product weighing less than 1.2 ounces taxed as if net weight is 1.2 ounces.	Tobacco products tax—same as cigarette tax.
Real estate conveyance tax.	$2.00 per $500 or fraction of consideration over $100.	No reports. Payment due when executing or presenting document for recording.

Tax	Basis—Rates	Due Dates
Sales and use tax.	7% of gross receipts from retail sales, rentals, and storage, use or consumption of all tangible personal property and selected services. Additional 5% of total consideration for transient room rentals. 1% local tax on meals and beverages. 1% local hotel tax.	Reports and payments—20th of each month. Quarterly reports and payments due if monthly liability is less than $200.
Public utilities taxes.	Based on gross earnings. Common carrier steamboat, ferryboat, steam or electric railroad, street railway, dining car, sleeping car, water and toll bridge companies, 1.25%; electric companies, 4%; express companies doing business on steamboats, railroads or street railways, 4%; telegraph corporations, 4%; telecommunications companies, 5%, plus a 911 surcharge of $1.00 per month; cable corporations, 8%; gas companies, 3%. Minimum tax, $100.	Reports and payments—March 1. Declaration of estimated tax due 15th day of 3rd month or 6th month of tax year; payments due with declaration and, if applicable, by 15th day of 6th month of tax year.
Insurance companies tax.	Domestic companies, 2% of gross premiums. Foreign companies, the greater of domestic rates or retaliatory tax rate. Captive insurers, 0.2% of first $20 million of gross premiums; 0.15% on next $20 million; 0.1% on next $20 million; thereafter 0.0375%. Captive insurance companies, 0.1125% on the first $20 million of assumed reinsurance premium, 0.075% on the next $20 million, 0.025% on the next $20 million, and 0.0125% of each dollar thereafter. Surplus lines brokers, 3% of gross premiums.	Domestic and foreign insurers, payment due March 1. Estimated tax declarations must be filed if estimated tax for taxable year is expected to exceed $500. Due dates vary. Surplus lines brokers, reports and payments due April 1.
Estate taxes.	Estate tax—Equal to the maximum credit for death taxes allowed under the IRC in effect as of January 1, 2001. (Decoupled from current federal estate tax laws.)	Estate tax—return and payment, within 9 months of death.
Generation-skipping transfer tax.	Generation-skipping transfer tax—Tax imposed to absorb federal generation-skipping transfer tax credit.	Generation-skipping transfer—Return and payment due at time federal return due.

South Carolina

Tax System.—The revenue system of South Carolina is founded upon a general property tax assessed uniformly according to value within each taxing district. There is no state levy. There are state taxes on incomes, franchises, retail sales, occupations and privileges, a part of the revenue from which is returned to the local governments. An outline of the South Carolina tax system follows:

Tax	Basis—Rates	Due Dates
Corporate organization and qualification fees.	Domestic and foreign corporations—$100 initial tax plus $10 for filing articles of incorporation or certificate of authority.	Initial tax—before filing documents; fee—when documents delivered for filing.
Corporation franchise tax.	Corporation license tax—$15 plus $1 for each $1,000 or fraction thereof of capital stock and surplus. Allocated for interstate corporation. Minimum, $25.	Corporation license tax and report—15th day of 3rd month following close of income year.
Income tax.	Individuals—**2006 rates:** Not over $2,570, 2.5% of taxable income; $2,570 to $5,140, 3% times the amount less $13; $5,140 to $7,710, 4% times the amount less $65; $7,710 to $10,280, 5% times the amount less $142; $10,280 to $12,850, 6% times the amount less $244; Over $12,850, 7% times the amount less $373.	Returns—corporations and associations: 15th day of 3rd month after close of income year; others, 15th day of 4th month after close of income year; organizations exempt under IRC Sec. 501 reporting unrelated business income, 15th day of 5th month; foreign corporations that do not maintain an office or place of business in the United States, 15th day of 6th month.
	General withholding is required.	
	Corporations—5% of entire net income.	
	Owner of pass-through business—6.5%; 6% in 2007; 5.5% in 2008; 5% thereafter.	Payment—corporations, with return and equally on or before the 15th day of 4th, 6th, 9th and 12th months following tax year if estimated tax exceeds $100. Individuals and fiduciaries: with return. Estimated personal income tax: payment, 15th day of the 4th, 6th, 9th and 13th months after beginning of taxable year.
Financial institutions tax.	Banks—4.5% of entire net income in the state. Savings and loan and similar associations, cooperative banks—6% of net income (not applicable in first three years of operation).	

Tax	Basis—Rates	Due Dates
General property tax.	Aggregate of local rates fixed to meet budget. Property is classified and assessed at the following percentages of fair market value: manufacturing and utility companies 4%; commercial and residential non-owner occupied real property 6%; privately owned agricultural real property 4%; commercially owned agricultural real property 6%; and all other personal property 10.5%.	Returns—April 30, except merchants, manufacturers and others required to report to the state must file by the last day of the 4th month after the close of the taxpayer's income year; real estate reported annually by March 1.
Payment—January 15 to the state. Due dates for local taxes vary.		
Primary forest product assessment.	Primary forest product assessment—50¢ per 1,000 board ft. for softwood, veneer logs and bolts and all other softwood products normally measured in board feet; 25¢ per 1,000 board ft. for hardwood and sawtimber, veneer and all other hardwood products normally measured in board feet; 20¢ per cord for softwood pulpwood and other softwood products normally measured in cords; and 7¢ per cord for hardwood pulpwood and other hardwood products normally measured in cords.	Payment—on or before the 25th day of the month following each quarter.
5% on paid admissions to places of amusement.	Reports and payments—20th day of each month.	
Alcoholic beverages tax.	Alcohol Beverages Tax: In addition to a $100 application fee, manufacturers, wholesalers, retail dealers, and special food manufacturers are required to pay a biennial license tax of $50,000, $20,000, $1,200, and $1,200 respectively.	Payment and returns—on or before the 20th day following the date of sale.
	Alcoholic beverages are taxed at a rate of 12¢ per 8 ounces or fractional quantity thereof (50.7¢ per liter), plus an additional tax 5¢ per 8 ounces or fractional quantity thereof (21.125¢ per liter). These rates do not apply to minibottles.	
	Minibottles of alcoholic liquor are taxed at a rate of 5% of the gross proceeds from the sale of alcoholic beverages by the drink for on-premises consumption.	
	A case tax of $1.81 is assessed on each standard case of alcoholic liquors. Additionally, wholesalers are required pay an additional case tax of 56¢ per standard case. Further, retailers are required to pay an additional case tax of $2.99 per standard case.	
	Finally, a surtax of 9% is assessed on all alcohol sold within the state.	
	Beer and wine tax: Beer, license tax of 0.6¢ per oz. Wines, license tax of 90¢ per gal., plus an additional tax of 18¢ per gal.; in quantities less than one gallon, 6¢ per 8 oz., plus an additional tax of 1.2¢ per 8 oz.; 25.35¢ per liter, plus and additional tax of 5.07¢ per liter. A biennial permit tax of $200 is due for each brewery or commercial winery.	

Tax	Basis—Rates	Due Dates
Motor fuels taxes.	Motor fuels tax—16¢ per gallon on all gasoline or diesel fuel used or consumed in the state in producing or generating power for propelling motor vehicles. 0.25¢ per gallon inspection fee and a 0.5¢ environmental impact fee.	Suppliers—reports and payments due the 22nd day of each month.
	Motor carriers' road tax—16¢ per gallon.	Motor carriers—reports and payments due the last day of April, July, October, and January.
	Motor oil fee—8¢ per gallon of motor oil or similar lubricants sold at wholesale or ex-tax motor oil or similar lubricants imported.	Payment—same as sales and use tax.
Retail license fee.	A $50 license fee is imposed for each retail license; $20 for artists and craftsmen.	Payment—at time of application.
Cigarette and tobacco tax.	Cigarette and tobacco tax—Cigarettes, 3.5 mills each (7¢ per pack of 20). Other tobacco products—5% of manufacturer's price.	Tobacco products—reports and payment due by the 20th day of each month for preceding month. Cigarettes—reports and payment due by the 20th day of each month for preceding month.
Recording fee.	$1.85 for each $500 of value of realty when transfer of deed is recorded.	Payment—at time of recording the deed.
Sales and use taxes.	5% of retail sales price of tangible personal property or tangible personal property stored, used, consumed, or rented (4% for persons over age 85).	Sales tax—returns and payments—20th day of month. Use tax—returns and payments—20th day of each month.
Public utilities tax; hydroelectric companies tax.	Public utilities license tax—1 mill per $1 of value of property owned and used in the state plus 3 mills per $1 of gross receipts. Minimum tax, $25.	Public utilities tax—reports and payments—15th day of 3rd month following income year.
	Electric power companies tax—persons selling electricity, 0.5 mill per kilowatt hour on sales for resale; electric cooperatives and public utilities, 0.5 mill per kilowatt hour of electricity sold to the ultimate user.	Electric companies tax—reports and payments—20th day of each month.
Insurance companies tax.	Life insurance companies, 0.75% of total premiums collected. All other companies, 1.25% of total premiums collected. Fire insurance companies, aggregate 2.35% on premiums written on fire insurance.	Reports—March 1.
	Foreign companies subject to retaliatory taxes.	Payments—on or before 1st day of March, June, September, and December.
Estate tax.	Estate tax—amount of the federal credit for state death taxes paid.	Estate tax—returns and payment due within 9 months of decedent's death.
Generation-skipping transfer tax.	Generation-skipping transfer—Tax imposed to absorb federal generation-skipping transfer tax credit.	Generation-skipping transfer—same date as federal return due date.

South Dakota

Tax System.—South Dakota imposes a general property tax on real and personal property at uniform rates in the taxing districts where such property is located. Personal property that is not centrally assessed is exempt. The property tax is supplemented by (1) state taxes on net incomes, privileges and occupations, including retail sales, and (2) municipal taxes and inspection fees. An outline of the South Dakota tax system follows:

Tax	Basis—Rates	Due Dates
Corporate organization and qualification fees.	For a domestic company, original articles of organization and issuing certificates of organization, $125. For a foreign company, $550.	Domestic—at time of incorporation. Foreign—at time of qualification.
Annual corporation report and tax.	Annual report (domestic and foreign)—$30.	Annual report due before the first day of the second month following the anniversary month of the corporation.
Bank and financial corporation excise tax.	6% on net income of $400 million or less; 5% on net income exceeding $400 million but not over $425 million; 4% on net income exceeding $425 million but not over $450 million; 3% on net income exceeding $450 million but not over $475 million; 2% on the net income exceeding $475 million but not over $500 million; 1% on the net income exceeding $500 million but not over $600 million; 0.5% on the net income exceeding $600 million but not over $1.2 billion; and 0.25% over $1.2 billion. Minimum, $200 per business location.	Reports and payments—quarterly estimates due on or before the 15th day following each quarter, with final report and payment due within 90 days after end of tax year.
General property tax.	General property tax—fixed locally to meet budget requirements. Based on true and full value (taxable value) of property. Personal property is exempt, except for centrally assessed operating property.	General property tax—Returns—general property, during first 6 months of year; public utilities, April 15, except railroads, May 1. Payment—January 1; delinquent on May 1 and November 1. Realty taxes totaling $50 or less are due in full by April 30. Entire amount of unpaid personal property taxes becomes delinquent May 1. Electronic funds transfer—first monthly installment, January 1; final monthly payment, October 1. Remittances not made by third day of month result in delinquent property taxes.

Tax	Basis—Rates	Due Dates
Alcoholic beverages tax.	Occupational—malt beverages, $8.50 per bbl.; light wines and diluted beverages (except sparkling wines) over 3.2% to 14% alcohol, 93¢ per gal., wines 15% to 20% alcohol, $1.45 per gal., 21% to 24% alcohol, and all natural and artificial sparkling wines containing alcohol, $2.07 per gal.; all cider containing alcohol by weight not more than 10%, 28¢ per gal.; other liquors, $3.93 per gal. Plus 2% of purchase price of alcoholic beverages, except beer, purchased by a wholesaler.	Reports and payments— 25th of second month following the month covered in the report.
Fuel excise tax.	Motor fuel and special fuel, 22¢ per gal.; ethanol blends and LPG, 20¢ per gal.; aviation gasoline, 6¢ per gal.; E85, M85, and compressed natural gas, 10¢ per gal.; jet fuel, E85 and M85 used in aircraft, 4¢ per gal.	Reports and payments—on or before the last day of each month (semiannually for liquid petroleum users); highway contractors report, last day of month following each quarter.
Mineral severance taxes.	4.5% of taxable value of any energy minerals severed and saved.	Returns and payments—30 days after end of each calendar quarter.
	Gold—$4 per ounce of gold severed in the state plus an additional tax on each ounce of gold severed as follows: $4 per ounce severed during a quarter if the average price of gold is $800 per ounce or greater; $3 per ounce severed during a quarter if the average price of gold is $700 per ounce or greater; $2 per ounce severed during a quarter if the average price of gold is $600 per ounce or greater; and $1 per ounce severed during a quarter if the average price of gold is $500 per ounce or greater. Gold and silver—10% of the net profits from the sale of gold and silver severed in the state. 8% of the value received for the right to sever gold and silver by an owner of a royalty interest, an overriding royalty, or a profits or working interest.	Returns—June 1. Payments—one-fourth of estimated tax for current year due on or before last days of January, April, July, and October. Balance of tax for preceding year due June 1.
Motor vehicle excise tax; motor vehicle rental tax.	3% of purchase price of vehicles used in state (in lieu of sales and use tax). 4.5% for vehicles rented 28 days or less (in addition to sales and use taxes but in lieu of the excise tax on the purchase price of motor vehicles).	Motor vehicle excise tax— upon transfer of title. Motor vehicle rental tax—at time of rental.
Mobile home excise tax.	Mobile home excise tax—Additional 3% tax is imposed on the purchase of mobile homes.	Mobile home excise tax— payment upon original registration of mobile home.
Large boat excise tax.	Large boat excise tax—Additional 3% tax is imposed on the purchase price of large boats.	Large boat excise tax— payment upon original registration of the boat.
Cigarette tax.	Cigarettes—26.5 mills each on cigarettes weighing 3 lbs. or less per 1,000; 26.5 mills each on cigarettes weighing over 3 lbs.	Reports—15th of each month by distributors. Payment—by affixing stamps or metered impression.

Tax	Basis—Rates	Due Dates
Tobacco products tax.	Tobacco products tax—10% of the wholesale purchase price of the tobacco products.	Reports and payments—15th of each month.
Real estate transfer tax.	50¢ per $500 or fraction of value payable by grantor.	Payment—by an inked stamping after recordation.
Sales and use taxes.	Sales, service and use taxes—4% of gross receipts.	Reports and payments—if the tax is less than $1,000 per year, on or before the last day of month following each 2-month period; if the tax is $1,000 or more per year, on or before the 20th of each month; if remitted via electronic funds transfer and the tax is $1,000 or more annually, report on or before the 23rd of following month, and payment on or before the second to the last day of following month.
	Additional sales, service and use taxes—1% seasonal tourism tax (June—September) on gross receipts of hotels, rooming houses, campground sites, and other lodging places, passenger car rentals, amusement parks, and miscellaneous amusement and recreational services.	
	Contractors' excise tax—2% of the gross receipts of all prime contractors engaged in realty improvement contracts and of the fair market value of buildings built for own use or lease with a value over $100,000.	
	Alternative contractors' excise tax—2% of gross receipts of all prime contractors and subcontractors engaged in realty improvement contracts for persons subject to the following taxes: railroad operating property, telephone companies, electric heating, water and gas companies, rural electric companies and rural water supply companies, or any municipal utility or telephone company but not to construction of a power generation facility that generates electricity with a nameplate capacity of at least 500 megawatts.	
Rural telephone companies tax.	Rural telephone companies tax—4% of gross revenue of companies having gross receipts of less than $50 million.	Reports—April 15. Payments—September 1.
Rural electric companies tax.	Rural electric companies—2% of gross receipts.	Reports—April 15. Payments—September 1.
Telephone, gas and electric utility tax.	Telephone companies, gas and electric utilities—not more than 0.0015% of annual gross receipts or $250, whichever is greater (exempt from the $250 minimum fee are telecommunications companies providing local exchange service or radio common carriers), from South Dakota customers.	Reports—April 1. Payments—July 15.

Tax	Basis—Rates	Due Dates
Insurance companies tax.	Domestic companies—2.5% of premiums and 1.25% of the consideration for annuity contracts.	Reports and payments— Generally, on or before March 1 or quarterly; surplus line brokers, payment with annual report on or before April 1; quarterly, if tax exceeds $5,000.
	Foreign companies—2.5% of premiums and 1.25% of the consideration for annuity contracts.	
	Foreign companies subject to retaliatory taxes (credits exist for companies with a regional home office in state).	
	Unlicensed insurers—2.5% of premiums and 1.25% of consideration for annuity contracts.	
	Fire companies pay additional tax of 0.5%.	
	Surplus line brokers, 3% of gross premiums.	
	Captive insurance companies—0.25% of gross premiums, less return premiums, on risks and property. Minimum tax, $5,000.	Payments—on or before March 1.
Estate tax.	Tax imposed equal to the maximum credit allowable under the federal estate tax.	Returns—within 9 months after decedent's death.
		Payments—when amount is determined; if not paid within 1 year after death, interest accrues from that date forward.

Tennessee

Tax System.—Tennessee imposes a general property tax on all real estate and tangible personal property at uniform rates in the taxing district where such property is located. There is no state levy. The property tax is supplemented by (1) state taxes on sales, use, income, franchises, privileges and occupations and (2) municipal taxes and inspection fees. An outline of the Tennessee tax system follows:

Tax	Basis—Rates	Due Dates
Corporation charter tax; privilege tax on foreign corporations.	Domestic—charter, $100; application for certificate of existence or authorization, $20.	Domestic—at time of incorporation.
	Foreign—application for certificate of authority, $600.	Foreign—at time of applying for certificate of authority.
Annual franchise tax; annual corporation report and tax.	Annual franchise tax—25¢ per $100 on greater of net worth or the value of real and tangible personal property; minimum, $100. Production credit associations—3.75% of net receipts. Investment companies—2% of gross profits.	Annual franchise tax report and payment—15th day of 4th month following close of fiscal year. Production credit associations—March 1. Investment companies—1st day of 4th month after close of fiscal year.
	Annual corporation report filing fee—$20.	Annual report—1st day of 4th month after the close of the corporation's fiscal year.
Excise (income) tax.	Excise tax—6.5% of net earnings from business done by corporations, limited liability entities, and banks doing business in the state.	Excise tax—15th day of 4th month after close of tax year. Estimated tax payments due on the 15th day of the 4th, 6th, and 9th months of the current year and on the 15th day of the first month of the succeeding year.
Tax on income from stocks and bonds.	Stocks and bonds income tax (applicable to individuals, partnerships, trusts, estates and associations)—6% of dividends from stocks or interest on bonds, notes and mortgages. No withholding.	Returns and payment—April 15. For fiscal year taxpayers, by the 15th day of the 4th month following the end of the fiscal year.
General property tax.	Sum of county, municipal and school rates fixed to meet budget. No state levy except central assessment of public utilities and telecommunications tower properties. Realty is assessed at 55% of actual value for utilities, at 40% for business and industry and at 25% for farm and residential property. Personal property is assessed at 55% for utilities and at 30% for business and industry. All other tangible personal property, 5% of appraised value.	Tangible personal property schedules—prior to March 1. Returns—public utilities, April 1. Payment—1st Monday in October. Cities—various dates.

Tax	Basis—Rates	Due Dates
Alcoholic beverage taxes.	Excise—beverages containing 5% alcohol or less, $4.29 per bbl.; wines not more than 21% alcohol, $1.21 per gal.; other spirits, $4.40 per gal. (except that beverages with an alcoholic content of 7% or less are taxed at $1.10 per gal.); on the wholesale sale of beer, 17% of the wholesale price; additional tax on sale of alcoholic beverages at wholesale, 15¢ per case. Persons selling mixed drinks and setups in localities where liquor sales are legal pay a privilege tax of 15% of gross receipts from such sales.	Excise—reports of wine, spirits and alcoholic beverage wholesalers, 15th of each month. Payment—per-barrel tax, 20th of each month; beer wholesale, 20th of each month; wines and spirits, with monthly report. The privilege tax on sales of mixed drinks and setups is due the 20th of each month.
Gasoline tax.	Gasoline tax—20¢ per gallon of gasoline sold, distributed or stored in Tennessee. Clear diesel, 17¢ per gallon.	Gasoline tax—suppliers and importers, 20th day of each month; terminal operators, last day of month following activity; interstate carriers, 25 days after month of delivery.
Alternative fuel taxes.	Compressed natural gas tax—13¢ per gallon on compressed natural gas.	Compressed natural gas tax—25th of month following activity.
	Liquefied gas tax—14¢ per gallon for commercial users and out-of-state vehicles. In-state users prepay tax annually from $70—$114 depending on vehicle weight classification.	Liquefied gas: Dealers—report and payment due on or before the 25th day of the month following each quarter. Users—annual prepayment due based on weight; annual report and payment due on or before July 25.
Special tax on petroleum products.	Special tax on petroleum products—1¢ per gallon levied in addition to gasoline tax. Additional 0.004¢ per gallon environmental assurance fee imposed on petroleum products.	Reports and payments—20th day of each month.
Automotive oil sales fee.	2¢ per quart.	Reports and payments—25th day of the month following each quarter.
Oil and gas severance tax.	3% of the sales price of oil and gas.	Reports and payments—20th of each month.
Coal severance tax.	20¢ per ton.	Reports and payments—15th of each month.
Cigarette and tobacco tax.	Tobacco products except cigarettes, 6.6% of wholesale cost price. Cigarettes, 10 mills per cigarette (20¢ per pack of 20), plus an enforcement and administration fee of 0.0005¢ per pack on dealers or distributors.	Reports—15th of each month. Payment—by purchase of stamps.
Mortgage tax.	Mortgage tax—11.5¢ on each $100 of mortgage indebtedness in excess of $2,000.	Mortgage tax—at time of recording.
Real estate transfer tax.	Real estate transfer tax—37¢ per $100 of consideration or value of the property, whichever is greater.	Real estate transfer tax—at time of recording.

Tax	Basis—Rates	Due Dates
Sales and use taxes.	7% of sales price or cost price of articles stored or used, gross proceeds from leases or rentals, and charges for services.	Reports and payments—20th of each month. Small taxpayers may be allowed to report and pay on or before the 20th day of the month following quarterly, semiannual or annual periods.
	An additional state tax rate of 2.75% is imposed on the amount in excess of $1,600, but less than or equal to $3,200, on the sale or use of any single article of personal property.	
	Instead of the general 7% rate, special rates apply to various items, including the following: 6% on food and food ingredients; 7.5% on interstate telecommunications services sold to businesses; 8.25% on certain cable television and satellite services; 1% on water used by qualified manufacturers (effective through 7/1/07); 1.5% on certain fuels used by manufacturers, farmers, and nurseries (effective through 7/1/07); 3.75% on certain property sold to common carriers for use outside the state; 4.5% on aviation fuel used in the operation of an aircraft; and 3.5% on manufactured homes.	
State business privilege tax.	Industrial loan and thrift companies—0.3% of gross income; minimum $450, maximum $1,500.	Reports and payments—March 1. Minimum taxes due December 31.
Public utility taxes.	All public utilities—3% of intrastate gross receipts. Gas companies—1.5%. Annual exemption electric and water companies—$5,000. Credit allowed for franchise and excise taxes paid.	All public utilities—Reports and payments due August 1. Tax may be paid in four equal installments due August 1, November 1, February 1 and May 1.
Insurance companies tax.	Domestic life insurance companies, 1.75% (minimum, $150) of gross premiums. Foreign life insurance companies, 1.75% of gross premiums received from citizens and residents of Tennessee (minimum, $150). Others, 2.5% of gross premiums on business done within the state (minimum, $150). Fire insurance companies pay an additional 0.75% tax on that portion of the premium applicable to the fire risk. Foreign companies are subject to retaliatory taxes. Surplus lines premiums, 2.5%, except 3.25% on fire premiums. Captive insurance companies, 1%. Title insurance companies, 2.5%; HMOs, including prepaid limited health service organizations, 2%.	Reports—March 1. Payments—HMOs and title insurers, March 1; self-insurers, June 30; All others, June 1, August 20, December 1, and March 1.
Inheritance tax.	5.5% to 9.5% of value of property transferred at death, or in contemplation of death. Exempt, spouses. Exemption, $1 million.	Reports and payments—9 months after death.
Estate tax.	An estate tax is imposed to absorb the credit allowed under the federal estate tax law if the inheritance tax does not equal the maximum credit. Not applicable to estates of decedents dying after December 31, 2004.	Reports and payments—at time of filing federal estate tax return.

Tax	Basis—Rates	Due Dates
Generation-skipping transfer tax.	Generation-skipping transfer—Tax imposed to absorb federal generation-skipping transfer tax credit. Not applicable to estates of decedents dying after December 31, 2004.	
Gift tax.	Class A—5.5% to 9.5% of appraised value at time of gift. Exempt, $10,000. Class B—6.5% to 16%. Exempt, $5,000.	April 15.

Texas

Tax System.—The Texas revenue system is founded on a general property tax at uniform rates within each taxing district. The general property tax has been supplemented by taxes on franchises, sales and use, occupations and privileges. It should be noted that no state ad valorem tax can be levied for general revenue purposes. An annual franchise tax is levied on domestic and foreign corporations. An outline of the Texas tax system follows:

Tax	Basis—Rates	Due Dates
Corporate organization and qualification fees; Business Corporation Act filing fees.	Domestic—articles and certificate of incorporation, $300; articles of amendment, $150; merger or consolidation, $300; registration or renewal of name, $75.	Domestic—Fees are paid when corresponding document is filed.
	Foreign—certificate of authority, $750; amended certificate of authority, $150; merger or consolidation, $300.	Foreign—Same.
Corporation franchise tax.	0.25% per year of privilege period of net taxable capital plus 4.5% of net taxable earned surplus.	Report and payment—May 15.
General property tax.	Aggregate of local rates fixed to meet budget. Texas has no state property tax. Taxable property is assessed at its market value as of January 1 of the tax year.	
	Imposed on all privately held real property and business tangible personal property, and on intangible property of certain savings and loan associations and insurance companies. Tangible personal property not held or used for production of income is exempt (there is a limited local option to tax such property).	Payment—December 1 and July 1, delinquent if not paid by following February 1.
Hotel occupancy tax.	6% of the cost of occupancy or the right to use a hotel room when charges are $15 or more each day; for local hotel taxes, charges of $2 or more each day. Local taxing authorities authorized to impose additional local hotel tax.	Reports and payments—on or before the 20th day of each month; if monthly liability is less than $500, on the 20th day after the end of the calendar quarter.
Alcoholic beverages tax.	Excise—beer, $6 per bbl.; ale and malt liquor, 19.8¢ per gal.; sparkling wine, 51.6¢ per gal.; vinous liquor of over 14% alcohol, 40.8¢ per gal.; vinous liquor not over 14% alcohol, 20.4¢ per gal.; distilled spirits, $2.40 per gal. (minimum tax of 5¢ if 2 oz. or less, 12.2¢ per package if more than 2 oz. but less than one-half pint). Permittees selling, preparing or serving mixed beverages, or ice or nonalcoholic beverages for use in mixed beverages, are taxed at 14% of gross receipts. Personal use importation fee—50¢.	Excise—Reports and payments—distilled spirits and vinous liquor, 15th day of each month following first sale (A 2% discount is given for the timely filing and payment of the tax on liquor); ale and malt liquor, 15th day of each month following first taxable sale; mixed beverage permittees, 20th day of each month; beer payment, 15th day of each month following first taxable sale.

Tax	Basis—Rates	Due Dates
Gasoline taxes, special fuel taxes.	Gasoline, 20¢ per gallon; liquefied gas, 15¢ per gallon; diesel fuel, 20¢ per gallon. Transit companies may request a refund for fuel used in qualified vehicles.	Reports and payments—Gasoline—25th day of each month for distributors, 25th day of the month following the end of each calendar quarter for interstate truckers. Liquefied gas—25th day of the month following the end of each calendar quarter for licensed dealers and interstate truckers. Diesel Fuel—25th day of each month for suppliers.
Petroleum products delivery fee.	Petroleum products delivery fee—Varies according to the net total gallons of all petroleum products withdrawn: $10.00 if less than 2,500 gallons; $20.00 if at least 2,500 but less than 5,000 gallons; $30.00 if at least 5,000 but less than 8,000 gallons; $40.00 if at least 8,000 but less than 10,000 gallons; and $20.00 for each 5,000 gallon increment on 10,000 gallons or more. For gasoline deliveries of at least 7,000 but less than 8,000 gallons (whether single product type or split load), special rules apply. If the gasoline portion of the delivery is less than 7,000 gallons, the fee is $30.00. If the gasoline portion of the delivery is at least 7,000 gallons, the total load is presumed to be at least 8,000 gallons and the fee is $40.00. The fee will expire on 9/1/07.	Reports and payments—25th day of each month.
Coastal protection fee.	Coastal protection fee—Eff. 9/1/2005, 1.333¢ per bbl. of crude oil imposed on persons owning crude oil in a vessel when oil is transferred to or from a marine terminal. Fee may be suspended or increased depending on fund balance.	Coastal protection fee—payment—last day of the month for the preceding month.
Severance taxes.	Oil—4.6¢ per bbl. (not less than 4.6% of market value); 2.3% of market value for oil produced from qualified new or expanded enhanced recovery projects.	Oil—Reports and payment—25th day of each month for oil produced during the preceding month.
	Natural gas—7.5% of market value.	Natural gas—Reports and payment—20th day of the second calendar month following production (August 15 for the production month of June of odd-numbered years); February 20 for small taxpayers.
	Sulphur—$1.03 per long ton or fraction thereof produced or manufactured.	Sulphur—Reports and payments—last day of January, April, July, and October.
	Cement—2.75¢ per 100 lbs., or fraction thereof, distributed in the state.	Cement—Reports and payments—25th of each month.

Tax	Basis—Rates	Due Dates
Motor vehicle sales or use tax.	6.25% of consideration paid; $90 per vehicle use tax for new residents. Exchange of vehicles, $5 on each party. Gift of vehicle, $10 on recipient.	Reports and payments—motor vehicle sales and use tax: 20th working day after delivery to the purchaser or after date motor vehicle brought into state.
	Manufactured home sales, 5% of 65% of the sales price, less shipping and delivery charges.	Reports and payment—last day of each month.
	Boat and boat motor sales and use tax, 6.25% of total consideration. New residents, $15 per boat or boat motor.	Payment—20th working day after delivery to the purchaser or entry into state.
Cigarette tax.	Cigarettes—$20.50 per 1,000 on cigarettes weighing 3 lbs. or less per 1,000 (41¢ per pack of 20); $22.60 per 1,000 on cigarettes weighing more than 3 lbs. per 1,000.	Cigarette reports—manufacturers and distributors, last day of each month. Payment—by means of stamps.
Tobacco products tax.	Cigars and tobacco products—cigars weighing not more than 3 lbs. per 1,000, 1¢ per 10; cigars weighing more than 3 lbs. per 1,000 and retailing for not more than 3.3¢ each, $7.50 per 1,000; cigars with substantially no nontobacco ingredients weighing more than 3 lbs. per 1,000 and retailing for over 3.3¢ each, $11 per 1,000; cigars with a substantial amount of nontobacco ingredients weighing more than 3 lbs. per 1,000 and retailing for over 3.3¢ each, $15 per 1,000; chewing tobacco, snuff, or smoking tobacco, 35.213% of factory list price.	Tobacco reports and payments—last day of month.
Sales and use taxes.	Sales—6.25% of retail sales price on sale at retail of taxable items and services.	Reports and payment—on the 20th day of each month or, if the taxpayer owes less than $500 for a month or $1,500 for a quarter, on or before the 20th day of the month following each quarter. May be prepaid on or before the 15th day of the second month of each calendar quarter or on or before the 15th day of the month for which prepayment is made.
	Use—6.25% of sales price upon the storage, use or consumption of taxable items or services purchased, leased or rented for use in the state.	
	Cities, counties, transit authorities, and special purpose districts may impose additional tax for a combined total rate not to exceed 8.25%.	
Public utilities tax.	Gas, electric light, power or waterworks: Towns of 1,000 to 2,500, 0.581%; Cities of 2,500 to 10,000, 1.07%; Cities of 10,000 or more, 1.997%; All utilities beginning business on or after 1st day of quarter, for 1st quarter $50.	Reports and payments—yearly on August 15, or quarterly on the 15th of August, November, February, and May.

Tax	Basis—Rates	Due Dates
Insurance companies tax.	Life, accident and health insurers are taxed at 1.75% of gross premiums; surplus lines insurers, 4.85%; insurance companies other than title, life, accident, and health, 1.6%; and title insurers, 1.35%. In addition, a 2.5% administrative services tax is imposed.	Licensed insurers—March 1; semiannual prepayments on March 1 and August 1. Independently procured—May 15 for previous calendar year. Surplus lines—March 1; prepayments due by 15th of month in which agent accrues $70,000 or more. Unauthorized insurance—March 1 for previous calendar year.
Estate tax.	Tax equal to basic federal estate tax credit for state death taxes. Not applicable to estates of decedents dying after December 31, 2004.	Returns and payment—9 months after death.
Generation-skipping transfer tax.	Generation-skipping transfer—Tax imposed to absorb federal generation-skipping transfer tax credit.	Returns and payment—same time as federal.

Utah

Tax System.—Utah imposes a general property tax on real and personal property in the taxing units where such property is located. Intangible property, exempted from general property tax, is taxed on the income therefrom. Maximum rates of taxation of intangible property are provided. Property taxes are supplemented by taxes on incomes, sales, use, occupations, and privileges. An outline of the Utah tax system follows:

Tax	Basis—Rates	Due Dates
Corporate organization and qualification fees.	Domestic and foreign corporations—articles of incorporation, $50.	Domestic—at time of incorporation or increase of stock. Foreign—at time of qualification or increase of stock.
Annual reports.	Domestic and foreign corporations—$10.	Reports—no later than the end of the 2nd month following the month the report form is mailed by the Division.
Corporate franchise and income taxes; corporate gross receipts tax.	Franchise tax: Domestic and foreign corporations—5% of Utah taxable income. Minimum tax, $100. Income tax: Nonexempt corporations that do not do business in Utah but derive income from sources within the state—5% of Utah taxable income not included in Utah franchise tax base. Unrelated business income is taxed at the 5% corporate tax rate.	Returns and payments—15th day of 4th month after close of tax year. Estimated payments due at same time as federal for corporations expecting to have current tax liability of $3,000 or more or that had a tax liability of $3,000 or more in the previous tax year. Unrelated business income tax returns due at same time as federal exempt organization business income tax returns.
	Corporate gross receipts tax on certain corporations not required to pay franchise or income tax—Corporations not required to pay state franchise or income tax or to declare dividends (Intermountain Power Agency and supplemental electricity-generating facilities)—0.6250% if gross receipts exceed $10 million but not $500 million; 0.9375% if gross receipts exceed $500 million but not $1 billion; 1.2500% if gross receipts exceed $1 billion.	Returns and payments—semiannually on or before the last day of July and January.
	Electrical corporations—0.2363% if gross receipts exceed $10 million but not $500 million; 0.3544% if gross receipts exceed $500 million but not $1 billion; 0.4725% if gross receipts exceed $1 billion.	Returns and payments—semiannually on or before the last day of July and January.

Tax	Basis—Rates	Due Dates
Personal income tax.	For taxable years beginning on or after January 1, 2006: resident or nonresident individuals— calculate and pay either a flat 5.35% tax or a multi-rate tax as follows: Individuals, married persons filing separately, trusts, and estates— under $1,000, 2.3% of taxable income; $1,000 to $2,000, $23 plus 3.3%; $2,000 to $3,000, $56 plus 4.2%; $3,000 to $4,000, $98 plus 5.2%; $4,000 to $5,500, $150 plus 6.0%; over $5,500, $240 plus 6.98%. For married couples filing jointly and heads of households—under $2,000, 2.3% of taxable income; $2,000 to $4,000, $46 plus 3.3%; $4,000 to $6,000, $112 plus 4.2%; $6,000 to $8,000, $196 plus 5.2%; $8,000 to $11,000, $300 plus 6.0%; over $11,000, $480 plus 6,98%.Withholding required.	Returns—calendar: April 15; fiscal: 3 months and 15 days after close of tax year.
		Payments—with returns. Prepayments may be required upon applications for extensions of time.
General property tax.	Aggregate of state and local rates fixed to meet budget.	Notices—general property, Nov. 1.
		Payments—personal property, within 30 days of notice; real property, November 30.
	Tangible personal property and real property, except residential property—Tax assessed at 100% of fair market value. Residential property owned by senior citizen claiming tax abatement for the poor—tax assessed at 35% of fair market value; other residential property—tax assessed at 55% of fair market value.	
Alcoholic beverages tax.	Excise—$12.80 per 31-gallon barrel on all beer; retail sales of wines and distilled liquor, 13% of retail sale price.	Excise—beer: reports and payments by the last day of each month; wine and liquor: tax included in total price of purchase from state liquor store.
Gasoline tax; fuel use tax.	Motor fuels and gasohol tax—24.5¢ per gallon of fuel sold or used. Aviation fuel—4¢ per gallon for fuel purchased for use by a federally certificated air carrier; 9¢ per gallon for fuel not purchased for use by a federally certificated air carrier. Clean fuels, including propane, compressed natural gas, and electricity—4¢ per gallon ($^{3}/_{19}$ of the motor fuel rate, rounded up to the nearest penny), plus $35 surcharge per clean fuel certificate from 2001-2010. Special fuel—same as motor fuel rate per gallon of special fuel sold or used.	Motor fuels and special fuel taxes—reports and payments, last day of the month following reporting period.
Environmental assurance fee.	Environmental assurance fee on petroleum products—0.005¢ per gallon on first sale or use of a petroleum product in Utah. Imposition depends on fund balance.	Assurance fee—returns and payments by last day of the month following month when sale occurs.
Recycling fee on lubricating oil.	Recycling fee on lubricating oil—4¢ per quart on the first sale of lubricating oil in the state.	Reports and payments—last day of month following end of each quarter.

Tax	Basis—Rates	Due Dates
Severance tax; oil and gas conservation tax.	3% of the value up to the first $13 per barrel for oil and up to and including $1.50 per MCF for natural gas, and 5% of the value from $13.01 and over per barrel for oil and $1.51 and over per MCF for natural gas. Liquid natural gas, 4% of value.	Reports and payments—June 1 for preceding year except on or before June 1, September 1, December 1, and March 1 if preceding year's tax liability was $3,000 or more.
	Mining severance tax—After an initial $50,000 gross value exemption, a tax of 2.6% is imposed on the taxable value of metalliferous minerals sold or shipped out of the state. Taxpayers must report to the Tax Commission any amounts of unsold, stockpiled minerals. Minerals remaining stockpiled for more than two years are subject to tax.	
	Conservation tax—2 mills per $1 of market value at the well of oil and gas.	Payments—45th day following quarter in which the fee accrued.
Cigarette tax.	Cigarettes—3.475¢ each on cigarettes weighing 3 lbs. or less per 1,000 (69.5¢ per pack of 20); 4.075¢ each on cigarettes weighing more. (The tax rate will be increased by the same amount as any amount of reduction in the federal cigarette excise tax.)	Reports: Cigarette tax—Tobacco products excise tax—last day of month following each quarterly period.
	Excise tax on tobacco products except cigarettes—35% of manufacturer's sales price.	Payments: Cigarette tax—by affixing stamps. Tobacco products excise tax—accompanies report.
Sales tax; use tax.	Sales and use taxes—4.75%, except rate is 2% on residential use of utility services. Effective 1/1/07, 2.75% on food and food ingredients. Sales tax based on total nonexempt cash and charge sales. Use tax based on total amount of cash and charge sales or purchases for storage, use, or other consumption in Utah. Purchase price excludes cash discounts taken and federal excise taxes imposed.	Sales tax—reports and payments—on or before the last day of the month following each calendar quarter. Taxpayers with a liability of $50,000 or more must report and pay the tax on or before the last day of each month. New businesses or businesses in good standing that expect or reported less than $1,000 in tax may file annually—due by January 31 following year end. Use tax—same as sales tax.
Public utilities tax.	Maximum rate—0.3% (0.15% for an electrical cooperative) of gross operating revenue from operations within the state; minimum tax, $50.	Reports—April 15. Payments—July 1.

Tax	Basis—Rates	Due Dates
Insurance companies tax.	Surplus line brokers—4.25%; others, 2.25% of gross premiums less premiums returned or credited to policyholders on direct taxable business, premiums received for reinsurance of property or risks located in Utah, and dividends paid or credited to policyholders; plus, for motor vehicle insurers, an additional 0.01% of total premiums less premiums returned or credited to policyholders from policies covering Utah motor vehicle risks. Title insurers, 0.45%. Effective January 1, 2006, on that portion of taxable premiums that is attributable to Utah variable life insurance premiums, 2.25% on the first $100,000 of Utah variable life insurance premiums paid and received by an admitted insurer in the preceding tax year and .08% of such premiums in excess of $100,000.	Reports—March 1.
		Payments—March 31; surplus line brokers, 25th day of each month. Quarterly payments from insurers owing $10,000 or more in the preceding year, due on April 30, July 31, October 31, and March 31.
	Foreign companies subject to retaliatory taxes.	
Estate tax.	An estate tax is assessed in an amount equal to the federal estate tax credit for state death taxes.	Returns and payments—due when federal estate tax return is due.

Vermont

Tax System.—Vermont derives its revenue from privilege, meals and rooms, sales and use, beverage, cigarettes and tobacco products, gasoline, income and estate and gift taxes, and from the taxation of other types of wealth. The state tax on real and personal property and intangibles has been superseded by the corporate and personal income taxes. The general property tax is for local purposes. An outline of the Vermont tax system follows:

Tax	Basis—Rates	Due Dates
Corporate organization and qualification fees.	Domestic—$75 fee for filing articles of incorporation.	At time of incorporation or qualification.
	Foreign—$100 for certificate of authority.	
	Annual report—$25 for domestic corporations; $150 for foreign corporations.	Annual report and fee—due within 2¹/₂ months after close of fiscal year.
General income tax.	**2006:** Corporations (domestic and foreign)—not over $10,000 of net income, 6%; $10,001 to $25,000, $600 plus 7% of excess over $10,000; $25,001 to $250,000, $1,650 plus 8.75% of excess over $25,000; $250,001 and over, $21,338 plus 8.9% of excess over $250,000. Minimum tax, $250.	Returns—15th day of 3rd month after end of taxable year. Estimated tax declaration due 15th day of 4th month of tax year if estimated tax is over $500; estimated tax due with the declaration on the 15th day of the 4th, 6th, 9th and 12th months of the tax year.
	After 2006: Corporations (domestic and foreign)—not over $10,000 of net income, 6%; $10,001 to $25,000, $600 plus 7% of excess over $10,000; $25,001 and over, $1,650 plus 8.5% of excess over $25,000. Minimum tax, $250.	
	The income tax on individuals: **2006 rates:** over $0 but not over $30,650, 3.6% of taxable income over $0; over $30,650, but not over $74,200, $1,103 plus 7.2% of taxable income over $30,650; over $74,200, but not over $154,800, $4,239 plus 8.5% of taxable income over $74,200; over $154,800, but not over $336,550, $11,090 plus 9.0% of taxable income over $154,800; over $336,550, $27,448 plus 9.5% of taxable income over $336,550. Separate schedules are set out for heads of household, married or civil union filing separately, and married, qualifying widow or widower, or civil union filing jointly.	Returns and payments—April 15; 15th day of 4th month following close of taxable year for fiscal-year taxpayers. Payment of estimated tax—15th day of 4th, 6th, 9th and 13th months.
	General withholding required.	
Bank franchise tax.	Banks and loan associations—0.000096 of the average monthly deposit held by the corporation.	Returns and payments—same as corporate income tax.
Property tax.	Education property tax—$1.10 (2007, $.95) per $100 of assessed value for residential property and $1.59 (2007, $1.44) per $100 of assessed value for nonresidential property (including businesses and vacation homes).	Payment—within 30 days of receipt of notice.
	Land use change tax—20% of fair market value of developed agricultural or managed forest lands previously receiving use value appraisal.	Payment—within 30 days of receipt of notice.

Tax	Basis—Rates	Due Dates
Meals and rooms tax.	Meals and rooms—9%. Alcoholic beverages—10%.	Reports and payments—if annual tax is $500 or less, 25th day of April, July, October and January; otherwise, 25th of each month (for February, the 23rd).
Alcoholic beverages tax.	Excise—malt beverages, 26.5¢ per gallon if not more than 6% alcohol by volume and 55¢ per gallon if more than 6% but not more than 8% alcohol by volume; vinous beverages, 55¢ per gallon; fortified wines and spirituous liquors, 25% of gross revenue.	Excise—beer, 10th of each month; liquor, collected from purchasers.
Gasoline and diesel fuel tax.	19¢ per gallon of gasoline sold or used within the state; 25¢ per gallon on diesel fuel; 3¢ per gallon on railroad fuel used in the state. Until April 1, 2011, an additional petroleum distributor licensing fee of 1¢ per gallon of gas or diesel fuel is levied on distributors, dealers or users.	Reports and payments—gasoline tax: 25th day of each month; diesel fuel tax: distributors and dealers report and pay on the last day of each month; railroad operators report and pay by the last day of October, January, April and July.
Motor vehicle purchase and use tax.	6% of the taxable cost of motor homes, motorcycles or pleasure cars or other vehicles weighing up to 10,099 pounds. For other motor vehicles, the lesser of 6% of the taxable cost or $1,680 (prior to July 1, 2006, $1,100).	Reports and payments due when registering or transferring registrations. Use tax report and payment at time of registration.
Cigarette tax; tobacco products tax.	Effective July 1, 2006, 89.5 mills ($1.79 per pack of 20); effective July 1, 2008, 99.5 mills ($1.99 per pack of 20) (prior to July 1, 2006, 59.5 mills for each cigarette or $1.19 per pack of 20). Tax is calculated for each 0.09 oz. of roll-your-own tobacco.	Cigarette tax report by wholesalers and distributors, 15th of each month; payment, by purchase and affixation of stamps.
	41% of wholesale price of tobacco products. 2% of tax may be deducted if tax is paid within 10 days of due date.	Tobacco products tax report and payment—15th of each month.
	Effective July 1, 2006, snuff is taxed at the rate of $1.49 per oz., or fractional part thereof; effective July 1, 2008, $1.66 per oz. or fractional part thereof.	
Capital gains tax on land.	From 5% to 80% of the gain, depending on (1) the number of years that the land was held and (2) the gain, calculated as a percentage of the basis.	Payment—buyers must withhold 10% of price if seller held land less than six years. Withheld tax due immediately. Returns and balance of tax due within 30 days after sale.
Realty transfer tax.	1.25% (minimum $1) of value of property transferred. Homes are taxed at 0.5% of the first $100,000 in value, and at 1.25% of value over $100,000. Qualified farms are taxed at 0.5%.	Payment—at the time of recording the deed.

Tax	Basis—Rates	Due Dates
Sales and use tax.	6% of taxable sales, purchases, services, charges, and rentals.	Returns and payment—tax due in one annual payment on or before January 25, if tax is less than $500. Tax must be paid and returns filed quarterly on or before 25th of April, July, October, and January if tax is more than $500 but less than $2,500. In all other cases, tax and returns are due monthly on or before the 25th (23rd of February) of the following month.
Telephone company tax.	Net book value rate of tax is 2.37%. Alternative tax (in lieu of income tax) on companies that received less than $50 million in annual gross operating revenues within the state in prior year: from 2.25% to 5.25% of gross operating revenue, depending on gross operating revenues during the quarter.	Net book value due in quarterly installments no later than the 25th day of the 3rd, 6th, 9th and 12th months of each taxable year; alternative tax—report, 25 days following the last day of the 3rd month of the tax year; payment—within 25 days following the last day of the 3rd, 6th, 9th, and 12th months of each tax year.
Insurance companies tax.	Domestic and foreign insurance companies, associations and societies, and surety and guaranty companies doing business in Vermont—2% of gross premiums *written* on Vermont business. Domestic and foreign life insurance companies doing business in Vermont—2% of gross premiums *collected* on Vermont business. Reinsurance premiums are not subject to premium tax.	Returns—reconciliation return due the last day of February for the preceding year ending December 31. Payment—due with the reconciliation return if tax is expected to be less than $500 for the year; otherwise, quarterly returns and payments must be made the last day of May, August, November, and February.
	Foreign mutual fire insurance companies insuring only factories or mills—2% of gross premiums covering risks within the state less unabsorbed portion of premiums deposits.	Returns and payments— during month of February.
	Surplus lines brokers—3% premium receipts tax.	Surplus lines brokers—end of the month following each calendar quarter.
	Foreign companies subject to retaliatory taxes.	
	Captive insurance companies—rate as determined under Sec. 6014, Title 8; minimum aggregate tax of $7,500 and maximum aggregate tax of $200,000.	Returns—last day of February. Payment—during month of February.
Estate tax.	Equal to the credit allowable under the federal estate tax law in effect on January 1, 2001.	Return and payment—at time of filing federal return.

Virginia

Tax System.—Virginia has adopted a tax system of complete segregation of state and local sources of revenue. By this method real estate, tangible personal property, machinery and tools used in a manufacturing or mining business and merchants' capital are segregated for local taxation exclusively, while the state revenue is derived from taxes on income, estate, corporate franchises, gasoline, cigarettes, sales and use, gross earnings of utilities, insurance companies and intangible personal property. An outline of the Virginia tax system follows:

Tax	Basis—Rates	Due Dates
Corporate organization and qualification fees.	Corporate Charter—If number of authorized shares is 1 million or less, $50 for each 25,000 shares; if more than 1 million shares, $2,500.	Domestic—at time of incorporation, or increase in capital stock.
	Fee for article of incorporation (domestic) or certificate of authority (foreign), $25.	Foreign—at time of qualification or increase in capital stock.
Annual registration fee.	$50 on first 5,000 authorized shares, $15 for each 5,000 shares or fraction over the first 5,000 shares, up to a maximum of $850.	Reports and payments—by last day of 12th month after incorporation or authorization, and on same date for following years.
		Payments—same.
Direct corporate income tax.	Corporate income—6% of net income from Virginia sources. Telecommunications companies are subject to a 0.5% minimum tax, if it is less than the corporate income tax, based on gross receipts for a calendar year. Certain electric suppliers are subject to a minimum tax if the corporate income tax net of any income tax credits is less than the minimum tax. The tax is 1.45% of gross receipts for the calendar year that ends during the taxable year minus the state's portion of the electric utility consumption tax billed to customers.	Returns and payments, corporations—15th day of 4th month after close of taxable year. Estimated corporate tax declaration and payments due 15th day of 4th, 6th, 9th and 12th months of taxable year.
Personal income tax.	Personal income—The tax is imposed on the taxpayer's federal adjusted gross income with modifications at rates ranging from 2% to 5.75% based on income level. The filing threshold for individuals who are single or married filing separately is $7,000 and the threshold for individuals married filing jointly is $14,000. Withholding required.	Returns—calendar: May 1; fiscal: 15th day of 4th month after close of income year. Estimated tax declaration due May 1.
		Payment—May 1. Estimated payments due April 15, June 15, September 15, and January 15.
Bank franchise tax.	$1 on each $100 of net capital.	Returns—March 1. Payments—June 1.
General property tax.	Aggregate of local rates fixed to meet budget; rates based on fair market value of real property, tangible personal property, machinery, tools and merchant's capital. All general reassessments and annual assessments in localities having annual assessments of realty are at 100% of fair market value.	Returns—May 1.
		Payment—December 5.

Tax	Basis—Rates	Due Dates
Railroad and private car companies property tax.	$1 per $100 value of rolling stock owned by railway companies, in lieu of local levies, and value of private cars used in the state.	Reports—April 15. Payment—June 1.
Alcoholic beverages tax.	Excise—beer and wine coolers, 25.65¢ per gallon per barrel; 7 oz. bottles or less, 2¢; bottles over 7 oz. but not over 12 oz., 2.65¢; bottles over 12 oz., 2.22 mills per oz. Wine, 40¢ per liter; additional 4% tax imposed on vermouth and wine produced by farm wineries and sold to consumers by the Alcoholic Beverage Control Board. Alcoholic beverages sold by the Board, 20% of price charged.	Excise—reports, 10th of each month. Payment—sale of wine to retailers and wholesalers, at time of purchase; others, with monthly report.
Gasoline tax.	17.5¢ per gallon of motor fuel sold and delivered or used by carriers of passengers; 5¢ per gallon of aviation motor fuel. Additional 0.2¢ per gallon imposed to keep Underground Petroleum Storage Tank Fund.	Motor fuel and fuels other than motor fuel—Returns and payments—postmarked by 15th day of the 2nd month following the month for which the return and payment are due.
Tax on fuels other than motor fuel.	16¢ per gallon of fuel (alternative fuels) used to propel motor vehicles except such fuel as is subject to the motor fuel tax; a tax rate equivalent to 16¢ per gallon is imposed on all other alternative fuel used to operate a highway vehicle.	
	Motor carrier road tax—19.5¢ per gallon of motor fuel used in state operations.	Motor carrier road tax—reports and payments due last day of April, July, October, and January.
Forest products tax.	Pine products—lumber, $1.15 per 1,000 ft. board measure or log scale, International 1/4" Kerf Rule; hardwood, cypress and all other species, 22.5¢ per 1,000 feet board measure. In the alternative, a taxpayer may elect to pay 20¢ per ton of pine log and 4¢ per ton of other type of logs received.	Reports and payments—quarterly, within 30 days after end of each calendar quarter. Flat taxes, due January 30.
	Small manufacturers—flat tax, $230 per year for 300,000 board feet or less, $460 for more than 300,000 and less than 500,000 board feet.	
Reclamation tax.	Reclamation tax—4¢ per clean ton of coal produced by permitted surface mining operation; 3¢ per ton of coal produced by permitted deep mining operation; 1.5¢ per ton of coal processed or loaded by permitted preparation or loading facilities. Payments cease when revenue generated exceeds specified amounts.	Reclamation tax—Payment—no later than 30 days after the end of each calendar quarter.
Aircraft sales and use tax.	Aircraft sales and use tax—2% of the sales price of aircraft licensed for use in Virginia (maximum tax, $2,000).	Payment—prior to applying for an aircraft license.
Motor vehicle sales tax, rental tax.	Sales and use tax—3% on the sale or use of motor vehicles, except 2% on the sale or use of mobile offices.	Sales and use tax—payable upon application for certificate of title.
	Vehicle rental tax—4% of gross proceeds of vehicle rentals, except 10% on daily rental passenger cars.	Rental tax—taxes and return due the 20th of each month.

Tax	Basis—Rates	Due Dates
Watercraft sales and use tax.	2% of sales price or current market value (maximum tax, $2,000).	Returns and payment— Dealers, 20th of each month. Purchasers, when applying for title.
Sales and use tax.	Sales tax—4% of sales price, gross proceeds or cost price of tangible personal property, rentals, services or accommodations. 1.5% on food for human consumption.	Sales and use tax—returns and payment due on or before the 20th of each month for preceding month.
Cigarette tax.	Cigarettes—1.5¢ per cigarette; 30¢ per pack of 20.	Reports—wholesalers by 20th of each month; retailers within one business day after receipt. Payment—by affixation of stamps, immediately upon receipt.
	10% of manufacturers sales price on distributors for privilege of selling or dealing in tobacco products.	Returns and payment—10th of each month.
Recordation tax; Realty transfer tax.	Conveyances—25¢ per $100 consideration or fraction thereof. Realty transfers—50¢ per $500 of value or fraction thereof.	Payment—at time of recording.
Water, heat, gas, light and power companies tax.	Water, heat, light, power and pipeline transmission companies tax—2% on all sources. Electric utilities subject to corporate income tax.	Reports—April 15. Estimated tax declaration due April 15.
	Special tax of up to 0.2% may be assessed on gross receipts from business in Virginia on corporations furnishing water, heat, light, or power, by means of gas or steam, except for electric suppliers, gas utilities and gas suppliers, and pipeline distribution companies.	Payment—June 1. Estimated taxes due on 15th day of April, June, September, and December.
Electric utility consumption tax.	2,500 kWh or less of electricity consumed, total rate is $0.00155/kWh (state rate $0.00102/kWh, special regulatory rate $0.00015/kWh, local rate $0.00038/kWh). 2,500 kWh but less than 50,000 kWh of electricity consumed, total rate is $0.00099/kWh (state rate $0.00065/kWh, special regulatory rate $0.00010/kWh, local rate $0.00024/kWh). 50,000 kWh or more of electricity consumed, total rate is $0.00075/kWh (state rate $0.00050/kWh, special regulatory rate $0.00007/kWh, local rate $0.00018/kWh).	Payment—last day of month after collection. State and regulatory tax paid to State Tax Commission; local tax to locality.
Natural gas utility consumption tax.	State consumption tax rate of $0.0135 per CCF; local consumption tax rate of $0.004 per CCF; and a special regulatory revenue tax rate of up to $0.002 per CCF.	Payment—last day of month after collection. State and regulatory tax paid to State Tax Commission; local tax to locality.

Tax	Basis—Rates	Due Dates
Insurance companies tax.	Life—2.25% of gross premiums, less return premiums, and premiums received for reinsurance on risks within the state.	Reports and payments— March 1. Declarations and payments of estimated taxes from insurers expecting to owe more than $3,000 are due on the 15th day of the 4th, 6th, 9th, and 12th months.
	Mutual and industrial sick benefit—1%.	
	Dental or optometric and health services plans, 0.75% of direct gross subscriber fee income from open enrollment contracts and 2.25% of other fee income.	
	Other—2.25%.	
	Foreign companies subject to retaliatory taxes.	
Estate tax.	Assessed in amount equal to federal credit for state death taxes under federal law as of January 1, 1978; reduced proportionately on account of property outside state. (Repealed for estates of persons who die on or after 7/1/07.)	Return and payment—within 9 months of decedent's death.
Generation-skipping transfer tax.	Generation-skipping transfer—Tax imposed to absorb federal generation-skipping transfer tax credit.	Return and payment—by date the federal return is due.

Washington

Tax System.—The revenue system of Washington is based primarily on the ad valorem assessment and taxation of property, but since 1933 the revenue needs of the state have been financed largely by occupation and other taxes. Although the state continues to receive a substantial income from property taxes, the greater part of such levies is used for the support of municipalities and other taxing districts. The yield from the revenue act taxes is devoted entirely to state purposes, and this is true of most of the other special taxes, the exceptions being the gasoline tax and the liquor taxes, a portion of each being redistributed locally. An outline of the Washington tax system follows:

Tax	Basis—Rates	Due Dates
Corporate organization and qualification fees.	Domestic and foreign corporations—for filing articles of incorporation and the first year's license, $175.	Domestic—at time of incorporation. Foreign—at time of qualification.
Corporation annual license tax.	Domestic and foreign corporations—$50 annual license fee.	Annual license tax—on or before the expiration of the corporate license.
Annual report.	No fee when filed concurrently with annual license fee.	Prior to expiration of corporate license.
Business and occupation tax.	Retailing (generally)—0.471% of gross proceeds of sales; Wholesaling—0.484% of gross proceeds of sales; Manufacturing—0.484% of value of products manufactured; Service and other activities—1.5% of gross income. Special rates applicable to certain industries.	Report and payment—25th of each month for monthly filers.
General property taxes.	Aggregate of state and local rates fixed to meet budget. Assessed value is 100% of true and fair cash value of real and tangible personal property, excluding open-space land, timber land, and agricultural land. Constitutional and statutory tax limitation, 1% of full, true and fair value.	Returns—real and personal property, between February 15 and April 30; public utilities, March 15; private car companies, May 1. Payment—in full by April 30 or in two equal installments on April 30 and October 31 if tax due is more than $50.
Leasehold excise tax.	Leasehold interests in exempt publicly owned real or personal property—12% plus 7% surtax of tax payable for a total state rate of 12.84%.	Return and payment—last day of following month.
Timber and forest lands taxes.	Timber harvesters pay a 5% tax on stumpage value of timber harvested.	Returns and payment—last day of month following calendar quarter.
Alcoholic beverages tax.	Excise—Total tax—beer (per barrel), $8.08; liquor (per liter), $2.4408; table wine (per liter), $0.2292; fortified wine (per liter), $0.4536; cider (per liter), $0.0814. These rates include any surcharge or additional taxes imposed.	Reports and payments—25th of each month.

Tax	Basis—Rates	Due Dates
Gasoline tax; special fuel tax.	34¢ per gallon motor fuel sold, distributed or used, effective July 1, 2006; 36¢ per gallon on July 1, 2007; 37.5¢ per gallon on July 1, 2008. Special fuel, 34¢ per gallon, effective July 1, 2006; 36¢ per gallon on July 1, 2007; 37.5¢ per gallon on July 1, 2008. Prior to July 1, 2006, the rate for motor fuel and special fuel was 28¢ per gallon. An annual license fee ranging from $45 to $250 is imposed in lieu of the special fuel tax upon the use of natural gas or liquefied petroleum gas (propane) in any motor vehicle. Aircraft fuel rate is 11¢ per gallon.	Reports and payments— gasoline and special fuel, 25th of following month. Payment of motor fuel and special fuel taxes by electronic funds transfer due on 26th of following month.
	Pollution liability insurance fee—1.2¢ per gallon of heating oil purchased within the state (until June 1, 2007).	Payment—with special fuel dealer return.
	Depending on revenues in the pollution liability reinsurance program trust account, an additional tax is imposed on the privilege of the first possession of petroleum products in the state at the rate of 0.5%.	Same as under the business and occupation tax.
	Depending on account balances, oil spill response tax imposed at 1¢ per barrel (suspended until further notice) and oil spill administration tax imposed at 4¢ per barrel on the privilege of off-loading crude oil or petroleum products at a marine terminal within Washington from a waterborne vessel or barge.	Reports and payments— 25th day of following month.
Uranium and thorium milling tax.	5¢ per pound of uranium and thorium compound milled out of raw ore.	Quarterly basis.
Enhanced food fish tax.	Chinook, coho and chum salmon, and anadromous game fish, 5.62% of value at the point of landing; pink and sockeye salmon, 3.37%; other food fish and shellfish except oysters, 2.25%; oysters, 0.09%; sea urchins and sea cucumbers, 4.92%. Rates include the additional 7% surtax.	Reports and payments— 25th day of following month.
Motor vehicle license fee.	Motor vehicle license fee—$30 per year regardless of year, value, make, or model. Includes cars, sport utility vehicles, motorcycles, and motor homes. Effective 1/1/06, annual weight fee imposed. Mobile homes affixed to realty are subject to property taxes.	Excise tax—paid at time of registration.
Cigarette tax; tobacco products tax.	Cigarettes—$2.025 per pack of 20 cigarettes.	Cigarettes—reports—15th of each month. Payment— stamps affixed upon receipt.
	Tobacco products—75% of taxable sales price. Maximum 50¢ per cigar.	Tobacco products— reports—25th of each month. Payment—with return.
Real estate excise tax.	State rate is 1.28% of selling price on each sale of real property, including transfers of controlling interests in entities that own property in the state. Combined state and local rate is 1.53% or 1.78% in most areas.	Payment—with filing of affidavit form.

Tax	Basis—Rates	Due Dates
Retail sales tax.	State rate—6.5% of retail sales price on taxable property and services plus additional 0.3% on motor vehicle sales and additional 5.9% on retail car rentals. Local sales taxes also imposed. Use tax imposed at same rate as sales tax.	Report and payment—25th of each month for monthly filers.
Public utility tax.	Express, sewer, telegraph, and gas distribution, 3.852%; light and power, 3.873%; urban transportation, vessels under 65 ft., 0.642%; water distribution, 5.029%; motor transportation, railroad, railroad car, tugboat business, and all other public service businesses, 1.926%. Rates include the additional 7% surtax.	Report and payment—25th of each month for monthly filers.
Insurance premiums tax.	Life and other insurance—2%.	Reports—March 1 annually.
	Marine and foreign trade insurance—0.95% of gross underwriting profit allocable to state.	Payment—March 1 annually. Prepayment due from taxpayers owing $400 or more for preceding year—15th of June, September and December. Remaining tax due with return on March 1.
	Foreign insurance companies are subject to a retaliatory tax.	
	Health maintenance organizations, health care service contractors, and certified health plans—2% of premiums and prepayments for health care services.	Report and payment—March 1. Prepayment—15th of June, September and December.
Estate tax.	Former estate tax assessed in amount equal to federal estate tax credit not applicable to decedents dying after December 31, 2004. New estate tax enacted May 17, 2005, applicable to estates exceeding $1.5 million for persons dying 5/17/05 to 12/31/05 and estates exceeding $2 million for persons dying on or after 1/1/06. Tax rates range between 10% and 19%, depending on amount of taxable estate.	Return and payment—at time federal return is filed (usually within nine months of decedent's death).
Generation-skipping transfer tax.	Repealed on May 17, 2005.	

West Virginia

Tax System.—The West Virginia tax system is founded on the ad valorem assessment and taxation of property, but this source of revenue has now been supplemented with other taxes affording a substantial yield. The revenue from property taxes is mainly devoted to the support of municipal governments and other local tax levying bodies, with only a small portion going to the State Treasury. The state receives the entire revenue from the inheritance tax, insurance company taxes, the privilege tax on gross income, the taxes on utilities, the gasoline tax and liquor taxes. Both the state and local bodies share in license fees, but the proceeds of the consumers sales and service tax are used entirely for support of the schools. The state collects both a personal income tax and a corporation net income tax. An outline of the West Virginia tax system follows:

Tax	Basis—Rates	Due Dates
Corporate organization and qualification fees.	Each certificate of incorporation or certificate of authority, $50 for domestic and foreign for-profit corporations. Each certificate of increase in capital stock or amendment of certificate of incorporation, $25.	Domestic—tax assessed and collected at time of incorporation. Foreign—tax assessed and collected at time of qualification.
	LLC Annual report (Foreign and Domestic)—$25	The first annual report must be delivered to the secretary of state between January 1 and April 1 of the year following the calendar year in which a limited liability company was organized or a foreign company was authorized to transact business. Subsequent annual reports must be delivered to the secretary of state between the first day of January and the first day of April of the ensuing calendar years.
Corporate license tax; annual corporation fee; business franchise tax; business registration tax.	Domestic—graduated from $20 on $5,000 or less to $2,500 on $15,000,000 or more of authorized capital stock. Foreign—75% higher than above rates. Minimum $250. No par stock valued at amount for which stock was issued but not less than $25 per share. Fee for Statutory Attorney-in-Fact—$25 on certain business entities whose principal places of business are outside the state.	Domestic and foreign corporations must pay corporate license tax (in addition to annual attorney-in-fact fee)—July 1. Annual corporation fee payable at same time license tax is paid.

232 Information by State

Tax	Basis—Rates	Due Dates
	Business franchise tax—greater of $50 or 0.70% of the value of taxpayer's capital.	Returns and payment—for corporations, on or before the 15th day of the 3rd month following the end of the tax year; for partnerships, on or before the 15th day of the 4th month following the end of the tax year. For unrelated business taxable income, 15th day of the 5th month following the end of the tax year. If annual liability is expected to exceed $12,000, declarations of estimated tax are due by the 15th day of the 4th month of tax year; payments of estimated tax are due by the 15th day of the 4th, 6th, 9th and 12th months of the tax year.
Corporation net income tax.	9% of taxable income.	Returns and payment—March 15 for calendar year returns; fiscal returns, 15th day of third month after close of fiscal year. For unrelated business taxable income of exempt corporations, 15th day of the 5th month following the close of the tax year. Estimated tax declarations and payments due 15th day of 4th, 6th, 9th or 12th month of taxable year if taxable income exceeds $10,000.
Personal income tax.	For individuals, individuals filing joint returns, heads of households, surviving spouses, and estates and trusts: Less than $10,000, 3%; $10,000—$25,000, $300 plus 4% of excess of $10,000; $25,000—$40,000, $900 plus 4.5% of excess of $25,000; $40,000—$60,000, $1,575 plus 6% of excess of $40,000; over $60,000, $2,775 plus 6.5% of excess of $60,000. For married individuals filing separate returns: less than $5,000, 3%; $5,000--$12,500, $150 plus 4% of excess over $5,000; $12,500--$20,000, $450 plus 4.5% of excess over $12,500; $20,000--$30,000, $787.50 plus 6% of excess over $20,000; over $30,000, $1,387.50 plus 6.5% of excess over $30,000. Minimum tax, the amount by which an amount equal to 25% of any federal minimum tax or alternative minimum tax for the tax year exceeds the total tax for the year.	Returns and payment—15th day of the 4th month after end of income year.

Tax	Basis—Rates	Due Dates
		Estimated tax due 15th of April, June, September, and , except for persons having total estimated tax of $40 or less or farmers, January 15.
	General withholding required.	
General property tax.	Determined annually. Maximum levies: Class 1—50¢ per $100 actual value of real and personal property; Class 2—$1 per $100; Class 3—$1.50 per $100; Class 4—$2 per $100. Property is assessed at 60% of value.	Returns—general property between July 1 and October 1; public utilities, May 1.
		Payment—September 1 and March 1.
Tax on corporations holding land.	5¢ for every acre over 10,000 acres.	Payment due before certificate of incorporation or of authority is issued.
Alcoholic beverages tax.	Excise—$5.50 per bbl. of beer not in excess of 4.2% alcohol, and proportionately on smaller amounts. Retail purchases of liquor, 5% of purchase price. Wine, 26.406¢ per liter.	Beer—estimated report and payment, 10th day of each month. Wine—report and payment, before 16th day of following month.
	Intoxicating liquors sold outside municipalities are taxed at 5% of the purchase price.	Intoxicating liquors—at time of purchase.
Motor fuels tax.	Motor fuels excise tax—20.5¢ (15.5¢, effective August 1, 2007) per gallon of motor fuel imported into the state, except for bulk transfers.	Gasoline—reports and payments—last day of the calendar month for the preceding calendar month.
Motor carrier road tax.	Motor carrier road tax—same as motor fuels tax on gallons of motor and other fuel used by carriers in the state.	Motor carrier road tax—reports, last day of April, July, October, and January; payments, last day of January.

Tax	Basis—Rates	Due Dates
Severance taxes.	Coal—5% (includes the 0.35% additional severance tax on coal for the benefit of counties and municipalities); minimum coal severance tax, 75¢ per ton; special tax on coal production, 2¢ per ton; limestone or sandstone—5%; natural gas or oil—5%; timber—3.22%; other natural resources—5%; coal refuse or gob piles, 2.5%.	Annual return and payments—last day of the month following the tax year. Payments of natural gas or oil, timber, or other natural resource severance taxes— on or before the last day of the month following each quarter; if estimated tax exceeds $1,000 per month, due on or before the last day of each month for the preceding month. Payments of the minimum severance tax on coal, limestone or sandstone severance taxes—on or before the last day of the month for the preceding month. All payments for May due June 15. Except for the privilege tax on severance of coal, limestone, and sandstone, if estimated tax due is $50 or less per month no installment payment is due.
	Additional taxes: clean coal—56¢ per ton; natural gas—4.7¢ per mcf; timber—2.78%.	
Motor vehicle privilege tax.	5% of the value of the vehicle at the time of certification or 5% of monthly payment for vehicles leased to residents (continues for entire term of initial lease period).	Tax on leased vehicles due monthly.
Cigarette tax.	55¢ on each 20 cigarettes or fraction thereof sold within state. Tobacco products are taxed at a rate of 7% of the wholesale price of each tobacco product.	Reports—15th day of each month by wholesalers, carriers, subjobbers, retail dealers and agents. Payment—by purchase of stamps or use of meters.
Document recording tax.	Realty transfers—$1.10 for each $500 value or fraction thereof plus an additional minimum county excise tax of 55¢ per $500 of value. In addition, county commissions may create a farmland protection program and impose an additional realty transfer tax with a maximum $1.10 for each $500 of value.	Payment—by affixing of documentary stamps at time of presentation for recording.

Tax	Basis—Rates	Due Dates
Consumer sales and service tax and use tax.	6% of sales price of tangible personal property or taxable services stored, consumed, or used within state excluding gasoline and special fuel sales; 6% on mobile homes to be used as the owner's principal year-round residence based on 50% of the sales price or value of the home.	Returns and payment—20 days after end of month. Large taxpayers must make accelerated payments for June no later than June 23. Quarterly returns—20th day of the 1st month in the next succeeding quarter (April 15, July 15, October 15). Annual return—sales tax—20th day of the month following the close of the annual reporting period.
	Gasoline and special fuel tax—From January 1, 2006, through December 31, 2006, 6.5¢ per gallon.	Gasoline sales tax—25th day of each month. Gasoline use tax—25th day of January, April, July, and October.
Utilities tax.	In general—street, interurban, and electric railways, 1.4%; water companies (except municipally owned), 4.4%; natural gas and toll bridge companies, 4.29%; all other public service or utility businesses, 2.86%.	
	Gross income—electric light and power companies and other producers of income, 4% of total sales; electric companies that supply but do not generate power, 3%; sales of electric power that exceed 200,000 kilowatts per hour per year, 2%. Tax is owed on the greater of the gross income tax or the alternate tax.	
	Alternate tax—For electricity generated in West Virginia, electric light and power companies, $22.78 multiplied by the taxable generating unit; if generating unit has flue and gas desulfurization system, $20.70. 5/100 of 1¢ times kilowatt hours sold where contract demands or usage at plant location exceeds 200,000 kilowatts per hour per year, whether electricity is produced in or out of state. For electricity sold in West Virginia but produced elsewhere, 19/100 of 1¢ times kilowatt hours sold. Tax is owed on the greater of the gross income tax or the alternate tax.	
	Gas storage business—gas injected into or withdrawn from a gas storage business, 5¢ multiplied by the sum of the net number of dekatherms of gas injected into or withdrawn from the reservoir during a tax month.	Reports—on or before the last day of the month following the end of the tax year. Payments—if estimated liability exceeds $1,000 per month, due on or before the last day of each month, except payment for May due June 15; if estimated liability is $1,000 or less per month, due on or before the last day of the month following each quarter.

Tax	Basis—Rates	Due Dates
Telecommunications tax.	Telegraph, telephone or other telecommunications service—4% of gross income from business beginning and ending in the state and gross income apportioned to the state from business that either begins or ends in the state.	Returns—on or before the last day of the month following the end of the tax year.
		Payments—if estimated liability less than $1,000, on or before the last day of the month following each quarter. If estimated liability exceeds $1,000 per month, due on or before the last day of each following month, except payment for May due June 15.
Insurance companies premiums tax.	2% of gross premiums less return premiums, plus additional 1% tax. Fire and casualty insurers, additional 1% of gross direct premiums. Excess line brokers, 4% of gross premiums. 1% of gross amount of annuity considerations less considerations returned; risk retention group, 2%; captive insurance companies, 5/10 of 1%.	Reports and payments—financial statement and annual tax return, March 1. Estimated quarterly payments and fire and casualty surcharge, 25th day of month following quarter, except March 1 for fourth quarter; an annual report for captive insurance companies, March 1.
	Additional fire marshal tax of 0.5% for insurance companies other than life.	
	Surcharge on fire and casualty policies—1% of gross direct premiums.	
	Minimum tax for aggregate taxes, $200 per year.	Minimum tax, March 1.
	Foreign companies subject to retaliatory taxes. Alternative minimum tax is imposed.	
Soft drinks tax.	1¢ per 16.9 oz. (one-half liter) or fraction thereof of bottled soft drinks; 80¢/gallon or 84¢ per four liters of soft drink syrup or fraction thereof; 1¢/ounce or 1¢/28.35 grams of dry mixture or fraction thereof.	Reports—15th day of each month showing preceding month's operations.
		Payment—tax crowns (stamps) affixed to each unit.
Health care provider tax.	1.75%—5.95% of gross receipts for enumerated health care services. For certain services, rates are phased out from July 1, 2001, through July 1, 2010. Effective July 1, 2005, rates range from 0.875%—2.75%. Effective July 1, 2006, rates range from 0.7%—2.2%.	Returns and payments—on or before January 31; with fiscal returns due by the last day of the 1st month following close of fiscal year.
Estate tax.	Basic federal estate tax credit for state death taxes reduced proportionately on account of property outside the state.	Payments and returns—within 9 months of death.

Wisconsin

Tax System.—The Wisconsin tax system is based on ad valorem levies on general property assessed by the state and its various taxing districts. Some specified businesses are taxed on other than an ad valorem basis and are not subject to the general property tax. Inheritance, estate, and gift taxes are in force. The state also levies personal and corporate income taxes, and sales and use taxes. An outline of the Wisconsin tax system follows:

Tax	Basis—Rates	Due Dates
Corporate organization and qualification fees.	Corporate organization and qualification fees—domestic, $100; foreign, $100 plus $2 per each $1,000 or fraction of the corporation's capital exceeding $60,000 employed in Wisconsin.	Domestic—upon incorporation or increase of capital stock. Foreign—upon qualification or increase of capital stock.
Annual corporation report fee.	Annual corporation report fee—foreign, $65 (plus $2 for every $1,000 or fraction thereof in excess of employed capital on which fee has been paid); domestic, $25.	Domestic—during the calendar quarter in which anniversary date of filing of articles of incorporation occurs. Foreign—annual report during first calendar quarter of each year following year when corporation can do business in Wisconsin.
Franchise and income taxes.	Single individuals, fiduciaries, and heads of households—2006 Rates: taxable income of $0 to $9,160, 4.6%; $9,160 to $18,320, 6.15% plus $421.36; $18,320 to $137,410, 6.5% plus $984.70; over $137,410, 6.75% plus $8,725.55. Separate schedules are set out for married filing separately and for married filing jointly. Corporations—7.9% of net income. Urban mass transportation companies—50% of gross income.	Returns and payments—corporation, calendar year, March 15; fiscal year, by 15th day of 3rd month following close of fiscal year; individuals, April 15.
General property tax.	General property tax—rates on real and tangible personal property of individuals, partnerships, corporations and intradistrict water, light, heat and power companies. Full cash value received in an arm's-length transaction. Assessment ratio set by Department of Revenue. Agricultural forest and undeveloped land are assessed at 50% of full value.	Returns—telephone companies, March 1; railroad, sleeping car, and express line companies, April 15; air carriers, pipeline, conservation, and regulation companies, May 1. Payment of taxes on real property due in full on or before January 31 or due in two equal installments, January 31 and July 31. If total real property tax is less than $100, full payment due January 31. Personal property tax—on or before January 31.
Vessels tax.	Vessels tax—1¢ per net registered tonnage of steam vessels, barges, boats or other watercraft owned within the state and employed regularly in interstate traffic, in lieu of property taxes.	Vessels tax—returns and payments, January 1.

Tax	Basis—Rates	Due Dates
Woodlands tax.	Woodlands tax—the tax computation is determined by whether the productive forest land is subject to (1) the forest crop law, or (2) the woodland tax law for land entered into the programs prior to 1986, or (3) the managed forest law, which replaced the two prior laws. Rates are: forest crop law—land entered prior to 1972, 10¢ (20¢ under special class) per acre per year; land entered after 1971, $1.66 per acre per year for 2003—2012; woodland tax law—through 1997, $1.67 per acre. Managed forest law—for 2003—2007, rates for lands entered under Managed Forest Law program before 2005 are 83¢ per acre for land designated as open to the public and $1.95 per acre for land designated as closed to the public; beginning in 2005, rates for lands entered under Managed Forest Law program from 2005 through 2007 are $1.30 per acre for open lands and $6.50 per acre for closed lands. Rates for lands entered before 2005 will continue to remain lower than rates for lands entered after 2004. In addition, owner pays a yield tax of 5% of the stumpage value of any harvested timber.	Returns and payments—January 31.
Coal docks tax.	Coal docks tax—Bituminous and subbituminous coal, coke, and briquettes, 5¢ per ton. Petroleum carbon, coke, and briquettes, 5¢ per ton. Anthracite coal, coke, and briquettes, 7¢ per ton.	Coal docks tax—returns, February 1; payments, January 31.
Grain tax.	Wheat and flax—0.5 mill per bushel received or handled by elevator or warehouse, in lieu of property tax. Other grain—0.25 mill per bushel.	Grain tax—returns, February 1; payments, January 31.
Iron ore tax.	Iron ore concentrates—5¢ per ton.	Iron ore concentrates—returns, May 1; payments, January 31.
Petroleum products tax.	Petroleum products tax—5¢ per ton of crude oil handled.	Petroleum products tax—returns, February 1; payments, January 31.
Alcoholic beverages tax.	Excise—intoxicating liquor containing 0.5% alcohol or more (including wine containing over 21% alcohol), 85.86¢ per liter; wines tax: containing 14% alcohol or less, 6.605¢ per liter; containing 14% to 21% alcohol, 11.89¢ per liter. 3¢-per-gallon administrative fee imposed on intoxicating liquor containing 0.5% alcohol or more. Fermented malt beverages (beer), $2 per 31-gallon barrel. Apple cider containing not less than 0.5% or more than 7% alcohol by volume, 1.71¢ per liter.	Reports and payments—15th day of each month.

Tax	Basis—Rates	Due Dates
Fuel taxes.	Motor vehicle fuel and alternate fuel—rates recomputed annually based on consumer price index and amount of fuel sold in the state. Effective April 1, 2006, motor vehicle and diesel fuels, 30.9¢ per gallon; liquefied petroleum gas, 22.6¢ per gallon; and compressed natural gas, 24.7¢ per gallon. General aviation fuel, 6¢ per gallon. Inspection fee—2¢ per gallon.	Reports—motor vehicle and alternate fuels, last day of each month; general aviation fuel, 20th day of each month. Payments—motor vehicle fuel, 15th day of each month; alternate and general aviation fuels, payments accompany report.
Metallic minerals occupation tax.	Percentage of net proceeds—-rates change yearly. For 2006 tax year: $0 to $477,700, 0%; $477,701 to $8,955,000, 3%; $8,955,001 to $17,909,800, 7%; $17,909,801 to $26,864,900, 10%; $26,864,901 to $35,820,100, 13%; $35,059,101 to $43,823,500, 14%; over $43,823,501, 15%.	Reports and payments—June 15 following applicable tax year.
	Oil and gas severance tax—7% of market value of total production of oil or gas during previous year.	Reports and payments—same as metallic minerals tax.
Timber yield tax.	5% of stumpage value of merchantable timber cut on managed forest lands.	Payment—last day of month following mailing of certificate of assessment.
Cigarette tax.	Cigarettes—38.5 mills each on cigarettes weighing 3 lbs. or less per 1,000 plus 8 mills per cigarette minus the federal tax; 77 mills each on cigarettes weighing more, plus 16.8 mills per cigarette minus the federal tax.	Reports—permittees, 15th day of each month; users, within 15 days of importing more than 400 cigarettes.
Tobacco products tax.	Tobacco products—25% of manufacturer's list price on domestic products; 25% of manufacturer's list price plus federal tax, duties and transportation costs to the U.S. on imported products.	Returns and payments—distributors, 15th day of each month.
Real estate transfer fee.	30¢ per $100 of value or fraction of realty transferred.	Reports and payments—at the time of recordation.
Sales and use taxes.	5% of gross receipts from selling or leasing tangible personal property and taxable services, or from the storage, use or other consumption in Wisconsin of tangible personal property or taxable services purchased from any retailer. 5% for rental vehicles.	Returns and payments—on or before the last day of the month following each calendar quarter. If the tax for a quarter exceeds $600, monthly returns and payments may be required, due on the last day of the following month. If the tax for a quarter exceeds $3,600, monthly returns and payments may be required, due on the 20th day of the following month.

Tax	Basis—Rates	Due Dates
Public utilities tax.	Telephone companies—tax imposed on real and tangible personal property; rate is prior year's net rate of the general property tax.	Reports—March 1. Payments—same for other public utilities, *i.e.,* May 10 and November 10. Companies owing less than $2,000 make one payment, due November 10 of the year of assessment.
	Car line companies—3% of gross earnings from intrastate business and proportionate mileage of interstate business done in Wisconsin (tax withheld and paid by railroad companies).	Reports—April 15. Payments—September 10 of year prior to assessment and April 15 of the year of assessment.
	Electric cooperatives—apportionment factor multiplied by gross revenues multiplied by 3.19%.	Reports—March 15. Payments—May 10 and November 10 on estimated basis for subsequent year, *i.e.,* one year in advance. Cooperatives with less than $2,000 liability pay full amount by May 10 of year of assessment.
	Light, heat, and power companies—0.97% of apportioned gross revenues from sale of gas services and 3.19% of all other apportioned gross revenues.	Reports—March 1. Payments—May 10 and November 10 on estimated basis for current calendar year. Companies with less than $2,000 liability pay full amount by May 10 of year of assessment.
	Note: A license fee for selling electricity at wholesale is scheduled to be imposed for calendar-year tax periods from 2004—2009; the fee amount is the apportionment factor multiplied by gross revenues from the sale of electricity at wholesale multiplied by 1.59%. Gross revenues subject to this fee will not be subject to the regular license fee.	
Insurance companies tax.	Foreign fire insurers—2.375%. Foreign marine insurers—0.5%. Surplus lines insurers—3%. Ocean marine insurers—0.5%.	Foreign fire, marine, casualty and life insurers reports—due March 1. Such insurers pay their estimated tax on or before the 15th day of April, June, September, and December.
	Fire companies also pay 2% on premiums on property located in municipalities entitled to fire department dues.	
	Casualty, surety, and mortgage guaranty—2%.	
	Life—domestic, 3.5%; foreign, 2%.	
	Foreign companies subject to retaliatory taxes.	

Tax	Basis—Rates	Due Dates
Estate tax.	Estate tax—For a decedent whose death occurs October 2002—December 2007, the federal credit and federal estate tax are computed under the federal estate tax law in effect on December 31, 2000. For a decedent whose death occurs after 2007, the federal credit and federal estate tax are computed under the federal estate tax law in effect on the date of the decedent's death.	Estate tax—beginning October 1, 2002, through December 31, 2007, report due 9 months after death. Payments, within 9 months after decedent's death.

Wyoming

Tax System.—Wyoming derives its public revenue from taxes imposed on real and certain personal property of individuals and corporations and from taxes imposed upon classes of individuals and corporations carrying on specified kinds of business or engaging in particular transactions. An outline of the Wyoming tax system follows:

Tax	Basis—Rates	Due Dates
Corporate organization and qualification fees.	Domestic and foreign—Domestic articles of incorporation, $100; foreign application for certificate of authority, $100. Annual report, $25.	Domestic—at time of incorporation. Foreign—at time of qualification.
Corporation franchise (license) tax.	Domestic and foreign—$50 or $2/10$ of one mill on the dollar ($.0002), whichever is greater, based upon the sum of its capital, property, and assets located and employed in Wyoming.	Report and payment—first day of month of registration.
General property tax.	State and local rates fixed to meet budget. Property is assessed at 100% of fair market value for gross mineral and mine products, 11.5% for property used for industrial purposes and 9.5% for all other property. Pipeline companies, electric utilities, railroad companies, rail car companies, and telecommunications companies—assessed on fair market value of property.	Returns—listing of taxable property, March 1; railroads, May 1; mines, February 25; public utilities, April 1. Payment—in installments, 50% by November 10 and remaining 50% by May 10, or payment in full by December 31.
Alcoholic beverages tax.	Excise—fermented liquor, $.0075 per 100 ml.; spirituous liquor, $.025 per 100 ml.; malt beverages, $.005 per liter; manufactured wine shipped into state, 12% of retail price.	No periodic reports requirement. Payment—at time liquors are sold to licensees by Liquor Division.
Motor fuel tax.	Gasoline and diesel, 13¢ per gallon, plus 1¢ additional tax to fund environmental clean-up costs. Aviation fuel, 4¢ per gallon, plus 1¢ additional tax to fund environmental clean-up costs.	Carriers—reports and payments—10th day of month. Others—last day of each month.
Oil and gas conservation charge.	Assessed on fair market value of all oil and gas produced, transported, or sold in Wyoming—currently $8/10$ of a mill ($0.0008).	Payment—25th of each month for the preceding month.
Severance taxes.	Gross products tax—6% on crude oil, lease condensate, and natural gas; 3.75% on value of underground coal; 4% of value of uranium and trona; 7% on surface coal; 2% on bentonite, sand and gravel, and oil shale or any other fossil fuel.	Reports and payments— monthly on 25th day of 2nd month following month of production; annually on February 25 if prior annual tax was under $30,000.
Cigarette tax.	30 mills per cigarette (60¢ per pack of 20 cigarettes) on sale by wholesaler or use or storage by consumer. 20% of wholesale purchase price of cigars, snuff, and other tobacco products.	Returns—20th day of each month for preceding month. Payments—Cigarette tax paid by purchase and affixation of stamps or use of meters.

Tax	Basis—Rates	Due Dates
Sales and use tax.	Both sales and use taxes are assessed at a state rate of 4% (3% general tax plus 1% additional temporary tax). Local rate may also apply.	Sales and use—reports and payments—last day of each month for preceding month, or if tax is less than $150 in any month, on or before last day of month following each quarter or year.
Insurance companies tax.	0.75% of net premiums, except 1% for annuity considerations.	Reports—and payments—quarterly on or before the last day of the month immediately following the end of the calendar quarter for which payment is due. However, payment for the quarter ending December 31 is payable on or before March 1.
	Wet marine and transportation insurers—0.75% of gross underwriting profit.	
	Brokers of surplus lines insurance transacted with unauthorized insurers—3% of premiums.	
	Foreign companies subject to retaliatory taxes.	
Estate tax.	Amount of the maximum state death tax credit allowed against the federal estate taxes.	Return and payment—within 9 months after death.

INCOME TAXES

The following pages contain summarizing facets of income-based taxes imposed by the state on corporations and individuals. Corporations are not subject to income-based taxes in Nevada, South Dakota (franchise tax on financial institutions only), Washington, and Wyoming. Individuals are not subject to income-based taxes in Alaska, Florida, Nevada, South Dakota, Texas, Washington, and Wyoming. Individuals in New Hampshire and Tennessee are taxed on interest and dividend income only.

Topics covered in this section include rates for corporations and individuals, allocation and apportionment (including UDITPA, MTC, and apportionment factors), certain credits against corporate income tax, combined returns, and consolidated filing.

Estimated tax, withholding, and information returns are also covered, as well as conformity with federal bonus depreciations, extended net operating loss carryback provisions, and various provisions of the federal American Jobs Creation Act of 2004 (AJCA) (P.L. 108-357).

In addition, there are charts dealing with the taxation of other types of entities, including limited liability companies, S corporation, utilities, insurance companies, and financial companies.

STATE CORPORATE INCOME TAXES

State	Return Due Dates		Will State Accept Federal Return Filing Extension?	Net Operating Losses Carryback years/ Carryforward years†	Federal Income Tax Deductible
	Calendar	Fiscal			
AL	3-15	15th, 3rd mo.	Yes*	0 back, 15 forward[10]	Yes
AK	(1)	(1)	Yes	2 back, 20 forward	No
AZ	4-15	15th, 4th mo.[2]	Yes*	0 back, 5 forward	No
AR	3-15[3]	(4)	Yes	0 back, 5 forward	No
CA	3-15	15th, 3rd mo.[2,5]	No	0 back, 10 forward[6]	No
CO	4-15	15th, 4th mo.	No	0 back, 20 forward	No
CT	4-1	1st, 4th mo.	No	0 back, 20 forward	No
DE	4-1	1st, 4th mo.	Yes	2 back, 20 forward[7]	No
DC	3-15	15th, 3rd mo.[2]	No	0 back, 20 forward	No
FL	4-1	1st, 4th mo.	No	0 back, 20 forward	No
GA	3-15	15th, 3rd mo.	Yes	2 back, 20 forward	No
HI	4-20	20th, 4th mo.	No	2 back, 20 forward	No
ID	4-15	15th, 4th mo.[5]	No	2 back, 20 forward[8]	No
IL	3-15	15th, 3rd mo.[2,5]	Yes	0 back, 12 forward[9]	No
IN	4-15	15th, 4th mo.[2]	Yes	2 back, 20 forward	No
IA	4-30	Last day, 4th mo.[5]	No	2 back, 20 forward	Yes[11]
KS	4-15	15th, 4th mo.	Yes	0 back, 10 forward	No
KY	4-15	15th, 4th mo.	Yes	0 back, 20 forward	No
LA	4-15	15th, 4th mo.	Yes	3 back, 15 forward	Yes
ME	3-15	15th, 3rd mo.	Yes	0 back, 20 forward	No
MD	3-15	15th, 3rd mo.	No	2 back, 20 forward	No
MA	3-15	15th, 3rd mo.	No	0 back, 5 forward	No
MI[12]	4-30	Last day, 4th mo.	No	0 back, 10 forward	No
MN	3-15	15th, 3rd mo.[2,5]	No	0 back, 15 forward	No
MS	3-15	15th, 3rd mo.	Yes*	2 back, 20 forward	No
MO	4-15	15th, 4th mo.	Yes	2 back, 20 forward	Yes[11]
MT	5-15	15th, 5th mo.	No	3 back, 7 forward	No
NE	3-15	15th, 3rd mo.	Yes	0 back, 5 forward	No
NH	3-15	15th, 3rd mo.[2,13]	No	3 back, 10 forward	No
NJ	4-15	15th, 4th mo.	No	0 back, 7 forward[14]	No
NM	3-15	15th, 3rd mo.	Yes	0 back, 5 forward	No
NY	3-15	15th, 3rd mo.	No	2 back, 20 forward[15]	No
NC	3-15	15th, 3rd mo.[5]	No	0 back, 15 forward	No
ND	4-15	15th, 4th mo.[2,5]	Yes	0 back, 20 forward[16]	Yes
OH	(17)	(17)	No	0 back, 20 forward	No
OK	3-15	15th, 3rd mo.	Yes*	2 back, 20 forward	No
OR	(18)	(18)	Yes	0 back, 15 forward	No
PA	4-15	(1)	No	0 back, 20 forward[19]	No
RI	3-15	15th, 3rd mo.	No	0 back, 5 forward	No
SC	3-15	15th, 3rd mo.[2]	Yes	0 back, 20 forward	No
TN	4-15	15th, 4th mo.	No	0 back, 15 forward	No
TX	5-15	5-15[20]	No	0 back, 5 forward	No
UT	4-15	15th, 4th mo.	No	3 back, 15 forward[21]	No
VT	3-15	15th, 3rd mo.	Yes*	0 back, 10 forward[51]	No
VA	4-15	15th, 4th mo.[22]	Yes	2 back, 20 forward	No
WV	3-15	15th, 3rd mo.	Yes	2 back, 20 forward[23]	No
WI	3-15	15th, 3rd mo.	Yes	0 back, 15 forward	No

2006 CORPORATE INCOME TAX REQUIREMENTS

Due Date for Report of Change In Federal Return	Federal Income Used as State Tax Base	Allow Federal ACRS or MACRS Depreciation	Allow Federal Asset Expense Election	Allow Federal Bonus Depreciation	Allow Federal Depletion	State
None	Yes	Yes	Yes	Yes	No[31]	AL
60 days	Yes	Yes	Yes	Yes	Yes[31]	AK
90 days	Yes	Yes	Yes[27]	No	Yes[24]	AZ
30 days	No	Yes	Yes[28]	No	Yes	AR
6 months	Yes	No	No	No	Yes	CA
30 days	Yes	Yes	Yes	Yes	Yes[26]	CO
90 days	Yes	Yes	Yes	No	Yes	CT
90 days	Yes	Yes	Yes	Yes	Yes[31]	DE
90 days	No	Yes	Yes[28]	No	Yes	DC
60 days	Yes	Yes	Yes	Yes	Yes	FL
180 days	Yes	Yes	Yes	No	Yes	GA
90 days	Yes	Yes	Yes[28]	No	Yes	HI
60 days	Yes	Yes	Yes	No	Yes	ID
120 days	Yes	Yes	Yes	No[52]	Yes	IL
120 days	Yes	Yes	Yes[28]	No	Yes	IN
None	Yes	Yes	Yes	No[40]	Yes[31]	IA
180 days	Yes	Yes	Yes	Yes	Yes	KS
30 days[29]	Yes	Yes	Yes[28]	No	Yes[30]	KY
60 days	Yes	Yes	Yes	Yes	Yes[31]	LA
90 days	Yes	Yes	Yes[28]	No[48]	Yes	ME
90 days	Yes	Yes	Yes[28]	No	Yes[32]	MD
3 months	Yes	Yes	Yes	No	Yes	MA
120 days	Yes[33]	No	No	No[49]	Yes	(12)MI
180 days	Yes	Yes	Yes	No[34]	No[35]	MN
30 days	No	Yes	Yes	No	Yes[35]	MS
90 days	Yes	Yes	Yes	No[40]	Yes	MO
90 days	Yes	Yes	Yes	Yes	Yes[35]	MT
90 days	Yes	Yes	Yes[36]	No[34]	Yes	NE
6 months	Yes	Yes	Yes[28]	No	Yes[31]	NH
90 days	Yes	Yes[37]	Yes[28]	No	Yes	NJ
90 days	Yes	Yes	Yes	Yes	Yes	NM
90 days[38]	Yes	Yes[39]	Yes[45]	No[47]	Yes	NY
6 months (previously 2 years)[50]	Yes	Yes	Yes	No[34]	Yes[31]	NC
90 days	Yes	Yes[41]	Yes	Yes	Yes	ND
1 year	Yes	Yes	Yes[28]	No[34]	Yes	OH
1 year	Yes	Yes	Yes	No[34]	Yes[42]	OK
90 days	Yes	Yes[43]	Yes	Yes	No[44]	OR
30 days	Yes	Yes[25]	Yes	No[48]	Yes	PA
60 days	Yes	Yes	Yes[28]	No	Yes	RI
180 days	Yes	Yes	Yes[28]	No	Yes	SC
None	Yes	Yes	Yes	No	Yes[35]	TN
120 days	Yes	Yes	Yes[28]	No[46]	Yes[31]	TX
90 days	Yes	Yes	Yes	Yes	Yes	UT
60 days	Yes	Yes	Yes	No	Yes	VT
1 year (previously 90 days)[50]	Yes	Yes	Yes	No	Yes	VA
90 days	Yes	Yes	Yes	Yes	Yes	WV
90 days	Yes	Yes	Yes[28]	No	No[31]	WI

[1] Due 30 days after federal return.

[2] Exempt organizations, 15th day of 5th month.

[3] Cooperatives, Sept. 15th.

[4] 2½months after fiscal year closing date. Cooperatives, 8½ months after fiscal year closing date.

[5] Cooperatives, Sept. 15th or 15th day of 9th month.

[6] NOL deduction suspended for 2002 and 2003. Normal carryover period is extended by one year for losses during 2002 and by two years for losses before 2002. After 2003, entire NOL may be carried forward.

[7] Carryback limited to $30,000.

[8] Carryback limited to $100,000 (or 0/20 provisions available).

[9] For taxable years ending on or after December 31, 1999, and prior to December 31, 2003, carry back was 2 years and carry forward was 20 years.

[10] NOL deduction is suspended for 2001. Normal carryover period is extended by one year.

[11] Federal income tax deduction is 50% of federal tax paid.

[12] Michigan imposes a single business tax instead of a corporate income tax.

[13] 15th day of 4th month for interest and dividend returns.

[14] NOL deduction is suspended for 2002 and 2003 and limited to 50% of entire net income for 2004 and 2005. Normal carryover period is extended by a period equal to the disallowance period.

[15] Carryback limited to $10,000.

[16] North Dakota allows a 2 year carryback only for NOL's incurred in taxable years beginning before 2003.

[17] Returns due between Jan. 1 and March 31. For tax years beginning on or after July 1, 2005, commercial activity tax (CAT) returns are due on February 10 or 40 days after end of tax period.

[18] Returns due 15th day of the month after due date of related federal return.

[19] Limited to $2 million. For taxable years beginning after 2006, limit will be $3 million or 12.5% of taxable income, whichever is greater.

[20] All Texas franchise tax reports must be filed on the basis of a calendar year; however, special rules apply for a corporation's first year subject to the tax.

[21] Carryback limited to $1 million.

[22] Exempt Organizations, 5th day of the 6th month.

[23] Carryback limited to $300,000.

[24] Except for mining exploration expenses.

[25] Straight-line depreciation required for realty.

[26] Except 27.5% rate for depletion of oil shale.

[27] Limits asset expense election to pre-Jobs and Growth Tax Relief Reconciliation Act of 2003 (JGTRRA) amount of $25,000 plus 20% of amounts exceeding the limit in years one through four.

[28] Limits asset expense election to pre-JGTRRA amount of $25,000.

[29] Notice required within 30 days after notice of federal examination and within 30 days after final determination.

[30] Special provisions for coal royalties.

[31] Except for oil and gas wells.

[32] Percentage depletion for oil not allowed.

[33] Major components of base are compensation, business income, and additions and subtractions to business income.

[34] Addback required for a portion of bonus depreciation and a subtraction allowed for a portion of the addback in subsequent years.

[35] Cost depletion only.

[36] Limits asset expense election to pre-JGTRRA amount of $25,000 plus 20% of amounts exceeding the limit beginning on or after January 1, 2006.

[37] MACRS may be used to depreciate property placed in service after July 7, 1993.

[38] 120 days for taxpayers filing combined returns.

[39] Except property placed in service in N.Y. after 1984 and before 1994.

[40] Allows 50% bonus depreciation for property purchased from May 6, 2003, through December 31, 2004, but disallows 30% bonus depreciation for property purchased after September 10, 2001 and before September 11, 2004.

[41] For assets placed in service after 1983.

[42] 22% allowance for oil and gas in lieu of federal depletion allowance, not to exceed 50% of net income for major oil companies.

[43] Conformity after 1994.

[44] Percentage depletion allowed only on metal mines.

[45] Except sport utility vehicles weighing over 6000 pounds.

[46] Allows bonus depreciation for corporations (including S corporations, close corporations, and corporations with taxable capital of less than $1 million) that qualify and elect to use the FIT (federal income tax) method of reporting taxable capital as long as the same method was used in the corporation's most recent federal income tax return.

[47] Except with respect to qualified Resurgence Zone property and qualified New York Liberty Zone property.

[48] Addback required for entire amount of bonus depreciation and a subtraction allowed for a portion of the addback in subsequent years.

[49] Allows bonus depreciation in computing federal taxable income amount that is the tax base for the Single Business Tax. However, federal depreciation deduction must be added to federal taxable income for purposes of determining Michigan tax base

[50] Effective on or after July 1, 2006.

[51] For 2007, Vermont NOL carryforward amount equals same proportion of the Vermont NOL as the proportion of the federal NOL that was carried forward in determining federal taxable income plus 10% of remaining Vermont NOL; for 2008, increased by 30% of remaining Vermont NOL; for 2009, increased by 40% of remaining Vermont NOL. For tax years prior to 2006, 2 back, 20 forward.

[52] Addback required. For tax years after 2000 and before 2006, subtraction allowed for 42.9% of regular depreciation until the bonus depreciation disallowance has been claimed. For tax years after 2005, subtraction allowed for 42.9% of regular depreciation on property for which 30% bonus depreciation was taken and 100% of regular depreciation on property for which 50% bonus depreciation deduction was taken.

* State imposes additional requirements.

† The federal Job Creation and Worker's Assistance Act extended the carryback from two to five years for NOLs arising in 2001 and 2002. Alaska, Delaware, Indiana, New York, North Dakota, Oklahoma, Vermont, and West Virginia conform to the extended federal provision.

Table of 2006 Corporate Income Tax Rates

ALABAMA[1]
. . . . 6.5%

ALASKA[2]
Less than $10,000 . . . 1%
Next $10,000 . . . . 2%
Next $10,000 . . . . 3%
Next $10,000 . . . . 4%
Next $10,000 . . . . 5%
Next $10,000 . . . . 6%
Next $10,000 . . . . 7%
Next $10,000 . . . . 8%
Next $10,000 . . . . 9%
$90,000 or more 9.4%

ARIZONA[3]
. . . . 6.968%

ARKANSAS
1st $3,000 . . . . 1%
2nd $3,000 . . . . 2%
Next $5,000 . . . . 3%
Next $14,000 . . . . 5%
Next $75,000 . . . . 6%
Over $100,000 . . . . . . 6.5%

CALIFORNIA[4]
. . . . 8.84%

COLORADO[5]
. . . . 4.63%

CONNECTICUT[6]
. . . . 7.5%

DELAWARE[7]
. . . . 8.7%

DISTRICT OF COLUMBIA[8]
. . . . 9.975%

FLORIDA[9]
. . . . 5.5%

GEORGIA
. . . . 6%

HAWAII[10]
First $25,000 . . . . 4.4%
Next $75,000 . . . . 5.4%
Over $100,000 . . . . . . 6.4%

IDAHO[11]
. . . . 7.6%

ILLINOIS[12]
. . . . 4.8%

INDIANA[13]
. . . . 8.5%

IOWA[14]
1st $25,000 . . . . 6%

Next $75,000 . . . . 8%
Next $150,000 . . . . . . 10%
Over $250,000 . . . . . . 12%

KANSAS[15]
. . . . 4%

KENTUCKY[16]
1st $50,000 . . . . 4%
Next $50,000 . . . . 5%
Over $100,000 . . . . . . 7%

LOUISIANA
1st $25,000 . . . . 4%
Next $25,000 . . . . 5%
Next $50,000 . . . . 6%
Next $100,000 . . . . . . 7%
Over $200,000 . . . . . . 8%

MAINE[17]
1st $25,000 . . . . 3.5%
Next $50,000 . . . . 7.93%
Next $175,000 . . . . . . 8.33%
Over $250,000 . . . . . . 8.93%

MARYLAND
. . . . 7%

MASSACHUSETTS[18]

MICHIGAN[19]
. . . . 1.9%

MINNESOTA[20]
. . . . 9.8%

MISSISSIPPI
1st $5,000 . . . . 3%
Next $5,000 . . . . 4%
Over $10,000 . . . . 5%

MISSOURI[21]
. . . . 6.25%

MONTANA[22]
. . . . 6.75%

NEBRASKA
1st $50,000 . . . . 5.58%
Over $50,000 . . . . 7.81%

NEW HAMPSHIRE[23]
. . . . 8.5%

NEW JERSEY[24]
Corporations with entire
net income of $50,000 or
less 6.5%
Corporations with entire
net income of $100,000 or
less 7.5%
All other corporations . . 9%

NEW MEXICO[25]
1st $500,000 . . . . 4.8%
2nd $500,000 . . . . 6.4%
Over $1 million 7.6%

NEW YORK[26]

NORTH CAROLINA
. . . . 6.9%

NORTH DAKOTA[27]
1st $3,000 . . . . 2.6%
Next $5,000 . . . . 4.1%
Next $12,000 . . . . 5.6%
Next $10,000 . . . . 6.4%
Over $30,000 . . . . 7%

OHIO[28]

OKLAHOMA
. . . . 6%

OREGON[29]
. . . . 6.6%

PENNSYLVANIA
. . . . 9.99%

RHODE ISLAND[30]
. . . . 9%

SOUTH CAROLINA[31]
. . . . 5%

TENNESSEE[32]
. . . . 6.5%

TEXAS[33]
. . . . 4.5%

UTAH[34]
. . . . 5%

VERMONT[35]
$0-$10,000 . . . . $0 plus 6.0%
$10,001-$25,000 . . . . $600 plus 7.0%
$25,001-$250,000 . . . $1,650 plus 8.75%
$250,001 and over . . . . $21,338 plus 8.9%

VIRGINIA[36]
. . . . 6%

WEST VIRGINIA
. . . . 9%

WISCONSIN[37]
. . . . 7.9%

[1] Alabama: Qualified taxpayers may elect alternative tax of 0.25% of gross sales in Alabama during the tax year. S corporations pay a 5% tax on net recognized built-in gains and excess net passive income.

[2] Alaska: Alternative minimum tax rate on capital gains is 4.5%. Alternative minimum tax on tax preference items is 18% of the applicable alternative minimum federal tax. The personal holding company tax rate is 12.6% of apportioned income; and the accumulated earnings tax rate is 4.95% of the first $100,000 and 6.93% of the excess.

[3] Arizona: Minimum tax, $50.

[4] California: Minimum tax, $800. Banks and financial corporations, excepting financial S corporations, are subject to a 10.84% tax rate (the general corporation rate, plus 2%). A 3.5% tax rate applies to financial S corporations, and a 1.5% rate applies to all other S corporations. A 6.65% alternative minimum tax is imposed.

[5] Colorado: Qualified taxpayers may pay an alternative tax of 0.5% of gross receipts from sales in or into Colorado.

[6] Connecticut: Tax is the greater of: (1) 7.5%; (2) $3^1/_{10}$ mills per dollar of capital holding; or (3) the minimum tax of $250. Financial institutions pay a tax equal to the greater of (1) 7.5% or (2) 4% of the interest of dividends credited on depositors' or account holders' savings accounts. A 20% surtax applies to corporations with tax liability greater than $250. After 2006, the surcharge is repealed. Corporations filing combined returns subject to additional tax of up to $250,000.

[7] Delaware: Headquarters management corporations pay minimum tax of $5,000 or tax at rate of 8.7% on taxable income, whichever is greater. Banking organizations taxed at rate of 8.7% for first $20 million, 6.7% for next $5 million, 4.7% for next $5 million, 2.7% for next $620 million, and 1.7% for amounts in excess of $650 million.

[8] District of Columbia: Minimum tax, $100. $5,500 ball park fee imposed on gross receipts of $5 million to $8 million, $10,800 on gross receipts of $8,000,001 to $12 million, $14,000 on gross receipts of $12,000,001 to $16 million, and $16,500 on gross receipts of $16,000,001 or more.

[9] Florida: Taxpayers who pay federal alternative minimum tax (AMT) are liable for the greater of the Florida corporate income tax or the 3.3% Florida AMT. An emergency excise tax applies to certain taxpayers that claimed the ACRs depreciation deduction during tax years 1980 through 1986.

[10] Hawaii: Qualified taxpayers with Hawaii sales of $100,000 or less may pay an alternative tax of 0.5% of Hawaii gross annual sales. Tax on banks and other financial corporations is imposed at the rate of 7.92% of net income. An alternative tax on capital gains is imposed at the rate of 4%.

[11] Idaho: Minimum tax, $20. Additional $10 tax on each corporation filing a return and having gross income during the tax year. Qualified taxpayers may pay alternative tax of 1% of dollar volume from Idaho sales.

[12] Illinois: Additional 2.5% personal property replacement tax imposed, for corporations other than S corporations. 1.5% for S corporations, partnerships, and trusts.

[13] Indiana: 5% on adjusted gross income derived from sources within a qualified area that contains an inactive or closed military base.

[14] Iowa: Financial institutions are subject to a 5% franchise tax. An alternative minimum tax is imposed at the rate of 60% of the highest corporate income tax rate, rounded to the nearest 0.1%.

[15] Kansas: A 3.35% surtax is imposed on taxable income in excess of $50,000. Qualified corporations may pay the alternative gross receipts tax allowed as an option by the Multistate Tax Compact; no tax rate has been set. Certain financial institutions pay a privilege tax at a rate of 2.25% of net income, plus a surtax of 2.125% (2.25% for trust companies and savings and loan associations with net income in excess of $25,000.)

[16] Kentucky: Minimum tax, $175. Corporations with over $3 million in gross receipts or gross profits from all sources must pay the greater of the tax based on taxable net income, the minimum tax, or an alternative minimum tax equal to the lesser of 9.5 cents per $100 of Kentucky gross receipts or 75 cents per $100 of Kentucky gross profits.

[17] Maine: Alternative minimum tax imposed equal to 5.4% of alternative minimum taxable income. The state franchise tax on financial institutions is the sum of 1% of the Maine net income of the financial institution for the taxable year, plus 8¢ per $1,000 of the institution's assets as of the end of its taxable year.

[18] Massachusetts: Corporations pay an excise equal to the greater of the following: (a) $2.60 (includes surtax) per $1,000 of value of Massachusetts tangible property not taxed locally or net worth allocated to Massachusetts, plus 9.5% (includes surtax) of net income; or (b) $456 (includes surtax), whichever is greater. (A surtax of 14% is imposed.) Special rates apply to security corporations, qualified subchapter S subsidiaries, financial institutions, utilities, and vessels.

[19] Michigan: Rate effective Jan. 1 provided the comprehensive annual report for the state shows an ending balance under $250 million. Insurance companies subject to the single business tax pay a surcharge that is the product of 1.26 times the taxpayer's tax liability before the application of any credits.

[20] Minnesota: Alternative minimum tax equal to the excess of 5.8% of Minnesota alternative minimum taxable income over the basic tax is imposed. Corporations are subject to an additional minimum tax ranging from $0 to $5,000 depending on the Minnesota property, payrolls, and sales or receipts and the type of corporation or partnership.

[21] Missouri: Financial institutions are taxed at a rate equal to the sum of (1) 0.05% of the par value of the institution's outstanding shares and surplus employed in Missouri and (2) 7% of the institution's net income for the income period minus the tax computed on their shares and surplus under (1) and the credits allowable for other state and local taxes.

[22] Montana: $50 minimum tax. Taxpayers making a water's-edge election are taxed at 7%. Qualified corporations may elect to pay an alternative tax of 1/2% of gross sales in Montana during the tax year.

[23] New Hampshire: 8.5% of taxable business profits if gross income over $50,000. For gross income over $150,000 or base over $75,000, the business enterprise tax also applies at a rate of .75% of business enterprise value base.

[24] New Jersey: Corporations must pay the greater of the tax based on taxable net income, an alternative minimum assessment, if applicable, based on gross receipts or gross profits, or a minimum tax of between $500 and $2000, depending on amount of gross receipts. $2,000 minimum tax for members of affiliated or controlled group with total payroll of $5 million or more. For privilege periods ending on or after July 1, 2006, and before July 1, 2009, surtax imposed at rate of 4%.

[25] New Mexico: Qualified taxpayers may pay an alternative tax of 0.75% of gross receipts from New Mexico sales.

[26] Corporations are subject to tax on the greatest of 7.5% of entire net income with adjustments, 2.5% alternative minimum tax base, 1.78 mills per dollar of allocated capital (up to $350,000 for manufacturers or $1 million for other taxpayers), or a minimum tax between $100 and $1,500, depending on payroll size. $800 minimum tax if gross payroll, total receipts, and average value of gross assets are each $1,000 or less. Additional 9/10 mill per dollar of allocated subsidiary capital is imposed. Special rates apply to small business taxpayers. S corporations are subject to the fixed dollar minimum tax.

[27] North Dakota: Corporations making a water's-edge election must pay an additional 3.5% tax. Financial institutions are subject to a financial institutions tax of 7% of taxable income with a minimum amount of $50 in lieu of the corporate income tax. Taxpayers with North Dakota sales of $100,000 or less may be eligible to pay the alternative gross receipts tax allowed as an option by the Multistate Tax Compact at the following rates: 0.6% of the first $20,000 of North Dakota sales, 0.8% of North Dakota sales above $20,000 and not exceeding $55,000, and 1% of all North Dakota sales above $55,000.

[28] Ohio: Franchise tax is 80% of the greater of (1) 5.1% on 1st $50,000 of net income and 8.5% on net income in excess of $50,000 or (2) 4 mills times net worth up to $150,000 maximum. Commercial activity tax (CAT) is $150 on gross receipts greater than $150,000 up to $1 million. For gross receipts exceeding $1 million, CAT is $150 plus 0.26% multiplied by (1) 23% for the measurement period from January 1 through March 31; and (2) 40% for for the measurement period from April 1 through December 31. Minimum franchise tax is $50 or $1,000 for corporations that have either (1) $5 million or more in worldwide gross receipts for the taxable year, or (2) 300 or more employees worldwide at any time during the taxable year.

[29] Oregon: Minimum tax, $10. Qualified taxpayers may elect to pay alternative tax of 0.25% of the dollar volume of sales in Oregon (0.0125% of the dollar volume of sales if the return on sales for the business is less than 5%).

[30] Rhode Island: Minimum tax, $500. The franchise tax, which is imposed to the extent that it exceeds the business corporation tax, is generally assessed at the rate of $2.50 for each $10,000 of authorized capital stock or fractional part thereof, or the sum of $500, whichever is greater. The annual tax on federally registered personal holding companies, RICs, and REITs is equal to the greater of $100 or 10 cents on each $100 of gross income. Special rates apply to public utilities.

[31] South Carolina: Banks are taxed at a rate of 4.5%. Associations are taxed at 6% on most net income after the first three years of operation.

[32] Tennessee: Corporations are also subject to the tax on dividends and interest and a franchise tax.

[33] Texas: The tax is equal to the greater of either 0.25% of its net taxable capital or 4.5% of its net taxable earned surplus.

[34] Utah: Minimum tax, $100. Nonprofit utilities are subject to an in lieu gross receipts tax.

[35] Vermont: Minimum tax, $250 ($75 for small farm corporations).

[36] Virginia: Telecommunication companies are subject to a minimum tax equal to 0.5% of a companies gross receipts for the calendar year, in lieu of the 6% corporate income tax rate if the corporate income tax liability is less than the minimum tax liability.

[37] Wisconsin: Corporations with at least $4 million in gross receipts for the taxable year must also pay recycling surcharge based on income tax liability without regard to tax credits.

STATE PERSONAL INCOME TAXES

State	Return Due Dates		State Accepts Federal Return Filing Extension	Optional Standard Deduction	Federal Income Used as State Tax Base	Federal Income Tax Deductible
	Calendar	Fiscal				
AL . . .	4-15	15th, 4th mo.	No	Yes	No	Yes
AZ . . .	4-15	15th, 4th mo.	Yes*	Yes	Yes	No
AR . .	4-15	3¹/₂ mos.	Yes*	Yes	No	No
CA . .	4-15	15th, 4th mo.	No(14)	Yes	Yes	No
CO . .	4-15	15th, 4th mo.	Yes	Yes(4)	Yes	No
CT . .	4-15	15th, 4th mo.	Yes(15)	No	Yes	No
DE . .	4-30	30th, 4th mo.	Yes(22)	Yes	Yes	No
DC . .	4-15	15th, 4th mo.	No	Yes(11)	Yes	No
GA . .	4-15	15th, 4th mo.	Yes	Yes(11)	Yes	No
HI . . .	4-20	20th, 4th mo.	No(23)	Yes	Yes	No
ID . . .	4-15	15th, 4th mo.	No(14)	Yes	Yes	No
IL . . .	4-15	15th, 4th mo.	Yes*,(14)	No	Yes	No
IN . . .	4-15	15th, 4th mo.	Yes*,(24)	No	Yes	No
IA . . .	4-30	Last day, 4th mo.	No(14)	Yes	No	Yes
KS . .	4-15	15th, 4th mo.	Yes	Yes	Yes	No
KY . .	4-15	15th, 4th mo.	Yes	Yes	Yes	No
LA . . .	5-15	15th, 5th mo.	Yes	No	Yes	Yes
ME . .	4-15	15th, 4th mo.	Yes*	Yes(4),(20)	Yes	No
MD . .	4-15	15th, 4th mo.	Yes(15)	Yes(11)	Yes	No
MA . .	4-15	15th, 4th mo.	No(25)	No	Yes	No
MI . . .	4-15	15th, 4th mo.	Yes*	No	Yes	No
MN . .	4-15	15th, 4th mo.	Yes	Yes(4)	Yes	No
MS . .	4-15	15th, 4th mo.	Yes(15)	Yes	No	No
MO . .	4-15	15th, 4th mo.	Yes	Yes(11)	Yes	Yes(8)
MT . .	4-15	15th, 4th mo.	No	Yes	Yes	Yes(8)
NE . .	4-15	15th, 4th mo.	Yes	Yes	Yes	No
NH(6) .	4-15	15th, 4th mo.	No(26)	No	No	No
NJ . . .	4-15	15th, 4th mo.	Yes*	No	No	No
NM . .	4-15	15th, 4th mo.(19)	No	Yes(4)	Yes	No
NY . .	4-15	15th, 4th mo.	Yes*,(15)	Yes	Yes	No
NC . .	4-15	15th, 4th mo.	No	Yes(16)	Yes	No
ND . .	4-15	15th, 4th mo.	Yes	Yes(4)	Yes	Yes(5)
OH . .	4-15	15th, 4th mo.	Yes	No	Yes	No
OK . .	4-15	15th, 4th mo.	Yes*	Yes(11)	Yes	Yes
OR . .	4-15	15th, 4th mo.	Yes	Yes	Yes	Yes(8)
PA . .	4-15	15th, 4th mo.	Yes*	No	No	No
RI . . .	4-15	15th, 4th mo.	Yes*	Yes(4),(20)	Yes	No
SC . .	4-15	15th, 4th mo.	Yes*	Yes(4)	Yes	No
TN(6) .	4-15	15th, 4th mo.	Yes	No(9)	No	No
UT . .	4-15	15th, 4th mo.	No(14)	Yes(4)	Yes	Yes(3)
VT . . .	4-15	15th, 4th mo.	No(14)	Yes(4)	Yes	No
VA . .	5-1	15th, 4th mo.	Yes	Yes(11)	Yes	No
WV . .	4-15	15th, 4th mo.	Yes*	No	Yes	No
WI . . .	4-15	15th, 4th mo.	Yes	Yes(12)	Yes	No

† The federal Job Creation and Worker's Assistance Act extended the carryback from two to five years for NOLs arising in 2001 and 2002. Colorado, Connecticut, Delaware, Illinois, Louisiana, Michigan, Minnesota, Montana, New York, North Carolina, North Dakota, Ohio, Oklahoma, Utah, and West Virginia conform to the extended federal provisions.

* State imposes additional requirements.

(1) Notice required after federal examination and after final determination.

(2) Failure to report suspends running of statute of limitations.

(3) One-half of federal tax paid is excluded.

(4) Federal standard deduction is allowed.

(5) Only if ND-2 (Optional Method) is filed.

(6) The tax applies only to interest and dividend income.

(7) Limited to taxes paid on compensation for personal services.

(8) Deductions limited.

(9) Each taxpayer is allowed a $1,250 exclusion ($2,500 for joint filers).

(10) Reports not required of resident individuals.

(11) Standard deduction must be claimed if federal return reflects a standard deduction.

(12) Deduction decreases as income rises.

(13) Limited credit for taxes paid on gain from the sale of a partnership interest where state of domicile does not allow credit for tax paid to MN on gain.

(14) 6-month automatic state extension allowed.

(15) If taxpayer expects to owe no tax for the taxable year.

(16) As federal taxable income is starting point for determining NC taxable income, standard deduction relevant only for determining difference between allowable federal and NC amounts for required add backs.

STATE PERSONAL INCOME TAX REQUIREMENTS

Net Operating Losses Carryback years/ Carryforward years †	Credit Allowed for Income Taxes Paid Other States		Due Date for Report of Change in	
	(a) Res.	(b) Nonres.	Federal Return	State
2 back, 15 forward	Yes	No	None	AL
2 back, 20 forward	Yes	Yes	90 days	AZ
0 back, 5 forward(27)	Yes	Yes	30 days	AR
0 back, 10 forward	Yes	Yes	6 months	CA
2 back, 20 forward	Yes	No	30 days	CO
2 back, 20 forward(21)	Yes	No	90 days	CT
2 back, 20 forward(17)	Yes	No	90 days	DE
2 back, 20 forward	Yes	No	90 days	DC
2 back, 20 forward	Yes	No	180 days	GA
2 back, 20 forward	Yes	No	90 days	HI
2 back, 20 forward(18)	Yes	No	60 days	ID
0 back, 12 forward	Yes	No	120 days	IL
2 back, 20 forward	Yes	Yes	120 days(10)	IN
2 back, 20 forward	Yes	Yes	None(2)	IA
0 back, 10 forward	Yes	No	180 days	KS
0 back, 20 forward	Yes	No	30 days(1)	KY
2 back, 20 forward	Yes	No	60 days	LA
0 back, 20 forward	Yes	No	90 days	ME
2 back, 20 forward	Yes	No	90 days	MD
None	Yes	No	1 year	MA
2 back, 20 forward	Yes	No	120 days	MI
0 back, 15 forward	Yes	No(13)	180 days	MN
2 back, 20 forward	Yes	No	30 days	MS
2 back, 20 forward	Yes	No	90 days	MO
2 back, 20 forward	Yes(29)	No	90 days	MT
2 back, 20 forward	Yes	No	90 days	NE
None	No	......	6 months	(6)NH
None	Yes	No	90 days	NJ
0 back, 5 forward	Yes	No	90 days	NM
2 back, 20 forward(21)	Yes	No	90 days	NY
2 back, 20 forward	Yes	No	2 yrs.	NC
2 back, 20 forward	Yes	No	90 days	ND
2 back, 20 forward	Yes	Yes	60 days	OH
2 back, 20 forward	Yes(7)	No	1 year	OK
2 back, 20 forward	Yes	Yes	90 days	OR
None	Yes	No	30 days	PA
0 back, 20 forward	Yes	No	90 days	RI
0 back, 20 forward	Yes	No	180 days	SC
None	No(28)	......	None	TN(6)
2 back, 20 forward	Yes	No	90 days	UT
2 back, 20 forward	Yes	No	30 days	VT
2 back, 20 forward	Yes	Yes	90 days(32)	VA
2 back, 20 forward	Yes	No(31)	90 days	WV
0 back, 15 forward	Yes(30)	No	90 days	WI

(17) Carryback limited to $30,000.
(18) Carryback limited to $100,000 (or 0/20 provisions available).
(19) Calendar year electronic filers, 30th, 4th, mo.
(20) Increased IRC Sec. 63 standard deduction for married couples filing jointly not allowed.
(21) Nonresidents with state NOL, but no federal NOL, 3 back, 15 forward.
(22) If balance due on return will be zero or less and federal extension has been filed.
(23) 4-month automatic state extension allowed.
(24) Taxpayer has 30 days beyond federal extension period to file state return.
(25) Taxpayers who do not expect to owe tax may submit copy of federal extension form in lieu of MA application for 6-month extension.
(26) Automatic 7-month extension to file state return granted upon full payment of tax by original due date.
(27) 10 year NOL carryforward for qualified steel manufacturers.
(28) Limited credit may be allowed if resident individual is a shareholder of an S corporation, provided there is a tax credit reciprocity agreement between TN and the other state.
(29) Credit not allowed if the other state allows MT residents a credit against tax imposed by the other state.
(30) Credit not allowed for taxes paid to a state with which Wisconsin has a reciprocity agreement (IL, IN, KY, MI, and MN).
(31) Credit allowed against WV tax for tax imposed by another state, of which the taxpayer is a resident, if there is a written reciprocal credit agreement between WV and the other state (KY, MD, OH, PA, and VA).
(32) Effective July 1, 2006, 1 year.

Personal Income Table of 2006 Rates

This chart provides the tax rates that the states and the District of Columbia impose on personal income. The graduated rate information is presented in a format that includes a subtraction amount, which is used to properly reflect the cumulative tax calculated for the lower graduated rates. The use of this format for all of the states allows the rate information to be presented in a uniform way.

States that do not impose a personal income tax are not included in this chart. The rates shown are state rates only. Local income taxes may apply.

* Brackets indexed for inflation annually.

† 2006 adjusted brackets not currently available. Bracketed rates listed are for 2005.

ALABAMA

Single, Married filed separately, Head of family

$0	– 500	×	2.000%	minus	$0
500	– 3,000	×	4.000%	minus	10
3,001 and over		×	5.000%	minus	40

Married filing jointly

$0	– 1,000	×	2.000%	minus	$0
1,000	– 6,000	×	4.000%	minus	20
6,001 and over		×	5.000%	minus	80

ARIZONA[1]

Single, Married filing separately

$0	– 10,000	×	2.730%	minus	$0
10,001	– 25,000	×	3.040%	minus	31
25,001	– 50,000	×	3.550%	minus	158.50
50,001	– 150,000	×	4.480%	minus	623
150,001 and over		×	4.790%	minus	1088

Married filing jointly, Head of household

$0	– 20,000	×	2.730%	minus	$0
20,001	– 50,000	×	3.040%	minus	62
50,001	– 100,000	×	3.550%	minus	317
100,001	– 300,000	×	4.480%	minus	1247
300,001 and over		×	4.790%	minus	2177

ARKANSAS[2]*†

$0	– 3,499	×	1.000%	minus	$0
3,500	– 6,999	×	2.500%	minus	52.49
7,000	– 10,499	×	3.500%	minus	122.48
10,500	– 17,499	×	4.500%	minus	227.47

State Tax Handbook

| 17,500 | – | 29,199 | × | 6.000% | minus | 489.96 |
| 29,200 and over | | | × | 7.000% | minus | 781.95 |

CALIFORNIA[1],[3]*

Single, Married filing separately

$0	–	6,622	×	1.000%	minus	$0
6,623	–	15,698	×	2.000%	minus	66.22
15,699	–	24,776	×	4.000%	minus	380.18
24,777	–	34,394	×	6.000%	minus	875.70
34,395	–	43,467	×	8.000%	minus	1,563.58
43,468 and over			×	9.300%	minus	2,218.65

Married filing jointly, Qualifying Widow/Widower

$0	–	13,244	×	1.000%	minus	$0
13,245	–	31,396	×	2.000%	minus	132.44
31,397	–	49,552	×	4.000%	minus	760.36
49,553	–	68,788	×	6.000%	minus	1751.40
68,789	–	86,934	×	8.000%	minus	3,127.16
86,935 and over			×	9.300%	minus	4,257.30

Head of household

$0	–	13,251	×	1.000%	minus	$0
13,252	–	31,397	×	2.000%	minus	132.51
31,398	–	40,473	×	4.000%	minus	760.45
40,474	–	50,090	×	6.000%	minus	1,569.91
50,091	–	59,166	×	8.000%	minus	2,571.71
59,167 and over			×	9.300%	minus	3,340.87

COLORADO[4]

4.63% of federal taxable income, regardless of filing status

CONNECTICUT[5]

Single, Married filing separately

| $0 | – | 10,000 | × | 3.000% | minus | $0 |
| 10,001 and over | | | × | 5.000% | minus | 200 |

Married filing jointly , Qualifying Widow/Widower

| $0 | – | 20,000 | × | 3.000% | minus | $0 |
| 20,001 and over | | | × | 5.000% | minus | 400 |

Head of household

| $0 | – | 16,000 | × | 3.000% | minus | $0 |
| 16,001 and over | | | × | 5.000% | minus | 320 |

DELAWARE

Single, Head of household, Married filing jointly, and Married filing separately

$0	–	2,000	× 0.000%	minus	$0
2,001	–	5,000	× 2.200%	minus	44.00
5,001	–	10,000	× 3.900%	minus	129.00
10,001	–	20,000	× 4.800%	minus	219.00
20,001	–	25,000	× 5.200%	minus	299.00
25,001	–	60,000	× 5.550%	minus	386.50
60,001 and over			× 5.950%	minus	626.50

DISTRICT OF COLUMBIA

Single, Head of household, Married filing jointly, and Married filing separately

$0	–	10,000	× 4.500%	minus	$0
10,001	–	40,000	× 7.000%	minus	250.00
40,001 and over			× 8.700%	minus	930.00

GEORGIA

Single

$0	–	750	× 1.000%	minus	$0
751	–	2,250	× 2.000%	minus	7.50
2,251	–	3,750	× 3.000%	minus	30.00
3,751	–	5,250	× 4.000%	minus	67.50
5,251	–	7,000	× 5.000%	minus	120.00
7,001 and over			× 6.000%	minus	190.00

Married filing jointly, Head of household

$0	–	1,000	× 1.000%	minus	$0
1,001	–	3,000	× 2.000%	minus	10.00
3,001	–	5,000	× 3.000%	minus	40.00
5,001	–	7,000	× 4.000%	minus	90.00
7,001	–	10,000	× 5.000%	minus	160.00
10,001 and over			× 6.000%	minus	260.00

Married filing separately

$0	–	500	× 1.000%	minus	$0
501	–	1,500	× 2.000%	minus	5.00
1,501	–	2,500	× 3.000%	minus	20.00
2,501	–	3,500	× 4.000%	minus	45.00
3,501	–	5,000	× 5.000%	minus	80.00
5,001 and over			× 6.000%	minus	130.00

HAWAII

Single and Married filing separately

$0	–	2,000	×	1.400%	minus	$0
2,001	–	4,000	×	3.200%	minus	36.00
4,001	–	8,000	×	5.500%	minus	128.00
8,001	–	12,000	×	6.400%	minus	200.00
12,001	–	16,000	×	6.800%	minus	248.00
16,001	–	20,000	×	7.200%	minus	312.00
20,001	–	30,000	×	7.600%	minus	392.00
30,001	–	40,000	×	7.900%	minus	482.00
40,001 and over			×	8.250%	minus	622.00

Married filing jointly, Qualifying Widow/Widower

$0	–	4,000	×	1.400%	minus	$0
4,001	–	8,000	×	3.200%	minus	72.00
8,001	–	16,000	×	5.500%	minus	256.00
16,001	–	24,000	×	6.400%	minus	400.00
24,001	–	32,000	×	6.800%	minus	496.00
32,001	–	40,000	×	7.200%	minus	624.00
40,001	–	60,000	×	7.600%	minus	784.00
60,001	–	80,000	×	7.900%	minus	964.00
80,001 and over			×	8.250%	minus	1,244.00

Head of household

$0	–	3,000	×	1.400%	minus	$0
3,001	–	6,000	×	3.200%	minus	54.00
6,001	–	12,000	×	5.500%	minus	192.00
12,001	–	18,000	×	6.400%	minus	300.00
18,001	–	24,000	×	6.800%	minus	372.00
24,001	–	30,000	×	7.200%	minus	468.00
30,001	–	45,000	×	7.600%	minus	588.00
45,001	–	60,000	×	7.900%	minus	723.00
60,001 and over			×	8.250%	minus	933.00

IDAHO[1][*][†]

Single and Married filing separately

$0	–	1,159	×	1.600%	minus	$0
1,160	–	2,318	×	3.600%	minus	23.18
2,319	–	3,477	×	4.100%	minus	34.77
3,478	–	4,636	×	5.100%	minus	69.54
4,637	–	5,794	×	6.100%	minus	115.90
5,795	–	8,692	×	7.100%	minus	173.84
8,693	–	23,178	×	7.400%	minus	199.92
23,179 and over			×	7.800%	minus	292.63

Married filing jointly, Head of household, Surviving Spouses

$0	–	2,318	× 1.600%	minus	$0.00
2,319	–	4,636	× 3.600%	minus	46.36
4,637	–	6,953	× 4.100%	minus	69.53
6,954	–	9,271	× 5.100%	minus	139.06
9,272	–	11,589	× 6.100%	minus	231.77
11,590	–	17,383	× 7.100%	minus	347.66
17,384	–	46,356	× 7.400%	minus	399.81
46,357 and over			× 7.800%	minus	585.24

ILLINOIS[6]

3.00% of federal adjusted gross income with modifications, regardless of filing status

INDIANA[7]

3.40% of adjusted gross income, regardless of filing status

IOWA[8]*

Single, Head of household, Married filing jointly, and Married filing separately

$0	–	1,300	× 0.360%	minus	$0
1,301	–	2,600	× 0.720%	minus	4.68
2,601	–	5,200	× 2.430%	minus	49.14
5,201	–	11,700	× 4.500%	minus	156.78
11,701	–	19,500	× 6.120%	minus	346.32
19,501	–	26,000	× 6.480%	minus	416.52
26,001	–	39,000	× 6.800%	minus	499.72
39,001	–	58,500	× 7.920%	minus	936.52
58,501 and over			× 8.980%	minus	1,556.62

KANSAS

Single, Head of household, and Married filing separately

$0	–	15,000	× 3.500%	minus	$0
15,001	–	30,000	× 6.250%	minus	412.50
30,001 and over			× 6.450%	minus	472.50

Married filing jointly

$0	–	30,000	× 3.500%	minus	$0
30,001	–	60,000	× 6.250%	minus	825.00
60,001 and over			× 6.450%	minus	945.00

KENTUCKY

Single, Head of household, Married filing jointly, and Married filing separately

$0	–	3,000	× 2.000%	minus	$0
3,001	–	4,000	× 3.000%	minus	30.00
4,001	–	5,000	× 4.000%	minus	70.00
5,001	–	8,000	× 5.000%	minus	120.00
8,001	–	75,000	× 5.800%	minus	184.00
75,001 and over			× 6.000%	minus	334.00

LOUISIANA[1]

Single, Head of household, and Married filing separately

$0	–	12,500	× 2.000%	minus	$0
12,501	–	25,000	× 4.000%	minus	250.00
25,001 and over			× 6.000%	minus	750.00

Married filing jointly, Qualifying Widow/Widower

$0	–	25,000	× 2.000%	minus	$0
25,001	–	50,000	× 4.000%	minus	500.00
50,001 and over			× 6.000%	minus	1,500.00

MAINE[9]*

Single and Married filing separately

$0	–	4,549	× 2.000%	minus	$0
4,550	–	9,099	× 4.500%	minus	113.73
9,100	–	18,249	× 7.000%	minus	341.20
18,250 and over			× 8.500%	minus	614.94

Married filing jointly

$0	–	9,149	× 2.000%	minus	$0
9,150	–	18,249	× 4.500%	minus	228.73
18,250	–	36,549	× 7.000%	minus	684.95
36,550 and over			× 8.500%	minus	1,233.19

Head of household

$0	–	6,849	× 2.000%	minus	$0
6,850	–	13,649	× 4.500%	minus	171.23
13,650	–	27,399	× 7.000%	minus	512.45
27,400 and over			× 8.500%	minus	923.44

MARYLAND

Single, Head of household, Married filing jointly, and Married filing separately

$0	–	1,000	× 2.000%	minus	$0
1,001		2,000	× 3.000%	minus	10.00
2,001		3,000	× 4.000%	minus	30.00
3,001 and over			× 4.750%	minus	52.50

MASSACHUSETTS[10]

Part A income (short–term capital gains)	12.00%
Part A income (interest and dividends) .	5.30%
Part B income	5.30%
Part C income	5.30%

MICHIGAN[11]

3.9% of taxable income, regardless of filing status

MINNESOTA[12]*
Single

$0	–	20,510	× 5.350%	minus	$0
20,511	–	67,360	× 7.050%	minus	348.66
67,361 and over			× 7.850%	minus	887.54

Married filing jointly

$0	–	29,980	× 5.350%	minus	$0
29,981	–	119,100	× 7.050%	minus	509.66
119,101 and over			× 7.850%	minus	1,462.46

Married filing separately

$0	–	14,990	× 5.350%	minus	$0
14,991	–	59,550	× 7.050%	minus	254.83
59,551 and over			× 7.850%	minus	731.23

Head of household

$0	–	25,250	× 5.350%	minus	$0
25,251	–	101,450	× 7.050%	minus	429.25
101,451 and over			× 7.850%	minus	1,240.85

MISSISSIPPI

Single, Head of household, Married filing jointly, and Married filing separately

$0	–	5,000	× 3.000%	minus	$0
5,001	–	10,000	× 4.000%	minus	50.00
10,001 and over			× 5.000%	minus	150.00

MISSOURI

Single, Head of household, Married filing jointly, and Married filing separately

$0	–	1,000	×	1.500%	minus	$0
1,001	–	2,000	×	2.000%	minus	5.00
2,001	–	3,000	×	2.500%	minus	15.00
3,001	–	4,000	×	3.000%	minus	30.00
4,001	–	5,000	×	3.500%	minus	50.00
5,001	–	6,000	×	4.000%	minus	75.00
6,001	–	7,000	×	4.500%	minus	105.00
7,001	–	8,000	×	5.000%	minus	140.00
8,001	–	9,000	×	5.500%	minus	180.00
9,001 and over			×	6.000%	minus	225.00

MONTANA[13]*

Single, Head of household, Married filing jointly, and Married filing separately

$0	–	2,399	×	1.000%	minus	$0
2,400	–	4,299	×	2.000%	minus	24.00
4,300	–	6,499	×	3.000%	minus	67.00
6,500	–	8,799	×	4.000%	minus	132.00
8,800	–	11,299	×	5.000%	minus	220.00
11,300	–	14,499	×	6.000%	minus	333.00
14,500 and over			×	6.900%	minus	464.00

NEBRASKA[14]

Single

$0	–	2,400	×	2.560%	minus	$0
2,401	–	17,500	×	3.570%	minus	24.24
17,501	–	27,000	×	5.120%	minus	295.49
27,001 and over			×	6.840%	minus	759.89

Married filing jointly, Surviving spouses

$0	–	4,000	×	2.560%	minus	$0
4,001	–	31,000	×	3.570%	minus	40.40
31,001	–	50,000	×	5.120%	minus	520.90
50,001 and over			×	6.840%	minus	1,380.90

Married filing separately

$0	–	2,000	×	2.560%	minus	$0
2,001	–	15,500	×	3.570%	minus	20.20
15,501	–	25,000	×	5.120%	minus	260.45
25,001 and over			×	6.840%	minus	290.45

Head of household

$0	–	3,800	× 2.560%	minus	$0
3,801	–	25,000	× 3.570%	minus	38.38
25,001	–	35,000	× 5.120%	minus	425.88
35,001 and over			× 6.840%	minus	1,027.88

NEW HAMPSHIRE

5% on interest and dividends only, regardless of filing status

NEW JERSEY

Single and Married filing separately

$0	–	20,000	× 1.400%	minus	$0
20,001	–	35,000	× 1.750%	minus	70.00
35,001	–	40,000	× 3.500%	minus	682.50
40,001	–	75,000	× 5.525%	minus	1,492.50
75,001	–	500,000	× 6.370%	minus	2,126.25
500,001 and over			× 8.970%	minus	15,126.25

Married filing jointly, Head of household, Qualifying Widow/Widower

$0	–	20,000	× 1.400%	minus	$0
20,001	–	50,000	× 1.750%	minus	70.00
50,001	–	70,000	× 2.450%	minus	420.00
70,001	–	80,000	× 3.500%	minus	1,155.00
80,001	–	150,000	× 5.525%	minus	2,775.00
150,001	–	500,000	× 6.370%	minus	4,042.50
500,001 and over			× 8.970%	minus	17,042.50

NEW MEXICO[1],[15]

Single

$0	–	5,500	× 1.700%	minus	$0
5,501	–	11,000	× 3.200%	minus	82.50
11,001	–	16,000	× 4.700%	minus	247.50
16,001 and over			× 5.300%	minus	343.50

Married filing jointly, Qualifying Widow/Widower

$0	–	8,000	× 1.700%	minus	$0
8,001	–	16,000	× 3.200%	minus	120.00
16,001	–	24,000	× 4.700%	minus	360.00
24,001 and over			× 5.300%	minus	504.00

Married filing separately

$0	–	4,000	× 1.700%	minus	$0
4,001	–	8,000	× 3.200%	minus	60.00
8,001	–	12,000	× 4.700%	minus	180.00
12,001 and over			× 5.300%	minus	252.00

Head of household

$0	–	8,000	×	1.700%	minus	$0
8,001	–	16,000	×	3.200%	minus	120.00
16,001	–	24,000	×	4.700%	minus	360.00
24,001 and over			×	5.300%	minus	504.00

NEW YORK[16]

Single and married filing separately

$0	–	8,000	×	4.000%	minus	$0
8,001	–	11,000	×	4.500%	minus	40.00
11,001	–	13,000	×	5.250%	minus	122.50
13,001	–	20,000	×	5.900%	minus	207.00
20,001 and over			×	6.850%	minus	397.00

Married filing jointly, Qualifying Widow/Widower

$0	–	16,000	×	4.000%	minus	$0
16,001	–	22,000	×	4.500%	minus	80.00
22,001	–	26,000	×	5.250%	minus	245.00
26,001	–	40,000	×	5.900%	minus	414.00
40,001 and over			×	6.850%	minus	794.00

Head of household

$0	–	11,000	×	4.000%	minus	$0
11,001	–	15,000	×	4.500%	minus	55.00
15,001	–	17,000	×	5.250%	minus	167.50
17,001	–	30,000	×	5.900%	minus	278.00
30,001 and over			×	6.850%	minus	563.00

NORTH CAROLINA

Single

$0	–	12,750	×	6.000%	minus	$0
12,751	–	60,000	×	7.000%	minus	127.50
60,001	–	120,000	×	7.750%	minus	577.50
120,001 and over			×	8.250%	minus	1,177.50

Married filing jointly, Qualifying Widow/Widower

$0	–	21,250	×	6.000%	minus	$0
21,251	–	100,000	×	7.000%	minus	212.50
100,001	–	200,000	×	7.750%	minus	962.50
200,001 and over			×	8.250%	minus	1,962.50

Married filing separately

$0	–	10,625	× 6.000%	minus	$0
10,626	–	50,000	× 7.000%	minus	106.25
50,001	–	100,000	× 7.750%	minus	481.25
100,001 and over			× 8.250%	minus	981.25

Head of household

$0	–	17,000	× 6.000%	minus	$0
17,001	–	80,000	× 7.000%	minus	170.00
80,001	–	160,000	× 7.750%	minus	770.00
160,001 and over			× 8.250%	minus	1,570.00

NORTH DAKOTA*

For Form ND–1
Single

$0	–	30,650	× 2.100%	minus	$0
30,651	–	74,200	× 3.920%	minus	557.83
74,201	–	154,800	× 4.340%	minus	869.47
154,801	–	336,550	× 5.040%	minus	1,953.07
336,551 and over			× 5.540%	minus	3,635.82

Married filing jointly, Surviving spouses

$0	–	51,200	× 2.100%	minus	$0
51,201	–	123,700	× 3.920%	minus	931.84
123,701	–	188,450	× 4.340%	minus	1,451.38
188,451	–	336,550	× 5.040%	minus	2,770.53
336,551 and over			× 5.540%	minus	4,453.28

Married filing separately

$0	–	25,600	× 2.100%	minus	$0
25,601	–	61,850	× 3.920%	minus	465.92
61,851	–	94,225	× 4.340%	minus	725.69
94,226	–	168,275	× 5.040%	minus	1,385.26
168,276 and over			× 5.540%	minus	2,226.64

Head of household

$0	–	41,050	× 2.100%	minus	$0
41,051	–	106,000	× 3.920%	minus	747.11
106,001	–	171,650	× 4.340%	minus	1,192.31
171,651	–	336,550	× 5.040%	minus	2,393.86
336,551 and over			× 5.540%	minus	4,076.61

For Form ND–2

$0	–	3,000	× 2.670%	minus	$0
3,001	–	5,000	× 4.000%	minus	39.90
5,001	–	8,000	× 5.330%	minus	106.40
8,001	–	15,000	× 6.670%	minus	213.60
15,001	–	25,000	× 8.000%	minus	413.10
25,001	–	35,000	× 9.330%	minus	745.60
35,001	–	50,000	× 10.670%	minus	1,214.60
50,001 and over			× 12.000%	minus	1,879.60

OHIO

Single, Head of household, Married filing jointly, and Married filing separately

$0	–	5,000	× 0.681%	minus	$0
5,001	–	10,000	× 1.361%	minus	34.00
10,001	–	15,000	× 2.722%	minus	170.10
15,001	–	20,000	× 3.403%	minus	272.25
20,001	–	40,000	× 4.083%	minus	408.25
40,001	–	80,000	× 4.764%	minus	680.65
80,001	–	100,000	× 5.444%	minus	1,224.65
100,001	–	200,000	× 6.32%	minus	2,100.65
200,001 and over			× 6.87%	minus	3,200.65

OKLAHOMA

Single and Married filing separately

$0	–	1,000	× 0.500%	minus	$0
1,001	–	2,500	× 1.000%	minus	5.00
2,501	–	3,750	× 2.000%	minus	30.00
3,751	–	4,900	× 3.000%	minus	67.50
4,901	–	7,200	× 4.000%	minus	116.50
7,201	–	8,700	× 5.000%	minus	188.50
8,701	–	10,500	× 6.000%	minus	275.50
10,501 and over			× 6.250%	minus	301.75

Married filing jointly, Qualifying Widow/Widower, Head of household

$0	–	2,000	× 0.500%	minus	$0
2,001	–	5,000	× 1.000%	minus	10.00
5,001	–	7,500	× 2.000%	minus	60.00
7,501	–	9,800	× 3.000%	minus	135.00
9,801	–	12,200	× 4.000%	minus	233.00
12,201	–	15,000	× .5.000%	minus	355.00
15,001	–	21,000	× 6.000%	minus	505.00
21,001 and over			× 6.250%	minus	557.50

OREGON*

Single and Married filing separately

$0	– 2,750	×	5.000%	minus	$0
2,751	– 6,850	×	7.000%	minus	55.00
6,851 and over		×	9.000%	minus	192.00

Married filing jointly, Qualifying Widow/Widower, Head of household

$0	– 5,500	×	5.000%	minus	$0
5,501	– 13,700	×	7.000%	minus	110.00
13,701 and over		×	9.000%	minus	384.00

PENNSYLVANIA

3.07% of taxable compensation, net profits, net gains from the sale of property, rent, royalties, patents or copyrights, income from estates or trusts, dividends, interest and winnings

RHODE ISLAND

25% of the federal income tax rates, including capital gains rates and any other special rates for other types of income, that were in effect prior to enactment of the Economic Growth and Tax Relief Reconciliation Act of 2001. Effective for the 2006 tax year, taxpayers may elect to compute income tax liability based on the graduated rate schedule or an alternative flat rate equal to 8%.

Single

$0	– 30,650	×	3.750%	minus	$0
30,651	– 74,200	×	7.000%	minus	996.13
74,201	– 154,800	×	7.750%	minus	1,552.63
154,801	– 336,550	×	9.000%	minus	3,487.63
336,551 and over		×	9.900%	minus	6,516.58

Married filing jointly, Surviving spouses

$0	– 51,200	×	3.750%	minus	$0
51,201	– 123,700	×	7.000%	minus	1,664.00
123,701	– 188,450	×	7.750%	minus	2,591.75
188,451	– 336,550	×	9.000%	minus	4,947.38
336,551 and over		×	9.900%	minus	7,976.33

Married filing separately

$0	– 25,600	×	3.750%	minus	$0
25,601	– 61,850	×	7.000%	minus	832.00
61,851	– 94,225	×	7.750%	minus	1,295.88
94,226	– 168,275	×	9.000%	minus	2,473.69
168,276 and over		×	9.900%	minus	3,988.16

Head of household

$0	– 41,050	×	3.750%	minus	$0
41,051	– 106,000	×	7.000%	minus	1,334.13
106,001	– 171,650	×	7.750%	minus	2,129.13
171,651	– 336,550	×	9.000%	minus	4,274.75
336,551 and over		×	9.900%	minus	7,303.70

SOUTH CAROLINA*

Single, Head of household, Married filing jointly, and Married filing separately

$0	– 2,570	× 2.500%	minus	$0
2,571	– 5,140	× 3.000%	minus	12.85
5,141	– 7,710	× 4.000%	minus	64.25
7,711	– 10,280	× 5.000%	minus	141.35
10,281	– 12,850	× 6.000%	minus	244.15
12,851 and over		× 7.000%	minus	372.65

TENNESSEE

6% upon interest and dividend income of individuals

UTAH

Single and Married filing separately

$0	– 1,000	× 2.300%	minus	$0
1,001	– 2,000	× 3.300%	minus	10
2,001	– 3,000	× 4.200%	minus	28
3,001	– 4,000	× 5.200%	minus	58
4,001	– 5,500	× 6.000%	minus	90
5,501 and over		× 6.980%	minus	143.90

Married filing jointly, Surviving Spouses, Head of household

$0	– 2,000	× 2.300%	minus	$0
2,001	– 4,000	× 3.300%	minus	20
4,001	– 6,000	× 4.200%	minus	56
6,001	– 8,000	× 5.200%	minus	116
8,001	– 11,000	× 6.000%	minus	180
11,001 and over		× 6.980%	minus	287.80

VERMONT[17]*

Single

$0	– 30,650	× 3.600%	minus	$0
30,651	– 74,200	× 7.200%	minus	1,103.40
74,201	– 154,800	× 8.500%	minus	2,068.00
154,801	– 336,550	× 9.000%	minus	2,842.00
336,551 and over		× 9.500%	minus	4,524.75

Married filing jointly, Qualifying Widow/Widower, Civil Union Filing Jointly

$0	– 51,200	× 3.600%	minus	$0
51,201	– 123,700	× 7.200%	minus	1,843.20
123,701	– 188,450	× 8.500%	minus	3,451.30
188,451	– 336,550	× 9.000%	minus	4,393.55
336,551 and over		× 9.500%	minus	6,076.30

Married filing separately, Civil Union Filing Separately

$0	–	25,600	× 3.600%	minus	$0
25,601	–	61,850	× 7.200%	minus	921.60
61,851	–	94,225	× 8.500%	minus	1,725.65
94,226	–	168,275	× 9.000%	minus	2,196.77
168,276 and over			× 9.500%	minus	3,038.15

Head of household

$0	–	41,050	× 3.600%	minus	$0
41,051	–	106,000	× 7.200%	minus	1,477.80
106,001	–	171,650	× 8.500%	minus	2,855.80
171,651	–	336,550	× 9.000%	minus	3,714.05
336,551 and over			× 9.500%	minus	5,396.80

VIRGINIA

Single, Head of household, Married filing jointly, and Married filing separately

$0	–	3,000	× 2.000%	minus	$0
3,001	–	5,000	× 3.000%	minus	30.00
5,001	–	17,000	× 5.000%	minus	130.00
17,001 and over			× 5.750%	minus	257.50

WEST VIRGINIA[18]

Single, Head of household, and Married filing jointly

$0	–	10,000	× 3.000%	minus	$0
10,001	–	25,000	× 4.000%	minus	100.00
25,001	–	40,000	× 4.500%	minus	225.00
40,001	–	60,000	× 6.000%	minus	825.00
60,001 and over			× 6.500%	minus	1,125.00

Married filing separately

$0	–	5,000	× 3.000%	minus	$0
5,001	–	12,500	× 4.000%	minus	50.00
12,501	–	20,000	× 4.500%	minus	112.50
20,001	–	30,000	× 6.000%	minus	412.50
30,001 and over			× 6.500%	minus	562.50

WISCONSIN[1,19]*

Single and Head of household

$0	–	9,160	× 4.600%	minus	$0
9,161	–	18,320	× 6.150%	minus	141.98
18,321	–	137,410	× 6.500%	minus	206.10
137,411 and over			× 6.750%	minus	549.63

Married filing jointly

$0	–	12,210	× 4.600%	minus	$0
12,211	–	24,430	× 6.150%	minus	189.26
24,431	–	183,210	× 6.500%	minus	274.76
183,211 and over			× 6.750%	minus	732.79

Married filing separately

$0	–	6,110	× 4.600%	minus	$0
6,111	–	12,210	× 6.150%	minus	94.71
12,211	–	91,600	× 6.500%	minus	137.44
91,601	and over		× 6.750%	minus	366.44

---

[1] Community property state in which, in general, one–half of the community income is taxable to each spouse.

[2] **Arkansas:** Tax liability is associated with a 3% tax surcharge based on existing rates. Married filing separately combined–status couples calculate taxes separately and add the results.

[3] **California:** An additional 1% tax is imposed on taxable income in excess of $1 million.

[4] **Colorado:** Alternative minimum tax imposed. Individual taxpayers are subject to an alternative minimum tax equal to the amount by which 3.47% of their Colorado alternative minimum taxable income exceeds their Colorado normal tax.

[5] **Connecticut:** Resident estates and trusts are subject to the 5% income tax rate on all of their income. Additional state minimum tax imposed on resident individuals, trusts and estates that are subject to the federal alternative minimum tax, equal to the amount by which the Connecticut minimum tax exceeds the Connecticut basic income tax (the lesser of (a) 19% of adjusted federal tentative minimum tax, or (b) 5.5% of adjusted federal alternative minimum taxable income). Separate provisions apply for non–and part–year resident individuals, trusts and estates.

[6] **Illinois:** Additional personal property replacement tax of 1.5% of net income is imposed on partnerships, trusts and S corporations.

[7] **Indiana:** Counties may impose an adjusted gross income tax on residents or on nonresidents, or a county option income tax. (Note: Rates have apparently changed.)

[8] **Iowa:** An alternative minimum tax of 6.7% of alternative minimum income is imposed if the minimum tax exceeds the taxpayer's regular income tax liability. The minimum tax is 75% of the maximum regular tax rate.

[9] **Maine:** Additional state minimum tax is imposed equal to the amount by which the tentative minimum tax exceeds regular income tax liability.

[10] **Massachusetts:** Part A income represents either interest and dividends or short–term capital gains. Part B income represents wages, salaries, tips, pensions, state bank interest, partnership income, business income, rents, alimony, winnings and certain other items of income. Part C income represents gains from the sale of capital assets held for more than one year.

[11] **Michigan:** Persons with business activity allocated or apportioned to Michigan are also subject to a single business tax on an adjusted tax base.

[12] **Minnesota:** A 6.4% alternative minimum tax is imposed.

[13] **Montana:** Minimum tax, $1.

[14] **Nebraska:** The tax rates in the schedules are determined by multiplying the primary rate set by the legislature by the following factors for the brackets, from lowest to highest bracket. For tax years beginning on or after January 1, 2003, the respective factors are: 0.6932, 0.9646, 1.3846, and 1.848. For tax years beginning before January 1, 2003, the respective factors are: 0.6784, 0.9432, 1.3541, and 1.8054. The figure obtained for each bracket is rounded to the nearest hundredth of 1%. One rate schedule is to be established for each federal filing status (Sec. 77–2715.02).

[15] **New Mexico:** Qualified nonresident taxpayers may pay alternative tax of 0.75% of gross receipts from New Mexico sales.

[16] **New York:** A supplemental tax is imposed to recapture the tax table benefit. The supplemental tax is calculated in accordance with N.Y. Tax Law Sec. 601(d).

[17] **Vermont:** The tax amount in the schedules is increased by 24% of a taxpayer's federal tax liability for: additional taxes assessed due to early withdrawals from qualified retirement plans, individual retirement accounts, and medical savings accounts; recapture of the federal investment tax credit; or tax on qualified lump–sum distributions of pension income not included in federal taxable income. The amount of tax is decreased by 24% of the reduction in the taxpayer's federal liability due to farm income averaging.

[18] **West Virginia:** Minimum tax equal to the excess by which 25% of any federal minimum tax or alternative minimum tax for the taxable year exceeds the sum of the primary tax for West Virginia personal income tax purposes for the taxable year.

[19] **Wisconsin:** A permanent recycling surcharge is imposed on individuals, estates, trusts and partnerships with at least $4 million in gross receipts at the rate of the greater of $25 or 0.2% of net business income as allocated or apportioned to Wisconsin. The maximum surcharge is $9,800. Farming is no longer treated preferentially.

Alternative Minimum Tax

This chart shows whether each state imposes a corporate income tax or personal income tax on preference items comparable to those imposed by IRC Secs. 55—59. States that impose neither a corporate income tax nor a personal income tax are not included in the chart.

State	Corporate	Personal
Alabama	No	No
Alaska	Yes	(*)
Arizona	No	No
Arkansas	No	No
California	Yes	Yes
Colorado	No	Yes
Connecticut	No	Yes
Delaware	No	No
District of Columbia	No	No
Florida	Yes	(*)
Georgia	No	No
Hawaii	No	No
Idaho	No	No
Illinois	No	No
Indiana	No	No
Iowa	Yes	Yes
Kansas	No	No
Kentucky	No[1]	No
Louisiana	No	No
Maine	Yes	Yes
Maryland	No	Yes
Massachusetts	No	No
Michigan	No	No
Minnesota	Yes	Yes
Mississippi	No	No
Missouri	No[2]	No
Montana	No	No
Nebraska	No	Yes
New Hampshire	No	(*)

State	Corporate	Personal
New Jersey	No[3]	No
New Mexico	No	No
New York	Yes	Yes
North Carolina	No	No
North Dakota	No	No
Ohio	No	No
Oklahoma	No	No
Oregon	No	No
Pennsylvania	No[4]	No
Rhode Island	No	Yes
South Carolina	No	No
Tennessee	No	(*)
Texas	No	(*)
Utah	No	No
Vermont	No	No
Virginia	No	No
West Virginia	No	Yes
Wisconsin	No	Yes

[1] For taxable years beginning after 2004 and before 2007, Kentucky imposes an alternative minimum tax calculation (AMC) based on gross receipts or gross profits. Corporations with gross receipts or gross profits of $3 million or less are excluded from the AMC for the 2006 tax year. After 2006, the AMC is replaced by an annual limited liability entity tax that must be paid by every corporation with $3 million or more in gross receipts or gross profits.

[2] Missouri allows a 50% deduction of federal income taxes paid, including the alternative minimum tax.

[3] New Jersey imposes an alternative minimum assessment based on gross profits or gross receipts.

[4] Some federal preference items are added back to federal taxable income.

* State does not impose a personal income tax to which the preference items apply.

Apportionment Formulas

Most states utilize a three-factor apportionment formula with property, payroll, and sales (or receipts) factors. Under UDITPA, each of these factors is equally weighted. However, few states still weight each factor equally.

The following chart shows the standard apportionment formulas used in each state. Special apportionment rules that apply to specific industries (such as financial institutions, insurance companies, and transportation companies) are not included.

States that do not impose a corporate income tax are not included in this chart.

State	Formula
Alabama	Evenly weighted three-factor formula.
Alaska	Evenly weighted three-factor formula.
Arizona	Three-factor formula with double-weighted sales factor. As long as one or more corporations, beginning June 1, 2005, commits to one or more capital investment projects with expenditures in excess of $1 billion, then effective for taxable years beginning after January 1, 2006, corporations may elect to use an apportionment formula with an enhanced sales factor equal to 60% for 2007, 70% for 2008, and 80% for tax years after 2008.
Arkansas	Three-factor formula with double-weighted sales factor.
California	Three-factor formula with double-weighted sales factor.
Colorado	Option between evenly weighted three-factor formula and evenly weighted two-factor formula of revenue and property.
Connecticut	Three-factor formula with double-weighted sales factor for income derived from the sale or use of tangible personal or real property; single-factor gross receipts formula for other income. Most manufacturers use single-factor gross receipts formula.
Delaware	Evenly weighted three-factor formula.
District of Columbia	Evenly weighted three-factor formula.
Florida	Three-factor formula with double-weighted sales factor.
Georgia	Three-factor formula with double-weighted sales factor (after December 31, 2005, 80-10-10 (sales, property, payroll); after December 31, 2006, 90-5-5 (sales property, payroll), after December 31, 2007, one-factor sales formula).
Hawaii	Evenly weighted three-factor formula.
Idaho	Three-factor formula with double-weighted sales factor.
Illinois	One-factor sales formula.
Indiana	Three-factor formula with double-weighted sales factor. Property and payroll factors phased out by 10% each year from 2007 through 2011. Single sales factor apportionment formula effective in tax year 2011.
Iowa	One-factor sales formula.
Kansas	Evenly weighted three-factor formula.

State	Formula
Kentucky	Three-factor formula with double-weighted sales factor.
Louisiana	Single-factor sales formula for manufacturers, merchandisers, and other corporations without a specified formula. Prior to 2006, three-factor formula with a double-weighted sales factor for manufacturers, merchandisers, and other corporations without a specified formula.
Maine	Three-factor formula with double-weighted sales factor.
Maryland	Three-factor formula with double-weighted sales factor; manufacturers use one-factor sales formula.
Massachusetts	Three-factor formula with double-weighted sales factor.
Michigan	Three-factor formula 90-5-5 (sales-payroll-property).
Minnesota	Three-factor formula 75-12.5-12.5 (sales-payroll-property). After 2006, 78-11-11 (sales, property, payroll); after 2007, 81-9.5-9.5 (sales, property, payroll); after 2008, 84-8-8 (sales, property, payroll); after 2009, 87-6.5-6.5 (sales, property, payroll); after 2010, 90-5-5 (sales, property, payroll); after 2011, 93-3.5-3.5 (sales, property, payroll); after 2012, 96-2-2 (sales, property, payroll); after 2013, single sales factor.
Mississippi	Retailers, wholesalers, service companies, lessors: one-factor sales formula; manufacturers selling at wholesale: evenly weighted three-factor formula; manufacturers selling at retail: three-factor formula with double-weighted sales.
Missouri	Corporations other than certain public utilities and transportation companies may choose between evenly weighted three-factor formula and one-factor sales formula.
Montana	Evenly weighted three-factor formula.
Nebraska	One-factor sales formula.
New Hampshire	Three-factor formula with double-weighted sales factor.
New Jersey	Three-factor formula with double-weighted sales factor.
New Mexico	Evenly weighted three-factor formula; certain manufacturers may elect to double-weight the sales factor.
New York	Three-factor formula 60-20-20 (receipts, property, payroll); after 2006, 80-10-10 (receipts, property, payroll); after 2007, single receipts factor formula. Three-factor formula with a double-weighted receipts factor for tax years prior to 2006.
North Carolina	Three-factor formula with double-weighted sales factor.
North Dakota	Evenly weighted three-factor formula.
Ohio	Three-factor formula with triple-weighted sales factor.
Oklahoma	Evenly weighted three-factor formula; corporations meeting investment criteria allowed to double-weight the sales factor.
Oregon	One-factor sales formula. Three-factor formula 80-10-10 (sales-property-payroll), before July 1, 2005
Pennsylvania	Three-factor formula with triple-weighted sales factor. Beginning with tax years after 2006, three-factor formula 70%-15%-15% (sales, property, payroll)
Rhode Island	Evenly weighted three-factor formula.

State	Formula
South Carolina	Three-factor formula with double-weighted sales for manufacturers or dealers in tangible personal property; others subject to single-factor gross receipts formula. Applicable to taxable years beginning after 2006, single-factor sales formula for manufacturers.
Tennessee	Three-factor formula with double-weighted sales factor.
Texas	One-factor gross receipts formula.
Utah	Evenly weighted three-factor formula (after 2005, optional three-factor formula with double-weighted sales factor).
Vermont	Evenly weighted three-factor formula. After 2005, three-factor formula with double-weighted sales factor.
Virginia	Three-factor formula with double-weighted sales factor.
West Virginia	Three-factor formula with double-weighted sales factor.
Wisconsin	Three-factor formula 60-20-20 (sales, property, payroll); after 2006, 80-10-10 (sales, property, payroll); after 2007, single sales factor formula. Three-factor formula with double-weighted sales factor for tax years prior to 2006.

Bad Debt Deduction

Under federal law (IRC § 166), a taxpayer may take a deduction for debts that become wholly or partially worthless within the income year. The amount of the deduction is calculated by reference to the adjusted basis for determining loss from the sale of property.

This chart shows each state's rules on the deduction for bad debts. States that do not impose a corporate income tax are not included in this chart below.

State	Bad Debt Deduction
Alabama	Same as federal
Alaska	Same as federal
Arizona	Same as federal
Arkansas	Same as federal
California	Same as federal, except modifications required for banks, saving and loan associations, and other financial corporations
Colorado	Same as federal
Connecticut	Same as federal
Delaware	Same as federal
District of Columbia	Same as federal
Florida	Same as federal
Georgia	Same as federal
Hawaii	Same as federal
Idaho	Same as federal
Illinois	Same as federal
Indiana	Same as federal
Iowa	Same as federal
Kansas	Same as federal
Kentucky	Same as federal
Louisiana	Same as federal
Maine	Same as federal
Maryland	Same as federal
Massachusetts	Same as federal
Michigan	Same as federal
Minnesota	Same as federal
Mississippi	Same as federal
Missouri	Same as federal
Montana	Same as federal, except MT does not allow the reserve method

State	Bad Debt Deduction
Nebraska	Same as federal
New Hampshire	Same as federal
New Jersey	Same as federal
New Mexico	Same as federal
New York	Same as federal
North Carolina	Same as federal
North Dakota	Same as federal
Ohio	Same as federal
Oklahoma	Same as federal
Oregon	Same as federal, except modifications required for financial institutions that change accounting methods
Pennsylvania	Same as federal
Rhode Island	Same as federal
South Carolina	Same as federal
Tennessee	Same as federal, except that large banks may use the reserve method
Texas	Same as federal
Utah	Same as federal
Vermont	Same as federal
Virginia	Same as federal, except modifications required for saving and loan associations
West Virginia	Same as federal, except reserve method allowed for all taxpayers
Wisconsin	Same as federal

Capital Loss Carryovers

The chart below deals with the states' position regarding capital loss carryovers under IRC § 1212. Under IRC § 1212, a corporation may carry back a capital loss to each of the three tax years preceding the loss year and any excess may be carried forward for five years following the loss year.

State	Answer	Comments
Alabama	Conforms	
Alaska	Conforms	
Arizona	Conforms	In addition, up to $1,000 of unused Arizona capital loss carryovers from taxable years beginning before 1988 may be subtracted from federal taxable income for Arizona purposes.
Arkansas	Does not conform	Capital losses must be deducted in full in year sustained.
California	Does not conform	Federal carryback provisions do not apply.
Colorado	Conforms	
Connecticut	Conforms	
Delaware	Conforms	
District of Columbia	Conforms	
Florida	Conforms	
Georgia	Conforms	A deduction is not allowed for losses that occurred in a year that the taxpayer was not subject to Georgia tax or for losses that were previously reported.
Hawaii	Conforms	

State	Answer	Comments
Idaho	Conforms	Capital loss carryovers incurred during a year in which a corporation transacts no business in Idaho must be added back to federal taxable income, unless the corporation was included in a group of corporations filing a combined report.
Illinois	Conforms	
Indiana	Conforms	
Iowa	Conforms	Capital loss carryforward must be modified.
Kansas	Conforms	
Kentucky	Conforms	
Louisiana	Conforms	
Maine	Conforms	
Maryland	Conforms	
Massachusetts	Does not conform	The full amount of the loss must be claimed and deductible in the year of loss; no carryover or carryback of any excess capital loss will be allowed
Michigan	Does not conform	Capital loss must be taken in full in year incurred.
Minnesota	Does not conform	While federal capital loss addback is required, Minnesota permits a separate state deduction, based on federal law, and carryforward period is 15 years.

State	Answer	Comments
Mississippi	Does not conform	Although Mississippi does not follow the federal provisions and capital losses must be computed separately for Mississippi purposes, the definition of relevant terms are the same as for federal purposes and losses may be carried over for five years.
Missouri	Conforms	
Montana	Does not conform	Capital losses must be deducted in full in year incurred.
Nebraska	Does not conform	
New Hampshire	Conforms	
New Jersey	Conforms	
New Mexico	Conforms	
New York	Conforms	Federal taxable income and entire net income must be recomputed to determine the amount to be carried back or forward, adding back any loss from subsidiary capital.
North Carolina	Does not conform	An addback is required for all federal capital loss carryovers and a subtraction is allowed for all capital losses in the taxable year that have not been taken federally.
North Dakota	Conforms	
Ohio	Conforms	
Oklahoma	Conforms	
Oregon	Conforms	
Pennsylvania	Conforms	
Rhode Island	Conforms	

State	Answer	Comments
South Carolina	Conforms	
Tennessee	Does not conform	Tennessee allows the full amount of capital losses to be deducted in the year sustained.
Texas	Conforms	
Utah	Conforms	
Vermont	Conforms	
Virginia	Conforms	
West Virginia	Conforms	
Wisconsin	Conforms	

Combined Reporting Requirements

The following chart indicates each state's position regarding the filing of combined returns.

State	State Has Combined Reporting	Required of Unitary Business	Foreign Affiliates Included
Alabama	No	N/A	N/A
Alaska	Yes	Yes	No, unless more than 20% of affiliate's property and payroll are assigned to a location within U.S. or affiliate is a tax-haven corporation.
Arizona	Yes	Yes, unless group files AZ consolidated return.	No
Arkansas	No	N/A	N/A
California	Yes	Yes, if activities both within and without CA	No—if water's edge election made; certain foreign affiliates included if water's edge election made.
Colorado	Yes	No*	Yes—except certain affiliates with 80% or more foreign property and payroll
Connecticut[3]	Yes	No	Yes
Delaware	No	N/A	N/A
District of Columbia	No	N/A	N/A
Florida	No	N/A	N/A
Georgia	No	N/A	N/A
Hawaii	Yes	Yes	No
Idaho	Yes	Yes, if more than 50% common ownership	Yes—if water's edge election is not made or if water's edge election is made and foreign affiliates meet certain conditions
Illinois	Yes	Yes	Yes, unless 80% or more of affiliate's business activity is conducted outside U.S.
Indiana	Yes	No*	Yes, except non-U.S. corporations and foreign operating corporations
Iowa	No	N/A	N/A
Kansas	Yes	Yes	No. However, may be required to include some U.S. possessions and Canadian companies if included in federal consolidated return.
Kentucky	No	N/A	N/A

State	State Has Combined Reporting	Required of Unitary Business	Foreign Affiliates Included
Louisiana	No	N/A	N/A
Maine	Yes	Yes	Yes, if required to file federal return
Maryland	No	N/A	N/A
Massachusetts	No	N/A	N/A
Michigan	Yes	No*	No
Minnesota	Yes	Yes	No (with exception of FSCs and DISCs; DISC income always combined with parent)
Mississippi	Yes[1]	No*	Only if affiliate is required to file a MS tax return
Missouri	No	N/A	N/A
Montana	Yes	Yes	Yes unless water's edge election made; some included even after election
Nebraska	Yes	Yes	Yes
New Hampshire	Yes	Yes, for business organizations that are part of a water's edge combined group	No—if water's edge election made and foreign affiliates meet certain other conditions
New Jersey	No	N/A	N/A
New Mexico	Yes	No	No
New York	Yes	No*	No—unless necessary to prevent distortion
North Carolina	No	N/A	N/A
North Dakota	Yes	Yes	Yes—if water's edge election is not made; certain foreign affiliates included even when election is made
Ohio	Yes	No*	No
Oklahoma	No	N/A	N/A
Oregon	No	N/A	N/A
Pennsylvania	No	N/A	N/A
Rhode Island	No	N/A	N/A
South Carolina	No	N/A	N/A
Tennessee	No[2]	No*,[2]	N/A
Texas	No	N/A	N/A

State	State Has Combined Reporting	Required of Unitary Business	Foreign Affiliates Included
Utah	Yes	Yes; must file a water's edge combined report unless worldwide election made	Yes, if they meet threshold level of U.S. activity or if worldwide election is made
Vermont	Yes, for taxable years beginning after 2005.	Yes, if more than 50% common ownership exists.	Yes, unless 80% or more of affiliate's property and payroll are assigned to locations outside U.S..
Virginia	Yes	No	Only to extent controlled foreign subsidiaries derive income from U.S. sources
West Virginia	Yes	No*	No
Wisconsin	No	N/A	N/A

[1] Only allowed where one or more group members are taxable outside Mississippi.
[2] Unitary financial corporations and some hospital companies must file combined.
[3] State uses the term "combined return" for what is usually called a consolidated return..
* State has the option to require combined reporting.

Composite Returns—LLCs

The following chart indicates whether composite returns may be filed for nonresident members.

State	Answer
Alabama	Yes
Alaska	N/A[1]
Arizona	Yes[2]
Arkansas	Yes[3]
California	Yes[4]
Colorado	Yes[5]
Connecticut	Yes[6]
Delaware	Yes[7]
District of Columbia	N/A[8]
Florida	N/A[1]
Georgia	Yes[9]
Hawaii	Yes[10]
Idaho	Yes[11]
Illinois	Yes[12]
Indiana	Yes[13]
Iowa	Yes[14]
Kansas	Yes[9]
Kentucky	No[15]
Louisiana	Yes[16]
Maine	Yes[17]
Maryland	Yes[10]
Massachusetts	Yes[18]
Michigan	Yes[19]
Minnesota	Yes[20]
Mississippi	Yes[21]
Missouri	Yes[9]
Montana	Yes[22]
Nebraska	No
New Hampshire	N/A[23]

State	Answer
New Jersey	Yes[24]
New Mexico	Yes
New York	Yes[25]
North Carolina	Yes[26]
North Dakota	Yes[7]
Ohio	Yes[27]
Oklahoma	Yes[9]
Oregon	Yes[28]
Pennsylvania	Yes[29]
Rhode Island	Yes[9]
South Carolina	Yes[30]
Tennessee	No[31]
Texas	N/A[32]
Utah	Yes[33]
Vermont	Yes[34]
Virginia	Yes[35]
West Virginia	Yes[36]
Wisconsin	Yes[37]

[1] Individuals not subject to income-based taxes.

[2] Must include at least 10 qualified members. Participants must have same tax year. Members must meet specified requirements to participate. Deceased members must be excluded.

[3] Must obtain prior approval. Members must meet specified requirements to participate. Effective for tax years beginning after 2005, composite returns may be filed on behalf of electing nonresident members.

[4] Participants in a "group nonresident return" must be individuals. Returns must be filed using calendar tax year. Members must meet certain requirements to participate.

[5] Participants must be individuals, estates, or trusts, or pass-through entities with such members. Members must meet specified requirements to participate.

[6] Entity may file "group return" on behalf of individuals that have same tax year and meet specified requirements. Composite return/payment required if member is nonresident individual, trust, estate, or pass-through entity that did not elect to be included on group return and whose share of CT income is $1,000 or more. After 2005, an LLC may no longer file a "group return"

[7] Participants must be individuals and have same tax year. Members must meet specified requirements to participate.

[8] Personal income tax not applicable to nonresidents.

[9] Members must meet specified requirements to participate.

[10] Participants must be individuals. Members must meet specified requirements to participate.

[11] Required to file return at entity level and must pay income tax on behalf of qualified individual members who elect not to file individual income tax returns.

[12] Participants must be individuals, trusts, or estates.

[13] Participants must be individuals. Members must meet specified requirements to participate. Members that are corporations, partnerships, or fiduciaries must be excluded.

[14] Return must be filed using tax year of majority of participants. Members must meet specified requirements to participate.

[15] For tax years beginning after 2003 and before 2005, withholding required and combined returns for nonresident members not allowed. For tax years beginning after 2004 and before 2007, LLCs subject to C corporation filing requirements. For tax years after 2006, LLCs are allowed to file composite returns on behalf of nonresident members.

[16] Composite returns and composite payments of tax are required on behalf of any or all nonresident individual members who do not agree to file an individual return. Members that are corporations or tax-exempt trusts must be excluded.

[17] Must obtain prior approval. Participants must be individuals or certain trusts. Members must meet specified requirements to participate.

[18] Participants must be individuals or estate/trust of deceased member. Members must meet specified requirements to participate.

[19] Participants must be individuals, estates, trusts, or flow-through entities with nonresident members.

[20] Election available only to full-year nonresident individuals who have no other income from state sources and, effective for tax years after 2004, estates or trusts distributing current income that do not claim a federal deduction under IRC Sec. 651 or IRC Sec. 661.

[21] Members must meet specified requirements to participate. Once filed, must continue to use composite return unless permission to change granted in writing by Commissioner.

[22] Participants must be individuals, out-of-state C corporations, or pass-through entities. Members must meet specified requirements to participate.

[23] Personal income tax applies only to interest and dividend income and is not applicable to nonresidents.

[24] Participants must be individuals. Members must meet specified requirements to participate. Fiscal year filers must be excluded. Returns with 25 or more participants must be filed on diskette.

[25] Must obtain prior approval and include at least 11 qualified members to file a "group return." Participants must have same accounting period. Members must meet specified requirements to participate.

[26] Nonresident individual member not required to file individual income tax return if only NC source income was from entity and entity reported nonresident's income on partnership return and paid tax due.

[27] C corporations that are direct or indirect investors must be excluded.

[28] Participants in a "multiple nonresident return" must be individuals or electing small business trusts (ESBTs). Return must be filed using tax year of majority of participants. Members must meet specified requirements to participate. For tax years beginning after 2005, composite returns required on behalf of electing nonresident owners.

[29] Participants must be individuals and use calendar tax year. Members must meet specified requirements to participate.

[30] Participants must be individuals or fiduciaries and have same tax year. Members must meet specified requirements to participate. Members that are corporations must be excluded.

[31] Personal income tax applies only to stock and bond income and is not applicable to nonresidents.

[32] Corporation franchise tax is imposed on LLCs at the entity level.

[33] Members must meet specified requirements to participate. Members entitled to Utah tax credits must be excluded.

[34] Must obtain prior approval and include at least 21 qualified members. Participants must be individuals. Members must meet specified requirements to participate.

[35] Must obtain prior approval to file a "unified return." Members must meet specified requirements to participate.

[36] Members must meet specified requirements to participate. Subject to $50 processing fee.

[37] Members must meet specified requirements to participate in a "combined return." Fiscal year filers, certain estates/trusts, partnerships, and corporations must be excluded.

Composite Returns—LLPs

The following chart indicates whether composite returns may be filed for nonresident partners.

State	Answer
Alabama	Yes
Alaska	N/A[1]
Arizona	Yes[2]
Arkansas	Yes[3]
California	Yes[4]
Colorado	Yes[5]
Connecticut	Yes[6]
Delaware	Yes[7]
District of Columbia	N/A[8]
Florida	N/A[1]
Georgia	Yes[9]
Hawaii	Yes[10]
Idaho	Yes[11]
Illinois	Yes[12]
Indiana	Yes[13]
Iowa	Yes[14]
Kansas	Yes[9]
Kentucky	No[15]
Louisiana	Yes[16]
Maine	Yes[17]
Maryland	Yes[10]
Massachusetts	Yes[18]
Michigan	Yes[19]
Minnesota	Yes[20]
Mississippi	Yes[21]
Missouri	Yes[9]
Montana	Yes[22]
Nebraska	No
New Hampshire	N/A[23]

State	Answer
New Jersey	Yes[24]
New Mexico	Yes
New York	Yes[25]
North Carolina	Yes[26]
North Dakota	Yes[7]
Ohio	Yes[27]
Oklahoma	Yes[9]
Oregon	Yes[28]
Pennsylvania	Yes[29]
Rhode Island	Yes[9]
South Carolina	Yes[30]
Tennessee	No[31]
Texas	N/A[32]
Utah	Yes[33]
Vermont	Yes[34]
Virginia	Yes[35]
West Virginia	Yes[36]
Wisconsin	Yes[37]

[1] Individuals not subject to income-based taxes.

[2] Must include at least 10 qualified partners. Participants must have same tax year. Partners must meet specified requirements to participate. Deceased partners must be excluded.

[3] Must obtain prior approval. Partners must meet specified requirements to participate. Effective for tax years beginning after 2005, composite returns may be filed on behalf of electing nonresident partners.

[4] Participants in a "group nonresident return" must be individuals. Returns must be filed using calendar tax year. Partners must meet certain requirements to participate.

[5] Participants must be individuals, estates, or trusts, or pass-through entities with such partners. Partners must meet specified requirements to participate.

[6] Entity may file "group return" on behalf of individuals that have same tax year and meet specified requirements. Composite return/payment required if member is nonresident individual, trust, estate, or pass-through entity that did not elect to be included on group return and whose share of CT income is $1,000 or more. After 2005, an LLP may no longer file a "group return" on behalf of individuals.

[7] Participants must be individuals and have same tax year. Partners must meet specified requirements to participate.

[8] Personal income tax not applicable for nonresidents.

[9] Partners must meet specified requirements to participate.

[10] Participants must be individuals. Partners must meet specified requirements to participate.

[11] Entity required to file partnership return and must pay income tax on behalf of qualified individual partners who elect not to file individual income tax returns.

[12] Participants must be individuals, trusts, or estates.

[13] Participants must be individuals. Partners must meet specified requirements to participate. Partners that are corporations, partnerships, or fiduciaries must be excluded.

[14] Return must be filed using tax year of majority of participants. Partners must meet specified requirements to participate.

[15] For tax years beginning after 2003 and before 2005, withholding required and combined returns for nonresident partners not allowed. For tax years beginning after 2004 and before 2007, LLPs subject to C corporation filing requirements. For tax years after 2006, LLPs are allowed to file composite returns on behalf of nonresident partners.

[16] Composite returns and composite payments of tax are required on behalf of any or all nonresident individual partners who do not agree to file an individual return. Partners that are corporations or tax-exempt trusts must be excluded.

[17] Must obtain prior approval. Participants must be individuals or certain trusts. Partners must meet specified requirements to participate.

[18] Participants must be individuals or estate/trust of deceased partner. Partners must meet specified requirements to participate.

[19] Participants must be individuals, estates, trusts, or flow-through entities with nonresident partners.

[20] Election available only to full-year nonresident individuals who have no other income from state sources and, effective for tax years after 2004, estates or trusts distributing current income that do not claim a federal deduction under IRC Sec. 651 or IRC Sec. 661.

[21] Partners must meet specified requirements to participate. Once filed, must continue to use composite return unless permission to change granted in writing by Commissioner.

[22] Participants must be individuals, out-of-state C corporations, or pass-through entities. Members must meet specified requirements to participate.

[23] Personal income tax applies only to interest and dividend income and is not applicable to nonresidents.

[24] Participants must be individuals. Partners must meet specified requirements to participate. Fiscal year filers must be excluded. Returns with 25 or more participants must be filed on diskette.

[25] Must obtain prior approval and include at least 11 qualified partners to file a "group return." Participants must have same accounting period. Partners must meet specified requirements to participate.

[26] Nonresident individual member not required to file individual income tax return if only NC source income was from entity and entity reported nonresident's income on partnership return and paid tax due.

[27] C corporations that are direct or indirect investors must be excluded.

[28] Participants in a "multiple nonresident return" must be individuals or electing small business trusts (ESBTs). Return must be filed using tax year of majority of participants. Partners must meet specified requirements to participate. For tax years beginning after 2005, composite returns required on behalf of electing nonresident owners.

[29] Participants must be individuals and use calendar tax year. Partners must meet specified requirements to participate.

[30] Participants must be individuals or fiduciaries and have same tax year. Partners must meet specified requirements to participate. Partners that are corporations must be excluded.

[31] Personal income tax applies only to stock and bond income and is not applicable to nonresidents.

[32] Corporation franchise tax is not imposed on partnerships. State does not impose income tax on individuals.

[33] Partners must meet specified requirements to participate. Partners entitled to Utah tax credits must be excluded.

[34] Must obtain prior approval and include at least 21 qualified partners. Participants must be individuals. Partners must meet specified requirements to participate.

[35] Must obtain prior approval to file a "unified return." Partners must meet specified requirements to participate.

[36] Partners must meet specified requirements to participate. Subject to $50 processing fee.

[37] Partners must meet specified requirements to participate in a "combined return." Fiscal year filers, certain estates/trusts, partnerships, and corporations must be excluded.

Composite Returns—Partnerships

The following chart indicates whether composite returns may be filed for nonresident partners.

State	Answer
Alabama	Yes
Alaska	N/A[1]
Arizona	Yes[2]
Arkansas	Yes[3]
California	Yes[4]
Colorado	Yes[5]
Connecticut	Yes[6]
Delaware	Yes[7]
District of Columbia	No[8]
Florida	N/A[1]
Georgia	Yes[9]
Hawaii	Yes[10]
Idaho	Yes[11]
Illinois	Yes[12]
Indiana	Yes[13]
Iowa	Yes[14]
Kansas	Yes[9]
Kentucky	Yes[15]
Louisiana	Yes[16]
Maine	Yes[17]
Maryland	Yes[10]
Massachusetts	Yes[18]
Michigan	Yes[19]
Minnesota	Yes[20]
Mississippi	Yes[21]
Missouri	Yes[9]
Montana	Yes[22]
Nebraska	No
New Hampshire	No[23]
New Jersey	Yes[24]

State	Answer
New Mexico	Yes
New York	Yes[25]
North Carolina	Yes[26]
North Dakota	Yes[7]
Ohio	Yes[27]
Oklahoma	Yes[9]
Oregon	Yes
Pennsylvania	Yes[28]
Rhode Island	Yes[29]
South Carolina	Yes[30]
Tennessee	No[31]
Texas	N/A[32]
Utah	Yes[33]
Vermont	Yes[34]
Virginia	Yes[35]
West Virginia	Yes[36]
Wisconsin	Yes[37]

---

[1] Individuals not subject to income-based taxes.

[2] Entity may file on behalf of nonresident individuals only. Must include at least 10 qualified partners. Participants must have same tax year. Partners must meet specified requirements to participate. Deceased partners must be excluded.

[3] Entity may file on behalf of nonresidents only. Must obtain prior approval. Partners must meet specified requirements to participate. Effective for tax years beginning after 2005, composite returns may be filed on behalf of electing nonresident partners.

[4] Entity may file a "group nonresident return" on behalf of nonresident individuals only. Returns must be filed using calendar tax year. Partners must meet certain requirements to participate.

[5] Partnerships, other than publicly traded partnerships, may file on behalf of nonresident individuals, nonresident estates/trusts, and certain pass-through entities. Partners must meet specified requirements to participate.

[6] Entity may file "group return" on behalf of nonresidents that have same tax year and meet specified requirements. Composite return/payment required if partner is nonresident individual, trust, estate, or pass-through entity that did not elect to be included on group return and whose share of CT income is $1,000 or more ($500 or more for publicly traded partnerships). After 2005, a partnership may no longer file a "group return" on behalf of nonresident individuals.

[7] Entity may file on behalf of nonresident individuals only. Participants must have same tax year. Partners must meet specified requirements to participate.

[8] Personal income tax not applicable to nonresidents.

[9] Entity may file on behalf of nonresidents only. Partners must meet specified requirements to participate.

[10] Entity may file on behalf of nonresident individuals only. Partners must meet specified requirements to participate.

[11] Entity required to file partnership return and must pay income tax on behalf of qualified resident and nonresident individual partners who elect not to file individual income tax returns.

[12] Entity may file on behalf of nonresident individuals, trusts, or estates. With prior approval, such returns may include residents.

[13] Entity may file on behalf of nonresident individuals only. Partners must meet specified requirements to participate. Partners that are corporations, partnerships, or fiduciaries must be excluded.

[14] Entity may file on behalf of nonresidents only. Return must be filed using tax year of majority of participants. Partners must meet specified requirements to participate.

[15] For tax years beginning on or after 2003 and before 2005, withholding required and combined returns for nonresident partners not allowed. For tax years beginning after 2004 and before 2007, limited partnerships are subject to C corporation filing requirements, while general partnerships may file composite return on behalf of electing nonresident individual partners and pay income tax at highest marginal rate on partners' pro rate share of partnership income. For tax years after 2006, composite returns allowed for all partnerships.

[16] Composite returns and composite payments of tax are required on behalf of any or all nonresident individual partners who do not agree to file an individual return. Partners that are corporations or tax-exempt trusts must be excluded.

[17] Entity may file on behalf of nonresident individuals or certain trusts. Must obtain prior approval. Partners must meet specified requirements to participate.

[18] Entity may file on behalf of nonresidents only. Participants must be individuals or estate/trust of deceased partner. Partners must meet specified requirements to participate.

[19] Entity may file on behalf of nonresidents only. Participants must be individuals, estates, trusts, or flow-through entities with nonresident members.

[20] Election available only to full-year nonresident individuals who have no other income from state sources and, effective for tax years after 2004, estates or trusts distributing current income that do not claim a federal deduction under IRC Sec. 651 or IRC Sec. 661.

[21] Entity may file on behalf of nonresidents only. Partners must meet specified requirements to participate. Once filed, must continue to use composite return unless permission to change granted in writing by Commissioner.

[22] Participants must be individuals, out-of-state C corporations, or pass-through entities. Members must meet specified requirements to participate.

[23] Personal income tax applies only to interest and dividend income and is not applicable to nonresidents.

[24] Entity may file on behalf of nonresident individuals only. Returns with 25 or more participants must be filed on diskette. Partners must meet specified requirements to participate. Fiscal year filers must be excluded.

[25] Entity may file a "group return" on behalf of nonresidents only. Must obtain prior approval and include at least 11 qualified partners. Participants must have same accounting period. Partners must meet specified requirements to participate.

[26] Nonresident individual partner not required to file individual income tax return if only NC source income was from partnership and partnership reported nonresident's income on partnership's return and paid tax due.

[27] C corporations that are direct or indirect investors must be excluded.

[28] Electing partners must all have the same taxable year.

[29] Entity may file on behalf of nonresident and part-year resident individuals. Participants must use calendar tax year. Partners must meet specified requirements to participate.

[30] Entity may file on behalf of nonresident individuals or fiduciaries. Participants must have same tax year. Partners must meet specified requirements to participate. Corporate partners must be excluded.

[31] Personal income tax applies only to stock and bond income and is not applicable to nonresidents.

[32] Corporation franchise tax is not imposed on partnerships. State does not impose income tax on individuals.

[33] Entity may file on behalf of nonresidents only. Partners must meet specified requirements to participate. Partners entitled to Utah tax credits must be excluded.

[34] Entity may file on behalf of nonresident individuals only. Must obtain prior approval and include at least 21 qualified partners. Partners must meet specified requirements to participate.

[35] Entity may file a "unified return" on behalf of nonresidents only. Must obtain prior approval. Partners must meet specified requirements to participate.

[36] Entity may file on behalf of nonresidents only. Partners must meet specified requirements to participate. Subject to $50 processing fee.

[37] Entity may file a "combined return" on behalf of nonresidents only. Partners must meet specified requirements to participate. Fiscal year filers, certain estates/trusts, partnerships, and corporations must be excluded.

Composite Returns—S Corporations

The following chart indicates whether composite returns may be filed for nonresident shareholders.

State	Answer
Alabama	Yes
Alaska	N/A[1]
Arizona	Yes[2]
Arkansas	No[3]
California	Yes[4]
Colorado	Yes[5]
Connecticut	Yes[6]
Delaware	Yes[7]
District of Columbia	N/A[8]
Florida	N/A[1]
Georgia	Yes[9]
Hawaii	Yes[10]
Idaho	Yes[11]
Illinois	Yes[12]
Indiana	Yes[13]
Iowa	Yes[14]
Kansas	Yes[9]
Kentucky	No[15]
Louisiana	No
Maine	Yes[16]
Maryland	Yes[10]
Massachusetts	Yes[17]
Michigan	Yes[18]
Minnesota	Yes[19]
Mississippi	Yes[20]
Missouri	Yes[9]
Montana	Yes[21]
Nebraska	No
New Hampshire	N/A[8]
New Jersey	Yes[22]

State	Answer
New Mexico	Yes
New York	Yes[23]
North Carolina	Yes
North Dakota	Yes[7]
Ohio	Yes[24]
Oklahoma	No
Oregon	Yes[25]
Pennsylvania	Yes[26]
Rhode Island	Yes[9]
South Carolina	Yes[27]
Tennessee	N/A[8]
Texas	N/A[28]
Utah	No
Vermont	Yes[29]
Virginia	Yes[30]
West Virginia	Yes[31]
Wisconsin	Yes[32]

[1] Individuals not subject to income-based taxes.

[2] Must include at least 10 qualified shareholders. Participants must have same tax year. Shareholders must meet specified requirements to participate.

[3] Effective for tax years beginning after 2005, composite returns may be filed on behalf of electing nonresident shareholders.

[4] Participants in a "group nonresident return" must be individuals. Return must be filed using calendar tax year. Shareholders must meet specified requirements to participate.

[5] Participants must be individuals, estates, or trusts, or pass-through entities with such members. Shareholders must meet specified requirements to participate.

[6] Entity may file "group return" on behalf of individuals that have same tax year and meet specified requirements. Composite return/payment required on behalf of shareholders that did not elect to be included on group return and whose share of CT income is $1,000 or more. After 2005, an S corporation may no longer file a "group return" on behalf of nonresident individuals.

[7] Participants must be individuals and have same tax year. Shareholders must meet specified requirements to participate.

[8] S corporations taxed in same manner as C corporations.

[9] Shareholders must meet specified requirements to participate.

[10] Participants must be individuals. Shareholders must meet specified requirements to participate.

[11] Entity required to file S corporation return and must pay income tax on behalf of qualified individual shareholders who elect not to file individual income tax returns.

[12] Participants must be individuals, estates, or trusts.

[13] Shareholders must meet specified requirements to participate. Shareholders that are corporations, partnerships, or fiduciaries must be excluded.

[14] Return must be filed using tax year of majority of participants. Shareholders must meet specified requirements to participate.

[15] For tax years beginning after 2003 and before 2005, withholding required and combined returns for nonresident shareholder not allowed. For tax years beginning after 2004 and before 2007, S corporations subject to C corporation filing requirements. For tax years after 2006, S corporations are allowed to file composite returns on behalf of nonresident shareholders.

[16] Must obtain prior approval. Participants must be individuals or certain trusts. Shareholders must meet specified requirements to participate.

[17] Participants must be individuals or estate/trust of deceased shareholder and have same tax year. Shareholders must meet specified requirements to participate.

[18] Participants must be individuals, estates, trusts, or flow-through entities with nonresident members.

[19] Election available only to full-year nonresident individuals who have no other income from state sources and, effective for tax years after 2004, estates or trusts distributing current income that do not claim a federal deduction under IRC Sec. 651 or IRC Sec. 661

[20] Shareholders must meet specified requirements to participate. Once filed, entity must continue to use composite filing method unless permission to change granted in writing by Commissioner.

[21] Participants must be individuals, out-of-state C corporations, or pass-through entities. Members must meet specified requirements to participate.

[22] Returns with 25 or more participants must be filed on diskette. Participants must be individuals. Shareholders must meet specified requirements to participate. Fiscal year filers must be excluded.

[23] Must obtain prior approval and include at least 11 qualified shareholders to file a "group return." Participants must have same accounting period. Shareholders must meet specified requirements to participate.

[24] C corporations that are direct or indirect investors must be excluded.

[25] Participants in a "multiple nonresident return" must be individuals or electing small business trusts (ESBTs). Return must be filed using tax year of majority of participants. Shareholders must meet specified requirements to participate. For tax years beginning after 2005, composite returns required on behalf of electing nonresident owners.

[26] Participants must be individuals and use calendar tax year. Shareholders must meet specified requirements to participate.

[27] Participants must be individuals or fiduciaries and have same tax year. Shareholders must meet specified requirements to participate. Corporate shareholders must be excluded.

[28] S corporations subject to corporate franchise tax in same manner as C corporations. Individuals not subject to income-based taxes.

[29] Must obtain prior approval and include at least 21 qualified shareholders. Participants must be individuals. Shareholders must meet specified requirements to participate.

[30] Must obtain prior approval to file a "unified return." Shareholders must meet specified requirements to participate.

[31] Shareholders must meet specified requirements to participate. Subject to $50 processing fee.

[32] Shareholders must meet specified requirements to participate in a "combined return." Fiscal year filers and certain estates/trusts must be excluded.

Consolidated Returns

A consolidated return is a single return in which the income of a group of affiliated corporations is reported. Most states provide for the filing of consolidated returns, although the qualifications for filing such returns may vary from state to state. For federal purposes, an "affiliated group" is defined as a group of corporations with a common parent that owns, directly, at least 80% of the voting stock and 80% of the value of all the stock of at least one member corporation, and in which the stock meeting the 80%-voting-and-value test in each of the members (except the parent) is owned directly by one or more of the other members. Most, though not all states, limit the filing of consolidated returns to corporate groups that qualify as an affiliated group under federal law.

The following chart indicates each state's positions regarding the filing of the consolidated returns. States that do not impose a corporate income tax are not included in the chart.

State	Permitted?	Conditions or Comments
Alabama	Yes	AL affiliated group filing or required to file a federal consolidated return may elect to file an AL consolidated return for same year.
Alaska	Yes	Required of affiliates that have filed federal consolidated return.
Arizona	Yes	Permitted for affiliated groups filing federal consolidated return. May be required.
Arkansas	Yes	Elective for members of federally defined affiliated group that have AR income.
California	No	Certain affiliated groups of railroad corporations may file consolidated returns.
Colorado	Yes	Permitted for federally defined affiliated group if all consent.
Connecticut	Yes	CT uses the term "combined" return for what usually is called a "consolidated" return. Affiliated corporations included in a federal consolidated return may file or be required to file a "combined" return.
Delaware	No	Permitted for affiliated group of headquarters management corporations.
District of Columbia	Yes	Permitted upon a binding election by all corporations that are part of a federally defined and electing affiliated group subject to D.C. franchise tax on some part of their gross income, where all corporations have nexus with the District, and the return does not include any corporation that uses a different accounting method and period. Exception applies regarding any Qualified High Technology Company.

State	Permitted?	Conditions or Comments
Florida	Yes	Permitted if parent and all members of affiliated group that filed federal consolidated return consent.
Georgia	No	Corporations filing a federal consolidated return must file separate returns, unless prior approval, is received.
Hawaii	Yes	Permitted for HI based affiliated groups with Hawaii source income where federal consolidated return requirements have been met.
Idaho	No	No provision requires or permits consolidated filing. However, unitary group may file a "group return" (also referred to as a "combined report").
Illinois	No	Corporations that are members of same unitary group must file "combined returns".
Indiana	Yes	Permitted if all filing members of the affiliated group have adjusted gross income derived from activities in IN and all qualifying members of the affiliated group are included in the consolidated group.
Iowa	Yes	Permitted (and may be required) for affiliated group members with nexus to IA who also file a federal consolidated return. Members of an affiliated group that are exempt from IA taxation cannot be included in the consolidated return.
Kansas	Yes	Required for affiliated groups that file a consolidated federal return and derive all their income from KS sources. Corporations that are members of an affiliated group that don't derive their entire income from KS sources and that have filed a federal return may file a KS consolidated return with Tax Director's permission.
Kentucky	Yes	For tax years beginning on or after January 1, 2005, required of members of affiliated group doing business in state if parent or any member has 80% direct or indirect control of the group. Not applicable to REITs, RICs, S corporations, and corporations that realize an NOL whose Kentucky apportionment factors are de minimis.
Louisiana	No	Not permitted, except as required by the Secretary of Revenue.
Maine	Yes	Permitted for those affiliated groups that have nexus with ME and that must determine their ME net income on a combined basis.

State	Permitted?	Conditions or Comments
Maryland	No	
Massachusetts	Yes	Affiliated groups that have filed a federal consolidated return may file "combined" return. MA "combined" returns permitted even though not all members filing the federal return are included in the MA return. However, all members of affiliated group subject to MA excise tax must be included.
Michigan	Yes	Affiliated groups that are MI taxpayers may be permitted or required to file a consolidated return if certain eligibility requirements are met.
Minnesota	No	
Mississippi	No	
Missouri	Yes	Permitted for an affiliated group that files a federal consolidated return.[1]
Montana	Yes	Permitted for federally defined affiliated groups that have common ownership of at least 80% of all classes of stock of each affiliated corporation, that have a unitary business operation, and that receive permission from the Dept. of Revenue.
Nebraska	No	
New Hampshire	No	
New Jersey	No	Required only for businesses holding a license pursuant to the Casino Control Act. Permitted for air carriers. May be required to prevent distortion of income.
New Mexico	Yes	Only permitted for corporations that have filed a federal consolidated return.
New York	No	Permitted only for corporate stockholders in a tax-exempt DISC.
North Carolina	No	Not permitted, but may be required if corporation's return does not disclose true net earnings through intercompany payments.
North Dakota	Yes	Taxpayers that compute their liability on a combined basis may elect to file a consolidated ND return. Two or more ND domestic corporations affiliated as parent and subsidiary that file a federal consolidated return must file a combined report and consolidated return for ND income tax purposes.
Ohio	No	

State	Permitted?	Conditions or Comments
Oklahoma	Yes	If federal return filed: permitted for two or more affiliated corporations that derive part of their income from OK sources; required if affiliates' income entirely from OK sources.
Oregon	Yes	Required for unitary members filing federal consolidated returns that are not permitted or required to (1) determine OR taxable income on a separate basis, or (2) use different apportionment factors than apply to other group members. Oregon "consolidated return" is what most states refer to as a "combined return."
Pennsylvania	No	
Rhode Island	Yes	Affiliated group may file a consolidated return if; (1) all affiliated corporations consent; (2) no member corporations are FSCs, DISCs, S corporations, or corporations buying, selling, dealing in, or holding securities on own behalf; (3) all members are subject to RI tax; and (4) all have the same fiscal year.
South Carolina	Yes	May be filed by (1) a parent and substantially-controlled subsidiary; (2) two or more corporations substantially under the control of the same interests; (3) a corporation doing business entirely within SC and a corporation doing a multistate business; or (4) two or more corporations doing multistate business.
Tennessee	No	Although a TN statute grants the Commissioner authority to allow corporations to file consolidated returns, as a matter of policy they have not been used.
Texas	No	
Utah	No	
Vermont	Yes	Permitted for corporations that receive any income allocated or apportioned to VT for the taxable year and that constitute a federally defined affiliated group of corporations.
Virginia	Yes	Permitted for federally defined affiliated corporation, but a consolidated return may not include corporations that are exempt from VA income tax, not affiliated, or that use different taxable years. Called a "combined return."
West Virginia	Yes	Permitted for affiliated groups with consent of all included corporations; may be required for affiliated corporations where necessary to clearly reflect the corporation's taxable income.

State	Permitted?	Conditions or Comments
Wisconsin	No	The Department may require whatever consolidated statements are necessary to determine the taxable income received by affiliated or related corporations.

[1] Provision permitting consolidated returns if at least 50% of the group's income is derived from MO was ruled invalid on 12-22-98 by the MO courts as violative of U.S. Commerce Clause.

Construction, Airlines, and Railroads

The chart below shows whether there are special industry apportionment factor rules in effect in the states for construction contractors, airlines, and railroads. States that do not impose a corporate income tax are not included in this chart.

State	Construction	Airlines	Railroads
Alabama	Yes	Yes	Yes
Alaska	Yes	Yes	Yes
Arizona	No	Yes	No
Arkansas	Yes	Yes	Yes
California	Yes	Yes	Yes
Colorado	Yes	Yes	Yes
Connecticut	No	Yes	No
Delaware	No	No	No
District of Columbia	No	Yes	Yes
Florida	No	Yes	Yes
Georgia	No	Yes	Yes
Hawaii	Yes	Yes	No
Idaho	Yes	Yes	Yes
Illinois	No	Yes	Yes
Indiana	No	Yes	Yes
Iowa	Yes	Yes	Yes
Kansas	No	Yes	Yes
Kentucky	Yes	Yes	Yes
Louisiana	No	Yes	Yes
Maine	No	No	No
Maryland	No	Yes	Yes
Massachusetts	No	Yes	No
Michigan	No	Yes	Yes
Minnesota	No	Yes	No
Mississippi	Yes	Yes	Yes
Missouri	Yes	Yes	Yes
Montana	Yes	Yes	Yes
Nebraska	No	Yes	No
New Hampshire	No	Yes	Yes

State	Construction	Airlines	Railroads
New Jersey	No	Yes	Yes[1]
New Mexico	Yes	Yes	Yes
New York	No	Yes[2]	No
North Carolina	Yes	Yes	Yes
North Dakota	No	Yes	Yes
Ohio	No	No	No
Oklahoma	No	Yes	Yes
Oregon	Yes	Yes	Yes
Pennsylvania	No	Yes	Yes
Rhode Island	No	Yes	No
South Carolina	No	Yes	Yes
Tennessee	No	Yes	Yes
Texas	No	No	No
Utah	Yes	No	No
Vermont	No	No	No
Virginia	Yes	No	Yes
West Virginia	No	No	No
Wisconsin	No	Yes	Yes

[1] Inland freight providers.
[2] Air freight forwarders.

304

Corporate Income Tax Filing Federal Form Attachment Requirements

This chart indicates whether the state imposes a generally applicable requirement that corporate income taxpayers attach their federal corporate income tax returns to their state corporate income tax returns. Additional or alternative attachment requirements are noted in the "Comments" column, including those states that require Schedule M-3 (Form 1120), Net Income (Loss) Reconciliation for Corporations With Total Assets of $10 Million or more, to be attached.

State	Requirement	Comments	Authority
AL	Yes	Complete copy of appropriate federal return with necessary supporting schedules must be attached to Form 20C. Members of affiliated group filing federal consolidated return must attach copy of Federal Form 851, copy of spreadsheet of income statement for every corporation in group, and copy of pages 1 through 4 of consolidated Federal Form 1120.	Form 20C Instructions
AK	Yes	Copy of signed federal return as filed with the IRS must be attached to Form 04-611. Corporations included in federal consolidated filing must attach copy of federal consolidated return. Affiliates filing Alaska consolidated return must attach complete copy of federal return for each affiliate. S corporations required to attach copy of pages 1 through 4 of federal 1120S.	Form 04-611 Instructions
AR	Yes	Copy of the completed federal Form 1120, 1120S, or other form, including all schedules and documents.	Form AR1100CT Instructions
AZ	Yes	Copy of the completed federal return (Form 1120, 1120A, etc.) must be attached to Form 120.	Form 120 Instructions
CA	Yes	Attach either (1) a copy of the Schedule M-3 (Form 1120) to the California Franchise or Income Tax Return; (2) a complete copy of the federal return; or (3) the Schedule M-3 (Form 1120) in a spreadsheet format. If federal reconciliation method is used, page 1 Form 1120 or 1120A and all pertinent schedules must be attached.	Form 100 Instructions
CO	No		Form 112 Instructions
CT	Yes	Complete copy of federal Form 1120 as filed with the IRS including all schedules must be attached to Form CT-1120.	Form CT-1120 Instructions
DC	No	Where applicable, federal Forms 4562, 4797, and Schedule D must be attached to Form D-20. If a federal Schedule M-3 (Form 1120) was filed with the federal return it must be attached to Form D-20.	Form D-20 Instructions

State	Requirement	Comments	Authority
DE	Yes	All federal schedules and exhibits must be attached to Form 1100 along with federal return. Members of federal affiliated groups must furnish spreadsheets of all income and deduction items reconciling each member's separate items with consolidated totals.	Form 1100 Instructions
FL	Yes	Copy of pages 1 through 4 of federal Form 1120, copy of pages 1 through 2 of federal Form 1120A, or copy of actual federal income tax return filed with the IRS must be attached to Form F-1120. Where applicable, federal Forms 4562, 851 (or Florida Form F-851), 1122, 4626, Schedule D, and any supporting details for Schedules M-1 and M-2.	Form F-1120 Instructions
GA	Yes	Federal return and all federal schedules supporting the federal return must be attached to Form 600.	Form 600 Instructions
HI	No	Corporations claiming a depreciation deduction must attach a completed federal Form 4562.	Form N-30 Instructions
IA	Yes	Complete copy of federal return as filed with IRS and federal Form 4626 must be attached to IA 1120. Federal affiliated group members filing consolidated federal returns that claim Iowa federal income tax deduction must attach pages 1 through 4 of consolidated federal return. Taxpayers reporting capital gains on Iowa Schedule D must file federal Schedule D.	Form IA 1120 Instructions
ID	Yes	Complete copy of federal return must be attached to the state return. First-time filers of Idaho Form 41S must attach copy of federal Form 2553 or federal notice approving S corporation election.	Form 41 Instructions

State	Requirement	Comments	Authority
IL	Yes	Copy of page 1, federal Form 1120 and Schedules L, M-1, M-2, and M-3, if applicable, or pages 1 and 2, federal Form 1120-A, must be attached to state return. Corporations included in federal consolidated return must attach pro forma copy of page 1, federal Form 1120 and Schedules L, M-1, M-2, and M-3, if applicable, as if they had filed separate federal returns. Life insurance companies, nonlife mutual, or nonlife stock insurance company must attach a copy of page 1, federal 1120L, or page 1, federal Form 1120-PC (and Schedule A if filed). Unitary business group members not required to attach page 1 federal Form 1120 or Schedules L, M-1, M-2, or M-3. Other federal forms and schedules required to support Illinois return must be attached.	Form IL-1120 Instructions
IN	Yes	Copies of pages 1 through 4 of federal return must be attached to Indiana IT-20	Form IT 20 Instructions
KS	Yes	Copy of pages 1 through 4 of federal return or consolidated return. If the return is a consolidated return, enclose a company-by-company spreadsheet of income and expense to total the consolidated federal taxable income and a company-by-company spreadsheet of the consolidated balance sheet including Schedules M-1 and M-2. Federal schedules to support any Kansas modifications claimed on page 1 of Form K-120, and federal Forms 851, 1118, and 5471, if applicable, must be attached to Form K-120.	Form K-120 Instructions
KY	Yes	Page 1, and Schedule L, including attached schedule, of federal Form 1120 must be attached to Form 720. Federal Schedule D and Forms 851, 4562, 4797, and 5884 must also be attached if applicable.	Form 720 Instructions
LA	No		Form CIFT-620 Instructions
MA	Yes	Exact copy of federal Form 1120 and applicable schedules and forms must be attached to Form 355.	Form 355 Instructions

State	Requirement	Comments	Authority
MD	Yes	Copy of pages 1 through 4 of actual federal return as filed with IRS must be attached to Form 500. Corporations included in federal consolidated filing must file separate Maryland returns with copy of pages 1 through 4 of consolidated federal return attached to each. Each filing must also include columnar schedules of income and expense and balance sheet items required for federal filing, reconciling separate items of each member to consolidated totals.	Form 500 Instructions
ME	Yes	Copy of pages 1 through 4 of federal Form 1120 must be attached to Maine return. Corporations included in federal consolidated filing must attach pages 1 through 4 of federal Consolidated Form 1120. S Corporations must attach federal return and federal Schedule K-1 to 1065-ME/1120S-ME.	Form 1120ME Instructions
MI	Yes	C corporations must attach copy of pages 1 through 4 of federal Form 1120 or 1120A to Single Business Tax Return C-8000. If filing as part of a consolidated federal return, attach a pro forma or consolidated schedule. S corporations must attach pages 1 through 4 of federal Form 1120S. Individuals must attach federal Form 1040, Schedules C, C-EZ, D, and E and Form 4797 if applicable.	Form C-8000 Instructions
MN	Yes	Copies of all 2004 returns filed with IRS and all supporting schedules except Form 5471 must be attached to M4.	Form M4 Instructions
MO	Yes	Federal return pages 1 through 4 and supporting schedules must be attached to MO-1120. Federal affiliated group members not filing Missouri consolidated returns must attach pro forma federal Form 1120 with all pertinent schedules, as well as pages 1 through 4 of actual consolidated federal income tax return. Taxpayers excluding gain from sale of low income housing project must attach federal Form 4797. Taxpayers required to recapture federal low income housing credit must attach federal Form 8611.	Form MO-1120 Instructions

State	Requirement	Comments	Authority
MS	Yes	Corporations excluding extraterritorial income on federal return must attach federal Form 8873 to Form 83-105. If federal 30% or 50% bonus depreciation claimed on federal return, federal Form 4562 must be completed twice and attached to Form 83-122. Taxpayers who elect installment method for federal income tax purposes should include both a federal Form 6252 and a schedule of any differences between the federal and Mississippi amounts.	2004 Form 83-122 and 83-105 Instructions
MT	Yes	Complete copy of federal Form 1120 must be attached to CLT-4	Form CLT-4 Instructions
NC	No	Complete federal return must be available to the North Carolina Department of Revenue upon request. Corporations included in federal consolidated filings must attach copy of separate federal taxable income.	Form CD-405 Instructions
ND	Yes	Complete copy of federal return as filed with IRS must be attached.	Form 40 Instructions
NE	Yes	Copy of actual federal return, including at least copies of the first four pages and supporting schedules, as filed with the IRS must be attached to 1120N. Exempt farm cooperatives must attach federal Form 990-C. Corporations included in consolidated federal filing must attach copy of federal Form 851 as well as consolidating schedules or workpapers for income and expenses, cost of goods sold, and balance sheet.	Form 1120N Instructions
NH	Yes		Form NH-1120 Instructions
NJ	No	Corporations included in consolidated federal filing must complete all schedules on own separate basis and attach copy of federal Form 851 to Form CBT 100. Federal S corporations that are not New Jersey S corporations must attach federal Form 1120S. Corporations filing unconsolidated federal Form 1120 with IRS may attach Schedules M-1 and M-2, federal Form 1120, in lieu of completing Schedules C and C-1, Form CBT 100. Corporations deducting IRC Sec. 78 gross-up must attach federal Form 1118. Federal Forms 4797 and 4562 must be attached if relevant.	Form CBT-100 Instructions
NM	Yes	Pages 1 through 4 of federal Form 1120 must be attached to Form CIT-1. Corporations filing as separate corporate entity or in a combined filing must attach pages I through 4 of simulated federal Form 1120.	Form CIT-1 Instructions

State	Requirement	Comments	Authority
NY	Yes	Complete copy of federal return must be attached to Form CT-3 or CT-4. Federal affiliated group members included in consolidated filings must complete and attach to New York return pro forma federal Form 1120 reflecting federal taxable income that would have been reported on separate federal return and attach copy of federal consolidated workpaper indicating separate taxable income before elimination of intercorporate transaction included in federal consolidated return.	Form CT-3 Instructions
OH	No	Schedule L, federal Form 1120, or other balance sheet reflecting books of taxpayer on separate company basis must be attached to FT 1120.	Form FT 1120 Form Instructions
OK	Yes	Complete copy of federal return must be attached to Form 512, Schedule A or Schedule B. Corporation deducting wages equal to federal Indian Employment Credit must attach federal Form 8845 and Form 3800 if applicable.	Form 512 Instructions
OR	Yes	Complete copy of federal return.	Form 20 Instructions
PA	Yes	Complete copy of federal return must be attached to Form RCT-101. Corporations reporting tax preference additions must attach federal Form 4626.	Form RCT-101 Instructions
RI	Yes	Copy of all pages and all schedules of federal return must be attached to Form RI-1120C.	Form RI-1120C Instructions
SC	Yes	Completed copy of federal return must be attached to SC 1120.	Form SC 1120 Instructions
TN	No	Corporations that have been audited by the IRS must attach copy of federal Revenue Agent's Report to Form FAE 170.	Form FAE 170 Instructions
TX	No		Form 05-142 and 05-143 Instructions
UT	Yes	First four pages of federal return must be attached to Form TC-20. Include federal Schedule M-3 (Form 1120), if applicable.	Form TC-20 Instructions
VA	Yes	Copy of federal return as filed with the IRS must be attached to Form 500. Corporations included in a consolidated federal filing must attach copy of consolidated federal return.	Form 500 Instructions

State	Requirement	Comments	Authority
VT	Yes	Pro forma federal Form 1120 if the corporations filed or are filing a consolidated federal return but separate Vermont returns. Provide a pro forma federal Form 1120/1120A or a detailed schedule of federal taxable income amount recomputed without the 30% or 50% special bonus depreciation.	Form CO-411 Instructions
WI	Yes	Copy of federal return must be attached to Wisconsin Form 4 even if corporation had no Wisconsin activity.	Form 4 Instructions
WV	Yes	Pages 1 through 4 of the signed federal income tax return as filed with the IRS. If a pro forma federal income tax return is attached, the following consolidated return data is also required: (1) a copy of pages 1 through 4 of the consolidated federal return plus supporting schedules showing the consolidation of the income statement, balance sheet, elimination and adjustments; (2) a copy of federal Form 851; and (3) a signed statement explaining any differences between federal filing and that reported for West Virginia. Include Schedule M-3 (Form 1120), if applicable.	Form WV/CNF-120 Instructions

Corporate Income Tax Return Filing Extensions

The following chart shows the return filing extension rules in effect for each state. Some states automatically provide a filing extension if the taxpayer has received a federal filing extension, while other states require taxpayers with a federal extension to apply separately for a state extension and fulfill additional requirements. A corporation that files a federal Form 7004 is entitled to an automatic six-month extension to file its federal income tax return. Taxpayers generally may apply for a state extension even if they did not apply for a federal extension. An extension to file a return is not an extension to pay the tax, and some states will not grant a filing extension unless a specified percentage or all tax due is paid by the original due date.

Unless otherwise indicated in the chart below, states that honor the federal extension require the taxpayer to attach a copy of the federal extension form to the state return. States that do not impose a corporate income tax are excluded.

State	Federal Extensions Honored	Independent State Extension
Alabama	Yes, if no AL tax due	Up to 6 months. Taxpayers file Form 20-E.
Alaska	Yes, plus 30 days	No
Arizona	Yes, provided a minimum of 90% of tax due is paid by original due date	6 months, provided a minimum of 90% of tax due is paid by original due date. Taxpayers file Form 120EXT
Arkansas	Yes	120 days; additional 60 days for extraordinary circumstances. Taxpayers file Form AR1055
California	No	Automatic 7 months for corporations in good standing; no written request required. Taxpayers file Form FTB 3539 if tax due
Colorado	No	Automatic 6 months. Taxpayers file Form DR 158-C if tax due
Connecticut	No	6 months. Taxpayers must file Form CT-1120 EXT and pay tax due by original due date
Delaware	Yes	6 months. Taxpayers must file Form 1100-EXT and pay tax due by original due date. Additional extensions for good cause upon written request
District of Columbia	No	Taxpayers must file Form FR-128 and pay tax due by original due date
Florida	No	6 months, upon written request for good cause shown. Taxpayers file form F-7004 and pay tentative tax by original due date
Georgia	Yes	6 months. Taxpayers must file Form IT-303
Hawaii	No	Automatic 6 months. Taxpayers file Form N-301 and must pay estimated tax by original due date.

State	Federal Extensions Honored	Independent State Extension
Idaho	No	6 months. Taxpayer file Form 41ES and must pay either 80% of total current year tax or 100% prior year tax by the original due date to obtain the extension
Illinois	Yes, plus 1 month	7 months. Taxpayers file Form IL-505-B, if tax due
Indiana	Yes, plus 30 days	60 days. Written requests filed by original due date accompanied by 90% of total current year tax or 100% of the prior year's tax
Iowa	No	6 months. Taxpayer must pay 90% of tax due to obtain the extension
Kansas	Yes	No
Kentucky	Yes	6 months. Taxpayers file Form 41A720SL
Louisiana	Yes	7 months. Taxpayers must file Form CIFT-620EXT and pay any tax due by original due date
Maine	Yes, plus 30 days	Automatic 7 months. No state form, but taxpayers may file Form 1120EXT-ME to pay at least 90% of tax owed by original due date
Maryland	No	Automatic 6 months. Taxpayers file Form 500E and must pay tax due by original due date. Extension requests may be submitted on-line or by telefile if no tax due. For tax years after 2005, 7-month extension may be granted for good cause.
Massachusetts	No	Automatic 6 months. Taxpayer must file Form 355-7004 and pay tax due by original due date. Additional time for good cause shown by written request
Michigan	No	Federal extension, plus an additional 60 days if copy of federal extension included, otherwise 180 days. Taxpayers must file Form 4 and pay any estimated tax due by original due date
Minnesota	No	Automatic 7 months. Taxpayers are not required to file a form for an extension but must pay 90% of the tax due by the original due date.
Mississippi	Yes, if no MS tax due	6 months. Taxpayers file Form 83-180 and must pay any tax due by original due date
Missouri	Yes	6 months. Taxpayers must file Form MO-7004 and pay any tax due by original due date
Montana	No	Automatic 6 months; additional time for good cause at discretion of Director
Nebraska	Yes	7 months. Taxpayer file Form 7004N and must pay any tax due by original due date

State	Federal Extensions Honored	Independent State Extension
New Hampshire	No	Automatic 7 months if 100% of tax paid by original due date. Taxpayers file Form BT-EXT
New Jersey	No	Automatic 6 months if taxpayer files Form CBT-200-T and pays tax due by original due date
New Mexico	Yes	Up to 12 months. Taxpayers file Form RPD-41096
New York	No	6 month extension if 90% of current year's tax due or 100% of prior year's tax due is paid and Form CT-5 is filed. Additional extensions, of up to two additional 3 month periods, available if Form CT-5.1 is filed
North Carolina	No	Automatic 7 months. Taxpayers must file Form CD-419
North Dakota	Yes	State extension same number of months as federal extension. Taxpayers file Form 101
Ohio	No	May 31 if the taxpayer files Form-1120ER by March 31 and pays second payment of three payments of estimated tax due. Second extension to 15th of month following month of federal extension if taxpayer pays remaining tax due and files Form-1120EX. Taxpayer must attach a copy of federal request
Oklahoma	Yes, if no OK tax owed	7 months. Taxpayers file Form 504 and must pay 90% of tax due by the original due date
Oregon	Yes	Use federal filing extension form and write "For Oregon only."
Pennsylvania	No	Extensions of up to 60 days may be granted. If federal extension allowed, extension may be the same period plus 30 days. Extension requests are made on-line
Rhode Island	No	Automatic 6 months if taxpayer pays estimated tax based on income or franchise, whichever is greater, and files Form RI-7004
South Carolina	Yes	Automatic 6 months. Taxpayers file Form SC 1120-T
Tennessee	No	6 months if taxpayer has paid 90% of estimated tax due by the original due date and attaches Form FAE-173 or copy of federal extension request to return filed by extended due date. If taxpayer is required to make tax payment with extension request and taxpayer does not file federal income tax return as member of consolidated group, FAE-173, or copy of federal extension request, must be filed with payment by due date of original return. If taxpayer is required to make tax payment with extension request and taxpayer files federal income tax return as member of consolidated group, FAE-173 must be filed with payment by due date of original return.

State	Federal Extensions Honored	Independent State Extension
Texas	No	6 months. Taxpayer must pay either 90% of tax due, or 100% of previous year's tax to obtain the extension. Taxpayers required to pay by EFT receive an initial 3 month extension upon application, instead of 6 months. Taxpayers file Form 05-110
Utah	No	6 months. Taxpayer must either pay 90% of tax due, or 100% of previous year's tax to obtain the extension
Vermont	Yes, plus 30 days provided taxpayer pays minimum tax due	30 days beyond federal provided taxpayer pays minimum tax due. Taxpayers file Form BA403
Virginia	Yes	6 months after due date or 30 days after extended due date, whichever is later, upon filing Form 500CP and paying estimated tax due.
West Virginia	Yes	Extension, if written request made
Wisconsin	Yes, plus 30 days	30 days. Taxpayers file Form IC-830

Credits for Investment/Research Activities

Many states offer corporate income or franchise tax credits to attract and increase new business investment and research and development (R&D) within the state. State credits often mirror or incorporate provisions of current of former credits under the Internal Revenue Code (IRC). Until 1986, businesses could claim a federal investment tax credit for investments in qualifying machinery and equipment under IRC Sec. 46. Currently, businesses can claim a federal credit for R&D expenses calculated under alternative formulas set forth in IRC Sec. 41, or can capitalize and amortize such expenditures under IRC Sec. 174.

The chart below sets forth the investment and research tax credits available in each state. States that do not impose an income-based tax on corporations are not included in the chart.

State	Investment Credit	Research Credit
Alabama	5% of capital costs for qualifying projects. Enterprise zone credit for new investments equal to 10% on first $10,000, 5% on next $90,000, 2% on remainder.	5% of capital costs for qualifying projects that will be used predominantly for research activity
Alaska	Allows federal credit under IRC Sec. 38 to extent attributable to AK property. Exploration incentive credits for mining operations (up to $20 million) and for oil and gas projects (up to $5 million per project). 10% of qualified capital investment, and 10% of costs related to investment, in gas exploration and development south of Brooks Range.	None
Arizona	None	Credit based on federal credit under IRC Sec. 41, limited to AZ research
Arkansas	7% credit for investment of at least $100 million before 2005 in a qualified paper manufacturing business; 5% of cost of biotechnology facility; 30% credit to build advanced biofuels manufacturing facility; 10% credit of land, buildings, M&E costs if certain payroll requirements are met; 5% of costs of equipment used to distribute biodiesel fuels	Biotechnology research credit for 20% of amount that cost of qualified research; 30% credit for higher education partnership conducting biotechnology research. 33% of cost of machinery or equipment donated to educational institutions, or if sold below cost, 33% of amount by which cost is reduced. 10% of qualified costs for in-house research (33% for targeted businesses or if in strategic research area).
California	For years before 2004, 6% manufacturer's credit for manufacturing, R&D, and pollution control equipment	Similar to federal credit; 24% basic research payments plus 15% qualified research expenses, or may elect alternative incremental credit
Colorado	1% of qualified pre-1990 IRC Sec. 38 property (3% in enterprise zones), maximum credit $1000 per year; separate credit for new business facility in enterprise zone	For businesses located in enterprise zones, 3% of CO R&D expenses over average expenses over 2-year period

State	Investment Credit	Research Credit
Connecticut	Three credits: 1) 10%-20% costs for industrial or urban redevelopment sites; 2) 5% "fixed capital" - tangible personal property with class life of more than 4 years, and 3) 5%-10% incremental machinery and equipment expenditures	Three credits: 1) 20% of incremental R&D expenditures qualifying under IRC Sec.174; 2) 1%-6% of Sec. 174 expenditures; and basic research payments under IRC Sec 41; and 3) 25% incremental increase in R&D grants to CT higher education institutions
Delaware	Economic development credit for corporation that has placed in service a qualified new/expanded facility, $400 per $100,000 investment and $400 per qualified employee hired (higher credit amount if facility located on "brownfield")	For tax years after 1999 and before 2006, credit equal to 1) 10% of excess DE R&D expenses over base amount, or 2) 50% of DE apportioned share of federal credit using alternative incremental method under IRC Sec. 41(c)(4)
District of Columbia	None	None
Florida	5% capital costs for qualified projects in high-impact industries (e.g. aerospace, silicon technology)	None (Exclusion from property/payroll factors for money or property dedicated to sponsored university R&D contracts)
Georgia	6% of cost of qualified investment property for use in construction or expansion of manufacturing facility (also, $5,250 per job created as result of construction/expansion). 1%-8% of cost of qualified investment property for use in construction/expansion of manufacturing or telecommunications facilities (rate varies based on facility location and type of property); or optional credit based on a 3-year tax liability average.	10% of excess qualified GA R&D expenses over base amount
Hawaii	4% of cost of eligible depreciable tangible personal property; 10%-35% of investment in high-technology business	20% credit based on federal credit under IRC Sec. 41 (beginning July 1, 2004, credit available only to qualified high-technology businesses)
Idaho	3% of investments in qualified depreciable property located in ID, including manufacturing equipment	Credit the sum of 1) 5% excess qualified ID R&D expenses over base amount, plus 2) 5% expenses allowed under IRC Sec. 41
Illinois	0.5% of investments in qualified tangible property by taxpayers engaged in manufacturing, mining or retailing; 0.5% of property invested in high-impact business	For tax years ending on or after 12/31/04, 6.5% of excess qualified IL R&D expenses over base amount over 3-year period
Indiana	For investments made during 2004 and 2005 tax years, lesser of the taxpayer's state tax liability growth or 30% of investment in new construction, infrastructure improvements, new equipment, or retooling of existing equipment	10% of excess qualified IN R&D expenses over base amount

State	Investment Credit	Research Credit
Iowa	10% of new investment made: (a) that directly relates to new jobs; (b) within a quality jobs enterprise zone; or (c) by the housing industry in an enterprise zone. Iowa also has credits available for equity investment in the Fund of Funds and the New Capital Investment Program.	6.5% of state's apportioned share of qualifying expenses under IRC Sec. 41. Credit for 30% of tax liability for business approved under University-Based Research Utilization Program.
Kansas	Credit for investments in qualified business facilities, calculated by investment amount/new employee formula	Credit equal to 6.5% of difference between actual qualified R&D expenses for tax year and average of actual expenditures made during the year and the 2 previous tax years. For tax years beginning after 2004, company engaged in R&D of bioscience products or processes may seek payment for up to 50% of KS NOL incurred during tax year.
Kentucky	Various economic development credits with investment components	5% of qualified costs of constructing, equipping, remodeling, and expanding research facilities
Louisiana	None	Credit similar to federal credit under IRC Sec. 41 (credit phased in, 75% of fully authorized credit can be taken for 2005, 100% for 2006, repealed on 12/31/06). Exemption, rebate, and/or credit by contract (30% cap) for cost of machinery and equipment for designated biomedical and university R&D parks. Credit equal to 35% of cash donation to dedicated research investment fund, if initial donation is at least $200,000.
Maine	Credit for equipment used in high-technology business; also credit based on federal investment credit	Credit the sum of 1) 5% excess qualified ME R&D expenses over base amount; plus 2) 7.5% basic research payments allowed under IRC Sec. 41
Maryland	Credit for qualified construction/ expansion of business premises equal to percentage (14%-28%) of property tax imposed on assessed value of premises	For tax years after 1999 and before 2005, basic credit equal to 3% of qualified MD R&D expenses up to base amount, and growth credit equal to 10% of MD R&D expenses that exceed base amount
Massachusetts	3% of cost of qualifying MA tangible personal property, after deduction of federal credit	Credit the sum of 1) 15% of basic MA R&D research payments under IRC Sec. 41, plus 2) 10% excess qualified expenses over base amount
Michigan	.85%-2.3% of costs for qualified tangible assets, based on adjusted gross receipts	None
Minnesota	None	Credit the sum of 1) 5% of excess qualified expenses (up to $2 million) over base amount, plus 2) 2.5% excess expenses over $2 million
Mississippi	None	$1,000 per employee for each job created requiring R&D skills

State	Investment Credit	Research Credit
Missouri	Until December 31, 2004, credit for new or expanding business facility, calculated by cost/new employee formula; increased credit in enterprise zones	Until December 31, 2004, 6.5% of excess qualified MO R&D expenses over 3-year base amount
Montana	35% of cost of IRC Sec. 48(a) energy property	5% of qualified MT R&D expenses under IRC Sec. 41
Nebraska	Various credits for investment/ employment in state, rural areas, and enterprise zones	None
New Hampshire	None	None
New Jersey	New Jobs Investment credit; manufacturing equipment credit; enterprise zone investment credit	Credit the sum of 1) 10% excess qualified NJ R&D expenses over base amount, plus 2) 10% basic research expenses allowed under IRC Sec. 41
New Mexico	One-half of the cost, up to $50,000 per project, incurred to restore, rehabilitate, or renovate buildings in enterprise zones for use in manufacturing, distribution, or service industry businesses	4% of qualified expenditures for research conducted at qualified facility
New York	4%-5% of investment credit base for qualified property, including buildings	9% R&D property if no employment incentive credit claimed
North Carolina	4–7% of excess of eligible investment amount over applicable threshold for qualified machinery & equipment (15%-20% for "technology commercialization" equipment)	Credit equal to 1) 5% of excess NC R&D expenditures under IRC Sec. 41; or 2) 25% NC apportioned share of federal credit under alternative incremental method
North Dakota	None	Credit the sum of 1) 8% of excess qualified ND expenses (up to $1.5 million) over base amount, and 2) 4% excess ND expenses over $1.5 million
Ohio	7.5%-13.5% credit for manufacturing machinery & equipment, applied over a 7-year period	After 2003, 7% of amount by which qualified research expenses exceed 3-year average of those expenses for preceding 3 years. Also, up to $150,000 for loan payments made by corporations that borrow money from an Ohio loan program for R&D projects that create and maintain technology jobs. Investors in certain OH- based R&D or technology transfer companies may be eligible for Edison center credit equal to 25% of investment (30% of investment in EDGE business enterprise).
Oklahoma	Greater of 1% of cost of qualified property in the year the property is placed in service or $500 for each new employee (certain manufacturers entitled to double credit)	After 2004, 50% of amount donated to independent biomedical research facility (credit adjusted annually beginning in 2007), $1,000 limit

State	Investment Credit	Research Credit
Oregon	None	Similar to federal credit, except amount equals 5% of qualified research expense over base amount, plus 5% of basic research payments; alternative credit equal to 5% of amount by which qualified research expenses exceed 10% of OR sales
Pennsylvania	None	10% of excess qualified PA R&D expenses over base amount
Rhode Island	4% and 10% credits for buildings and qualified property, including manufacturing equipment	10% of tangible personal property (including buildings); 22.5% of first $25,000 of RI R&D expenses; 16.9% of expenses over $25,000
South Carolina	1%-5% of manufacturing and production equipment in economic impact zone	5% of qualified SC research expenditures if federal credit under IRC. Sec. 174 claimed
Tennessee	1% cost of industrial machinery and equipment, includes certain computer equipment	None
Texas	7.5% cost of machinery and equipment in designated strategic investment areas	5% of excess qualified TX R&D expenses over base amount, plus basic research payments under IRC Sec. 41(e)(1)(A)
Utah	For qualified manufacturing businesses in enterprise zones, 10% of the first $250,000 and 5% of the next $1 million investment in plant, equipment, and other depreciable property	6% cost of machinery and equipment used primarily to conduct qualified research; 6% of excess qualified UT R&D expenses over base amount
Vermont	5%-10% of plant, facilities, machinery & equipment costs over $150,000; also, for sustainable technology businesses, 30% of qualified expenditures or an export credit based on difference between standard apportionment formula and special formula; High-tech growth credit – 6% of qualified investment	10% of qualified VT R&D expenses under IRC. Sec. 41; 30% of qualified sustainable R&D expenditures
Virginia	50% capital investment in information technology or biotechnology company in a tobacco-dependent locality; 10%-50% of costs of recycling, agricultural, and waste motor-oil burning equipment.	50% of eligible R&D activity in a tobacco-dependent locality, max. $500,000 per year
West Virginia	5% of qualified manufacturing investment, applied over 10-year period; Economic opportunity tax credits—amount of investment in property multiplied by new jobs percentage, applied over 10-year period	Greater of 3% of annual combined qualified research and development expenditure, or 10% of excess of annual combined qualified research and development expenditure over base amount; High growth business investment—50% of investment in qualified R&D companies

State	Investment Credit	Research Credit
Wisconsin	Development zones investment credit-2.5% of depreciable tangible property or 1.75% of property if expensed under IRC Sec. 179; Technology Zone credit – 25% of investment; 10% for investment in dairy farm modernization/expansion	5% of excess qualified WI R&D expenses over base amount; 5% of WI capital expenditures for new or expanded R&D facilities

Depletion Deduction

Under federal law (IRC § § 611—614), in the case of mines, oil and gas wells, other natural deposits, and timber, there is allowed as an income tax deduction a specified allowance for depletion. This chart shows each state's rules on the depletion deduction.

States that do not impose a corporate income tax are not included in the chart.

State	Deduction Rules
Alabama	Oil and gas: 12% of the gross income of the property, but not less than the federal allowance.
Alaska	Same as federal, except federal percentage depletion not allowed for oil and gas
Arizona	Same as federal, except for mining exploration expenses
Arkansas	Same as federal
California	Same as federal, except for the suspension of income limitation for oil and gas production from marginal properties.
Colorado	Same as federal, except 27.5% rate for oil shale
Connecticut	Same as federal
Delaware	Same as federal, except federal percentage depletion not allowed for oil and gas
District of Columbia	Same as federal
Florida	Same as federal
Georgia	Same as federal
Hawaii	Same as federal
Idaho	Same as federal
Illinois	Same as federal
Indiana	Same as federal
Iowa	Same as federal, except cost depletion only for oil, gas, and geothermal wells
Kansas	Same as federal
Kentucky	Same as federal, except for disposal of coal or iron ore
Louisiana	Same as federal, except for oil and gas: greater of cost depletion under federal law, or percentage depletion under Louisiana law, up to 50% of net income from property
Maine	Same as federal
Maryland	Same as federal, except federal percentage depletion not allowed for oil
Massachusetts	Same as federal
Michigan	Same as federal

State	Deduction Rules
Minnesota	Cost depletion only; special rules apply to mining companies
Mississippi	Same as federal, except that aggregate deductions for depletion may not exceed cost basis
Missouri	Same as federal
Montana	Same as federal, except cost depletion only for purposes of computing the MT NOL
Nebraska	Same as federal
New Hampshire	Same as federal, except for the income limitation on marginal properties
New Jersey	Same as federal
New Mexico	Same as federal
New York	Same as federal
North Carolina	Same as federal, except cost depletion only for mines, oil and gas wells, and other natural deposits located outside the state
North Dakota	Same as federal
Ohio	Same as federal
Oklahoma	22% across-the-board allowance for oil and gas, at the taxpayer's option, in lieu of the federal depletion allowance. For major oil companies, allowance may not exceed 50% of the corporation's net income
Oregon	Cost depletion only, except for metal mines. Metal mines: Cost depletion or 15% of gross income from the property during the taxable year, not to exceed 50% of net income
Pennsylvania	Same as federal
Rhode Island	Same as federal
South Carolina	Same as federal. Multistate taxpayers have the option of allocating the federally computed allowance with respect to South Carolina deposits only, up to 50% of apportioned net income
Tennessee	Same as federal, but no deduction allowed in excess of the cost basis of the property
Texas	Same as federal, except for the income limitation on marginal properties
Utah	Same as federal
Vermont	Same as federal
Virginia	Same as federal
West Virginia	Same as federal
Wisconsin	Cost depletion only

Depreciation Rules

The following chart shows each state's policy on depreciation. As reflected below, many states follow the federal provisions set forth in IRC Sec. 167 and IRC Sec. 168 ("same as federal"). Although a state may follow federal rules, there may be adjustments necessary to reflect a difference in federal and state bases.

The federal Job Creation and Worker Assistance Act of 2002 (JCWAA) (P.L. 107-147) allowed taxpayers an additional first-year depreciation deduction equal to 30% of the adjusted basis of qualified property acquired after September 10, 2001 and placed in service before May 6, 2003. The federal Jobs and Growth Tax Relief Reconciliation Act of 2003 (JGTRRA) (P.L. 108-27) increased the additional first-year depreciation allowance to 50% for qualified property acquired after May 5, 2003 and placed in service before January 1, 2005.

States that otherwise follow federal depreciation rules but do not conform to the "bonus" depreciation provisions either because they have statutes affirmatively not conforming or they conform to the Internal Revenue Code as of a date prior to the enactment of the JCWAA and JGTRRA are noted below with an asterisk (*).

State conformity with provisions of the Working Families Tax Relief Act of 2004 (WFTRA) (P.L. 108-311) and the American Jobs Creation Act of 2004 (AJCA) (P.L. 108-357) amending federal depreciation rules for certain property, including noncommercial aircraft and restaurant property, is covered in a separate chart.

States that do not impose a corporate income tax are not included in this chart.

State	Current Policy
Alabama	Same as federal
Alaska	Same as federal, except depreciation disallowed for oil and gas producers and pipelines
Arizona	Same as federal, except for certain specialized assets entitled to optional treatment[1]
Arkansas	Same as federal, as in effect on January 1, 1999*
California	Pre-ACRS rules for all property
Colorado	Same as federal
Connecticut	Same as federal*
Delaware	Same as federal
District of Columbia	Same as federal*
Florida	Same as federal
Georgia	Same as federal, except for safe harbor leases*
Hawaii	Same as federal , except Hawaii does not follow federal depreciation rules for Native American reservation property*

State	Current Policy
Idaho	Same as federal*
Illinois	Same as federal*
Indiana	Same as federal*
Iowa	Same as federal, except for speculative shell buildings and safe harbor leases[2]
Kansas	Same as federal, except for buildings for which Kansas disabled access credit was claimed
Kentucky	Same as federal, except for safe harbor leases*
Louisiana	Same as federal
Maine	Same as federal*
Maryland	Same as federal*
Massachusetts	Same as federal, except when optional deductions elected*
Michigan	No depreciation deduction allowed[3]
Minnesota	Same as federal[4]
Mississippi	Same as federal*
Missouri	Same as federal[5]
Montana	Same as federal, except for title plants[6]
Nebraska	Same as federal[7]
New Hampshire	Same as federal, as in effect on December 31, 2000*
New Jersey	Same as federal, except for safe-harbor leases and property placed in service after 1980 and before the taxpayer's tax year beginning after 6/30/93*
New Mexico	Same as federal
New York	Same as federal, except for property placed in service prior to 1994 and safe-harbor leases[8]
North Carolina	Same as federal, except for certain ecological and sewage facilities and certain utility plants[9]
North Dakota	Same as federal, except for safe-harbor leases and property placed in service in 1981 and 1982
Ohio	Same as federal[10]
Oklahoma	Same as federal[11]
Oregon	Same as federal, except for safe-harbor leases and prior law basis differences
Pennsylvania	Same as federal except straight-line required on real property*
Rhode Island	Same as federal, except when deductions for research and development and pollution control facilities elected*
South Carolina	Same as federal*
Tennessee	Same as federal , except for safe-harbor leases*

State	Current Policy
Texas	Same as federal[12]
Utah	Same as federal, except for safe-harbor leases
Vermont	Same as federal*
Virginia	Same as federal, except deduction may be increased for certain utility companies*
West Virginia	Same as federal, except for certain water and air pollution control facilities.
Wisconsin	Same as federal, except for safe-harbor leases and prior law differences[13]

[1] Applicable to tax years after 1999, all depreciation deducted under IRC Sec. 167(a) for federal purposes must be added back. A subtraction may be claimed for IRC Sec. 167(a) depreciation as if the taxpayer had not elected Sec. 168(k) bonus depreciation.

[2] Iowa disallows 30% bonus depreciation on property placed in service between September 11, 2001, and September 11, 2004, but allows 50% bonus depreciation for qualified property acquired after May 5, 2003, and before 2005.

[3] Amount claimed on federal return must be added to federal taxable income for purpose of determining the Michigan tax base. A business investment credit is available in lieu of depreciation.

[4] Minnesota requires that 80% of any bonus depreciation be added back. The add back amount may be deducted over the next five years.

[5] Missouri disallows 30% bonus depreciation deduction for property purchased between July 1, 2002 and June 30, 2003, but allows the 50% bonus depreciation for property purchased from May 6, 2003, through December 31, 2004.

[6] Montana specifically adopts IRC Sec. 167 without referencing IRC Section 168. However, it has been the state's long-standing practice to follow Sec. 168 treatment if that method is chosen by the taxpayer.

[7] Nebraska requires that 85% of any bonus depreciation be added back. The add back amount may later be deducted over five years beginning with tax year 2005.

[8] Addback required for federal bonus depreciation claimed in tax years beginning after 2002 on property placed in service on or after June 1, 2003, except for qualified resurgence zone/New York Liberty Zone property.

[9] Effective beginning with the 2005 taxable year, subtraction allowed for 20% of amount of any bonus depreciation addback required in taxable years 2001 to 2004. Taxpayers were previously required to make an addition equal to 100% of federal bonus depreciation claimed in 2001 and 2002 and 70% of federal bonus depreciation claimed in 2003 and 2004.

[10] Ohio requires that 5/6 of any bonus depreciation be added back. The add back amount may be deducted over the next five years. Special rules apply to taxpayers who claimed bonus depreciation in a tax year ending prior to June 5, 2002.

[11] Oklahoma requires that 80% of any 30% bonus depreciation be added back. The add back amount may then be deducted in equal amounts over the next four years. Oklahoma conforms to the 50% bonus depreciation, therefore no adjustment is required.

[12] Texas generally does not allow bonus depreciation because it adopts the IRC in effect for the federal tax year beginning on or after January 1, 1996, and before January 1, 1997. However, for corporations that qualify and elect to use the FIT (federal income tax) method of reporting taxable capital (including S corporations, close corporations with not more than 35 shareholders, and corporations with taxable capital of less than $1 million), the bonus depreciation will be allowed as long as the same method was used in the corporation's most recent federal income tax return.

[13] Adopts IRC depreciation provisions as amended to December 31, 2000. Addback required if amount of federal deduction exceeds amount of allowable state deduction. Subtraction allowed if amount of state deduction exceeds federal deduction.

Determining Nonbusiness Income

Under the Uniform Division of Income for Tax Purposes Act (UDITPA), a corporation's income is divided into business income, which is subject to formula apportionment, and nonbusiness income, which is subject to allocation. UDITPA defines "business income" as income arising from transactions and activity in the regular course of the taxpayer's trade or business, including income from tangible and intangible property if the acquisition, management and disposition of the property constitute integral parts of the taxpayer's regular trade or business operations. "Nonbusiness income" is defined as all income other than business income.

Many states follow the UDITPA method with respect to the treatment of nonbusiness income, though some states do not follow it, or apply only certain aspects of UDITPA nonbusiness rules. The chart below shows the nonbusiness income rules in effect for each state. A response that a state "follows UDITPA approach" indicates that its provisions are substantially similar to the uniform Act, but not necessarily that the state has specifically adopted the Act.

States that do not impose a corporate income tax are not included in this chart.

State	Provision
Alabama	Follows UDITPA approach.
Alaska	Follows UDITPA approach.
Arizona	Follows UDITPA approach.
Arkansas	Follows UDITPA approach.
California	Follows UDITPA approach.
Colorado	Depending on option selected, either follows UDITPA, or all income is apportionable.
Connecticut	Corporation's entire net income subject to apportionment; no distinction between types of income.
Delaware	Rents, royalties, interest, and gains and losses from the sale of capital assets and real property are allocated; other income apportionable.
District of Columbia	Follows UDITPA approach, except that some interest and dividends from District sources are specifically excluded.
Florida	Follows UDITPA approach.
Georgia	Business income subject to apportionment; investment income (income from interest, intangibles, and real property rental) and sales of noninventory items considered allocable income.
Hawaii	Follows UDITPA approach.
Idaho	UDITPA, with minor variations.
Illinois	All income that may be constitutionally treated as apportionable business income is business income.

State	Provision
Indiana	Follows UDITPA approach; eliminates presumptions that income is business income.
Iowa	Same as UDITPA, but adds "operationally related" and "unitary business" tests.
Kansas	Same as UDITPA, except for business income election regarding income from property transactions.
Kentucky	Follows UDITPA approach.
Louisiana	Rents, royalties, income from construction services, dividends from corporate stock, income from estates, trusts, and partnerships, profits/losses from nonbusiness sales of property considered "allocable income"; other items of income considered "apportionable income".
Maine	Entire net income subject to apportionment.
Maryland	Entire net income subject to apportionment.
Massachusetts	"Income derived from unrelated activities" is not subject to apportionment; income of Massachusetts-domiciled corporation that nondomiciliary states constitutionally barred from taxing is allocated to Massachusetts all other income apportioned.
Michigan	Entire tax base subject to apportionment.
Minnesota	Income that cannot constitutionally be apportioned, including capital transactions serving solely as investments, must be allocated; all other income apportioned.
Mississippi	Follows UDITPA approach.
Missouri	Follows UDITPA approach.
Montana	Follows UDITPA approach.
Nebraska	Entire federal taxable income is presumed to be subject to apportionment; presumption may be rebutted.
New Hampshire	All taxable income constitutes business income.
New Jersey	All operational income is subject to "allocation" (NJ uses this term instead of "apportionment"); nonoperational income assigned to particular state.
New Mexico	Follows UDITPA approach; adds business or segment liquidation to definition of business income.
New York	Business income (net income minus investment income) is apportioned.
North Carolina	All income apportionable under U.S. Constitution.
North Dakota	Follows UDITPA approach.
Ohio	Rents, royalties, capital gains/losses, and some dividends are allocable; other net income subject to apportionment.
Oklahoma	Similar to UDITPA, by specifying allocable items.
Oregon	Follows UDITPA approach.
Pennsylvania	Follows UDITPA approach.

State	Provision
Rhode Island	All net income subject to apportionment.
South Carolina	Dividends from corporate stocks, gains and losses on real property, and income from personal services always allocable; interest from intangible property, rents, gains and losses on intangible property, and royalties allocable if not connected with business; all other income apportionable.
Tennessee	Follows UDITPA approach.
Texas	Income nonapportionable due to insufficient unitary connection allocable; all other income apportionable.
Utah	Follow UDITPA approach, with presumption that dividends and capital gains are business income.
Vermont	Entire net income is subject to apportionment.
Virginia	Dividends allocable; all other income apportionable.
West Virginia	Follows UDITPA approach.
Wisconsin	Rents/royalties from nonbusiness property, income (gain/loss) from sale of nonbusiness property, and income (gain/loss) from intangibles owned by personal holding company are allocated; all other income apportioned.

Dividends Received Deduction

This chart shows whether a state follows the federal rules on the deduction for dividends received pursuant to IRC Secs. 243 through 245 and provides a brief description of state provisions having no federal counterpart.

States that do not impose a corporate income tax are not included in this chart.

State	Federal deduction allowed	Special state provisions
Alabama	Addition required for dividends received from non-20% owned corporations to extent deducted from federal taxable income.	Subtraction allowed for dividends received from a non-U.S. corporation in which the recipient owns at least 20% of stock, by vote and value, but only to extent dividends would be deductible under federal law if received from U.S. corporation.
Alaska	Yes	Elimination of intercompany dividends by unitary groups filing combined returns. 80% of dividends from foreign corporations are also eliminated. Limited to dividends taxable by Alaska.
Arizona	Addition required for amount of federal deduction.	Subtraction allowed for 100% of dividends received from foreign corporations or 50% or more controlled domestic corporations
Arkansas	No	Subtraction allowed for 100% of dividends received from 80% subsidiaries and on stock of capital development corporations
California	No	Subtraction allowed on Schedule H equal to 100% of dividends received from unitary subsidiaries to extent paid from unitary earnings and profits accumulated while both payee and payer were members of a combined report; and 75% of dividends received by water's edge group (100% for dividends derived from a construction project) from any 50%-or-more-owned corporation with less than 20% U.S. factors. Deduction for 80% of dividends (85% for tax years after 2007) from insurance company subsidiaries. California's prior dividends received deduction declared unconstitutional in 2003. The California Franchise Tax Board has taken the position that California law requires that the deduction be disallowed for all open years.
Colorado	Yes	Additional subtraction allowed for a portion of dividends received that qualify as excludable foreign source income.
Connecticut	No	Subtraction allowed for 100% of all dividends, except that no exclusion is allowed for 30% of dividends from domestic corporation in which taxpayer owns less than 20%; specific exclusions for REIT and RIC dividends. Subtraction calculated on Form CT-1120 ATT, Schedule I.
Delaware	Yes	Additional subtraction allowed for 100% of foreign dividends on which foreign tax paid
District of Columbia	No	Subtraction from gross income tax base allowed equal to 100% of dividends from wholly-owned subsidiaries and dividends from foreign sources not attributable to trade or business income.

State	Federal deduction allowed	Special state provisions
Florida	Yes	Additional subtraction allowed for 100% of foreign source dividends included in federal taxable income.
Georgia	Yes	Subtraction allowed for 100% of foreign source dividends, dividends on Georgia obligations, and federal bank dividends. Dividends received by affiliated corporations excluded if corporation receiving dividend engaged in business in Georgia
Hawaii	No	Subtraction allowed for 70% of dividends received from all corporations. A corporation that is part of an affiliated group may claim a 100% dividends received deduction for dividends received from a group member that is a. foreign affiliate, a small business investment company, or a national banking association
Idaho	Addition required for amount of federal deduction.	Subtraction allowed equal to 80% of dividends received from foreign corporations or 85% of dividends received by water's-edge filers from foreign corporations. Subtraction computed on Form 42.
Illinois	Yes	Subtraction allowed for remaining portion of federally taxable dividends equal to 100% of dividends received from wholly owned foreign subsidiaries; 80% of dividends received from 20%-or-more-owned foreign corporations; and 70% of dividends received from less-than-20%-owned foreign corporations. Subtraction computed on Schedule J..
Indiana	Yes	Subtraction allowed for remaining foreign dividends included in federal taxable income, equal to 100% of dividends received from 80%-or-more-owned foreign corporations; 85% of dividends received from less-than-80% but more-than-50%-owned foreign corporations; and 50% of dividends received from less-than-50%-owned foreign corporations.
Iowa	Yes	Subtraction allowed for remaining portion of federally taxable dividends equal to 100% of dividends received from 80%-or-more-owned foreign corporations; 80% of dividends received from less-than-80% but more-than-20%-owned foreign corporations; and 70% of dividends received from less-than-20%-owned foreign corporations.
Kansas	Yes	Subtraction allowed for 80% of remaining portion of federally taxable dividends.
Kentucky	No	All dividends excluded
Louisiana	Yes	Subtraction allowed equal to 100% of remaining foreign dividends included in federal taxable income. Prior to 2005, addition required for dividends received from foreign corporations.
Maine	Yes	Subtraction allowed for 50% of remaining federally taxable dividends, unless stock ownership is less than 50% or affiliated corporation is included in combined report.

State	Federal deduction allowed	Special state provisions
Maryland	Yes	Additional subtraction allowed equal to 100% of dividends from 50%-or-more-owned foreign corporations.
Massachusetts	No	Subtraction allowed for 95% of dividends except for dividends from (1) less-than-15% owned corp., (2) MA corp. trust, (3) non-wholly owned DISCs, and (4) RICs and REITs.
Michigan	Addition required for amount of federal deduction.	Subtraction allowed for 100% of dividends other than dividends from non-Michigan state obligations.
Minnesota	No	Subtraction allowed equal to 80% of dividends received from 20%-or-more-owned corporations; and 70% of dividends received from less-than-20%-owned corporations. Subtraction computed on Form DIV. Addition required for deemed dividends from foreign operating corporations (FOCs).
Mississippi	No	Subtraction allowed for 100% of dividend income already subject to MS income tax that can be specifically identified to recipient. Exclusion available for dividends received by holding company from a subsidiary corporation other than a REIT.
Missouri	Yes	Additional subtraction allowed for dividends apportioned to state sources using single or three-factor apportionment formula, equal to 100% of dividends received from wholly owned foreign subsidiaries; 80% of dividends received from 20%-or-more-owned corporations; and 70% of dividends received from less-than-20%-owned corporations. Subtraction computed on Schedule MO-C if using single sales-factor apportionment formula.
Montana	Yes	None
Nebraska	Yes	Additional subtraction allowed equal to 100% of foreign dividends included in federal taxable income.
New Hampshire	No	Subtraction allowed for 100% of dividends received by parent if subsidiary subject to tax or not unitary; special provisions under water's edge election.
New Jersey	No	100% of dividends from 80%-owned subsidiaries; 50% of dividends from 50% to 80%-owned subsidiaries.
New Mexico	Yes	Subtraction allowed for remaining portion of federally taxable dividends for separate filers equal to 100% of dividends received from 80%-or-more-owned foreign corporations; 80% of dividends received from less-than-80% but more-than-20%-owned foreign corporations; and 70% of dividends received from less-than-20%-owned foreign corporations. Subtraction computed on Form CIT-D.

State	Federal deduction allowed	Special state provisions
New York	No	100% deductible if from more-than-50%-owned subsidiary; 50% deductible otherwise excluding amounts from specified types of organizations.
North Carolina	Yes	Additional subtraction allowed equal to 100% of foreign dividends included in federal taxable income.
North Dakota	Addition required for amount of federal deduction.	None
Ohio	No	Subtraction allowed equal to 100% of dividends received from corporations that neither transact any substantial portion of business nor regularly maintain any substantial portion of assets within the U.S..
Oklahoma	Yes	None
Oregon	No	Subtraction allowed equal to 100% of dividends if the recipient and the payer corporations are both members of the same unitary group filing an state consolidated tax return; 80% of dividends received from 20%-or-more-owned corporations; and 70% of dividends received from less-than-20%-owned corporations. Schedule and explanation for subtraction must be attached to state return.
Pennsylvania	Subtraction allowed on Schedule C-2 for amount of federal deduction.	Additional subtraction allowed for foreign dividends included in federal taxable income, equal to 100% of dividends received from 80%-or-more-owned foreign corporations; 80% of dividends received from less-than-80% but more-than-20%-owned foreign corporations; and 70% of dividends received from less-than-20%-owned foreign corporations.
Rhode Island	Subtraction allowed for amount of federal deduction.	Additional subtraction allowed for foreign dividends included in federal taxable income equal to 100% of dividends received from 100%-owned foreign corporations; 80% of dividends received from more-than-20%-owned foreign corporations; and 70% of dividends received from less-than-20%-owned foreign corporations.
South Carolina	Yes	Additional subtraction allowed for foreign dividends included in federal taxable income, equal to 100% of dividends received from 80%-or-more-owned foreign corporations; 80% of dividends received from less-than-80% but more-than-20%-owned foreign corporations; and 70% of dividends received from less-than-20%-owned foreign corporations.
Tennessee	No	Subtraction allowed equal to 100% of dividends received from 80%-or-more-owned foreign corporations.

State	Federal deduction allowed	Special state provisions
Texas	No	Subtraction allowed for 100% of dividends received from a subsidiary, associate, or affiliated corporation that does not transact a substantial portion of its business or regularly maintain a substantial portion of its assets in the U.S..
Utah	No	Subtraction allowed for 50% of dividends from 50% owned corporations, unitary foreign subsidiaries that are not included in a combined report, and certain insurance companies.
Vermont	Yes	None
Virginia	Yes	Additional subtraction allowed for 100% of dividends received from 50%-owned subsidiaries to the extent included federally.
West Virginia	Yes	None
Wisconsin	No	Subtraction allowed for 100% of dividends received from 70%-owned subsidiaries.

Enterprise Zone Tax Incentives

In order to encourage development in economically distressed areas, a number of states provide tax incentives to businesses that locate and operate in geographical areas designated as "enterprise zones". Enterprise zones vary in size and required economic condition depending on the state. Some states use differing nomenclature for these zones (e.g. "Renaissance Zones" in North Dakota), while other offer similar development programs in addition to enterprise zones.

The chart below summarizes by tax type the major enterprise zone tax incentives in each state. The following abbreviations are used for incentives: C=Credit; E=Exemption/Exclusion' D=Deduction; R=Rebate/Refund; A=Assessment Reduction/Abatement; G=Grant.

State	Income/Franchise Tax	Sales & Use Tax	Property Tax
Alabama	C,E	E	
Alaska	No enterprise zones		
Arizona	C		A[1]
Arkansas	C	R	
California	C,D[2]	C	
Colorado	C	E	†
Connecticut	C	E	E
Delaware	No enterprise zones		
District of Columbia	C		
Florida	C,R	C,E,R	E,R
Georgia	C		†
Hawaii	C	E	†
Idaho	No enterprise zones		
Illinois	C,D	E	A
Indiana	C		C,D
Iowa	C	R	E
Kansas		E	†
Kentucky	C	E	A[3]
Louisiana	C	E,R	
Maine	No enterprise zones		
Maryland	C		C
Massachusetts	C		A
Michigan[4]	C[5]	E	E
Minnesota	C	E	E
Mississippi		E	†
Missouri			E
Montana	C		
Nebraska	C	R	
Nevada		C[6]	
New Hampshire	No enterprise zones		

State	Income/Franchise Tax	Sales & Use Tax	Property Tax
New Jersey	C	E	A
New Mexico	C		†
New York	C	E,C,R	†
North Carolina	C	R	E[7]
North Dakota	C		
Ohio	C,E[8]		†
Oklahoma	C	E	†
Oregon	C		E
Pennsylvania	C	E	A
Rhode Island	C	E[9]	†
South Carolina	C		
South Dakota	No enterprise zones		
Tennessee			†
Texas	C,D,R	R	†
Utah	C	R	
Vermont..........	C		
Virginia	C,G[10]		†
Washington		E[11]	E[12]
West Virginia	No enterprise zones		
Wisconsin	C		
Wyoming	No enterprise zones		

† No state incentives offered but local governments authorized to create local property tax incentives.

[1] Assessment reduction for small manufacturing businesses expires July 1, 2006.
[2] Net operating loss carryover also authorized.
[3] Reassessment moratorium also authorized.
[4] In addition to enterprise zone incentives, Michigan has Renaissance Zones in which designated state and local taxes are waived.
[5] Credits taken against the Single Business Tax.
[6] Credit taken against Local School Support Tax.
[7] Property owned by the Global TransPark Development Zone exempt.
[8] Improvements excluded from corporation franchise tax net worth basis and from payroll/property apportionment factors.
[9] Local exemptions only.
[10] Credits available to qualified businesses using enterprise zone tax credits before July 2, 2005. Grants available under the Enterprise Zone Grant Program Act, effective July 1, 2005.
[11] Sales and use tax deferral/forgiveness program offered.
[12] Property tax exemption available for qualified new housing construction, conversion, and rehabilitation improvements to multiple housing unit.

Estimated Tax Requirements

This chart sets forth the estimated tax requirements of each state for the payment of corporate income tax. While some states also may include S corporations, financial institutions, and other business entities in its requirements, only C corporations are discussed in this chart. For comparison purposes, the federal requirements for the payment of estimated corporate income tax are included in this chart.

This chart indicates the threshold that triggers a corporation's obligation to make estimated tax payments, provides payment due dates, shows how a corporation's estimated tax payment must be calculated, and gives the estimated tax payment form or voucher number. Note the following: (1) in the "Due Date" column, four installment dates signify equal payments, unless otherwise noted; (2) the information provided in the "Calculation" column must be compared with the information in the column entitled "Interest/Penalty Threshold for Underpayments," because a state's interest/penalty threshold may be lower than the state's definition of what constitutes a required annual payment; and (3) any mention of a prior year is intended to refer to a 12-month taxable year in which there actually was a tax liability.

This chart also indicates whether a state provides alternative payment methods for corporations that meet the estimated tax threshold requirement after a certain date; whether a state will accept lower estimated tax payments for corporations that calculate their income using an annualized method (AIM) or adjusted seasonal income method (ASIM); the state's interest/penalty threshold for determining underpayments; the state's electronic filing transfer (EFT) payment provisions, if any; and miscellaneous notes

States that do not impose a corporate income tax are not included in this chart.

FEDERAL

Payment Threshold	$500 or more (IRC Sec. 6655(f))
Due Dates	Four equal installments on the 15th of April, June, September, and December (IRC Sec. 6655(c))
Calculation	Required annual payment except as otherwise provided, is the lessor of (1) 100% of tax shown on return for taxable year or if no return filed, 100% of the tax for such year; or (2) 100% of the tax shown on the corporation's return for preceding taxable year (IRC Sec. 6655(d)(1)(b))
Form	1120-W
Alternative Payment Methods	Yes
AIM/ASIM Allowed	Yes
Interest/Penalty Threshold for Underpayment	Amount of underpayment is excess of the required installment over the amount, if any, of the installment payment (IRC Sec. 6655(b)(1))

EFT Payment Required . . . . Yes. A corporation required to deposit taxes in excess of $200,000 must transfer tax deposits electronically. Each remittance must be accompanied by a Federal Tax Deposit form (IRC Reg. Sec. 1.6302-1)

Miscellaneous . . . . Large corporations are required to pay 100% of current year's tax. However, a large corporation can use the preceding taxable year's liability to determine its first installment. Any reduction in the first installment must be captured by increasing the amount of the next required installment by the amount of such reduction (IRC Sec. 6655(d)(2))

ALABAMA

Payment Threshold . . . . Estimated liability $5,000 or more

Due Dates . . . . Same as federal

Calculation . . . . Same as federal

Form 20-CD

Alternative Payment Methods . . . . . . Yes

AIM/ASIM Allowed . . . . Yes

Interest/Penalty Threshold for
Underpayments . . . . Penalties if estimated tax payments do not equal (1) 100% of prior year's liability or (2) 100% of current year's liability

EFT Payment Required . . . . Yes, if payment amounts to $25,000 or more

Miscellaneous . . . . For the first two years for which an Alabama affiliated group files a federal and an Alabama consolidated return, it may make payments of estimated tax on either a consolidated or separate basis. Alabama follows federal law concerning treatment of large corporations.

ALASKA

Payment Threshold . . . . Same as federal

Due Dates . . . . Same as federal

Calculation . . . . Lesser of 100% of current year's estimated liability or 100% of tax paid in prior year

Form 04-711

Alternative Payment Methods . . . . . . None

AIM/ASIM Allowed . . . . Yes

Interest/Penalty Threshold for
Underpayments . . . . Same as federal

EFT Payment Required . . . . Yes, if estimated tax payment is $100,000

Miscellaneous . . . . A large corporation may base only its first required installment on 100% of its prior year's tax liability

ARIZONA

Payment Threshold	Estimated liability $1,000 or more
Due Dates	Same as federal
Calculation	90% of current year's estimated liability or, under certain conditions and for certain tax filers, 100% of prior year's liability
Form	120-ES and 120W
Alternative Payment Methods	None
AIM/ASIM Allowed	Yes
Interest/Penalty Threshold for Underpayments	Penalty if tax shown on return is $1,000 or more and taxpayer did not timely pay at least the smaller of: 90% of current year's tax or 100% tax shown on prior year's return
EFT Payment Required	Yes, if corporate income tax liability during prior tax year was $20,000 or more
Miscellaneous	Federally defined large corporations must pay 90% of current year's tax liability. A large corporation may base only its first required installment on prior year's liability

ARKANSAS

Payment Threshold	Estimated liability over $1,000
Due Dates	Same as federal
Calculation	90% of current year's estimated liability
Form	1100-ESCT
Alternative Payment Methods	Yes
AIM/ASIM Allowed	Yes
Interest/Penalty Threshold for Underpayments	Penalty if taxpayer fails to pay at least 90% of amount due. No penalty if payment equals or exceeds amount of tax shown on prior year's return or in instances of casualties, disasters, or other extraordinary circumstances
EFT Payment Required	Yes, if corporate income tax liability based on average quarterly liability for prior year is $20,000 or more
Miscellaneous	Exceptions apply to qualified corporations with farming income

CALIFORNIA

Payment Threshold	No threshold; all general corporations
Due Dates	Same as federal

Calculation . . . . For general corporations and exempt organizations subject to tax on unrelated income, amount estimated to be imposed by the Corporation Tax law for current year; for banks and financial corporations, amount estimated to be due for income tax year for bank or financial corporation plus amount due for each wholly owned subsidiary; may not be less than the minimum tax

Form 100-ES

Alternative Payment Methods . . . . . . Yes

AIM/ASIM Allowed . . . . Yes

Interest/Penalty Threshold for
Underpayments . . . . Penalty if amount paid does not equal or exceed 100% of current year's liability or previous year's liability, installments calculated on annualized basis, installments calculated on adjusted seasonal basis. Large corporations may only use previous year's liability for purposes of first installment. Other exceptions or relief available if required percentage of tax was paid by withholding, taxpayer was involved in bankruptcy proceedings, or underpayment was created by legislation enacted and operative for the taxable year. Exceptions computed on a cumulative basis

EFT Payment Required . . . . Yes, if corporation required to remit a payment over $20,000 or has a total tax liability of over $80,000

Miscellaneous . . . . None

COLORADO

Payment Threshold . . . . None

Due Dates . . . . Same as federal

Calculation . . . . Lesser of: (1) 70% of liability; or (2) 100% of preceding year's liability

Form 112-EP

Alternative Payment Methods . . . . . . No

AIM/ASIM Allowed . . . . Yes

Interest/Penalty Threshold for
Underpayments . . . . Penalty if corporation fails to pay: (1) 70% of current year's tax liability; or (2) 100% of prior year's liability; Penalty waived if tax liability less than $5,000

EFT Payment Required . . . . No

Miscellaneous . . . . Large corporations can base their first quarter estimated tax payment on 25% of the previous year's tax liability

CONNECTICUT

Payment Threshold . . . . Estimated liability exceeds $1,000

Income Taxes

Due Dates	The 15th of 3rd, 6th, 9th, and 12th mos. The amount of the payments are 30%, 40%, 10%, and 20% respectively, of the lesser of 90% of the tax estimated to be due for the current year or 100% of preceding full year's tax liability without regard to any credits
Calculation	Lesser of: (1) 90% of tax estimated to be due for current income year; or (2) 100% of preceding full year's tax liability without regard to any credits
Form	CT-1120 ESA; CT-1120 ESB; CT-1120 ESC; CT-1120 ESD
Alternative Payment Methods	None
AIM/ASIM Allowed	Yes
Interest/Penalty Threshold for Underpayments	Penalty if the taxpayer fails to pay the lesser of: (1) 90% of current year's tax liability; or (2) 100% of prior year's liability
EFT Payment Required	Yes, if tax liability was more than $10,000 for the previous tax year and taxpayer is notified by Department of Revenue
Miscellaneous	None

DELAWARE

Payment Threshold	Every corporation
Due Dates	50% on 1st of 4th mo.; 20% on 15th of 6th and 9th mos.; 10% on 15th of 12th mo.
Calculation	100% of current year's estimated tax liability
Form	1100T
Alternative Payment Methods	No
AIM/ASIM Allowed	Yes
Interest/Penalty Threshold for Underpayments	Penalty if the taxpayer fails to pay: (1) 80% of current year's liability; or (2) for corporations with less than $200,000 in taxable income for the last three preceding taxable years, 100% of prior year's liability
EFT Payment Required	None
Miscellaneous	None

DISTRICT OF COLUMBIA

Payment Threshold	Estimated liability over $1,000
Due Dates	Same as federal
Calculation	90% of current year's tax (100% if no return filed) or 100% of prior year's tax
Form	D-20-ES
Alternative Payment Methods	Yes

AIM/ASIM Allowed . . . .   Yes

Interest/Penalty Threshold for
Underpayments . . . .   Underpayment if taxpayer fails to pay lesser of: (1) 90% of current year's tax (100% if no return filed) or (2) 100% of prior year's tax

EFT Payment Required . . . .   Beginning with District of Columbia corporation business (franchise) tax returns due March 15, 2005, and unincorporated franchise tax returns due April 15, 2005, electronic filing and payment required for all taxpayers filing annual tax returns with outstanding tax liability exceeding $25,000

Miscellaneous . . . .   Taxpayers may request a six month extension to pay estimated tax

FLORIDA

Payment Threshold . . . .   Expected liability exceeds $2,500

Due Dates . . . .   1st of 5th, 7th, and 10th mos., and 1st mo. of next tax year

Calculation . . . .   100% of current year's estimated tax liability

Form F-1120ES

Alternative Payment Methods . . . . . .   Yes

AIM/ASIM Allowed . . . .   No

Interest/Penalty Threshold for
Underpayments . . . .   Underpayment if any installment is less than 90% of the amount prescribed for payment. No penalty or interest imposed if total payments at least equal the amount which would have been required to be paid if tax the lesser of: (1) an amount equal to a tax computed at current year's rates, but otherwise on the basis of prior year's facts and law; or (2) an amount equal to 90% of tax due for taxable year

EFT Payment Required . . . .   Yes, if preceding year's tax liability was $30,000 or more

Miscellaneous . . . .   None

GEORGIA

Payment Threshold . . . .   Expected net income over $25,000

Due Dates . . . .   Same as federal

Calculation . . . .   100% of current year's estimated tax liability

Form 602-ES

Alternative Payment Methods . . . . . .   Yes

AIM/ASIM Allowed . . . .   Yes

Interest/Penalty Threshold for
Underpayments . . . . No penalty if taxpayer pays: (1) prior year's liability; (2) tax computed on basis of facts and law of prior year, using rates and status of current year's liability for the months in the taxable year ending the month before the installment is due date; (3) 70% of the current year's tax determined on an annualized basis

EFT Payment Required . . . . Yes, for corporate estimated taxpayers with quarterly payments of $10,000 or more

Miscellaneous . . . . None

HAWAII

Payment Threshold . . . . Expected liability exceeds $500

Due Dates . . . . 20th of the 4th, 6th, and 9th mos. and 20th of the first mo. of the next taxable year

Calculation . . . . 100% of current year's tax liability

Form N-3

Alternative Payment Methods . . . . . . Yes

AIM/ASIM Allowed . . . . Yes

Interest/Penalty Threshold for
Underpayments . . . . Penalty if taxpayer fails to pay: (1) 100% of current year's tax liability; or (2) 100% of prior year's tax liability

EFT Payment Required . . . . Yes, if liability exceeds $100,000 or more for the year

Miscellaneous . . . . Hawaii's treatment of large corporations is same as federal law. Foreign corporations that have less than 15% of their income attributable to Hawaii are exempt from estimated tax requirements

IDAHO

Payment Threshold . . . . If required to make federal estimated tax payments and estimated tax liability, plus permanent building fund tax, less credits is $500 or more

Due Dates . . . . Same as federal

Calculation . . . . 90% of current year's liability or 100% of prior year's liability

Form 41ES

Alternative Payment Methods . . . . . . No

AIM/ASIM Allowed . . . . Yes, if used for federal

Interest/Penalty Threshold for
Underpayments . . . . Interest imposed if taxpayer fails to pay the lesser of: (1) 100% of prior year's tax liability; or (2) 90% of current year's liability

EFT Payment Required . . . . Yes, if payment amounts to $100,000 or more

Miscellaneous . . . .   Estimated payments not required if corporation wasn't required to file an Idaho tax return the previous year

ILLINOIS

Payment Threshold . . . .   Estimated income and replacement tax, less credits, exceeds $400

Due Dates . . . .   Same as federal

Calculation . . . .   (1) 90% of the tax shown on the current year's return or if no return filed, 90% of the tax due; or (2) 100% of the tax shown on the prior full-year's return

Form IL-1120-ES

Alternative Payment Methods . . . . . .   Yes

AIM/ASIM Allowed . . . .   Yes

Interest/Penalty Threshold for
Underpayments . . . .   Penalty if taxpayer fails to pay in required installments the lesser of: (1) 90% of current year's tax liability; or (2) 100% of previous year's tax liability

EFT Payment Required . . . .   Yes, for taxpayers with an annual tax liability of $200,000 or more

Miscellaneous . . . .   None

INDIANA

Payment Threshold . . . .   AGI tax liability exceeds $1,000

Due Dates . . . .   20th of 4th, 6th, 9th, and 12th mos.

Calculation . . . .   100% of AGI for taxable year, less the credit for gross income tax payment

Form IT-6

Alternative Payment Methods . . . . . .   No

AIM/ASIM Allowed . . . .   No

Interest/Penalty Threshold for
Underpayments . . . .   No penalties if AGI quarterly estimated tax installment equals or exceeds: (1) 20% of final tax liability for taxable year; or (2) 25% of final tax liability for previous taxable year

EFT Payment Required . . . .   Yes, if a corporation's (1) estimated quarterly AGI tax liability for current year or (2) average estimated quarterly AGI tax liability for prior year exceeds/exceeded $10,000

Miscellaneous . . . .   None

IOWA

Payment Threshold . . . .   Estimated liability, less credits, exceeds $1,000

Due Dates . . . .   Last day of 4th, 6th, 9th, and 12th mos.

Calculation . . . .   100% of current year's estimated liability

Form	IA 1120ES
Alternative Payment Methods	Yes
AIM/ASIM Allowed	Yes
Interest/Penalty Threshold for Underpayments	Penalty if payments do not equal or exceed: (1) tax shown on prior year's return; (2) amount computed by using current year's tax rates on basis of facts and law applicable to prior year; or (3) amount equal to 90% of current tax year, as computed on an annualized basis
EFT Payment Required	Yes, if tax liability exceeds $80,000 for the year prior to tax year just completed (no declaration form required with EFT payment)
Miscellaneous	None

KANSAS

Payment Threshold	Estimated liability exceeds $500
Due Dates	Same as federal
Calculation	100% of current year's estimated tax liability
Form	K-120ES
Alternative Payment Methods	Yes
AIM/ASIM Allowed	Yes
Interest/Penalty Threshold for Underpayments	No penalty or interest if the estimated tax paid amounts to at least (1) the prior year's tax liability or (2) 90% of the current year's tax, as computed on an annualized basis
EFT Payment Required	No
Miscellaneous	None

KENTUCKY

Payment Threshold	Estimated liability exceeds $5,000
Due Dates	50% on 15th day of 6th mo.; 25% on 15th day of 9th and 12th mos.
Calculation	100% of current year's liability, less statutory $5,000 floor
Form	720ES
Alternative Payment Methods	Yes
AIM/ASIM Allowed	No
Interest/Penalty Threshold for Underpayments	Penalty if taxpayer fails to pay at least 70% of tax liability, less $5,000 and any overpayments credited forward
EFT Payment Required	No

Miscellaneous . . . . None

LOUISIANA

Payment Threshold . . . . Estimated liability, less credits, $1,000 or more

Due Dates . . . . Same as federal

Calculation . . . . 100% of tax due for current period, less credits

Form CIFT-620ES

Alternative Payment Methods . . . . . . Yes

AIM/ASIM Allowed . . . . Yes

Interest/Penalty Threshold for
Underpayments . . . . No penalty if the total amount of all payments made on or before last date prescribed for payment equals or exceeds amount which would have been required to be paid on or before such date if the estimated tax were the lesser of: (1) tax shown on prior year's return; (2) amount equal to tax computed at rates applicable to taxable year, but otherwise on basis of the facts shown and law applicable to prior tax year; or (3) amount equal to 80% of tax for taxable year as computed on an annualized basis

EFT Payment Required . . . . Yes, if tax due with return, report, or other document exceeds $15,000 or if payments during prior 12-month period averaged $15,000 or more. The $15,000 is lowered to $10,000 for filing periods beginning January 1, 2006, through December 31, 2007, and to $5,000 for filing periods beginning after 2007

Miscellaneous . . . . None

Payment Threshold . . . . Estimated liability for current or prior year exceeds $1,000

Due Dates . . . . Same as federal

Calculation . . . . Lesser of: (1) 100% of prior year's liability; or (2) 90% of current year's estimated liability. Large corporations, as defined in IRC Sec. 6655(g)(2)(a), must pay 90% of current year's estimated liability without taking into account the investment tax credit

Form 1120ES-ME

Alternative Payment Methods . . . . . . No

AIM/ASIM Allowed . . . . No. In general, the estimated tax must be paid in four equal installments, unless the taxpayer establishes by adequate records that the actual distribution of its tax liability and allowable credits supports a different allocation of the tax throughout the year

Interest/Penalty Threshold for
Underpayments . . . . Penalty if taxpayer fails to pay the lesser of: (1) 100% of tax liability for previous year; or (2) 90% of current year's liability

EFT Payment Required . . . . Yes, for taxpayers with tax liability of $400,000 or more

Miscellaneous	A federally defined large corporation may elect to determine its first required installment based on prior year's tax liability. Large corporations must pay 90% of current year's liability to avoid penalty

MARYLAND

Payment Threshold	Estimated liability exceeds $1,000
Due Dates	Same as federal
Calculation	90% of current year's tax liability or 110% of prior year's tax liability
Form	500D
Alternative Payment Methods	No
AIM/ASIM Allowed	No
Interest/Penalty Threshold for Underpayments	Penalty if payment is less than 90% of current year's estimated tax liability or less than 110% tax paid in the prior year, less allowable credit
EFT Payment Required	Yes, for taxpayers making payments exceeding $10,000
Miscellaneous	None

MASSACHUSETTS

Payment Threshold	Estimated liability exceeds $1,000
Due Dates	40% on the 15th day of the 3rd mo.; 25% on 15th day of 6th and 9th mos.; 10% on 15th day of 12th mo.
Calculation	Lesser of (1) 90% of tax shown on return for current taxable year; (2) for taxpayers other than federally defined large corporations, 100% of tax shown on return for preceding taxable year; (3) 90% of the tax due for the taxable year; or (4) 90% of the required tax for the taxable year calculated using the income apportionment percentage for the preceding taxable year
Form	355-ES
Alternative Payment Methods	Yes
AIM/ASIM Allowed	No
Interest/Penalty Threshold for Underpayments	No underpayment penalty if total of payments equal or exceed the lesser of: (1) 90% of current year's estimated taxes; (2) 100% of tax due in previous year; (3) 90% of the tax for the taxable year, or (4) 90% of the tax that would be required to be shown on the return for the taxable year if the tax were determined by using the income apportionment percentage determined for the preceding taxable year
EFT Payment Required	Yes, if for the preceding taxable year, the corporation had gross receipts or sales exceeding $100,000 or more.

Miscellaneous . . . . New corporations in their first full taxable year with fewer than 10 employees pay installments based on the following percentages: 30%-25%-25%-20%

MICHIGAN

Payment Threshold . . . . Estimated liability exceeds $600.

Due Dates . . . . Last day of the 4th, 7th, and 10th mos. and 1st mo. of following tax year. Generally payments equal 25% of amount due for the year, however, adjustments in quarterly payments may be necessary to correct underpayments or overpayments from previous quarterly payments to reflect a revised estimate of the annual tax liability

Calculation . . . . Each quarter's payment must represent the estimated income for the quarter or 25% the estimated tax liability for the year

Form C-8002

Alternative Payment Methods . . . . . . No

AIM/ASIM Allowed . . . . Yes

Interest/Penalty Threshold for
Underpayments . . . . Interest assessed if amount paid with estimated tax returns is less than 85% of annual liability or 1% of gross receipts, and amount of estimated payment does not equal or approximate the quarter's liability

EFT Payment Required . . . . No

Miscellaneous . . . . Taxpayers whose SBT in prior year was $20K or less may qualify for prior year exception; taxpayer may use amount of prior year's tax liability as current year's estimated annual tax

MINNESOTA

Payment Threshold . . . . Estimated liability exceeds $500

Due Dates . . . . 15th day of 3rd, 6th, 9th, and 12th mos.

Calculation . . . . Lesser of 100% of current or prior year's tax liability. For federally defined large corporations, required annual payment is 100% of current year's tax liability. For first quarter only, a large corporation may base its installment on 100% of prior year's liability

Form M-18

Alternative Payment Methods . . . . . . No

AIM/ASIM Allowed . . . . Yes

Interest/Penalty Threshold for
Underpayments . . . . Underpayment penalty avoided by payment of either 100% of current or prior year's tax liability

EFT Payment Required . . . . Yes, corporations whose aggregate prior year estimated tax payments amounted to at least $20,000 must make current year estimated payments via EFT

Miscellaneous . . . . A corporation is not required to pay estimated taxes the first year it is subject to tax in Minnesota. Large corporations avoid an underpayment penalty only if they pay 100% of current year's estimated liability

MISSISSIPPI

Payment Threshold . . . . Estimated liability exceeds $200

Due Dates . . . . Same as federal

Calculation . . . . 90% of current year's tax liability

Form 83-300

Alternative Payment Methods . . . . . . Yes

AIM/ASIM Allowed . . . . Yes

Interest/Penalty Threshold for
Underpayments . . . . Underpayment if total estimated taxes paid is less than 90% of tax actually due; however, no interest is imposed for underpayments if the payments equal prior year's liability

EFT Payment Required . . . . No

Miscellaneous . . . . Large corporations cannot use prior year tax measure except as basis for determining first installment

MISSOURI

Payment Threshold . . . . Estimated liability $250 or more

Due Dates . . . . Same as federal

Calculation . . . . 100% of current year's tax liability

Form MO-1120ES

Alternative Payment Methods . . . . . . No

AIM/ASIM Allowed . . . . Yes

Interest/Penalty Threshold for
Underpayments . . . . No penalty if payments equal or exceed (1) 90% of tax shown on current year's return; (2) 100% of prior year's liability; (3) 90% of tax, as computed on an annualized installment basis; (4) 90% of tax, as computed on basis of actual taxable income for month in which the installment is required to be paid, as if such months constituted the taxable year; (5) tax figured by using current year's rates, but based on prior year's return and law; or (6) 90% of the tax for the taxable year computed by placing on an annualized basis the taxable income for the months in the taxable year ending before the month in which the installment is required to be paid

EFT Payment Required . . . . No

Miscellaneous . . . . Large corporations may not use 100% of prior year's liability or the tax figured by using current year's rates based on the prior year's return and law as a penalty threshold

MONTANA

Payment Threshold	Estimated corporate license or corporate income tax liability $5,000 or more
Due Dates	Same as federal
Calculation	Required annual payment is the lesser of: (1) 80% of current year's tax liability; or (2) 100% of prior year's tax liability (based on 12-month year)
Form	CLT-4-EST
Alternative Payment Methods	Yes
AIM/ASIM Allowed	Yes
Interest/Penalty Threshold for Underpayments	No interest penalty is imposed if the corporation pays the lesser of: (1) 80% of current year's tax liability; or (2) 100% of preceding year's liability
EFT Payment Required	Yes, if amount of tax due is $500,000 or more
Miscellaneous	None

NEBRASKA

Payment Threshold	Estimated liability, less credits, $400 or more
Due Dates	Same as federal
Calculation	100% of current year's estimated tax liability
Form	1120N-ES
Alternative Payment Methods	Yes
AIM/ASIM Allowed	Yes
Interest/Penalty Threshold for Underpayments	Penalty if estimated tax payment is less than (1) 100% of tax shown on return for year after reduction by credits other than estimated payments; (2) the tax shown on the Nebraska return for the preceding taxable year; or (3) a tax amount based on the tax rate for the current taxable year using the facts and law applicable to the return for the preceding taxable year
EFT Payment Required	Tax commissioner may require it for payments over $100,000
Miscellaneous	Large corporations are prohibited from using their prior year's tax liability in determining the first installment of its tax year

NEW HAMPSHIRE

Payment Threshold	Estimated liability $200 or more
Due Dates	Same as federal
Calculation	100% of current year's estimated tax liability

Form	NH-1120-ES
Alternative Payment Methods	No
AIM/ASIM Allowed	Yes
Interest/Penalty Threshold for Underpayments	Underpayment if total of estimated tax payments is less than 90% of the year's tax liability. No penalty imposed, however, if payments equal lesser of: (1) amount of prior year's tax liability; (2) amount equal to tax computed at rates applicable to the taxable year, but otherwise on the basis of facts shown on prior year's return; or (3) 90% of current year's tax computed on an annualized basis
EFT Payment Required	Yes, for taxpayers with a tax liability of $100,000 or more
Miscellaneous	None

NEW JERSEY

Payment Threshold	Taxpayers whose tax liability for previous year exceeds $500 make payments as outlined below. Taxpayers whose tax liability was $500 or less, have the option of making a single payment of estimated tax equal to 50% of the prior year's tax liability. The payment must be made by the due date of the original return for the prior year
Due Dates	Same as federal, other than those taxpayers with gross receipts of $50 million or more for the prior privilege period. Such taxpayers pay 25% on the 15th of the fourth month, 50% on the 15th of the sixth month, and 25% on the 15th of the 12th month
Calculation	100% of current year's liability)
Form	CBT-150
Alternative Payment Methods	No
AIM/ASIM Allowed	Yes
Interest/Penalty Threshold for Underpayments	Underpayment if installment payment is less than: (1) 90% of current year's liability; or (2) 100% of prior year's liability
EFT Payment Required	Yes, if prior year's tax liability was $10,000 or more
Miscellaneous	None

NEW MEXICO

Payment Threshold	Estimated liability exceeds $5,000
Due Dates	Payments are due on the 15th day of the 6th, 9th, and 12th months of the current taxable year and the 15th day of the 3rd month following the close of the taxable year

Calculation	Lesser of: (1) 80% of current year's liability; (2) 100% of prior year's liability, if prior year was at least 12 months; (3) 100% of the tax due for the taxable year immediately preceding the previous taxable year if it was a full 12-month year, the return for the previous year has not been filed, and the extended due date for filing the return has not occurred when the first installment is due for the taxable year; or (4) 80% of the current year's tax liability due determined by each fiscal quarter
Form	CIT-ES
Alternative Payment Methods	No
AIM/ASIM Allowed	Yes
Interest/Penalty Threshold for Underpayments	Penalty if the taxpayer fails to pay the lesser of: (1) 80% of current year's liability; or (2) 100% of prior year's liability, if prior year was at least 12 months; (3) 100% of the tax due for the taxable year immediately preceding the previous taxable year if it was a full 12-month year, the return for the previous year has not been filed, and the extended due date for filing the return has not occurred when the first installment is due for the taxable year; or (4) 80% of the current year's tax liability due determined by each fiscal quarter
EFT Payment Required	No
Miscellaneous	None

NEW YORK

Payment Threshold	Estimated liability exceeds $1,000
Due Dates	First installment when return due and remaining installments due on the 15th day of the 6th, 9th, and 12th mos.
Calculation	100% of current year's estimated tax liability
Form	CT-400-MN
Alternative Payment Methods	Yes
AIM/ASIM Allowed	Yes
Interest/Penalty Threshold for Underpayments	First installment underpaid if less than 25% of prior year's tax liability. Other installments are underpaid if less than 91% of current year's tax liability. Taxpayers with underpaid estimated taxes may avoid penalties if they qualify by paying estimated tax equal to: (1) the tax shown on prior year's return; (2) the tax equal to current tax rates applies to last year's facts and law; or (3) amount equal to 91% of current year's tax as computed on annualized basis; or (4) amount equal to 91% of tax estimated to be due by calculating on a recurring seasonable income basis
EFT Payment Required	No

| Miscellaneous | For taxable years beginning before January 1, 2006, the first installment amount is increased to 30% in cases where the preceding year's tax exceeds $100,000. Corporations doing business in the Metropolitan Commuter Transportation District that are required to make a declaration of estimated franchise tax also must make a declaration of estimated metropolitan transportation business tax and make installment payments. Large corporations must calculate their taxes on the basis of 100% of current year's liability. Lower penalties apply for corporations that pay 80% of the current year's tax liability |

NORTH CAROLINA

Payment Threshold	Estimated liability $500 or more
Due Dates	Same as federal
Calculation	100% of current year's estimated tax liability
Form	CD-429
Alternative Payment Methods	Yes
AIM/ASIM Allowed	Yes
Interest/Penalty Threshold for Underpayments	Underpayment if paid less than 90% of current year's estimated liability. No interest if total payments at least equal: (1) prior year's tax liability; (2) tax computed at current year's rate, but otherwise on basis of facts and law and applicable to prior year; or (3) 90% of current year's estimated liability, as computed on an annualized basis
EFT Payment Required	Corporations required to pay their federal-estimated corporate income tax by EFT also must pay their NC tax via EFT
Miscellaneous	For federally defined large corporation, no penalty if payment is at least 90% of current year's estimated liability, as computed on an annualized basis

NORTH DAKOTA

Payment Threshold	Current and prior year's liability exceeds $5,000
Due Dates	15th day of the 4th, 6th, and 9th mos. and 1st mo. of next tax year
Calculation	Lesser of: (1) 90% of current year's net tax liability; and (2) 100% of corporation's preceding year's net tax liability. "Net tax liability" is the amount of income tax for taxable year less any allowable credits
Form	40-ES
Alternative Payment Methods	No
AIM/ASIM Allowed	Yes
Interest/Penalty Threshold for Underpayments	No interest if estimated tax payments for any quarter is less than: (1) 90% of the quarterly tax liability; or (2) prior year's liability

EFT Payment Required . . . .   No

Miscellaneous . . . .   None

OHIO

Payment Threshold . . . .   Estimated payments due if franchise tax report not filed and tax not paid in Jan.

Due Dates . . . .   If estimated tax does not exceed minimum tax, entire amount due by Jan. 31. If Form FT-1120 not filed and full tax not paid in Jan. of tax year, FT-1120E and 1/3rd of tax due by Jan. 31. If second 1/3rd of tax paid and FT-1120ER filed by March 31, automatic extension for filing FT-1120 granted until May 31. If FT-1120EX filed and balance of tax paid by May 31, further extension granted to 15th day of month following month that IRS has granted an extension for filing federal return

Calculation . . . .   100% of qualified net tax, less credits, but not less than minimum tax

Form FT-1120E/ER/EX

Alternative Payment Methods . . . . . .   No

AIM/ASIM Allowed . . . .   No

Interest/Penalty Threshold for
Underpayments . . . .   Lesser of: 100% of the previous year's tax liability or 90% of the current year's liability

EFT Payment Required . . . .   Taxpayer must submit franchise tax payments by EFT if the taxpayer's total liability after reduction for nonrefundable credits exceeded $50,000 for the second preceding tax year

Miscellaneous . . . .   None

OKLAHOMA

Payment Threshold . . . .   Estimated liability, less credits, $500 or more

Due Dates . . . .   15th day of 4th, 6th, and 9th mos. and 1st mo. of next tax year

Calculation . . . .   Lesser of 70% of current year's liability or 100% of prior year's liability

Form OW-8-ESC

Alternative Payment Methods . . . . . .   No

AIM/ASIM Allowed . . . .   Yes

Interest/Penalty Threshold for
Underpayments . . . .   Underpayment is the lesser of: (1) 70% of current year's tax liability; (2) 100% of preceding year's liability; or (3) 70% of the current year's liability computed on an annualized basis. No underpayment of estimated tax is imposed if the tax on the return is less than $1,000

EFT Payment Required . . . .   No

Miscellaneous . . . . For corporations, the annualization provisions found in IRC Sec. 6655(e)(2)(c) and (e)(3) may not be used. The provisions allowed for computing estimated taxes on an annualized basis is permitted only for a taxable year of 12 mos.

OREGON

Payment Threshold . . . . Estimated liability, less credits, $500 or more

Due Dates . . . . Same as federal

Calculation . . . . 100% of corporation excise or income tax less allowable credit

Form 20-ES

Alternative Payment Methods . . . . . . No

AIM/ASIM Allowed . . . . Yes

Interest/Penalty Threshold for
Underpayments . . . . No penalty if each installment equal to or more than any one of the following: (1) 25% of the tax shown on the return for the year or, if no return filed, 25% of tax for the year; (2) 25% of the tax shown on the previous year's return if the preceding taxable year was a 12-month year; or (3) 100% of the tax computed on annualized taxable income or seasonal income, calculated by using the same annualization periods as used for federal tax purposes

EFT Payment Required . . . . Yes, if the taxpayer is required to make federal estimated tax payments electronically

Miscellaneous . . . . Large corporations may use the tax shown on prior year's return only to calculate first quarterly estimated tax installment

PENNSYLVANIA

Payment Threshold . . . . Every corporation subject to corporate net income tax

Due Dates . . . . 15th day of the 3rd, 6th, 9th, and 12th mos.

Calculation . . . . 90% of current year's liability

Form PA-40ESR

Alternative Payment Methods . . . . . . No

AIM/ASIM Allowed . . . . No

Interest/Penalty Threshold for
Underpayments . . . . Underpayment is the excess of the amount of the estimated tax installment equal to: (1) 90% of the tax shown on the report for the current tax year, except if settled or resettled taxes; or (2) the cumulative amount of installments paid on or before the last date prescribed for payment

EFT Payment Required . . . . Yes, if a payment is $20,000 or more

Miscellaneous . . . . None

RHODE ISLAND

Payment Threshold	Estimated income or franchise tax liability exceeds $500
Due Dates	40% on the 15th day of the 3rd mo.; 60% on the 15th day of the 6th mo.
Calculation	100% of tax estimated to be due
Form	RI-112-ES
Alternative Payment Methods	Yes
AIM/ASIM Allowed	No
Interest/Penalty Threshold for Underpayments	No penalty or interest assessed if the estimated payments made are at least equal to: (1) 80% of the tax due for the year; or (2) 100% of the tax calculated at the current year's rate, but at a prior year's taxable base
EFT Payment Required	Yes, if the amount of the tax payment exceeds $10,000
Miscellaneous	None

SOUTH CAROLINA

Payment Threshold	Estimated tax, less credits, $100 or more
Due Dates	Same as federal law
Calculation	Lesser of (1) 100% of tax shown on the current year's return or 100% of tax due if no return filed or (2) 100% of tax shown on return for preceding full taxable year
Form	SC1120-CDP
Alternative Payment Methods	No
AIM/ASIM Allowed	Yes, same as federal
Interest/Penalty Threshold for Underpayments	Same as federal
EFT Payment Required	Yes, if taxpayer's liability is $15,000 or more during a filing period
Miscellaneous	None

TENNESSEE

Payment Threshold	Combined franchise and excise tax liability for current year exceeds $5,000
Due Dates	15th day of the 4th, 6th, and 9th mos. and 1st month of next taxable year
Calculation	Lesser of: (1) 100% of prior year's combined liability, annualized if the preceding tax year was for less than 12 months; or (2) 100% of current year's combined liability
Form	FAE-172

Alternative Payment Methods . . . . . . No

AIM/ASIM Allowed . . . . No

Interest/Penalty Threshold for
Underpayments . . . . No penalty if taxpayer makes timely, quarterly estimated franchise and excise tax payments, each of which equals at least 25% of the current year's franchise and excise tax liability

EFT Payment Required . . . . If the taxpayer's average payment is $10,000 or more, the Department of Revenue notifies the corporation if it is required to make EFT payments

Miscellaneous . . . . None

UTAH

Payment Threshold . . . . Current or preceding year's corporation franchise or income tax $3,000 or more

Due Dates . . . . Same as federal

Calculation . . . . 90% of current year's liability or 100% of prior year's liability

Form TC-559

Alternative Payment Methods . . . . . . No

AIM/ASIM Allowed . . . . Yes

Interest/Penalty Threshold for
Underpayments . . . . No penalty if taxpayer makes timely, quarterly estimated tax payments, equal to 22.5% of current year's liability or 25% of the prior year's liability

EFT Payment Required . . . . No

Miscellaneous . . . . Estimated tax payments not required for the first tax year if taxpayer makes payment on or before return due date equal or greater to minimum tax

VERMONT

Payment Threshold . . . . Estimated liability exceeds $500

Due Dates . . . . Same as federal

Calculation . . . . 100% of current year's estimated tax liability

Form CO-414

Alternative Payment Methods . . . . . . Yes

AIM/ASIM Allowed . . . . No

Interest/Penalty Threshold for
Underpayments . . . . Underpayment occurs if amount of any installment is less than: (1) 80% of appropriate portion of tax shown on current year's return; or (2) the prior year's income at current year's tax rate

EFT Payment Required . . . . Commissioner may require EFT payment if taxpayer required under federal law to remit federal EFT tax payment

Miscellaneous . . . . None

VIRGINIA

Payment Threshold . . . . Estimated tax liability exceeds $1,000

Due Dates . . . . Same as federal

Calculation . . . . 100% of current year's liability

Form 500-ES

Alternative Payment Methods . . . . . . Yes

AIM/ASIM Allowed . . . . Yes

Interest/Penalty Threshold for
Underpayments . . . . Penalty on underpayments in excess of the installment amount required to be paid if the estimated tax is 90% of the liability on the return. Penalties abated if installments equal lesser of (1) 100% of tax shown on the return for the preceding year as long as preceding year was 12 months; (2) tax rate for current year applied to the income reported for the prior year, or (3) 90% of the tax for the taxable year computed on an annualized basis

EFT Payment Required . . . . Yes, for corporations with an average monthly tax liability that exceeds $20,000

Miscellaneous . . . . None

WEST VIRGINIA

Payment Threshold . . . . Estimated taxable income of $10,000 or more

Due Dates . . . . Same as federal

Calculation . . . . 100% of current year's estimated tax liability

Form WV/CNT-112ES

Alternative Payment Methods . . . . . . Yes

AIM/ASIM Allowed . . . . Yes

Interest/Penalty Threshold for
Underpayments . . . . No penalty if payment on estimated tax is or exceeds the lesser of: (1) the amount shown on the return for the prior year; or (2) the annualized income installment

EFT Payment Required . . . . Taxpayers making payments of $100,000 per tax type per taxable year or reporting period may be required to make payments by EFT

Miscellaneous . . . . None

WISCONSIN

Payment Threshold . . . . Estimated tax payments required, unless corporation's net tax less than $500 or, if in prior year, corporation had no liability and a net income of less than $250,000

Due Dates . . . . 15th day of the 3rd, 6th, 9th, and 12th mos. of taxable year

Calculation . . . . 100% of current year's estimated tax liability plus surcharge

Form 4-ES

Alternative Payment Methods . . . . . . Yes

AIM/ASIM Allowed . . . . Yes

Interest/Penalty Threshold for
Underpayments . . . . No penalty if each installment payment is timely and the total tax and surcharge paid is at least equal to: (1) 90% of current year's liability; (2) 100% of prior year's tax liability for taxpayer's with less than $250,000; or (3) 90% of liability and surcharge figured on annualized basis

EFT Payment Required . . . . Yes, if a corporation's net tax, less refundable credits, on prior year's returns was $40,000 or more

Miscellaneous . . . . Underpayment interest is increased or decreased based on any changes made to the tax and surcharge originally reported

Federal Bonus Depreciation Conformity

The federal Job Creation and Worker Assistance Act of 2002 (JCWAA) (P.L. 107-147) allowed taxpayers an additional first-year depreciation deduction equal to 30% of the adjusted basis of qualified property acquired after September 10, 2001 and placed in service before May 6, 2003. The federal Jobs and Growth Tax Relief Reconciliation Act of 2003 (JGTRRA) (P.L. 108-27) increased the additional first-year depreciation allowance to 50% for qualified property acquired after May 5, 2003 and placed in service before January 1, 2005. State response to the bonus depreciation provisions of the JCWAA and JGTRRA has varied and the chart below reflects the states' corporate income tax treatment of bonus depreciation.

Conforming States—The following states allow the bonus depreciation for state corporate income tax purposes.

Alabama	*Kansas*	*North Dakota*
Alaska	*Louisiana*	*Oregon*
Colorado	*Montana*	*Utah*
Delaware	*New Mexico*	*West Virginia*
Florida		

Nonconforming States—The following states do not allow the bonus depreciation for state corporate income tax purposes.

Arizona	*Idaho*	*New Jersey*
Arkansas	*Indiana*	*Rhode Island*
California	*Kentucky*	*South Carolina*
Connecticut	*Maryland*	*Tennessee*
District of Columbia	*Massachusetts*	*Vermont*
Georgia	*Mississippi*	*Virginia*
Hawaii	*New Hampshire*	*Wisconsin*

States with Special Situations—

Nevada, South Dakota, Washington, and *Wyoming* do not impose a general corporate income tax.

Illinois requires that bonus depreciation to be added back. For tax years after 2000 and before 2006, subtraction allowed for 42.9% of regular depreciation until the bonus depreciation disallowance has been claimed. For tax years after 2005, subtraction allowed for 42.9% of regular depreciation on property for which 30% bonus depreciation was taken and 100% of regular depreciation on property for which 50% bonus depreciation deduction was taken.

Iowa disallows 30% bonus depreciation on property placed in service between September 11, 2001, and September 11, 2004, but allows 50% bonus depreciation for qualified property acquired after May 5, 2003, and before 2005.

Maine requires an add-back of the net increase in depreciation. For property placed in service in a tax year after 2002, a subtraction is allowed beginning in the tax year after the property was placed in service, equal to 5% of the amount added back for the first year in which a subtraction is allowed. In later years, the subtraction is equal to 95% of the amount added back divided by the number of years in the recovery period for the property minus two.

Michigan allows the bonus depreciation deduction in computing the federal taxable income amount that is the tax base for the Single Business Tax. However, the federal depreciation deduction must be added to federal taxable income for purposes of determining the Michigan tax base.

Minnesota will allow the bonus depreciation subject to an 80% add-back provision, and the add-back amount is allowed as a subtraction for the five tax years following the add-back.

Missouri requires an add-back for the amount that any bonus depreciation claimed under the JCWAA exceeds what would have been claimed without the bonus for property purchased on or after July 1, 2002, but before July 1, 2003. A subtraction is allowed in each year for the amount that would have been deducted for that property if the bonus depreciation was not claimed. Additional subtraction if assets subject to bonus depreciation disposed of before end of depreciable life. JGTRAA 50% bonus depreciation is allowed.

Montana has a longstanding practice to follow IRC § 168 treatment if that is the method chosen by the taxpayer.

Nebraska requires that 85% of any bonus depreciation be added back. The amount may later be deducted over five years beginning with tax year 2005.

New York requires an addback for federal bonus depreciation claimed in tax years beginning after 2002 on property placed in service on or after June 1, 2003. An add-back is not required for qualified resurgence zone/New York Liberty Zone property.

North Carolina required an add-back of 100% of federal bonus depreciation claimed for tax years 2001 and 2002 and 70% of bonus depreciation claimed for tax years 2003 and 2004. In each of the first five tax years beginning after 2004, taxpayers are allowed a subtraction equal to 20% of the add-back.

Ohio requires taxpayers to add back 5/6 of the amount of bonus depreciation taken for federal purposes. Taxpayers may deduct the add-back amount in equal installments over the following five tax years.

Oklahoma requires an add-back of 80% of the amount of the bonus depreciation claimed under the JCWAA. In the tax year following the add-back, and in each of the next three years, 25% of the amount added back may be subtracted. JGTRAA 50% bonus depreciation is allowed.

Pennsylvania requires an add-back of the bonus depreciation, but allows a subtraction equal to 3/7 of the regular depreciation deduction, which may be claimed in later taxable years until the entire amount of the add-back has been claimed.

Texas generally does not allow bonus depreciation except for the FIT method of reporting taxable capital.

Federal Conformity—Asset Expense Election (IRC §179)

The federal American Jobs Creation Act of 2004 (AJCA) (P.L. 108-357) extended the increased IRC Sec. 179 asset expense and investment limitations, which were due to expire December 31, 2005, to December 31, 2007. The Jobs and Growth Tax Relief Reconciliation Act of 2003 (JGTRRA) (P.L. 108-27) increased the expense limitation from $25,000 to $100,000 and the investment limitation from $200,000 to $400,000. The AJCA also provides that off-the-shelf computer software qualifies for expensing. Finally, for vehicles placed in service after October 22, the AJCA limits the cost of a sport utility vehicle (SUV) that may be expensed under IRC Sec. 179 to $25,000 if the SUV is exempt from the IRC Sec. 280F depreciation limitations (e.g., SUV's weighing more than 6,000 pounds). The state response has varied and the chart below reflects the states' positions regarding the new IRC Sec. 179 rules. NOTE: For those states that previously decoupled from the $100,000 expense limitation, the SUV provisions of the AJCA are moot, e.g., expensing of SUV's is already limited to $25,000.

State	Answer	Comments	Authority
Alabama	Conforms		Alabama Code §40-18-1.1
Alaska	Conforms		Alaska Stat. §43.20.021(a)
Arizona	Does not conform		Ariz. Rev. Stat. §43-105(A) Ariz. Rev. Stat. §43-1121(1)
Arkansas	Does not conform		Ark. Code. Ann. §26-51-428
California	Does not conform		Cal. Rev. & Tax Code §24356(b)
Colorado	Conforms		Colo. Rev. Stat. §39-22-103(5.3)
Connecticut	Conforms		Conn. Gen. Stat. §12-213(a)(23)
Delaware	Conforms		Del. Code Ann. tit. 30, §1901(5) Del. Code Ann. tit. 30, §1903(a)
District of Columbia	Does not conform		D.C. Code Ann. §47-1803.03
Florida	Conforms		Fla. Stat. Ch. 220.03(3)
Georgia	Conforms	For taxable years beginning on or after January 1, 2005	Ga. Code Ann. §48-1-2(14)
Hawaii	Does not conform		Haw. Rev. Stat. §235-2.4(g)
Idaho	Conforms		Idaho Code §63-3004
Illinois	Conforms		35 ILCS 5/102

State	Answer	Comments	Authority
Indiana	Does not conform		Ind. Code §6-3-1-3.5(b)(7)
Iowa	Conforms		Iowa Code §422.32(7)
Kansas	Conforms		Kan. Stat. Ann. §79-32,109
Kentucky	Does not conform		Ky. Rev. Stat. Ann. §141.010(3)
Louisiana	Conforms		La. Rev. Stat. Ann. §47:287.701A
Maine	Does not conform		Me. Rev. Stat. Ann. tit. 36, §5200-A(1)(N)(3)
Maryland	Does not conform	Maryland has its own provision regarding SUVs	Sec. 10-210.1(b) T.G.A
Massachusetts	Conforms		Mass. Gen. Laws ch. 63, §30(4) Technical Information Release 03-25, Massachusetts Department of Revenue, April 29, 2004
Michigan	Does not conform	Michigan does not allow depreciation, amortization, or accelerated write-offs. The state provides an investment credit in lieu of these deductions.	Instructions, 2004 Form C-8000, Michigan Single Business Tax Annual Return
Minnesota	Does not conform		Minn. Stat. §290.01(19c) and (19d)
Mississippi	Conforms		Miss. Reg. 504
Missouri	Conforms		Mo. Rev. Stat. §143.091
Montana	Conforms		2004 Form CLT-4, Montana Corporation License Tax Return
Nebraska	Does not conform	Nebraska allows an offsetting deduction in later years	Neb. Rev. Stat. §77-2716
New Hampshire	Does not conform		N.H. Rev. Stat. Ann. §77-A:1
New Jersey	Does not conform		N.J. Stat. Ann. §54:10A-4(k) (13) (A)

State	Answer	Comments	Authority
New Mexico	Conforms		N.M. Stat. Ann. § 7-2A-2(G)
New York	Conforms	New York allows no deduction for SUVs over 6,000 pounds	Instructions, 2004 Form CT-3, New York General Business Corporation Franchise Tax Return Sec. 208(9), Tax Law
North Carolina	Conforms		N.C. Gen. Stat. § 105-228.90
North Dakota	Conforms		N.D. Cent. Code § 57-38-01(5)
Ohio	Does not conform	Ohio allows a subtraction for amounts that have to be added back	Ohio Rev. Code Ann. § 5733.04(I)
Oklahoma	Conforms		Okla. Stat. tit. 68, § 2353(2)
Oregon	Conforms		Or. Rev. Stat. § 317.010
Pennsylvania	Conforms		72 P.S. § 7401(3)1(a)
Rhode Island	Does not conform		R.I. Gen. Laws § 44-61-1.1(a)
South Carolina	Conforms	Effective for taxable years beginning after December 31, 2003. Addback required for tax year 2003.	S.C. Code Ann. § 12-6-40(A)(1)(b) Revenue Ruling 05-2 Temporary Revenue Ruling 05-2
Tennessee	Conforms		Tenn. Code Ann. § 67-4-2006 Important Notice No. 04-27, Tennessee Department of Revenue
Texas	Does not conform		Tex. Tax Code Ann. § 171.001(b)(5)
Utah	Conforms		Utah Code Ann. § 59-7-101(16)
Vermont	Conforms		Vt. Stat. Ann. tit 32, § 5824
Virginia	Conforms		Va. Code. Ann. § 58.1-301
West Virginia	Conforms		W.Va. Code § 11-24-3

State	Answer	Comments	Authority
Wisconsin	Does not conform		Wis. Stat. § 71.22(4)(r) Instructions, 2004 Form 4, Wisconsin Corporation Franchise or Income Tax Return

Federal Conformity—Depreciation (IRC § 167 & IRC § 168)

The federal Working Families Tax Relief Act of 2004 (WFTRA) (P.L. 108-311) and the American Jobs Creation Act of 2004 (AJCA) (P.L. 108-357) made numerous changes to IRC § 167 and § 168, concerning depreciation. Some of the most significant changes include: bonus depreciation for noncommercial aircraft placed in service after September 10, 2001; a 15-year recovery period for qualified leasehold improvements and qualified restaurant property placed in service after October 22, 2004 and before January 1, 2006; increased recovery periods for land-clearing costs and electric utility property; and extension of shortened recovery periods for Indian reservation property through December 31, 2005. The AJCA also made changes that affect the film and television industry. The state response has varied and the chart below reflects the states' positions regarding the new federal depreciation rules.

State	Answer	Comments	Authority
Alabama	Conforms		Alabama Code § 40-18-1.1
Alaska	Conforms		Alaska Stat. § 43.20.021(a)
Arizona	Conforms	Arizona does not allow bonus depreciation.	Ariz. Rev. Stat. § § 43-105(A), 43-1121(1)
Arkansas	Does not conform	Adopts IRC depreciation sections as in effect on January 1, 1999.	Ark. Code. Ann. § 26-51-428
California	Does not conform		Cal. Rev. & Tax Code § 24349
Colorado	Conforms		Colo. Rev. Stat. § 39-22-103(5.3)
Connecticut	Conforms	Connecticut does not allow bonus depreciation.	Conn. Gen. Stat. § 12-217(b)
Delaware	Conforms		Del. Code Ann. tit. 30, § 1901(5)
District of Columbia	Conforms	The District of Columbia does not allow bonus depreciation.	D.C. Code Ann. § 47-1803.03

State	Answer	Comments	Authority
Florida	Conforms		Fla. Stat. Ch. 220.03(3)
Georgia	Conforms	Georgia does not allow bonus depreciation.	Ga. Code Ann. § 48-1-2(14)
Hawaii	Conforms	Hawaii does not allow bonus depreciation.	Haw. Rev. Stat. § 235-2.4
Idaho	Conforms	Idaho does not allow bonus depreciation.	Idaho Code § 63-3004 Idaho Code § 63-3022O
Illinois	Conforms	Illinois does not allow bonus depreciation.	35 ILCS 5/203
Indiana	Conforms	Indiana does not allow bonus depreciation.	Ind. Code § 6-3-1-11(b)
Iowa	Conforms	Iowa does not allow the 30% bonus depreciation, but does allow 50% bonus depreciation	Iowa Code § 422.3(5)
Kansas	Conforms		Kan. Stat. Ann. § 79-32,109
Kentucky	Conforms	Kentucky does not allow bonus depreciation.	Ky. Rev. Stat. Ann. § 141.010(3)
Louisiana	Conforms		La. Rev. Stat. Ann. § 47:287.701A
Maine	Conforms	Maine does not allow bonus depreciation.	36 M.R.S.A. § 111(1-A) 36 M.R.S.A. § 5200-A(1)(N)
Maryland	Conforms	Maryland does not allow bonus depreciation.	Tax Gen. Art. § 10-108, Tax Gen. Art. § 10-210.1
Massachusetts	Conforms	Massachusetts does not allow bonus depreciation.	Mass. Gen. Laws ch. 63, § 30(4)

State	Answer	Comments	Authority
Michigan	Does not conform	Michigan does not allow depreciation, amortization, or accelerated write-offs. The state provides an investment credit in lieu of these deductions.	Mich. Comp. Laws § 208.9(4)(c)
Minnesota	Conforms	Minnesota requires modifications for bonus deprecation	Minn. Stat. § 290.01(19), § 290.01(19c) (16)
Mississippi	Conforms	Mississippi does not allow bonus depreciation.	2004 Form 83-122, Mississippi Computation of Net Taxable Income Schedule Miss. Reg. 504
Missouri	Conforms	Missouri does not allow 30% bonus depreciation, for assets purchased between July 1, 2002, and June 30, 2003, but allows 50% bonus depreciation to same extent as federal law.	Mo. Rev. Stat. § 143.091 Mo. Rev. Stat. § 143.121
Montana	Conforms		2004 Form CLT-4, Montana Corporation License Tax Return
Nebraska	Conforms	Nebraska does not allow bonus depreciation.	Neb. Rev. Stat. § 77-2714 Neb. Rev. Stat. § 77-2716
New Hampshire	Does not conform	Adopts IRC depreciation provisions as in effect on December 31, 2000.	N.H. Rev. Stat. Ann. § 77-A:1
New Jersey	Conforms	New Jersey does not allow bonus depreciation.	N.J. Stat. Ann. § 54:10A-4(k)

State	Answer	Comments	Authority
New Mexico	Conforms		N.M. Stat. Ann. §7-2A-2(G)
New York	Conforms	New York does not allow bonus depreciation for tax years beginning after 2002, except with respect to qualified Resurgence Zone property and qualified New York Liberty Zone property.	Instructions, 2004 Form CT-3, New York General Business Corporation Franchise Tax Return Sec. 208(9), Tax Law
North Carolina	Conforms	North Carolina does not allow bonus depreciation.	N.C. Gen. Stat. §105-228.90 N.C. Gen. Stat. §105-130.5(a)(15)
North Dakota	Conforms		N.D. Cent. Code §57-38-01(5)
Ohio	Conforms	Ohio does not allow bonus depreciation.	Ohio Rev. Code Ann. §5733.04(G) Ohio Rev. Code Ann. §5733.04(I)
Oklahoma	Conforms	Oklahoma does not allow the 30% bonus depreciation, but does allow the 50% bonus depreciation.	Okla. Stat. tit. 68, §2353(2) Okla. Stat. tit. 68, §2358.6(A)
Oregon	Conforms		Or. Rev. Stat. §317.010
Pennsylvania	Conforms	Pennsylvania does not allow bonus depreciation.	72 P.S. §7401
Rhode Island	Conforms	Rhode Island does not allow bonus depreciation.	R.I. Gen. Laws §44-11-11 R.I. Gen. Laws §44-61-1
South Carolina	Conforms	South Carolina does not allow bonus depreciation.	S.C. Code Ann. §12-6-40(A)(1) S.C. Code Ann. §12-6-50

State	Answer	Comments	Authority
Tennessee	Conforms	Tennessee does not allow bonus depreciation.	Tenn. Code Ann. § 67-4-2006
Texas	Does not conform	Texas does not allow bonus depreciation.	Tex. Tax Code Ann. § 171.001(b)(5) Form 05-386, Instructions for Completing Annual Franchise Tax Reports Originally Due May 16, 2005
Utah	Conforms		Utah Code Ann. § 59-7-101(16)
Vermont	Does not conform	Vermont does not allow bonus depreciation.	Vt. Stat. Ann. tit 32, § 5811(18)
Virginia	Conforms	Virginia does not allow bonus depreciation.	Va. Code. Ann. § 58.1-301
West Virginia	Conforms		W. Va. Code § 11-24-3
Wisconsin	Does not conform	Adopts IRC depreciation provisions as amended to December 31, 2000.	Wis. Stat. § 71.26(3)(y)

Federal Conformity—Manufacturer's Deduction (IRC § 199)

The federal American Jobs Creation Act of 2004 (P.L. 108-357) created a new deduction for manufacturers (i.e., IRC § 199) that will effectively reduce the federal corporate income tax rate for domestic manufacturing by 3 percent, from a top rate of 35 percent down to 32 percent. When fully phased in by 2010, the deduction will be equal to 9% of the lesser of qualified production activities income for the year, or taxable income for the year. The state response has varied and the chart below reflects the states' positions regarding this new deduction.

State	Manufacturers' Deduction (IRC § 199)	Comments	Citation
Alabama	Conforms	Deduction passes through to entity owners and shareholders. Deduction not allowed for entity owners and shareholders who are individuals and financial institutions. However, deduction allowed for corporate entity owners or shareholders.	Alabama Code § 40-18-1.1
Alaska	Conforms		Alaska Stat. § 43.20.021(a)
Arizona	Conforms		Ariz. Rev. Stat. § 43-105(A)
Arkansas	Does not conform		Ark. Code. Ann. § 26-51-401 et seq.
California	Does not conform	Addition required for amount of federal deduction.	Cal. Rev. & Tax Code § 23051.5 Cal. Rev. & Tax Code § 24341
Colorado	Conforms		Colo. Rev. Stat. § 39-22-103(5.3)
Connecticut	Conforms		Conn. Gen. Stat. § 12-213(a)(23)

State	Manufacturers' Deduction (IRC §199)	Comments	Citation
Delaware	Conforms	IRC not incorporated by reference, but starting point for computing taxable income is federal taxable income as currently defined by the IRC.	Del. Code Ann. tit. 30, §1901(5) Del. Code Ann. tit. 30, §1903(a)
District of Columbia	Conforms		D.C. Code Ann. §47-1801.04(28A)
Florida	Conforms		Fla. Stat. Ch. 220.03(3)
Georgia	Does not conform		Ga. Code Ann. §48-1-2(14)
Hawaii	Does not conform		Haw. Rev. Stat. §235-2.3
Idaho	Conforms		Idaho Code §63-3004
Illinois	Conforms		35 ILCS 5/102
Indiana	Does not conform		Ind. Code §6-3-1-3.5(b)(8)
Iowa	Conforms		Iowa Code §422.3(5)
Kansas	Conforms		Kan. Stat. Ann. §79-32,109
Kentucky	Conforms		Ky. Rev. Stat. Ann. §141.010(3)
Louisiana	Conforms		La. Rev. Stat. Ann. §47:287.701A
Maine	Does not conform		Me. Rev. Stat. Ann. tit. 36, §5200–A(1) (S)
Maryland	Does not conform		Sec. 2, H.B. 147, Law 2005
Massachusetts	Does not conform	Massachusetts has decoupled from IRC Sec. 199 (Ch. 466, Laws 2005).	Mass. Gen. Laws ch. 63, §30(4)

State	Manufacturers' Deduction (IRC § 199)	Comments	Citation
Michigan	Conforms for taxpayers who elect to use the IRC as in effect for the tax year; Does not conform for taxpayers who use the 1999 incorporation date for single business tax purposes		Mich. Comp. Laws § 208.5(4)
Minnesota	Does not conform	Addition required for amount of federal deduction.	Minn. Stat. § 290.01(19c) (17)
Mississippi	Does not conform		Unofficial department guidance
Missouri	Conforms		Mo. Rev. Stat. § 143.091
Montana	Conforms		2004 Form CLT-4, Montana Corporation License Tax Return
Nebraska	Conforms		Neb. Rev. Stat. § 77-2714 Unofficial department guidance
New Hampshire	Does not conform		N.H. Rev. Stat. Ann. § 77-A:1
New Jersey	Does not conform		N.J. Stat. Ann. § 54:10A-4(k) (2) (J)
New Mexico	Conforms		N.M. Stat. Ann. § 7-2A-2(G)
New York	Conforms		Instructions, 2004 Form CT-3, New York General Business Corporation Franchise Tax Return
North Carolina	Does not conform		N.C. Gen. Stat. § 105-228.90
North Dakota	Does not conform		N.D. Cent. Code § 57-38-01.3(1) (i)

State	Manufacturers' Deduction (IRC §199)	Comments	Citation
Ohio	Conforms		Ohio Rev. Code Ann. §5733.04(G)
Oklahoma	Conforms		Okla. Stat. tit. 68, §2353(2)
Oregon	Does not conform	Addback required for amount of federal deduction.	Sec. 41, S.B. 31, Laws 2005
Pennsylvania	Conforms		72 P.S. §7401(3)1(a)
Rhode Island	Conforms		R.I. Gen. Laws §44-11-11
South Carolina	Does not conform		S.C. Code Ann. §12-6-40(A)(1)
Tennessee	Does not conform		Tenn. Code Ann. §67-4-2006
Texas	Does not conform		Tex. Tax Code Ann. §171.001(b)(5)
Utah	Conforms		Utah Code Ann. §59-7-101(16)
Virginia	Conforms		Va. Code. Ann. §58.1-301
Vermont	Conforms		Vt. Stat. Ann. tit 32, §5811(18)
West Virginia	Does not conform		W. Va. Code §11-24-3
Wisconsin	Conforms		Wis. Stat. §71.22(4)(r)

Federal Conformity—Repeal of ETI Regime (IRC §114)

The federal American Jobs Creation Act of 2004 (P.L. 108-357) repeals IRC §114, which provides an exclusion from gross income for extraterritorial income (ETI). The state response has varied and the chart below reflects the states' positions regarding the repeal of the ETI regime.

State	Repeal of ETI Regime (IRC §114)	Comments	Citation
Alabama	Does not conform	IRC Sec. 114 never adopted, so repeal is moot.	Alabama Code §40-18-1.1
Alaska	Conforms	Water's edge filers must add back extraterritorial income excluded for federal purposes.	Alaska Stat. §43.20.021(a)
Arizona	Conforms		Ariz. Rev. Stat. §43-105(A)
Arkansas	Does not conform	IRC Sec. 114 never adopted, so repeal is moot.	Ark. Code. Ann. §26-51-401 et seq.
California	Does not conform	IRC Sec. 114 was never adopted, so repeal is moot.	Cal. Rev. & Tax Code §23051.5 Cal. Rev. & Tax Code §24341
Colorado	Conforms		Colo. Rev. Stat. §39-22-103(5.3)
Connecticut	Conforms		Conn. Gen. Stat. §12-213(a)(23)
Delaware	Conforms	IRC not incorporated by reference, but starting point for computing taxable income is federal taxable income as currently defined by the IRC.	Del. Code Ann. tit. 30, §1901(5) Del. Code Ann. tit. 30, §1903(a)
District of Columbia	Conforms		D.C. Code Ann. §47-1801.04(28A)
Florida	Conforms		Fla. Stat. Ch. 220.03(3)

State	Repeal of ETI Regime (IRC §114)	Comments	Citation
Georgia	Does not conform		Ga. Code Ann. §48-1-2(14)
Hawaii	Does not conform	IRC Sec. 114 never adopted, so repeal is moot.	Haw. Rev. Stat. §235-2.3
Idaho	Conforms		Idaho Code §63-3004
Illinois	Conforms		35 ILCS 5/102
Indiana	Conforms		Ind. Code §6-3-1-11(b)
Iowa	Conforms		Iowa Code §422.3(5)
Kansas	Conforms		Kan. Stat. Ann. §79-32,109
Kentucky	Conforms		Ky. Rev. Stat. Ann. §141.010(3)
Louisiana	Conforms		La. Rev. Stat. Ann. §47:287.701A
Maine	Conforms		2004 Form 1120ME, Maine Corporate Income Tax Return
Maryland	Conforms		Instructions, 2004 Form 500, Corporation Income Tax Return
Massachusetts	Conforms		Mass. Gen. Laws ch. 63, §30(4)
Michigan	Conforms for taxpayers who elect to use the IRC as in effect for the tax year; Does not conform for taxpayers who use the 1999 incorporation date for single business tax purposes		Mich. Comp. Laws §208.5(4)
Minnesota	Does not conform	Decoupled from IRC Sec. 114, so repeal is moot.	Minn. Stat. §290.01(19c)(13)

State	Repeal of ETI Regime (IRC §114)	Comments	Citation
Mississippi	Does not conform	IRC Sec. 114 never adopted, so repeal is moot.	Unofficial department guidance
Missouri	Conforms		Mo. Rev. Stat. §143.091
Montana	Does not conform	IRC Sec. 114 never adopted, so repeal is moot.	2004 Form CLT-4, Montana Corporation License Tax Return
Nebraska	Conforms		Neb. Rev. Stat. §77-2714 Unofficial department guidance
New Hampshire	Does not conform		N.H. Rev. Stat. Ann. §77-A:1
New Jersey	Does not conform	Income from all sources, whether within or without the United States is taxable.	N.J. Stat. Ann. §54:10A-4(k)
New Mexico	Conforms		N.M. Stat. Ann. §7-2A-2(G)
New York	Conforms		Instructions, 2004 Form CT-3, New York General Business Corporation Franchise Tax Return
North Carolina	Conforms		N.C. Gen. Stat. §105-228.90
North Dakota	Does not conform		N.D. Cent. Code §57-38-01.3 (1)(j)
Ohio	Conforms		Ohio Rev. Code Ann. §5733.04(G)
Oklahoma	Conforms		Okla. Stat. tit. 68, §2353(2)
Oregon	Conforms		Or. Rev. Stat. §317.010
Pennsylvania	Conforms		72 P.S. §7401(3)1(a)

State	Repeal of ETI Regime (IRC §114)	Comments	Citation
Rhode Island	Conforms		R.I. Gen. Laws §44-11-11
South Carolina	Conforms		S.C. Code Ann. §12-6-40(A)(1)
Tennessee	Conforms		Tenn. Code Ann. §67-4-2006
Texas	Does not conform		Tex. Tax Code Ann. §171.001(b)(5)
Utah	Conforms		Utah Code Ann. §59-7-101(16)
Virginia	Conforms		Va. Code. Ann. §58.1-301
Vermont	Conforms	The federal extraterritorial income exclusion is not required to be added back to federal taxable or federal adjusted gross income.	Vt. Stat. Ann. tit 32, §5811(18)
West Virginia	Conforms	The federal extraterritorial income exclusion is not required to be added back to federal taxable or federal adjusted gross income.	W. Va. Code §11-24-3
Wisconsin	Does not conform	IRC Sec. 114 never adopted, so repeal is moot.	Wis. Stat. §71.22(4)(r)

Federal Conformity—Start-Up and Organizational Expenditures (IRC §195, §248, and §709)

The federal American Jobs Creation Act of 2004 (P.L. 108-357) allows taxpayers to elect to deduct up to $5,000 of start-up or organizational expenses incurred in the tax year in which a trade, business, corporation, or partnership begins (IRC §195, §248, and §709). The $5,000 must be reduced (but not below zero) by any amount in excess of $50,000. Start-up or organizational expenses that cannot be deducted may be amortized over a 15-year period. Previously, such expenses could only be amortized over a 5-year period. The new deduction and amortization period generally applies to expenses incurred after October 22, 2004. The state response has varied and the chart below reflects the states' positions regarding start-up and organizational expenditures.

State	Answer	Comments	Authority
Alabama	Conforms		Alabama Code §40-18-1.1
Alaska	Conforms		Alaska Stat. §43.20.021(a)
Arizona	Conforms		Ariz. Rev. Stat. §43-105(A)
Arkansas	Conforms	Arkansas conforms to AJCA changes made to IRC §248 and §709, but not to IRC §195.	Ark. Code. Ann. §26-51-439
California	Conforms		Cal. Rev. & Tax Code §24407 Cal. Rev. & Tax Code §24414 Cal. Rev. & Tax Code §17851
Colorado	Conforms		Colo. Rev. Stat. §39-22-103(5.3)
Connecticut	Conforms		Conn. Gen. Stat. §12-213(a)(23)
Delaware	Conforms		Del. Code Ann. tit. 30, §1601(c), Del. Code Ann. tit. 30, §1901(5), Del. Code Ann. tit. 30, §1903(a)

State	Answer	Comments	Authority
District of Columbia	Conforms		D.C. Code Ann. § 47-1801.04(28A)
Florida	Conforms		Fla. Stat. Ch. 220.03(3)
Georgia	Conforms		Ga. Code Ann. § 48-1-2(14)
Hawaii	Conforms		Haw. Rev. Stat. § 235-2.3
Idaho	Conforms		Idaho Code § 63-3004 Idaho Code § 63-3006B
Illinois	Conforms		35 ILCS 5/102
Indiana	Conforms		Ind. Code § 6-3-1-11(b)
Iowa	Conforms		Iowa Code § 422.3(5)
Kansas	Conforms		Kan. Stat. Ann. § 79-32,109
Kentucky	Conforms		Ky. Rev. Stat. Ann. § 141.010(3)
Louisiana	Conforms		La. Rev. Stat. Ann. § 47:287.701A
Maine	Conforms		Me. Rev. Stat. Ann. tit. 36, § 111 (1-A)
Maryland	Conforms		Md. Code Ann. § 10–304(1)
Massachusetts	Conforms		Mass. Gen. Laws ch. 63, § 30(4)
Michigan	Conforms for taxpayers who elect to use the IRC as in effect for the tax year; Does not conform for taxpayers who use the 1999 incorporation date for single business tax purposes.		Mich. Comp. Laws § 208.5(4)

State	Answer	Comments	Authority
Minnesota	Conforms		Minn. Stat. § 290.01(19)
Mississippi	Conforms		Instructions, 2004 Form 83-105, Mississippi Corporate Income and Franchise Tax Return Instructions, 2004 Form 86-105, Mississippi Partnership Income Tax Return
Missouri	Conforms		Mo. Rev. Stat. § 143.091 Mo. Rev. Stat. § 143.401
Montana	Conforms	Only specific IRC provisions incorporated as currently amended, but taxable income computation starts with federal taxable income.	2004 Form CLT-4, Montana Corporation License Tax Return
Nebraska	Conforms		Neb. Rev. Stat. § 77-2714
New Hampshire	Does not conform		N.H. Rev. Stat. Ann. § 77-A:1
New Jersey	Conforms		N.J. Stat. Ann. § 54:10A-4(k)
New Mexico	Conforms		N.M. Stat. Ann. § 7-2A-2(G)
New York	Conforms	IRC not incorporated by reference, but taxable income computation starts with federal taxable income.	Instructions, 2004 Form CT-3, New York General Business Corporation Franchise Tax Return
North Carolina	Conforms		N.C. Gen. Stat. § 105-228.90

State	Answer	Comments	Authority
North Dakota	Conforms		N.D. Cent. Code §57-38-01(5)
Ohio	Conforms		Ohio Rev. Code Ann. §5733.04(G)
Oklahoma	Conforms		Okla. Stat. tit. 68, §2353(2)
Oregon	Conforms		Or. Rev. Stat. §317.010 Or. Rev. Stat. §314.712
Pennsylvania	Conforms		72 P.S. §7401(3)1(a) 72 P.S. §7301(n.0)
Rhode Island	Conforms		R.I. Gen. Laws §44-11-11
South Carolina	Conforms		S.C. Code Ann. §12-6-40(A)(1) S.C. Code Ann. §12-6-600
Tennessee	Conforms		Tenn. Code Ann. §67-4-2006
Texas	Does not conform		Tex. Tax Code Ann. §171.001(b)(5)
Utah	Conforms		Utah Code Ann. §59-7-101(16)
Vermont	Conforms		Vt. Stat. Ann. tit 32, §5811(18)
Virginia	Conforms		Va. Code. Ann. §58.1-301
West Virginia	Conforms		W.Va. Code §11-24-3
Wisconsin	Conforms		Wis. Stat. §71.22(4)(r)

Federal Conformity—Temporary Dividends Received Deduction (IRC § 965)

The IRC § 965 temporary dividends received deduction enacted under the federal American Jobs Creation Act of 2004 (P.L. 108-357) allows corporate taxpayers to deduct 85% of the cash dividends received during the tax year by the corporate shareholder from controlled foreign corporations that are invested in the United States. The taxpayer may elect to apply the IRC § 965 deduction for repatriated dividends to either the taxpayer's last tax year that begins before October 22, 2004 or the taxpayer's first tax year that begins during the one-year period beginning on October 22, 2004. The IRC § 965 deduction is entered on federal Form 1120, Schedule C and included with the total federal special dividends received deduction taken on line 29b of the federal return. States that have a federal form 1120, line 30 (or line 28 minus line 29b) starting point for computing taxable income of corporate taxpayers, generally allow the IRC § 965 deduction, although a few such states have addback requirements. States that have a line 28 starting point generally do not allow the IRC § 965 deduction, unless a subtraction adjustment is allowed for the federal special dividends received deduction. The chart below reflects the states' positions regarding the IRC § 965 deduction.

State	Temporary Dividends Received Deduction (IRC § 965)	Comments	Citation
Alabama	Does not conform	Addition required if less than 20% stock ownership.	Alabama Code §§ 40-18-33, 40-18-34(d) Form 20C Instructions
Alaska	Does not conform		Form 04-611 Instructions
Arizona	Conforms		Ariz. Rev. Stat. § 43-105(A), Form 120 Instructions
Arkansas	Does not conform		Ark. Code. Ann. § 26-51-404.
California	Does not conform		Cal. Rev. & Tax Code § 25106 Form 100 Instructions
Colorado	Conforms		Colo. Rev. Stat. § 39-22-103(5.3) Form 112 Instructions
Connecticut	Does not conform		Form CT-1120 Instructions

State	Temporary Dividends Received Deduction (IRC §965)	Comments	Citation
Delaware	Conforms		Form 1100 Instructions
District of Columbia	Does not conform		Form D-20 Instructions
Florida	Conforms		Fla. Stat. Ch. 220.03(1)(n) Form F-1120N Instructions
Georgia	Conforms		Ga. Code Ann. §48-1-2(14)
Hawaii	Does not conform	Does not adopt IRC Subchapter N (IRC Sec. 861–IRC Sec. 999) with respect to tax based on income from sources within or without United States, except IRC Sec. 985–IRC Sec. 989 with respect to foreign currency transactions.	Haw. Rev. Stat. §235-2.3(b)(26)
Idaho	Conforms		Idaho Code §63-3004 Form 41 Instructions
Illinois	Conforms		35 ILCS 5/102 Form IL-1120 Instructions
Indiana	Conforms		Ind. Code §6-3-1-11(b) Form IT-20 Instructions
Iowa	Conforms		Iowa Code §422.3(5) Form IA 1120 Instructions
Kansas	Conforms		Kan. Stat. Ann. §79-32,109 Form K-120 Instructions

State	Temporary Dividends Received Deduction (IRC §965)	Comments	Citation
Kentucky	Does not conform		Form 720 Instructions
Louisiana	Conforms		La. Rev. Stat. Ann. §47:287.738(F)(1) Form CIFT-620 Instructions
Maine	Conforms		Me. Rev. Stat. Ann. tit. 36, §111(1-A) Form 1120ME Instructions
Maryland	Conforms		Form 500 Instructions
Massachusetts	Does not conform		Form 355 Instructions
Michigan	Does not conform	Addition required for federal dividends deduction.	Mich. Comp. Laws §208.9(4)(d) and (7)(a)
Minnesota	Does not conform		Form M4 Instructions
Mississippi	Does not conform		Miss. Code. Ann. §27-7-15(1) Form 83-100 Instructions
Missouri	Does not conform	Addition required on Schedule MO-C for amount of federal deduction. Subtraction allowed for 85% of dividends apportioned to state sources using single or three-factor apportionment formula.	Mo. Rev. Stat. §143.091, Mo. Rev. Stat. §143.531(2) Form MO-1120 Instructions, Form MO-C
Montana	Does not conform		Form CLT-4 Instructions
Nebraska	Conforms		Neb. Rev. Stat. §77-2714 Form 1120N Instructions

State	Temporary Dividends Received Deduction (IRC § 965)	Comments	Citation
New Hampshire	Does not conform		N.H. Rev. Stat. Ann. § 77-A:1(III)
New Jersey	Does not conform		N.J. Stat. Ann. § 54:10A-4(k)
New Mexico	Conforms		N.M. Stat. Ann. § 7-2A-2(C) and (G) Form CIT-Instructions
New York	Does not conform		N.Y. Tax Law § 208(9)(b)(2) Form CT-3 Instructions
North Carolina	Conforms		N.C. Gen. Stat. § 105-228.90(b)(1b) Form CD-405 Instructions
North Dakota	Does not conform	Addition required for federal special dividends deduction.	N.D. Cent. Code § 57-38-01.3(1)(g) Form 40, Schedule SA
Ohio	Does not conform		Ohio Rev. Code Ann. § 5733.04(I) Form FT 1120 Instructions
Oklahoma	Conforms		Okla. Stat. tit. 68, § 2353(2)
Oregon	Conforms	Subtraction allowed for amount of federal deduction.	Form 20 Instructions, Form 20-I Instructions
Pennsylvania	Conforms	Subtraction allowed on Schedule C-2 for amount of federal deduction.	Form RCT-101 Instructions
Rhode Island	Conforms	Subtraction allowed for full amount of federal special dividends deduction.	Form RI 1120C, Schedule A

State	Temporary Dividends Received Deduction (IRC § 965)	Comments	Citation
South Carolina	Does not conform	Does not adopt IRC Sec. 944 to IRC Sec. 989 relating to taxation of foreign income. Addition required for amount of federal deduction.	S.C. Code Ann. § 12-6-50(11)
Tennessee	Does not conform		Tenn. Code Ann. § 67-4-2006(a) Form FAE 170 Instructions
Texas	Does not conform		Tex. Tax Code Ann. § 171.001(b)(5)
Utah	Does not conform		Utah Code Ann. § 59-7-101(27)
Vermont	Conforms		Vt. Stat. Ann. tit 32, § 5811(18) Form CO-411 Instructions
Virginia	Conforms		Va. Code. Ann. § 58.1-301(B) 23 Va. Admin. Code § 10-120-100 Form 500 Instructions
West Virginia	Conforms		W. Va. Code § 11-24-3(a) Form WV/CNF-120 Instructions
Wisconsin	Does not conform		Form 4 Instructions

Federal Extended NOL Carryback Conformity

The federal Job Creation and Worker Assistance Act of 2002 (P.L. 107-147) extends the net operating loss (NOL) carryback from two years to five years for NOLs arising in 2001 and 2002. The full amount of NOLs arising in or carried forward to 2001 and 2002 can be used to reduce the alternative minimum tax. The state response has varied.

Conforming States—The following states incorporate the extended carryback period for state corporate income tax purposes either because they automatically conform to the current federal NOL provisions or they have enacted legislation conforming as of a date subsequent to enactment of P.L. 107-147.

Alaska	*Oklahoma*
*Delaware**	*Vermont*
Indiana	*West Virginia**
*New York**	

* Although **Delaware, New York,** and **West Virginia** incorporate the extended NOL carrybacks, they limit the amount that may be carried back. Delaware limits NOL carrybacks to $30,000 and New York limits NOL carrybacks to $10,000 per year. West Virginia limits NOL carrybacks to $300,000.

Nonconforming States—The following states do not allow the extended NOL carryback for state corporate income tax purposes, either because they do not conform to federal NOL carryback provisions or they conform as of a date prior to enactment of P.L. 107-147.

Alabama	*Kansas*	*New Mexico*
Arizona	*Kentucky*	*North Carolina*
Arkansas	*Louisiana*	*Ohio*
California	*Maine*	*Oregon*
Colorado	*Maryland*	*Pennsylvania*
Connecticut	*Massachusetts*	*Rhode Island*
District of Columbia	*Michigan*	*South Carolina*
Florida	*Minnesota*	*South Dakota*
Georgia	*Mississippi*	*Tennessee*
Hawaii	*Missouri*	*Texas*
Idaho	*Montana*	*Utah*
Illinois	*Nebraska*	*Virginia*
Iowa	*New Hampshire*	*Wisconsin*
	New Jersey	

States with Special Situations—

Nevada, Washington, and *Wyoming* do not impose a corporate income tax.

North Dakota allows the carryback only for NOL's incurred in taxable years beginning before 2003.

Federal Return Attached—LLCs

The following chart indicates whether a federal return must be attached to an LLC's state tax return.

State	Answer
Alabama	Yes
Alaska	Yes
Arizona	Yes
Arkansas	No[1]
California	No
Colorado	No
Connecticut	Yes
Delaware	Yes
District of Columbia	Yes
Florida	Yes
Georgia	Yes
Hawaii	No
Idaho	Yes
Illinois	No[1]
Indiana	Yes
Iowa	Yes
Kansas	Yes
Kentucky	Yes
Louisiana	No
Maine	Yes
Maryland	No
Massachusetts	Yes
Michigan	Yes
Minnesota	Yes
Mississippi	Yes
Missouri	Yes
Montana	Yes
Nebraska	Yes
New Hampshire	Yes
New Jersey	Yes
New Mexico	Yes

State	Answer
New York	Yes
North Carolina	No
North Dakota	Yes
Ohio	Yes
Oklahoma	Yes
Oregon	Yes
Pennsylvania	Yes
Rhode Island	Yes
South Carolina	Yes
Tennessee	No[2]
Texas	No
Utah	No[1]
Vermont	Yes
Virginia	No[3]
West Virginia	Yes
Wisconsin	Yes

[1] Partnerships (LLCs) are not required to attached copies of the federal return to their state return.

[2] At the Commissioner of Revenue's discretion, taxpayers may be required to file a copy of the federal tax forms filed with the IRS.

[3] Partnerships (LLCs) are not required to file reports. However, the Tax Commissioner has authority to require copies of federal partnership returns and attached schedules.

Federal Return Attached—LLPs

The following chart indicates whether a federal return must be attached to an LLP's state tax return.

State	Answer
Alabama	Yes
Alaska	Yes
Arizona	Yes
Arkansas	No[1]
California	No
Colorado	No
Connecticut	Yes
Delaware	Yes
District of Columbia	Yes
Florida	Yes
Georgia	Yes
Hawaii	No
Idaho	Yes
Illinois	No[1]
Indiana	Yes
Iowa	Yes
Kansas	Yes
Kentucky	Yes
Louisiana	No
Maine	Yes
Maryland	No
Massachusetts	Yes
Michigan	Yes
Minnesota	Yes
Mississippi	Yes
Missouri	Yes
Montana	Yes
Nebraska	Yes
New Hampshire	Yes
New Jersey	Yes

State	Answer
New Mexico	Yes
New York	Yes
North Carolina	No
North Dakota	Yes
Ohio	Yes
Oklahoma	Yes
Oregon	Yes
Pennsylvania	Yes
Rhode Island	Yes
South Carolina	Yes
Tennessee	No[2]
Texas	No
Utah	No[1]
Vermont	Yes
Virginia	No[3]
West Virginia	Yes
Wisconsin	Yes

[1] Partnerships are not required to attached copies of the federal return to their state return.

[2] At the Commissioner of Revenue's discretion, taxpayers may be required to file a copy of the federal tax forms filed with the IRS.

[3] Partnerships are not required to file reports. However, the Tax Commissioner has authority to require copies of federal partnership returns and schedules.

Federal Return Attached—Partnerships

The following chart indicates whether a federal return must be attached to a partnership's state tax return.

State	Answer
Alabama	Yes
Alaska	Yes
Arizona	Yes
Arkansas	No[1]
California	No
Colorado	No
Connecticut	Yes
Delaware	Yes
District of Columbia	Yes
Florida	Yes
Georgia	Yes
Hawaii	No
Idaho	Yes
Illinois	No[1]
Indiana	Yes
Iowa	Yes
Kansas	Yes
Kentucky	Yes
Louisiana	No
Maine	Yes
Maryland	No
Massachusetts	Yes
Michigan	Yes
Minnesota	Yes
Mississippi	Yes
Missouri	Yes
Montana	Yes
Nebraska	Yes
New Hampshire	Yes
New Jersey	Yes

State	Answer
New Mexico	Yes
New York	Yes
North Carolina	No
North Dakota	Yes
Ohio	Yes
Oklahoma	Yes
Oregon	Yes
Pennsylvania	Yes
Rhode Island	Yes
South Carolina	Yes
Tennessee	No[2]
Texas	No
Utah	No[1]
Vermont	Yes
Virginia	No[3]
West Virginia	Yes
Wisconsin	Yes

[1] Partnerships are not required to attached copies of the federal return to their state return.

[2] At the Commissioner of Revenue's discretion, taxpayers may be required to file a copy of the federal tax forms filed with the IRS.

[3] Partnerships are not required to file reports. However, the Tax Commissioner has authority to require copies of federal partnership returns and attached schedules.

Federal Return Attached—S Corporations

The following chart indicates whether a federal return must be attached to an S corporation's state tax return.

State	Answer
Alabama	Yes
Alaska	Yes
Arizona	Yes
Arkansas	Yes
California	No
Colorado	No
Connecticut	Yes
Delaware	Yes
District of Columbia	Yes
Florida	Yes
Georgia	Yes
Hawaii	No
Idaho	Yes
Illinois	No
Indiana	Yes
Iowa	Yes
Kansas	Yes
Kentucky	Yes
Louisiana	No
Maine	Yes
Maryland	No
Massachusetts	Yes
Michigan	Yes
Minnesota	Yes
Mississippi	Yes
Missouri	Yes
Montana	Yes
Nebraska	Yes
New Hampshire	Yes
New Jersey	Yes
New Mexico	Yes

State	Answer
New York	Yes
North Carolina	No
North Dakota	Yes
Ohio	Yes
Oklahoma	Yes
Oregon	Yes
Pennsylvania	Yes
Rhode Island	Yes
South Carolina	Yes
Tennessee	No[1]
Texas	No
Utah	Yes
Vermont	Yes
Virginia	Yes
West Virginia	Yes
Wisconsin	Yes

[1] At the Commissioner of Revenue's discretion, taxpayers may be required to file a copy of the federal tax forms filed with the IRS.

Financial Corporations, Athletics and Others

The chart below shows whether there are special industry apportionment factor rules in effect in the states for financial corporations, athletic teams, and other industries that are not covered. Nevada, Washington, and Wyoming do not impose a corporate income tax and are not included in the chart below.

State	Financial Corps.	Athletics	Others
Alabama	Yes	No	TV & radio broadcasters; publishers
Alaska	Yes	No	Oil and gas production
Arizona	No	No	No
Arkansas	Yes	No	Publishers; TV and radio broadcasters; passive intangible holding companies
California	Yes	Yes	Franchisors; commercial fishing; film & TV; publishers; unitary businesses with foreign operations; corporate partners; franchisors
Colorado	Yes	No	Publishers; television and radio broadcasters; public utilities
Connecticut	No	No	Life insurance companies; regulated investment company service providers; securities brokerages; credit card companies; corporate partner; broadcasters
Delaware	No	No	No
District of Columbia	Yes	No	No
Florida	Yes	No	Insurance; citrus growers
Georgia	No	No	Service providers; public service corporations; credit card processing services; corporate partners
Hawaii	Yes	No	TV and radio broadcasters; publishers; utilities
Idaho	Yes	No	TV & radio broadcasters; publishers
Illinois	Yes	No	Insurance companies
Indiana	No	No	Domestic insurance companies
Iowa	Yes	No	Telecommunications; radio & TV broadcasters; publishers; electric and gas companies
Kansas	Yes	No	Insurance companies; telecommunications companies; investment companies

State	Financial Corps.	Athletics	Others
Kentucky	Yes	No	Telecommunications companies; RIC sales and enterprise zone brokerage service sales
Louisiana	Yes	No	Service businesses; radio & TV broadcasters; manufacturers & merchandisers
Maine	No	No	Mutual fund service providers; corporate partners
Maryland	Yes	No	Processing services; leasing and rental enterprises; film and TV producers/ broadcasters; manufacturers; brokerage & RIC services; print publishers
Massachusetts	No	No	Courier and package delivery services; manufacturers; mutual fund service corporations; corporate trusts
Michigan	Yes	No	Insurers
Minnesota	Yes	No	Certain mail-order and telephone solicitation businesses; insurance companies; investment companies
Mississippi	Yes	No	Utilities; natural resource producers; non-life insurance companies; wholesalers, retailers, merchants, services, lessors; manufacturers
Missouri	Yes	No	Bridge companies; telecommunication companies
Montana	No	No	No
Nebraska	No	No	Insurance
New Hampshire	Yes	No	TV and radio broadcasters; publishers
New Jersey	Yes	No	No
New Mexico	Yes	No	TV and radio broadcasters
New York	Yes	No	Owners of cable TV rights; TV & radio broadcasters; newspaper & periodical advertisers; government contractors; securities and commodities brokers; RIC management service providers; corporate partners

State	Financial Corps.	Athletics	Others
North Carolina	Yes	No	Telephone companies; telegraph companies; public utilities ; dealers in intangibles
North Dakota	Yes	No	TV and radio broadcasters; publishers; public utilities
Ohio	No	No	No
Oklahoma	No	No	Telecommunication companies; limited presence manufacturers
Oregon	Yes	No	Insurance companies; movie and TV film producers; interstate broadcasters; timber; public utilities; installment sales; lobbying expenses
Pennsylvania	No	No	Natural gas companies; RIC services
Rhode Island	Yes	No	Manufacturers; manufacturers of medical products; broadcasters; RIC service providers; securities brokerage services; pension plan service companies
South Carolina	No	No	Telephone companies; recycling facilities; new or expanded facilities
South Dakota	Yes	N/A	N/A
Tennessee	Yes	No	N/A
Texas	Yes	No	RIC services; radio and TV broadcasters; stockbrokers; telephone companies; newspapers; commission DISCs and FSCs
Utah	Yes	No	Publishers; telecommunication companies
Vermont	No	No	No
Virginia	Yes	No	No
West Virginia	Yes	No	Public utilities
Wisconsin	Yes	Yes	Telecommunications and cable television companies; domestic insurance companies

Incorporation of Internal Revenue Code

The following chart indicates which states have incorporated the Internal Revenue Code (IRC) by reference and thus use federal taxable income as the starting point for calculating state corporate taxable income. Some states do not incorporate the code by reference, but instead adopt specific provisions of the code and/or use federal taxable income as the starting point for determining state corporate taxable income.

States that conform to the IRC generally may specifically exclude certain IRC sections, such as those relating to depreciation and net operating loss deductions. Such exceptions to general conformity provisions are not discussed in the chart below.

States that do not impose a corporate income tax are not included in this chart.

State	IRC Incorporated by Reference
Alabama	Yes, as currently amended.
Alaska	Yes, as currently amended.
Arizona	Yes, as of January 1, 2006 for tax years after 2005. January 1, 2005 for tax years after 2004.
Arkansas	No, but certain IRC provisions are incorporated as amended through specified dates.
California	Yes, as of January 1, 2005, with specified modifications.
Colorado	Yes, as currently amended.
Connecticut	Yes, as currently amended.
Delaware	No, but the starting point for the computation of DE taxable income is federal taxable income as currently defined by the IRC.
District of Columbia	Yes, as currently amended.
Florida	Yes, as of January 1, 2006 for tax years beginning after 2005. January 1, 2005 for tax years beginning after 2004.
Georgia	Yes, as of January 1, 2006, except IRC Sec. 168(k) bonus depreciation, the IRC Sec. 199 domestic production activities deduction, IRC Sec. 1400L New York liberty zone tax benefits, and IRC Sec. 1400N Gulf Opportunity (GO) zone benefits.
Hawaii	Yes, as of December 31, 2005 with some provisions specifically not adopted.
Idaho	Yes, as of January 1, 2006.
Illinois	Yes, as currently amended.
Indiana	Yes, as of January 1, 2006.
Iowa	Yes, as of January 1, 2006 for tax years after 2004. January 31, 2005 for tax years after 2002.
Kansas	Yes, as currently amended.
Kentucky	Yes, as of December 31, 2004.

State	IRC Incorporated by Reference
Louisiana	Yes, as currently amended.
Maine	Yes, as of December 31, 2005.
Maryland	No, but the starting point for the computation of MD taxable income is federal taxable income as currently defined by the IRC.
Massachusetts	Yes, as currently amended.
Michigan	Yes, as of January 1, 1999 or, at taxpayer's option, IRC in effect for the tax year.
Minnesota	Yes, as of May 18, 2006.
Mississippi	To the extent IRC provisions are incorporated by reference, those provisions are adopted as amended to date.
Missouri	Yes, as currently amended.
Montana	Only specific provisions incorporated as currently amended.
Nebraska	Yes, as currently amended.
New Hampshire	Yes, as of December 31, 2000.
New Jersey	No, except as specifically adopted, but computation of NJ income begins with federal taxable income.
New Mexico	Yes, as currently amended.
New York	Not incorporated by reference, but NY uses federal taxable income as starting point for calculating state income.
North Carolina	Yes, as of January 1, 2006.
North Dakota	Yes, as currently amended.
Ohio	Yes, as of March 30, 2006.
Oklahoma	Yes, as currently amended.
Oregon	Yes, as of December 31, 2004.
Pennsylvania	No, but PA adopts various provisions of the IRC on a current basis and uses federal taxable income as the starting point for calculating state taxable income.
Rhode Island	No, but the starting point for determining RI income is federal taxable income as currently defined by the IRC.
South Carolina	Yes, as of December 31, 2005.
Tennessee	No, but the starting point for determining TN taxable income is federal taxable income as currently defined by the IRC.
Texas	Yes, IRC in effect for federal tax year beginning after 1995 and before 1997.
Utah	To the extent IRC provisions are incorporated by reference those provisions are adopted as amended to date.
Vermont	Yes, as in effect for 2005 taxable year.
Virginia	Yes, as of December 31, 2005.

State	IRC Incorporated by Reference
West Virginia	No, except as specifically adopted. The starting point for the computation of WV taxable income is federal taxable income. WV has adopted federal tax laws in effect after December 31, 2004, but prior to January 1, 2006, for purposes of computing taxable income.
Wisconsin	Yes, as of December 31, 2004, with modifications.

Information Returns

Some states require the filing of information returns by individuals and entities that have made payments to others for which no withholding was required. These payments may be for salaries and wages, or for non-wage payments such as interest, dividends, rents, or royalties.

The chart below summarizes the threshold amount at which payments must be reported as well as the due dates for filing information returns. Information returns required of pass-through entities are not covered by this chart.

State	Salaries and Wages Minimum Required	Non-wage Amounts Minimum Required	Due Date
Alabama	$1,500	$1,500	Mar. 15
Arizona	None	None	n/a
Arkansas	$2,500	$2,500	May 15
California[1]	$600	$10 (interest/dividends)/ $600 (other)	Feb. 28
Colorado[1]	None	None	n/a
Connecticut	$600	$10 (interest/dividends)/ $600 (other)	Feb. 28[2]
Delaware	$600	$600	Feb. 28
District of Columbia	$600	$10 (interest/dividends)/ $600 (other)	Feb. 28
Georgia	$1,500	$1,500	Apr. 15
Hawaii	$600	$600	Feb. 28
Idaho[3]	$600	$10 (interest/dividends)/ $600 (other)	Feb. 28[2]
Illinois	State Request	State Request	n/a
Indiana	State Request	State Request	n/a
Iowa[3]	$600	$10 (interest/dividends)/ $600 (other)	Feb. 28[2]
Kansas	$600	$10 (interest/dividends)/ $600 (other)	Mar. 1
Kentucky[4]	None	None	n/a
Louisiana[4]	None	None	n/a
Maine[1]	None	None	n/a
Maryland[5]	None	None	n/a
Massachusetts	$600	$10 (interest/dividends)/ $600 (other)	Feb. 28
Michigan	State Request	State Request	n/a
Minnesota[1]	None	None	n/a
Mississippi	$3,000	$600	Mar. 15
Missouri	$1,200	$100 (interest/ dividends)/$1200 (other)	Feb. 28
Montana	$600	$10 (interest/dividends)/ $600 (other)	Apr. 15
Nebraska[4]	None	None	n/a
New Jersey	$1,000	$1,000	Feb. 15
New Mexico[6]	None	None	n/a
New York[4]	None	None	n/a
North Carolina[4]	None	None	n/a

State	Salaries and Wages Minimum Required	Non-wage Amounts Minimum Required	Due Date
North Dakota	$600	$600[7]	Feb. 28
Ohio	None	None	n/a
Oklahoma	$750	$750[8]	Feb. 28
Oregon	State Request	State Request	n/a
Pennsylvania	None	None	Feb. 28[9]
Rhode Island	$100	$100	Feb. 28
South Carolina	$800	$200 (interest/ dividends)/$800 (other)	Mar. 15
Tennessee	None	None	n/a
Utah	None	None	n/a
Vermont	None	None	n/a
Virginia	None	None	n/a
West Virginia[4]	None	None	n/a
Wisconsin	$600	$600	Feb. 28

[1] State has the option to require taxpayer to file.
[2] February 29 when applicable.
[3] Certain information returns filed federally are not required to be filed.
[4] Statute authorizes state to require filing; currently does not.
[5] Statute requires filing for any amounts not reflected on federal return; no due date specified.
[6] Only required to file if federal return is filed for oil and gas rents or royalties; due June 15.
[7] Interest, dividends, and pension and annuity payments not reported unless state income tax withheld.
[8] State authorized to require filing for any amount of interest or dividends; currently uses $750 threshold.
[9] If there is a premature distribution of a pension or profit sharing plan, copy of federal Form 1099-R must be provided to the state. Submission of other 1099's, including 1099-A, 1099-B, 1099-INT, 1099-DIV, 1099-MISC., not required unless there is income tax withheld.

Insurance Companies

Most states do not impose a corporate income tax on insurance companies doing business in their state, but rather impose a tax on gross premiums. Those states that do impose corporate income tax on insurance companies are set out on the chart below, as well as whether there are specific provisions governing the starting point for determining the taxable income of insurance companies, whether there are special modifications to taxable income applicable to such companies, and whether special apportionment provisions apply.

States that do not impose a corporate income tax on insurance companies are not included in this chart.

State	Tax	Taxable Income Starting Point	Special Modifications	Special Apportionment
Florida	Corporate income with credit against premiums tax	Specifically defined for insurance companies	No	Single premium factor, modified for reinsurers
Illinois	Corporate income	Specifically defined for insurance companies, inter-insurers, and reciprocal underwriters	No	Single premium factor
Indiana	Election between adjusted gross income or premiums tax	Specifically defined for insurance companies	No	Single premium factor
Louisiana	Corporate income with credit for premium tax paid	Specifically defined for insurance companies	Yes; varies by insurance type	None
Michigan	Single business tax and surcharge	Specifically defined for insurance companies; limited exemption for disability premiums	No	Single premium factor
Mississippi	Corporate income	Specifically defined for insurance companies	Yes; also credit for assessment by state association	For non-life insurers as specified by regulation
Nebraska	Corporate income with credit for premiums tax paid	Same as other corporations	No	Single premium factor with specific provisions for reinsurance
New Hampshire	Business profits tax with credit for premiums tax paid	Same as other corporations	No	None
Oregon	Corporate excise tax with credit for premiums taxes paid	Specifically defined for insurance companies	Yes	Three factor apportionment; insurance sales, wages and commissions, real estate income and interest

State	Tax	Taxable Income Starting Point	Special Modifications	Special Apportionment
Wisconsin	Corporate franchise/income tax for certain insurers; foreign insurers, domestic life insurers exempt	Same as other corporations	Yes	Two factor apportionment; premiums and payroll. Single premium factor for tax years after 2005

Limitation Periods for Assessment and Refund

The following chart reflects the general statute of limitation (SOL) periods for deficiency assessments by the state as well as the general limitations period for refund claims by taxpayers. Also noted are special provisions relating to the limitation periods associated with changes to federal taxable income for those states that have a provision addressing federal changes. States may also have specific provisions relating to certain types of claims (e.g. NOL carrybacks, capital losses, and bad debts) that are not reflected in the chart below.

Entries below referring to "25% understatement" generally refer to a 25% or greater understatement of gross income. Some states use net income or tax liability instead of gross income.

States that do not impose a corporate income tax are not included in this chart.

State	Assessment Period	Refund Period
Alabama	3 yrs from later of due date or date filed; 6 yrs in case of 25% understatement; No limit in cases of fraud or failure to file. 1 year from date of learning of final federal change	Later of 3 yrs from date filed or 2 yrs from date paid; 2 yrs from date paid if return not timely filed. Later of 1 year from date of final federal change or general SOL
Alaska	3 yrs from date filed; 6 yrs in case of 25% understatement; No limit in cases of fraud.	Later of 3 yrs from date filed or 2 yrs from date paid. If no return filed, two years from date paid.
Arizona	4 yrs from later of due date or date filed; 6 yrs in case of 25% understatement; No limit in cases of fraud or failure to file.	Later of 4 yrs from date due, 4 yrs from date filed, or 6 mos from payment of deficiency
Arkansas	3 yrs from later of due date or date filed; 6 yrs in case of 25% understatement; No limit in cases of fraud or failure to file. 1 yr. from filing federal change report; if amended return not filed 8 yrs. from later of due date or date filed; 3 yrs. from final decision or tax payment if federal assessment appealed.	Later of 3 yrs from date filed or 2 yrs from date paid
California	4 yrs from date filed; 6 yrs in case of 25% understatement;No limit in cases of fraud. Federal change reported after 6 mos. of final determination—4 yrs. from notification; reported within 6 mos—the later of 2 yrs. or standard SOL; no limit if taxpayer does not notify FTB	Later of 4 yrs from date filed (if timely), 4 yrs from due date, or 1 yr from date paid. If taxpayer notifies FTB of federal change, later of 2 yrs from date of final federal determination, 4 yrs from return filing deadline, or the SOL for deficiency assessments

State	Assessment Period	Refund Period
Colorado	4 yrs from date filed; 7 yrs in case of 25% understatement; No limit in cases of fraud or failure to file. 1 yr. from receipt or discovery of federal change	Later of 4 yrs from date due or 3 yrs from date paid. Can not be less than period for assessing deficiencies
Connecticut	3 yrs from later of due date or date filed; No limit in cases of failure to file.	3 yrs from date due.
Delaware	3 yrs from date filed; 6 yrs in case of 25% understatement; No limit in cases of fraud or failure to file or to report federal change. 2 yrs from date federal change reported.	Later of 3 yrs from date filed or 2 yrs from date paid. Refunds related to federal changes, 2 yrs from due date for reporting federal change.
District of Columbia	3 yrs from date filed; 6 yrs in case of 25% understatement; No limit in cases of fraud or failure to file. 6 mos for federal changes reported by taxpayer, otherwise SOL suspended if taxpayer fails to report federal changes.	Later of 3 yrs from date due or 3 yrs from date paid. For refunds related to federal changes, 6 mos from date change made or ordered.
Florida	3 yrs from later of payment due date, filing due date, or date return filed. No limit in cases of fraud or failure to file or pay (unless Taxpayer contacts Dept. first) or for failure to report federal change. 5 yrs. from federal change if taxpayer reports federal change.	3 yrs from date paid. 2 yrs. from date federal change required to be reported.
Georgia	3 yrs from date filed; 6 yrs in case of 25% understatement; No limit in cases of fraud or failure to file. (GA Supreme Ct. held 7 year limit for failure to file) 1 yr. from date taxpayer notifies Dept. of federal change; 5 yrs. if info received from IRS.	3 yrs from date paid.
Hawaii	3 yrs from later of due date or date filed; No limit in cases of fraud or failure to file.	Later of 3 yrs from date filed, 3 yrs from due date, or 2 yrs from date paid.
Idaho	3 yrs from later of due date or date filed; No limit in cases of fraud or failure to file. Assessments related to federal changes, later of 1 yr from filing of amended return or general SOL. If no amended return filed, 3 yrs from date finally filed.	Later of 3 yrs from date due or 3 yrs from date filed. Refunds related to federal changes, later of 1 yr from filing of amended return or 3 yrs from date due or date filed.

State	Assessment Period	Refund Period
Illinois	3 yrs from date filed; 6 yrs in case of 25% understatement; No limit in cases of fraud or failure to file or to report federal change. 2 yrs from date taxpayer reports federal change.	Later of 3 yrs from date filed or 1 yr from date paid. 2 yrs from date notification of federal change was due.
Indiana	3 yrs from later of due date or date filed; 6 yrs in case of 25% understatement; No limit in cases of fraud or failure to file. 6 mos. from report of federal change.	Later of 3 yrs from date due or 3 yrs from date paid; or 6 mos. after taxpayer is notified by IRS of federal change.
Iowa	Later of 3 yrs from due date or date filed or 6 mos. from date taxpayer reports federal change. 6 yrs in case of 25% understatement; No limit in cases of fraud or failure to file.	Later of 3 yrs. from due date, 1 yr. from date paid, or 6 mos. from taxpayer's report of federal change.
Kansas	Later of 3 yrs. from date filed or date paid, or 1yr. from filing of amended return. No limit in cases of fraud. 6 mos. from receipt of federal change.	3 yrs. from date due (if timely); later of 3 yrs from date filed or 2 yrs. from date paid (if not timely). Later of 6 mos. from receipt of federal change or 2 yrs. from date tax paid.
Kentucky	Later of 4 yrs. from date filed or due or 6 mos. from taxpayer's report of federal change. 6 yrs. in case of 25% understatement. No limit in cases of fraud or failure to file.	Later of 4 yrs. from date due or date paid or 6 mos. from federal audit conclusion.
Louisiana	3 yrs. from end of calendar year in which due (prescriptive period). No limit in cases of fraud or failure to file. Prescriptive period suspended for 1 yr. from report of federal change.	Later of 3 yrs from end of calendar year in which due or 1 yr from year in which paid. Prescriptive period suspended for 1 yr. from report of federal change.
Maine	3 yrs from later of due date or date filed; 6 yrs in case of liability shown less than 50% due; No limit in cases of fraud or failure to file.	Later of 3 yrs from date filed or date paid. Refunds related to federal changes, 2 yrs from due date of amended return.
Maryland	3 yrs from later of due date or date filed; No limit in cases of fraud, failure to file, filing of incomplete returns, or failure to report federal change. 1 yr. from date Dept. receives report of federal change.	3 yrs from date due. Refunds related to federal changes, 1 yr. from date of final federal change.

State	Assessment Period	Refund Period
Massachusetts	3 yrs from later of due date or date filed; No limit in cases of fraud or failure to file. 1 yr. from taxpayer's report of federal change. 2 yrs. from IRS' report of federal change.	Later of 3 yrs from date due, 2 yrs from date assessed, or 1 yr from date paid.
Michigan	4 yrs from later of due date or date filed; 2 yrs from discovery of fraud or failure to file. SOL suspended during pendency of final federal determination plus 1 yr.	4 yrs from date due. SOL suspended during pendency of final federal determination plus 1 yr.
Minnesota	3.5 yrs from date filed; 6.5 yrs in case of 25% understatement; No limit in cases of fraud or failure to file. Assessments related to federal changes, later of regular SOL or 1 yr. from taxpayer's report of federal change. If no taxpayer report, 6 yrs. from due date of federal change report.	Later of 3.5 yrs from due date or 1 yr from assessment order date.
Mississippi	3 yrs from later of due date or date filed; No limit in cases of fraud. 3 yrs. from final federal determination.	3 yrs. from later of due date or date paid. Refunds related to federal issues, 3 yrs. from disposal of federal issue.
Missouri	3 yrs from date filed; 6 yrs in case of 25% understatement; No limit in cases of fraud or failure to file. 1 yr. from the time the Dept. becomes aware of federal change	Later of 3 yrs from date filed or 2 yrs from date paid. Refunds related to federal changes, 1 yr. from due date of federal change report.
Montana	3 yrs from date filed; No limit in cases of fraud or failure to file. If federal period is suspended, the same suspension applies, or 1 yr. from final federal change or filing of federal amended return, whichever is later.	Later of 3 yrs. from return due date or 1 yr. from date paid.
Nebraska	3 yrs from date filed; 6 yrs in case of 25% understatement; No limit in cases of fraud or failure to file, or failure to report federal change. If taxpayer reports federal change, 2 yrs. from filing of report.	Later of 3 yrs from date filed or 2 yrs from date paid. Refunds relating to federal changes, 2 yrs. from due date of federal change report.
New Hampshire	3 yrs from later of due date or date filed; 6 yrs in case of 25% understatement; No limit in cases of fraud or failure to file.	Later of 3 yrs from date filed or 2 yrs from date paid.

State	Assessment Period	Refund Period
New Jersey	4 yrs from date filed; No limit in cases of fraud or failure to file. 4 yrs. from date of federal change/correction.	4 yrs from date paid. Refunds resulting from federal changes, 4 yrs. from date of change.
New Mexico	3 yrs. from end of calendar year tax due. 6 yrs in case of 25% understatement; 7 yrs in case of failure to file; 10 yrs in case of fraud.	Later of 3 yrs. from end of calendar year tax due. Assessments relating to federal changes, 3 yrs from end of calendar Year in which report of federal change due.
New York	Later of 3 yrs. from end of calendar year tax due 6 yrs in case of 25% understatement; No limit in cases of fraud or failure to file or failure to report federal change. If federal changes are reported, 2 yrs from filing report or amended return.	Later of 3 yrs from date filed or 2 yrs from date paid. Refunds resulting from federal changes, 2 yrs. from due date of federal change report.
North Carolina	3 yrs from later of due date or date filed; No limit in cases of fraud or failure to file. Assessments related to federal changes, later of 1 yr from date federal change reported or regular SOL. If federal change not reported, 3 yrs. from Date of final federal determination	Later of 3 yrs from due date or 6 mos from date paid. Refunds related to federal changes, later of 1 yr from return reporting federal change or 3 yrs from date return filed or due to be filed.
North Dakota	3 yrs from later of due date or date filed; 6 yrs in case of 25% understatement; 10 yrs in case of failure to file; No limit in cases of fraud, or failure to report federal change. If federal change reported, 2 yrs from filing of report or amended return.	Later of 3 yrs from due date or 3 yrs from date filed. 6 yrs in cases of 25% overstatement. No limit if taxpayer timely files report of federal change, otherwise 2 yrs from date of final federal determination.
Ohio	3 yrs from later of due date or date filed; No limit in cases of fraud or failure to file.	3 yrs from date paid. Refunds related to federal changes, 1 yr. from date of adjustment to federal return.
Oklahoma	3 yrs from later of due date or date filed; No limit in cases of fraud or failure to file return. Assessments related to federal changes, 2 yrs. from filing date of amended return.	3 yrs from due date. 2 yrs. from timely filing of amended return for refunds related to federal changes
Oregon	3 yrs from date filed; 5 yrs in case of 25% understatement; No limit in cases of fraud or failure to file. Assessments related to federal changes, later of 2 yrs. from date DOR receives info or the 3-yr of 5-yr limits above.	Later of 3 yrs from date filed or 2 yrs from date paid.

State	Assessment Period	Refund Period
Pennsylvania	3 yrs from date of settlement. Anytime federal change is made.	3 yrs. from date paid. If resulting from assessment, determination, or settlement, 6 mos. from notice thereof.
Rhode Island	Later of 3 yrs from date filed or date due 6 yrs in case of 25% understatement; No limit in cases of fraud or failure to file.	3 yrs from date paid. Refunds related to federal changes, 3 yrs. after receiving notice of federal change.
South Carolina	3 yrs from later of due date or date filed; 6 yrs in case of 20% understatement; No limit in cases of fraud or failure to file. Assessments related to federal changes, later of 3-yr limit or 6 mos. from date taxpayer reports federal change	Later of 3 yrs from date filed or 2 yrs from date paid. Refunds related to federal changes, 6 mos. from final federal determination.
Tennessee	3 yrs from end of calendar year in which filed; No limit in cases of fraud or failure to file. Assessments related to federal changes, 2 yrs. from date Rev. Comm'r receives notice of federal change.	3 yrs from end of calendar year in which paid. Refunds related to federal changes, 3 yrs. from final federal determination.
Texas	4 yrs from date due; No limit in cases of 25% understatement or in cases of fraud or failure to file. Assessment related to federal change , 1 yr from later of date federal change report due or filed or final federal determination discovered.	4 yrs from date due or 1 yr. from date of final federal determination.
Utah	3 yrs from date filed; No limit in cases of fraud or failure to file. For taxpayers that fail to report federal change, 3 yrs. from date of federal change.	3 yrs from date paid. Refunds related to federal changes, anytime before deficiency limitations period expires.
Vermont	3 yrs from date due or 3 yrs from date filed (if not timely); No limit in cases of fraud. Assessments related to federal changes, later of 3 yrs. from date due or 6 mos. from taxpayer's written notification of change.	Later of 3 yrs from date due or 6 mos from receipt of federal refund for same year.
Virginia	3 yrs from date filed; No limit in cases of fraud or failure to file or failure to report federal change. If taxpayer timely reports federal change, 1 yr. from report.	Later of 3 yrs from due date, 1 yr. from federal determination, 2 yrs. from filing amended return increasing tax due, or 2 yrs. from assessment.

State	Assessment Period	Refund Period
West Virginia	3 yrs from date filed; No limit in cases of fraud or failure to file. Assessments related to federal changes, later of 3 yr. limit or 90 days from date taxpayer reports federal change.	Later of 3 yrs from date due or 2 yrs from date paid. Refunds related to federal changes, 6 mos. from final federal determination.
Wisconsin	4 yrs from date filed; 6 yrs in case of 25% understatement; No limit in cases of fraud or failure to file. Assessments related to federal changes, 90 days from date taxpayer files timely report/ amended return, otherwise 4 yrs. from date of discovery.	4 yrs from date due. Refunds related to federal changes, 90 days from final federal determination.

Limited Liability Companies

All states have adopted legislation governing the treatment of limited liability companies (LLCs). Every state, except New Jersey and Texas, that impose a corporate or franchise income tax follow federal income tax law in their tax treatment of LLCs. Under federal income tax regulations, certain types of business entities are classified for federal tax purposes as corporations. If a business entity is not required to classified as a corporation under those provisions, the entity is eligible to elect its own federal income tax classification. An eligible entity with at least two members may elect to be classified as an association, which is classified as a corporation under Treasury Regulations, or as a partnership.

States that follow federal classification treat state-incorporated LLCs and foreign LLCs doing business in the state as partnerships for purposes of applying state law.

The chart below summarizes the LLC treatment by the states that do not follow federal law.

State	Statutory Provisions	Tax Treatment
AL	LLC Act	Follows federal
AK	LLC Act	Follows federal
AZ	LLC Act	Follows federal
AR	Small Business Entity Tax Pass-Through Act	Follows federal eff. after 2002 LLCs with 2 or more members treated as partnership prior to 2003
CA	LLC Act	Follows federal
CO	LLC Act	Follows federal
CT	LLC Act	Follows federal
DE	LLC Act	Follows federal
DC	LLC Act	Follows federal
FL	LLC Act	Follows federal
GA	LLC Act	Follows federal
HI	Uniform LLC Act	Follows federal
ID	LLC Act	Follows federal
IL	LLC Act	Follows federal
IN	Business Flexibility Act	Follows federal
IA	LLC Act	Follows federal
KS	LLC Act	Follows federal

State	Statutory Provisions	Tax Treatment
KY	LLC Act	For taxable years beginning after 2004 and before 2007, state subjects LLCs to the corporate income tax and its requirements
LA	LLC Law	Follows federal
ME	LLC Act	Follows federal
MD	LLC Act	Follows federal
MA	LLC Act	Follows federal
MI	LLC Act	Follows federal
MN	LLC Act	Follows federal
MS	LLC Act	Follows federal
MO	LLC Act	Follows federal
MT	LLC Act	Follows federal
NE	LLC Act	Follows federal
NH	LLC Act	Follows federal. State subjects LLCs to business taxes at entity level whether classified as partnership or LLC
NJ	LLC Act	Generally follows federal
NM	LLC Act	Follows federal
NY	LLC Act	Follows federal
NC	LLC Act	Follows federal
ND	LLC Act	Follows federal
OH	LLC Law	Follows federal. LLCs subject to commercial activity tax (CAT)
OK	LLC Act	Follows federal
OR	LLC Act	Follows federal
PA	LLC Act	Follows federal
RI	LLC Act	Follows federal
SC	Uniform LLC Act	Follows federal
SD	LLC Act	LLCs are exempt from franchise tax on financial institutions
TN	LLC Act	Follows federal
TX	LLC Act	LLCs treated as corporations, regardless of federal income tax status

State	Statutory Provisions	Tax Treatment
UT	LLC Act	Follows federal
VT	LLC Act	Follows federal
VA	LLC Act	Generally follows federal
WV	Uniform LLC Act	Follows federal
WI	Statutory provisions	Follows federal

Lump Sum Distributions

Federal law offers taxpayers over age 65 who receive lump-sum distributions from qualified retirement plans the choice of (1) including the entire taxable portion of the distribution in their federal adjusted gross income (AGI) for the year or (2) calculating a separate tax on the entire taxable portion of the distribution by applying a 10-year averaging method. Taxpayers who elect to apply the 10 year averaging method must use federal form 4972 to calculate the amount of federal tax due on their distribution and then add that amount to the amount of tax otherwise due on federal form 1040 after federal AGI and federal taxable income are determined. Thus, since most states begin the calculation of personal income tax liability with federal AGI or federal taxable income, lump-sum distributions for which federal 10-year averaging has been elected would not be included in the state tax base in those states, and would be effectively exempted at the state level, unless the state required that the distributions be added to federal AGI or taxable income as part of the state personal income tax calculation.

The chart below identifies how each of the states imposing a personal income tax responds to the federal treatment of lump-sum distributions, that is, whether the state (1) imposes no addback requirement, thus effectively exempting lump-sum distributions from its personal income tax, (2) requires that lump-sum distributions be added back to federal AGI, or (3) has lump-sum distribution provisions that are unrelated to the federal provisions.

States that do not impose a personal income tax are not included in this chart.

State	Tax Treatment of Lump-Sum Distributions
Alabama	Lump-sum distributions reported on federal 4972 included in Alabama gross receipts.
Arizona	Ordinary income portion of distribution added to federal AGI.
Arkansas	10-year averaging option. Calculation patterned on federal. Arkansas AR1000TD required.
California	10-year averaging option. Calculation patterned on federal. California Schedule G-1 required.
Colorado	Lump-sum distributions reported on federal 4972 added to federal taxable income. Subtraction may be claimed for amount of state pension exclusion.
Connecticut	Lump-sum distributions reported on federal 4972 added to federal AGI.
Delaware	10-year averaging option. Calculation patterned on federal. Delaware Form 329 required.
District of Columbia	Lump-sum distributions reported on federal 4972 added to federal AGI.
Georgia	Lump-sum distributions reported on federal 4972 added to federal AGI.

State	Tax Treatment of Lump-Sum Distributions
Hawaii	10-year averaging option. Calculation patterned on federal. Hawaii N-152 required. Portions of distribution attributable to noncontributory plans exempt.
Idaho	Lump-sum distributions reported on federal 4972 added to federal AGI.
Illinois	No requirement to add distributions reported on Federal 4972 to federal AGI. Distributions reflected in federal AGI are subtracted for Illinois purposes.
Indiana	Lump-sum distributions reported on federal 4972 added to federal AGI.
Iowa	Tax equals 25% of federal tax on Form 4972.
Kansas	Tax equals 13% of federal tax on Form 4972.
Kentucky	10-year averaging option. Calculation patterned on federal. Subtraction may be claimed for amount of state pension exclusion. Addition required for portion of distribution on which capital gains rate elected for federal tax purposes. Kentucky 4972-K and Schedule P required.
Louisiana	No requirement to add distributions reported on Federal 4972 to federal AGI.
Maine	Tax equals 15% of federal tax on Form 4972.
Maryland	Ordinary income portion and 40% of capital gains portion of amount reported on federal 4972 added to federal AGI.
Massachusetts	Lump-sum distributions reported on federal 4972 added to federal AGI.
Michigan	No requirement to add distributions reported on Federal 4972 to federal AGI.
Minnesota	5-year averaging only. Minnesota Form M-1LS required.
Mississippi	Retirement income exempt.
Missouri	Tax equals 10% of federal tax on Form 4972.
Montana	Tax equals 10% of federal tax on Form 4972.
Nebraska	29.6% minimum tax applies to sum of federal AMT, federal tax on lump-sum distribution, and federal tax on early distributions from retirement plans.
New Jersey	Lump-sum distributions reported on federal 4972 included in New Jersey gross income.
New Mexico	5-year averaging only.
New York	Calculation similar to former federal 5-year averaging. New York IT-230 required.
North Carolina	Lump-sum distributions reported on federal 4972 added to federal AGI.
North Dakota	Lump-sum distributions reported on federal 4972 added to federal taxable income.

State	Tax Treatment of Lump-Sum Distributions
Ohio	No requirement to add distributions reported on Federal 4972 to federal AGI. Credit available for lump-sum distributions from qualified employee benefit plans.
Oklahoma	Lump-sum distributions reported on federal 4972 added to federal AGI. Subtraction may be claimed for amount of state pension exclusion.
Oregon	Lump-sum distributions reported on federal 4972 added to federal AGI.
Pennsylvania	Retirement income exempt.
Rhode Island	Tax equals 25% of federal tax on Form 4972.
South Carolina	10-year averaging. Calculation patterned on federal. South Carolina 4972 required.
Utah	Lump-sum distributions reported on federal 4972 added to federal AGI.
Vermont	Tax equals 24% of federal tax on Form 4972.
Virginia	Lump-sum distributions reported on federal 4972 added to federal AGI.
West Virginia	Lump-sum distributions reported on federal 4972 added to federal AGI.
Wisconsin	Lump-sum distributions reported on federal 4972 added to federal AGI.

Net Operating Loss Deduction

This chart shows each state's rules on the net operating loss deduction.

For federal purposes net operating losses can generally be carried back two years and forward 20 years. However, the federal Job Creation and Worker's Assistance Act of 2002 (P.L. 107-147) extended the carryback from two years to five years for NOLs arising in 2001 and 2002. Those states that conform to the extended federal NOL carryback provisions are noted by an asterisk (*).

States that do not impose a corporate income tax are not included in the chart below.

State	Carryback/Carryforward periods
Alabama	0 back , 15 forward[1]
Alaska	2 back*, 20 forward
Arizona	0 back, 5 forward
Arkansas	0 back, 5 forward
California	0 back, 10 forward[2]
Colorado	0 back, 20 forward
Connecticut	0 back, 20 forward
Delaware	2 back * ($30,000 limit), 20 forward
District of Columbia	0 back, 20 forward
Florida	0 back, 20 forward
Georgia	2 back, 20 forward
Hawaii	2 back, 20 forward
Idaho	2 back ($100,000 limit), 20 forward, or 0 back, 20 forward
Illinois	0 back, 12 forward[3]
Indiana	2 back*, 20 forward
Iowa	2 back, 20 forward
Kansas	0 back, 10 forward
Kentucky	0 back, 20 forward[4]
Louisiana	3 back, 15 forward
Maine	0 back, 20 forward
Maryland	2 back, 20 forward
Massachusetts	0 back, 5 forward
Michigan	0 back, 10 forward
Minnesota	0 back, 15 forward
Mississippi	2 back, 20 forward

State	Carryback/Carryforward periods
Missouri	2 back, 20 forward
Montana	3 back, 7 forward
Nebraska	0 back, 5 forward
New Hampshire	0 back, 10 forward ($1 million limit)[5]
New Jersey	0 back, 7 forward[6]
New Mexico	0 back, 5 forward
New York	2 back * (1st $10,000 of loss), 20 forward
North Carolina	0 back, 15 forward
North Dakota	0 back[7], 20 forward.
Ohio	0 back , 20 forward
Oklahoma	2 back *[8], 20 forward
Oregon	0 back, 15 forward
Pennsylvania	0 back, 20 forward ($2 million limit for taxable years before 2007)[9]
Rhode Island	0 back, 5 forward
South Carolina	0 back, 20 forward
Tennessee	0 back, 15 forward
Texas	0 back, 5 forward
Utah	3 back (limited to $1 million), 15 forward
Vermont	0 back, 10 forward[10]
Virginia	2 back, 20 forward
West Virginia	2 back * (limited to $300,000), 20 forward
Wisconsin	0 back, 15 forward

[1] NOL deduction suspended for 2001. Normal carryover period is extended by one year.
[2] NOL deduction suspended for 2002 and 2003. Normal carryover period is extended by one year for losses during 2002 and by two years for losses before 2002. After 2003, entire NOL may be carried forward.
[3] For tax years prior to 2004 the carryforward period was 20 years, and the carryback period was two years.
[4] For tax years prior to 2005, the carryback period was two years.
[5] For tax years ending prior to July 1, 2005, the carryback period was three years. $750,000 carryover limit for tax years ending after June 30, 2004; $550,000 limit for tax years ending after June 30, 2003; $250,000 limit for tax years ending after June 30, 2002.
[6] NOL deduction is suspended for 2002 and 2003 and limited to 50% of entire net income for 2004 and 2005. Normal carryover period is extended by a period equal to the period the NOL was suspended.
[7] North Dakota allows the carryback only for NOLs incurred in taxable years beginning before 2003.

[8] Oklahoma carrybacks only conform for losses incurred in tax years beginning on or after Jan. 1, 2001. Therefore, NOLs incurred in fiscal years beginning in 2000 and ending in 2001 would be ineligible for the five-year carryback for Oklahoma purposes.

[9] For taxable years beginning after 2006, limit will be $3 million or 12.5% of taxable income, whichever is greater.

[10] For 2007, Vermont NOL carryforward amount equals same proportion of the Vermont NOL as the proportion of the federal NOL that was carried forward in determining federal taxable income plus 10% of remaining Vermont NOL; for 2008, increased by 30% of remaining Vermont NOL; for 2009, increased by 40% of remaining Vermont NOL. For tax years prior to 2006, 2 back, 20 forward.

Payroll Factor Rules

The following chart reflects whether each state uses a payroll factor in apportioning income, whether compensation for officers is included in the factor, as well as whether contributions to a 401(k) plan are included in the factor. An entry of "U/A" in the 401(k) column indicates information is not available about the inclusion of such earnings in the payroll factor.

States that do not impose a corporate income tax are not included in this chart.

State	Factor used	Officers' compensation included	401(k) earnings included
Alabama	Yes	Yes	Yes
Alaska	Yes	Yes	No
Arizona	Yes	Yes	Yes
Arkansas	Yes	Yes	No
California	Yes	Yes	Yes
Colorado	Yes[1]	Yes	Yes
Connecticut	Yes	Yes	Yes
Delaware	Yes	No	U/A
District of Columbia	Yes	Yes	Yes
Florida	Yes	Yes	Yes
Georgia	Yes	Yes	No
Hawaii	Yes	Yes	Yes
Idaho	Yes	Yes	Yes
Illinois	No	n/a	n/a
Indiana	Yes	Yes	No
Iowa	No	n/a	n/a
Kansas	Yes	Yes	Yes
Kentucky	Yes	Yes[2]	Yes
Louisiana	Yes	Yes	Yes
Maine	Yes	Yes	Yes
Maryland	Yes	Yes([2])	Yes
Massachusetts	Yes	Yes	Yes
Michigan	Yes	Yes	Yes
Minnesota	Yes	Yes	Yes
Mississippi	Yes	No	U/A
Missouri	Yes	Yes	Yes

State	Factor used	Officers' compensation included	401(k) earnings included
Montana	Yes	Yes	Yes
Nebraska	No	n/a	n/a
New Hampshire[3]	Yes	Yes	Yes
New Jersey	Yes	Yes[4]	Yes
New Mexico	Yes	Yes	No
New York	Yes	No	Yes
North Carolina	Yes	No	Yes
North Dakota	Yes	Yes	Yes
Ohio	Yes	Yes([2])	Yes
Oklahoma	Yes	No	U/A
Oregon	Yes	Yes	Yes
Pennsylvania	Yes	Yes	No
Rhode Island	Yes	Yes	U/A
South Carolina	Yes	No	Yes
Tennessee	Yes	Yes	No
Texas	No	n/a	n/a
Utah	Yes	Yes	Yes
Vermont	Yes	No[5]	No
Virginia	Yes	Yes	Yes
West Virginia	Yes	Yes	No
Wisconsin	Yes	Yes([2])	Yes

[1] No payroll factor if two-factor formula used.
[2] Not specifically excluded.
[3] Business profits tax apportionment.
[4] Director compensation not included.
[5] Compensation to general executive officers for acting as such not included.

Personal Income Tax Filing Federal Form Attachment Requirements

This chart indicates whether the state imposes a generally applicable requirement that resident taxpayers attach their federal personal income tax return to their state personal income tax return. Additional or alternative attachment requirements are noted in the "Comments" column.

State	Requirement	Comments	Authority
AL	No	Alabama does not provide the following forms and schedules and taxpayers must use and attach the appropriate federal form/schedule when making Alabama modifications: Schedules C and F; Forms 2106, 3903, 4684, 4797, 6252, and 8283.	2004 Form 40 Instructions
AR	Yes	Nonresidents and part-year residents must attach Federal Form 1040, 1040A, or 1040EZ. Taxpayers claiming child care credit must attach a copy of federal form 2441 or 1040A.	2004 AR1000 Instructions
AZ	No	Taxpayers who itemize must attach copy of federal Schedule A.	2004 Form 140 Instructions
CA	No	Taxpayers who attached federal forms or schedules other than Schedule A or B to federal Form 1040 must attach Federal 1040 to California Form 540.	2004 Form 540 Instructions
CO	No		2004 Form 104 Instructions
CT	No		2004 Form CT-1040 Instructions
DC	No	Taxpayers filing any of the following federal forms/schedules with their federal returns must attach a copy to their Form DC-40: Form 1065 K-1, 1120S K-1, 2441, 4797, 4972, or 8814, or Schedule C, C-EZ, D, E, or F. Taxpayers claiming D.C. Low Income or Earned Income Credits must attach federal Form 1040, 1040A, or 1040 EZ.	2004 DC-40 Instructions.

State	Requirement	Comments	Authority
DE	No	Copies of all schedules required to be filed with federal return must be attached to Form 200. Taxpayers claiming a Child and Dependent Care Expense Credit must attach federal Form 2441 or Schedule 2.	2004 Form 200-01 Instructions
GA	No	Taxpayers making depreciation adjustments must attach federal Form 4562 to Form 500. Taxpayers claiming Combat Zone Pay Exclusion must attach copy of federal return.	2004 Form IT-511 Individual Income Tax Booklet.
HI	No	Taxpayers claiming dependent who was supported by multiple taxpayers must attach signed federal Form 2120 (Multiple Support Declaration) to Form N-11 or Form N-12. Taxpayers claiming depreciation deduction must attach completed federal Form 4562. Taxpayers claiming casualty or theft losses must attach copy of federal Form 4684. Taxpayers claiming employee business expenses must attach copy of federal Form 2106. Taxpayers claiming foreign tax credit must attach copy of federal Form 1116. Taxpayers reporting like-kind exchanges must attach federal Form 8824. Copies of all federal forms used as substitutes for Hawaii forms must be attached.	2004 Forms N-11 and N-12 Instructions
IA	No	Copies of federal Forms 3903 and 4797 must be attached to IA 1040 if relevant. Taxpayers claiming nonresident/part-year resident credit, and Illinois residents claiming a refund of Iowa income tax withheld in error, must attach federal return.	2004 IA 1040 Instructions
ID	Yes		2004 Form 40 Instructions

State	Requirement	Comments	Authority
IL	No	Taxpayers subtracting Social Security and government disability benefits and retirement income, those deducting interest from federal obligations, and those deducting for recovery of items previously deducted on federal 1040, must attach federal 1040, or 1040A, page 1.	2004 Form IL-1040 Instructions
IN	No	Taxpayers claiming a net operating loss must attach federal Form 1045 Schedule A. Those claiming county tax credit for the elderly must attach federal Schedule R. Those claiming foreign tax credit must attach federal Form 1116, 1099-INT, or 1099-DIV.	2004 Form IT-40 Instructions
KS	No	Taxpayers filing K-40 using address outside Kansas must attach federal Form 1040EZ, 1040A, or 1040 and Schedules A through F if applicable.	2004 Form K-40 Instructions
KY	No	Federal Schedule D and Forms 2106, 2120, 2441, 4562, 4684, 4952, 8283, 8332 must be attached to Form 740 if applicable. Taxpayers reporting farm, business or rental income must attach federal return, unless they filed federal Form 1040A or 1040EZ.	2004 Form 740 Instructions
LA	No	If Louisiana income tax withheld exceeds 10% of federal adjusted gross income, federal return must be attached.	2004 Form IT-540 Instructions
MA	No		2004 Form 1 Instructions
MD	No		2004 Form 502 Instructions

State	Requirement	Comments	Authority
ME	No	Part-year residents and nonresidents must attach copy of federal return to Maine return. Taxpayers making fiduciary adjustment must attach federal Schedule K-1.	2004 Form 1040ME Instructions
MI	No	Taxpayers filing any of the following federal forms/schedules with their federal returns must attach a copy to Form MI-1040: Form 1040NR, 2555, 3903, 3903-F, 4797, 4868, 6198, 8829, or 8839, or Schedule B, C, C-EZ, E, F, or R or 1040A Schedule 3. Taxpayers claiming credit for repayment of amounts previously reported as income must attach portion of federal return showing deduction or credit.	2004 Form MI-104 Instructions
MN	Yes	Copy of federal return and schedules must be attached to Form M1. Taxpayers required to complete Schedule M1MT must complete and attach federal Form 6251.	2004 Form M1 Instructions
MO	Yes	Taxpayers claiming pension exemption must also attach federal form 1099-R and/or Form W-2P. Federal Forms 4255, 8611, and 8828 must be attached if applicable.	2004 Form MO-1040 Instructions
MS	No	Taxpayers filing federal Schedules C, C-EZ, E, and/or F with a federal return must attach a copy to Form 80-105. If an amount of state taxable income entered on Form 80-105 differs from the amount of federal taxable income entered on a federal return, separate reconciling schedules must be attached. Taxpayers deducting moving expenses must attach Form 3903 or 3903F.	2004 Form 80-105 Instructions
MT	Yes	Applicable federal forms and schedules must be attached to Form 2.	2004 Form 2 Instructions

State	Requirement	Comments	Authority
NC	No	Copy of federal return must be attached to Form D-400 if federal return bears out-of-state address and taxpayer did not file electronically. Taxpayers with gross income meeting North Carolina filing threshold who were not required to file federal return must complete and attach federal return. Taxpayers filing separate North Carolina return who filed joint federal return must complete and attach federal return as married filing separately or schedule showing computation of separate federal taxable income and include copy of joint federal return if that return bears out-of-state address.	2004 Form D-400 Instructions
ND	Yes	Complete copy of federal return, including supplemental forms and schedules, must be attached to North Dakota return.	2004 Form ND-1 Instructions
NE	No	If applicable, federal Forms 4972, 5329 (1040 if taxpayer received early retirement plan distribution and was not required to file Federal 5329) and 6251 recalculated for Nebraska using Nebraska Revenue Ruling 22-03-1 must be attached to 1040N. Taxpayers claiming special capital gain deduction must attach federal Schedule D. Taxpayers claiming elderly or disabled credit must attach Federal Schedule R, pages 1 and 2, or Federal Schedule 3.	2004 Form 1040N Instructions
NH	No		Form DP-10 Instructions

State	Requirement	Comments	Authority
NJ	No	Taxpayers excluding reimbursements for employee business expenses included on W-2 must attach copy of federal Form 2106. Those excluding moving expense reimbursements included on W-2 must attach copy of federal Form 3903. Those subtracting early-withdrawal penalties from interest income must attach federal Form 1040 Schedule B or Form 1040A Schedule 1. Part-year residents with income below annual filing threshold ($10,000 single or married filing separately, $20,000 married filing jointly) must attach copy of federal return to NJ-1040. In addition, the following federal forms and schedules must be attached if relevant: Forms 4868, 8283, and 8853; Schedules C, C EZ, F, and K-1.	2004 NJ-1040 Instruction
NM	No	New Mexico Taxation and Revenue Department may require a taxpayer to furnish copy of federal return and all attachments.	2004 Form PIT-1 Instructions
NY	No	The following federal forms and schedules must be attached to state return if relevant: Form 4797; Schedules C, C-EZ, D, E, and F.	2004 IT-201 Instructions
OH	No	Taxpayers with zero or negative federal adjusted gross income must attach copy of page 1 of federal return to state return. Investors in pass-through entities claiming credit for tax paid on Ohio Form IT-4708 or IT-1140 must attach federal Form K-1 that reflect amount of Ohio tax paid.	2004 IT 1040 Instructions
OK	No	If Oklahoma adjusted gross income differs from federal adjusted gross income, or if taxpayer claims Oklahoma earned income credit, copy of federal return must be attached to Form 511. Taxpayers claiming Oklahoma child care credit must attach federal Form 2441 and page 2 federal Form 1040 or Form 1040A, Including Schedule 2.	2004 Form 511 Instructions

State	Requirement	Comments	Authority
OR	Yes		2004 Form 40 Instructions
PA	No		2004 Form PA-40 Instructions
RI	No		2004 Form RI-1040 Instructions
SC	No	Taxpayers reporting income or loss on federal Schedule C, D, E, or F or who filed South Carolina Schedule NR, Form SC1040TC, or Form I-319 must attach copy of federal return to SC 1040.	2004 Form SC1040 Instructions
TN	No		2004 Form INC 250 Instructions
UT	No	Taxpayers claiming nonresident shareholder's withholding tax credit must attach federal Form K-1 to Form TC-40.	2004 Form TC-40 Instructions
VA	No	Federal Schedules C, C-EZ, E and F must be attached to Form 760 if applicable.	2004 Form 760 Instructions

State	Requirement	Comments	Authority
VT	Yes	Copy of pages 1 and 2 of federal return must be attached to Form IN-113 (Income Adjustment Schedules). Civil union partners filing jointly must complete federal return on married filing jointly basis (partners filing separately complete federal return on married filing separately basis) and attach recomputed federal return to IN-111 along with copy of federal return actually filed. If married filing separately and one spouse is nonresident and has no Vermont income, federal return must be completed on married filing separately basis and attached along with copy of federal return as actually filed. Taxpayers electing to pay Vermont tax on entire gain from installment sale or real estate in year of sale must attach copy of federal Form 6252.	2004 IN-111 Instructions
WI	Yes	Complete copy of federal return with supporting schedules and forms must be attached to Form 1. Taxpayers itemizing deductions on federal, but not Wisconsin, return are not required to attach federal Schedule A.	2004 Form 1
WV	No		2004 Form IT-140 Instructions

Property Factor Rules

The following chart reflects the property factor rules in effect for each state for purposes of apportionment. All states currently use an average value of property rather than an existing value when determining the factor. In addition, no state currently includes intangible property in the factor, except for certain drilling and development costs in a few states (AK, CA, HI, KY).

States that do not impose a corporate income tax are not included in this chart.

State	Rented Property Included at 8x Rentals	Original Cost or Net Book Value
Alabama	Yes	Original Cost
Alaska	Yes	Original Cost
Arizona	Yes	Original Cost
Arkansas	Yes	Original Cost
California	Yes	Original Cost
Colorado	Yes	Original Cost[1]
Connecticut	Yes	Net Book Value
Delaware	Yes	Original Cost
District of Columbia	Yes	Original Cost
Florida	Yes	Original Cost
Georgia	Yes	Original Cost
Hawaii	Yes	Original Cost
Idaho	Yes	Original Cost
Illinois	No property factor	
Indiana	Yes	Original Cost
Iowa	No property factor	
Kansas	Yes	Original Cost
Kentucky	Yes	Original Cost
Louisiana	Not included	Net Book Value
Maine	Yes	Original Cost
Maryland	Yes	Original Cost
Massachusetts	Yes	Original Cost
Michigan	Yes	Original Cost
Minnesota	Yes	Original Cost
Mississippi	Yes	Net Book Value
Missouri	Yes	Original Cost

State	Rented Property Included at 8x Rentals	Original Cost or Net Book Value
Montana	Yes	Original Cost
Nebraska	No property factor	
New Hampshire[2]	Yes	Original Cost
New Jersey	Yes	Net Book Value
New Mexico	Yes	Original Cost
New York	Yes	Federal Adjusted Basis[3]
North Carolina	Yes	Original Cost
North Dakota	Yes	Original Cost
Ohio	Yes	Original Cost
Oklahoma	Yes	Original Cost
Oregon	Yes	Original Cost
Pennsylvania	Yes	Original Cost
Rhode Island	Yes	Net book value
South Carolina	Yes	Original Cost
Tennessee	Yes	Original Cost
Texas	No property factor	
Utah	Yes	Original Cost
Vermont	Yes	Original Cost
Virginia	Yes	Original Cost
West Virginia	Yes	Original Cost
Wisconsin	Yes	Original Cost

[1] Federal adjusted basis option if two-factor formula is used.
[2] Business profits tax apportionment.
[3] A one-time revocable election can be made to use fair market value instead of federal adjusted basis.

Public Utilities and Financial Corporations

The following chart indicates which states subject public utilities and financial corporations to corporate income taxation and which states impose some other tax on them. Some states specify various institutions that come within the definition of "public utility" or "financial corporation," which differ from state to state. Reference in the chart to "usual income tax" means that the state taxes the corporations in question in the same way as other corporations.

Nevada, Washington, and Wyoming do not impose a corporate income tax and are not included in this chart.

State	Public Utilities	Financial Corporations
Alabama	Usual income tax, also tax measured by gross receipts (except freight lines)	Excise tax on net income
Alaska	Usual income tax	Usual income tax
Arizona	Usual income tax	Usual income tax
Arkansas	Usual income tax	Usual income tax
California	Usual franchise (income) tax	Usual franchise (income) tax
Colorado	Usual income tax	Usual income tax
Connecticut	Usual business (income) tax	Usual business (income) tax
Delaware	Usual income tax	Bank franchise tax on net income
District of Columbia	Franchise tax and additional gross receipts tax	Usual franchise income tax
Florida	Annual gross receipts tax	Bank franchise tax measured by net income
Georgia	Usual income tax and net worth tax	Usual income and net worth taxes; gross receipts tax on depository institutions
Hawaii	Usual income tax; also public service company tax (determined according to ratio of net income to gross income)	Franchise tax on entire net income
Idaho	Usual income or franchise tax	Usual income or franchise tax
Illinois	Usual income and personal property replacement income taxes	Usual income and personal property replacement income taxes
Indiana	Usual income tax and utilities receipts tax	Franchise tax on adjusted gross or apportioned income
Iowa	Usual income tax	Franchise tax measured by net income
Kansas	Usual income tax	Privilege tax on "net income"; tax on cessation of business
Kentucky	Usual income tax	Intangibles tax for specified financial institutions; usual income tax for remainder

State	Public Utilities	Financial Corporations
Louisiana	Usual income and franchise taxes	Shares tax (some foreign corporations subject to income tax)
Maine	Usual income tax	Franchise tax on net income and assets
Maryland	Usual income tax	Usual income tax
Massachusetts	Franchise tax on net income	Financial institution excise tax on net income
Michigan	Usual Single Business Tax	Usual Single Business Tax (some nonresident institutions exempt)
Minnesota	Usual franchise (income) tax	Usual franchise (income) tax
Mississippi	Usual income tax plus privilege tax and regulatory fees	Usual income tax (mutual savings banks and some others exempt)
Missouri	Usual income tax (express companies taxed on gross receipts)	Financial institutions franchise tax and (except for credit unions, savings and loans, and building and loans) the general corporate income tax;
Montana	Usual income (license) tax	Usual income (license) tax
Nebraska	Usual franchise tax on income	Franchise tax based on percentage of deposits
New Hampshire	Usual business profits (income) tax	Usual business profits (income) tax
New Jersey	Usual corporation business (franchise) tax; sewerage and water corps. subject to gross receipts excise and franchise taxes	Usual corporation business (franchise) tax
New Mexico	Usual income tax	Usual income tax (credit unions exempt)
New York	usual franchise tax	Bank franchise tax
North Carolina	Usual income tax	Usual income tax
North Dakota	Usual income tax	Financial institution (income) tax
Ohio	Gross receipts excise tax; usual franchise (income) tax for electric companies and telephone companies, eff. 2005. Excluded from commercial activities tax (CAT)	Franchise tax on net worth. Excluded from commercial activities tax (CAT)
Oklahoma	Usual income tax	Privilege tax based on net income; banks and credit unions also subject to franchise taxes
Oregon	Usual excise tax	Usual excise tax
Pennsylvania	Gross receipts tax	Mutual thrift institution excise tax; banks, trust companies, title insurance companies, bank and trust company shares tax; private bankers, gross receipts tax

State	Public Utilities	Financial Corporations
Rhode Island	Tax on gross earnings with exemption from business corporation tax	Bank excise tax measured by net income or capital stock
South Carolina	Usual income tax (some specifically exempt)	Special tax on entire net income
South Dakota	Tax on gross earnings or gross receipts	Franchise tax on net income
Tennessee	Usual excise tax	Usual excise tax
Texas	Usual franchise tax (certain cooperatives exempt) and gross receipts tax	Usual franchise tax
Utah	Usual franchise tax on net income	Usual franchise tax on net income
Vermont	Usual income tax and gross revenues tax	Franchise tax measured by average monthly deposits held in Vermont
Virginia	License tax on gross receipts	Bank franchise tax
West Virginia	Usual income tax	Usual income tax for most institutions
Wisconsin	Usual franchise tax on income (certain electric cooperatives exempt)	Usual franchise tax on income

Reciprocal Personal Income Tax Agreements

Various states have adopted reciprocal personal income tax agreements with one or more states, including the District of Columbia, that allow income to be taxed in the state of residence even though it is earned in another state, as long as the income-source state is a party to the reciprocity agreement. States enter into such agreements because, in addition to greatly reducing the administrative reporting burden, no revenue loss is anticipated. Even taking into account such variables as the number of nonresidents working in a state, the tax rate, and taxpayer income levels, the taxable revenue shared may be roughly equivalent in both states.

Reciprocity agreements put into operation an exception to the source-tax rule that the state in which income is earned has the primary right to tax that income.

Generally, reciprocal agreements apply only to compensation, which may be limited to wages, salaries, tips commissions, and/or bonuses received for personal and/or professional services. Thus, even though New Jersey has a reciprocity agreement with Pennsylvania, income such as that arising from self-employment or a gain from a sale of property would be subject to tax under the source-tax rule in the income-source state. However, states may specify that certain income is not covered under reciprocity agreements, such as lottery winnings.

States that do not impose a personal income tax are not included in this chart. Personal income tax in New Hampshire and Tennessee applies only to interest and dividend income.

State	Agreement With
Alabama	None
Arizona	None
Arkansas	None
California	None
Colorado	None
Connecticut	None
Delaware	None
District of Columbia	MD, VA
Georgia	None
Hawaii	None
Idaho	None
Illinois	IA, KY, MI, WI
Indiana	KY, MI, OH, PA, WI
Iowa	IL
Kansas	None
Kentucky	IL, IN, MI, OH, VA, WV, WI
Louisiana	None
Maine	None
Maryland	DC, PA, VA, WV
Massachusetts	None
Michigan	IL, IN, KY, MN, OH, WI
Minnesota	MI, ND, WI
Mississippi	None
Missouri	None

State	Agreement With
Montana	ND
Nebraska	None
New Hampshire	None
New Jersey	PA
New Mexico	None
New York	None
North Carolina	None
North Dakota	MN, MT
Ohio	IN, KY, MI, PA, WV
Oklahoma	None
Oregon	None
Pennsylvania	IN, MD, NJ, OH, VA, WV
Rhode Island	None
South Carolina	None
Tennessee	None
Utah	None
Vermont	None
Virginia	DC, KY, MD, PA, WV
West Virginia	KY, MD, OH, PA, VA
Wisconsin	IL, IN, KY, MI, MN

Related Party Expense Addback Requirements

In a number of states, interest and intangible expenses and costs paid to related parties must be added back in the computation of state taxable income. Exceptions to the addback requirements vary significantly from state to state, some of which are intended to exempt income resulting from arms-length transactions or to minimize the possibility that the same income is taxed by more than one jurisdiction. This chart both identifies the states that impose related party expense addback requirements and sets forth the exceptions to the addback requirements.

State	Answer	Comments	Authority
Alabama	Yes. Addback required for interest and intangible expenses and costs paid to related member.	Not applicable if (1) amount taxed by any state or foreign nation with U.S. treaty; (2) principal purpose not tax avoidance and related member not engaged in disposition of intangibles; (3) transaction has substantial business purpose; (4) adjustments are unreasonable; or (5) taxpayer agrees in writing to alternative adjustments and computations.	Alabama Code § 40-18-35(b); Ala. Admin. Code r. 810-3-35-.02
Alaska	No		
Arizona	No		
Arkansas	Yes. Addback required for interest and intangible expenses and costs paid to related party. unless amount taxed by Arkansas, another state, or foreign nation with U.S. treaty.	Not applicable if (1) transaction not intended to avoid tax and made at arm's-length; (2) taxpayer enters into written agreement; or (3) related member is in non-tax location, employs 50 there, owns property valued over $1,000,000 there, and generates revenue over $1,000,000 there.	Ark. Code. Ann. § 26-51-423(g)

State	Answer	Comments	Authority
California	No		
Colorado	No		
Connecticut	Yes. Addback required for interest and intangible expenses and costs paid to related member.	Not applicable if (1) principal purpose not tax avoidance and related member paid the expenses or costs to unrelated party; (2) taxpayer establishes addback is unreasonable; (3) taxpayer enters into written agreement for alternative apportionment; (4) related member taxed by Connecticut, another state, or foreign nation, tax applies to paid expenses or costs, and tax rate not less than Connecticut rate minus 3 percentage points; or (5) related member is subject to Connecticut or other state insurance premiums tax.	Conn. Gen. Stat. § 12-218c Sec. 78(b), Act 03-6 (H.B. 6808, Special Session, Laws 2003
Delaware	No		
District of Columbia	Yes. Addback required for costs or expenses paid to related entity, the activities of which are primarily limited to the maintenance and management of trademarks, patents, or other intangible assets or investments.		D.C. Code Ann. § 47-1803.03(b)(7)
Florida	No		

State	Answer	Comments	Authority
Georgia	Yes. Effective for tax years after December 31, 2005, addback required for interest and intangible expenses and costs paid to related members. Addback reduced if arm's length transaction, (1) income allocated or apportioned to state imposing income tax on related member income other than state where combined return filed with related member, (2) related member domiciled in foreign nation with U.S. tax treaty, (3) transaction has valid business purpose other than tax avoidance or reduction, and (4) taxpayer discloses information about transaction.	Addback requirement not applicable to expenses and costs that related member during same taxable year paid to unrelated party and that arose from transaction with valid business purpose.	Ga. Code Ann. § 48-7-28.3(b)
Hawaii	No		
Idaho	No		

State	Answer	Comments	Authority
Illinois	Yes. Addback required for interest and intangible expenses and costs paid to 80-20 company that would be member of same unitary business group but for activities outside U.S. Addback reduced to extent dividends included in taxable income of unitary group for same taxable year and received by taxpayer or by member of unitary group with respect to stock of recipient.	Addback not required if (1) item paid to recipient subject to net income tax on item by foreign country or U.S. state that does not mandate unitary reporting; (2) taxpayer establishes that recipient paid the item to unrelated person during same taxable year and avoidance of Illinois income tax not principal purpose of transaction and item paid pursuant to arm's-length agreement; (3) taxpayer establishes that adjustments are unreasonable; or (4) taxpayer enters agreement for alternative apportionment.	35 ILCS 5/203(b)(E-12),(E-13)

State	Answer	Comments	Authority
Indiana	Yes. Addback required for intangible expenses and any directly related intangible interest expenses that reduced the corporation's taxable income for federal income tax purposes.	Not applicable if: (1) taxpayer and recipient in same consolidated or combined return; (2) income tax imposed on item of income corresponding to intangible expense by any state or foreign country that is recipient's commercial domicile; (3) purpose of transaction not tax avoidance; (4) transaction made at commercially reasonable rate and terms comparable to arm's length; (5) recipient engages in transactions involving intangible property with unrelated parties on terms identical to transaction; (6) payment received from unrrelated party and on behalf of unrelated party in arm's length transaction; (7) recipient paid liability to unrelated party during taxable year for an equal or greater amount; (8) recipient engaged in substantial business activities from acquisition,use, or other dispostion of intangible property or other substantial business activities separate from those business activities;	Ind. Code §§6-3-1-3.5(b)(9), 6-3-2-20

State	Answer	Comments	Authority
		(9) adjustments are unreasonable; or (10) taxpayer agrees to alternative adjustments and computations.	
Iowa	No		
Kansas	No		

State	Answer	Comments	Authority
Kentucky	Yes. Deduction of intangible expenses, intangible interest expenses or management fees paid to related members disallowed.	Addback not required (1) taxpayer and recipient included in consolidated corporate income tax return; (2) taxpayer agrees to use alternative apportionment formula; (3) recipient engages in transactions involving intangible property with unrelated parties on terms identical to transaction; (4) transaction made at commercially reasonable rate and at arm's-length, or; (5) payment made to recipient subject to income-based tax in another state or country, recipient engaged in substantial business activities unrelated to intangible property or financing of related members that require maintenance of permanent office space and full-time employees dedicated to the maintenance and protection of intangible property, and transaction made at commercially reasonable rate and arm's-length.	Ky. Rev. Stat. Ann. § 141.205
Louisiana	No		
Maine	No		

State	Answer	Comments	Authority
Maryland	Yes. Addback required for interest or intangible expense if paid to related member.	Not applicable if (1) tax avoidance not principle purpose of transaction; (2) expense paid pursuant to arm's length contract at arm's length interest rate or price; and (3) during same taxable year, related member paid the expense to an unrelated person; the related member subject to income tax in Maryland, another state, U.S. possession or foreign nation with U.S. tax treaty and measure of tax included expense received by related member taxpayer and aggregate effective tax rate paid on amount received by related member is at least 4%; or in the case of interest expense, taxpayer and related party are banks.	Md. Code Ann. § 10-306.1

State	Answer	Comments	Authority
Massachusetts	Yes. Addback for interest expenses related to intangible property and intangible expenses incurred in connection with transaction with related member, including expenses related to the acquisition, maintenance, management, ownership, sale, exchange, or disposition of intangible property.	Addback not require if (1) adjustment unreasonable; (2) taxpayer enters agreement for alternative apportionment; or (3) during same taxable year, related member paid the expenses to unrelated person, and principal purpose of transaction giving rise to the expenses between taxpayer and related member not tax avoidance.	Mass. Gen. Laws ch. 63, §31I Mass. Gen. Laws ch. 63, §31J
Michigan	No		
Minnesota	No		
Mississippi	Yes. Addback required for the following expenses if paid to related member: (1) intangible and interest expenses for maintenance or management, ownership, sale, exchange, or other disposition of intangible property; (2) royalty, patent, technical, and copyright fees, licensing fees, and other similar expenses; and (3) expenses associated with factoring or discounting transactions.	Addback not required if related member not primarily engaged in acquisition, use, maintenance, management, ownership, sale, exchange, or other disposition of intangible property and transaction done for valid business purpose.	Miss. Code. Ann. §27-7-17(2)
Missouri	No		
Montana	No		

State	Answer	Comments	Authority
Nebraska	No		
New Hampshire	No		

State	Answer	Comments	Authority
New Jersey	Yes. Addback required for (1) interest and other expenses, losses and costs for acquisition, use, maintenance or management, ownership, sale, exchange, or other disposition of intangible property; (2) losses related to factoring or discounting transactions; (3) royalty, patent, technical and copyright fees; (4) licensing fees; and (5) other similar expenses and costs. Addback required also for interest paid to related member.	Addback not required if (1) interest and intangible expenses paid to related member in foreign nation with U.S. tax treaty; (2) taxpayer establishes addback is unreasonable; (3) taxpayer enters alternative apportionment agreement; or (4) during income year, related member paid, received, accrued or incurred the portion to or from unrelated person and principal purpose of transaction giving rise to interest or intangible expense between taxpayer and related member not tax avoidance. Addback for interest paid to related member not required if (1) principal purpose of transaction giving rise to interest payment not tax avoidance; (2) interest paid pursuant to arm's length contracts at arm's length interest rate; and (3) related member subject to tax on net income or receipts in New Jersey or other state, U.S. possession, or foreign nation, measure of tax includes interest received by related	N.J. Stat. Ann. §54:10A-4 N.J. Stat. Ann. §54:10A-4.4

State	Answer	Comments	Authority
		member, and tax rate equal to or greater than 3% less than New Jersey rate. Addback also not required if (1) taxpayer establishes that disallowance unreasonable; (2) taxpayer enters into alternative apportionment agreement; or (3) taxpayer establishes that interest was paid to related member in foreign nation with U.S. tax treaty or to an independent lender and taxpayer guaranteed the debt.	
New Mexico	No		
New York	Yes. Add-back required for royalty payments made to related member.	Add-back not required if (1) related member during same taxable year paid the amount to unrelated party, transaction done for valid business purpose, and payment made at arm's length; or (2) payment is paid to related member organized under the laws of foreign nation, is subject to comprehensive income tax treaty between foreign nation and U.S., and is taxed by foreign at rate at least equal to New York rate.	N.Y. Tax Law, §208.9(o)

State	Answer	Comments	Authority
North Carolina	Yes. Add-back required for royalty payments made to a related member for use of trademarks, patents, or copyrights in the state.	Not applicable if: (1) related member includes the amount as income on a North Carolina return for same taxable year that amount is deducted by taxpayer; (2) the related member does not deduct the amount; or (3) related member organized in foreign country with a U.S. income tax treaty that taxes the payments at a rate equal or greater than North Carolina corporate income tax rate.	N.C. Gen. Stat. § 105-130.7A
North Dakota	No		

State	Answer	Comments	Authority
Ohio	Yes. Add-back required for interest and intangible expenses paid to related members.	Add-back not required if (1) taxpayer establishes that adjustments unreasonable; (2) taxpayer enters alternative apportionment agreement; or (3) taxpayer establishes that related member during the same taxable year paid the expense to unrelated person, or to related person that in turn paid the expense to unrelated person, and tax avoidance not principal purpose of transaction giving rise to expense between taxpayer and related member. Add-back requirement not applicable to the extent that the increased tax attributable to addback would have been avoided if both taxpayer and related member had made election to file combined report.	Ohio Rev. Code Ann. §5733.042
Oklahoma	No		

State	Answer	Comments	Authority
Oregon	Yes. Addback required if intangible asset owned by one entity and used by another for royalty or other fee; both owner and the user owned by same interests as defined by federal law; owner and user not included in same Oregon tax return; and separation of ownership of intangible asset from user of intangible asset results in either (1) evasion of tax or (2) a computation of Oregon taxable income not clearly reflective of Oregon business activity in comparison to business activity as a whole.		Or. Admin. R. 150-314.295
Pennsylvania	No		
Rhode Island	No		

State	Answer	Comments	Authority
South Carolina	Yes. Applicable to taxable years beginning after 2005, deduction not allowed for accrual of expense or interest if payee is related person and payment not made in taxable year of accrual or before payer's income tax return due, without regard to extensions, for taxable year of accrual. Disallowed deductions allowed when payment made. Holder must include payment in income in year the debtor is entitled to take deduction. Interest deduction not allowed for accrual or payment of interest on obligations issued as dividends or paid instead of paying dividends, unless the Director of the South Carolina Department of Revenue is satisfied that tax avoidance is not a significant purpose of the transaction.		S.C. Code Ann. § 12-6-1130
Tennessee	Yes. Addback required for intangible expenses paid, accrued, or incurred in connection with transaction involving affiliates if expenses not disclosed to Commissioner of Revenue.		Tenn. Code Ann. § 67-4-2006(d)

State	Answer	Comments	Authority
Texas	No		
Utah	No		
Vermont	No		

State	Answer	Comments	Authority
Virginia	Yes. Addback required for interest expenses and costs associated with transaction with related member.	Addback not required if (1) related member has substantial business operations relating to the interest-generating activities and pays at least five full-time employees to manage and administer the interest-generating activities, (2) the interest expenses and costs are not associated with activities related to intangible property, (3) the transaction has valid business purposes other than avoidance or reduction of tax and the payments made at arm's length rates and terms; and (4) item of income received by related member subject to net-income or capital-based tax imposed by Virginia, other state, or foreign government; payments made pursuant to pre-existing contract entered into when parties were not related members and the payments continue to be made at arm's length rates and terms; related member engages in transactions with nonrelated members that generate revenue	Va. Code. Ann. §58.1-402B

State	Answer	Comments	Authority
		in excess of $2 million annually; or transaction undertaken at arm's length rates and terms and related member uses funds that are either borrowed from or paid by a nonrelated member or debt incurred involves specified business purposes.	
West Virginia	No		
Wisconsin	No		

Return Due Dates

Under federal law (IRC § 6012), returns of corporations operating on a calendar year basis must be filed by March 15th following the close of the calendar year, while returns of corporations operating on a fiscal year basis must be filed by the 15th day of the third month following the close of the fiscal year.

This chart shows the state return due dates for corporations in effect for each state. States that do not impose a corporate income tax are not included in this chart.

State	Due Date
Alabama	Same as federal
Alaska	30 days after federal
Arizona	By April 15th following close of calendar year or 15th day of 4th mo. after fiscal year
Arkansas	By March 15 following close of calendar year or 2.5 mos. after fiscal year
California	Same as federal
Colorado	15th day of 4th mo. after tax year
Connecticut	By April 1 following close of calendar year or return 1st day of month following due date of federal return. 1st day of fourth month after income year if no federal return is filed
Delaware	By April 1 following close of calendar year or 1st day of 4th mo. after fiscal year
District of Columbia	Same as federal
Florida	By April 1 following close of calendar year or 1st day of 4th mo. after fiscal year
Georgia	Same as federal
Hawaii	20th day of 4th mo. after tax year
Idaho	15th day of 4th mo. after tax year
Illinois	Same as federal
Indiana	15th day of 4th mo. after tax year
Iowa	Last day of 4th mo. after tax year
Kansas	15th day of 4th mo. after tax year
Kentucky	By April 15th following close of calendar year or 15th day of 4th mo. after fiscal year
Louisiana	By April 15th following close of calendar year or 15th day of 4th mo. after tax year
Maine	Same as federal
Maryland	Same as federal
Massachusetts	Same as federal
Michigan	Last day of 4th mo. after tax year

State	Due Date
Minnesota	Same as federal
Mississippi	Same as federal
Missouri	15th day of 4th mo. after tax year
Montana	15th day of 5th mo. after tax year
Nebraska	Same as federal
New Hampshire	Same as federal
New Jersey	15th day of 4th mo. after tax year
New Mexico	Same as federal
New York	Same as federal
North Carolina	Same as federal
North Dakota	By April 15th following close of calendar year or 15th day of 4th mo. after close of fiscal tax year
Ohio	Between Jan. 1 and Mar. 31. For tax years beginning on or after July 1, 2005, commercial activity tax (CAT) returns are due on February 10 or 40 days after end of tax period.
Oklahoma	Same as federal
Oregon	15th day of the month following due date of related federal return
Pennsylvania	By April 15th following close of calendar year, or 30 days after federal return due for fiscal year
Rhode Island	Same as federal
South Carolina	Same as federal
Tennessee	15th day of 4th mo. after tax year
Texas	May 15 (except initial and second reports)
Utah	15th day of 4th mo. after tax year
Vermont	Same as federal
Virginia	15th day of 4th mo. after tax year
West Virginia	Same as federal
Wisconsin	Same as federal

S Corporations

With regard to those states that recognize S corporation status, qualified small corporation shareholders that elect to be taxed as an S corporation are subject to state personal income tax on their pro rata shares of the S corporation's income and losses, (whether distributed or not) and deductions and credits, rather than being taxed at the corporate level. S corporations are exempt from these states' corporate income tax to the same extent that they are exempt from the federal income tax. Several states, however, do not recognize S corporations for state income tax purposes. In these states, the S corporation may be required to pay tax at the corporate level.

The following chart indicates states that recognize federal S corporation status, states that require separate S corporation elections, and states that impose any entity-level tax.

Nonresident shareholder withholding requirements, estimated tax payment requirements, and composite return requirements are covered in multistate pass-through entity quick answer charts. States that do not impose an income-based tax on corporations are not included in this chart.

State	S Corporation Status Recognized	Separate State Election Required
AL	Yes.	No.
AK	Yes.	No.
AZ	Yes.	No.
AR	Yes.	Yes.
CA	Yes, but most S corporations continue to pay franchise tax at 1.5% rate (3.5% for financial S corporations).	No.
CO	Yes.	No.
CT	Yes.	No.
DE	Yes.	No.
DC	No. S corporations taxed in same manner as other corporations.	N/A
FL	Yes.	N/A
GA	Yes, so long as all shareholders are subject to tax in GA.	No.
HI	Yes.	No.
ID	Yes.	No.
IL	Yes, but S corporations are subject to the IL's personal property replacement income tax (currently 1.5%).	No.
IN	Yes, if corporation withholds tax on amounts paid to nonresidents.	No.
IA	Yes.	No.

State	S Corporation Status Recognized	Separate State Election Required
KS	Yes.	No.
KY	Yes, but for tax years beginning after 2004 and before 2007, S corporations taxed in same manner as C corporations.	No.
LA	No, S corporation taxed in the same manner as other corporations.	N/A
ME	Yes.	No.
MD	Yes.	No.
MA	Yes; however, S corporations with total receipts of $6 million or more subject to tax at graduated rate.	No.
MI	No. S corporations subject to Single Business Tax, though they are entitled to an increased statutory exemption and special credit.	No.
MN	Yes.	No.
MS	Yes.	No.
MO	Yes.	No.
MT	Yes.	No.
NE	Yes.	No.
NH	No. S corporations required to pay business profits tax.	N/A
NJ	Yes.	Yes.
NM	Yes.	No.
NY	Yes; however, S corporations are subject to a corporate-level tax.	Yes.
NC	Yes.	No.
ND	Yes.	No.
OH	Yes.	Yes.
OK	Yes.	No.
OR	Yes.	No.
PA	Yes. Federal election automatically applies unless S corporation elects out with approval of all shareholders.	No. For tax years prior to 2005, separate state election required.
RI	Yes. S corporations subject to annual franchise tax.	No.
SC	Yes.	No.

State	S Corporation Status Recognized	Separate State Election Required
SD	No; however, SD imposes neither a general corporate income tax nor a personal income tax. Financial corporations electing federal Sub S corporation status do pay franchise tax.	No.
TN	No. S corporations taxed in same manner as other corporations.	N/A
TX	No, S corporations taxed in the same manner as other corporations.	N/A
UT	Yes.	No.
VT	Yes.	No.
VA	Yes.	No.
WV	Yes, provided the S corporation files an Information Return.	No.
WI	Yes.	No, unless S corporation elects out of tax-option corporations status.

Sales Factor Rules

The following chart reflects each state's use of the various tests involved in apportioning sales.

Destination Test: Assigns to the numerator receipts from sales of tangible personal property if the property is delivered or shipped to a purchaser, other than the U.S. government, located in the taxing state.

Throwback Rule: Assigns to the numerator receipts from sales of tangible personal property if the property is shipped from a location in the taxing state to a purchaser in a state where the taxpayer is not taxable.

Sales to U.S. Throwback: Assigns to the numerator receipts from sales of tangible personal property to the U.S. Government if the property is shipped from a location in the taxing state.

Income-Producing Activity Test: Assigns to the numerator receipts other than those from sales of tangible personal property if the receipts are attributable to income-producing activity performed by the taxpayer in the taxing state.

States that do not impose a corporate income tax are not included in this chart.

State	Destination Test	Throwback Rule	Sales to U.S. Throwback	Income-Producing Activity Test
Alabama	Yes	Yes	Yes	Yes
Alaska	Yes	Yes	Yes	Yes
Arizona	Yes	No	No	Yes
Arkansas	Yes	Yes	Yes	Yes
California	Yes	Yes	Yes	Yes
Colorado[1]	Yes	Yes	Yes	Yes
Connecticut	Yes	No	No	No
Delaware	Yes	No	No	No
District of Columbia	Yes	Yes	Yes	Yes
Florida	Yes	No	No	Yes
Georgia	Yes	No	No	No
Hawaii	Yes	Yes	Yes	Yes
Idaho	Yes	Yes	Yes	Yes
Illinois	Yes	Yes	Yes	Yes
Indiana	Yes	Yes	Yes	Yes
Iowa	Yes	No	No	No
Kansas	Yes	Yes	Yes	Yes
Kentucky	Yes	No	Yes	Yes

State	Destination Test	Throwback Rule	Sales to U.S. Throwback	Income-Producing Activity Test
Louisiana	Yes	No	No	No
Maine	Yes	Yes	Yes	Yes
Maryland	Yes	No	No	No
Massachusetts	Yes	Yes	Yes	Yes
Michigan	Yes	No	No	Yes
Minnesota	Yes	No	No	No
Mississippi	Yes	Yes	Yes	Yes
Missouri	Yes	Yes	Yes	Yes
Montana	Yes	Yes	Yes	Yes
Nebraska	Yes	No	Yes	Yes
New Hampshire[2]	Yes	Yes	Yes	Yes
New Jersey	Yes	No	No	No
New Mexico	Yes	Yes	Yes	Yes
New York	Yes	No	No	No
North Carolina	Yes	No	Yes	Yes
North Dakota	Yes	Yes	Yes	Yes
Ohio	Yes	No	No	No
Oklahoma	Yes	Yes	Yes	No
Oregon	Yes	Yes[3]	Yes	Yes
Pennsylvania	Yes	No	No	Yes
Rhode Island	Yes	No	No	No
South Carolina	Yes	No	No	Yes
Tennessee	Yes	No	Yes	Yes
Texas	Yes	Yes	Yes	Yes
Utah	Yes	Yes	Yes	Yes
Vermont	Yes	Yes	Yes	Yes
Virginia	Yes	No	No	Yes
West Virginia	Yes	No	Yes	Yes
Wisconsin	Yes	Yes[4]	Yes[(4)]	Yes[(5)]

[1] Destination test is only test if two-factor formula used.
[2] Business profits tax apportionment.
[3] The test is modified in some circumstances.
[4] Throwback sales are single-weighted.
[5] For taxable years beginning on or after January 1, 2005, receipts from services are in Wisconsin if the purchaser receives the benefit of the services in Wisconsin, and receipts from the use of computer software are in Wisconsin if the purchaser or licensee uses the software at a Wisconsin location.

Social Security Benefits

Under federal law, taxpayers may be required to include a portion of their Social Security benefits in their taxable adjusted gross income (AGI). Most states begin the calculation of state personal income tax liability with federal AGI, or federal taxable income, and in those states, the portion of Social Security benefits subject to federal personal income tax is subject to state personal income tax, unless state law allows taxpayers to subtract the federally taxed portion of their benefits from their federal AGI in the computation of their state AGI.

The chart below identifies how each of the states imposing a personal income tax responds to the federal treatment of Social Security benefits, that is, whether the state (1) allows taxpayers to subtract the benefits from federal AGI, thus effectively exempting them from its personal income tax, (2) does not allow taxpayers to subtract the benefits, thus subjecting them to its personal income tax, or (3) has provisions concerning Social Security benefits that are unrelated to the federal provisions.

States that do not impose a personal income tax are not included in this chart.

State	Tax Treatment of Social Security Benefits
Alabama	State computation not based on federal. Social Security benefits excluded from taxable income.
Arkansas	State computation not based on federal. Social Security benefits excluded from taxable income.
Arizona	Social Security Benefits subtracted from federal AGI.
California	Social Security Benefits subtracted from federal AGI.
Colorado	Pension income, including Social Security benefits, up to $24,000 may be subtracted from federal taxable income by those 65 and older, and up to $20,000 by those 55 and older or those who are second party beneficiaries of someone 55 or older.
Connecticut	Joint filers and heads of households with AGIs under $60,000 and individuals with AGIs under $50,000 deduct from federal AGI all Social Security income included for federal income tax purposes. Joint filers and heads of households with AGIs over $60,000 and individuals with AGIs over $50,000 deduct the difference between the amount of Social Security benefits included for federal income tax purposes and the lesser of 25% of Social Security benefits received or 25% of the excess of the taxpayer's provisional income in excess of the specified base amount under IRC Sec. 86(b)(1).
Delaware	Social Security benefits subtracted from federal AGI.
District of Columbia	Social Security benefits subtracted from federal AGI.
Georgia	Social Security benefits subtracted from federal AGI.
Hawaii	Social Security benefits subtracted from federal AGI.
Idaho	Social Security benefits subtracted from federal AGI.
Illinois	Social Security benefits subtracted from federal AGI.
Indiana	Social Security benefits subtracted from federal AGI.

State	Tax Treatment of Social Security Benefits
Iowa	No more than 50% of Social Security benefits taxable. Subtraction allowed for 32% of taxable benefits for tax years 2007 and 2008; 43% in 2009; 55% in 2010; 67% in 2011; 77% in 2012, and 89% in 2013. For tax years after 2013, Social Security benefits are fully exempt.
Kansas	State computation begins with federal AGI. No subtraction.
Kentucky	Social Security benefits subtracted from federal AGI.
Louisiana	Social Security benefits subtracted from federal AGI.
Maine	Social Security benefits subtracted from federal AGI.
Maryland	Social Security benefits subtracted from federal AGI.
Massachusetts	Social Security benefits subtracted from federal AGI.
Michigan	Social Security benefits subtracted from federal AGI.
Minnesota	State computation begins with federal taxable income. No subtraction.
Mississippi	State computation not based on federal. Social Security benefits exempt in total.
Missouri	State computation begins with federal AGI. Up to $6.000 of retirement income, including Social Security benefits exempt, if annual income less taxable Social Security benefits is $25,000 or less ($32,000 for married taxpayers filing jointly).
Montana	Separate calculation to determine taxable Social Security benefits. Benefits exempt if income is $16,000 or under for single filers, $25,000 or under for heads of households, or $32,000 and under for married taxpayers filing jointly.
Nebraska	State computation begins with federal AGI. No subtraction.
New Jersey	State computation not based on federal. All Social Security benefits are excluded by statute from gross income.
New Mexico	State computation begins with federal AGI. No subtraction.
New York	Social Security benefits subtracted from federal AGI.
North Carolina	Social Security benefits subtracted from federal taxable income.
North Dakota	State computation begins with federal taxable income. No subtraction.
Ohio	Social Security benefits subtracted from federal AGI.
Oklahoma	Social Security benefits subtracted from federal AGI.
Oregon	Social Security benefits subtracted from federal taxable income.
Pennsylvania	State computation not based on federal. Social Security benefits not included in Pennsylvania taxable income.
Rhode Island	State computation begins with federal taxable income. No subtraction.
South Carolina	Social Security benefits subtracted from federal taxable income.

State	Tax Treatment of Social Security Benefits
Utah	State computation begins with federal taxable income. No subtraction, except Social Security income eligible for inclusion in retirement income deduction for taxpayers under age 65 of up to $4,800 and retirement income exemption for taxpayers age 65 and older of up to $7,500. Deduction and exemption reduced by 50 cents of each dollar of income exceeding $32,000 for married taxpayers filing jointly, $16,000 for married taxpayers filing separately, and $25,000 for single taxpayers.
Vermont	State computation begins with federal taxable income. No subtraction.
Virginia	Social Security benefits subtracted from federal AGI.
West Virginia	State computation begins with federal AGI. No subtraction.
Wisconsin	Partial exclusion (no more than 50% of Social Security benefits taxable). Full exclusion effective beginning in tax year 2008.

State and Foreign Income Tax Deduction

This chart shows each state's rules on the state and foreign income tax deduction. Most states deny a deduction for state taxes measured by corporate net income, whether imposed by the taxing state or its subdivisions or by another state. In these states, the state income taxes deducted on the federal return must be added back to determine state taxable income. Of the states that permit a deduction for state income taxes, most deny a deduction for their own income tax. A number of states allow a deduction for the Michigan Single Business Tax ("SBT"), which is not considered a tax on income.

Many states deny a deduction for foreign (non-U.S.) income taxes. Those that allow a deduction for foreign income taxes do so by adopting federal taxable income as a starting point; therefore, the allowable deduction is limited to that portion claimed on the federal return.

States that do not impose a corporate income tax are not included in this chart.

State	State Tax Deductible	Foreign Tax Deductible
Alabama	No, except MI SBT	Yes, adjustment required if federal foreign tax credit claimed
Alaska	No	No
Arizona	No, except MI SBT	No
Arkansas	Yes, except AR tax	Yes
California	No, except MI SBT	No
Colorado	Yes, except CO tax	No
Connecticut	No, except MI SBT	Yes
Delaware	No	Same as federal
District of Columbia	No	No
Florida	No, except MI SBT and local taxes	Yes
Georgia	No, except GA tax and MI SBT	No
Hawaii	Same as federal	Same as federal
Idaho	No, except MI SBT	Same as federal
Illinois	Yes, except IL tax	Same as federal
Indiana	No	No
Iowa	Yes, except IA tax	Same as federal
Kansas	No, except KS privilege tax	No
Kentucky	No, except portion of MI SBT	No
Louisiana	Yes, except LA tax	Same as federal
Maine	No, except MI SBT	Same as federal

State	State Tax Deductible	Foreign Tax Deductible
Maryland	No, except portion of MI SBT	Same as federal
Massachusetts	No	No
Michigan	No	No
Minnesota	No, except portion of MI SBT	No
Mississippi	No, except MI SBT	No
Missouri	No, except MI SBT	Same as federal
Montana	No, except MI SBT	No
Nebraska	Same as federal	Same as federal
New Hampshire	No, except MI SBT	No
New Jersey	No	No
New Mexico	Same as federal	Same as federal
New York	No	No
North Carolina	No, except MI SBT	No
North Dakota	No, except portion of MI SBT	No
Ohio	Same as federal	Same as federal
Oklahoma	No	No
Oregon	No, except MI SBT	No
Pennsylvania	No, except portion of MI SBT	No
Rhode Island	Yes, except RI tax	Same as federal
South Carolina	No, except MI SBT	No
Tennessee	Yes, except TN tax	Same as federal
Texas	Same as federal	Same as federal
Utah	No	No
Vermont	No	Same as federal
Virginia	No	No
West Virginia	No	No
Wisconsin	No	Yes

States Utilizing Multistate Allocation/Apportionment Provisions

In the chart below, the states listed as having adopted the Uniform Division of Income for Tax Purposes Act (UDITPA) and the Multistate Tax Compact (MTC) regulations include not only those that have formally adopted them, but also those that have enacted statutory or regulatory provisions that substantially duplicate them. The UDITPA is a model act adopted by the Commissioners on Uniform State Laws and the American Bar Association to promote uniformity in the application of allocation and apportionment rules across the states. UDITPA divides income into "business income," which is apportioned among states by means of a three-factor formula, and "non-business income," which is allocated to a specific state according to the type of income and the type of property giving rise to the income. The MTC regulations are model regulations adopted by the Multistate Tax Compact that interpret the UDITPA provisions.

States that do not impose a corporate income tax are not included in this chart.

State	Adoption of UDITPA	Adoption of MTC Regs.
Alabama	Yes	Substantially all
Alaska	Yes	Substantially all
Arizona	Yes	Substantially all
Arkansas	Yes, with modifications	Adopted the business/non-business income regs.
California	Yes, with modifications	Substantially all
Colorado	Yes, for corporations electing to apportion income by using the MTC apportionment schedule, as opposed to the method prescribed by the Colo. income tax act.	Yes, for corporations electing to apportion income by using the MTC apportionment schedule, as opposed to the method prescribed by the Colo. income tax act.
Connecticut	No	None
Delaware	No, but similar statute	None
District of Columbia	No, but substantially similar provisions	None, but generally consistent provisions
Florida	No, but many similar provisions	None
Georgia	No, but many similar provisions	None, but several similar provisions
Hawaii	Yes, with some modifications	Substantially all
Idaho	Yes	All except airlines reg.
Illinois	No	None
Indiana	No, but many similar provisions	None, but generally consistent provisions
Iowa	No, but statute contains some similar provisions	Only business rents/royalty income reg.
Kansas	Yes, with some modifications	Most

State	Adoption of UDITPA	Adoption of MTC Regs.
Kentucky	Yes, with many variations	None, but many similar provisions
Louisiana	No, but similar statutory provisions	None
Maine	Yes, with modifications (e.g., use of double-weighted sales factor)	Abbreviated version
Maryland	No, but similar apportionment factor rules	None
Massachusetts	No	None
Michigan	No, but similar apportionment provisions	None
Minnesota	No	None, but generally consistent provisions
Mississippi	No, but many similar provisions	None
Missouri	Yes, but option to apply state's one-factor formula or separate accounting	Substantially all
Montana	Yes, except provisions dealing with exemptions for financial organizations and public utilities	Substantially all
Nebraska	No, but several similar provisions	None, but some similar provisions
New Hampshire	No, but several similar provisions	None, but similar factor provisions
New Jersey	No	None
New Mexico	Yes	None, but generally consistent provisions
New York	No	None, but several comparable NY regs.
North Carolina	No, but substantially similar provisions	None
North Dakota	Yes, except provisions dealing with financial organizations, public utilities, broadcasting, and some transportation	Substantially all
Ohio	No, but many similar provisions	None
Oklahoma	No, but many similar provisions	None
Oregon	Yes, with modified sales factor	Substantially all
Pennsylvania	Yes, with some exceptions	None, but generally consistent allocation and apportionment provisions
Rhode Island	No, but some similar provisions	None
South Carolina	No	Generally consistent provisions; no UDITPA option
Tennessee	Yes	Yes, substantially similar version
Texas	No	None

State	Adoption of UDITPA	Adoption of MTC Regs.
Utah	Yes, with some modifications	Most
Vermont	No, but some similar provisions	None
Virginia	No	None
West Virginia	No	None
Wisconsin	No, but many similar provisions	Some, including business/nonbusiness income regs.

Taxability of Bond Interest

The following chart indicates the position of each state and the District of Columbia on the taxation of state and federal bond interest. Except where noted, this information applies equally to corporate and personal income taxation. Where a state treats interest income differently based on tax type, the following is used: FI=franchise income tax, CI=corporate income tax, and PI=personal income tax.

Further, while states are prohibited from taxing federal obligations, federal law provides an exception to the prohibition for states that characterize a corporate taxing scheme as a nondiscriminatory corporate franchise tax. States that impose neither a corporate income tax nor a personal income tax are not included in this chart.

State	State's Own Bonds		Other States' Bonds	U.S. Bond Interest
Alabama		Exempt	Taxable	Exempt
Alaska	CI:	Exempt	Exempt (No personal income tax)	Exempt
Arizona		Exempt	Taxable	Exempt
Arkansas		Exempt	Taxable	Exempt
California	FI:	Taxable	Taxable	Taxable[1]
	CI:	Exempt	Taxable	Exempt
	PI:	Exempt	Taxable	Exempt
Colorado		Exempt[2]	Taxable	Exempt
Connecticut	CI:	Taxable	Taxable	Taxable[1]
	PI:	Exempt	Taxable	Exempt[3]
Delaware		Exempt	Taxable	Exempt
District of Columbia	CI:	Exempt	Taxable	Exempt
	PI:		Exempt	Exempt
Florida	CI:	Taxable	Taxable (No personal income tax)	Taxable[1]
Georgia		Exempt	Taxable	Exempt
Hawaii		Exempt	Taxable	Exempt
Idaho		Exempt	Taxable	Exempt
Illinois		Taxable[4]	Taxable	Exempt
Indiana		Exempt	Exempt	Exempt

State	State's Own Bonds		Other States' Bonds	U.S. Bond Interest
Iowa		Taxable[4]	Taxable	Exempt
Kansas		Exempt[5]	Taxable	Exempt
Kentucky		Exempt	Taxable	Exempt
Louisiana[6]		Exempt	Taxable[7]	Exempt[3]
Maine		Exempt	Taxable	Exempt[3]
Maryland		Exempt	Taxable	Exempt
Massachusetts	CI:	Taxable	Taxable	Taxable[1]
	PI:	Exempt	Taxable	Exempt
Michigan		Exempt	Taxable	Exempt
Minnesota	CI:	Taxable	Taxable	Taxable[1]
	PI:	Exempt	Taxable	Exempt
Mississippi		Exempt	Taxable	Exempt
Missouri		Exempt	Taxable	Exempt
Montana	CI:	Taxable[4]	Taxable	Taxable[1]
	PI:	Exempt	Taxable	Exempt
Nebraska		Exempt	Taxable	Exempt
New Hampshire	CI:	Exempt	Exempt	Exempt
	PI:		Taxable	
New Jersey	CI:	Taxable	Taxable	Taxable[1]
	PI:	Exempt	Taxable	Exempt
New Mexico		Exempt	Taxable[8]	Exempt
New York	CI:	Taxable	Taxable	Taxable[1]
	PI:	Exempt	Taxable	Exempt
North Carolina		Exempt	Taxable	Exempt
North Dakota		Exempt	Taxable	Exempt
Ohio	CI:	Exempt	Exempt	Exempt
	PI:	Exempt	Taxable	Exempt
Oklahoma		Taxable[4]	Taxable	Exempt
Oregon	FI:	Taxable	Taxable	Taxable[1]
	CI:	Exempt[9]	Taxable	Exempt
	PI:	Exempt	Taxable	Exempt

State		State's Own Bonds	Other States' Bonds	U.S. Bond Interest
Pennsylvania	CI:	Exempt	Exempt	Exempt
	PI:	Exempt	Taxable	Exempt
Rhode Island		Exempt	Taxable	Exempt
South Carolina		Exempt	Taxable	Exempt
Tennessee	CI:	Taxable	Taxable	Taxable[1]
	PI:	Exempt	Taxable	Exempt
Texas	CI:	Exempt	Exempt (No personal income tax)	Exempt
Utah	CI:	Taxable[10]	Taxable	Taxable[10]
	PI:	Exempt	Exempt[11]	Exempt
Vermont		Exempt	Taxable	Exempt
Virginia		Exempt	Taxable	Exempt[3]
West Virginia	CI:	Taxable[4]	Taxable	Exempt[3]
	PI:	Exempt	Taxable	Exempt
Wisconsin	CI:	Taxable[4]	Taxable	Exempt
	FI:	Taxable	Taxable	Taxable[1]
	PI:	Taxable[4]	Taxable	Exempt

[1] Nondiscriminatory franchise or privilege tax.
[2] Interest income on obligations of Colorado or a political subdivision thereof issued on or after 5/01/80 is exempt. Interest from obligations issued prior thereto is exempt only if specifically made exempt by statute.
[3] Interest on obligations of federal authorities, commissions, or instrumentalities that is exempt for federal tax but not from state tax is taxable.
[7] Income from certain specified obligations is exempt. Interest from all other obligations is taxable.
[5] Interest income on obligations of Kansas or a political subdivision thereof issued after 1987 is exempt. Interest from obligations issued prior to 1988 is exempt only if specifically made exempt by statute.
[6] After 2005, interest income from federal or state bonds is exempt from corporation income tax.
[7] For personal income tax purposes, interest on obligations of non-Louisiana state and local government obligations is table only for obligations purchased after 1979.
[8] Interest on obligations of Puerto Rico, Guam, and other U.S. territories and possessions are exempt.
[9] Interest on obligations of Oregon are exempt for obligations issued after May 24, 1961.
[10] Utah does not provide a subtraction for interest on Utah and U.S. obligations, but does allow a partial credit.
[11] Interest on non-Utah sate and local bonds acquired after 2002 is taxable only if the other state or locality imposes an income-based tax on Utah government bonds.

Withholding Returns and Deposits

All states that impose a personal income tax require withholding of tax by employers. The frequency of remittance of tax to the state varies, as does the frequency of returns.

In addition to the information detailed below, a few states allow remittance on an annual basis, but the threshold is generally quite low. Many states also require remittance on a more frequent basis than monthly (including semi-monthly, weekly, and semi-weekly) depending on the amount of tax withheld by the employer.

"Last day" entries below indicate the last day of the month following the end of the period (quarter or month), while other entries indicate the day of the month following the end of the period (e.g. 15th day of following month or 15th day of month following end of the quarter).

State	Annual Reconciliation (form)	Quarterly Return (form)	Monthly Deposit (form)
AL	Last day of February (A-3)	Last day (A-1)	15th day (A-6)
AR	February 28 (AR3MAR)	none	15th day (AR941M)
AZ	February 28 (A-1R)	10th day (A1-QTR)	15th day (A1-WP)
CA	January 31 (DE 7)	Last day (DE 6)	15th day (DE 88)
CO	Last day of February (DR 1093)	Last day (DR 1094)	15th day (DR 1094)
CT	Last day of February (CT-W3)	Last day (CT-941)	15th day (CT-WH)
DC	January 31 (FR-900B)	none	20th day (FR-900M)
DE	1st day of March (W-3)	Last day (W1Q)	15th day (W1)
GA	Last day of February (G-1003)	Last day (G-7)	15th day (GA-V)
HI	Last day of February (HW-3)	15th day (HW-14)	15th day (HW-14)[1]
IA	Last day of February (44-007/VSP)	Last day (44-095)[2]	15th day (44-101)
ID	January 31 (956)	Last day (910)	20th day (910)
IL	Last day of February (IL-W-3)	Last day (IL-941)	15th day (IL-501)
IN	1st day of March (WH-3)	Last day (WH-1)[3]	20th/30th day (WH-1)[4]
KS	Last day of February (KW-3)	25th day (KW-5)	15th day (KW-5)
KY	January 31 (K-3)	Last day (K-1)	15th day (K-1)
LA	First business day after February 27 (L-3)	Last day (L-1)	Last day (L-1)
MA	none	Last day (M-941)	15th day (M-942)
MD	February 28 (MW-508)	15th day (MW-506)	15th day (MW-506)[15]
ME	February 28 (W-3ME)	Last day (941/C1-ME)	none

State	Annual Reconciliation (form)	Quarterly Return (form)	Monthly Deposit (form)
MI	February 28 (165)	15th day (3862)[3]	15th day (3862)
MN	February 28 (2004 WH Instructions)	Last day (MW-5 WH)[5]	15th day (MW-5)
MO	February 28 (MO W-3)	Last day (MO-941)[3]	15th day (MO-941)
MS	January 31 (89-115)	15th day (89-105)[3]	15th day (89-105)
MT	February 28 (MW-3)	none	15th day (MW-1)[14]
NC	February 28 (NC-3/NC-3M)	Last day (NC-5)[3]	15th day (NC-5)[6]
ND	February 28 (307)	Last day (306)	none
NE	March 15 (W-3N)	Last day (941N)	15th day (501N)
NJ	February 28 (NJ-W-3M)[17]	30th day (NJ-927/NJ-927-W)[16,17]	15th day (NJ-500)[7,17]
NM	March 1 (RPD-41072)[8]	25th day (CRS-1)[3]	25th day (CRS-1)
NY	February 28 (NYS-45-ATT)	Last day (NYS-45)[9]	none
OH	January 31 (IT-941)	Last day (IT-501)[3]	15th day (IT-501)
OK	none[10]	15th day (OW-9)[3]	15th day (OW-9)
OR	February 28 (WR)	Last day (OQ)	15th day (OTC)
PA	none	Last day (W-3)[11]	15th day (PA-501)[6]
RI	February 28 (RI-W3)	Last day (RI-941Q)	20th day (RI-941M)
SC	February 28 (WH-1606)	Last day (WH-1605)	15th day (WH-1601)
UT	February 28 (TC-96R)	Last day (TC-96Q)	Last day (TC-96M)
VA	February 28 (VA-6)	Last day (VA-5)[3]	20th day (VA-5)
VT	February 28 (WH-434)	25th day (WH-431)	25th day (WH-431)[12]
WI	January 31 (WT-7)	Last day (WT-6)[3]	Last day (WT-6)
WV	February 28 (WV/IT-103)	Last day (WV/IT-101)	20th day (WV/IT-101)[6,13]

[1] Semiweekly if annual withholding exceeds $40K
[2] Semimonthly if withholding exceeds $5K in semimonthly period
[3] Quarterly deposit rather than return
[4] 20th if average monthly withholding greater than $1K
[5] Last day of February for 4th quarter
[6] Deposit for December due January 31
[7] 30th day of month following end of quarter
[8] Semi-annual return (CRS-1) due 25th day after end of six-month period
[9] February 28 (NYS-45-ATT) if extended due date used
[10] Necessary year-end adjustments must be made on OW-9
[11] Quarterly withholders file PA-501/W3
[12] Deposit for January due February 23
[13] Monthly depositors who withhold more than $100K per month must file WV/IT-101 and deposit withheld taxes for first 15 days of June by June 23
[14] Monthly schedule required for new employers and those without complete lookback period (12-month period from July 1 of preceding year to June 30 of present year). Employers with more than $12,000 of WH in lookback period must use accelerated schedule for deposits, which is the same as their federal deposit schedule.

[15] Employers with $15,000 or more of withholding in the 12-month lookback period and that have also accumulated $700 of withholding in any pay period must remit the withholding payment within 3 business days following that payroll. Applicable to all calendar years beginning after December 31, 2006, employers subject to the accelerated schedule may seek a waiver permitting monthly filing if allowed to do so for federal withholding tax purposes.

[16] Online filing allowed.

[17] Paperless telefiling allowed.

Withholding—LLCs

The following chart indicates whether limited liability companies (LLCs) are required to withhold on nonresident member income. A growing number of states require withholding from nonresident members and some of these states provide exceptions, for, among other items, distributive income that is less than a specified threshold amount, partners included in composite returns, or partners agreeing to comply with state income tax requirements. State specific conditions or limitations placed on the withholding requirement are noted in the footnotes. The chart does not reflect whether nonresident withholding is subject to estimated tax payment requirements.

State	Answer
Alabama	No
Alaska	N/A[1]
Arizona	No
Arkansas	Yes[2]
California	Yes[3]
Colorado	Yes[4]
Connecticut	No[5]
Delaware	No
District of Columbia	No[6]
Florida	N/A[1]
Georgia	Yes[7]
Hawaii	No
Idaho	No[8]
Illinois	No
Indiana	Yes[9]
Iowa	Yes[10]
Kansas	Yes[11]
Kentucky	No[12]
Louisiana	No
Maine	Yes[13]
Maryland	Yes[14]
Massachusetts	No[15]
Michigan	Yes[16]
Minnesota	Yes[17]
Mississippi	No[18]

State	Answer
Missouri	Yes[19]
Montana	Yes[20]
Nebraska	Yes[21]
New Hampshire	N/A[21]
New Jersey	Yes[23]
New Mexico	Yes[24]
New York	No
North Carolina	Yes[25]
North Dakota	Yes[26]
Ohio	Yes[27]
Oklahoma	Yes[28]
Oregon	No[29]
Pennsylvania	Yes[30]
Rhode Island	Yes[31]
South Carolina	Yes[32]
Tennessee	N/A[33]
Texas	N/A[1]
Utah	No
Vermont	No
Virginia	No
West Virginia	Yes[34]
Wisconsin	Yes[35]

[1] No personal income tax.

[2] Effective for tax years beginning after 2005, withholding required at highest individual income tax rate, unless, among other exceptions, distributive income is less than $1000, the nonresident participates in a composite return, the entity files an agreement by the nonresident to comply with state income tax requirements.

[3] Withholding required at 7% on distributions to domestic nonresident members, unless annual total distributions of income are $1,500 or less, the member or the income is tax exempt, or the distribution was previously reported on partner's California return. Withholding required at highest individual or corporate tax rate on distributions to foreign (non-U.S.) nonresident members.

[4] Withholding required at highest marginal individual tax rate, unless member signs agreement to pay tax or is included in composite return.

[5] Composite payment required if member is nonresident individual, trust, estate, or pass-through entity that did not elect to be included on group return and whose share of state income is $1,000 or more. After 2005 tax year, composite payment required if member is nonresident individual, trust, estate, or pass-through entity whose share of state income is $1,000 or more.

[6] Personal income tax not applicable to nonresidents.

[7] LLCs owning property or doing business in Georgia required to withhold at 4% on distributions paid or credited to nonresident members attributable to property owned or business done in state. Not required on deemed distributions, or if LLC files composite return on behalf of nonresident partners, if aggregate annual distributions to partner are less than $1,000, if distribution is attributable to return of capital, or if partnership is publicly traded partnership.

[8] Individual LLC members may elect to have LLC file return and pay income tax at corporate rate. LLC liable for income tax of members who do not elect to have LLC file and pay and who fail to file and pay tax individually.

[9] Withholding required on distributive shares of income derived from Indiana sources paid or credited to nonresident individual and corporate members. Not required if nonresident member domiciled for entire year in reverse credit state with higher tax rate and Indiana source income is taxed in domiciliary state.

[10] LLCs required to withhold at 5%, or according to Taxpayer Services schedule, on Iowa source income of nonresident members unless member pays estimated tax.

[11] Withholding on distributed or nondistributed taxable income required at maximum individual rate, unless member provides statement of federally-exempt status or files affidavit agreeing to pay tax.

[12] For tax years beginning on or after January 1, 2004 and before January 1, 2005, withholding on nonresident income required. For tax years beginning on or after January 1, 2005, LLCs taxed in same manner as C Corporations.

[13] Withholding required at highest tax rate imposed on corporations, individuals, trusts or estates, unless member's share of annual income is less than $1,000.

[14] Withholding required equal to sum of highest marginal individual tax rate and the lowest county tax rate applied to each nonresident individual member's distributive share of pass-through income plus corporation income tax rate applied to each nonresident entity member's distributive share of pass-through income.

[15] Commissioner may require non-employers to withhold on payments made to residents, nonresidents, and part-year residents other than exempt organizations.

[16] Withholding required at personal income tax rate, after deducting personal and dependency exemptions, unless distributive income is exempt or aggregated quarterly income available for distribution to all nonresident members subject to withholding is less than $1,000.

[17] Withholding required at highest individual tax rate if distributive income from state sources is $1,000 or more and nonresident is not included in composite return. Certain income from entity termination or liquidation, discharge of indebtedness, or sale of property is excluded from withholding requirements.

[18] Individual members liable for tax. LLC liable if member fails to pay unless partnership withholds 5% of partnership net gain or profit. Commissioner may require withholding on a nonresident partner.

[19] Withholding required at highest individual tax rate on payment to nonresidents of dividends and shares of undistributed taxable income, unless assignable income from LLC is less than $1200, nonresident is included in composite return, or nonresident agrees to file return and pay tax. Amount of withholding tax may be determined based on withholding tables if nonresident submits withholding allowance certificate.

[20] Withholding required at highest marginal individual tax rate imposed on resident taxpayers, unless nonresident agrees to file return and pay tax or is included in composite return.

[21] Withholding required at highest individual income tax rate, unless member signs agreement to file return and pay tax.

[22] Personal income tax applies only to interest and dividend income and is not applicable to nonresidents.

[23] Tax must be paid on behalf of nonresident members with New Jersey-allocated income at rate of 6.37% for nonresident individual members and 9% for nonresident entity members. Qualified investment partnerships, investment clubs, and publicly traded partnerships are exempt.

[24] Withholding required on nonresident member's share of net income. Not required if nonresident agrees to file return and pay tax. Not applicable to entities taxed federally as corporations and to certain gas proceeds and investment partnerships.

[25] Managing members required to pay income tax on nonresident member's share of entity's North Carolina income and are authorized to withhold on nonresident's share. Managing members not required to pay tax if member is corporation, partnership, trust, or estate and signs affirmation that it will pay tax.

[26] For tax years beginning after 2005, withholding required at highest individual tax rate unless distributive share of income is less than $1,000, an election is made to pay tax as part of a composite return, or the pass-through entity is a publicly traded partnership. Withholding requirement applies to lower-tier pass-through entities.

[27] Withholding required at 5% of adjusted qualifying amounts over $1,000, unless entity files composite return on behalf of all nonresident individual members and estates.

[28] Withholding required at 5%, unless nonresident files affidavit agreeing to be subject to personal jurisdiction of Tax Commission or if entity is publicly traded partnership that has agreed to file information return.

[29] Withholding required at 5%, unless nonresident files affidavit agreeing to be subject to personal jurisdiction of Tax Commission or entity is publicly traded partnership that has agreed to file information return.

[30] LLCs with income sources in Pennsylvania must withhold at 3.07% of income allocable to nonresident members.

[31] Withholding required at corporate tax rate or highest individual tax rate, unless distributive share of income is less than $1,000 or member elects to pay tax as part of composite return.

[32] LLCs treated as partnerships required to withhold at 5% of nonresident's share of LLC's South Carolina income whether distributed or undistributed. Not required if nonresident agrees to be subject to South Carolina personal jurisdiction, if nonresident is included in composite return, or if income is attributable to sale of real property subject to withholding.

[33] Personal income tax applies only to stock and bond income and is not applicable to nonresidents.

[34] Withholding required at 4% of actual and deemed distributions, unless member is tax exempt or withholding would cause undue hardship.

[35] For taxable years beginning on or after January 1, 2005, withholding required at highest corporate tax rate or highest individual income tax rate for individuals, estates, or trusts, unless distributable share is less than $1,000, nonresident is exempt or has no other income attributable to state sources. Exemptions also available for joint ventures.

Withholding—LLPs

The following chart indicates whether limited liability partnerships (LLPs) are required to withhold on nonresident partner income. A growing number of states require withholding from nonresident partners and some of these states provide exceptions, for, among other items, distributive income that is less than a specified threshold amount, partners included in composite returns, or partners agreeing to comply with state income tax requirements. State specific conditions or limitations placed on the withholding requirement are noted in the footnotes. The chart does not reflect whether nonresident withholding is subject to estimated tax payment requirements.

State	Answer
Alabama	No
Alaska	N/A[1]
Arizona	No
Arkansas	Yes[2]
California	Yes[3]
Colorado	Yes[4]
Connecticut	No[5]
Delaware	No
District of Columbia	No[6]
Florida	N/A[1]
Georgia	Yes[7]
Hawaii	No
Idaho	No[8]
Illinois	No
Indiana	Yes[9]
Iowa	Yes[10]
Kansas	Yes[11]
Kentucky	No[12]
Louisiana	No
Maine	Yes[13]
Maryland	Yes[14]
Massachusetts	No[15]
Michigan	Yes[16]
Minnesota	Yes[17]
Mississippi	No[18]

State	Answer
Missouri	Yes[19]
Montana	Yes[20]
Nebraska	Yes[21]
New Hampshire	N/A[22]
New Jersey	Yes[23]
New Mexico	Yes[24]
New York	No
North Carolina	Yes[25]
North Dakota	Yes[26]
Ohio	Yes[27]
Oklahoma	Yes[28]
Oregon	No[29]
Pennsylvania	Yes[30]
Rhode Island	Yes[31]
South Carolina	Yes[32]
Tennessee	N/A[33]
Texas	N/A[1]
Utah	No
Vermont	No
Virginia	No
West Virginia	Yes[34]
Wisconsin	No[35]

---

[1] No personal income tax.

[2] Withholding required at highest individual income tax rate, unless, among other exceptions, distributive income is less than $1000, the nonresident participates in a composite return, the entity files an agreement by the nonresident to comply with state income tax requirements, or the entity files an agreement by the nonresident to comply with state income tax requirements.

[3] Withholding required at 7% on distributions to domestic nonresident partners, unless annual total distributions of income are $1,500 or less, the partner or the income is tax exempt, or the distribution was previously reported on partner's California return. Withholding required at highest individual or corporate tax rate on distributions to foreign (non-U.S.) nonresident partners.

[4] Withholding required at highest marginal individual tax rate, unless partner signs agreement to pay tax or is included in composite return.

[5] Composite payment required if partner is nonresident individual, trust, estate, or pass-through entity that did not elect to be included on group return and whose share of state income is $1,000 or more. After 2005 tax year, composite payment required if partner is nonresident individual, trust, estate, or pass-through entity whose share of state income is $1,000 or more.

[6] Personal income tax not applicable to nonresidents.

[7] Partnerships owning property or doing business in Georgia required to withhold at 4% on distributions paid or credited to nonresident partners attributable to property owned or business done in state. Not required on deemed distributions, or if partnership files composite return on behalf of nonresident partners, if aggregate annual distributions to partner are less than $1,000, if distribution is attributable to return of capital, or if partnership is publicly traded partnership.

[8] Individual LLP may elect to have LLP file return and pay income tax at corporate rate. LLP liable for income tax of partners who do not elect to have LLP file and pay and who fail to file and pay tax individually.

[9] Withholding required on distributive shares of income derived from Indiana sources paid or credited to nonresident individual and corporate members. Not required if nonresident member domiciled for entire year in reverse credit state with higher tax rate and Indiana source income is taxed in domiciliary state.

[10] LLPs required to withhold at 5%, or according to Taxpayer Services schedule, on Iowa source income of nonresident partners unless partner pays estimated tax.

[11] Withholding on distributed or nondistributed taxable income required at maximum individual rate, unless partner provides statement of federally-exempt status or files affidavit agreeing to pay tax.

[12] For tax years beginning on or after January 1, 2004 and before January 1, 2005, withholding on nonresident income required. For tax years beginning on or after January 1, 2005, LLPs taxed in same manner as C Corporations.

[13] Withholding required at highest tax rate imposed on corporations, individuals, trusts or estates, unless partner's share of annual income is less than $1,000.

[14] Withholding required equal to sum of highest marginal individual tax rate and the lowest county tax rate applied to each nonresident individual partner's distributive share of pass-through income plus corporation income tax rate applied to each nonresident entity partner's distributive share of pass-through income.

[15] Commissioner may require non-employers to withhold on payments made to residents, nonresidents, and part-year residents other than exempt organizations.

[16] Withholding required at personal income tax rate, after deducting personal and dependency exemptions, unless distributive income is exempt or aggregated quarterly income available for distribution to all nonresident partners subject to withholding is less than $1,000.

[17] Withholding required at highest individual tax rate if distributive income from state sources is $1,000 or more and nonresident is not included in composite return. Certain income from entity termination or liquidation, discharge of indebtedness, or sale of property is excluded from withholding requirements.

[18] Individual members liable for tax. LLP liable if member fails to pay unless partnership withholds 5% of partnership net gain or profit. Commissioner may require withholding on a nonresident partner.

[19] Withholding required at highest individual tax rate on payment to nonresidents of dividends and shares of undistributed taxable income, unless assignable income from LLP is less than $1200, nonresident is included in composite return, or nonresident agrees to file return and pay tax. Amount of withholding tax may be determined based on withholding tables if partner submits withholding allowance certificate.

[20] Withholding required at highest marginal individual tax rate imposed on resident taxpayers, unless nonresident agrees to file return and pay tax or is included in composite return.

[21] Withholding required at highest individual income tax rate, unless member signs agreement to file return and pay tax. For taxable years beginning after January 1, 2005, publicly traded partnerships treated as partnerships for federal income tax purposes that agree to file annual information returns are exempt from withholding requirement.

[22] Personal income tax applies only to interest and dividend income and is not applicable to nonresidents.

[23] Tax must be paid on behalf of nonresident partners with New Jersey-allocated income at rate of 6.37% for nonresident individual partners and 9% for nonresident entity partners. Qualified investment partnerships, investment clubs, and publicly traded partnerships are exempt.

[24] Withholding required on nonresident member's share of net income. Not required if nonresident agrees to file return and pay tax. Not applicable to entities taxed federally as corporations and to certain gas proceeds and investment partnerships.

[25] Managing partners required to pay income tax on nonresident partner's share of entity's North Carolina income and are authorized to withhold on nonresident's share. Managing partners not required to pay tax if partner is corporation, partnership, trust, or estate and signs affirmation that it will pay tax.

[26] For tax years beginning after 2005, withholding required at highest individual tax rate unless distributive share of income is less than $1,000, an election is made to pay tax as part of a composite return, or the pass-through entity is a publicly traded partnership. Withholding requirement applies to lower-tier pass-through entities.

[27] Withholding required at 5% of adjusted qualifying amounts over $1,000, unless entity files composite return on behalf of all nonresident individual partners and estates.

[28] Withholding required at 5%, unless nonresident files affidavit agreeing to be subject to personal jurisdiction of Tax Commission or if entity is publicly traded partnership and has agreed to file information return.

[29] Effective for tax years after 2005, withholding required at highest marginal rate for nonresident individuals and corporation rate for nonresident corporations, if distributive income is $1000 or more, nonresident does not participate in composite return or does not agree to file individual return and pay tax.

[30] LLPs with income sources in Pennsylvania must withhold at 3.07% of income allocable to nonresident partners.

[31] Withholding required at corporate tax rate or highest individual tax rate, unless distributive share of income is less than $1,000, partner elects to pay tax as part of composite return, or entity is publicly traded partnership.

[32] LLPs required to withhold at 5% of nonresident's share of LLP's South Carolina income whether distributed or undistributed. Not required if nonresident agrees to be subject to South Carolina personal jurisdiction, if nonresident is included in composite return, or if income is attributable to sale of real property subject to withholding.

[33] Personal income tax applies only to stock and bond income and is not applicable to nonresidents.

[34] Withholding required at 4% of actual and deemed distributions, unless partner is tax exempt or withholding would cause undue hardship.

[35] For taxable years beginning on or after January 1, 2005, withholding required at highest corporate tax rate or highest individual income tax rate for individuals, estates, or trusts, unless distributable share is less than $1,000, nonresident is exempt or has no other income attributable to state sources. Exemptions also available for joint ventures.

Withholding—Partnerships

The following chart indicates whether partnerships are required to withhold on nonresident partner income. A growing number of states require withholding from nonresident partners and some of these states provide exceptions, for, among other items, distributive income that is less than a specified threshold amount, partners included in composite returns, or partners agreeing to comply with state income tax requirements. State specific conditions or limitations placed on the withholding requirement are noted in the footnotes. The chart does not reflect whether nonresident withholding is subject to estimated tax payment requirements.

State	Answer
Alabama	No
Alaska	N/A[1]
Arizona	No
Arkansas	Yes[2]
California	Yes[3]
Colorado	Yes[4]
Connecticut	No[5]
Delaware	No
District of Columbia	No[6]
Florida	N/A[1]
Georgia	Yes[7]
Hawaii	No
Idaho	No[8]
Illinois	No
Indiana	Yes[9]
Iowa	Yes[10]
Kansas	Yes[11]
Kentucky	No[12]
Louisiana	No
Maine	Yes[13]
Maryland	Yes[14]
Massachusetts	No[15]
Michigan	Yes[16]
Minnesota	Yes[17]
Mississippi	No[18]

State	Answer
Missouri	Yes[19]
Montana	Yes[20]
Nebraska	Yes[21]
New Hampshire	N/A[22]
New Jersey	Yes[23]
New Mexico	Yes[24]
New York	No
North Carolina	Yes[25]
North Dakota	Yes[26]
Ohio	Yes[27]
Oklahoma	Yes[28]
Oregon	No[29]
Pennsylvania	Yes[30]
Rhode Island	Yes[31]
South Carolina	Yes[32]
Tennessee	N/A[33]
Texas	N/A[1]
Utah	No
Vermont	No
Virginia	No
West Virginia	Yes[34]
Wisconsin	Yes[35]

[1] No personal income tax.

[2] Withholding required at highest individual income tax rate, unless, among other exceptions, distributive income is less than $1000, the nonresident participates in a composite return, the entity files an agreement by the nonresident to comply with state income tax requirements, or the entity is a publicly held partnership that has agreed to file a return reporting information for each partner with income greater than $500.

[3] Withholding required at 7% on distributions to domestic nonresident partners, unless annual total distributions of income are $1,500 or less, the partner or the income is tax exempt, or the distribution was previously reported on partner's California return. Withholding required at highest individual or corporate tax rate on distributions to foreign (non-U.S.) nonresident partners.

[4] Withholding required at highest marginal individual tax rate, unless partner signs agreement to pay tax or is included in composite return.

[5] Composite payment required if partner is nonresident individual, trust, estate, or pass-through entity that did not elect to be included on group return and whose share of state income is $1,000 or more. After 2005 tax year, composite payment required if partner is nonresident individual, trust, estate, or pass-through entity whose share of state income is $1,000 or more.

[6] Personal income tax not applicable to nonresidents.

[7] Partnerships owning property or doing business in Georgia required to withhold at 4% on distributions paid or credited to nonresident partners attributable to property owned or business done in state. Not required on deemed distributions, or if partnership files composite return on behalf of nonresident partners, if aggregate annual distributions to partner are less than $1,000, if distribution is attributable to return of capital, or if partnership is publicly traded partnership.

[8] Individual partners may elect to have partnership file return and pay income tax at corporate rate. Partnership liable for income tax of partners who do not elect to have partnership file and pay and who fail to file and pay tax individually.

[9] Withholding required on distributive shares of income paid or credited to nonresident partners. Not required if nonresident partner domiciled for entire year in reverse credit state with higher tax rate and Indiana source income is taxed in domiciliary state.

[10] Partnerships required to withhold at 5%, or according to Taxpayer Services schedule, on Iowa source income of nonresident partners unless partner pays estimated tax.

[11] Withholding on distributed or nondistributed taxable income required at maximum individual rate, unless partner provides statement of federally-exempt status or files affidavit agreeing to pay tax.

[12] Withholding required at highest marginal individual rate, unless distributive income is less than $1,000, entity demonstrates share not subject to tax, or entity is publicly traded partnership. For tax years beginning on or after January 1, 2005, limited partnerships taxed in the same manner as C Corporations.

[13] Withholding required at highest tax rate imposed on corporations, individuals, trusts or estates, unless partner's share of annual income is less than $1,000.

[14] Withholding required equal to sum of highest marginal individual tax rate and the lowest county tax rate applied to each nonresident individual partner's distributive share of pass-through income plus corporation income tax rate applied to each nonresident entity partner's distributive share of pass-through income.

[15] Commissioner may require non-employers to withhold on payments made to residents, nonresidents, and part-year residents other than exempt organizations.

[16] Withholding required at personal income tax rate, after deducting personal and dependency exemptions, unless distributive income is exempt or aggregated quarterly income available for distribution to all nonresident partners subject to withholding is less than $1,000.

[17] Withholding required at highest individual tax rate if distributive income from state sources is $1,000 or more and nonresident is not included in composite return. Certain income from entity termination or liquidation, discharge of indebtedness, or sale of property is excluded from withholding requirements.

[18] Individual members liable for tax. Partnership liable if member fails to pay unless partnership withholds 5% of partnership net gain or profit. Commissioner may require withholding on a nonresident partner.

[19] Withholding required at highest individual tax rate on payment to nonresidents of dividends and shares of undistributed taxable income, unless assignable income from partnership is less than $1200, nonresident is included in composite return, or nonresident agrees to file return and pay tax. Amount of withholding tax may be determined based on withholding tables if partner submits withholding allowance certificate.

[20] Withholding required at highest marginal individual tax rate imposed on resident taxpayers, unless nonresident agrees to file return and pay tax or is included in composite return.

[21] Withholding required at highest individual income tax rate, unless member signs agreement to file return and pay tax. For taxable years beginning after January 1, 2005, publicly traded partnerships treated as partnerships for federal income tax purposes that agree to file annual information returns are exempt from withholding requirement.

[22] Personal income tax applies only to interest and dividend income and is not applicable to nonresidents.

[23] Tax must be paid on behalf of nonresident partners with New Jersey-allocated income at rate of 6.37% for nonresident individual partners and 9% for nonresident entity partners. Qualified investment partnerships, investment clubs, and publicly traded partnerships are exempt.

[24] Withholding required on nonresident member's share of net income. Not required if nonresident agrees to file return and pay tax. Not applicable to entities taxed federally as corporations and to certain gas proceeds and investment partnerships.

[25] Managing partners required to pay income tax on nonresident partner's share of entity's North Carolina income and are authorized to withhold on nonresident's share. Managing partners not required to pay tax if partner is corporation, partnership, trust, or estate and signs affirmation that it will pay tax.

[26] For tax years beginning after 2005, withholding required at highest individual tax rate unless distributive share of income is less than $1,000, an election is made to pay tax as part of a composite return, or the pass-through entity is a publicly traded partnership. Withholding requirement applies to lower-tier pass-through entities.

[27] Withholding required at 5% of adjusted qualifying amounts over $1,000, unless entity files composite return on behalf of all nonresident individual partners and estates.

[28] Withholding required at 5%, unless nonresident files affidavit agreeing to be subject to personal jurisdiction of Tax Commission or entity is publicly traded partnership that has agreed to file information return.

[29] Effective for tax years after 2005, withholding required at highest marginal rate for nonresident individuals and corporation rate for nonresident corporations, if distributive income is $1000 or more, nonresident does not participate in composite return or does not agree to file individual return and pay tax.

[30] Partnerships with income sources in Pennsylvania must withhold at 3.07% of income allocable to nonresident partners.

[31] Withholding required at corporate tax rate or highest individual tax rate, unless distributive share of income is less than $1,000, partner elects to pay tax as part of composite return, or entity is publicly traded partnership.

[32] Partnerships required to withhold at 5% of nonresident's share of partnership's South Carolina income whether distributed or undistributed. Not required if nonresident agrees to be subject to South Carolina personal jurisdiction, if nonresident is included in composite return, or if income is attributable to sale of real property subject to withholding.

[33] Personal income tax applies only to stock and bond income and is not applicable to nonresidents.

[34] Withholding required at 4% of actual and deemed distributions, unless partner is tax exempt or withholding would cause undue hardship.

[35] For taxable years beginning on or after January 1, 2005, withholding required at highest corporate tax rate or highest individual income tax rate for individuals, estates, or trusts, unless distributable share is less than $1,000, nonresident is exempt or has no other income attributable to state sources. Exemptions also available for joint ventures.

Withholding—S Corporations

The following chart indicates whether S corporations are required to withhold on nonresident shareholder income. A growing number of states require withholding from nonresident shareholders and some of these states provide exceptions, for, among other items, distributive income that is less than a specified threshold amount, shareholders included in composite returns, or shareholders agreeing to comply with state income tax requirements. State specific conditions or limitations placed on the withholding requirement are noted in the footnotes. The chart does not reflect whether nonresident withholding is subject to estimated tax payment requirements.

State	Answer
Alabama	No
Alaska	N/A[1]
Arizona	No
Arkansas	Yes[2]
California	No[3]
Colorado	Yes[4]
Connecticut	No[5]
Delaware	No
District of Columbia	No[6]
Florida	N/A[1]
Georgia	Yes[7]
Hawaii	No[8]
Idaho	No[9]
Illinois	No
Indiana	Yes[10]
Iowa	Yes[11]
Kansas	Yes[12]
Kentucky	No[13]
Louisiana	N/A[14]
Maine	Yes[15]
Maryland	Yes[16]
Massachusetts	No[17]
Michigan	Yes[18]
Minnesota	Yes[19]
Mississippi	No[20]

State	Answer
Missouri	Yes[21]
Montana	Yes[22]
Nebraska	Yes[23]
New Hampshire	N/A[24]
New Jersey	No[25]
New Mexico	Yes[26]
New York	No
North Carolina	No[27]
North Dakota	Yes[28]
Ohio	Yes[29]
Oklahoma	Yes[30]
Oregon	No[31]
Pennsylvania	Yes[32]
Rhode Island	Yes[33]
South Carolina	Yes[34]
Tennessee	N/A[35]
Texas	N/A[1]
Utah	Yes[36]
Vermont	No
Virginia	No
West Virginia	Yes[37]
Wisconsin	Yes[38]

---

[1] No personal income tax.

[2] Withholding required at highest individual income tax rate, unless, among other exceptions, distributive income is less than $1000, the nonresident participates in a composite return, or entity files an agreement by the nonresident to comply with state income tax requirements.

[3] Although the Franchise Tax Board is authorized by law to require withholding on distributive income of nonresident shareholders, the FTB does not currently require it.

[4] Withholding required at highest marginal individual tax rate, unless shareholder signs agreement to pay tax or is included in composite return.

[5] Composite payment required if shareholder is nonresident individual, trust, or estate that did not elect to be included on group return and whose share of state income is $1,000 or more. After 2005 tax year, composite payment required if shareholder is nonresident individual, trust, estate, or pass-through entity whose share of state income is $1,000 or more.

[6] Personal income tax not applicable to nonresidents.

[7] S Corporations owning property or doing business in Georgia required to withhold at 4% on distributions paid or credited to nonresident shareholders attributable to property owned or business done in state. Not required on deemed distributions, or if S Corporations files composite return on behalf of nonresident shareholders, if aggregate annual distributions to shareholders are less than $1,000, if distribution is attributable to return of capital, or if federal S Corporation fails to meet state requirements and is taxed as C.

[8] Withholding from nonresident shareholders required at 8.25%, unless shareholder has provided an agreement to file a return and pay tax.

[9] Individual S Corporation shareholders may elect to have S Corporation file return and pay income tax at corporate rate. S Corporation liable for income tax of shareholders who do not elect to have S Corporation file and pay and who fail to file and pay tax individually.

[10] Withholding required on payment to nonresidents of dividends and shares of undistributed taxable income. Not required when nonresidents shareholder domiciled for entire year in reverse credit state with higher tax rate and Indiana source income is taxed in domiciliary state.

[11] S Corporations required to withhold at 5%, or according to Taxpayer Services schedule, on Iowa source income of nonresident shareholders unless shareholder pays estimated tax.

[12] Withholding on distributed or nondistributed taxable income required at maximum individual rate, unless shareholder provides statement of federally-exempt status or files affidavit agreeing to pay tax.

[13] For tax years beginning on or after January 1, 2004 and before January 1, 2005, withholding on nonresident income required. For tax years beginning on or after January 1, 2005, S Corporations taxed in same manner as C Corporations.

[14] Louisiana does not recognize S Corporation status.

[15] Withholding required at highest tax rate imposed on corporations, individuals, trusts or estates, unless shareholder's share of annual income is less than $1,000.

[16] Withholding required equal to sum of highest marginal individual tax rate and the lowest county tax rate applied to each nonresident individual shareholder's distributive share of pass-through income plus corporation income tax rate applied to each nonresident entity shareholder's distributive share of pass-through income.

[17] Commissioner may require non-employers to withhold on payments made to residents, nonresidents, and part-year residents other than exempt organizations.

[18] Withholding required at personal income tax rate, after deducting personal and dependency exemptions, unless distributive income is exempt or aggregated quarterly income available for distribution to all nonresident shareholders subject to withholding is less than $1,000.

[19] Withholding required at highest individual tax rate if distributive income from state sources is $1,000 or more and nonresident is not included in composite return. Certain income from entity termination or liquidation, discharge of indebtedness, or sale of property is excluded from withholding requirements.

[20] Nonresident shareholders required to sign agreement to file return and pay tax. If shareholder fails to agree or to file return and pay tax, S Corporation required to pay tax on shareholder's pro rata share of S Corporation Mississippi income at highest individual rate.

[21] Withholding required at highest individual tax rate on payment to nonresidents of dividends and shares of undistributed taxable income, unless assignable income from S corporation is less than $1200, nonresident is included in composite return, or nonresident agrees to file return and pay tax. Amount of withholding tax may be determined based on withholding tables if shareholder submits withholding allowance certificate.

[22] Withholding required at highest marginal individual tax rate imposed on resident taxpayers, unless nonresident agrees to file return and pay tax or is included in composite return.

[23] Withholding required at highest individual income tax rate, unless member signs agreement to file return and pay tax.

[24] Personal income tax applies only to interest and dividend income and is not applicable to nonresidents.

[25] Withholding required at highest marginal gross income tax rate if nonresident fails to consent to New Jersey S Corporation election. Tax may be collected from corporation, if nonconsenting shareholder objects to withholding.

[26] Withholding required on nonresident shareholder's share of net income. Not required if nonresident agrees to file return and pay tax. Not applicable to oil and gas proceeds subject to the Oil and Gas Proceeds Withholding Tax Act.

[27] S Corporations required to file nonresident shareholder agreements to file return and pay tax. If agreement not filed, S Corporation required to pay tax on shareholder's pro rata share of S Corporation North Carolina income.

[28] For tax years beginning after 2005, withholding required at highest individual tax rate, unless distributive share of income is less than $1,000 or an election is made to pay tax as part of a composite return. Withholding requirement applies to lower-tier pass-through entities.

[29] Withholding required at 5% of adjusted qualifying amounts over $1,000, unless entity files composite return on behalf of all nonresident individuals and estates.

[30] Withholding required at 5%, unless nonresident files affidavit agreeing to be subject to personal jurisdiction of Tax Commission.

[31] Effective for tax years after 2005, withholding required at highest marginal rate for nonresident individuals and corporation rate for nonresident corporations, if distributive income is $1000 or more, nonresident does not participate in composite return or does not agree to file individual return and pay tax.

[32] Pennsylvania S corporations with income sources in Pennsylvania must withhold at 3.07% of income allocable to nonresident shareholders.

[33] Withholding required at corporate tax rate or highest individual tax rate, unless distributive share of income is less than $1,000 or shareholder elects to pay tax as part of composite return. Withholding requirements apply to lower-tier pass through entities.

[34] S Corporations required to withhold at 5% of nonresident's share of S Corporation's South Carolina income whether distributed or undistributed. Not required if nonresident agrees to be subject to South Carolina personal jurisdiction, if nonresident is included in composite return, or if income is attributable to sale of real property subject to withholding.

[35] S corporations taxed in same manner as C corporations.

[36] Withholding required at applicable corporate and individual tax rates, unless entity is exempt.

[37] Withholding required at 4% of actual and deemed distributions of West Virginia source income to nonresident shareholders. Option of filing composite return annually for one or more nonresidents and paying tax due with return.

[38] For taxable years beginning on or after January 1, 2005, withholding required at highest corporate tax rate or highest individual income tax rate for individuals, estates, or trusts, unless distributable share is less than $1,000, nonresident is exempt or has no other income attributable to state sources. Exemptions also available for joint ventures.

SALES AND USE TAXES

The following pages contain charts summarizing facets of sales and use taxes imposed by the states. The charts include not only states with sales and use taxes, but also those imposing transaction privilege or gross receipts taxes. Alaska, Delaware, Montana, New Hampshire, and Oregon do not impose a general, statewide sales and use tax.

Topics covered include state rates, the tax basis (including the components), exempt transactions (arranged by topic), statutes of limitations, validity periods for exemption and resale certificates, taxpayer remedies, and collection discounts.

Sales and Use Tax Table of Rates

State tax rates generally applicable to the retail sale of tangible personal property are listed below. Special rates may apply to specific categories of tangible personal property, and are not noted in this chart. Most states also authorize local jurisdictions to adopt sales and use taxes in addition to the state tax set forth below.

The following states do not impose a general sales and use tax: Alaska, Delaware, Montana, New Hampshire, and Oregon. Delaware imposes a merchants' and manufacturers' license tax and a use tax on leases.

	Sales	Use		Sales	Use
Alabama	4%	4%	Rhode Island[1]	7%	7%
Arizona	5.6%	5.6%	South Carolina	5%[8]	5%[8]
Arkansas	6%	6%	South Dakota	4%	4%
California	6.25%	6.25%	Tennessee	7%	7%
Colorado	2.9%	2.9%	Texas	6.25%	6.25%
Connecticut[1]	6%	6%	Utah	4.75%	4.75%
District of Columbia[1]	5.75%	5.75%	Vermont	6%	6%
Florida	6%	6%	Virginia	4%	4%
Georgia	4%	4%	Washington	6.5%	6.5%
Hawaii	4%[2]	4%[2]	West Virginia[1]	6%	6%
Idaho	6%[3]	6%[3]	Wisconsin	5%	5%
Illinois	6.25%	6.25%	Wyoming	4%	4%
Indiana[1]	6%	6%			
Iowa	5%	5%			
Kansas	5.3%	5.3%			
Kentucky	6%	6%			
Louisiana	4%	4%			
Maine[1]	5%	5%			
Maryland[1]	5%	5%			
Massachusetts[1]	5%	5%			
Michigan[1]	6%	6%			
Minnesota	6.5%	6.5%			
Mississippi[1]	7%	7%			
Missouri	4.225%	4.225%[4]			
Nebraska	5.5%	5.5%			
Nevada	6.5%[5]	6.5%[5]			
New Jersey[1]	7%[6]	7%[6]			
New Mexico	5%	5%			
New York	4%	4%			
North Carolina	4.5%[7]	4.5%[7]			
North Dakota	5%	5%			
Ohio	5.5%	5.5%			
Oklahoma	4.5%	4.5%			
Pennsylvania	6%	6%			

[1] Local general sales/use taxes not authorized or imposed. (Local governments may be authorized, however, to levy miscellaneous local taxes on specific types of transactions.)
[2] Hawaii: Rate for wholesalers/manufacturers is 0.5%.
[3] Idaho: State rate increased from 5% to 6% effective October 1, 2006.
[4] Missouri: Rate reduced to 4.125% on November 8, 2008. Total rate of 4.225% consists of general sales/use tax of 4%, additional sales tax of 0.10% for soil/water conservation and state parks (expires 11/8/08), and additional sales tax of 0.125% for wildlife conservation.
[5] Nevada: Tax rate consists of a 2% state rate under the general Sales and Use Tax Act, a 2.25% state rate under the Local School Support Tax Law, and a 2.25% state-mandated local rate under the City-County Relief Tax Law.
[6] New Jersey: State rate increased from 6% to 7% effective July 15, 2006.
[7] North Carolina: Rate is lowered to 4.25% on December 1, 2006, and to 4% on July 1, 2007.
[8] South Carolina: Effective June 1, 2007, rate increases from 5% to 6% (except on accommodations and grocery food).

Agricultural Exemptions

The following chart details the taxability of sales to farmers and ranchers for use in the commercial production of food and commodities.

In the majority of states, feed, seed, and fertilizer sold for use in commercial agriculture are not taxable. Such sales are considered to be made for resale because their product is ultimately destined to be sold at retail, at which time the tax will be payable.

For purposes of this chart, "T" stands for taxable and "E" for exempt; but the designations are of a general nature, and exceptions unnoted in the chart may exist.

States that do not impose a sales and use tax are not included in this chart.

State	Insecticides and Pesticides	Fertilizer, Seed and Feed	Seedlings, Plants and Shoots
Alabama	E	E	E
Arizona	T	E[1]	E
Arkansas	E	E	E
California	T	E	E
Colorado	E[2]	E	E
Connecticut	E	E	E
District of Columbia	T	T	T
Florida	E	E	E
Georgia	E	E	E
Hawaii	T[3]	T[3]	T[3]
Idaho	E	E	E
Illinois	E	E	E
Indiana	E	E	E
Iowa	E	E	E
Kansas	E	E	E
Kentucky	E	E	E
Louisiana	E	E	E
Maine	E	E	E
Maryland	E	E	E
Massachusetts	E	E	E
Michigan	E	E	E
Minnesota	E	E	E
Mississippi	E	E	E

State	Insecticides and Pesticides	Fertilizer, Seed and Feed	Seedlings, Plants and Shoots
Missouri	E	E	E
Nebraska	E	E[4]	E
Nevada	E[5]	E[5]	E
New Jersey	E	E	E
New Mexico	E	E	E
New York	E	E	E
North Carolina	E	E	E
North Dakota	E	E	E
Ohio	E	E	E
Oklahoma	E	E	E
Pennsylvania	E	E	E
Rhode Island	E	E	E
South Carolina	E	E	E
South Dakota	E	E[6]	E
Tennessee	E	E	E
Texas	E	E	E
Utah	E	E	E
Vermont	E	E	E
Virginia	E	E	E
Washington	E	E	E
West Virginia	E	E	E
Wisconsin	E	E	E
Wyoming	E	E	E

[1] Exemption allowed for seed and feed.
[2] Pesticides for production of agricultural and livestock products are exempt. Fungicides, germicides and herbicides are taxable.
[3] Taxed at reduced "wholesale" rate.
[4] Fee imposed on commercial fertilizers.
[5] Fertilizer used for nonfood crops is taxable, as well as fertilizer mixed with insecticides and herbicides if proportions cannot be determined.
[6] Exemption applies if 500 pounds of fertilizer are purchased in a single sale. Exemption applies to seed if 25 pounds or more of seed are purchased in a single sale for use exclusively for agricultural purposes.

Clothing

While many states tax all sales of clothing, some states exempt specific types (*e.g.*, children's clothes or worker safety apparel), and a few states exempt most items of clothing. The chart below sets forth the exemptions available, if any, in each state.

Several states have instituted "sales tax holidays" (intended to offset the cost of back-to-school purchases), which provide a limited exemption for clothing sales during a specified period in August. Sales tax holidays typically last for one week and are restricted to items priced under a certain amount. Sales tax holidays are covered in a separate chart.

States that do not impose a general sales and use tax are not included in this chart.

State	Taxability of Clothing
Alabama	Taxable
Arizona	Taxable
Arkansas	Taxable
California	Exemptions allowed for (1) new children's clothing sold to a nonprofit organization for its distribution without charge to elementary school children and (2) used clothing sold by certain thrift stores benefiting the chronically ill.
Colorado	Taxable
Connecticut	Clothing and footwear costing less than $50 are exempt (protective or athletic items and accessories not included). Employee safety apparel and bicycle helmets are exempt.
District of Columbia	Taxable
Florida	Taxable
Georgia	Taxable
Hawaii	Taxable
Idaho	Taxable, except purchases of clothes and footwear by nonsale clothiers that provide free clothes to the needy.
Illinois	Taxable
Indiana	Taxable
Iowa	Taxable
Kansas	Taxable
Kentucky	Taxable
Louisiana	Taxable
Maine	Taxable
Maryland	Taxable

State	Taxability of Clothing
Massachusetts	An exemption is provided for up to $175 of the sales price of any article of clothing or footwear, unless designed for athletic activity or protective use.
Michigan	Taxable
Minnesota	Sales of clothing and wearing apparel (excluding jewelry, fur, perfumes, sporting and recreational articles) are exempt. Certain safety and protective articles are also exempt.
Mississippi	Taxable. Clothing, shoes, jewelry, and accessories used as wardrobes in production of motion pictures exempt.
Missouri	Taxable
Nebraska	Taxable
Nevada	Taxable
New Jersey	Clothing and footwear are generally exempt. Accessories and athletic goods/equipment are taxable. Effective July 15, 2006, fur clothing is taxable. Protective equipment is only exempt when purchased for the daily work of the user and worn as part of a work uniform or work clothing.
New Mexico	Taxable
New York	A temporary exemption period for clothing, footwear, and items used to make or repair clothing or footwear, costing less than $110 per item was authorized beginning January 30 and ending February 5, 2006. Beginning April 1, 2006, there is a year-round exemption from state sales and use tax for such items. A year-round exemption from New York City sales and use tax took effect for such items beginning on September 1, 2005.
North Carolina	Taxable. Separately stated alteration charges in connection with the sale of clothing are exempt.
North Dakota	Taxable
Ohio	Taxable (narrow exemption for protective clothing used exclusively in a regulated manufacturing area).
Oklahoma	Taxable
Pennsylvania	Generally exempt. Accessories, fur articles, ornamental and formal wear, and sports clothing are taxable.
Rhode Island	Generally exempt, unless designed primarily for athletic activity or protective use.
South Carolina	Taxable
South Dakota	Taxable
Tennessee	Taxable, except for used clothing sold by certain nonprofit organizations.
Texas	Taxable
Utah	Taxable
Vermont	Clothing and footwear costing $110 or less and specially protective steel or Kevlar-toed footwear are exempt. Accessories and items designed primarily for athletic activity or protective use are taxable.

State	Taxability of Clothing
Virginia	Taxable
Washington	Taxable. The exemption for wearing apparel used as a sample for display was repealed, effective July 1, 2006.
West Virginia	Taxable
Wisconsin	Taxable, unless the clothing is used for an exempt purpose. Cloth diapers used for sanitary purposes are expressly exempt.
Wyoming	Taxable

Collection Discounts Allowed Seller

A number of states have enacted provisions that allow the seller reimbursement in one form or another for expenses incurred in acting as the collecting agent and remitting sales tax before it becomes delinquent.

For taxpayers that have multiple business locations in a state, the chart below reflects whether a single discount is allowed for all locations combined or whether each location qualifies for a discount.

Those states that do not impose sales and use taxes are not included in this chart.

State	Discount Amount	Multiple Locations
Alabama	5% of first $100 of tax due and 2% of excess; $400 maximum per month; no discount for rental tax.	Single discount
Arizona	Credit allowed equal to 1% of tax due, not to exceed $10,000 per calendar year.	Single discount
Arkansas	Lesser of $1,000 or 2% of amount of tax due per month.	Single discount
California	None	N/A
Colorado	3.33% of tax due (2.33% for sales made from 7/1/03 through 6/30/05). No deduction of a vendor's fee is allowed for vending machine sales.	(*)
Connecticut	None	N/A
District of Columbia	None	N/A
Florida	2.5% of the first $1,200 of tax due. Dealers in mail-order sales may be allowed up to 10% of the tax remitted. No discount for rental car surcharge.	Each registered location
Georgia	3% of the first $3,000 and 0.5% of excess; 3% of sales taxes on motor fuels; 0.5% for second motor fuel tax.	Each registered location
Hawaii	None	N/A
Idaho	None	N/A
Illinois	1.75% of tax due, or $5 per calendar year, whichever is greater. Same discount for service occupation (and use) tax.	(*)
Indiana	Retail merchants allowed a collection allowance of 0.83%. Certain utilities not entitled to allowance.	(*)
Iowa	None	N/A
Kansas	None	N/A
Kentucky	1.75% of first $1,000 of tax due and 1% of excess; maximum of $1,500 per month.	(*)
Louisiana	1.1% of tax due.	(*)

State	Discount Amount	Multiple Locations
Maine	None. However, retailers are allowed to retain "breakage" as compensation for collection of tax. Under the bracket system, when the tax due in a sales tax return is less than the actual tax collected from customers, the excess collected is "breakage".	N/A
Maryland	Credit equal to 1.2% of first $6,000 of tax due and 0.9% of excess. Credit does not apply to any sales and use tax that a vendor is required to pay for any taxable purchase or use made by the vendor.	Single discount
Massachusetts	None	N/A
Michigan	Vendor may deduct greater of (1) for payments made before the 12th day of the month, 0.75% of tax due at a rate of 4% for the preceding month (maximum $20,000 of tax due); for payments made between the 12th and the 20th, 0.5% of the tax due at a rate of 4% for the preceding month (maximum $15,000 of tax due); or (2) the tax collected at a rate of 4% on $150 of taxable purchase price for prior month.	(*)
Minnesota	None	N/A
Mississippi	2% of tax due, but not to exceed $50 per reporting period or $600 per calendar year. Not applicable to taxes on contracting, cotton ginning, or public utilities, or to collections by government agencies, or to certain wholesale taxes.	Each business location
Missouri	2% of total tax due	(*)
Nebraska	2.5% of first $3,000 remitted each month.	Each sales location
Nevada	0.5% of sales tax due.	(*)
New Jersey	None	N/A
New Mexico	None	N/A
New York	Credit equal to 3.5% of the state sales tax remitted with a return for a quarterly or longer period, but not to exceed $150 per return period.	(*)
North Carolina	None	N/A
North Dakota	1.5% of tax due; $85 monthly maximum.	Each business location
Ohio	0.9% of tax due (0.75%, effective 7/1/07).	(*)
Oklahoma	1.25% of tax due (2.25% for participants in electronic filing/payment program), up to $3,300 per month. Deduction not allowed with respect to a direct payment permit.	Each permit
Pennsylvania	1% of tax due.	(*)

State	Discount Amount	Multiple Locations
Rhode Island	None	N/A
South Carolina	2% of tax due; maximum discount of $3,000 per state fiscal year ($3,100 for electronic filers and $10,000 for out-of-state taxpayers filing voluntarily). If total tax liability is less than $100, discount is 3%.	(*)
South Dakota	Effective July 1 following the date when $10 million is accumulated in the tax relief fund created from additional revenue received by the state from sellers that voluntary register to collect under the Streamlined Sales and Use Tax (SST) Agreement, monthly filers are allowed a credit of 1.5% of the gross amount of tax due, as compensation for the cost of collection. Credit may not exceed $70 per month.	(*)
Tennessee	2% of the first $2,500 due on each report and 1.15% of excess. Only available to out-of-state vendors who are not required to register, but register voluntarily.	(*)
Texas	0.5% of tax due plus 1.25% of the amount of any prepaid tax. Discounts for timely filing do not apply to holders of direct pay permits.	(*)
Utah	Vendors paying monthly may retain up to 1.31% of state tax and 1% of local, public transit, and municipal energy sales and use tax. Effective July 1, 2007, monthly filers who remit the 2.75% tax collected on sales of food and food ingredients may retain an amount equal to the sum of (1) 1.31% of the amount the seller is required to remit under the provision imposing a 2.75% tax on food and food ingredients and (2) 1.31% of the difference between the amounts the seller would have remitted under the provision imposing a general 4.75% tax and the amounts the seller must remit under the provision imposing a 2.75% tax on food and food ingredients.	(*)
Vermont	Retailers may retain any amount lawfully collected under the prescribed bracket system that is in excess of the amount of tax due.	(*)
Virginia	Dealer allowed discount at the following percentages, depending on volume of total taxable sales, of the first 3% of the tax due for a given period: 3% (4% food tax) if monthly taxable sales are less than $62,501; 2.25% (3% food tax) if $62,501 to $208,000; 1.5% (2% food tax) if over $208,000. Dealer discount factors above apply for returns filed for sales on and after 7/1/05.	Single discount
Washington	None	N/A
West Virginia	None	N/A

State	Discount Amount	Multiple Locations
Wisconsin	0.5% of the tax payable on retail sales or $10, whichever is greater, not to exceed tax liability.	(*)
Wyoming	None	N/A

* Statutes/regulations do not address the issue

Components of Basis

The following chart sets forth common items that may or may not be included in basis, or may actually reduce the basis on which the sales tax is paid. When to include payments made over time and when to deduct payments on returned items are also included. The treatment of trade-ins and delivery charges is discussed in separate charts.

ALABAMA

Bad Debt Deduction . . . . allowed as refund or credit

Coupons, Cash Discounts . . . . cash discounts, retailers coupons not included; manufacturers coupons included

Installation Charges . . . . included unless separately stated

Federal, State, Local Excise Taxes . . . . included, except for federal taxes retailers must collect from consumers, certain separately stated state taxes on alcoholic beverages, and municipal privilege tax

Installment, Lay-Away, Conditional Sales . . . . . credit sales—payments reported as received; lay-away sales—payments taxable at transfer of title

Finance Charges . . . . included unless separately stated

Returned Goods, Repossessions . . . . returned goods—deductible, if full sales price refunded; deduction allowed for unpaid purchase price of repossessed property

ARIZONA

Bad Debt Deduction . . . . allowed

Coupons, Cash Discounts . . . . cash discounts, retailers coupons not included; manufacturers coupons included

Installation Charges . . . . included unless separately stated

Federal, State, Local Excise Taxes . . . . included except for federal retail excise tax on autos, heavy trucks, and fuel

Installment, Lay-Away, Conditional Sales . . . . . conditional and credit sales—payments reported when received; lay-away payments—taxable at transfer of title or when transaction nonrefundable

Finance Charges . . . . included unless separately stated

Returned Goods, Repossessions . . . . returns not included in gross receipts; no specific provisions on repossessions

ARKANSAS

Bad Debt Deduction . . . . allowed

Coupons, Cash Discounts . . . . cash discounts, retailers coupons, membership discounts not included; manufacturers coupons, motor vehicle rebates included

Installation Charges . . . . included unless separately stated

Federal, State, Local Excise Taxes . . . . separately stated manufacturers federal excise tax not included; federal luxury excise tax, import tariff or duty included

Installment, Lay-Away, Conditional Sales . . . . . no specific provisions

Finance Charges . . . . no specific provisions

Returned Goods, Repossessions . . . . returned goods—deductible, if full purchase price and tax were returned to customer; deduction not allowed for property that has been repossessed or voluntarily returned without a full refund

CALIFORNIA

Bad Debt Deduction	allowed
Coupons, Cash Discounts	cash discounts not included
Installation Charges	not included
Federal, State, Local Excise Taxes	federal excise taxes on retail sales, local rapid transit district sales and use taxes, state motor vehicle fees and taxes that are added to or measured by a vehicle's price, and diesel fuel excise tax not included; federal manufacturers and importers excise taxes on gasoline, diesel, or jet fuel for which the purchaser is entitled to a direct income tax credit or refund also not included; import duties not included if the importer of record is a consignee and the consignee is the buyer; state motor vehicle fuel license taxes included; other manufacturers and importers excise taxes included
Installment, Lay-Away, Conditional Sales	credit and installment sales—payment reported when sale made; lay-away sales—payments taxable at transfer of title
Finance Charges	included unless separately stated
Returned Goods, Repossessions	returns - deductible, if the purchaser receives a full refund of the sales price including tax, and the purchaser is not required to purchase other property at a price greater than the returned merchandise in order to obtain a refund or credit; repossessions - deductible if the entire amount paid by the purchaser is refunded, or if a credit for a worthless account is allowable

COLORADO

Bad Debt Deduction	allowed
Coupons, Cash Discounts	discounts, retailers coupons, rebates, credits not included; manufacturers coupons, early payment discounts included
Installation Charges	included unless separately stated
Federal, State, Local Excise Taxes	direct federal taxes and state sales and use taxes not included; indirect federal manufacturers taxes included
Installment, Lay-Away, Conditional Sales	for payments made over a period longer than 60 days, reported when received
Finance Charges	included unless separately stated
Returned Goods, Repossessions	returned goods—deductible, if full sale price and tax refunded; deduction allowed for uncollected sale price of repossessed property

CONNECTICUT

Bad Debt Deduction	allowed as credit
Coupons, Cash Discounts	cash discounts and manufacturers and retailers coupons not included; rebate amounts included
Installation Charges	included unless separately stated
Federal, State, Local Excise Taxes	federal taxes imposed on retail sales, state cabaret tax not included; federal manufacturers or importers excise taxes and all taxes imposed on a basis other than the proceeds from retail sales included

Installment, Lay-Away, Conditional Sales . . . . . total sales price reported at time of sale
Finance Charges . . . . interest paid included
Returned Goods, Repossessions . . . . returns not included in gross receipts, if property is returned within 90 days from the purchase date; no specific provisions on repossessions

DISTRICT OF COLUMBIA

Bad Debt Deduction . . . . allowed
Coupons, Cash Discounts . . . . cash discounts at time of sale, trade discounts, and quantity discounts at time of sale not included
Installation Charges . . . . included unless separately stated and the property was not installed as a repair or replacement part
Federal, State, Local Excise Taxes . . . . federal retailers excise tax not included if separately stated
Installment, Lay-Away, Conditional Sales . . . . . total sales price reported at time of sale
Finance Charges . . . . included unless separately stated
Returned Goods, Repossessions . . . . returned goods—refund allowed if property returned within 90 days of sale and full purchase price including tax is refunded to purchaser; no deduction or refund allowed for repossessed property

FLORIDA

Bad Debt Deduction . . . . allowed as credit or refund if claimed within 12 months following month in which the bad debt was charged off a federal return
Coupons, Cash Discounts . . . . cash discounts at time of sale, retailers coupons not included; manufacturers coupons included
Installation Charges . . . . included
Federal, State, Local Excise Taxes . . . . separately stated federal retailers excise taxes, separately stated municipal public service taxes, separately stated motor vehicle warranty fee not included; federal manufacturers excise tax, municipal utility fees, state tire and battery fees, rental car surcharge included, state utility gross receipts tax included if the cost is separately itemized and passed on to customers; other taxes included
Installment, Lay-Away, Conditional Sales . . . . . total sales price reported at time of sale
Finance Charges . . . . included unless separately stated
Returned Goods, Repossessions . . . . returned goods—deductible if tax has not been remitted, credit allowed if tax has been remitted; deduction allowed for unpaid balance of repossessed property

GEORGIA

Bad Debt Deduction . . . . allowed if accrual method of accounting used
Coupons, Cash Discounts . . . . cash discounts not included
Installation Charges . . . . included unless separately stated
Federal, State, Local Excise Taxes . . . . separately stated federal retailers excise tax and state motor fuel and cigarette excise tax not included; federal excise taxes on cigarettes, fuel, tires, tubes and accessories included
Installment, Lay-Away, Conditional Sales . . . . . no specific provisions
Finance Charges . . . . not included

Returned Goods, Repossessions . . . . returns - deductible, if property is returned within 90 days from the sale date, and the entire sales price is refunded to the purchaser; after 90 days must apply for credit; repossessions – no specific provisions

HAWAII

Bad Debt Deduction . . . . allowed

Coupons, Cash Discounts . . . . cash discounts not included

Installation Charges . . . . included

Federal, State, Local Excise Taxes . . . . state tobacco excise and nursing home facility taxes, federal fuel, retail, excise, sugar, and luxury taxes not included

Installment, Lay-Away, Conditional Sales . . . . . no specific provisions

Finance Charges . . . . included

Returned Goods, Repossessions . . . . returns - amount refunded not included in gross proceeds; repossessions – no specific provisions

IDAHO

Bad Debt Deduction . . . . allowed as credit or refund

Coupons, Cash Discounts . . . . retailer discounts (to the extent they represent price adjustments), trade discounts, discounts offered as inducement to continue telecommunications services, retailers coupons, retailers rebates, and manufacturers rebates on motor vehicle sales not included; manufacturers coupons, manufacturers rebates (other than motor vehicle rebates), cash discounts offered as inducements for prompt payment included

Installation Charges . . . . included unless separately stated

Federal, State, Local Excise Taxes . . . . federal manufacturers and importers excise taxes included; federal taxes on retail sales not included

Installment, Lay-Away, Conditional Sales . . . . . total sales price reported at time of sale; lay-away sales taxable at transfer of title

Finance Charges . . . . not included

Returned Goods, Repossessions . . . . returns - deductible, if the sale price is refunded, and the purchaser is not required to purchase other merchandise at a greater price; repossessions – bad debt adjustment allowed for property repossessed and seasonably resold

ILLINOIS

Bad Debt Deduction . . . . allowed as deduction or credit

Coupons, Cash Discounts . . . . ROT, SOT: discounts, retailers coupons not included; reimbursed coupons included

Installation Charges . . . . included unless separately contracted

Federal, State, Local Excise Taxes . . . . ROT: federal taxes collected from customer, federal excise taxes on retail sales, state motor fuel tax, state tire fee not included; federal excise taxes on manufacture, import taxes, tax on non-retail sale, state liquor tax, cigarette tax included

Installment, Lay-Away, Conditional Sales . . . . . payments reported when received

Finance Charges . . . . not included in ROT or UT basis

Returned Goods, Repossessions	returned goods—deductible, if amount charged including tax is refunded to purchaser; credit allowed for uncollected portion of sale price of repossessed property

INDIANA

Bad Debt Deduction	allowed
Coupons, Cash Discounts	cash and term discounts, retailers coupons not included; manufacturers coupons included
Installation Charges	included unless separately stated
Federal, State, Local Excise Taxes	federal or state taxes collected as agent, federal retailers tax if imposed solely on sale of personal property and collected by a merchant as a separate item in addition to the price, manufacturers excise tax, and federal and state fuel tax not included
Installment, Lay-Away, Conditional Sales	no specific provisions
Finance Charges	included unless separately stated
Returned Goods, Repossessions	no specific provisions

IOWA

Bad Debt Deduction	allowed
Coupons, Cash Discounts	discounts, retail coupons, motor vehicle rebates to purchaser not included; manufacturers coupons included
Installation Charges	included unless separately contracted
Federal, State, Local Excise Taxes	taxes imposed on sales subject to Iowa sales and use tax, federal excise tax on first retail sale of a vehicle not included, federal excise tax on communication services of local and toll telephone and teletypewriter exchange services not included; federal excise taxes on alcohol, tobacco, fuel, and tires, and state cigarette tax included
Installment, Lay-Away, Conditional Sales	total payment reported at time of delivery
Finance Charges	included unless separately stated
Returned Goods, Repossessions	returned goods—amount refunded not included in gross receipts; seller may claim bad debt credit for repossessed merchandise

KANSAS

Bad Debt Deduction	allowed
Coupons, Cash Discounts	discounts at time of sale, retailers coupons not included; manufacturers coupons included
Installation Charges	included; certain installation services related to construction are excluded
Federal, State, Local Excise Taxes	federal manufacturers excise tax included; state excise taxes not specifically excluded
Installment, Lay-Away, Conditional Sales	payment reported when received or, for accrual accounting, at time of sale
Finance Charges	included unless separately stated
Returned Goods, Repossessions	returned goods—amount refunded to customer deductible from gross receipts; deduction allowed for repossessed property if retailer's records are kept on accrual basis so that total selling price of property was previously reported

KENTUCKY

Bad Debt Deduction . . . . allowed if accrual method of accounting used

Coupons, Cash Discounts . . . . cash discounts, retailers coupons not included; reimbursed coupons included

Installation Charges . . . . included unless separately stated

Federal, State, Local Excise Taxes . . . . federal tax on retail sale not included; federal excise tax on retailer, manufacturer, or importer included

Installment, Lay-Away, Conditional Sales . . . . . cash basis retailers—payments reported when received; if accrual basis—payments reported at time of sale

Finance Charges . . . . included unless separately stated

Returned Goods, Repossessions . . . . returned goods—amount refunded not included in gross receipts; deduction allowed for unpaid balance of repossessed property, if full sales price had been previously included in retailer's receipts and the tax paid

LOUISIANA

Bad Debt Deduction . . . . allowed as refund

Coupons, Cash Discounts . . . . cash discounts, retailers coupons, motor vehicle rebates offered as price reductions not included; manufacturers coupons included

Installation Charges . . . . included unless separately stated

Federal, State, Local Excise Taxes . . . . excise taxes included

Installment, Lay-Away, Conditional Sales . . . . . payments reported at time of sale

Finance Charges . . . . not included

Returned Goods, Repossessions . . . . returned goods—deductible before tax has been remitted, refund allowed after tax has been remitted; no deduction or refund allowed for repossessed property

MAINE

Bad Debt Deduction . . . . allowed as credit

Coupons, Cash Discounts . . . . discounts, retailers coupons not included; manufacturers coupons, manufacturers rebates included

Installation Charges . . . . included unless separately stated

Federal, State, Local Excise Taxes . . . . federal tax on retail sales not included; federal manufacturers, importers, alcohol, and tobacco excise taxes included

Installment, Lay-Away, Conditional Sales . . . . . payments reported at time of sale

Finance Charges . . . . included unless separately stated

Returned Goods, Repossessions . . . . returns - deductible, if full sale price is refunded; repossessions – a deduction is not allowed for repossessed property unless the retailer incurs a loss, based on either the fair market value of the property or the resale price

MARYLAND

Bad Debt Deduction	allowed as credit or refund
Coupons, Cash Discounts	discounts at time of sale and retailers coupons not included; early payment discounts, reimbursed coupons included
Installation Charges	included unless separately stated
Federal, State, Local Excise Taxes	consumer excise taxes imposed directly on buyer, certain county utility taxes, and certain taxes imposed on leased property not included if separately stated
Installment, Lay-Away, Conditional Sales	payments reported at time of sale
Finance Charges	included unless separately stated
Returned Goods, Repossessions	returned goods—deductible; credit allowed for repossessed property (amount is difference between tax on unpaid balance and tax on value of item at time of repossession)

MASSACHUSETTS

Bad Debt Deduction	allowed as refund
Coupons, Cash Discounts	cash discounts at time of sale, trade discounts, manufacturers and retailers coupons not included; discounts for early payment
Installation Charges	not included
Federal, State, Local Excise Taxes	federal retail excise tax on trucks not included; taxes with incidence on vendor included
Installment, Lay-Away, Conditional Sales	payment reported at time of sale
Finance Charges	included unless separately stated
Returned Goods, Repossessions	returns - deductible, if the property is returned within 90 days from the sale date (180 days for motor vehicles), and the entire amount charged, less vendor's handling fees, has been refunded; repossessions – no specific provisions

MICHIGAN

Bad Debt Deduction	allowed
Coupons, Cash Discounts	retailers coupons, discounts not included; manufacturers coupons, manufacturers rebates included
Installation Charges	included unless separately stated
Federal, State, Local Excise Taxes	federal tax on retail sales and state and local convention and tourism marketing taxes not included; federal excise taxes on vehicles, tires, fishing equipment, and firearms included
Installment, Lay-Away, Conditional Sales	payment reported at time of sale
Finance Charges	included unless separately stated
Returned Goods, Repossessions	returns - deducted from gross proceeds; repossessions -no specific provisions

MINNESOTA

Bad Debt Deduction	allowed
Coupons, Cash Discounts	discounts not reimbursed by third party, such as retailer coupons, not included; discounts reimbursed by third party, such as manufacturer coupons, included
Installation Charges	included
Federal, State, Local Excise Taxes	federal excise tax on retailers and separately stated taxes imposed directly on consumers not included; federal manufacturers excise tax included
Installment, Lay-Away, Conditional Sales	payment reported when received or, for accrual accounting, at time of sale
Finance Charges	included unless separately stated
Returned Goods, Repossessions	returned goods—deductible, if sales tax is refunded to purchaser; repossession is not considered a deductible return

MISSISSIPPI

Bad Debt Deduction	allowed as credit
Coupons, Cash Discounts	cash discounts, retailers coupons not included; manufacturers coupons included
Installation Charges	included
Federal, State, Local Excise Taxes	federal retailers excise tax, tax levied on income from transportation, telegraphic dispatches, telephone conversations, and electric energy, and certain state gasoline tax not included
Installment, Lay-Away, Conditional Sales	payments reported at time of sale
Finance Charges	included unless credit extended by third-party creditor
Returned Goods, Repossessions	returns - deductible, if the total sales price is refunded to the purchaser; repossessions - deduction is allowed for the uncollected portion of the selling price of repossessed property

MISSOURI

Bad Debt Deduction	allowed as credit or refund
Coupons, Cash Discounts	cash discounts, retailers coupons not included; manufacturers coupons included
Installation Charges	included unless separately stated
Federal, State, Local Excise Taxes	federal manufacturers excise tax, excise tax on retail sales of fuel, vehicles, sporting goods, firearms, communications, and certain transportation, state tobacco tax not included; local tobacco tax imposed on seller included
Installment, Lay-Away, Conditional Sales	payments reported when received or, for accrual accounting, at time of sale; lay-away sales taxed when sale complete
Finance Charges	not included
Returned Goods, Repossessions	returns - deductible, if the full price including tax is refunded to the purchaser; repossessions - no specific provisions

NEBRASKA

Bad Debt Deduction	allowed
Coupons, Cash Discounts	cash discounts, retailers coupons, motor vehicle rebates used to reduce the selling price not included; manufacturers coupons, cash rebates included
Installation Charges	included if sale of property subject to tax
Federal, State, Local Excise Taxes	excise taxes, property taxes included
Installment, Lay-Away, Conditional Sales	cash basis retailers report payments as received; accrual basis retailers report payments at time of sale or elect to report payments as received
Finance Charges	included unless separately stated
Returned Goods, Repossessions	returned goods—deductible, if full sales price including tax is refunded to purchaser; credit allowed for unpaid balance of repossessed property, credit not allowed if retailer remitted the tax on a cash accounting basis or collected the full tax from purchaser at time of purchase

NEVADA

Bad Debt Deduction	allowed (prior to January 1, 2006, a bad debt credit was authorized)
Coupons, Cash Discounts	reimbursed coupons included; cash discounts, retailers coupons not included
Installation Charges	included unless separately stated
Federal, State, Local Excise Taxes	federal taxes on retail sale not included; manufacturers and importers excise taxes included)
Installment, Lay-Away, Conditional Sales	no specific provisions
Finance Charges	included unless separately stated
Returned Goods, Repossessions	returns - deductible, if the full sales price is refunded, and the purchaser is not required to purchase other property at a greater price than the returned property in order to obtain a refund; repossessions - no specific provisions

NEW JERSEY

Bad Debt Deduction	allowed
Coupons, Cash Discounts	discounts that represent price reductions, retailers coupons not included; reimbursed coupons, early payment discounts, rebates included
Installation Charges	included, unless installation constitutes addition or capital improvement to real property
Federal, State, Local Excise Taxes	excise taxes imposed on consumers not included; other federal, state, and local excise taxes included
Installment, Lay-Away, Conditional Sales	payments reported at time of sale
Finance Charges	not included
Returned Goods, Repossessions	returns - not deductible; a regulation allowing a deduction has been authorized but not implemented; repossessions - a retailer may file a refund claim for overpaid sales tax on repossessed property; a deduction is not allowed

NEW MEXICO

Bad Debt Deduction	allowed
Coupons, Cash Discounts	cash discounts, retailers coupons not included; manufacturers coupons included
Installation Charges	included
Federal, State, Local Excise Taxes	gross receipts taxes, federal communication excise tax, air transportation excise tax not included; federal manufacturers excise tax, cigarette tax included
Installment, Lay-Away, Conditional Sales	payments reported when received
Finance Charges	not included
Returned Goods, Repossessions	returns goods—deductible; retailer that reports on an accrual basis may deduct amounts written off as uncollectible debt for amount credited to buyer from whom property repossessed

NEW YORK

Bad Debt Deduction	allowed as refund or credit
Coupons, Cash Discounts	discounts that represent a price reduction, retailers coupons not included; reimbursed coupons, early payment discounts included
Installation Charges	included, unless installation constitutes addition or capital improvement to real property
Federal, State, Local Excise Taxes	excise taxes imposed directly on consumers (other than cigarette taxes) not included; taxes imposed on manufacturers, importers, distributors, producers, or distillers, which the vendor passes on to consumer and state and New York City cigarette taxes included
Installment, Lay-Away, Conditional Sales	payments reported at time of sale
Finance Charges	not included
Returned Goods, Repossessions	returns—tax that has not been remitted may be deducted during current reporting period; credit or refund allowed for tax that has already been remitted; repossessions - no specific provisions

NORTH CAROLINA

Bad Debt Deduction	allowed
Coupons, Cash Discounts	cash discounts, trade discounts, retailers coupons not included; manufacturers coupons included)
Installation Charges	included unless separately stated
Federal, State, Local Excise Taxes	separately stated taxes imposed directly on consumers not included; federal excise taxes imposed on manufacturer included
Installment, Lay-Away, Conditional Sales	payments reported as received or, for accrual accounting, at time of sale
Finance Charges	included unless separately stated
Returned Goods, Repossessions	returns - a refund or a credit is allowed if the entire amount charged including tax is refunded to the purchaser; repossessions - no deduction allowed

NORTH DAKOTA

Bad Debt Deduction	allowed
Coupons, Cash Discounts	discounts, retailers coupons not included; manufacturers coupons, manufacturers rebates included
Installation Charges	included unless separately stated
Federal, State, Local Excise Taxes	federal manufacturers excise tax included except for separately stated charges in a direct manufacture-to-customer sale
Installment, Lay-Away, Conditional Sales	payments made over a period of more than 60 days reported when received
Finance Charges	included unless separately stated
Returned Goods, Repossessions	returned goods—credit allowed, if purchase price including tax is refunded to purchaser; repossessions—credit allowed for tax paid on unpaid balance of repossessed property

OHIO

Bad Debt Deduction	allowed
Coupons, Cash Discounts	cash and term discounts, retailers coupons not included; reimbursed coupons included
Installation Charges	included
Federal, State, Local Excise Taxes	excise taxes imposed on consumers not included; excise taxes imposed on manufacturers, distributors, wholesalers, and retailers included
Installment, Lay-Away, Conditional Sales	payments reported at time of sale
Finance Charges	included unless separately stated
Returned Goods, Repossessions	returns—amounts refunded not included in receipts; repossessions - no specific provisions

OKLAHOMA

Bad Debt Deduction	allowed
Coupons, Cash Discounts	cash and term discounts and retailers coupons not included; reimbursed coupons included
Installation Charges	included unless separately stated
Federal, State, Local Excise Taxes	federal excise taxes levied on retailers and manufacturers included; any separately stated taxes imposed directly on consumers not included
Installment, Lay-Away, Conditional Sales	payments reported at time of sale
Finance Charges	included unless separately stated
Returned Goods, Repossessions	returned goods—deductible, if full purchase price including tax is refunded to purchaser; credit allowed for unpaid portion of repossessed property

PENNSYLVANIA

Bad Debt Deduction	allowed as refund
Coupons, Cash Discounts	discounts at time of sale and retailers and manufacturers coupons not included if separately stated; discounts after sale included
Installation Charges	included
Federal, State, Local Excise Taxes	state taxes and taxes that represent cost to vendor, including manufacturers excise, gross receipts, and mercantile taxes, included

Installment, Lay-Away, Conditional Sales	seller collects tax on full purchase price within 30 days of sale; lay-away sales taxed upon first payment after property appropriated
Finance Charges	included unless separately stated
Returned Goods, Repossessions	returned goods—deductible, if sale amount and tax have been refunded to purchaser; deduction not allowed for repossessed property

RHODE ISLAND

Bad Debt Deduction	allowed
Coupons, Cash Discounts	cash discounts at time of sale, retailers coupons not included; discounts after sale, early payment discounts, manufacturers coupons included
Installation Charges	included unless separately stated
Federal, State, Local Excise Taxes	federal taxes on retail sales not included; manufacturers and importers excise taxes included
Installment, Lay-Away, Conditional Sales	no specific provisions
Finance Charges	included unless separately stated
Returned Goods, Repossessions	returned goods—deductible, if full sale price including tax but excluding handling charges is refunded to purchaser, and the merchandise is returned within 120 days from purchase date; deduction not allowed for repossessed property

SOUTH CAROLINA

Bad Debt Deduction	allowed
Coupons, Cash Discounts	cash discounts at time of sale, retailers coupons not included; timely payment discounts deductible on subsequent report; manufacturers coupons and rebates included
Installation Charges	included unless separately stated
Federal, State, Local Excise Taxes	federal taxes imposed on retail sales, local sales and use taxes, and local hospitality taxes and accommodations fees imposed directly on customers not included; federal manufacturers and importers excise taxes, local hospitality taxes and accommodations fees imposed on retailers included
Installment, Lay-Away, Conditional Sales	taxpayer elects reporting payments at time of sale or as received for conditional, installment sales; lay-away sales—payments reported when received
Finance Charges	included unless separately stated
Returned Goods, Repossessions	returns—amount refunded not included in gross proceeds; repossessions—no specific provisions

SOUTH DAKOTA

Bad Debt Deduction	allowed
Coupons, Cash Discounts	discounts, retailers coupons not included; reimbursed coupons included
Installation Charges	included
Federal, State, Local Excise Taxes	separately stated taxes imposed directly on consumers not included
Installment, Lay-Away, Conditional Sales	payments made over a period of more than 60 days reported when received

Finance Charges	included unless separately stated
Returned Goods, Repossessions	returns - amounts refunded not included in gross receipts; repossessions - no specific provisions

TENNESSEE

Bad Debt Deduction	allowed as credit
Coupons, Cash Discounts	cash discounts not included
Installation Charges	included
Federal, State, Local Excise Taxes	separately stated federal excise taxes imposed on consumers and state and local taxes not included
Installment, Lay-Away, Conditional Sales	payments reported at time of sale; lay-away sales taxable upon delivery to customer
Finance Charges	included unless separately stated
Returned Goods, Repossessions	returned goods—deductible, if purchase price including tax is refunded to purchaser; repossessions—if unpaid purchase price of repossessed property exceeds $500, dealer may claim credit equal to difference between sales tax paid at time of original purchase and the amount of sales tax that would be owed for the portion of the purchase price that was paid by purchaser, plus the sales tax on the first $500 of unpaid balance

TEXAS

Bad Debt Deduction	allowed as deduction or refund
Coupons, Cash Discounts	retailers and manufacturers coupons, cash discounts not included
Installation Charges	included
Federal, State, Local Excise Taxes	certain federal excise taxes included
Installment, Lay-Away, Conditional Sales	payments reported as received or, for accrual accounting, at time of sale
Finance Charges	included unless separately stated
Returned Goods, Repossessions	returned goods—credit allowed for tax on fully refunded amount; credit allowed for unpaid portion of purchase price of repossessed property

UTAH

Bad Debt Deduction	allowed
Coupons, Cash Discounts	cash discounts, retailers coupons, and term discounts not included; manufacturers coupons included
Installation Charges	included unless separately stated
Federal, State, Local Excise Taxes	separately stated taxes imposed directly on consumer not included; taxes imposed on seller included
Installment, Lay-Away, Conditional Sales	payments reported at time of sale
Finance Charges	included unless separately stated

Returned Goods, Repossessions . . . . returns—adjustment and credit allowed if tax reported and paid in full (credit amount may not exceed sales tax on portion of purchase price remaining unpaid at time the goods are returned); repossessions—credit allowed to seller of a motor vehicle for tax that the seller collected on vehicle that has been repossessed and that the seller resells (credit equal to product of the portion of the vehicle's purchase price that was subject to tax and remains unpaid after resale of the vehicle, and the tax rate).

VERMONT

Bad Debt Deduction . . . . allowed as refund or credit

Coupons, Cash Discounts . . . . cash discounts, retailers coupons not included; early payment discounts, manufacturers coupons included

Installation Charges . . . . included unless separately stated

Federal, State, Local Excise Taxes . . . . taxes applied before retail sale included; federal excise taxes added to customer telecommunications service bills not included

Installment, Lay-Away, Conditional Sales . . . . . total sales price reported at time of sale; taxpayer may request to report payments as received

Finance Charges . . . . included unless separately stated

Returned Goods, Repossessions . . . . returns - deductible, if the full price including tax is refunded to the purchaser; repossessions - a vendor may apply for a refund for tax paid on the unpaid balance of repossessed property

VIRGINIA

Bad Debt Deduction . . . . allowed as credit

Coupons, Cash Discounts . . . . cash, trade, and early payment discounts, and retailers coupons not included; manufacturers coupons included

Installation Charges . . . . included unless separately stated

Federal, State, Local Excise Taxes . . . . separately stated federal retailers excise tax, state and local sales and use taxes, and local excise taxes on meals and lodging not included; federal manufacturers excise tax and taxes on alcoholic beverages and tobacco included

Installment, Lay-Away, Conditional Sales . . . . . payments reported at time of sale; lay-away sales taxable when property delivered to customer

Finance Charges . . . . included unless separately stated

Returned Goods, Repossessions . . . . returned goods—deductible, if sales price is refunded to purchaser; unpaid balance on repossessed property is deductible

WASHINGTON

Bad Debt Deduction . . . . allowed as credit or refund

Coupons, Cash Discounts . . . . discounts, retailers coupons not included; manufacturers coupons included

Installation Charges . . . . included

Federal, State, Local Excise Taxes . . . . any separately stated tax imposed on consumers not included; taxes imposed on sellers included

Installment, Lay-Away, Conditional Sales . . . . . payments reported in the tax period in which the sale is made

Finance Charges	included unless separately stated
Returned Goods, Repossessions	returned goods—deductible, if full sale price including tax is refunded to purchaser (if property is not returned within the guaranty period or if the full sale price is not refunded, a presumption is raised that the property returned is not returned goods but rather an exchange or repurchase by the vendor); repossessions—deduction allowed for unpaid portion of the balance of repossessed property

WEST VIRGINIA

Bad Debt Deduction	allowed
Coupons, Cash Discounts	Cash discounts at time of sale, retailers coupons not included; discounts after sale, manufacturers coupons included
Installation Charges	included
Federal, State, Local Excise Taxes	Federal, state, and local taxes simultaneously imposed on the property or service purchased not included; any excise tax imposed before imposition of West Virginia sales tax included
Installment, Lay-Away, Conditional Sales	conditional, installment sales—tax accrues upon transfer of property to buyer and must be paid within 30 days after possession transferred; lay-aways—payments reported when property delivered to buyer
Finance Charges	included unless separately stated
Returned Goods, Repossessions	returns - amount refunded/credited deducted from gross proceeds; repossessions - no specific provisions

WISCONSIN

Bad Debt Deduction	allowed
Coupons, Cash Discounts	cash discounts, retailers coupons not included; manufacturers coupons included
Installation Charges	included unless separately stated and installation constitutes addition to or capital improvement of real property
Federal, State, Local Excise Taxes	federal, state, and local taxes imposed on retail sales not included if the tax is measured by a percentage of sales price or gross receipts and the retailer is required to remit the tax; federal communications tax imposed on intrastate telecommunications also not included; any tax added to or included in purchase price, federal manufacturers excise tax included
Installment, Lay-Away, Conditional Sales	payments reported when purchaser takes possession of property
Finance Charges	included unless separately stated
Returned Goods, Repossessions	returned goods—deductible, if amount charged including tax is refunded to purchaser; deduction for repossessed property not allowed unless entire consideration paid by purchaser is refunded, or a deduction for worthless accounts is allowable

WYOMING

Bad Debt Deduction	allowed as credit
Coupons, Cash Discounts	cash and term discounts and retailers coupons not included; manufacturers coupons included
Installation Charges	included
Federal, State, Local Excise Taxes	separately stated taxes imposed directly on consumers not included; other taxes included
Installment, Lay-Away, Conditional Sales	payments reported at time of sale; if title passes at a future date, payments taxed when received
Finance Charges	included unless separately stated
Returned Goods, Repossessions	returned goods—deductible, if full sales price including tax is refunded to purchaser; deduction not allowed for repossessed property

Computer Software

Generally, computer hardware is taxable, with certain exceptions for computers used in manufacturing, production, and research. Similar exceptions may exist for software that would otherwise be taxable. "Canned" or prewritten software is also taxable; however, in some states the sale of any software that is digitally delivered is not taxable.

The methods by which the states apply their sales and use taxes to sales of computer software vary greatly. Most states impose their sales taxes on transfers of tangible personal property, but computer software is not easily classified as "tangible" or "intangible."

Many states distinguish between "canned" or "prewritten" software, which can be purchased off the shelf and used in a customer's computer without any modification, and "custom" software, which is generally a program created to meet a specific customer's needs. In some states, a canned program modified to meet a particular customer's needs qualifies as a nontaxable custom program. Definitions of "custom" programs vary widely among the states.

For purposes of this chart, "T" stands for taxable and "E" for exempt; but the designations are of a general nature, and exceptions unnoted in the chart may exist.

States that do not impose a sales and use tax are not included in this chart.

State	Custom Software	Modified Canned Software	Downloaded Software
Alabama	E	T[1]	T[2,3]
Arizona	E	T[4]	T[2]
Arkansas	T[3]	T	E[5]
California	E	T[1]	E[6]
Colorado	E	E	E
Connecticut	T[7]	T[8]	T[9]
District of Columbia	T	T	T
Florida	E	E	E
Georgia	E	T[10]	E[11]
Hawaii	T	T	T
Idaho	E	T[1]	T[2]
Illinois	E	E[12]	T[2]
Indiana	E	T[13]	T[2]
Iowa	E	T[14]	E
Kansas	E[15]	T[16]	T[2]
Kentucky	E	E[17]	T[2,18]

State	Custom Software	Modified Canned Software	Downloaded Software
Louisiana	E[19]	T[20]	T[2]
Maine	E	T[1]	T[2]
Maryland	E	E[21]	E[22]
Massachusetts	E	E[23]	T[24]
Michigan	E	T[25]	T[2]
Minnesota	E	T[1]	T[2]
Mississippi	T	T	T
Missouri	E	T[26]	E
Nebraska	T	T[27]	T
Nevada	E	T[17]	E
New Jersey	E	T[28]	T[29]
New Mexico	T	T	T
New York	E	T[30,31]	T[2]
North Carolina	E	T[17]	E
North Dakota	E	T[17]	T[2]
Ohio	T[32]	T[30]	T[2]
Oklahoma	E	T[30]	E
Pennsylvania	E	T[33]	T[2,34]
Rhode Island	E	T	E[35]
South Carolina	T	T[36]	E[35]
South Dakota	T	T	T
Tennessee	T[37]	T	T[37]
Texas	T[38]	T[39]	T
Utah	E	T[40]	T[2]
Vermont	E	E	E
Virginia	E	T[41]	E[35]
Washington	E	E	T[2]
West Virginia	T[42]	T[42]	T[42]
Wisconsin	E[43]	T[44]	T[2]
Wyoming	E	T	T[2]

[1] Separately stated charges for modifications to canned software prepared exclusively for a particular customer exempt only to extent of modification.
[2] Downloaded custom software is exempt.

[3] Exempt if it is designed specifically for, and necessary for the operation of, machinery used in manufacturing.

[4] Charges for modification of prewritten software for the specific use of an individual customer are exempt if separately stated on the sales invoice and records.

[5] Downloading of software, transmitted electronically, is considered excluded from tax because there is no tangible personal property involved.

[6] Prewritten program transferred by remote telecommunications exempt, provided that purchaser does not obtain possession of any tangible personal property (such as storage media) in the transaction.

[7] Design, creation, or development of custom software taxable at reduced rate of 1% for computer and data processing services. Separately stated charges for mere use and possession of software (such as license fees) not taxable.

[8] Taxable at reduced rate for computer and data processing services.

[9] If no tangible personal property delivered to purchaser along with downloaded software, software is taxed at 1% rate applicable to computer and data processing services.

[10] Prewritten computer software, even though modified or enhanced to the specifications of a purchaser, remains prewritten computer software. However, if there is a separately stated charge on the dealer's invoice for the modification or enhancement, the charge is not subject to sales and use tax.

[11] Software delivered electronically is not subject to sales and use tax because it is not a sale of tangible personal property. Documentation must indicate the method of delivery. If not, then delivery will be presumed to have been made through a tangible medium, and the burden will be on the taxpayer to establish the software was delivered electronically. If software is delivered both electronically and through a tangible medium, the transaction is treated as a taxable sale of tangible personal property unless the software qualifies as custom software.

[12] Modified software held for general or repeated sale/lease is taxable.

[13] If modification or enhancement is designed and developed to the specifications of a specific purchaser, software remains prewritten computer software. Where there is a reasonable, separately stated charge for such a modification or enhancement, the modification or enhancement is not prewritten computer software and is exempt.

[14] Separately stated charges for modifications to canned software prepared exclusively for a particular customer exempt only to extent of modification. If charges are not separately stated, then tax applies to entire charge unless modification is so significant that the new program qualifies as a custom program.

[15] Effective January 1, 2005, custom software and the services of modifying, altering, updating, or maintaining custom software are exempt.

[16] Separately stated charges for modifications to canned software prepared exclusively for a particular customer exempt.

[17] Exempt if charges for modification are separately stated.

[18] Effective July 1, 2004, downloaded "prewritten computer software" taxable.

[19] Tax on custom software phased out (July 1, 2002-June 30, 2003: 75% of sales price taxed; July 1, 2003- June 30, 2004: 50% taxed; July 1, 2004- June 30, 2005: 25% taxed; exempt after June 30, 2005).

[20] All canned software incorporated into custom software that is sold after June 30, 2005, is fully taxable. (Prior to that date, due to the phase-out of tax on custom software, purchases of canned software for use in custom programs were treated as purchases for resale according to a certain percentage of custom software's sales price based on sales date of custom software.)

[21] Exempt if the service aspect of the transaction predominates over sale of canned software.

[22] Exempt as long as transaction does not include the transfer of any tangible personal property.

[23] Exempt if sales price of canned software is an inconsequential element of the cost of the transaction and is not separately stated. If separately stated, charges for modification are exempt and charges for canned software are taxable.

[24] Effective April 1, 2006, all transfers of canned software are considered taxable transfers of tangible personal property (including, but not limited to, electronic, telephonic, or similar transfers; downloaded software from the Internet; or transfers by "load and leave"). Sales of custom software are generally exempt as professional service transactions.

[25] Exempt if separately stated and identified.

[26] Exempt if true object of transaction is provision of technical professional service.

[27] Software that alters existing software is considered separate from the existing software and is taxable.

[28] A separately stated, commercially reasonable charge for the professional service of modifying canned software for a customer is exempt.

[29] Effective October 1, 2006, downloaded software is exempt only if used exclusively and directly in the purchaser's business, trade, or occupation, and if the purchaser does not receive a CD or disc or other tangible item in connection with the sale.

[30] Reasonable, separately stated charges for modifications to canned software prepared exclusively for a particular customer exempt only to extent of modification.

[31] Modified software may be exempt if used directly and predominantly in production of property for sale or for research and development.

[32] Ohio taxes purchases of "computer services" purchased for business use. "Computer services" includes custom programming of system software. Programming of custom application software is not a taxable sale.

[33] Reasonable, separately stated charges for modifications to canned software prepared exclusively for a particular customer exempt.

[34] Effective for invoices dated after October 2005, the sale or use of canned software is taxable, regardless of the method of delivery. See Graham Packaging Co. v. Commonwealth of Pennsylvania, Pennsylvania Commonwealth Court, No. 652 F.R. 2002, September 15, 2005. Downloaded custom software exempt as long as the transaction does not include the transfer of any tangible personal property.

[35] Exempt as long as the transaction does not include the transfer of any tangible personal property.

[36] Modifications to canned software prepared exclusively for a particular customer are considered to be taxable custom programs.

[37] Exemptions may apply for the use of software developed and fabricated by an affiliated company or for fabrication of software by a person for that person's own use or consumption.

[38] Charges to create a computer program from scratch for a customer who is given all and exclusive rights to the program are exempt.

[39] Taxable if performed by person who sold the canned software. Charges to customize canned software not sold by the person doing the customization are exempt.

[40] Charges for modifications to canned software that are reasonable and separately stated and identified on the invoice are exempt.

[41] Canned software that is modified to any degree does not become exempt custom software.

[42] Exemptions may apply for high technology businesses, certain education software, software directly used in communications or incorporated into a manufactured product, or software used to provide data processing services.

[43] There is a rebuttable presumption that any program with a cost of $10,000 or less is not custom software. Custom software does not include basic operational programs.

[44] Exempt if vendor significantly modifies canned software to meet a customer's specific hardware and software needs.

Drop Shipments

A drop shipment is a shipment of tangible personal property from a seller directly to the purchaser's customer at the direction of the purchaser. These sales also are known as third-party sales because they require that there be, at arm's length, three parties and two separate sales transactions. Generally, a retailer accepts an order from an end purchaser, places this order with a third party, usually a manufacturer or wholesale distributor (for purposes of this chart, "supplier"), and directs the third party to ship the goods directly to the customer. The transaction between the supplier and retailer constitutes the "primary sale"; the transaction between the retailer and the customer constitutes the "secondary" sale.

The following chart summarizes the status of drop shipments when both the supplier and customer are in-state and the retailer is out-of-state. Note that many states view the drop shipment scenario as two separate, potentially taxable events. Some states, however, collapse the three-party, two-transaction scenario into a single taxable event. In the latter case, the theory advanced is that in the primary transaction, the supplier has no obligation to collect sales tax from the out-of-state retailer if there is no nexus between the retailer and the customer's state. Consequently, the customer is liable for the payment of use tax.

State	Taxability of Drop Shipment
Alabama	Primary sale exempt where retailer furnishes a resale exemption from retailer's state. Customer subject to use tax on secondary transaction.
Arizona	Primary sale exempt where retailer furnishes resale certificate from retailer's state. Customer subject to use tax on secondary transaction.
Arkansas	Primary sale exempt where retailer furnishes resale certificate. Customer subject to compensating (use) tax on secondary transaction.
California	Party making the drop shipment is deemed the retailer and is thus responsible for collecting and remitting sales and use tax from the customer, unless the customer furnishes the party making the drop shipment with a resale certificate.
Colorado	Primary sale exempt where retailer furnishes a resale certificate from retailer's state. Customer pays use tax on secondary transaction.
Connecticut	Party making the drop shipment is deemed the retailer and is thus responsible for collecting and remitting sales and use tax from the customer, unless the customer furnishes the party making the drop shipment with a resale certificate.
District of Columbia	Supplier must collect sales or use tax from retailer unless retailer furnishes a valid DC certificate of resale. Resale certificate from home state not accepted, nor is a resale certificate furnished to the retailer by the customer.
Florida	Supplier must collect sales tax from retailer on the theory that retailer, being out-of-state and unregistered in Florida for sales tax purposes, cannot furnish the Florida supplier with a Florida resale certificate.
Georgia	Primary sale exempt where retailer furnishes a resale certificate from retailer's state. Customer liable for use tax on secondary transaction.

State	Taxability of Drop Shipment
Hawaii	Supplier is liable for collecting Hawaii's general excise tax (GET) of 4% on the sale to the customer, and 0.5% use tax from the customer on the sale for resale.
Idaho	Primary sale is not taxable on the theory that there is no nexus between the retailer and Idaho. Customer responsible for payment of use tax.
Illinois	Primary sale exempt where retailer furnishes an Illinois resale number or other evidence that the sale is for resale. Customer liable for payment of use tax on secondary transaction.
Indiana	Primary sale exempt where retailer furnishes exemption form or required documentation of resale. Retailer liable for collecting sales or use tax from customer.
Iowa	Consumer liable for payment of use tax.
Kansas	Party making the drop shipment is deemed the retailer and is thus responsible for collecting and remitting sales and use tax from the customer, unless the customer furnishes the party making the drop shipment with a resale certificate.
Kentucky	Primary sale exempt where retailer furnishes a Kentucky resale certificate. A nonresident retailer uses a Kentucky certificate, but makes a notation on the face to the effect that it is a nonresident purchaser not required to register in Kentucky. Customer liable for payment of use tax on secondary transaction.
Louisiana	If manufacturer located outside LA and delivers from inventory located outside LA but is registered with state, manufacturer not required to collect tax from retailer. Retailer can provide letter to manufacturer that retailer is not registered in LA and is not required to be registered. If manufacturer is located in LA or delivers from inventory located within LA, manufacturer must collect sales tax on retailer's purchase for resale as a result of the intrastate delivery to the consumer. The retailer may then claim a refund for advanced taxes paid when retailer files LA return for period in which transaction occurred. The retailer must also collect tax from consumer on the sale.
Maine	Primary sale exempt if supplier furnished sufficient documentation to sustain burden of proving that sale is for resale. Customer liable for payment of use tax.
Maryland	Supplier may either (1) require retailer to register as a Maryland vendor and furnish a resale certificate, or (2) collect tax from the retailer based on the wholesale price paid.
Massachusetts . .	Supplier must include the retail selling price charged by the retailer in its gross receipts and must collect tax imposed from the retailer.
Michigan	Primary sale exempt where retailer furnishes supplier with an exemption certificate from retailer's state. Customer liable for payment of use tax.
Minnesota	Primary sale exempt where retailer furnishes supplier with an exemption certificate from Minnesota or retailer's state. Customer liable for payment of use tax.
Mississippi	Primary sale exempt if retailer furnishes supplier with Mississippi sales or use tax account number.
Missouri	Primary sale exempt where retailer furnishes supplier with a Missouri Resale Exemption Certificate with its out-of-state registration listed. Customer liable for payment of use tax.
Nebraska	Supplier must collect sales tax from retailer based on the wholesale price. Resale certificate not accepted from out-of-state retailer unless retailer registers to collect sales and use tax for Nebraska. Nebraska also requires customer to pay use tax on the basis of the retail price paid.

State	Taxability of Drop Shipment
Nevada	Supplier treated as retailer and is responsible for collecting sales tax from the out-of-state retailer based on the wholesale price. Resale certificate not accepted from out-of-state retailer unless retailer registers to collect sales and use tax for Nevada.
New Jersey	Primary sale exempt if retailer furnishes supplier with evidence that the sale is for resale. Customer liable for payment of use tax.
New Mexico	Primary sale exempt where retailer furnishes supplier with nontaxable transaction certificate. Customer liable for payment of use tax.
New York	Primary sale exempt where retailer furnishes a New York resale certificate. Customer liable for payment of use tax.
North Carolina	Primary sale exempt if retailer furnishes supplier with an exemption certificate from North Carolina or retailer's state. Customer liable for payment of use tax.
North Dakota	Primary sale exempt where retailer furnishes a North Dakota resale certificate or one from the retailer's state. Customer liable for payment of use tax.
Ohio	Primary sale exempt where retailer furnishes a resale certificate from the retailer's state. Customer liable for payment of use tax.
Oklahoma	Primary sale exempt where retailer furnishes a resale exemption form from its state or an MTC resale certificate. Customer liable for payment of use tax.
Pennsylvania	Primary sale exempt where retailer furnishes a PA or MTC resale certificate. Consumer liable for payment of use tax.
Rhode Island	Supplier is considered to be making a retail sale on the theory that he or she is the former owner of, or has a factor's interest in, the goods. Supplier is thus required to collect and pay tax based on the retail selling price of the property delivered.
South Carolina	Primary sale exempt if retailer furnishes supplier with a South Carolina exemption certificate, an MTC uniform exemption certificate, or an exemption certificate from the retailer's state. Customer liable for payment of use tax.
South Dakota	Supplier must collect sales tax from retailer based on the wholesale price, unless retailer furnishes resale certificate. A resale exemption certificate may be accepted from retailers registered in any state. Consumer also responsible for payment of use tax on secondary transaction.
Tennessee	Supplier must collect sales tax from the retailer based on the wholesale receipts, unless retailer furnishes Tennessee exemption certificate.
Texas	Primary sale exempt where retailer furnishes properly executed Texas resale certificate validated with a registration number issued by retailer's home state. On secondary sale, customer liable for payment of use tax.
Utah	Primary sale exempt where retailer furnishes resale certificate from retailer's state. Customer liable for payment of use tax on secondary transaction.
Vermont	Supplier must collect sales tax from retailer, unless retailer furnishes Vermont exemption certificate or exemption certificate from retailer's state. Secondary sale not taxable since retailer has no nexus with Vermont.
Virginia	Primary sale exempt where retailer furnishes resale certificate from retailer's state. Customer liable for payment of use tax on secondary transaction.
Washington	Primary sale exempt where retailer furnishes resale certificate from retailer's state. Customer liable for payment of use tax in secondary transaction.
West Virginia	Primary sale exempt where retailer furnishes resale certificate from retailer's state. Customer liable for payment of use tax on secondary transaction.

State	Taxability of Drop Shipment
Wisconsin	Supplier must collect tax from the customer based on the retail price of the property delivered. However, if the Wisconsin purchaser furnishes a properly completed exemption certificate the delivery is not a taxable sale.
Wyoming	Primary sale exempt where retailer furnishes a resale certificate from retailer's state. Customer liable for payment of use tax on secondary transaction.

Exemption and Resale Certificates' Validity Periods

State-by-state validity periods for exemption and/or resale certificates are listed below. In many states, the exemption certificate is also used as a resale certificate. Although many certificates do not have expiration dates, most states recommend the certificates be verified or updated periodically.

State	Resale Certificates	Exemption Certificates
Alabama	Resale certificates not required.	Valid until change in character of purchaser's operation.
Arizona	Valid for the period set out on certificate.	Valid for the period set out on certificate.
Arkansas	No stated expiration period.	State does not use exemption certificates.
California	Until revoked in writing.	Until revoked in writing, unless issued for specific transaction.
Colorado	Two years (expiring at end of odd-numbered years).	Charitable exemption certificates do not expire. Contractor's exemption certificates expire at the end of the job.
Connecticut	Valid indefinitely, but should be renewed at least every three years.	Must be renewed annually.
District of Columbia	Until cancelled by customer.	Until recalled by the District.
Florida	Must be renewed annually.	Expires five years after issuance.
Georgia	Until revoked in writing.	Until revoked in writing.
Hawaii	Until revoked in writing.	Does not expire. New application must be filed if there is material change in facts.
Idaho	No stated expiration period.	No stated expiration period.
Illinois	Valid indefinitely, but should be updated at least every three years.	Expires five years after issuance.
Indiana	Does not expire.	Does not expire.
Iowa	Must be reviewed periodically by seller.	Must be reviewed periodically by seller.
Kansas	Valid until purchaser's status changes.	Valid until purchaser's status changes.
Kentucky	Valid until change in character of purchaser's operation.	Valid until withdrawn by purchaser.
Louisiana	Valid indefinitely. Department recommends updating every three years.	Valid indefinitely. Department recommends updating every three years.
Maine	Valid until revoked in writing.	Valid until revoked in writing.
Maryland	Valid until revoked by either taxpayer or Comptroller.	Expires five years after issuance. Governmental entity certificates do not expire.
Massachusetts	No stated expiration period.	No stated expiration period.
Michigan	Expires after four years unless shorter period agreed to.	Expires after four years unless shorter period agreed to.

State	Resale Certificates	Exemption Certificates
Minnesota	Valid indefinitely, but should be renewed at least every three years.	Does not expire; should be updated every three years.
Mississippi	State does not use resale certificates. Contractor's Material Purchase Certificate is valid for the job identified on the certificate.	State does not use exemption certificates.
Missouri	Valid until change in character of purchaser's operation.	Valid until change in character of purchaser's operation.
Nebraska	Valid for three years from issuance.	Valid for three years from issuance.
Nevada	Valid until revoked in writing. Department recommends updating every two to three years.	Valid for five years.
New Jersey	No stated expiration period.	No stated expiration period.
New Mexico	Valid during 12-year period.	Valid during 12-year period.
New York	Valid as long as information remains accurate.	Valid until revoked in writing.
North Carolina	Valid until change in ownership/ structure. Department recommends updating every few years.	No stated expiration period.
North Dakota	New certificate should be taken every two years.	Valid until exemption no longer applies.
Ohio	No stated expiration period.	No stated expiration period.
Oklahoma	Valid for three years.	Valid for three years.
Pennsylvania	Valid indefinitely. Department recommends periodic updating. Sales tax license must be renewed every five years.	Valid indefinitely. Department recommends periodic updating. Exempt status must be renewed every three years.
Rhode Island	Valid indefinitely. Department recommends updating every three years.	No stated expiration period.
South Carolina	Valid as long as the business is in operation.	Valid as long as the business is in operation.
South Dakota	New certificate should be requested each year.	New certificate should be requested each year.
Tennessee	Valid until change in status/character.	Valid until change in status/character.
Texas	Valid until revoked in writing.	No stated expiration period.
Utah	Valid indefinitely. Department recommends updating every year.	Valid indefinitely. Department recommends updating every year.
Vermont	Valid indefinitely.	Valid indefinitely.
Virginia	Valid as long as business remains in operation; unless cancelled by Department.	Valid as long as business remains in operation; unless cancelled by Department. Construction contractors certificate has expiration date on its face.
Washington	Valid for four years from effective date.	No stated expiration period.

State	Resale Certificates	Exemption Certificates
West Virginia	New certificate should be requested each year.	New certificate should be requested each year. New certificate should be taken for each contracting project.
Wisconsin	Valid indefinitely, but should be reviewed periodically.	Valid indefinitely.
Wyoming	No stated expiration period.	No stated expiration period. Certain exempt organizations must also present letter of authority

Food and Meals

The exemptions for sales of nonprepared food from a grocery store ("grocery food") are quite broad, with the most common restrictions requiring that the food products be intended for human consumption away from the retailer's premises. Alcoholic beverages are generally excluded from the exemptions, and a few states exclude soft drinks or confections.

Sales of meals or food prepared for on-premises consumption are almost always taxable, as are sales of meals by caterers.

For purposes of this chart, "T" stands for taxable and "E" stands for exempt; but the designations are of a general nature, and exceptions unnoted in the chart may exist.

States that do not impose a sales and use tax are not included in the chart.

State	Grocery Food	Meals	Sales by Caterers
Alabama	T	T	T
Arizona	E	T	T
Arkansas	T	T	T
California	E	T[1]	T
Colorado	E	T	T
Connecticut	E	T	T
District of Columbia	E	T	T
Florida	E	T	T
Georgia	E	T	T
Hawaii	T	T	T
Idaho	T	T	T
Illinois	T[2]	T	T
Indiana	E	T	T
Iowa	E	T	T
Kansas	T[3]	T	T
Kentucky	E	T	T
Louisiana	E[4]	T	T
Maine	E[5]	T	T
Maryland	E[6]	T	T
Massachusetts	E	T	T
Michigan	E	T	T
Minnesota	E	T	T
Mississippi	T	T	T
Missouri	T[7]	T	T

State	Grocery Food	Meals	Sales by Caterers
Nebraska	E	T	T
Nevada	E	T	T
New Jersey	E	T	T
New Mexico	E[8]	T	T
New York	E	T	T
North Carolina	E[9]	T	T
North Dakota	E	T	T
Ohio	E	T	T
Oklahoma	T	T	T
Pennsylvania	E[10]	T	T
Rhode Island	E	T	T
South Carolina	T[11]	T	T
South Dakota	T	T	T
Tennessee	T[12]	T	T
Texas	E	T	T
Utah	T[13]	T[13]	T
Vermont	E	E[14]	E[14]
Virginia	T[15]	T	T
Washington	E	T	T
West Virginia	T[16]	T	T
Wisconsin	E[17]	T	T
Wyoming	T[18]	T	T

[1] Meals and food products furnished or served by any nonprofit veterans' organizations for fund-raising purposes is exempt.
[2] Taxed at reduced rate of 1%.
[3] Limited tax refund available to disabled, elderly, and low-income households.
[4] Exemption applies to food sold for preparation and consumption in the home.
[5] The exemption for food products for home consumption is limited to "grocery staples".
[6] Sales of food for consumption off-premises exempt when sold by a substantial grocery or market business, where at least 10% of all food sales are sales of grocery or market food items.
[7] Taxed at reduced rate of 1.225%.
[8] Effective January 1, 2005, receipts from sales of food at a retail food store may be deducted from gross receipts.
[9] Exempt from state sales and use tax but subject to local food taxes.
[10] The sale of food may be taxable or exempt depending upon the type of food or upon the location from which food is sold.
[11] Effective October 1, 2006, the state rate on unprepared food that can be purchased with federal food stamps is reduced from 5% to 3%.
[12] Taxed at reduced rate of 6%.
[13] Effective January 1, 2007, reduced rate of 2.75% imposed on food and food ingredients. In a bundled transaction involving both food/food ingredients and another item of tangible personal property, the rate is 4.75%.
[14] Subject to meals and rooms tax.
[15] Taxed at reduced rate of 1.5% (1% local option tax also applies).
[16] Effective January 1, 2006, taxed at reduced rate of 5%.
[17] Some snack foods may be excluded from exemption.
[18] Food for domestic home consumption is exempt from July 1, 2006, through June 30, 2008.

Leases and Rentals

Most states clearly tax the renting or leasing of tangible personal property if the same property would be taxable if sold at retail. States often give retailers an option either to report and remit tax on rental receipts as they are collected or to pay the sales or use tax at the outset on the cost or retail value of property that is purchased for subsequent leasing. If the first method is used, the initial purchase of the property is considered a tax-exempt purchase for resale. Where rental receipts are *not* subject to the tax, however, the lessor is considered the user of the leased property and, when purchasing property intended for rental purposes, must pay either the sales or the use tax. Some states may impose a separate motor vehicle tax on the rental or leasing of motor vehicles in lieu of, or in addition to, the sales or use tax.

Most states tax the rental receipts from rooms or lodgings furnished by hotel or motel operators. However, exemptions are usually allowed for accommodations rented for a specified continuous period, accommodations furnished by hospitals, nursing homes, camps operated by nonprofit organizations, etc., and accommodations furnished to the federal or state government. Many states that exempt lodgings from their sales or use taxes will impose an occupancy tax on such lodgings; some states that impose a sales or use tax on lodgings may impose an additional occupancy tax on the same lodgings.

For purposes of this chart, "T" stands for taxable and "E" for exempt; but the designations are of a general nature, and exceptions unnoted in the chart may exist.

State	Motor Vehicles	Other Tangible Personal Property	Rooms and Lodgings
Alabama	T[1]	T	E[2]
Arizona	T[3]	T	T[4]
Arkansas	T[5,6]	T[7]	T[8]
California	T	T	E[9]
Colorado	T	T[10]	T
Connecticut	T[11]	T	T[1,12]
District of Columbia	T[1]	T	T[1,13]
Florida	T[14]	T	T[15]
Georgia	T	T	T[16]
Hawaii	T[17]	T	T[18]
Idaho	T	T	T[19]
Illinois	T[20]	E[21]	E[2]
Indiana	T[6]	T	T[22]
Iowa	T[23]	T	E[2]
Kansas	T[24]	T[25]	T
Kentucky	E[26]	T	T[22]
Louisiana	T[27]	T	T[28]
Maine	T[29]	T[30]	T[31]
Maryland	T[32]	T	T[33]

State	Motor Vehicles	Other Tangible Personal Property	Rooms and Lodgings
Massachusetts	T[34]	T	E[2]
Michigan	T[35]	T[36]	T[35,37]
Minnesota	T[38]	T	T[22]
Mississippi	T[39]	T	T[40]
Missouri	T[41]	T	T[22,42]
Montana*	T[43]	N/A	T[22]
Nebraska	T[44]	T	T[22,45]
Nevada	T[46]	T[47]	E[9]
New Jersey	T[48]	T	T[16,49]
New Mexico	T[50]	T	T
New York	T[51]	T	T[16,52]
North Carolina	E[53]	T	T[16,54]
North Dakota	E[55]	T	T[22,56]
Ohio	T	T	T[22]
Oklahoma	T[57]	T	T
Pennsylvania	T[58]	T	E[2]
Rhode Island	T[59]	T[60]	T[12]
South Carolina	T[61]	T	T[16,62]
South Dakota	T[63]	T	T[64]
Tennessee	T[61]	T	T[16]
Texas	E[65]	T	E[2]
Utah	T[66]	T	T[22]
Vermont	E[67]	T[68]	E[2]
Virginia	E[69]	T	T[16]
Washington	T[70]	T	T[22]
West Virginia	T[71]	T	T[12]
Wisconsin	T[72]	T	T[73]
Wyoming	T[74]	T	T[22]

* Montana does not impose any form of sales, gross receipts, occupational license, or consumption tax based upon the sale or use of tangible personal property within the state. However, Montana does impose a limited sales and use tax on the base rental charge for rental vehicles, a limited sales and use tax on accommodations and campgrounds, and a lodging facility use tax. A limited sales tax may also be imposed by Montana resort communities.

[1] Special tax rate applies.

[2] Exempt from general sales/use tax, but subject to separate state occupancy tax.

[3] Rentals for 180 days or less subject to additional surcharge.

[4] For rooms rented for less than 30 consecutive days. Owner-occupied bed-and-breakfast establishments that lease no more than four rooms are exempt if average annual occupancy rate is 50% or less. For calendar years 2006 through 2010, leases or rentals of lodging space to a motion picture production company may qualify for exemption.

[5] For rentals of 30 days or more, lessor may pay sales/use tax upon registration or collect sales/use tax and long-term rental tax on periodic lease payments.

[6] Additional tax on rentals of less than 30 days.

[7] For rentals of less than 30 days, tax paid on basis of rental payments to lessor, regardless of whether lessor paid sales or use tax at time of purchase of property.

[8] For rooms rented on less than a month-to-month basis. Subject to additional tourism gross receipts tax.

[9] Exempt from general sales/use tax, but local transient lodging taxes may apply.

[10] Exempt if lease/rental for 3 years or less and lessor paid sales/use tax upon acquisition.

[11] Rentals for less than 31 days subject to additional surcharges. Leases/rentals of certain passenger cars utilizing hybrid technology exempt.

[12] For rooms rented for 30 consecutive days or less.

[13] For rooms rented for 90 consecutive days or less.

[14] Additional surcharge applies to first 30 days of term of any lease/rental.

[15] For rooms rented for 6 months or less.

[16] For rooms rented for less than 90 consecutive days.

[17] Subject to additional surcharge.

[18] Subject to general excise tax and transient accommodations tax.

[19] For rooms rented for 30 consecutive days or less. Additional 2% travel and convention tax imposed. However, if room rented for purpose other than sleeping, travel and convention tax does not apply.

[20] Rentals for one year or less subject to automobile renting occupation tax and use tax.

[21] Lessors pay use tax upon acquisition. Purported lease to nominal lessee that is actually a sale may be subject to retailers' occupation tax.

[22] For rooms rented for less than 30 consecutive days.

[23] Rentals for 60 days or less subject to additional automobile rental excise tax. Leases for 12 months or more exempt from general use tax, but subject to long-term lease tax.

[24] Rentals for 28 days or less subject to additional motor vehicle rental excise tax.

[25] Transaction in form of lease but treated as sale for federal income tax purposes is considered installment sale.

[26] Exempt from general sales/use tax if motor vehicle usage tax paid. Vehicles not subject to motor vehicle usage tax are subject to general sales/use tax.

[27] Subject to general sales/use tax, and automobile rental tax.

[28] For rooms rented for less than two consecutive months. If more than half of guests are permanent or if establishment has less than 6 sleeping rooms at a single location, establishment is not classified as a hotel for sales tax purposes.

[29] Long-term rentals subject to tax at 5%. Short-term auto rental tax imposed on rentals for period of less than one year at rate of 10%.

[30] Only leases deemed by state tax assessor to be in lieu of purchase are treated as sales. In a "straight" lease, lessor pays tax on purchase price, no tax charged to lessee.

[31] Rentals for 28 consecutive days or more exempt if occupant does not maintain primary residence at another location or is away from primary residence for employment or education. As of July 1, 2005, casual rentals of living quarters for more than 14 days in a calendar year taxable.

[32] Leases for 180 days or less taxed at special rate. Leases for one year or more exempt.

[33] Rentals on monthly basis or to permanent residents exempt. All rentals for 4 months or less in resort areas taxable.

[34] Rentals in Boston subject to additional surcharge.

[35] Subject to use tax.

[36] Lessor may elect to pay use tax on rental/lease receipts in lieu of payment of sales/use tax on cost of property upon acquisition.

[37] For rooms rented for one month or less.

[38] Rentals for 28 days or less subject to additional motor vehicle rental fee and tax.

[39] Subject to general sales tax at special rates. Additional rental vehicle tax imposed on rentals for a period of 30 days or less.

[40] Charges for non-transient guests exempt. To be considered non-transient guest, guest must enter into a contract at beginning of stay for a period of at least three consecutive complete months or for a minimum of 90 consecutive days.

[41] Lessor/renter who paid tax on previous purchase, lease, or rental of vehicle, should not collect tax on subsequent lease/rental or sublease/subrental.

[42] Room rentals on permanent basis to certain businesses, including airlines, taxable.

[43] Rentals of not more than 30 days.

[44] For leases of one year or more, lessors may elect to pay tax on cost of vehicle in lieu of collecting tax on lease proceeds. Rentals for 31 days or less subject to additional fee.

[45] Additional tax on total consideration for hotel room occupancy.

[46] Short-term leases subject to additional fees.

[47] Only leases deemed by Tax Commission to be in lieu of a transfer of title, exchange, or barter are treated as sales.

[48] Rentals for 28 days or less subject to additional fee. Leases/rentals of new or used zero-emission vehicles exempt.

[49] Exempt if total amount of rent is $2 per day or less. Additional hotel/motel occupancy fee applies.

[50] Subject to additional leased vehicle gross receipts tax and additional surcharge.

[51] Subject to additional special tax on passenger car rentals. Accelerated sales tax payment provisions apply to long-term leases.

[52] Exempt if total amount of rent is less than $2 per day.

[53] Exempt from general sales/use tax, but subject to highway use tax or alternate gross receipts tax.

[54] Private residences or cottages rented for less than 15 days in calendar year exempt.

[55] Leases for one year or more exempt from general sales/use tax, but subject to motor vehicle excise tax. Rentals for less than 30 days subject to general sales/use tax and surcharge.

[56] From January 1, 2006, through June 30, 2007, a 1% temporary lodging tax is imposed on the lease or rental of hotel, motel, or tourist court accommodations for periods of fewer than 30 consecutive days. The tax is not imposed on the lease or rental of licensed bed and breakfast accommodations.

[57] Leases for 12 months or more exempt from general sales/use tax if owner paid motor vehicle excise tax. Rentals of 90 days or less subject to general sales tax, motor vehicle rental tax, and tourism promotion tax.

[58] Leases for 30 days or more subject to additional motor vehicle lease tax. Rentals for 29 days or less subject to additional rental tax and fee.

[59] For rentals of 30 days or less, car rental companies must collect additional surcharge.

[60] Lessor may elect to pay tax on cost of property upon acquisition or collect tax on total rental/lease charges.

[61] Maximum tax is $300 for each lease (for South Carolina). Rentals for 31 days or less subject to additional surcharge.

[62] Exempt if facility is individual's residence in which fewer than 6 sleeping rooms are rented.

[63] Rentals for 28 days or less subject to additional vehicle rentals tax. Leases/rentals for more than 28 days exempt.

[64] For rooms rented for less than 28 consecutive days. Rentals for 10 days or less in calendar year exempt. In June-September, additional seasonal tax imposed.

[65] Leases for more than 180 days exempt from general sales/use tax, but subject to motor vehicle sales/use tax. Rentals for 30 days or less subject to gross rental receipts tax at rate of 10% (6.25% for rentals longer than 30 days).

[66] Leases/rentals for 30 days or less subject to additional motor vehicle rental tax.

[67] Charges at end of lease for excess wear and tear or excess mileage taxable. Rentals for less than one year subject to rental car use tax.

[68] Rentals of furniture in furnished apartments or houses for residential use are exempt.

[69] Rentals for less than 12 months exempt from general sales/use tax, but subject to motor vehicle sales/use tax. Rental of any daily rental vehicle subject to additional tax (also subject to additional fee, effective July 1, 2004).

[70] Additional motor vehicle sales tax on every rental in the state at rate of 0.3% of net price paid, used to finance transportation improvements. In addition to retail sales tax, rental car tax paid by consumer on rental of passenger car for period of less than 30 days at rate of 5.9%.

[71] Leases for 30 days or more exempt.

[72] Additional fee on rentals for 30 days or less.

[73] For rooms rented for less than one month.

[74] Exempt where rental is computed from gross receipts of the operation, provided operator has a valid interstate authority or permit. Additional surcharge imposed on rentals of passenger or U-Drive-It motor vehicles for 29 days or less.

Manufacturing and Machinery

Many states exempt machinery used in manufacturing or agriculture, while others tax such sales at a reduced rate. Most states require the machinery to be *directly used or consumed* in the process. However, states differ in their definition of *directly used or consumed.* All states currently tax purchases of office equipment.

Most states exempt raw material used in manufacturing. At present, only Hawaii taxes such purchases.

While many states exempt utilities or fuel used in the manufacturing process, some limit what percentage of manufacturing costs can be included as exempt utilities/fuel.

For purposes of this chart, "T" stands for taxable and "E" stands for exempt; but the designations are general and exceptions unnoted on the chart may exist. States that do not impose a sales and use tax are not included in the chart.

State	Manufacturing Machinery	Utilities/Fuel	Farm Machinery
Alabama	T*	E	T*
Arizona	E	T	E
Arkansas	T[1]	T[2]	E
California	E	E	T*
Colorado	E	E	E
Connecticut	E	E	E
District of Columbia	T	E	T
Florida	T[2]	E[3]	E
Georgia	E[4]	T	E
Hawaii	T	T	T
Idaho	E	E	E
Illinois	E	T	E
Indiana	E	E	E
Iowa	E	E	E
Kansas	E	E	E
Kentucky	T[4]	E	E
Louisiana	T[5]	T[1]	T[5]
Maine	E	T*	E
Maryland	E	E	E
Massachusetts	E	E	E
Michigan	E	E	E
Minnesota	T[6]	E[7]	E
Mississippi	T*	T*	T*
Missouri	E	E	E
Nebraska	T[8]	E	E
Nevada	T	T	T[9]
New Jersey	E	T	E
New Mexico	T[10]	T	T*
New York	E	E	E
North Carolina	T[11]	T[11]	T[11]
North Dakota	T[4]	T[4]	T*
Ohio	E	E	E

State	Manufacturing Machinery	Utilities/Fuel	Farm Machinery
Oklahoma	E	E	E
Pennsylvania	E	E	E
Rhode Island	E	E	E
South Carolina	E	E	E
South Dakota	T	T	T*
Tennessee	E	E[12]	E
Texas	E	E	E
Utah	E	E	E
Vermont	E	E	E
Virginia	E	E	E
Washington	E	T	T
West Virginia	E	E[13]	E
Wisconsin	E	T[14]	E
Wyoming	E	E	E[1]

[1] A limited exemption/exclusion available.

[2] Exemption/exclusion available for certain manufacturers or businesses.

[3] Certain fuels are exempt.

[4] Machinery used for "new and expanded industry" is exempt.

[5] Exclusion being phased in.

[6] Refunds available for tax paid on certain capital equipment.

[7] Transportation, transmission, or distribution of certain fuels through pipes, lines, tanks, or mains is taxable.

[8] Effective January 1, 2006, sales of manufacturing machinery and equipment are exempt.

[9] Sales of farm machinery and equipment to a forwarding agent for shipment out of state are exempt. Sales of farm machinery and equipment are also exempt from local school support tax.

[10] A partial credit is available for certain machinery.

[11] Effective January 1, 2006, these sales are exempt.

[12] Manufacturers eligible for a reduced rate for energy, fuel, and water purchases, and a full exemption for separately metered or accounted for energy, fuel and water used directly in the manufacturing process.

[13] Gasoline and special fuels not exempt.

[14] Effective January 1, 2006 fuel and electricity consumed in manufacturing tangible personal property in Wisconsin are exempt.

* Taxed at a reduced rate.

Medicines, Medical Services, and Devices

In all states except Illinois, prescription medicines are exempt from sales and use taxes, and in some states, nonprescription medicines are also exempt. In most states, services provided by licensed medical professionals are specifically excluded from sales and use taxes. However, medical professionals are generally considered consumers of the items used in performing their services and are subject to tax on their purchases.

The types of medical devices that are exempt vary greatly from state to state, and many states require a prescription from a licensed medical professional for the exemption to apply. Some states limit the exemption to prosthetic devices (which replace organic material), while others include durable medical equipment and mobility enhancing equipment in the exemption.

The following chart sets forth the taxability of nonprescription medicines, medical services, and medical devices in each state. For purposes of the chart below, "T" stands for taxable and "E" stands for exempt, while an asterisk after an entry ("E*") indicates that the exemption is limited to devices sold pursuant to a prescription; but the designations are of a general nature, and exceptions unnoted on the chart may exist.

State	Nonprescription Medicines	Medical Services	Medical Devices
Alabama	T	E	T[1]
Arizona	T	E	E *
Arkansas	T	E	E *
California	T	E	E*
Colorado	T	E	E[2]
Connecticut	T[3]	E	E
District of Columbia	E	E	E[4]
Florida	T[3]	E	E*
Georgia	T	E	E*[1]
Hawaii	T	T	E*
Idaho	T	E	E*
Illinois	T[5]	E	T[5]
Indiana	T	E	E*
Iowa	T	E	E[4]
Kansas	T	E	E*
Kentucky	T	E	E[4]
Louisiana	T	E	E*
Maine	T[6]	E	E

State	Nonprescription Medicines	Medical Services	Medical Devices
Maryland	E	E	E
Massachusetts	T	E	E[4]
Michigan	T	E	E*
Minnesota	E	E	E[7]
Mississippi	T[8]	E	T[9]
Missouri	T[10]	E	E
Nebraska	T	E	E*
Nevada	T[8]	E	E*
New Jersey	E	E	E
New Mexico	T	T[1,11]	T[12]
New York	E	E	E
North Carolina	T	E	E[4]
North Dakota	T	E	E
Ohio	T	E	E*
Oklahoma	T	E	T[9]
Pennsylvania	E	E	E
Rhode Island	E	E	E
South Carolina	T[13]	E	E*
South Dakota	T[8]	E	E*
Tennessee	T	E	E
Texas	E	E	E[4]
Utah	T	E	E*
Vermont	E	E	E
Virginia	E	E	E
Washington	T[14]	E	T[15]
West Virginia	T	E	E*
Wisconsin	T[8]	E	E
Wyoming	T	E	E

[1] Exempt if payment under Medicare or Medicaid.
[2] Exempt if $100 or less or, if greater, exempt if sold under prescription.
[3] Specified items exempt.
[4] Prescription required for some types of devices.
[5] Taxed at a reduced rate.
[6] Exempt if purchased by a doctor for use in practice.
[7] Effective July 1, 2005, durable medical equipment exempt only if sold to an individual for home use.
[8] Exempt if furnished by medical personnel.
[9] Exempt if prescribed and payment made under Medicare/Medicaid.

[10] Sales of non-prescription drugs to or for use by disabled persons are exempt.

[11] Effective January 1, 2005, New Mexico removed the gross receipts tax on certain health care services by allowing health care practitioners to deduct from gross receipts payments they receive from managed health care providers or health care insurers for commercial contract services or Medicare Part C services provided by a health care practitioner. Receipts from fee-for-service payments by a health care insurer do not qualify. (Ch. 116 (H.B. 625), Laws 2004)

[12] Only exempt if delivered directly by licensed practitioner incidental to, and included in the cost of providing a service.

[13] Exempt if sold to health care clinic that provides free medical and dental care to all of its patients.

[14] Naturopathic medicines dispensed or used by a licensed naturopath in the treatment of a patient are exempt.

[15] Some devices are taxable while others are exempt if sold under a prescription.

Newspapers and Periodicals

The method of taxing receipts from the sales of newspapers and periodicals varies greatly among the states. In some states, publishers of newspapers are considered to be rendering a service and the gross receipts from the sales of newspapers are, as a result, not taxable. In other states that tax services, newspapers, magazines and periodicals are granted specific exemption from the tax, while, in a few states, newspapers and periodicals are regarded as tangible personal property and are subject to tax.

For purposes of this chart, "T" stands for taxable and "E" stands for exempt, but the designations are of a general nature and exceptions unnoted in the chart may exist.

States that do not impose a sales and use tax are not included in this chart.

State	Newspapers	Periodicals
Alabama	T	T
Arizona	T	T
Arkansas	E	T[1]
California	T[2]	T[2]
Colorado	E	T
Connecticut	E	E
District of Columbia	T	T
Florida	T[3]	T[3]
Georgia	T	T
Hawaii	T	T
Idaho	T[4]	T[4]
Illinois	E	E
Indiana	E	T[5]
Iowa	E	T
Kansas	T	T
Kentucky	T	T
Louisiana	T[6]	T
Maine	T[7]	T[7]
Maryland	T[8]	T
Massachusetts	E	E[9]
Michigan	E[10]	E[10]
Minnesota	E	T[7]

State	Newspapers	Periodicals
Mississippi	E[11]	T[12]
Missouri	T	T
Nebraska	E[13]	T
Nevada	E[14]	T
New Jersey	E	E
New Mexico	E	T
New York	E	E
North Carolina	E[15]	E[15]
North Dakota	E	T[16]
Ohio	E	T[17]
Oklahoma	E	E
Pennsylvania	E[18]	T[1]
Rhode Island	E	T
South Carolina	E	T
South Dakota	T	T
Tennessee	E[19]	E[19]
Texas	E	T[20]
Utah	E	T
Vermont	E	T
Virginia	E[21]	E[21]
Washington	E	T[22]
West Virginia	T[23]	T
Wisconsin	E	E[24]
Wyoming	E	T

[1] Exempt if sold by subscription.
[2] Exemptions provided for certain newspapers and periodicals distributed at no charge, published by exempt organizations, or sold by subscription and delivered by mail or common carrier.
[3] Subscriptions delivered by mail are exempt, as are advertising periodicals delivered free of charge.
[4] Subscriptions to and single-copy sales of newspapers and magazines are taxed if the single-copy price exceeds 11¢. Free distribution publications exempt.
[5] Periodicals distributed as part of a newspaper are exempt.
[6] The exemption for newspapers is suspended through June 30, 2009.
[7] Publications regularly issued at average intervals not exceeding 3 months are exempt.
[8] Newspapers that are distributed by a publisher at no charge are exempt.
[9] Exemption limited to magazines and publications of certain nonprofit organizations.
[10] Exempt if publication is: (1) accepted as second-class mail or as a controlled circulation publication, (2) qualified to accept legal notices for publication in Michigan, or (3) of general circulation established at least two years and published at least weekly.

[11] Sales of daily or weekly newspapers exempt.

[12] Certain periodicals of exempt scientific, literary, or educational organizations and subscription sales of all magazines are exempt.

[13] Exemption limited to newspapers regularly issued at average intervals not exceeding one week.

[14] Newspapers regularly issued at intervals not exceeding one week.

[15] Exemption applies to newspapers sold by street vendors, by carriers making door-to-door deliveries, or through vending machines and to magazine vendors making door-to-door sales.

[16] Periodicals furnished by a nonprofit to members without charge are exempt.

[17] Magazine subscriptions and sales or transfers of magazines distributed as controlled circulation publications are exempt.

[18] Exemption applies to newspapers of general circulation qualified to carry a legal advertisement.

[19] Exemption applies to periodicals printed entirely on newsprint or bond paper and regularly distributed twice monthly or on a biweekly or more frequent basis. Magazines that are distributed and sold to consumers through U.S. mail or common carrier are exempt if the only activities carried on by the seller or distributor in Tennessee are the printing, storage, labeling, and delivery to the mail or carrier.

[20] Subscriptions to magazines are exempt if sold for a semiannual or longer period and if entered as second-class mail.

[21] Newsstand sales are taxable. Exemption applies to any publication issued daily, or regularly at intervals not exceeding 3 months.

[22] Certain sales for fundraising purposes are exempt.

[23] Exempt if delivered to consumers by route carriers.

[24] Exemption applies to periodicals sold by subscription and regularly issued at average intervals not exceeding 3 months (6 months for educational associations and certain nonprofit corporations), certain controlled circulation publications, and shoppers guides that distribute no less than 48 issues in a 12-month period.

Occasional Sales

This chart notes the taxability of occasional (isolated or casual) sales by persons not engaged in business, such as private individuals and nonprofit corporations. An exemption for sales by persons engaged in business but selling property not sold in the regular course of their business is noted. Many states have, either explicitly, or through their definition of "occasional sale," imposed limits on their occasional sales exemption, such as limiting the exempt sales to family members or to a maximum dollar amount or limiting the number of days in a year such sales can be held. With regard to motor vehicles, vessels, and aircraft, in many states the transaction is subject to use tax rather than sales tax.

For purposes of this chart, "T" stands for taxable and "E" stands for exempt. However, the designations are of a general nature, and exceptions unnoted in the chart may exist.

States that do not impose a general sales or use tax are not included in this chart.

State	Motor Vehicles, Vessels and Aircraft	All Other Sales
Alabama	E[1]	E[2]
Arizona	E	E[2]
Arkansas	T	E
California	T[3]	E
Colorado	T	T
Connecticut	T[3]	E[2]
District of Columbia	E[1]	E
Florida	T[4]	E[2]
Georgia	E	E[2]
Hawaii	E	E[2]
Idaho	T[4]	E
Illinois	E[5]	E[2]
Indiana	T[4]	E[2]
Iowa	T[6,7]	E[2]
Kansas	T[4]	E[2]
Kentucky	E[1]	E
Louisiana	T	E[2]
Maine	T[4]	E[2]
Maryland	E[1,8]	E[9]

State	Motor Vehicles, Vessels and Aircraft	All Other Sales
Massachusetts	T[4]	E[2]
Michigan	T[4]	E[2,6]
Minnesota	E[1]	E[2]
Mississippi	T[4,10]	E
Missouri	T	E[2,11]
Nebraska	T[4]	E[2]
Nevada	T[4]	E
New Jersey	T[4]	E
New Mexico	E[1]	E[2]
New York	T[4]	E[12]
North Carolina	E[1]	E
North Dakota	E[1]	E[2]
Ohio	T[4]	E[2]
Oklahoma	E[1]	T
Pennsylvania	T[4]	E[2]
Rhode Island	T[4]	E[2]
South Carolina	E[1]	E
South Dakota	E[1]	E
Tennessee	T[4]	E[2]
Texas	E[1]	E
Utah	T	E[2]
Vermont	E[1]	E
Virginia	E[1]	E[2]
Washington	T	E[2,6]
West Virginia	E	E[2]
Wisconsin	T[4]	E[2,13]
Wyoming	T	T[14]

[1] Exempt from general sales/use tax, but subject to separate tax.
[2] Includes exemption provisions for a retailer selling property, if the transaction is not in the regular course of business.
[3] Motor vehicle sales specifically excluded from occasional sales exemption. Separate sales tax exemption exists for sales by non-dealers, but purchaser subject to use tax. Use tax exemptions may apply for certain family and/or corporate transfers/sales.
[4] Exemptions may apply for certain family and/or business entity transfers/sales.

[5] Sales by individuals and non-dealers are exempt from retailers' occupation tax and general use tax, but are subject to vehicle use tax.

[6] Exempt from sales tax, but purchaser liable for payment of use tax.

[7] Use tax exemptions may apply for certain family and/or corporate transfers/sales. Motor vehicle sales specifically excluded from occasional sales exemption.

[8] Short-term rentals are taxable.

[9] Exemption applies only if the sale price is less than $1,000 and the sale is not made through an auctioneer or dealer.

[10] Taxed at reduced rate.

[11] Exemption does not apply if gross receipts from all such sales in calendar year exceed $3,000.

[12] Exemption applies only to first $600 of receipts from such sales in calendar year.

[13] Exemption applies to persons not required to hold a seller's permit only if gross receipts for calendar year are less than $1,000 ($1,000 threshold does not apply to nonprofit organizations). Includes exemption provisions for a retailer selling property, if the transaction is not in the regular course of business.

[14] Exemption applies only to occasional sales by religious or charitable organizations.

Optional Warranty Agreements

The following chart details the taxability of optional warranties, as well as the parts used to fulfill those warranties. Optional warranties are service agreements purchased in addition to an item that provide for the repair or maintenance of that item. Such warranties typically augment the coverage of the non-optional manufacturers warranty, which is included with the item at no additional cost to the purchaser. Most states impose either sales tax on the sale of the optional warranty or use tax on the cost of the parts used to repair or maintain an item under the warranty.

For purposes of the chart, "Yes" denotes that the item is taxable and "No" indicates that the item is non-taxable, but the designations are of a general nature, and exceptions unnoted in the chart may exist. States that do not impose a sales and use tax are not included in the chart.

State	Sales Tax on Optional Warranty Agreement	Use Tax on Parts Under Optional Warranty
Alabama	No	Yes, except manufacturer warranty
Arizona	No	Yes
Arkansas	Yes	No
California	No	Yes
Colorado	No	Yes
Connecticut	Yes	No
District of Columbia	Yes	Yes
Florida	Yes	No
Georgia	No	Yes
Hawaii	Yes	Yes
Idaho	No	Yes
Illinois	No	Yes
Indiana	No	Yes
Iowa	Yes (50%-computer service warranty), except residential service contracts	No, except residential maintenance contracts
Kansas	Yes, except residential maintenance contracts	No, except residential maintenance contracts
Kentucky	No	Yes
Louisiana	No	Yes
Maine	No	Yes
Maryland	No	Yes
Massachusetts	No	Yes
Michigan	No	Yes
Minnesota	No	Yes
Mississippi	Yes, except motor vehicle third-party warranties	No
Missouri	No	Yes
Nebraska	Yes, except fixtures	No, except fixtures

State	Sales Tax on Optional Warranty Agreement	Use Tax on Parts Under Optional Warranty
Nevada	No	Yes
New Jersey	Yes	No
New Mexico	No	Yes
New York	Yes	No
North Carolina	No	Yes
North Dakota	No	Yes
Ohio	Yes	No
Oklahoma	No	Yes
Pennsylvania	Yes	No
Rhode Island	No, except leases	Yes
South Carolina	Yes, except motor vehicles or if warranty purchased after sale	Yes
South Dakota	Yes, unless an insurance policy	No
Tennessee	Yes	No
Texas	Yes, except motor vehicles	No
Utah	Yes	No
Vermont	No	Yes
Virginia	Yes (on 50% of total charge for contract), where both parts and services covered	No
Washington	Yes	No
West Virginia	Yes	No
Wisconsin	Yes	No
Wyoming	No	Yes

Pollution Control Equipment

Pollution control equipment and machinery are exempt from sales and use tax in many states, either as part of the processing exemption or as a separate exemption.

For purposes of this chart, "T" stands for taxable and "E" stands for exempt; but the designations are of a general nature, and exceptions unnoted in this chart may exist. States that do not impose a general sales and use tax are not included in this chart.

State	Air	Water
Alabama	E	E
Arizona	E	E
Arkansas	E[1]	E[1]
California	T[2]	T[2]
Colorado	T[3]	T[3]
Connecticut	E	E
District of Columbia	T	T
Florida	E	E
Georgia	E	E
Hawaii	E	T
Idaho	E[1]	E[1]
Illinois	T	T
Indiana	E[1]	E[1]
Iowa	E	E
Kansas	E	E
Kentucky	E[4]	E[4]
Louisiana	E	E
Maine	E	E
Maryland	E[1]	E[1]
Massachusetts	T	T
Michigan	E	E
Minnesota	T[5]	T[5]
Mississippi	E[1]	E[1]
Missouri	E	E
Nebraska	T[6]	T[6]

State	Air	Water
Nevada	T	T
New Jersey	T	T
New Mexico	T	T
New York	E	E
North Carolina	T[7]	T[7]
North Dakota	T	T
Ohio	E	E
Oklahoma	T[8]	T[8]
Pennsylvania	E	E
Rhode Island	E	E
South Carolina	E[1]	E[1]
South Dakota	T	T
Tennessee	E	E
Texas	E[1]	E[1]
Utah	E[9]	E[9]
Vermont	T	T
Virginia	E[10]	E[10]
Washington	T[11]	T
West Virginia	E	E
Wisconsin	T[12]	T[12]
Wyoming	T	T

[1] Exempt only if required by federal or state law.
[2] Transfers of property constituting any project or pollution control facility to or from the California Pollution Control Financing Authority are exempt.
[3] Qualified taxpayers are allowed a sales and use tax refund if state revenues exceed a certain threshold.
[4] After June 2005, equipment that reduces emissions at a power plant may qualify for exemption as environmental upgrade equipment.
[5] Pollution control equipment purchased by steel reprocessors or used at a resource recovery facility may be exempt.
[6] Tax is refundable.
[7] May qualify for reduced rate of tax applicable to manufacturing machinery.
[8] Exemption is provided for certain equipment used in the process of reducing hazardous waste at treatment facilities permitted under the Hazardous Waste Disposal Act.
[9] Exempt if certification of pollution control facility obtained.
[10] Exempt if certified by the Department of Taxation as being in conformity with the state program or requirements
[11] Sales of tangible personal property for construction or installation of air pollution control facilities at a thermal electric generation facility may be exempt.
[12] The sale or use of tangible personal property that becomes a component part of certain industrial waste treatment facilities is exempt.

Sales for Resale

Generally, a sales tax is levied on retail transactions, and as a result, sales made for resale (i.e., "wholesale" sales) fall outside the purview of the tax. Hawaii is the only state that taxes sales for resale, with the exception of imports.

The burden of proving that a sale is made for resale generally rests upon the seller. In some states, the only evidence required and acceptable is a certificate of resale (or, in some states, an exemption certificate) obtained *in good faith* from the buyer. Where continual sales of the same type are being made to the same buyer, blanket certificates of resale are usually permitted.

The following chart indicates whether the state allows sellers to accept the Multistate Tax Compact (MTC) Uniform Multijurisdiction Exemption Certificate and/or the Border States Uniform Sales for Resale Certificate (BSC) for purposes of sales made for resale. Some states place limitations on acceptance of the MTC Certificate. These limitations are noted on the Certificate Instructions. States with noted limitations are indicated with an asterisk below (MTC*).

States that do not impose a sales and use tax are not included in this chart.

State	Multistate Certificate Accepted?
Alabama	MTC*
Arizona	BSC, MTC*
Arkansas	MTC
California	BSC, MTC*
Colorado	MTC*
Connecticut	MTC*
District of Columbia	MTC*
Florida	MTC*
Georgia	MTC*
Hawaii	MTC*
Idaho	MTC
Illinois	MTC*
Indiana	No
Iowa	MTC
Kansas	MTC
Kentucky	MTC*
Louisiana	No
Maine	MTC*
Maryland	MTC*
Massachusetts	No
Michigan	MTC*
Minnesota	MTC*
Mississippi	No
Missouri	MTC*
Nebraska	MTC*
Nevada	MTC
New Jersey	MTC
New Mexico	BSC, MTC*
New York	No

State	Multistate Certificate Accepted?
North Carolina	MTC*
North Dakota	MTC
Ohio	MTC*
Oklahoma	MTC*
Pennsylvania	MTC*
Rhode Island	MTC*
South Carolina	MTC
South Dakota	MTC*
Tennessee	MTC
Texas	BSC, MTC*
Utah	MTC
Vermont	MTC
Virginia	No
Washington	MTC*
West Virginia	No
Wisconsin	MTC*
Wyoming	No

Services

Most states impose their sales taxes primarily on retail transactions that involve the transfer of tangible personal property, and tax applies only to those services specifically subjected to taxation. A few states impose their taxes more generally on all sales of property and services or on the privilege of doing business, and under such a scheme charges for the provision of services (with certain exceptions) are taxable. Note also that an otherwise nontaxable service may be subject to tax if it is construed to be part of a taxable sale of tangible personal property.

Property and services purchased by service providers: Generally, a service provider must pay tax when purchasing property that he or she will use or consume in the business of providing a service. If taxable items will also be sold to customers in the regular course of business, however, the service provider's initial purchases of those particular items should qualify as exempt purchases for resale. In addition, a number of states have provisions specifically allowing a service provider to purchase *services* for resale.

Services chart: The "General Treatment" column indicates the tax scheme followed in each state:

"NT" means "not taxable"— the state taxes only a few specified services, or no services;

"MT" means "many taxable"— the law provides that only specified services are taxable, but the state has chosen to tax a number of them; and

"GT" means "generally taxable"— tax imposed generally on the provision of services, although certain specific services may be exempt.

The four columns to the right indicate more specifically how each state treats a few particular types of services (cleaning, intrastate transportation, repair, and professional/personal services (excluding medical services). In these columns, "T" stands for "taxable" and "E" stands for "exempt." Note, however, that these designations are of a general nature; exceptions may exist that are not reflected in the chart.

State	General Treatment	Cleaning Services	Transportation Services	Repair Services	Professional/ Personal Services
Alabama	NT	E	E[1]	E	E
Arizona	MT[2]	E	T[3]	E[4]	E
Arkansas	MT	T	E	T[5]	E[6]
California	NT	E	E	E	E
Colorado	NT	E	E	E	E
Connecticut	MT	T[7]	E	T[5]	T
District of Columbia .	MT	T	E	T	E[6]

State	General Treatment	Cleaning Services	Transportation Services	Repair Services	Professional/ Personal Services
Florida	MT	T[8]	E	E[9]	E[6]
Georgia	NT	E	T[10]	E	E
Hawaii	GT	T	T[11]	T	T
Idaho	NT	E	T[12]	E	E
Illinois	NT[13]	E	E	E	E
Indiana	NT	E	E	E	E
Iowa	MT	T	E[14]	T[15]	T[16]
Kansas	MT	E	E	T	E
Kentucky	NT	E	E	E	E
Louisiana	NT	E[17]	E	T[5]	E
Maine	NT	E	E	E	E
Maryland	NT	T[18]	E	E	E[6]
Massachusetts	NT	E	E	E	E
Michigan	NT	E	E	E	E
Minnesota	MT	T	E	E	E[6]
Mississippi	GT	E	E	T[19]	E[6]
Missouri	NT	E	T[20]	E	E
Nebraska	NT	T	E	T[21]	E[6]
Nevada	NT	E	E	E	E
New Jersey	MT	T	E[43]	T	E[44]
New Mexico	GT	T	T	T	T
New York	MT	T[22]	E	T[5]	E[6]
North Carolina	NT	E	E	E	E
North Dakota	NT	E	E[23]	E	E
Ohio	MT	T	T[24]	T[25]	E[6]
Oklahoma	MT	E	T[26]	E	E
Pennsylvania	MT	T	E	T[27]	E[6]
Rhode Island	NT	E	E	E	E
South Carolina	NT	E	E	E	E
South Dakota	GT	T	T[28]	T	T[29]
Tennessee	NT	E[30]	E	T	E
Texas	MT	T	E[31]	T[32]	T[16]

State	General Treatment	Cleaning Services	Transportation Services	Repair Services	Professional/ Personal Services
Utah	MT	E[33]	T[34]	T[35]	E
Vermont	NT	E	E	E	E
Virginia	NT	E	E[36]	E	E
Washington	MT	E	E[37]	T	E[6]
West Virginia	GT	T	T[38]	T[39]	E[6]
Wisconsin	MT	E[40]	E	T	E[6]
Wyoming	NT	E[41]	T[42]	T	E

[1] Exemption limited to transportation services of the kind and nature that would be regulated by the state Public Service Commission or similar regulatory body if sold by a public utility.

[2] Tax is imposed on a number of distinct business *classifications*, including certain services.

[3] Taxpayers subject to motor carrier fee or light motor vehicle fee exempt. Certain transportation services provided by railroads, ambulances, dial-a-ride programs, or special needs programs exempt.

[4] Repairs to tangible personal property permanently attached to real property are taxable under the contracting classification.

[5] Special exemptions apply.

[6] A limited number of services are taxable.

[7] Janitorial or maintenance services performed on a casual-sale basis are not taxable. Janitorial services for the disabled may be exempt.

[8] Nonresidential cleaning services, including janitorial services on a contract or fee basis, are taxable. Residential cleaning services exempt.

[9] Repairer's records must establish that no tangible personal property was furnished and incorporated into or attached to the repaired item.

[10] Passenger transportation by public transit exempt. Charges for transportation of tangible personal property, including refrigeration, switching, storage, and demurrage exempt.

[11] Certain stevedoring and towing services, inter-island transport of agricultural commodities, and passenger transport by helicopter or county mass transit system are generally exempt.

[12] Air transportation generally taxable; ground transportation services exempt.

[13] Special service occupation tax is imposed on the price of property transferred incident to a service, but not on the service itself.

[14] Limousine services taxable.

[15] The tax applies to labor for "enumerated services". Most repairs of tangible personal property fall under an enumerated service. Where the repair is not an enumerated service, the charge for labor is exempt if separately stated.

[16] In general, personal services are taxable, professional services are exempt.

[17] Cleaning furniture, carpeting, and rugs is taxable.

[18] Cleaning of a commercial or industrial building is taxable. Cleaning for individuals is exempt.

[19] Charges for repair services are excluded from gross income for sales and use tax purposes when the property on which the service was performed is delivered to the customer in another state by common carrier or in the seller's equipment.

[20] Exempt if provided on contract basis, when no ticket is issued. Transport by limousines, taxis, and buses that are not required to be licensed by the Division of Motor Carrier and Railroad Safety exempt.

[21] Most charges for labor to repair motor vehicles are not taxable. Charges for repair labor performed on a nontaxable item of tangible personal property are not taxable.

[22] Interior cleaning and maintenance service agreements of 30 days or more are taxable.

[23] Passenger transportation exempt.

[24] Transportation of persons by aircraft or motor vehicle, exempt ambulance or transit bus, taxable. Charges by delivery companies that are not making sales of tangible personal property generally exempt.

[25] Certain exemptions apply to ships, rail rolling stock, motor vehicles, and aircraft.

[26] Fares of $1 or less; passenger transportation within corporate limits of municipality, except by taxi; and certain transportation services provided by tourism service brokers or funeral establishments exempt.

[27] Certain exemptions exist for the repair of clothing, shoes, manufacturing machines, and repairs involving real estate.

[28] Certain railroad, river/canal, and air transportation; trucking and courier services; and local and suburban passenger transportation, except limousine service, exempt.

[29] Health services exempt.

[30] Cleaning real property, such as windows, walls, and carpeting is exempt. Cleaning personal property, including furniture, rugs, and draperies, is taxable.

[31] Transportation services provided on a stand alone basis exempt. Transportation services that are incident to the performance of a taxable service are taxable.

[32] Certain exemptions exist for the repair of aircraft, certain ships and boats, motor vehicles, and computer programs.

[33] However, cleaning tangible personal property is taxable.

[34] Effective July 1, 2006, transportation provided by common carrier is exempt.

[35] May be exempt if the tangible personal property being repaired is exempt.

[36] Separately stated transportation charges are exempt.

[37] Automotive transportation services, including towing , are taxable unless taxpayer is subject to public utilities tax. Charges for moving existing structures/buildings is taxable.

[38] Businesses regulated by the Public Service Commission exempt.

[39] Repairs that result in a capital improvement to a building or other structure or to real property are tax-exempt contracting services.

[40] Routine and repetitive janitorial services exempt. Specialized cleaning of tangible personal property taxable; specialized cleaning of real property exempt.

[41] However, generally, services for repair, alteration, or improvement of tangible personal property are taxable.

[42] Transportation by ambulance or hearse and certain transportation of freight/property, raw farm products, and drilling rigs exempt. Transportation of employees to/from work exempt when paid or contracted for by employee or employer.

[43] Effective October 1, 2006, transportation services provided by limousine operators are taxable.

[44] Effective October 1, 2006, a limited number of professional/personal services are taxable.

Shipping

The following chart indicates whether shipping fees charged in connection with the delivery of tangible personal property are included in the tax base for sales and use tax purposes. The term "shipping" refers to any charge incurred for the transportation of property from the seller to the purchaser, commonly refered to as delivery, freight, and transportation charges.

In many states, freight charges are excluded from tax when title transfers prior to shipment, and the buyer assumes liability during shipment (F.O.B. origin). If however, title transfers at the point of delivery (F.O.B. destination), such as in the case of most retail goods, then the seller must include shipping charges in the taxable sales price. States that exclude shipping charges from the tax base generally require that the charges be stated separately from the purchase price for the exclusion to apply.

States that do not impose a sales and use tax are not included in the chart.

State	Shipping Charges Included in Basis
Alabama	Excluded where (1) charges are separately stated and paid by the purchaser, and (2) delivery is by common carrier or the U.S. Postal Service.[1]
Arizona	Excluded where charges are separately stated.
Arkansas	Included[2,3]
California	Excluded where (1) charges are separately stated and (2) delivery is by common carrier or the U.S. Postal Service.
Colorado	Excluded where charges are (1) separable from the sales transaction, and (2) separately stated.[4]
Connecticut	Included[5]
District of Columbia	Included[6]
Florida	Excluded where charges are (1) separately stated, and (2) optional.[4]
Georgia	Included[4]
Hawaii	Included[7]
Idaho	Excluded where charges are separately stated.[8]
Illinois	Excluded where charges are separately contracted.
Indiana	Included[3]
Iowa	Excluded where charges are separately contracted for and separately stated.[3]
Kansas	Included[3]

State	Shipping Charges Included in Basis
Kentucky	Included[3]
Louisiana	Included[6]
Maine	Excluded where (1) shipment is made direct to the purchaser, (2) charges are separately stated, and (3) the transportation occurs by means of common carrier, contract carrier or the United States mail.
Maryland	Excluded where charges are separately stated.[9]
Massachusetts	Excluded where charges (1) reflect the costs of preparing and delivering goods to a location designated by the buyer, (2) are separately stated on the invoice to the buyer, and (3) are set in good faith and reasonably reflect the actual costs incurred by the vendor.
Michigan	Excluded if separately stated and incurred after the transfer of ownership to the purchaser.[3,10]
Minnesota	Included[3]
Mississippi	Included
Missouri	Excluded where charges are (1) separately stated, and (2) optional.
Nebraska	Included[3,11]
Nevada	Included[3,12]
New Jersey	Included[3,13]
New Mexico	Included
New York	Included[14]
North Carolina	Included[3]
North Dakota	Included[3,15]
Ohio	Included[3,16]
Oklahoma	Included[3,17]
Pennsylvania	Included[18]
Rhode Island	Included[19]
South Carolina	Included[4]
South Dakota	Included[3,20]
Tennessee	Included[4,21]
Texas	Included[22]
Utah	Excluded if separately stated.[3,23]

State	Shipping Charges Included in Basis
Vermont	Excluded where (1) charges are separately stated, and (2) the transportation occurs by means of common carrier, contract carrier or the United States mail.
Virginia	Excluded where separately stated
Washington	Included[5],[24]
West Virginia	Excluded where (1) delivery is by common carrier, and (2) the customer pays the delivery charge directly to the carrier.[3]
Wisconsin	Included[3],[6]
Wyoming	Excluded[3]

[1] Transportation charges are not separate and identifiable if included with other charges and billed as "shipping and handling" or "postage and handling."

[2] Charges billed to buyer by a carrier other than the seller are excluded.

[3] If shipment includes both exempt and taxable property, the seller should allocate the delivery charge on the basis of the sales price or weight of the property being delivered and must tax the percentage allocated to the taxable property.

[4] Charges for transportation after title passes to the buyer are excluded.

[5] Charges to deliver tax-exempt items are excluded.

[6] Excluded where (1) charges are separately stated and (2) delivery occurs after the sale.

[7] Charges for items shipped outside the state are excluded.

[8] Charges by a manufactured homes dealer to transport the home to a buyer are included.

[9] Charges for delivering goods to seller or between various locations of seller are taxable.

[10] Charges incurred prior to the transfer of ownership are taxable, unless the retailer is engaged in a separate delivery business.

[11] Shipping charges paid to a person other than the retailer are exempt.

[12] Excluded where (1) charges are separately stated, and (2) title passes to the purchaser before shipment pursuant to a written agreement.

[13] Prior to October 1, 2006, delivery charges were excluded if separately stated.

[14] Exceptions apply for charges to ship promotional materials under certain circumstances.

[15] Shipping charges are excluded if the product being shipped is exempt.

[16] Charges paid by customer to delivery company (not imposed/collected by retailer) are not taxable.

[17] Excluded where separately stated.

[18] Charges made in conjunction with nontaxable transactions are excluded. Charges for delivery made and billed by someone other than seller of item being delivered not taxable.

[19] Separately stated charges for transportation after title has passed to the purchaser are excluded.

[20] Freight charges paid directly to freight company (not to seller) by purchaser are exempt.

[21] Provisions conforming to the Streamlined Sales and Use Tax Agreement take effect July 1, 2007.

[22] Shipping charges incident to the sale or lease/rental of taxable tangible personal property or the performance of taxable services that are billed by the seller/lessor to the purchaser/lessee are taxable. A third-party carrier that only provides transportation and does not sell the item being delivered is not responsible for collecting tax.

[23] Effective July 1, 2006, all transportation by common carrier is exempt.

[24] Charges incurred after purchaser has taken receipt of the goods are excluded.

Statutes of Limitations

This chart provides the statute of limitations periods for all states and the District of Columbia. The periods reflect the time within which states must take action to assess additional sales and use taxes after a return is filed or if no return is filed.

States that do not impose a sales and use tax are not included in this chart.

State	Statute of Limitations Period		
	If a Return Is Filed	If No Return Is Filed	If a False or Fraudulent Return Is Filed
Alabama	Later of 3 years from date filed or 3 years from due date. If base understated by more than 25%, later of 6 years from date return was due or date return was filed.	No limitation	No limitation
Arizona	Later of 4 years from date filed or 4 years from date due. If receipts understated by more than 25%, 6 years from the date the return was filed.	No limitation	No limitation
Arkansas	Later of 3 years from date filed or 3 years from date due. If tax understated by 25% or more, later of 6 years from date return was due or date return was filed.	No limitation	No limitation
California	Later of 3 years from the end of the calendar month following the end of the quarterly period to which the deficiency determination relates or 3 years from the date filed	8 years after the end of the calendar month following the quarterly period	No limitation
Colorado	3 years from date due	No limitation	No limitation
Connecticut	The later of 3 years from the last day of the month following the period to which the deficiency relates or 3 years from the date filed	No limitation	No limitation
District of Columbia ..	3 years from date filed. 6 years from the date the return was filed if tax understated by more than 25%.	No limitation	No limitation

State	Statute of Limitations Period		
	If a Return Is Filed	**If No Return Is Filed**	**If a False or Fraudulent Return Is Filed**
Florida	Later of 3 years (5 years for taxes due before July 1, 1999) from the date the return is due, filed, or the tax is due; or 6 years from the later of the date a substantial underpayment of tax is made or a substantially incorrect return is filed	No limitation	No limitation
Georgia	Later of 3 years from date filed or 3 years from date due	No limitation	No limitation
Hawaii	Later of 3 years from date filed or 3 years from date due	No limitation	No limitation
Idaho	The later of 3 years from date filed or 3 years from date due	7 years from date due	No limitation
Illinois	3 years from the month or period in which the taxable gross receipts were received (assessments issued on January 1 or July 1)	No limitation	No limitation
Indiana	Later of 3 years from date return was filed or 3 years from end of calendar year containing the period for which the return was filed	No limitation	No limitation
Iowa	5 years after a return is filed, for quarterly periods beginning before the year 2000; 4 years for quarterly periods beginning in 2000; and 3 years for quarterly periods beginning after 2000	No limitation	No limitation
Kansas	3 years from date filed	No limitation	2 years from the discovery of the fraud
Kentucky	Later of 4 years from date filed or 4 years from date due	No limitation	No limitation
Louisiana	3 years from the 31st day of December in the year the taxes were due	No limitation	No limitation

State	Statute of Limitations Period		
	If a Return Is Filed	**If No Return Is Filed**	**If a False or Fraudulent Return Is Filed**
Maine	Later of 3 years from date filed or 3 years from date due; 6 years from date filed where substantial underreporting of liability	No limitation	No limitation
Maryland	4 years from date due	No limitation if due to gross negligence	No limitation
Massachusetts	Later of 3 years from date filed or 3 years from date due	No limitation	No limitation
Michigan	The later of 4 years from date filed or 4 years from date due	Liable for all taxes due for the entire period for which the person would be subject to the taxes	Assessment of up to 2 years after the discovery of the fraud
Minnesota	Later of 3.5 years from date return was due or 3.5 years from date return was filed. If taxes underreported by more than 25%: later of 6.5 years from date return was due or the return was filed.	No limitation	No limitation
Mississippi	3 years from date filed	No limitation	No limitation
Missouri	Later of 3 years from date filed or 3 years from date due	No limitation	No limitation
Nebraska	Later of 3 years from date filed or 3 years from the last day of the calendar month following the period to which the deficiency relates	5 years after the last day of the calendar month following the period to which the deficiency relates	Not specifically addressed in statutes or regulations
Nevada	Later of 3 years from date filed or 3 years from the last day of the calendar month following the period to which the deficiency relates	8 years after the calendar month following the period for which the assessment is proposed to be determined	No limitation
New Jersey	4 years from date filed	No limitation	No limitation
New Mexico	3 years from the end of the calendar year in which payment was due. If taxes underreported by more than 25%, 6 years from the end of the calendar year in which the tax payment was due.	7 years from the end of the calendar year in which payment was due	10 years from the end of the calendar year in which payment was due

State	Statute of Limitations Period		
	If a Return Is Filed	**If No Return Is Filed**	**If a False or Fraudulent Return Is Filed**
New York	Later of 3 years from date filed or 3 years from date due	No limitation	No limitation
North Carolina	Later of 3 years from date filed or 3 years from date due	No limitation	No limitation
North Dakota	Later of 3 years from date filed or 3 years from date due. If tax understated by 25% or more, 6 years from the later of date return was due or date return was filed.	6 years after due date	No limitation
Ohio	Later of 4 years from date filed or 4 years from date due	No limitation	No limitation
Oklahoma	Later of 3 years from date filed or 3 years from date due	No limitation	No limitation
Pennsylvania	Later of 3 years from date filed or the end of the year in which the liability arose	No limitation	No limitation
Rhode Island	Later of 3 years from date filed or 3 years from the 15th day of the month on which the return is due	No limitation	No limitation
South Carolina	Later of 3 years from date filed or 3 years from date due. If tax understated by 20% or more, later of 6 years from date return was due or date return was filed.	No limitation	No limitation
South Dakota	3 years from date filed	No limitation	No limitation
Tennessee	3 years from December 31 of the year in which filed	No limitation	No limitation
Texas	The later of 4 years from date filed or 4 years after last day of month following close of regular reporting period. If tax understated by 25% or more, no limitations period.	No limitation	No limitation
Utah	3 years from date filed	No limitation	No limitation

State	Statute of Limitations Period		
	If a Return Is Filed	If No Return Is Filed	If a False or Fraudulent Return Is Filed
Vermont..........	The later of 3 years from date filed or 3 years from date due. If tax understated by 20% or more, 6 years from date return was filed.	No limitation	No limitation
Virginia	3 years from date due	6 years from date due	6 years from date due
Washington	4 years after the close of the tax year	Not specifically addressed in statutes or regulations	No limitation
West Virginia	Later of 3 years from date filed or 3 years from date due	No limitation	No limitation
Wisconsin	4 years from date filed	No limitation	No limitation
Wyoming	Within 3 years following the delinquency	No limitation	Not specifically addressed in statutes or regulations

568

Taxpayer Remedies—Administrative Remedies

A taxpayer who has been issued a notice of additional taxes, delinquent taxes, interest, or penalties has a limited time within which to petition for a correction or review. The chart below notes how long a taxpayer has in which to file the request for administrative review and to which department the request should be directed.

State	Petition Due	Petition Filed With
Alabama	Within 30 days after the date of entry of the assessment	Department of Revenue, Administrative Law Division
Arizona	Within 45 days after receipt of notice of deficiency assessment or within such additional time as the Department may allow	Department of Revenue
Arkansas	Within 30 days after receipt of notice of assessment	Director of Department of Finance and Administration
California	Within 30 days after service of notice of deficiency assessment if petition for redetermination	State Board of Equalization
Colorado	Within 30 days after mailing notice of deficiency	Executive Director of Department of Revenue
Connecticut	Within 60 days after service of notice	Commissioner of Revenue Services
District of Columbia	Within 30 days after notice of deficiency	Office of Administrative Hearings (serve copy on Mayor of District of Columbia)
Florida	Within 60 days after issuance of proposed assessment	Department of Revenue
Georgia	Within 30 days after date of notice of assessment, or within another time limit specified with the notice	Revenue Commissioner
Hawaii	Within 30 days from the date of the proposed notice of assessment	Appeal directly to District Board of Review
Idaho	Within 63 days after mailing notice of deficiency	Tax Commission
Illinois	Within 60 days after issuance of notice of deficiency	Department of Revenue
Indiana	Within 60 days after date of notice of assessment	Department of Revenue
Iowa	Within 60 days after date of notice of assessment	Director of Revenue
Kansas	Informal conference may be requested within 60 days after mailing of notice	Secretary of Revenue
Kentucky	Within 45 days after date of notice of assessment	Revenue Cabinet

©2006 CCH. All Rights Reserved.

State	Petition Due	Petition Filed With
Louisiana	Within 30 days after notice of deficiency or assessment (15 days if notice based on failure to file return)	Secretary of Revenue and Taxation
Maine	Within 30 days after receipt of notice of assessment	State Tax Assessor
Maryland	Within 30 days after mailing notice of Comptroller's action	Comptroller
Massachusetts	Informal conference may be requested within 30 days of notice	Commissioner of Revenue
Michigan	Informal conference within 30 days after receipt of notice of intent to assess	Department of Treasury
Minnesota	Within 60 days after date of notice of action	Commissioner of Revenue
Mississippi	Within 30 days from date of assessment	Board of Review
Missouri	Informal review within 60 days after the assessment is delivered or sent by certified mail, whichever is earlier	Director of Revenue
Nebraska	Within 30 days after service of notice of deficiency	Tax Commissioner
Nevada	Within 45 days after service of notice of assessment	Department of Taxation
New Jersey	Within 90 days after service of notice of assessment	Director of Division of Taxation
New Mexico	Within 30 days after mailing notice of assessment or 30 days after return mailed or filed	Secretary of Taxation and Revenue
New York	Within 90 days after mailing notice of determination	Division of Tax Appeals
North Carolina	Within 30 days after mailing or delivery of notice of proposed assessment	Secretary of Revenue
North Dakota	Within 30 days after notice of determination	Tax Commission
Ohio	Within 60 days after service of notice of assessment	Tax Commissioner
Oklahoma	Within 60 days after mailing notice of assessment	Tax Commission
Pennsylvania	Within 30 days after mailing notice of assessment	Department of Revenue
Rhode Island	Within 30 days after mailing notice of assessment	Tax Administrator
South Carolina	Within 90 days after issuance of proposed assessment	Department of Revenue

State	Petition Due	Petition Filed With
South Dakota	Within 30 days after date of certification of assessment	Secretary of Revenue
Tennessee	Informal conference within 30 days after date of notice of assessment	Commissioner of Revenue
Texas	Within 30 days after issuance of notice of determination	Comptroller of Public Accounts
Utah	Within 30 days after mailing notice of deficiency	Tax Commission
Vermont	Within 60 days after notice of determination	Commissioner of Taxes
Virginia	Within 90 days after notice of assessment	Tax Commissioner
Washington	Within 30 days after issuance of notice of assessment	Department of Revenue
West Virginia	Within 60 days after service of notice of assessment	Appeal directly to Office of Tax Appeals
Wisconsin	Within 60 days after receipt of notice of determination	Department of Revenue
Wyoming	Within 30 days of decision	Appeal directly to Board of Equalization

Taxpayer Remedies—First Formal Appeal

In many states, a taxpayer may appeal an administrative denial of a petition or a determination to a board of tax appeal or tax appeals commission before going to the courts. The chart below notes how long a taxpayer has in which to file a review of the action and with what body.

State	Petition Due	Petition Filed With
Alabama	N/A	No tax appeal board—seek judicial review of administrative determination
Arizona	Within 30 days after receipt of final decision or order	State Board of Tax Appeals
Arkansas	N/A	No tax appeal board—seek judicial review of administrative determination
California	N/A	No tax appeal board—seek judicial review of administrative determination
Colorado	N/A	No tax appeal board—seek judicial review of administrative determination
Connecticut	N/A	No tax appeal board—seek judicial review of administrative determination
District of Columbia	N/A	No tax appeal board—seek judicial review of administrative determination
Florida	N/A	No tax appeal board—seek judicial review of administrative determination
Georgia	N/A	No tax appeal board—seek judicial review of administrative determination
Hawaii	Within 30 days after mailing date of notice of assessment	District Board of Review
Idaho	Within 91 days after notice of redetermination is received	Board of Tax Appeals
Illinois	Within 180 days after notice of tax liability becomes final (only to seek relief from penalties and interest or for offer-in-compromise)	Board of Appeals
Indiana	N/A	No tax appeal board—seek judicial review of administrative determination
Iowa	Within 30 days after decision rendered	State Board of Tax Review
Kansas	Within 30 days after a final decision	Board of Tax Appeals
Kentucky	Within 30 days after date of decision	Board of Tax Appeals

State	Petition Due	Petition Filed With
Louisiana	Within 60 days after notice of deficiency or decision	Board of Tax Appeals
Maine	N/A	No tax appeal board—seek judicial review of administrative determination
Maryland	Within 30 days after mailing notice of decision	Tax Court
Massachusetts	Within 60 days after date of notice of decision or within six months after application for abatement is deemed to be denied	Appellate Tax Board
Michigan	Within 35 days after decision	Tax Tribunal
Minnesota	Within 60 days after decision	Tax Court
Mississippi	Within 30 days after notice of decision	Tax Commission
Missouri	Within 60 days after mailing or delivery of decision, whichever is earlier	Administrative Hearing Commission
Nebraska	N/A	No tax appeal board—seek judicial review of administrative determination
Nevada	Within 30 days after service of decision	Tax Commission
New Jersey	N/A	No tax appeal board—seek judicial review of administrative determination
New Mexico	N/A	No tax appeal board—seek judicial review of administrative determination
New York	Within 30 days after notice of decision	Tax Appeals Tribunal
North Carolina	Within 60 days after notice of intent filed (notice of intent to file a petition must be submitted within 30 days after final decision)	Tax Review Board
North Dakota	N/A	No tax appeal board—seek judicial review of administrative determination
Ohio	Within 60 days after service of notice of decision	Board of Tax Appeals
Oklahoma	N/A	No tax appeal board—seek judicial review of administrative determination
Pennsylvania	Within 60 days after notice of decision (within 90 days after notice of decision on a petition for refund)	Board of Finance and Revenue

State	Petition Due	Petition Filed With
Rhode Island	N/A	No tax appeal board—seek judicial review of administrative determination
South Carolina	Within 30 days after decision mailed or delivered	Administrative Law Judge
South Dakota	N/A	No tax appeal board—seek judicial review of administrative determination
Tennessee	N/A	No tax appeal board—seek judicial review of administrative determination
Texas	N/A	No tax appeal board—seek judicial review of administrative determination
Utah	N/A	No tax appeal board—seek judicial review of administrative determination
Vermont	N/A	No tax appeal board—seek judicial review of administrative determination
Virginia	N/A	No tax appeal board—seek judicial review of administrative determination
Washington	Within 30 days after mailing notice of decision	Board of Tax Appeals
West Virginia	Within 60 days of receipt of assessment notice	Office of Tax Appeals
Wisconsin	Within 60 days after receipt of notice of decision	Tax Appeals Commission
Wyoming	Within 30 days after the date of final decision	Board of Equalization

13

Taxpayer Remedies—Judicial Review

Appeals for judicial review may be taken from decisions of the board of tax appeals or the tax appeals commission (or, in some cases, directly from the department of revenue). The following chart notes how long a taxpayer has in which to file for judicial review and what court has jurisdiction.

State	Appeal Due	Court
Alabama	Within 30 days after the date of final assessment	Circuit Court
Arizona	Within 30 days after the date of final decision	Tax Court
Arkansas	Within one year after date of final determination	Circuit Court
California	Within 90 days after mailing of notice of board's action	Court of competent jurisdiction in city or county in which Attorney General has office
Colorado	Within 30 days after the mailing of the determination	District Court
Connecticut	Within one month after service of notice	Superior Court for the District of New Britain
District of Columbia	Within six months after date of final determination or denial of refund claim	Superior Court
Florida	Within 60 days after date of final assessment (30 days after rendition of order under Administrative Procedures Act)	Circuit Court
Georgia	Within 30 days after date of decision	Superior Court
Hawaii	Within 30 days after mailing date of assessment (30 days after Board of Review decision filed)	Tax Appeal Court
Idaho	Within 91 days after notice of redetermination is received or within 28 days after board's decision is mailed	District Court
Illinois	Within 35 days after date administrative decision served	Circuit Court
Indiana	Within 180 days of issuance of letters of finding	Tax Court
Iowa	Within 30 days after date of state board's decision	District Court
Kansas	Within 30 days after rehearing order entered or denied by Board	District Court
Kentucky	Within 30 days after notice of appeal was filed with Board (notice of appeal to Board required within 30 days of final order)	Circuit Court

State	Appeal Due	Court
Louisiana	Within 30 days after decision of Board	District Court
Maine	Within 30 days after receipt of notice	Superior Court
Maryland	Within 30 days after the latest of date of action, date of agency's notice of action, or date taxpayer received notice	Circuit Court
Massachusetts	Within 60 days of entry of judgement of the Board	Appeals Court
Michigan	Within 90 days after assessment, decision, or order	Court of Claims
Minnesota	Within 60 days after Tax Court order entered	State Supreme Court
Mississippi	Within 30 days after decision	Chancery Court
Missouri	Within 30 days after notice of final decision mailed or delivered	Court of Appeals
Nebraska	Within 30 days after service of final decision	District Court
Nevada	Within 30 days of the Commission's decision	District Court
New Jersey	Within 90 days of Director's decision	Tax Court
New Mexico	Within 30 days after mailing or delivery of administrative hearing decision (with 90 days of denial of claim or 90 days after expiration of Secretary's time for action if administrative hearing not held)	Court of Appeals (District Court for Santa Fe County)
New York	Within four months after notice of determination	Appellate Division of Supreme Court, Third Department
North Carolina	Within 30 days after receipt of decision	Superior Court
North Dakota	Within 30 days after notice of decision or denial of rehearing request	District Court
Ohio	Within 30 days after entry of decision on Board's journal	Court of Appeals or State Supreme Court
Oklahoma	Within 30 days after mailing of decision	State Supreme Court
Pennsylvania	Within 30 days after entry of the order of the Board	Commonwealth Court
Rhode Island	Within 30 days after mailing notice of final decision	Sixth Division, District Court
South Carolina	Within 30 days of receipt of Law Judge's decision	Circuit Court

State	Appeal Due	Court
South Dakota	Within 30 days after notice of final decision served	Circuit Court
Tennessee	Within 90 days after mailing notice of assessment	Chancery Court
Texas	Within 30 days after denial of rehearing motion or within 90 days after filing protest	District Court
Utah	Within 30 days after mailing notice of agency action	District Court
Vermont	Within 30 days after decision or action of Commissioner	Superior Court
Virginia	Within later of three years after assessment or one year after Commissioner's determination	Circuit Court
Washington	Within 30 days after decision	Superior Court
West Virginia	Within 60 days after receipt of notice of decision	Circuit Court
Wisconsin	Within 30 days after service of decision or disposition of rehearing request	Dane County Circuit Court
Wyoming	Within 30 days after service of decision	District Court

Trade-Ins

In certain industries, it is a common practice to allow buyers a credit for articles traded in against the purchase price of similar articles. From the seller's standpoint, the trade-in represents part of the value received on the sale of the new article. However, there is a wide variation in the sales tax laws and regulations concerning the treatment of such transactions.

There are three principal methods employed by the states in determining taxable gross receipts with respect to sales involving trade-ins:

(1) the acceptance of a trade-in has no effect on the tax due on the sale. In states that follow this rule, the tax is due on the full selling price of the property sold without deduction for any credit allowed the buyer for the trade-in. When the trade-in is subsequently resold at retail, tax is due on its full selling price;

(2) the new article sold is taxed on the full selling price without deduction for the value of the trade-in. On resale of the trade-in at retail, no tax is due; and

(3) the sale of the new article is taxed on the cash or credit received by the seller, the value of the trade-in being excluded. On resale of the trade-in, tax is due on the full selling price.

States that tax the value of trade-ins generally utilize the first method to determine taxable gross receipts.

The following chart indicates whether each state taxes the value of trade-ins. States that do not impose a sales and use tax are not listed in the chart below.

State	Trade-In Taxed or Excluded
Alabama	Taxed[1]
Arizona	Excluded
Arkansas	Taxed[2]
California	Taxed
Colorado	Excluded
Connecticut	Excluded
District of Columbia	Taxed
Florida	Excluded
Georgia	Excluded
Hawaii	Excluded
Idaho	Excluded[3]
Illinois	Excluded
Indiana	Excluded
Iowa	Excluded
Kansas	Excluded
Kentucky	Excluded
Louisiana	Excluded
Maine	Taxed[4]
Maryland	Taxed
Massachusetts	Taxed[5]
Michigan	Taxed
Minnesota	Excluded
Mississippi	Excluded

State	Trade-In Taxed or Excluded
Missouri	Excluded[6]
Nebraska	Excluded
Nevada	Taxed[7]
New Jersey	Excluded[8]
New Mexico	Excluded[9]
New York	Excluded
North Carolina	Taxed
North Dakota	Excluded[10]
Ohio	Taxed[11]
Oklahoma	Taxed[12]
Pennsylvania	Excluded
Rhode Island	Taxed[13]
South Carolina	Excluded
South Dakota	Excluded
Tennessee	Excluded
Texas	Excluded
Utah	Excluded
Vermont	Excluded
Virginia	Excluded
Washington	Excluded
West Virginia	Excluded
Wisconsin	Excluded[14]
Wyoming	Excluded

[1] Exclusion generally allowed only on motor vehicles (including parts), trailers, and agricultural machinery.
[2] Exclusion allowed only on aircraft, mobile homes, motor vehicles, trailers, and semitrailers.
[3] Exclusion not allowed on the sale of a newly manufactured home or a modular building.
[4] Exclusion allowed only on motor vehicles, aircraft, boats, livestock trailers, camper trailers, chain saws, or special mobile equipment.
[5] Exclusion allowed only on aircraft, boats, motor vehicles, snowmobiles, recreational vehicles, and trailers.
[6] Exclusion not applicable to certain manufactured home sales.
[7] Partial exclusion allowed on certain vehicle trade-ins.
[8] Exclusion not allowed on certain sales of manufactured or mobile homes.
[9] Exclusion not allowed for trade-in of manufactured homes.
[10] Exclusion not allowed on trade-in of used mobile home.
[11] Exclusion allowed only on watercraft and new motor vehicles.
[12] Limited exclusion for certain used or trade-in parts.
[13] Exclusion allowed on sales of certain items, e.g., private passenger automobiles.
[14] Exclusion not allowed on sale of manufactured building.

Use Tax Collection Responsibility Created by Trade Show Participation

The chart below describes the states' positions on use tax collection responsibility created by participation in a trade show in their state.

The chart is based upon responses from the states to a CCH survey about trade show participation. The survey was conducted in September and October 2002, via e-mail and telephone. Those states that declined to respond to the survey are noted below, as are those states that do not impose sales and use (or similar) taxes.

The chart below indicates whether use tax collection responsibility is created by certain types of participation at a trade show in the subject state. Types of participation include: attending as a consumer and not as an exhibitor or seller; attending as an exhibitor, but neither making sales nor taking orders; attending as an exhibitor and taking orders or making sales only to other out-of-state parties; and participating as an exhibitor and taking orders or making sales to in-state parties.

States that do not impose sales and use tax are not included in this chart.

State	Consumer	Exhibit Only	Exhibit with Out-of-State Sales	Exhibit with In-State Sales
Alabama	No	Yes	No[1]	Yes
Arizona	No	No	Yes[2]	Yes[2]
Arkansas	No	No	No	Yes
California	No	No[3]	Yes	Yes
Colorado	No	No	Yes	Yes
Connecticut	([4])	Yes	Yes	Yes
District of Columbia	No	No	Yes	Yes
Florida	No	Yes	Yes	Yes
Georgia	No	No	Yes	Yes
Hawaii	No	No	No[1]	Yes
Idaho	([4])	No	No[1]	Yes[5]
Illinois	No	No	Yes	Yes
Indiana	Yes	No	Yes	Yes
Iowa	Yes	Yes[6]	Yes[6]	Yes[6]
Kansas	No	No	Yes	Yes
Kentucky	No	Yes[7]	Yes[7]	Yes
Louisiana	No	Yes	Yes	Yes
Maine	No[5]	Yes	No[1]	Yes
Maryland	No	Yes[6]	Yes[6]	Yes[6]
Massachusetts	State did not answer survey questions, rather referred to administrative guidance.			
Michigan	No	No[8]	Yes[9]	Yes[9]
Minnesota	No	No	Yes	Yes
Mississippi	No	No	Yes	Yes
Missouri	No	No	Yes	Yes
Nebraska	State did not answer survey questions, rather referred to administrative guidance.			

State	Consumer	Exhibit Only	Exhibit with Out-of-State Sales	Exhibit with In-State Sales
Nevada	No	No	Yes[2]	Yes[2]
New Jersey	No	Yes	Yes	Yes
New Mexico	State did not answer survey questions, rather referred to administrative guidance.			
New York	State declined to respond to survey.			
North Carolina	No	Yes[10]	Yes[10]	Yes[10]
North Dakota	Yes	Yes	Yes	Yes
Ohio	No	Yes[11]	Yes[11]	Yes[11]
Oklahoma	No	Yes	Yes	Yes
Pennsylvania	No[12]	Yes	Yes	Yes
Rhode Island	No	No	No	Yes[13]
South Carolina	State declined to respond to survey.			
South Dakota	No	No[2]	No	No[2]
Tennessee	No	Yes	Yes	Yes
Texas	No	No	Yes	Yes
Utah	No	No	Yes	Yes
Vermont	No	No	No	Yes
Virginia	State declined to respond to survey.			
Washington	No	Yes[14]	Yes[14]	Yes
West Virginia	No	No	No[1]	Yes
Wisconsin	State declined to respond to survey.			
Wyoming	No	No[15]	No[15]	Yes[16]

[1] As long as delivery is outside of state.
[2] A single visit to state within a 12-month period will not give rise to nexus.
[3] Unless participation for more than 15 days in 12-month period or sales over $100K in state in prior calendar year.
[4] Additional facts required for determination.
[5] Eligible for temporary permit if participation limited to three shows per calendar year.
[6] Although number of visits may determine substantial physical presence is not met.
[7] Although overall activity may determine physical presence insignificant.
[8] Provided that presence in state is less than 10 days per year.
[9] Employee present in state for two days creates nexus (for that month and following 11 months).
[10] Whether exhibitor's presence is more than *de minimis* is determined on case-by-case basis.
[11] Not enforced if less than seven instances of nexus creating activity in calendar year and not more than $25K in gross sales in state for same year.
[12] Unless solicitation of business occurs.
[13] Only for orders accepted at the trade show.
[14] Unless attendance did not create/expand market for goods in the state.
[15] Unless agent present in state more than four times in 12-month period.
[16] May be relieved of responsibility if agent present in state less than four times in 12-month period.

Vending Machine Sales

Receipts from vending machines sales are taxable in most states. Persons selling through such machines are generally considered to be retailers and must conform to the requirements of the state with respect to retailers. Tax liability usually falls on the person having access to the monies earned by the machine or machines. The chart below notes whether vending machine sales of food and vending machine sales in general are taxable but does not specify upon whom the liability for the tax falls.

For purposes of this chart, "T" stands for taxable and "E" for exempt; but the designations are of a general nature, and exceptions unnoted in the chart, for example exemptions for sales of food through bulk vending machines, may exist.

States that do not impose a sales and use tax are not included in this chart.

State	Food Sales	All Other Sales
Alabama	T[1]	T
Arizona	E[2]	T
Arkansas	E[3]	E[3,4]
California	T[5]	T
Colorado	E	T[6]
Connecticut	E[7,8]	T[8]
District of Columbia	T	T
Florida	T[9,10]	T[9]
Georgia	T	T
Hawaii	T	T
Idaho	T[11]	T[11]
Illinois	T[12,13]	T[13]
Indiana	T[14]	T[14]
Iowa	T[15]	T
Kansas	T	T
Kentucky	T[16]	T[16]
Louisiana	E[17]	E[17]
Maine	T[18]	T[19]
Maryland	T[20,21]	T[20]
Massachusetts	T[22]	T[23]
Michigan	T[24,25]	T
Minnesota	T	T
Mississippi	E[26]	T
Missouri	T[27]	T[27,28]
Nebraska	T	T
Nevada	T[24]	T
New Jersey	T[29,30]	T[29]
New Mexico	T	T
New York	T[31]	T[32]
North Carolina	T[33]	T[33,34]
North Dakota	T[6]	T[6]
Ohio	T[35]	T
Oklahoma	T[36]	T[36]
Pennsylvania	T[37]	T
Rhode Island	T[38]	T[39]
South Carolina	T[40]	T[40]

State	Food Sales	All Other Sales
South Dakota	T	T
Tennessee	T[41]	T[41]
Texas	T[42,43]	T[43]
Utah	T[44]	T
Vermont............................	T[35,45]	T
Virginia	T[46]	T[46]
Washington	T[47]	T
West Virginia	T	T
Wisconsin	E[48]	T
Wyoming...........................	T	T[49]

[1] Food and food products, coffee, milk and milk products, and substitutes for these products are taxed at reduced rate.

[2] Food for consumption on premises is taxable.

[3] Registered vending device operators exempt from general gross receipts tax, but subject to either special vending device sales/use tax or vending device decal fee.

[4] Devices that sell only cigarettes, newspapers, magazines, or postage stamps not taxable as vending devices.

[5] 33% of cold food receipts taxable.

[6] Sales for 15 cents or less exempt.

[7] Candy, carbonated and alcoholic beverages, cigarettes, tobacco products, and items not intended for human consumption are not considered food products and are taxable.

[8] Sales for 50 cents or less exempt.

[9] Sales for less than 10 cents exempt. Receipts from machines operated by churches exempt.

[10] Food/drink sales in school cafeterias and food/drink sales for 25 cents or less through coin-operated machines sponsored by certain charitable organizations exempt.

[11] Sales for 11 cents or less exempt. Sales for 12 cents through $1 taxed at 117% of vendor's acquisition cost. Sales for more than $1 taxed on retail sales price.

[12] Reduced rate on food applies to food sales through vending machines, except soft drinks and hot foods.

[13] Bulk vending machine sales exempt.

[14] Sales for 8 cents or less exempt. Sales may be exempt because of tax-exempt status of person or organization that makes the sale.

[15] Applies to items sold for consumption on premises, items prepared for immediate consumption off premises, candy, candy-coated items, candy products, and certain beverages.

[16] Sales of 50 cents or less through coin-operated bulk vending machines exempt.

[17] Sales to dealer for resale through coin-operated vending machines taxable. Subsequent resale exempt.

[18] Exemption for sales of products for internal human consumption when sold through vending machines operated by a person more than 50% of whose retail gross receipts are from sales through vending machines.

[19] Items sold through vending machines (other than items for internal human consumption) are taxable retail sales. Chewing gum is not considered an item for internal human consumption.

[20] Taxed at special rate. Sales for 25 cents or less through bulk vending machines exempt.

[21] Snack food, milk, fresh fruit/vegetables, and yogurt exempt.

[22] Exempt if machine sells only snacks and/or candy with a sales price of less than $3.50.

[23] Sales for 10 cents or less exempt.

[24] Prepared food intended for immediate consumption taxable.

[25] Milk, juices, fresh fruit, candy, nuts, chewing gum, cookies, crackers, chips, and nonalcoholic beverages in sealed container exempt.

[26] Food/drinks sold through vending machines serviced by full-line vendors exempt.

[27] Sales made on religious, charitable, and public elementary or secondary school premises exempt.

[28] Photocopies and tobacco products exempt.

[29] Sales for 25 cents or less by retailer primarily engaged in coin-operated machine sales exempt.

[30] Taxed at 70% of retail vending machine price. Food/drink sold in school cafeterias and milk exempt.

[31] Sales for 10 cents or less by vendor primarily engaged in vending machine sales exempt. Candy and certain beverages sold for 75 cents or less exempt. Certain sales intended for off-premises consumption and certain bulk vending machine sales exempt.

[32] Sales for 10 cents or less and bulk vending machine sales for 50 cents or less exempt if vendor primarily engaged in vending machine sales.

[33] Taxed at 50% of sales price. Sales for one cent exempt.

[34] Tobacco products fully taxable. Newspapers exempt.

[35] Sales of food for off-premises consumption exempt.

[36] Sales from coin-operated devices for which certain license fees have been paid are exempt.

[37] Specific items taxable, including soft drinks, meals, sandwiches, hot beverages, and items dispensed in heated form or served cold but normally heated in operator-provided oven/microwave. Sales on school or church premises exempt.

[38] Sales in school areas designated primarily for students/teachers exempt.

[39] Sales made from machines located in certain facilities by licensed operators who are blind are exempt.

[40] Vendors making sales solely through vending machines are deemed to be users or consumers of certain property they purchase for sale through vending machines (not cigarettes or soft drinks in closed containers, which are subject to business license tax at wholesale level).

[41] Certain nonprofit entities may pay gross receipts tax in lieu of sales tax.

[42] Taxed on 50% of receipts.

[43] Candy and soft drinks fully taxable. Sales of food, candy, gum, or items designed for a child's use/play for 50 cents or less through coin-operated bulk vending machines exempt.

[44] For food, beverages, and dairy products sold for $1 or less, operators may pay tax on total sales or 150% of cost of goods sold.

[45] Sales through vending machines located on premises of a restaurant subject to meals tax.

[46] Rate and base vary depending on placement/use of machine.

[47] Taxed on 57% of receipts. Hot prepared foods fully taxable.

[48] Generally, exempt as food sold for off-premises consumption. Meals, sandwiches, heated food/beverages, candy, chewing gum, lozenges, popcorn, and confections taxable.

[49] Postage stamps exempt.

PROPERTY TAX

The following pages contain charts summarizing facets of property taxes imposed by the states. Topics covered include personal property rendition filing requirements, the basis of assessment, the taxation of inventory, the taxation of intangible property, and the taxation of tangible personal property.

Administrative Appeals

The following chart indicates the period within which property owners must initially appeal their property valuations.

State	Appeal Period
Alabama	A taxpayer may appeal any final assessment entered by the department by filing a notice of appeal with the administrative law division within 30 days from the date of entry of the final assessment.
Alaska	An appeal from a state oil or gas tax assessment must be filed within 20 days after an assessment notice is mailed; a municipal property tax assessment must be appealed no later than 30 days after a property tax statement is mailed.
Arizona	Petitions must be filed within 60 days after the date of mailing of the valuation notice.
Arkansas	Assessments must be appealed to the county board of equalization by the third Monday in August.
California	An appeal of an assessment on the regular tax roll must be filed between July 2 and September 15; appeals of supplemental taxes and of taxes for which a timely notice was not sent must be filed within 60 days of the notice or the mailing of the tax bill.
Colorado	Petitions must be filed by May 27, if made in writing, or by June 1, if made in person; personal property petitions must be filed by June 30, if made in writing, or by July 5, if made in person.
Connecticut	Appeals must be filed by February 20, for the March hearing or March 20 if the Assessor or the Board of Assessors has received and extension.
Delaware	The Board of Assessment for Kent County hears appeals from April 1 through April 15; in Sussex County, the Board of Assessment Review hears appeals from February 15 through March 1; and the Board of Assessment Review in New Castle County hears appeals from March 15 through April 1. Appeals of quarterly supplemental assessments may be made within 30 days from the date the notice is sent.
District of Columbia	Petitions must be filed by April 1 of the tax year to request an administrative review.
Florida	A petition for review of valuation issues must be filed no later than the 25th day following mailing of the notice of assessment; a petition for review of denial of an exemption, an application for agricultural or high-water recharge classification, or deferral must be filed no later than the 30th day following notice.
Georgia	Appeals must be filed within 45 days from the date the county board of equalization notifies the taxpayer of any changes in a return. Appeals must be filed within 30 days when a county or municipality provides for collection and payment in installments.
Hawaii	An appeal to a county board of review must be filed no later than April 9 preceding the tax year.
Idaho	An appeal of an assessment listed on the real or personal property roll must be filed by the fourth Monday of June; an appeal of an assessment listed on the subsequent property roll must be filed by the fourth Monday of November.

State	Appeal Period
Illinois	Appeals of a decision by a local board of review in a county with a population of 150,000 or less must be filed the later of August 10 or 30 days after the date of publication of the assessment changes; appeals of a decision by a local board in a county with a population of 150,000, but less than 3 million, must be filed the later of September 10 or 30 days after the date of publication of assessment changes; and appeals of a decision by a local board in a county with a population of 3 million or more must be filed within 20 days after the date of publication of time and date for filing assessment complaints. Appeals of a local board's decision may be appealed to the state property tax appeal board within 30 days of the notice of the board's written decision.
Indiana	If a taxpayer disagrees with the determination reached by a county property tax assessment board of appeals, and has gone through a preliminary conference with the county property tax assessment board of appeals, the taxpayer may file a petition for review by the Indiana Board within 30 days on a form prescribed by the Indiana Board.
Iowa	Written protests must be filed between April 16 and May 5.
Kansas	As a prerequisite for a formal protest, an appeal to a county appraiser must first be filed within 30 days after receipt of the notice of valuation for real property or by May 15 for personal property. An appeal of a county appraiser may be filed with a hearing officer or board within 18 days of the date that the final determination of the appraiser was mailed. A written appeal of an officer's or board's decision must be filed with the state board of tax appeals within 30 days after the date of the order from which the appeal is taken.
Kentucky	Before a formal appeal may be filed, a conference with the property valuation administrator must be filed within the 13-day tax roll inspection period, which begins on the first Monday in May. An appeal of the administrator must be filed with the board of assessment appeals within one workday following the conclusion of the tax roll inspection period.
Louisiana	Appeals of the board of review must be filed with the tax commission within 10 business days of the board's decision.
Maine	Written appeals must be filed with the board of assessment review (or to the county commissioners if no board is adopted) within 60 days after the notice of the decision from which the appeal is taken or after the application is denied.
Maryland	Appeals to an assessment supervisor must be made within 45 days from receipt of the assessment notice.
Massachusetts	Appeals of a local board of assessors must be filed with the county commissioners within three months after the assessor's decision or the date the application is denied. Appeals of the commissioners' decision must be filed with the appellate tax board within three months of the decision.
Michigan	An initial appeal of a valuation is taken to the local board of review, which meets during the week beginning on the second Monday in March. Written petitions of the local review board's decision must be filed with the tax tribunal within 30 days after the final decision.
Minnesota	Petitions must be filed with the local board of appeal and equalization during the board's annual April and May meetings.
Mississippi	Written objections to a municipal or county tax assessment must be filed with the governing body of the municipality or county board of supervisors during the August annual meeting.
Missouri	Appeals are heard by the county board of equalization and must be filed with the county clerk before the third Monday in June.

State	Appeal Period
Montana	Protests must be filed with the county tax appeal board within 30 days after receipt of notice or the first Monday in June.
Nebraska	Protests must be filed with the county board of equalization by May 1.
Nevada	Appeals must be made to the county board of equalization by January 15. Appeals from the county board to the state board of equalization must be made by March 10.
New Hampshire	Appeals to the board of tax and land appeals must be filed by September 1. Motions for rehearing of the board's decision must be filed within 30 days of the clerk's date on the board's order or decision.
New Jersey	Petitions must be filed with county board of taxation the later of April 1 or 45 days from the date the taxing district completes the bulk mailing of the notification of assessment.
New Mexico	A prepayment protest must be filed within 30 days after the notice of valuation is mailed.
New York	A complaint may be filed any time before the time fixed for review by the local board of assessment review, which is generally the fourth Tuesday in May.
North Carolina	Review by the county board of equalization must be filed within 15 days after the assessor's notice of decision.
North Dakota	Appeals of an assessment must be filed with the township board, normally by the first Monday in April, or the city board, normally by the second Tuesday in April. Appeals of the local board must be filed with the county board of equalization during the county board's meeting in the first 10 days in June. Appeals of the county board must be filed with the state board of equalization during the state board's meeting the second Tuesday in August.
Ohio	When county auditor assesses property that has been omitted from return, or assesses listed property in excess of value listed or without allowing a deduction from depreciated book value of personal property used in business, the taxpayer must be notified by mail. Within 60 days after notice is mailed, taxpayer may file petition for reassessment with Tax Commissioner. At the hearing, Commissioner may make such correction in the assessment that is considered proper. If no appeal is taken from Commissioner's decision, the determination becomes final subject to appeal to the Board of Tax Appeals.
Oklahoma	Written complaints must be filed with the county assessor 20 days from the date that a notice of valuation was mailed; if the valuation has not increased from the prior year, complaints must be filed by the first Monday in May. Appeals of an assessor's decision must be filed within 10 working days of the date of the final action notice.
Oregon	A value reduction petition must be filed after tax statements are mailed before December 31.
Pennsylvania	Appeal deadlines vary by locality.
Rhode Island	Appeals to local assessors must be made within 90 days of the first tax payment due date.
South Carolina	Written objections must be filed with the county assessor within 90 days after the assessment notice is mailed provided the objection is for a tax year when a notice is sent; otherwise, written objections must be filed by March 1. Appeals of an assessor's decision to the county board of appeals must be filed within 30 days after the date of the assessor's response.

State	Appeal Period
South Dakota	Appeals must be filed with the clerk of the local board of equalization by the Thursday preceding the third Monday in March. Appeals to the county board of equalization must be filed with the county auditor by the third Tuesday in April.
Tennessee	To protest an assessment, taxpayers must appear before the county board of equalization during its meeting, which begins June 1. Appeals to the state board of equalization must be filed the later of August 1 or 45 days after notice of the local board's decision was mailed.
Texas	Written notice to the appraisal review board must be filed the later of June 1 or 30 days after the appraisal notice is delivered.
Utah	Appeals must be filed with the county board of equalization the later of 45 days after the valuation notice is mailed or September 15; for personal property, appeals must be filed within 30 days after the notice is mailed. Appeals to the state tax commission must be filed with the county auditor within 30 days of the board's final action.
Vermont	Appeals to the local board of civil authority must be filed with the town clerk within 14 days of the lister's decision. Appeals to the director of the division of property valuation and review must be filed within 30 days of the local board's decision notice.
Virginia	Appeal dates vary by locality; appeal date must be a minimum of 30 days from the final date for the assessing officer to hear objections.
Washington	Appeals to the county board of equalization must be filed by the later of (1) July 1, (2) within 30 days after a notice is mailed, or (3) within a time limit of 60 days adopted by the county legislative authority. Appeals to the board of tax appeals must be filed within 30 days after the county board's notice is mailed.
West Virginia	Applications must be made before the county commission during its annual February 1 meeting.
Wisconsin	After an informal review by the local assessor, the taxpayer can seek review with the board of review, which meets for 30 days beginning on the 2nd Monday of May. Written or oral notice to the clerk at least 48 hours prior to the scheduled meeting required. Written complaints to the Department of Revenue must be filed within 20 days after receipt of the board's determination notice or within 30 days of the date specified on the affidavit if no notice is received. Appeals to the state tax commission must be filed within 60 days of the determination.
Wyoming	Appeals to the county or state board of equalization must be made within 30 days of the notification of assessment. Appeals to the state board of equalization must be made within 30 days of the local board's decision.

Assessment Date

The following chart indicates the date property taxes are assessed in each state.

State	Assessment Date
Alabama	October 1.
Alaska	January 1.
Arizona	January 1.
Arkansas	January 1.
California	January 1.
Colorado	January 1.
Connecticut	October 1.
Delaware	Varies by county.
District of Columbia	January 1.
Florida	January 1.
Georgia	January 1.
Hawaii	January 1.
Idaho	January 1.
Illinois	January 1.
Indiana	March 1 (January 15 for certain mobile homes).
Iowa	January 1.
Kansas	January 1.
Kentucky	January 1.
Louisiana	January 1.
Maine	April 1.
Maryland	January 1.
Massachusetts	January 1.
Michigan	December 31.
Minnesota	January 2.
Mississippi	January 1 for real property, March 1 for personal property.
Missouri	January 1.
Montana	January 1.
Nebraska	January 1.
Nevada	July 1.
New Hampshire	April 1.
New Jersey	October 1 for real property, and January 1 for business personal property.

State	Assessment Date
New Mexico	January 1.
New York	Property generally is assessed on March 1 on the basis of its value as of July 1; however, cities and villages may modify these dates.
North Carolina	January 1.
North Dakota	February 1.
Ohio	January 1.
Oklahoma	January 1.
Oregon	January 1.
Pennsylvania	Varies by locality.
Rhode Island	December 31.
South Carolina	December 31.
South Dakota	November 1.
Tennessee	January 1.
Texas	January 1.
Utah	January 1.
Vermont	April 1.
Virginia	January 1.
Washington	January 1.
West Virginia	July 1.
Wisconsin	January 1.
Wyoming	January 1.

Construction Work in Progress

The following chart identifies the manner in which each state values improvements to real estate that are not completed as of the general assessment (lien) date.

State	Treatment of New Construction
Alabama	An improvement to real property that is incomplete as of October 1 of a tax year must be reported to the local tax assessor no later than the following January 1 and is assessed on a percentage of completion basis.
Alaska	Property committed primarily to the production or pipeline transportation of oil or gas or to the operation or maintenance of oil or gas production or transportation facilities must be assessed at its full and true value as of the date that construction commences. Additionally, a two or four year exemption from municipal property taxes is authorized for certain real property improvements.
Arizona	Construction work in progress becomes taxable when the work has progressed to a degree that it is useful for its eventual purpose.
Arkansas	No specific statutory provisions.
California	Property under construction is taxable throughout the construction process, with the value of the construction being determined as of the lien date.
Colorado	Property under construction after January 1 is assessed on July 1 of that year. If construction is completed by July 1, the valuation is prorated at the same ratio as the number of months it is completed bears to the full year. If completed after July 1, the valuation added is one-half the difference between the valuation on January 1 and on July 1.
Connecticut	Assessment is made on a prorated basis for construction completed after the assessment date.
Delaware	No specific statutory provisions.
District of Columbia	Construction work in progress is taxable at estimated market value when 65% of the estimated construction is completed.
Florida	Any improvement to real property that is not substantially completed on January 1 has no value placed on it.
Georgia	Taxpayers are responsible for filing timely returns when improvements have been made to real property since it was last returned for taxation.
Hawaii	In assessing a building, consideration must be given to any new construction, improvement, modification, or repair that results in a higher assessed value. However, any increase in value attributable to work undertaken pursuant to the requirements of an urban redevelopment, rehabilitation, or conservation project may not increase the building's assessed value for a period of seven years from the date of certification by the appropriate official.
Idaho	An occupancy tax is imposed in lieu of property taxes during the construction year. The amount of tax is the same as it would have been if the structures were on the assessment rolls on January 1, but prorated for the portion of the year the structures were actually occupied.
Illinois	When the construction of new or added buildings or other improvements on property are completed or initially occupied or used after January 1, the property owner is liable for an increased assessment on a proportionate basis.
Indiana	Construction work in progress is valued at 10% of the true tax value of the cost of the property.

State	Treatment of New Construction
Iowa	No specific statutory provisions.
Kansas	Construction incomplete as of the January 1 assessment date is valued at the cost as of that date.
Kentucky	No specific statutory provisions.
Louisiana	Assessment is to be made on the basis of the condition of the buildings on the first day of January.
Maine	The valuation of construction in progress varies by district.
Maryland	Improvements adding at least $50,000 in value will be taxable on the date of finality, the semiannual date of finality, or quarter date of finality, following substantial completion.
Massachusetts	Construction work in progress becomes taxable once an occupancy permit is issued and is assessed on a prorated basis.
Michigan	Value of new construction is 50% of the true cash value.
Minnesota	Construction work in progress is assessed annually to the extent completed on January 2.
Mississippi	A newly constructed home remains exempt from property tax until it is first leased, rented, sold, or occupied.
Missouri	Partially completed construction valued on a percentage completed basis on January 1.
Montana	Construction of improvements does not become taxable until completed, with partial exemptions further applying during the first four years following completion.
Nebraska	Improvements become taxable to the extent completed on the December 31st prior to the January 1 assessment date.
Nevada	A closed assessment roll may be reopened to reflect changes in improvements resulting from new construction occurring before July 1. The Commission establishes the valuation of (1) new construction reported from January 1 to June 30 of the preceding fiscal year, and enters that valuation of the central assessment roll for the next fiscal year; and (2) new construction reported for the entire preceding fiscal year for supplemental tax bills for the current fiscal year.
New Hampshire	No specific statutory provisions.
New Jersey	Construction work in progress on the October 1 assessment date of any year and completed before January 1 is assessed on the basis of the property's value on the first day of the month following completion.
New Mexico	Construction work in progress in connection with business property is valued at 50% of the actual amounts expended as of December 31.
New York	No specific statutory provisions.
North Carolina	No specific statutory provisions.
North Dakota	Construction work in progress is exempt for up to five years if approved by a city or county governing body.
Ohio	Construction work in progress is valued based on its value or percentage of completion as it existed on January 1.
Oklahoma	Construction work in progress is assessed at the fair cash value of the materials used in construction as of the January 1 assessment date.

State	Treatment of New Construction
Oregon	A new commercial building or structure, or an addition to an existing commercial building or structure is generally not taxable until construction is complete; however, noncommercial property may be assessed before construction is complete.
Pennsylvania	Pennsylvania encourages the renovation of deteriorating residential and commercial properties by permitting the exemption of a portion of the value attributable to new construction or improvements.
Rhode Island	Completed construction work in progress becomes taxable either from the date that the certificate of occupancy is issued or the date that it is first used, whichever occurs first, prorated for the assessment year in which the construction is completed.
South Carolina	New structures are taxable when completed.
South Dakota	Newly constructed improvements are taxable when the improvements reach a value of $10,000 or $30,000 depending on the structure.
Tennessee	An improvement that is incomplete on January 1 is assessed based on the fair market value of the materials used. If the improvement is subsequently completed and ready for use before the following September 1, the assessment is corrected to reflect the value of the structure at the time of completion. The corrected assessment is then prorated for the portion of the year following the date of completion.
Texas	No specific statutory provisions.
Utah	Construction work in progress is valued at full cash value projected upon completion.
Vermont	Towns may exempt for up to three years construction work in progress up to the first $75,000 of appraised value of homes, dwelling houses, or farms.
Virginia	New buildings are assessed at their actual value at the time of assessment, whether entirely completed or not.
Washington	New construction is assessed each year up until August 31.
West Virginia	Buildings become taxable when they are fit for use, but construction materials are taxed as personal property.
Wisconsin	The value of a structure as if it were completed, multiplied by the percentage of completion; or a blanket percentage reduction in value throughout a development in progress.
Wyoming	Although improvements are taxable, no specific statutory provisions directly address construction work in progress.

Freeport Exemptions

The following chart indicates in which states a freeport exemption is allowed for property temporarily stored in state as of the assessment date.

State	Scope of Exemption
Alabama	Exemption for a period of up to 36 months following consignment or storage in a public or private warehouse or other storage facility for shipment outside Alabama.
Alaska	No exemption is specified by Alaska law.
Arizona	Exemptions apply to (1) property moving through Arizona to a destination outside the state, (2) property consigned to an Arizona warehouse from a point outside Arizona for storage or assembly in transit to a destination outside Arizona, and (3) commodities held in an Arizona warehouse for resale on a contract subject to the rules of a regulated commodity market.
Arkansas	Exemption for tangible personal property in transit through the state and for property manufactured, processed, or refined in the state and stored for out-of-state shipment.
California	Exemption for property moving in interstate or foreign commerce, whether entering or leaving the state, while in transit.
Colorado	While no property law provision specifically addresses in-transit property, apparently property in-transit traveling out of state would not be taxable whereas property in-transit traveling into the state would be taxable at its destination.
Connecticut	Exemptions apply to (1) merchandise shipped into Connecticut and held in storage in its original package in the name of, or for the account of, the producer or manufacturer in a public commercial storage warehouse and (2) merchandise produced or manufactured in Connecticut that is in a public commercial warehouse or wharf and that is intended to be shipped outside the state in the package or container in which it is stored.
Delaware	Not applicable because personal property is not taxable (except for captive insurance companies).
District of Columbia	Exemption for property held in a public warehouse for shipment outside the District.
Florida	Exemptions for items manufactured or produced in another state and brought into Florida only for transshipment to a foreign country, or items manufactured or produced in another country and brought into Florida for transshipment to other states provided the in-state storage does not exceed 180 days, in addition to tangible personal property physically present in the state on or after January 1 for temporary purposes only, which property is in the state for 30 days or less.
Georgia	Foreign merchandise in transit is exempt while located at the port of original entry or port of export even if it is held in a warehouse where it is assembled, bound, joined, processed, disassembled, divided, cut, broken in bulk, relabeled, or repackaged.
Hawaii	Not applicable because personal property is not taxable.
Idaho	Exemptions apply to personal property that is shipped into Idaho, stored in warehouses, and designated for reshipment out of the state and to property that is shipped into the state, stored in its original package in a warehouse, and owned by a person who has no domicile or business situs in the state.
Illinois	Not applicable because personal property is not taxable.

State	Scope of Exemption
Indiana	Exemptions for property manufactured for out-of-state shipment, property shipped into Indiana for transshipment, property transshipped by nonresidents, property to be shipped out of state, and property transported by a common carrier.
Iowa	No specific exemption is authorized; however, most personal property is exempt.
Kansas	Exemptions for in-transit property moving through the state in interstate commerce even if it is warehoused in Kansas prior to reaching its final destination outside the state.
Kentucky	Exemption for personal property shipped into Kentucky and placed in a warehouse or distribution center for the purpose of further shipment to an out-of-state destination.
Louisiana	Exemptions apply to property that (1) is moving through Louisiana to a destination outside the state, (2) is consigned to a Louisiana warehouse from a point outside Louisiana for storage or assembly in transit to a destination outside Louisiana, or (3) is a commodity held in a Louisiana warehouse for resale on a contract subject to the rules of a regulated commodity market.
Maine	Exemption for in-transit property that is moving through the state in interstate commerce.
Maryland	No specific exemption is authorized, although local governing bodies may authorize payments in lieu of property taxes for business stock consisting of foreign imports if the foreign imports are in their original packages and are in the possession of a business engaged in importing.
Massachusetts	Personal property that is stored in its original package in a public warehouse is exempt if owned by a person who does not have a domicile or place of business in the state.
Michigan	Exemption for products, materials, and goods (except alcoholic beverages) in a public warehouse, U.S. customs port of entry bonded warehouse, dock, or port facility if designated as in transit to out-of-state destinations.
Minnesota	Exemption for goods in transit that are shipped into the state.
Mississippi	Exemption from state, county, and municipal taxes for commodities that are: (1) in transit; (2) assembled or stored on wharves, in railway cars, or in warehouses at ports of entry designated by the federal government; and (3) intended for import or export into, through, or from Mississippi. At the discretion of a county or municipality, exemption for personal property from local taxes for property that is (1) moving in interstate commerce through the state or (2) consigned or transferred to a licensed free port warehouse in the state for storage in transit to a final destination outside the state.
Missouri	Exemption for property moving through the state in interstate commerce, even if it is warehoused in the state prior to reaching its final destination outside the state.
Montana	Exemption for merchandise produced outside Montana that is in transit through the state and that is consigned to a storage facility in the state prior to shipment to a final destination outside the state.
Nebraska	Exemption for in-transit property moving through the state in interstate commerce.
Nevada	Exemption for property moving in interstate commerce through or over Nevada or consigned to a Nevada warehouse from outside the state for storage in transit to a final destination outside the state.
New Hampshire	Not applicable because personal property is not taxable.

State	Scope of Exemption
New Jersey	Not applicable because personal property generally is not taxable.
New Mexico	Exemption for property being transported in interstate commerce to a destination outside the state even if it is consigned to an in-state warehouse or factory.
New York	Not applicable because personal property generally is not taxable.
North Carolina	Exemptions apply to: (1) property that has been imported from a foreign country through a North Carolina seaport terminal and which is stored at the terminal while awaiting further shipment for the first 12 months of storage; (2) property shipped into North Carolina for the purpose of repair, alteration, maintenance, or servicing and reshipment to the owner outside the state; (3) Motor vehicle chassis belonging to nonresidents and temporarily in-state to have a body mounted upon them.
North Dakota	No specific exemption is authorized; however, most personal property is exempt.
Ohio	Exemption for merchandise and agricultural products shipped into Ohio for storage purposes only (without further manufacturing or processing), held in a facility not owned or controlled by the owner of the merchandise, and subsequently shipped out of Ohio to anyone.
Oklahoma	Exemption for property moving through the state if it is (1) forwarded at through rates from the point of origin to the point of destination and (2) not detained in Oklahoma for more than 90 days.
Oregon	Exemption for property moving in interstate or foreign commerce, whether entering or leaving the state, while it remains in transit.
Pennsylvania	Not applicable because tangible personal property is not taxable.
Rhode Island	None; however, tax is not imposed on manufactured property brought into the state for finishing and returned to a non-resident owner.
South Carolina	Exemption for property moving in interstate commerce through the state or consigned to an in-state warehouse from outside the state for storage while in transit to an out-of-state destination.
South Dakota	No specific exemption is authorized; however, most personal property is exempt.
Tennessee	Exemptions apply to (1) property moving in interstate commerce, (2) property consigned to an in-state warehouse for storage while in transit to a final destination outside the state, and (3) property transported from outside the state to an in-state plant, warehouse, or establishment for storage or repackaging and held for eventual sale or other disposition outside the state.
Texas	Exemption applies to property that is (1) acquired in or imported into the state to be forwarded outside the state, (2) detained in state for assembling, storing, manufacturing, processing, or fabricating purposes, and (3) transported outside the state within 175 days.
Utah	Exemption applies to property that is held for shipment to a final destination outside the state within 12 months.
Vermont	None.
Virginia	Exemptions apply to domestic merchandise scheduled for export while in inventory located in a foreign trade zone within Virginia and cargo merchandise, and equipment in transit that is stored, located or housed temporarily in a marine or airport terminal in Virginia prior to being transported by vessels or aircraft to a point outside Virginia.

State	Scope of Exemption
Washington	Proportional exemption allowed to account for property in transit.
West Virginia	Exemption for property moving in interstate commerce through the state.
Wisconsin	Goods and merchandise located in storage in a commercial storage warehouse or on a public wharf are assessed to the property owner, not the warehouse owner. For inventories, a merchant's stock-in-trade, manufacturers' materials and finished products, and livestock are exempt, but property held for rental is taxable.
Wyoming	Exemption applies to manufactured goods, wares, seed, feed, fertilizer, tools, supplies, and merchandise, or Wyoming assembled or manufactured products being held for out-of-state sale that is consigned or placed in any Wyoming storage area for storage, repackaging, processing, fabricating, milling, disassembly, or assembly in transit to a final destination outside the state, irrespective of whether the destination is specified before or after the transportation begins.

Intangible Property

The following chart indicates in which states intangible property generally is subjected to ad valorem taxation.

State	Intangible property taxable
Alabama	Specified intangibles, such as certain bonds and hoarded money, are taxable.
Alaska	No.
Arizona	No.
Arkansas	No.
California	No.
Colorado	No.
Connecticut	No.
Delaware	No.
District of Columbia	No.
Florida	No. A separate tax is imposed on specified intangibles.
Georgia	No. A separate intangible recording tax applies only to long-term notes secured by real estate.
Hawaii	No.
Idaho	No.
Illinois	No.
Indiana	No.
Iowa	No, except for a tax on credit unions, loan agencies, and investment companies.
Kansas	No.
Kentucky	Specified intangible property, such as money in hand, notes, bonds, accounts, and other credits, is taxable.
Louisiana	No, except for bank stocks and certain credit assessments.
Maine	No.
Maryland	No.
Massachusetts	No.
Michigan	No.
Minnesota	No.
Mississippi	Money on hand and evidence of indebtedness bearing interest in excess of the maximum rate allowed by law is taxable.
Missouri	No.
Montana	No.
Nebraska	No.

State	Intangible property taxable
Nevada	No.
New Hampshire	No.
New Jersey	No.
New Mexico	No.
New York	No.
North Carolina	No, other than leasehold interests in exempted real property.
North Dakota	No.
Ohio	Only intangibles held by a dealer in intangibles are taxable.
Oklahoma	No.
Oregon	No.
Pennsylvania	Specified intangibles owned by resident individuals and corporations are taxable.
Rhode Island	No.
South Carolina	No.
South Dakota	No.
Tennessee	Only certain intangibles of insurance companies, loan and investment companies, and cemetery companies are taxable.
Texas	Only certain intangibles of insurance companies and savings and loan associations are taxable.
Utah	No.
Vermont	No.
Virginia	No.
Washington	No.
West Virginia	No.
Wisconsin	No.
Wyoming	No.

Legal Basis for Assessment

The following chart identifies the legal standard employed by each state in valuing property for purposes of ad valorem taxation. Assessment ratios are noted, when applicable.

State	Tax is applied to:
Alabama	Specified percentages of fair and reasonable market value.
Alaska	Full and true value.
Arizona	Specified percentages of either full cash value or limited property value.
Arkansas	No more than 20% of true and full market or actual value.
California	Full cash value.
Colorado	Specified percentages (29% for all nonresidential property) of actual value.
Connecticut	Fair market value.
Delaware	True value in money.
District of Columbia	Estimated market value for real property.
Florida	Just value.
Georgia	Specified percentages (generally 40%) of fair market value.
Hawaii	Fair market value.
Idaho	Market value.
Illinois	33 1/3% of fair cash value; special percentages apply within Cook County.
Indiana	True tax value.
Iowa	100% of actual value except for certain classes of property.
Kansas	Fair market value in money.
Kentucky	Fair cash value.
Louisiana	Specified percentages of fair market value, or for certain property types, use value.
Maine	Just value, which is 100% of current market value.
Maryland	Specified percentages of full cash value.
Massachusetts	Specified percentages of fair cash value.
Michigan	50% of true cash value.
Minnesota	Specified percentages of market value.
Mississippi	Specified percentages of true value.
Missouri	Specified percentages of true value in money.
Montana	100% of market value.
Nebraska	Actual value for real property, net book value for personal property.
Nevada	Value as determined by using cost, income, and market approaches.

State	Tax is applied to:
New Hampshire	Market Value.
New Jersey	Fair market value.
New Mexico	Market value.
New York	Value of property in its current use.
North Carolina	True value in money.
North Dakota	Specified percentages of true and full value.
Ohio	Specified percentages of true value in money.
Oklahoma	Specified percentages of fair cash value.
Oregon	100% of real market value.
Pennsylvania	Actual value.
Rhode Island	Full and fair cash value.
South Carolina	Specified percentages of true value in money.
South Dakota	True and full value in money.
Tennessee	Specified percentages of appraised or market value.
Texas	Fair cash market value.
Utah	Specified percentages of fair market value.
Vermont	1% of listed value.
Virginia	Fair market value.
Washington	100% of true and fair value in money.
West Virginia	True and actual value.
Wisconsin	Full cash value.
Wyoming	Specified percentages of fair market value.

Payment Dates

The following chart indicates the date or dates by which property taxes generally are payable. The due date for the payment also is the date after which the taxes become delinquent if a later delinquency date is not specified.

State	Payment Dates
Alabama	Payment is due October 1 and become delinquent if not paid by the following January 1. The dates that municipal taxes are due and become delinquent vary by municipality.
Alaska	Payment and delinquency dates are fixed by each municipality.
Arizona	The first half of secured property tax is due October 1 and the second half is due March 1.
Arkansas	Property taxes, except taxes held in escrow, due October 10.
California	Payment of first half of taxes for property on secured roll is due November 1 and becomes delinquent on December 10; second half of payment is due on February 1 and becomes delinquent on April 10. Payments of taxes for property on the unsecured roll is due January 1.
Colorado	The first half of property tax is due February 28 and the second half is due June 15.
Connecticut	Payment is due July 1, although municipalities may provide for single, semiannual, or quarterly payments. Unpaid tax or tax installments become delinquent on the first day of the month following the month the taxes were due (August 1 for the first or sole payment).
Delaware	Payment is due July 1 in New Castle County, June 1 in Kent County, and May 1 in Sussex County. Taxes in all three counties become delinquent after September 30.
District of Columbia	The first half of the real property tax is due March 31 and the second half is due September 15; personal property tax is due July 31.
Florida	Taxes are due on November 1 and become delinquent on the following April 1, although an election to pay in quarterly installments is available.
Georgia	Payment is due December 20, subject to variation in some counties.
Hawaii	Installment payments are due on August 20 and February 20 of the year following the assessment.
Idaho	Payment is due December 20; however, the taxes may be paid in two equal installments, the first by December 20 and the second by June 20 of the following year.
Illinois	First installment of property tax is due June 1 and the second installment is due September 1; however, counties may provide different deadlines.
Indiana	Installment payments are due on May 10 and November 10 of the year following the assessment.
Iowa	Installment payments are due on September 1 and March 1 of the year following the assessment..
Kansas	Installment payments must be made by December 20 and May 10 of the year following the assessment to avoid delinquency.
Kentucky	Subject to some local variations, payment is due on September 15 and becomes delinquent on January 1.
Louisiana	Payment is due November 15 and becomes delinquent December 31.

State	Payment Dates
Maine	Payment and delinquency dates are fixed by locality.
Maryland	Property taxes are due on July 1 of each taxable year, and are delinquent after September 30.
Massachusetts	Payment is due July 1, although there are provisions for semi-annual and quarterly tax payments.
Michigan	Payment is due February 14 and become delinquent on February 15; payment is due September 14 and become delinquent on September 15 for the summer levy; different provisions apply to villages and fourth class cities.
Minnesota	Installments are due on May 15 and October 15 and become delinquent if not timely paid.
Mississippi	Payment is due February 1, although a locality may allow installment payments.
Missouri	Payment is due December 31, although a locality may allow installment payments.
Montana	Installments are due on November 30 (or 30 days after the postmark of the tax notice, if later) and May 31.
Nebraska	Payment is due December 31, with installment payments due on May 1 and September 1 (April 1 and August 1 in larger counties) to avoid delinquency.
Nevada	Payment is due third Monday in August, although quarterly installment payments may be made.
New Hampshire	Payment is due December 1, although a locality may allow semiannual installment payments.
New Jersey	Quarterly installments are due on February 1, May 1, August 1, and November 1. Municipalities may allow a grace period for payments of up to an additional ten calendar days.
New Mexico	Installments are due on November 10 and April 10, although a prepayment option may be available that results in four installments.
New York	Payment is due the later of January 31 or 30 days of the date of receipt of the tax roll and warrant, although a locality may allow installment payments.
North Carolina	Payment is due September 1, with the taxes becoming delinquent if not paid before January 6.
North Dakota	Payment is due January 1, although installment payments may be made.
Ohio	Payment is due December 31 for real property taxes or one-half payment on December 31 and one-half payment on June 20, although installment payments may be made. Personal property tax is payable in two installments, the first of which is due when the return is filed between February 15 and April 30, and the second of which is due on September 20.
Oklahoma	Payment is due November 1, or in installments that are due on January 1 and April 1.
Oregon	Payment is due on November 15, or in equal installments due on November 15, February 15, and May 15.
Pennsylvania	Payment and delinquency dates vary by locality.
Rhode Island	Payment and delinquency dates vary by locality.

State	Payment Dates
South Carolina	Payments is due between September 30 and January 15, although actual date varies by locality.
South Dakota	Payment is due January 1, become delinquent if not paid by May 1 and October 31.
Tennessee	County taxes are due on the first Monday of October and become delinquent if not paid by the following March 1; the payment and delinquency dates for municipal taxes vary by municipality.
Texas	Payment is due January 31 or in installments due December 1 and July 1, if the governing body of the taxing unit has adopted the split-payment option.
Utah	Payment is due November 30.
Vermont	Payment and delinquency dates vary by locality.
Virginia	Payment is due December 5, unless another date is set by the locality.
Washington	Payment is due between February 15 and April 30 or in installments due on April 30 and October 31.
West Virginia	Installment payments are due on September 1 and March 1 and become delinquent on October 1 and April 1, respectively.
Wisconsin	Payment is due January 31 or in equal installments due on January 31 and July 31.
Wyoming	Installment payments are due on November 10 and May 10.

Personal Property Renditions

The following chart indicates the generally applicable due date for filing personal property returns or renditions with respect to general business property. Dates applicable to specific industries (e.g., centrally assessed utilities) are not included in this chart.

States that do not impose a personal property tax are designated as "Exempt." In some states, taxpayers may apply for an extension for filing returns or renditions.

State	Return Due Date
Alabama	January 1.
Alaska	Varies locally.
Arizona	April 1.
Arkansas	May 31.
California	April 1.
Colorado	April 15.
Connecticut	November 1.
Delaware	Personal property exempt except for certain property owned by captive insurance companies.
District of Columbia	July 31.
Florida	April 1.
Georgia	Varies locally, but between January 1 and April 1.
Hawaii	Exempt.
Idaho	March 15.
Illinois	Exempt.
Indiana	May 15.
Iowa	Exempt.
Kansas	March 15.
Kentucky	May 15.
Louisiana	Later of April 1 or within 45 days of receipt of forms from assessor. In Jefferson Parish, 45 days after receipt of forms from assessor.
Maine	Varies locally.
Maryland	April 15.
Massachusetts	March 1.
Michigan	February 20.
Minnesota	Exempt.
Mississippi	April 1.
Missouri	March 1.

State	Return Due Date
Montana	30 days following receipt of reporting forms.
Nebraska	May 1.
Nevada	July 31.
New Hampshire	Exempt.
New Jersey	Exempt.
New Mexico	Last day of February.
New York	Exempt.
North Carolina	First business day in January through January 31.
North Dakota	Exempt.
Ohio	April 30.
Oklahoma	March 15.
Oregon	March 1.
Pennsylvania	Exempt.
Rhode Island	March 15.
South Carolina	April 30.
South Dakota	Exempt.
Tennessee	March 1.
Texas	April 15.
Utah	30 days following request.
Vermont	April 1.
Virginia	May 1.
Washington	April 30.
West Virginia	October 1.
Wisconsin	March 1.
Wyoming	March 1.

State Real Property Tax Calendar

The following chart details the various recurring dates of interest within state real property tax schedules. When multiple dates are listed under the Payment Date and Delinquent columns, the fractions preceding dates indicate the amount of partial payment due or delinquent. Local due dates are not included.

ALABAMA

Real Property Tax Year	October-September
Assessment/Valuation Date	October 1
Payment Date	October 1
Delinquency Date	January 1
Lien Date	October 1

ALASKA

Real Property Tax Year	Calendar Year
Assessment/Valuation Date	January 1
Payment Date	Varies Locally
Delinquency Date	Varies Locally
Lien Date	Varies Locally

ARIZONA

Real Property Tax Year	Calendar Year
Assessment/Valuation Date	January 1
Payment Date	1/2 October 1, 1/2 March 1
Delinquency Date	1/2 November 1, 1/2 May 1
Lien Date	January 1

ARKANSAS

Real Property Tax Year	Calendar Year
Assessment/Valuation Date	January 1
Payment Date	From the third Monday in February through October 10
Delinquency Date	October 11
Lien Date	First Monday in January

CALIFORNIA

Real Property Tax Year	July-June
Assessment/Valuation Date	January 1
Payment Date	1/2 November 1, 1/2 February 1
Delinquency Date	1/2 December 10, 1/2 April 10
Lien Date	January 1

COLORADO

Real Property Tax Year	Calendar Year
Assessment/Valuation Date	January 1
Payment Date	1/2 February 28, 1/2 June 15
Delinquency Date	June 16
Lien Date	January 1

CONNECTICUT

Real Property Tax Year	October-September
Assessment/Valuation Date	October 1
Payment Date	Fixed Locally
Delinquency Date	Fixed Locally
Lien Date	October 1

DELAWARE

Real Property Tax Year	Varies Locally
Assessment/Valuation Date	Varies Locally
Payment Date	Varies Locally
Delinquency Date	September 30
Lien Date	Varies Locally

DISTRICT OF COLUMBIA

Real Property Tax Year	Calendar Year
Assessment/Valuation Date	January 1
Payment Date	1/2 March 31, 1/2 September 15
Delinquency Date	1/2 April 1, 1/2 September 16
Lien Date	July 1

FLORIDA

Real Property Tax Year	Calendar Year
Assessment/Valuation Date	January 1
Payment Date	November 1
Delinquency Date	April 1
Lien Date	January 1

GEORGIA

Real Property Tax Year	Calendar Year
Assessment/Valuation Date	January 1
Payment Date	December 20
Delinquency Date	December 21
Lien Date	Varies Locally

HAWAII

Real Property Tax Year	July 1 to June 30
Assessment/Valuation Date	January 1
Payment Date	1/2 August 20, 1/2 February 20
Delinquency Date	1/2 August 21, 1/2 February 21
Lien Date	July 1

IDAHO

Real Property Tax Year	Calendar Year
Assessment/Valuation Date	January 1
Payment Date	1/2 December 20, 1/2 June 20
Delinquency Date	1/2 December 21, 1/2 June 21
Lien Date	January 1

ILLINOIS

Real Property Tax Year	Calendar Year
Assessment/Valuation Date	January 1
Payment Date	1/2 June 1, 1/2 September 1
Delinquency Date	1/2 June 2, 1/2 September 2
Lien Date	January 1

INDIANA

Real Property Tax Year	Calendar Year
Assessment/Valuation Date	March 1
Payment Date	1/2 May 10, 1/2 November 10
Delinquency Date	1/2 May 11, 1/2 November 11
Lien Date	March 1

IOWA

Real Property Tax Year	Calendar Year
Assessment/Valuation Date	January 1
Payment Date	1/2 September 1, 1/2 March 1
Delinquency Date	1/2 October 1, 1/2 April 1
Lien Date	June 30

KANSAS

Real Property Tax Year	Calendar Year
Assessment/Valuation Date	January 1
Payment Date	1/2 December 20, 1/2 June 20
Delinquency Date	1/2 December 21, 1/2 June 21
Lien Date	November 1

KENTUCKY

Real Property Tax Year	Calendar Year
Assessment/Valuation Date	January 1
Payment Date	September 15
Delinquency Date	January 1
Lien Date	January 1

LOUISIANA

Real Property Tax Year	Calendar Year
Assessment/Valuation Date	January 1
Payment Date	December 31
Delinquency Date	January 1
Lien Date	December 31

MAINE

Real Property Tax Year	April-March
Assessment/Valuation Date	April 1
Payment Date	Varies Locally
Delinquency Date	Varies Locally
Lien Date	8 to 12 months from commitment date

MARYLAND

Real Property Tax Year	July-June
Assessment/Valuation Date	January 1
Payment Date	July 1
Delinquency Date	October 1
Lien Date	July 1

MASSACHUSETTS

Real Property Tax Year	Calendar Year
Assessment/Valuation Date	January 1
Payment Date	July 1
Delinquency Date	November 1
Lien Date	January 1

MICHIGAN

Real Property Tax Year	Calendar Year
Assessment/Valuation Date	December 31
Payment Date	February 14, September 14 (summer levy)
Delinquency Date	February 15, September 15 (summer levy)
Lien Date	December 1, July 1 (summer levy)

MINNESOTA
Real Property Tax Year .... Calendar Year
Assessment/Valuation Date .... January 2
Payment Date .... 1/2 May 15, 1/2 October 15
Delinquency Date .... 1/2 May 16, 1/2 October 16
Lien Date .... January 2

MISSISSIPPI
Real Property Tax Year .... Calendar Year
Assessment/Valuation Date .... January 1
Payment Date .... February 1
Delinquency Date .... February 2
Lien Date .... January 1

MISSOURI
Real Property Tax Year .... Calendar Year
Assessment/Valuation Date .... January 1
Payment Date .... December 31
Delinquency Date .... January 1
Lien Date .... January 1

MONTANA
Real Property Tax Year .... Calendar Year
Assessment/Valuation Date .... January 1
Payment Date .... 1/2 May 31, 1/2 November 30
Delinquency Date .... 1/2 June 1, 1/2 December 1
Lien Date .... January 1

NEBRASKA
Real Property Tax Year .... Calendar Year
Assessment/Valuation Date .... January 1
Payment Date .... 1/2 May 1, 1/2 September 1
Delinquency Date .... 1/2 May 2, 1/2 September 2
Lien Date .... December 31

NEVADA
Real Property Tax Year .... July-June
Assessment/Valuation Date .... July 1
Payment Date .... Third Monday in August or 1/4 third Monday in August and 1/4 on each of the first Mondays in October, January, March
Delinquency Date .... Third Monday in August
Lien Date .... July 1

NEW HAMPSHIRE
Real Property Tax Year .... April-March
Assessment/Valuation Date .... April 1
Payment Date .... December 1
Delinquency Date .... December 2
Lien Date .... October 1

NEW JERSEY
Real Property Tax Year .... Calendar Year
Assessment/Valuation Date .... October 1
Payment Date .... 1/4 February 1, 1/4 May 1, 1/4 August 1, 1/4 November 1
Delinquency Date .... 1/4 February 2, 1/4 May 2, 1/4 August 2, 1/4 November 2
Lien Date .... January 1

NEW MEXICO

Real Property Tax Year	Calendar Year
Assessment/Valuation Date	January 1
Payment Date	1/2 November 10, 1/2 April 10
Delinquency Date	30 days after due date
Lien Date	January 1

NEW YORK

Real Property Tax Year	July to June
Assessment/Valuation Date	March 1 (Assessment), January 1 (Valuation)
Payment Date	Varies Locally
Delinquency Date	Varies Locally
Lien Date	Varies Locally

NORTH CAROLINA

Real Property Tax Year	Calendar Year
Assessment/Valuation Date	January 1
Payment Date	September 1
Delinquency Date	January 6
Lien Date	January 1

NORTH DAKOTA

Real Property Tax Year	Calendar Year
Assessment/Valuation Date	February 1
Payment Date	January 1
Delinquency Date	1/2 March 1, 1/2 October 15
Lien Date	January 1

OHIO

Real Property Tax Year	Calendar Year
Assessment/Valuation Date	Varies Locally
Payment Date	1/2 December 31, 1/2 June 20
Delinquency Date	1/2 January 1, 1/2 June 21
Lien Date	January 1

OKLAHOMA

Real Property Tax Year	Calendar Year
Assessment/Valuation Date	January 1
Payment Date	November 1 or 1/2 December 31, 1/2 March 31
Delinquency Date	1/2 January 1, 1/2 April 1
Lien Date	November 1

OREGON

Real Property Tax Year	Calendar Year
Assessment/Valuation Date	January 1
Payment Date	November 15 or 1/3 November 15, 1/3 February 15, 1/3 May 15
Delinquency Date	May 16
Lien Date	July 1

PENNSYLVANIA

Real Property Tax Year	Varies Locally
Assessment/Valuation Date	Varies Locally
Payment Date	Varies Locally
Delinquency Date	Varies Locally
Lien Date	Varies Locally

RHODE ISLAND

Real Property Tax Year . . . . Calendar Year
Assessment/Valuation Date . . . . December 31
Payment Date . . . . Varies Locally
Delinquency Date . . . . Varies Locally
Lien Date . . . . December 31

SOUTH CAROLINA

Real Property Tax Year . . . . Calendar Year
Assessment/Valuation Date . . . . December 31
Payment Date . . . . September 30 through January 15
Delinquency Date . . . . January 16
Lien Date . . . . December 31

SOUTH DAKOTA

Real Property Tax Year . . . . Calendar Year
Assessment/Valuation Date . . . . November 1
Payment Date . . . . January 1 or 1/2 April 30, 1/2 October 31
Delinquency Date . . . . 1/2 May 1, 1/2 November 1
Lien Date . . . . January 1

TENNESSEE

Real Property Tax Year . . . . Calendar Year
Assessment/Valuation Date . . . . January 1
Payment Date . . . . First Monday in October
Delinquency Date . . . . March 1
Lien Date . . . . January 1

TEXAS

Real Property Tax Year . . . . Calendar Year
Assessment/Valuation Date . . . . January 1
Payment Date . . . . January 31 or 1/2 November 30, 1/2 June 30
Delinquency Date . . . February 1 or 1/2 December 1, 1/2 July 1 (if locality has elected split payment option)
Lien Date . . . . January 1

UTAH

Real Property Tax Year . . . . Calendar Year
Assessment/Valuation Date . . . . January 1
Payment Date . . . . November 30
Delinquency Date . . . . November 30
Lien Date . . . . January 1

VERMONT

Real Property Tax Year . . . . April-March
Assessment/Valuation Date . . . . April 1
Payment Date . . . . Varies Locally
Delinquency Date . . . . Varies Locally
Lien Date . . . . Varies Locally

VIRGINIA

Real Property Tax Year . . . . Calendar Year
Assessment/Valuation Date . . . . January 1
Payment Date . . . . December 5 in most localities
Delinquency Date . . . . December 6 in most localities
Lien Date . . . . December 6

WASHINGTON

Real Property Tax Year . . . . Calendar Year
Assessment/Valuation Date . . . . January 1
Payment Date . . . . February 15 through April 30 or 1/2 April 30, 1/2 October 31
Delinquency Date . . . . May 1 or November 1
Lien Date . . . . January 1

WEST VIRGINIA

Real Property Tax Year . . . . July-June
Assessment/Valuation Date . . . . July 1
Payment Date . . . . 1/2 September 1, 1/2 March 1
Delinquency Date . . . . 1/2 October 1, 1/2 April 1
Lien Date . . . . July 1

WISCONSIN

Real Property Tax Year . . . . Calendar Year
Assessment/Valuation Date . . . . January 1
Payment Date . . . . January 31 or 1/2 January 31, 1/2 July 31
Delinquency Date . . . . February 1 or 1/2 February 1, 1/2 August 1
Lien Date . . . . January 1

WYOMING

Real Property Tax Year . . . . Calendar Year
Assessment/Valuation Date . . . . January 1
Payment Date . . . . December 31 or 1/2 November 10, 1/2 May 10
Delinquency Date . . . . May 10
Lien Date . . . . January 1

Tangible Personal Property

The following chart sets forth which states subject tangible personal property to ad valorem taxation. In most cases, the tax is limited to business-related property due to exemptions for personal effects or household goods. Such exemptions are noted when applicable in the chart below.

State	Tangible personal property taxable
Alabama	Yes, absent a specific exemption. Most personal-use property is exempt.
Alaska	Yes, absent a specific exemption. Household furniture and personal effects are exempt.
Arizona	Yes, absent a specific exemption. Household goods are exempt.
Arkansas	Yes, absent a specific exemption. Personal property used within the home is exempt.
California	Yes, absent a specific exemption. Household goods and personal effects are exempt.
Colorado	Yes, absent a specific exemption. Household goods and $2,500 of otherwise taxable property are exempt.
Connecticut	Yes, absent a specific exemption. Specific household and personal effects are exempt.
Delaware	No, other than property of captive insurance companies.
District of Columbia	Yes, but only property used in a trade or business.
Florida	Yes, absent a specific exemption. Household goods and personal effects are exempt.
Georgia	Yes, absent a specific exemption. Personal effects and other items used within the home and the first $700 of other taxable property are exempt.
Hawaii	No.
Idaho	Yes, absent a specific exemption. Household goods and personal effects are exempt.
Illinois	No.
Indiana	Yes, absent a specific exemption. Household goods are exempt.
Iowa	Most personal property is exempt, although some items of personal property are deemed to be real property.
Kansas	Yes, absent a specific exemption. Household items and business inventories are exempt.
Kentucky	Yes, absent a specific exemption. Household goods used in the home are exempt.
Louisiana	Yes, absent a specific exemption. Personal property used in the home is exempt.
Maine	Yes, absent a specific exemption. Exemptions are provided for household goods, apparel, farming utensils, mechanics' tools, and de minimis property (less than $1,000).
Maryland	Only personal property used in connection with a business or profession is taxable.

State	Tangible personal property taxable
Massachusetts	Yes, absent a specific exemption. Household effects of residents kept at their domiciles are exempt.
Michigan	Yes, absent a specific exemption. Household goods are exempt.
Minnesota	Only specified items of personal property are taxable. Household goods are exempt.
Mississippi	Yes, absent a specific exemption. Specified household goods are exempt.
Missouri	Yes, absent a specific exemption. Household goods are exempt.
Montana	Yes, absent a specific exemption. Household goods and furniture are exempt.
Nebraska	Only depreciable property that is used in a trade or business or for the production of income and that has a determinable life longer than one year is taxable.
Nevada	Yes, absent a specific exemption. Household goods and furniture used by a single household and owned by a member of that household are exempt.
New Hampshire	No.
New Jersey	Only business personal property used by specified utilities and petroleum refineries is taxable.
New Mexico	Only specified items of personal property are taxable. Household items are not included in the list of taxable property.
New York	No.
North Carolina	Yes, absent a specific exemption. Nonbusiness property generally is not taxable.
North Dakota	Only centrally assessed property of certain entities is taxable.
Ohio	Personal property tax on business inventory, machinery and equipment used in business, and furniture and fixtures is being phased out; for tax year 2005, 25% of true value, to tax year 2008, 0% of true value. The personal property tax on the personal property of telephone companies, telegraph companies, and interexchange telecommunications companies is also phased out; for tax year 2007 20% of true value, to tax year 2010, 0% of true value.
Oklahoma	Yes, absent a specific exemption. Household goods are exempt, subject to a $100 cap, although counties may enact a full exemption.
Oregon	Only personal property used in a trade or business is taxable.
Pennsylvania	No.
Rhode Island	Yes, absent a specific exemption. Household goods and furniture are exempt.
South Carolina	Yes, absent a specific exemption. Household goods, wearing apparel, and furniture used in the owner's home are exempt.
South Dakota	Only personal property of centrally assessed utilities and railroads is taxable.
Tennessee	Only personal property used in a business or profession is taxable.

State	Tangible personal property taxable
Texas	Unless a locality elects otherwise, only income-producing personal property is taxable.
Utah	Yes, absent a specific exemption. Household goods used exclusively by their owner in maintaining a home are exempt.
Vermont	Yes, absent a specific exemption. Personal wearing apparel, household furniture, and equipment are exempt.
Virginia	Yes, absent a specific exemption. Household goods and personal effects are exempt only if a local authority enacts the exemption.
Washington	Yes, absent a specific exemption. Household goods and personal effects are exempt.
West Virginia	Yes, absent a specific exemption. Household goods and personal effects are exempt; $200 exemption for property used for profit.
Wisconsin	Yes, absent a specific exemption. Household goods and personal effects are exempt.
Wyoming	Yes, absent a specific exemption. Personal property used for personal or family use (excluding mobile homes) is exempt.

Taxation of Inventories

The following chart indicates the states' treatment of business inventories, including those of manufacturers, wholesalers, and retailers, for ad valorem tax purposes. The designations are of a general nature and exceptions unnoted in the chart may exist.

State	Taxability of Inventory
Alabama	Stocks of goods, wares, and merchandise are exempt.
Alaska	Inventory exemption may be enacted by each municipality.
Arizona	Inventory is exempt.
Arkansas	Inventory of merchants and manufacturers is taxable.
California	Inventory is exempt.
Colorado	Inventory is constitutionally exempt.
Connecticut	Inventory generally is exempt.
Delaware	Inventory is exempt.
District of Columbia	Inventory is exempt.
Florida	Inventory is exempt.
Georgia	Inventory is generally taxable, unless locality enacts exemption.
Hawaii	Inventory is exempt.
Idaho	Inventory is exempt.
Illinois	Inventory is exempt.
Indiana	Beginning in 2006 for taxes payable in 2007, 100% exempt.
Iowa	Inventory generally is exempt.
Kansas	Inventory is exempt.
Kentucky	Inventory is taxable.
Louisiana	Inventory is taxable, unless it is being held in the state for storage purposes only.
Maine	Inventory is exempt.
Maryland	Business stock of person engaged in a manufacturing or commercial business is exempt.
Massachusetts	Inventories held by corporations are exempt; inventories held by unincorporated businesses is taxable.
Michigan	Inventory is exempt, unless it is held for lease or federal depreciation or depletion deductions have been claimed.
Minnesota	Inventory is exempt.
Mississippi	Inventory is taxable.
Missouri	Inventory is exempt.
Montana	Inventory is exempt.

State	Taxability of Inventory
Nebraska	Inventory is exempt.
Nevada	Inventory is exempt.
New Hampshire	Inventory is exempt.
New Jersey	Inventory is exempt.
New Mexico	Inventory generally exempt, unless federal depreciation or depletion deductions have been claimed.
New York	Inventory is exempt.
North Carolina	Inventory generally is exempt.
North Dakota	Inventory is exempt.
Ohio	Personal property tax on business inventory is being phased out; for tax year 2005, 25% of true value, to tax year 2008, 0% of true value.
Oklahoma	Inventory is taxable.
Oregon	Inventory is exempt.
Pennsylvania	Inventory is exempt.
Rhode Island	Manufacturers' inventory is exempt, and the tax on wholesale and retail inventory is being phased out.
South Carolina	Inventory is exempt.
South Dakota	Inventory is exempt unless it is owned by a centrally assessed utility.
Tennessee	Inventory of merchandise held for sale or exchange by persons subject to the state business and occupation tax is exempt.
Texas	Inventory is taxable.
Utah	Inventory is exempt.
Vermont	Inventory is taxable, although municipalities may elect an exemption.
Virginia	Inventory generally is taxable as merchants capital, although local taxing authorities may enact an exemption.
Washington	Inventory is exempt.
West Virginia	Inventory is taxable.
Wisconsin	Inventory is exempt.
Wyoming	Inventory is exempt.

PRACTICE AND PROCEDURE

The following pages contain charts summarizing facets of state tax practice and procedure. Topics covered include interest rates for 2006, electronic income tax filing options, and requirements, electronic payment requirements, record retention, and abatement of penalties/interest. Also included are managed audits and collection of out-of-state taxes.

Abatement of Penalties and Interest

The state taxing authority of most states, including the District of Columbia, or its director secretary, or authority representative, has the authority to abate or waive penalties or interest due on delinquent taxes if certain criteria are met. The criteria for abatement vary from state to state but generally fall within one of four categories, as discussed below.

Good cause (GC)—Some states allow abatement of penalties or interest if the taxpayer can show good cause for the failure to pay the tax or file the return or report. Some states use one of the following phrases to convey the same concept: reasonable cause, reasonable diligence, good faith, or excusable failure. While many states with these types of provisions provide statutory or regulatory guidance, many leave interpretation of the terms up to the taxing authority.

Department fault (DF)—Many states allow abatement of penalties or interest if the penalty or interest was incurred as a result of the taxpayer's reliance on the erroneous advice of taxing authority personnel. In such cases, the taxpayer must have supplied the personnel with all of the necessary facts to render the advice given. In addition, abatement is also allowed where the taxing authority unreasonably delayed the taxpayer and caused penalties or interest to be incurred.

Uncollectible (UC)—Penalties and interest may sometimes be abated when the taxing authority determines that the amounts due are uncollectible or that the cost of collecting the outstanding amount outweighs the amount that would be collected.

Compromise/closing agreement (CC)—The final method of abatement of penalties or interest is in conjunction with a compromise of tax or a closing agreement related to disputed outstanding amounts. While this is more in the nature of a settlement of a dispute rather than an abatement, some states limit their abatement provisions to these agreements.

Although most states treat abatements of penalties and interest similarly for all taxes, property taxes are generally the exception. The chart below does not necessarily reflect the States' positions on abatements relating to property taxes.

State	Penalties	Interest
Alabama	GC or DF	No
Alaska	CC	No
Arizona	GC or DF	DF
Arkansas	DF	DF
California	GC or DF	DF or UC
Colorado	GC	GC
Connecticut	UC	UC
Delaware	UC, GC or DF	UC, GC or DF

State	Penalties	Interest
District of Columbia	GC or DF	DF
Florida	GC, UC or CC	UC or CC
Georgia	GC or CC	GC or DF
Hawaii	GC or UC	GC or UC
Idaho	GC or CC	No
Illinois	GC or DF	GC or DF
Indiana	GC	No
Iowa	DF	DF
Kansas	GC, DF or UC	GC or DF[1]
Kentucky	GC or DF	DF
Louisiana	GC or DF	GC or DF[3]
Maine	GC	GC
Maryland	GC	GC
Massachusetts	GC or DF	GC
Michigan	GC	No
Minnesota	GC or DF	GC or DF
Mississippi	GC	GC
Missouri	GC or DF	DF
Montana	GC or UC	GC or UC[4,5]
Nebraska	GC	DF
Nevada	GC or DF	GC or DF
New Hampshire	GC, DF or UC	GC, DF or UC
New Jersey	GC or DF	GC or DF
New Mexico	DF or CC	DF or CC
New York	GC or DF	DF
North Carolina	GC	No
North Dakota	GC	GC
Ohio	GC	No
Oklahoma	GC or UC	GC or UC
Oregon	GC or UC	GC, DF or UC
Pennsylvania	GC or DF[6]	DF
Rhode Island	UC, DF or CC	UC, DF or CC

State	Penalties	Interest
South Carolina	GC or DF	Yes[7]
South Dakota	GC or DF	GC or DF
Tennessee	GC or DF	No
Texas	GC	GC
Utah	GC	GC
Vermont	Any reason	Any reason
Virginia	GC or DF	DF
Washington	GC	DF
West Virginia	DF, CC or UC	DF[4]
Wisconsin	DF	DF[8]
Wyoming	GC	No

[1] Limited to taxes that are not more than 90 days, delinquent.
[2] Interest rate may be reduced on showing of good cause, but may be abated on showing of department fault.
[3] Penalties and interest imposed on personal income tax may be waived, reduced or compromised. Interest imposed on corporate income tax may be waived if the interest is the result of a required change to the separate method of accounting.
[4] Interest abatement only allowed if penalty is abated.
[5] Maximum of $100 may be abated.
[6] Income tax penalties eligible for abatement limited to $300 or less.
[7] Up to 30 days interest may be abated for administrative convenience.
[8] Rates also may be reduced for equitable reasons. Applies to income tax only.

Credit Card Payment of State Taxes

A number of states, including the District of Columbia, allow taxpayers to make tax payments by major credit card. While some states accept credit card payments for all types of taxes, other states accept this method of payment for personal or corporate income taxes only. Certain states restrict credit card payments to delinquent taxes, and a few states accept credit card payments only with electronically filed returns.

The number and type of credit cards accepted varies among the states, and most states impose a service charge to offset the cost of accepting credit card payments. This chart does not include such information.

State	Credit Card Payment Accepted	State	Credit Card Payment Accepted
Alabama	Yes[1]	Missouri	Yes
Alaska	Yes[2]	Montana	Yes
Arizona	No	Nebraska	Yes
Arkansas	Yes[1]	Nevada	Yes
California	Yes	New Hampshire	No
Colorado	No	New Jersey	Yes
Connecticut	Yes	New Mexico	Yes
Delaware	Yes	New York	Yes[1]
District of Columbia	Yes	North Carolina	Yes[1]
Florida	No	North Dakota	Yes[1]
Georgia	No	Ohio	Yes[1]
Hawaii	Yes	Oklahoma	Yes
Idaho	Yes	Oregon	Yes[2]
Illinois	Yes	Pennsylvania	Yes[3]
Indiana	Yes	Rhode Island	Yes
Iowa	Yes[4]	South Carolina	Yes
Kansas	Yes	South Dakota	No
Kentucky	Yes	Tennessee	Yes
Louisiana	Yes	Texas	Yes[2]
Maine	No	Utah	No
Maryland	Yes	Vermont	Yes
Massachusetts	Yes	Virginia	Yes
Michigan	No	Washington	Yes
Minnesota	Yes[4]	West Virginia	Yes
Mississippi	Yes[5]	Wisconsin	Yes
Wyoming	No		

[1] Accepted for payment of personal income taxes only.
[2] Accepted for payment of delinquent taxes only.
[3] Accepted for payment of sales and use tax and personal income tax.
[4] Accepted for personal income and property tax payments and delinquent taxes.
[5] Accepted for payment of delinquent personal income taxes only.

Electronic Filing

Alabama

ELF Coordinator	Tavares Mathews
ELF Coordinator e-mail	tavares.mathews@revenue.alabama.gov
ELF Coordinator Phone	334-353-9497
ELF Coordinator FAX	334-353-8068
PATS Name	Tavares Mathews
Internet Address	http://www.ador.state.al.us
E-Filing Requirement	Yes
E-Filing Requirement Threshold	100 returns
ERO Application Requirements	Automatic acceptance into state program if accepted by IRS.
Taxpayer Opt-out	yes
State E-File Deadline	15-Oct
Retain or Mail 8453	Retained by ERO
On-Line Filing Availability	Yes
On-Line Filing Retention Requirement	Retained by Taxpayer
On-Line Filing Separate 8453-OL Required	Yes
Self-Prepared Returns Permitted	No
Paperless Filing Options	No
Acknowledgment/Acceptance	Accept
Conditional Acceptance	No
Credit Card Payment Allowed	Yes
Balance Due Returns Allowed	Yes
ACH Debit of Balance Due Allowed	No
Forms Allowed	Resident Only
Federal and State/State Only	State-Only allowed
Corporate Income Tax Electronic Filing Options/ Requirements	Alabama will participate in the Federal/State 1120 e-file project for purposes of electronically filing Alabama corporation income tax returns for tax year 2005. The program includes Form 20C, Alabama Corporation Income Tax Return, and most of the major supporting schedules. Estimated taxes may also be e-filed.

Alaska

ELF Coordinator	Does not impose a personal income tax
Corporate Income Tax Electronic Filing Options/ Requirements	None

Arizona

ELF Coordinator	DonnaJean Muccilli
ELF Coordinator e-mail	EFile@revenue.state.az.us DMuccilli@azdor.gov
ELF Coordinator Phone	602-716-6513
ELF Coordinator FAX	602-716-7986
PATS Name	Karen Sertich-reviewer
Internet Address	http://www.revenue.state.az.us/
E-Filing Requirement	No
ERO Application Requirements	Automatic acceptance into state program if accepted by IRS.
State E-File Deadline	22-Oct

Retain or Mail 8453	Retained by ERO
On-Line Filing Availability	Yes
On-Line Filing Retention Requirement	Retained by Taxpayer
On-Line Filing Separate 8453-OL Required	No
Self-Prepared Returns Permitted	No
Paperless Filing Options	The taxpayer(s) has the option to use the same self-selected PIN used for the federal return as for AZ electronic filing. In this case, the form AZ-8879 will be produced instead of Form AZ-8453. The document is to be treated exactly as the IRS version of the document (signed if the taxpayer does not enter their own PIN, otherwise not signed, retained for 4 years by the ERO). However, if Form AZ-8453 is required for one of the reasons stated above, the electronic signature option is not available, Form AZ-8453 is produced and must be mailed to the ADOR. For online returns, the paperless filing option is available also but no signature document is produced because none is required. For state-only returns, the paperless filing option is not available.
Acknowledgment/Acceptance	Accept
Conditional Acceptance	No
Credit Card Payment Allowed	No
Direct Refund Deposit Timeframe	3-4 days
Balance Due Returns Allowed	Yes
ACH Debit of Balance Due Allowed	Yes
Forms Allowed	Resident, Non-Resident, Part-Year
Federal and State/State Only	State-Only allowed
Corporate Income Tax Electronic Filing Options/ Requirements	None

Arkansas

ELF Coordinator	Dan Brown
ELF Coordinator e-mail	Dan.Brown@rev.state.ar.us
ELF Coordinator Phone	501-682-7070
ELF Coordinator FAX	501-682-7393
Internet Address	http://www.state.ar.us/dfa/income_tax/ tax_efile.html
E-Filing Requirement	No
ERO Application Requirements	Automatic acceptance into state program if accepted by IRS.
Application Deadline	http://www.state.ar.us/efile
State E-File Deadline	15-Oct
Retain or Mail 8453	Retained by ERO
On-Line Filing Availability	Yes
On-Line Filing Retention Requirement	Mail
On-Line Filing Separate 8453-OL Required	Yes
Self-Prepared Returns Permitted	No
Paperless Filing Options	No
Acknowledgment/Acceptance	Acknowledge
Credit Card Payment Allowed	Yes
Balance Due Returns Allowed	Yes
ACH Debit of Balance Due Allowed	No
Forms Allowed	Resident, Non-Resident Only

Federal and State/State Only . . . . State-Only allowed
Corporate Income Tax Electronic Filing Options/
Requirements . . . . None

California

ELF Coordinator	Sean McDaniel
ELF Coordinator e-mail	sean.mcdaniel@ftb.ca.gov
ELF Coordinator Phone	916-845-6180
ELF Coordinator FAX	916-845-5340
Internet Address	http://www.ftb.ca.gov/efileSRD/index.asp
E-Filing Requirement	Yes
E-Filing Requirement Threshold	100 returns
ERO Application Requirements	Form CA-8633 is required for new participants. If previously accepted with the FTB, should be fine to file with no new 8633. Uses the same EFIN as the IRS. You can go to http://www.ftb.ca.gov/online/8633/index.html to enroll on-line.
Taxpayer Opt-out	yes
State E-File Deadline	15-Oct
Retain or Mail 8453	Retained by ERO
On-Line Filing Availability	Yes
On-Line Filing Retention Requirement	Retained by Taxpayer
On-Line Filing Separate 8453-OL Required	Yes
Acknowledgment/Acceptance	Accept
Credit Card Payment Allowed	Yes
Balance Due Returns Allowed	Yes
ACH Debit of Balance Due Allowed	Yes
Forms Allowed	Resident, Non-Resident, Part-Year
Federal and State/State Only	State-Only allowed
Corporate Income Tax Electronic Filing Options/ Requirements	For tax year 2005, only the Form 100, California Corporation Franchise or Income Tax Return, and 15 supporting forms and schedules are accepted under the business e-file program. For tax year 2006, the list of acceptable forms is expanded to include Form 100S, California Corporation Franchise or Income Tax Return, Form 565, Partnership Return of Income, Form 568, Limited Liability Company Return of Income, and additional schedules.

Colorado

ELF Coordinator	Steve Asbell
ELF Coordinator e-mail	sasbell@spike.dor.state.co.us
ELF Coordinator Phone	303-866-3889
ELF Coordinator FAX	303-866-3050
PATS Name	Steve Asbell
Internet Address	http://www.taxcolorado.com
E-Filing Requirement	No
ERO Application Requirements	Automatic acceptance into state program if accepted by IRS.
State E-File Deadline	15-Oct
Retain or Mail 8453	Retained by ERO
On-Line Filing Availability	Yes
On-Line Filing Retention Requirement	Retained by Taxpayer

On-Line Filing Separate 8453-OL Required . . . . No
Paperless Filing Options . . . . PIN not accepted, no mailing requirement for CO DR 8453
Acknowledgment/Acceptance . . . . Acknowledge
Credit Card Payment Allowed . . . . No
Direct Refund Deposit Timeframe . . . . for 2002
Balance Due Returns Allowed . . . . Yes
ACH Debit of Balance Due Allowed . . . . No
Forms Allowed . . . . Resident, Non-Resident, Part-Year
Federal and State/State Only . . . . State-Only allowed
Corporate Income Tax Electronic Filing Options/
Requirements . . . . None

Connecticut

ELF Coordinator . . . . Jim Annino
ELF Coordinator e-mail . . . . jim.annino@po.state.ct.us
ELF Coordinator Phone 860-297-4713
ELF Coordinator FAX 860-297-4761
PATS Name . . . . Jim Annino
Internet Address . . . . http://www.ct.gov/DRS
E-Filing Requirement . . . . Yes
E-Filing Requirement Threshold . . . . 100 returns
ERO Application Requirements . . . . Automatic acceptance into state program if accepted by IRS.
Taxpayer Opt-out . . . . yes
State E-File Deadline 15-Oct
Signature Documents . . . . None Required
On-Line Filing Availability . . . . Yes
On-Line Filing Retention Requirement . . . . Mail
Self-Prepared Returns Permitted . . . . Yes
Paperless Filing Options . . . . If the taxpayer elects to use the IRS self-select PIN for the e-file Program, and the IRS accepts it, the DRS will now accept this PIN as the electronic signature for the Connecticut tax return. By adopting this PIN alternative, the DRS has effectively removed the need for Form CT-8453.
Acknowledgment/Acceptance . . . . Acknowledge
Credit Card Payment Allowed . . . . Yes
Direct Refund Deposit Timeframe . . . . 4 days
Balance Due Returns Allowed . . . . Yes
ACH Debit of Balance Due Allowed . . . . Yes
Forms Allowed . . . . Resident, Non-Resident, Part-Year
Federal and State/State Only . . . . State-Only allowed
Corporate Income Tax Electronic Filing Options/
Requirements . . . . None

Delaware

ELF Coordinator . . . . James Stewart III
ELF Coordinator e-mail . . . . james.stewart@state.de.us
ELF Coordinator Phone 302-577-8170
ELF Coordinator FAX . . . . 302-577-8202 . . . .
PATS Name . . . . Lisa Jones . . . .

Internet Address	http://www.state.de.us/revenue . . . .
E-Filing Requirement	No . . . .
ERO Application Requirements	Automatic acceptance into state program if accepted by the IRS. . . . .
Application Deadline	http://www.state.de.us/revenue . . . .
State E-File Deadline	15-Oct . . . .
Retain or Mail 8453	Retained by ERO
On-Line Filing Availability	Yes
On-Line Filing Retention Requirement	Retained by Taxpayer
On-Line Filing Separate 8453-OL Required	Yes
Acknowledgment/Acceptance	Acknowledge
Credit Card Payment Allowed	Yes
Balance Due Returns Allowed	Yes
ACH Debit of Balance Due Allowed	Yes
Forms Allowed	Resident, Non-Resident, Part-Year
Federal and State/State Only	State-Only allowed
Corporate Income Tax Electronic Filing Options/ Requirements	None

District of Columbia

ELF Coordinator	Sonja Thornburg
ELF Coordinator e-mail	sonja.peterson@dc.gov
ELF Coordinator Phone	202-442-6392
ELF Coordinator FAX	202-442-6330
Internet Address	http://otr.cfo.dc.gov/otr/site/default.asp
E-Filing Requirement	No
ERO Application Requirements	Automatic acceptance into state program is accepted by IRS.
State E-File Deadline	15-Oct
Retain or Mail 8453	Retained by ERO
On-Line Filing Availability	Yes
On-Line Filing Retention Requirement	Retained by Taxpayer
On-Line Filing Separate 8453-OL Required	No
Acknowledgment/Acceptance	Accept
Conditional Acceptance	No
Credit Card Payment Allowed	Yes
Balance Due Returns Allowed	Yes
ACH Debit of Balance Due Allowed	No
Forms Allowed	Resident, Part-Year Only
Federal and State/State Only	State-Only allowed
Corporate Income Tax Electronic Filing Options/ Requirements	Beginning with corporation business tax returns due March 15, 2005 and unincorporated business tax returns due April 15, 2005, electronic filing required for taxpayers filing quarterly estimated tax returns with outstanding tax liability for the period exceeding $25,000. Beginning June 15, 2005, Entities with District of Columbia gross receipts of $5 million or more during preceding tax year and thus liable for paying District professional baseball ballpark fee must file applicable return electronically.

Florida

ELF Coordinator	Does not impose a personal income tax
Corporate Income Tax Electronic Filing Options/ Requirements	Federal/State 1120 E-File Program optional. State accepts Forms F-1120 and F-1120A for the 2006 tax year.

Georgia

ELF Coordinator	Michelle Oden
ELF Coordinator e-mail	gaelf@dor.ga.gov
ELF Coordinator Phone	404-417-6644
ELF Coordinator FAX	404-362-6437
PATS Name	Michelle Oden
Internet Address	http://www.etax.dor.ga.gov/inctax/efile/electronicfile.shtml
E-Filing Requirement	No
ERO Application Requirements	Automatic acceptance into state program if accepted by the IRS.
State E-File Deadline	15-Oct
Retain or Mail 8453	Retained by ERO
On-Line Filing Availability	Yes
On-Line Filing Retention Requirement	Retained by Taxpayer
On-Line Filing Separate 8453-OL Required	Yes
Paperless Filing Options	There is no form that needs mailed in but the return isn't truely paperless because the form must still be signed.
Acknowledgment/Acceptance	Acknowledge
Credit Card Payment Allowed	Yes
Balance Due Returns Allowed	Yes
ACH Debit of Balance Due Allowed	No
Forms Allowed	Resident, Non-Resident, Part-Year
Federal and State/State Only	State-Only allowed
Corporate Income Tax Electronic Filing Options/ Requirements	Federal/State 1120 E-File Program optional. State accepts current year Forms 600 and 600S.

Hawaii

ELF Coordinator	Susan Adamson (interim)
ELF Coordinator e-mail	Tax.Efile@hawaii.gov
ELF Coordinator Phone	808-587-1741 or 808-587-1740
ELF Coordinator FAX	808-587-1488
Internet Address	http://www.state.hi.us/tax
E-Filing Requirement	No
ERO Application Requirements	Automatic acceptance into state program if accepted by the IRS. EROs not located in Hawaii must provide a copy of IRS Form 8633 upon the Coordinator's request.
State E-File Deadline	15-Oct
Signature Documents	None Required
On-Line Filing Availability	Yes
On-Line Filing Separate 8453-OL Required	No
Paperless Filing Options	No signature documents are required.

Acknowledgment/Acceptance	Accept
Conditional Acceptance	No
Credit Card Payment Allowed	No
Direct Refund Deposit Timeframe	4 weeks
Balance Due Returns Allowed	Yes
ACH Debit of Balance Due Allowed	No
Forms Allowed	Resident Only
Federal and State/State Only	State-Only not allowed
Corporate Income Tax Electronic Filing Options/Requirements	None

Idaho

ELF Coordinator	Dawn Glazier
ELF Coordinator e-mail	dglazier@tax.idaho.gov
ELF Coordinator Phone	208-334-7822
ELF Coordinator FAX	208-334-7650
PATS Name	Robin Allen
Internet Address	http://tax.idaho.gov/
E-Filing Requirement	No
ERO Application Requirements	Automatic acceptance into state program if accepted by the IRS.
State E-File Deadline	15-Oct
Signature Documents	None Required
On-Line Filing Availability	Yes
On-Line Filing Separate 8453-OL Required	No
Acknowledgment/Acceptance	Acknowledge
Credit Card Payment Allowed	Yes
Balance Due Returns Allowed	No
ACH Debit of Balance Due Allowed	No
Forms Allowed	Resident, Non-Resident, Part-Year
Federal and State/State Only	State-Only allowed
Corporate Income Tax Electronic Filing Options/Requirements	None

Illinois

ELF Coordinator	Kevin Richards
ELF Coordinator e-mail	krichards@revenue.state.il.us
ELF Coordinator Phone	217-524-4767 or 217-524-4097
ELF Coordinator FAX	217-782-7992
PATS Name	Debbie Bartholomew
Internet Address	http://www.revenue.state.il.us
E-Filing Requirement	No
ERO Application Requirements	Form IL-8633-I is required for new participants. In addition, if there are any business information changes, previous applicants are required to file a revised Form IL-8633-I and check the "Revised" box. Participation in the IL program is based upon acceptance into the IRS program. The participant must have a valid EFIN that has been assigned and approved by the IRS.
State E-File Deadline	15-Oct
Retain or Mail 8453	Retained by ERO
On-Line Filing Availability	Yes

On-Line Filing Retention Requirement . . . .   Retained by Taxpayer

On-Line Filing Separate 8453-OL Required . . . .   No

Self-Prepared Returns Permitted . . . .   For online filing (Complete Tax), the IL-PIN is required. The IL-PIN is assigned by IDOR and is NOT reissued annually.
In addition, users can submit any of the following extra information for IL to use to validate a return in case the IL-PIN fails:
(a) Prior year AGI (prior year Form IL-1040, line 1)
(b) Driver's license number
(c) Nine digit ZIP code from taxpayer's most recent address on file at IDOR

Paperless Filing Options . . . .   Even with PINs IL is not completely paperless but they require you to retain the signature form for no less than 3 years.

Acknowledgment/Acceptance . . . .   Accept

Conditional Acceptance . . . .   No

Credit Card Payment Allowed . . . .   Yes

Direct Refund Deposit Timeframe . . . .   7 days

Balance Due Returns Allowed . . . .   Yes

ACH Debit of Balance Due Allowed . . . .   Yes

Forms Allowed . . . .   Resident, Non-Resident, Part-Year

Federal and State/State Only . . . .   State-Only allowed

Corporate Income Tax Electronic Filing Options/
Requirements . . . .   Federal/State 1120 E-File Program optional

Indiana

ELF Coordinator . . . .   Bill Dunbar

ELF Coordinator e-mail . . . .   bldunbar@dor.state.in.us

ELF Coordinator Phone 317.615.2508

ELF Coordinator FAX 317.615.2520

Internet Address . . . .   http://www.in.gov/dor

E-Filing Requirement . . . .   No

ERO Application Requirements . . . .   Automatic acceptance into state program if accepted by the IRS.

Application Deadline . . . .   http://www.in.gov/dor

State E-File Deadline 15-Oct

Retain or Mail 8453 . . . .   Retained by ERO

On-Line Filing Availability . . . .   Yes

On-Line Filing Retention Requirement . . . .   Retained by Taxpayer

On-Line Filing Separate 8453-OL Required . . . .   No

Paperless Filing Options . . . .   Indiana adopted the PIN signature alternative that follows Federal IRS Guidelines. Provide the taxpayer Date of Birth and Prior Year AGI for authentication. Electronic signatures are not allowed for state only filers.

Acknowledgment/Acceptance . . . .   Accept

Conditional Acceptance . . . .   No

Credit Card Payment Allowed . . . .   Yes

Balance Due Returns Allowed . . . .   Yes

ACH Debit of Balance Due Allowed . . . .   No

Forms Allowed . . . .   Resident Only

Federal and State/State Only . . . .   State-Only allowed

Corporate Income Tax Electronic Filing Options/
Requirements . . . .   None

Iowa

ELF Coordinator	Richard Jacobs
ELF Coordinator e-mail	idrefile@iowa.gov
ELF Coordinator Phone	515-281-8453
ELF Coordinator FAX	515-242-6040
PATS Name	Peter Johann
	Judy Neal
Internet Address	http://www.state.ia.us/tax
E-Filing Requirement	No
ERO Application Requirements	Automatic acceptance into state program if accepted by the IRS.
State E-File Deadline	15-Oct
Retain or Mail 8453	Retained by ERO
On-Line Filing Availability	Yes
On-Line Filing Retention Requirement	Retained by Taxpayer
On-Line Filing Separate 8453-OL Required	Yes
Paperless Filing Options	Iowa adopted the PIN signature alternative as implemented by the IRS. Provide the prior years Fed AGI then a 5 digit PIN. Electronic signatures are not allowed on Iowa state-only returns.
Acknowledgment/Acceptance	Acknowledge
Credit Card Payment Allowed	Yes
Balance Due Returns Allowed	Yes
ACH Debit of Balance Due Allowed	No
Forms Allowed	Resident, Non-Resident, Part-Year
Federal and State/State Only	State-Only allowed
Corporate Income Tax Electronic Filing Options/ Requirements	None

Kansas

ELF Coordinator	Terry Hunt
ELF Coordinator e-mail	Terry_Hunt@kdor.state.ks.us
ELF Coordinator Phone	785-296-4066
ELF Coordinator FAX	785-291-3614
PATS Name	Terry Hunt
Internet Address	http://www.ksrevenue.org/
E-Filing Requirement	No
ERO Application Requirements	Automatic acceptance into state program if accepted by the IRS.
State E-File Deadline	15-Oct
Signature Documents	None Required
On-Line Filing Availability	Yes
On-Line Filing Separate 8453-OL Required	No
Paperless Filing Options	Signature process used for federal return accepted for Kansas Signature requirement-No KS PIN Signature option.
Acknowledgment/Acceptance	Accept
Conditional Acceptance	No
Credit Card Payment Allowed	Yes
Direct Refund Deposit Timeframe	5-7 days
Balance Due Returns Allowed	Yes

ACH Debit of Balance Due Allowed . . . .   Yes
Forms Allowed . . . .   Resident, Non-Resident, Part-Year
Federal and State/State Only . . . .   State-Only allowed
Corporate Income Tax Electronic Filing Options/
Requirements . . . .   Federal/State 1120 E-File Program Optional

Kentucky

ELF Coordinator . . . .   Judy Ritchie
ELF Coordinator e-mail . . . .   Judy.Ritchie@ky.gov
ELF Coordinator Phone   502-564-5370
                                                          ext 300
ELF Coordinator FAX   502-564-9897
PATS Name . . . .   Peggy Barber

                                                          Aaron Hicks
Internet Address . . . .   http://revenue.ky.gov/
E-Filing Requirement . . . .   No
ERO Application Requirements . . . .   Automatic acceptance into state program if
                                                          accepted by the IRS.
State E-File Deadline 15-Oct
Retain or Mail 8453 . . . .   Retained by ERO
On-Line Filing Availability . . . .   Yes
On-Line Filing Retention Requirement . . . .   Retained by Taxpayer
On-Line Filing Separate 8453-OL Required . . . .   No
Paperless Filing Options . . . .   If using federal PIN authorization form then no
                                                          KY-8453 is required. If On-Line filers use PIN then
                                                          they are required to retain KY-8453 for 3 years
Acknowledgment/Acceptance . . . .   Accept
Conditional Acceptance . . . .   No
Credit Card Payment Allowed . . . .   Yes
Direct Refund Deposit Timeframe . . . .   7-10 days
Balance Due Returns Allowed . . . .   Yes
ACH Debit of Balance Due Allowed . . . .   Yes
Forms Allowed . . . .   Resident Only
Federal and State/State Only . . . .   State-Only allowed
Corporate Income Tax Electronic Filing Options/
Requirements . . . .   None

Louisiana

ELF Coordinator . . . .   Kay Wilson
ELF Coordinator e-mail . . . .   kay.wilson@la.gov
ELF Coordinator Phone 225 219-2492
ELF Coordinator FAX   225-219-2651
PATS Name . . . .   Patricia Garcia

Internet Address . . . .   http://www.revenue.louisiana.gov
E-Filing Requirement . . . .   Yes - in conjunction with 2-D
E-Filing Requirement Threshold . . . .   100 returns
ERO Application Requirements . . . .   Automatic acceptance into state program if
                                                          accepted by the IRS.
State E-File Deadline 15-Oct
Retain or Mail 8453 . . . .   Retained by ERO
On-Line Filing Availability . . . .   Yes

On-Line Filing Retention Requirement	Retained by Taxpayer
On-Line Filing Separate 8453-OL Required	Yes
Paperless Filing Options	no
Acknowledgment/Acceptance	Acknowledge
Conditional Acceptance	No
Credit Card Payment Allowed	Yes
Direct Refund Deposit Timeframe	Yes
Balance Due Returns Allowed	Yes
ACH Debit of Balance Due Allowed	Yes
Forms Allowed	Resident, Non-Resident, Part-Year
Federal and State/State Only	State-Only allowed
Corporate Income Tax Electronic Filing Options/ Requirements	None

Maine

ELF Coordinator	Mike Thompson
ELF Coordinator e-mail	Michael.J.Thompson@maine.gov
ELF Coordinator Phone	207-624-9730
ELF Coordinator FAX	207-624-9740
Internet Address	http://www.state.me.us/revenue/developers
E-Filing Requirement	Considering
ERO Application Requirements	Automatic acceptance into state program if accepted by FED. If Out of State ERO then the preparer needs to fax a copy of the Federal Acceptance Letter indicating EFIN to fax number 207-624-9740 for the state to set it up in the system.
Application Deadline	http://www.state.me.us/revenue/developers
State E-File Deadline	21-Oct
Signature Documents	None Required
On-Line Filing Availability	Yes
On-Line Filing Separate 8453-OL Required	No
Paperless Filing Options	Maine ECN
Acknowledgment/Acceptance	Accept
Conditional Acceptance	No
Credit Card Payment Allowed	No
Balance Due Returns Allowed	Yes
ACH Debit of Balance Due Allowed	Yes
Forms Allowed	Resident, Non-Resident, Part-Year
Federal and State/State Only	State-Only allowed
Corporate Income Tax Electronic Filing Options/ Requirements	None

Maryland

ELF Coordinator	Jeane Olson
ELF Coordinator e-mail	jolson@comp.state.md.us
ELF Coordinator Phone	410-260-7753 or 410-260-7617
ELF Coordinator FAX	410-974-2967 or 410-974-2274
Internet Address	http://www.marylandtaxes.com
E-Filing Requirement	No
ERO Application Requirements	Automatic acceptance into state program if accepted by the IRS

Application Deadline . . . . http://www.marylandtaxes.com
State E-File Deadline 15-Oct
Retain or Mail 8453 . . . . Retained by ERO
On-Line Filing Availability . . . . Yes
On-Line Filing Retention Requirement . . . . Mail
On-Line Filing Separate 8453-OL Required . . . . No
Self-Prepared Returns Permitted . . . . Must be noted as 'TAXPAYER' for preparer name and 'SAME' for preparer address.
Paperless Filing Options . . . . Available only for online filers, only if not a first-time MD filer, and only if filed a timely return the previous year. The federal self-selected PIN(s) are not used for this purpose, PIN(s) for MD must be entered. The MD PIN is the FAGI from the taxpayer's prior year return. If a joint return, a PIN must be entered for both the taxpayer and spouse, unless only one spouse filed a timely MD return the previous year. In this case, only one spouse if required to enter a PIN in the applicable primary or secondary PIN field and no Form EL101 is required. Negative amounts for the PIN require no sign, only the numeric value. If the amount was zero, "0" should be entered. When the taxpayer(s) filed a prior year MD return, but do not know the amount of prior year FAGI, they can call taxpayer services at 1-800-MDTAXES or 410-260-7980 from central Maryland to request it.
Acknowledgment/Acceptance . . . . Accept
Conditional Acceptance . . . . No
Credit Card Payment Allowed . . . . Yes
Direct Refund Deposit Timeframe . . . . 2-5 days
Balance Due Returns Allowed . . . . Yes
ACH Debit of Balance Due Allowed . . . . Yes
Forms Allowed . . . . Resident, Non-Resident, Part-Year
Federal and State/State Only . . . . State-Only allowed
Corporate Income Tax Electronic Filing Options/ Requirements . . . . Federal/State 1120 E-File Program optional

Massachusetts

ELF Coordinator . . . . Barry White

or Eddie Lepore
ELF Coordinator e-mail . . . . WHITEB@dor.state.ma.us

LEPORE@dor.state.ma.us
ELF Coordinator Phone 617-887-5174
617-887-5084

617-887-6367 Customer Service
PATS Name . . . . Vinod Aggarwal

Secondary Contacts:
Edward Dockhame

Anthony Fruciano
Internet Address . . . . http://www.dor.state.ma.us/
E-Filing Requirement . . . . Yes
E-Filing Requirement Threshold . . . . 100 returns
ERO Application Requirements . . . . Automatic acceptance into state program if accepted by the IRS.

Taxpayer Opt-out	yes
State E-File Deadline	15-Oct
Retain or Mail 8453	Retained by ERO
On-Line Filing Availability	Yes
On-Line Filing Retention Requirement	Retained by Taxpayer
On-Line Filing Separate 8453-OL Required	No
Self-Prepared Returns Permitted	No
Acknowledgment/Acceptance	Accept
Conditional Acceptance	No
Credit Card Payment Allowed	No
Direct Refund Deposit Timeframe	?
Balance Due Returns Allowed	Yes
ACH Debit of Balance Due Allowed	Yes
Forms Allowed	Resident, Non-Resident, Part-Year
Federal and State/State Only	State-Only allowed
Corporate Income Tax Electronic Filing Options/ Requirements	Beginning January 1, 2006, corporations with more than $100,000 in gross receipts or sales must file corporate excise tax returns electronically. A taxpayer must continue to file electronically even if it does not meet the electronic filing threshold in later years.

Michigan

ELF Coordinator	Scott Bunnell
ELF Coordinator e-mail	MIefile2D@michigan.gov
ELF Coordinator Phone	517-636-4450 x517-636-4418
ELF Coordinator FAX	517-636-4444
PATS Name	Sandy Platte
Internet Address	http://www.mifastfile.org
E-Filing Requirement	Yes
E-Filing Requirement Threshold	200 returns
ERO Application Requirements	Automatic acceptance into state program if accepted by the IRS.
Taxpayer Opt-out	no
Application Deadline	http:/www.treasury.state.mi.us
State E-File Deadline	15-Oct
Retain or Mail 8453	Retained by ERO
On-Line Filing Availability	Yes
On-Line Filing Retention Requirement	Retained by Taxpayer
On-Line Filing Separate 8453-OL Required	No
Paperless Filing Options	No signature document is required when paperless filing is selected for federal/Michigan.
Acknowledgment/Acceptance	Accept
Credit Card Payment Allowed	No
Direct Refund Deposit Timeframe	7 days
Balance Due Returns Allowed	Yes
ACH Debit of Balance Due Allowed	No
Forms Allowed	Resident, Non-Resident, Part-Year
Federal and State/State Only	State-Only allowed

Corporate Income Tax Electronic Filing Options/
Requirements .... SBT returns prepared using a computer software program must be filed through Michigan's Internet portal. Balance due SBT returns eligible for electronic filing.

Minnesota

ELF Coordinator	Justine Schindeldecker
ELF Coordinator e-mail	justine.schindeldecker@state.mn.us
ELF Coordinator Phone	651-556-4818 651-296-2153 (for preparers and software developers only)
ELF Coordinator FAX	651-556-3130 651-556-5130
PATS Name	Justine Schindeldecker/Bill Grewe
Internet Address	http://www.taxes.state.mn.us
E-Filing Requirement	Yes
E-Filing Requirement Threshold	100 returns
ERO Application Requirements	Automatic acceptance into state program if accepted by the IRS and if the preparer is located in Minnesota. Preparers located outside of Minnesota must fax a copy of IRS Form 8633 and the current year's letter of acceptance from the IRS to be enrolled as e-filers with the State of Minnesota. It usually takes one business day (excluding weekends) to get set up after the ERO has faxed in the information.
Taxpayer Opt-out	yes
State E-File Deadline	15-Oct
Signature Documents	None Required
On-Line Filing Availability	Yes
On-Line Filing Separate 8453-OL Required	No
Acknowledgment/Acceptance	Accept
Conditional Acceptance	No
Credit Card Payment Allowed	Yes
Balance Due Returns Allowed	Yes
ACH Debit of Balance Due Allowed	Yes
Forms Allowed	Resident, Non-Resident, Part-Year
Federal and State/State Only	State-Only allowed
Corporate Income Tax Electronic Filing Options/ Requirements	None

Mississippi

ELF Coordinator	Lisa Chism
ELF Coordinator e-mail	efile@mstc.state.ms.us, lchism@mstc.state.ms.us
ELF Coordinator Phone	601.923.7055
ELF Coordinator FAX	601.923.7039
PATS Name	Niki Meadows or Ravaughn Robinson
Internet Address	http://www.mstc.state.ms.us
E-Filing Requirement	No
ERO Application Requirements	Automatic acceptance into state program if accepted by the IRS.
Application Deadline	1-Dec

State E-File Deadline 15-Oct
Retain or Mail 8453 . . . .   Retained by ERO
On-Line Filing Retention Requirement . . . .   Mail
On-Line Filing Separate 8453-OL Required . . . .   Yes
Acknowledgment/Acceptance . . . .   Acknowledge
Credit Card Payment Allowed . . . .   Yes
Balance Due Returns Allowed . . . .   Yes
ACH Debit of Balance Due Allowed . . . .   No
Forms Allowed . . . .   Resident, Non-Resident, Part-Year
Federal and State/State Only . . . .   State-Only allowed
Corporate Income Tax Electronic Filing Options/
Requirements . . . .   None

Missouri

ELF Coordinator . . . .   Jerry Wingate
ELF Coordinator e-mail . . . .   elecfile@dor.mo.gov
ELF Coordinator Phone   573-522-4300
ELF Coordinator FAX   573-526-5915
PATS Name . . . .   Jerry Wingate
Internet Address . . . .   http://www.dor.mo.gov/tax
E-Filing Requirement . . . .   No
ERO Application Requirements . . . .   Automatic acceptance into state program if accepted by the IRS.
State E-File Deadline 15-Oct
Retain or Mail 8453 . . . .   Retained by ERO
On-Line Filing Availability . . . .   Yes
On-Line Filing Retention Requirement . . . .   Retained by Taxpayer
On-Line Filing Separate 8453-OL Required . . . .   No
Paperless Filing Options . . . .   If federal form 8879 used - Mo does not print the state 8453. If fed 8453 used - MO8453 will print and should be retained by the taxpayer.
Acknowledgment/Acceptance . . . .   Acknowledge
Conditional Acceptance . . . .   No
Credit Card Payment Allowed . . . .   Yes
Direct Refund Deposit Timeframe . . . .   10-12 days
Balance Due Returns Allowed . . . .   Yes
ACH Debit of Balance Due Allowed . . . .   No
Forms Allowed . . . .   Resident, Non-Resident, Part-Year
Federal and State/State Only . . . .   State-Only allowed
Corporate Income Tax Electronic Filing Options/
Requirements . . . .   None

Montana

ELF Coordinator . . . .   David Berg
ELF Coordinator e-mail . . . .   daberg@state.mt.us
ELF Coordinator Phone   406-444-6957
ELF Coordinator FAX   406-444-4556
PATS Name . . . .   David Berg
Internet Address . . . .   http://discoveringmontana.com/revenue
E-Filing Requirement . . . .   No
ERO Application Requirements . . . .   Automatic acceptance into state program if accepted by the IRS.

State E-File Deadline 15-Oct
Signature Documents . . . . None Required
On-Line Filing Availability . . . . Yes
On-Line Filing Separate 8453-OL Required . . . . No
Acknowledgment/Acceptance . . . . Acknowledge
Conditional Acceptance . . . . No
Credit Card Payment Allowed . . . . Yes
Direct Refund Deposit Timeframe . . . . 3 days
Balance Due Returns Allowed . . . . Yes
ACH Debit of Balance Due Allowed . . . . Yes
Forms Allowed . . . . Resident, Non-Resident, Part-Year
Federal and State/State Only . . . . State-Only allowed
Corporate Income Tax Electronic Filing Options/
Requirements . . . . None

Nebraska

ELF Coordinator . . . . Larry Chapman
ELF Coordinator e-mail . . . . lchapman@rev.state.ne.us
ELF Coordinator Phone . . . . 402-471-5619 or 800-433-8631
ELF Coordinator FAX 402-471-5608
PATS Name . . . . Brian Catlin
Internet Address . . . . http://www.revenue.state.ne.us
E-Filing Requirement . . . . No
ERO Application Requirements . . . . Automatic acceptance into the state program if accepted by the IRS.
State E-File Deadline . . . . October 15, retransmits through October 17
Retain or Mail 8453 . . . . Retained by ERO
On-Line Filing Availability . . . . Yes
On-Line Filing Separate 8453-OL Required . . . . No
Paperless Filing Options . . . . NE PIN no longer required.
Acknowledgment/Acceptance . . . . Accept
Conditional Acceptance . . . . No
Credit Card Payment Allowed . . . . Yes
Direct Refund Deposit Timeframe . . . . 7-10 days
Balance Due Returns Allowed . . . . Yes
ACH Debit of Balance Due Allowed . . . . Yes
Forms Allowed . . . . Resident, Non-Resident, Part-Year
Federal and State/State Only . . . . State-Only allowed
Corporate Income Tax Electronic Filing Options/
Requirements . . . . None

Nevada

ELF Coordinator . . . . Does not impose a personal income tax
Corporate Income Tax Electronic Filing Options/
Requirements . . . . Does not impose a corporate income tax

New Hampshire . . . .

ELF Coordinator . . . . E-filing allowed for interest and dividends tax
Corporate Income Tax Electronic Filing Options/
Requirements . . . . None

New Jersey

ELF Coordinator	Tim Bachman
ELF Coordinator e-mail	Tim.Bachman@treas.state.nj.us
ELF Coordinator Phone	609-292-7508
ELF Coordinator FAX	609-292-1777
Internet Address	http://www.state.nj.us/treasury/revenue
E-Filing Requirement	Yes - in conjunction with 2-D
E-Filing Requirement Threshold	100 Partners or more
ERO Application Requirements	Initial registration is mandatory for any participant whose business address is outside the state of New Jersey. EROs must file Form NJ Registration Form. New Jersey obtains registration information from the IRS registration file for businesses located within the state of New Jersey.
Taxpayer Opt-out	yes
State E-File Deadline	15-Oct
Signature Documents	None Required
On-Line Filing Availability	Yes
On-Line Filing Retention Requirement	Mail
On-Line Filing Separate 8453-OL Required	No
Paperless Filing Options	The 5-digit IRS PIN is required.
Acknowledgment/Acceptance	Accept
Conditional Acceptance	Yes
Credit Card Payment Allowed	Yes
Balance Due Returns Allowed	Yes
ACH Debit of Balance Due Allowed	Yes
Forms Allowed	Resident, Non-Resident, Part-Year
Federal and State/State Only	State-Only allowed
Corporate Income Tax Electronic Filing Options/ Requirements	Corporate income tax electronic filing option.

New Mexico

ELF Coordinator	Bernie Candelaria
ELF Coordinator e-mail	BCandelaria@state.nm.us
ELF Coordinator Phone	505-476-1708
ELF Coordinator FAX	505-827-0469
PATS Name	1120-Bernie.
Internet Address	http://www.state.nm.us/tax
E-Filing Requirement	No
ERO Application Requirements	Automatic acceptance into state program if accepted by the IRS. All preparers, whose business resides in New Mexico must have a New Mexico CRS Identification Number. A CRS registration form can be downloaded from the "Forms" section at http://www.state.nm.us/tax. Out-of-state preparers are to use their SSN or PTIN.
State E-File Deadline	15-Oct
Retain or Mail 8453	Retained by ERO
On-Line Filing Availability	Yes
On-Line Filing Separate 8453-OL Required	No
Acknowledgment/Acceptance	Acknowledge
Credit Card Payment Allowed	No
Direct Refund Deposit Timeframe	7-10 days

Balance Due Returns Allowed . . . . Yes
ACH Debit of Balance Due Allowed . . . . Yes
Forms Allowed . . . . Resident, Non-Resident, Part-Year
Federal and State/State Only . . . . State-Only allowed
Corporate Income Tax Electronic Filing Options/
Requirements . . . . None

New York

ELF Coordinator . . . . Ping Wu
ELF Coordinator e-mail . . . . Ping_Wu@tax.state.ny.us
ELF Coordinator Phone 518-457-4064
ELF Coordinator FAX 518-485-0449
PATS Name . . . . Ping Wu
Internet Address . . . . http://www.tax.state.ny.us/elf
E-Filing Requirement . . . . Yes - in conjunction with 2-D
E-Filing Requirement Threshold . . . . 200 returns
ERO Application Requirements . . . . Automatic acceptance into state program if
                                                      accepted by the IRS.
Taxpayer Opt-out . . . . yes
State E-File Deadline 15-Oct
Retain or Mail 8453 . . . . Retained by ERO
On-Line Filing Availability . . . . Yes
On-Line Filing Retention Requirement . . . . Retained by Taxpayer
On-Line Filing Separate 8453-OL Required . . . . No
Paperless Filing Options . . . . NY requires PINs. Returns will not qualify without
                                                      them. Form TR-579 should be signed by both
                                                      taxpayers (if applicable) and retained by the ERO.
Acknowledgment/Acceptance . . . . Accept
Conditional Acceptance . . . . No
Credit Card Payment Allowed . . . . Yes
Balance Due Returns Allowed . . . . Yes
ACH Debit of Balance Due Allowed . . . . Yes
Forms Allowed . . . . Resident, Non-Resident, Part-Year
Federal and State/State Only . . . . State-Only allowed
Corporate Income Tax Electronic Filing Options/
Requirements . . . . None

North Carolina

ELF Coordinator . . . . Johnetta Baugham
ELF Coordinator e-mail . . . . Johnetta.Baugham@
                                                      dornc.com
ELF Coordinator Phone 919-733-1674
ELF Coordinator FAX 919-715-3165
Internet Address . . . . http://www.dornc.com/

E-Filing Requirement . . . . No
ERO Application Requirements . . . . Automatic acceptance into state program if
                                                      accepted by the IRS.
State E-File Deadline 15-Oct
Signature Documents . . . . None Required
On-Line Filing Availability . . . . Yes
On-Line Filing Separate 8453-OL Required . . . . No
Paperless Filing Options . . . . No signature documents are required.

Acknowledgment/Acceptance	Acknowledge
Credit Card Payment Allowed	Yes
Direct Refund Deposit Timeframe	7 days
Balance Due Returns Allowed	Yes
ACH Debit of Balance Due Allowed	No
Forms Allowed	Resident, Non-Resident, Part-Year
Federal and State/State Only	State-Only allowed
Corporate Income Tax Electronic Filing Options/ Requirements	Returns may be electronically filed only when the Department has established and implemented procedures permitting electronic filing of a specific tax return. The Department will allow the electronic filing of corporate franchise tax and income tax returns filed under the federal/state electronic filing program.

North Dakota

ELF Coordinator	Chuck Picard
ELF Coordinator e-mail	cpicard@state.nd.us
ELF Coordinator Phone	701-328-3129 or 701-328-3102
ELF Coordinator FAX	701-328-1032
PATS Name	Chuck Picard
Internet Address	http://www.nd.gov/tax/
E-Filing Requirement	No
ERO Application Requirements	File ND-8633 for new participants. Subsequent filing of this form is NOT required unless changes exist. ERO must also be accepted by the IRS.
State E-File Deadline	15-Oct
Retain or Mail 8453	Retained by ERO
On-Line Filing Availability	Yes
On-Line Filing Retention Requirement	Mail
On-Line Filing Separate 8453-OL Required	Yes
Paperless Filing Options	no signature document required
Acknowledgment/Acceptance	Accept
Conditional Acceptance	No
Credit Card Payment Allowed	No
Direct Refund Deposit Timeframe	7 days
Balance Due Returns Allowed	Yes
ACH Debit of Balance Due Allowed	No
Forms Allowed	Resident, Non-Resident, Part-Year
Federal and State/State Only	State-Only allowed
Corporate Income Tax Electronic Filing Options/ Requirements	None

Ohio

ELF Coordinator	Karen Fisk
ELF Coordinator e-mail	Karen_Fisk@tax.state.oh.us
ELF Coordinator Phone	614-466-0197 DO NOT GIVE TO TAXPAYERS
ELF Coordinator FAX	614-466-0019 FAX
PATS Name	Same
Internet Address	http://tax.ohio.gov/
E-Filing Requirement	No

ERO Application Requirements	No separate application is required; however, Ohio will conduct their own suitability testing and notify any applicant who is ineligible.
State E-File Deadline	15-Oct
Retain or Mail 8453	Retained by Taxpayer
On-Line Filing Availability	Yes
On-Line Filing Separate 8453-OL Required	No
Paperless Filing Options	Ohio uses the IRS Self-Select PIN. If the federal 8453 is used, an Ohio copy of the federal 8453 is produced and it should be retained by the taxpayer.
Acknowledgment/Acceptance	Acknowledge
Credit Card Payment Allowed	Yes
Direct Refund Deposit Timeframe	7-10 days
Balance Due Returns Allowed	Yes
ACH Debit of Balance Due Allowed	Yes
Forms Allowed	Resident, Non-Resident, Part-Year
Federal and State/State Only	State-Only allowed
Corporate Income Tax Electronic Filing Options/ Requirements	Not available for OH-1120, available for annual commercial activities tax filers, but mandated for quarterly CAT filers.

Oklahoma

ELF Coordinator	Darla Young
ELF Coordinator e-mail	dyoung@tax.ok.gov
ELF Coordinator Phone	405-521-3124 405-522-5696
ELF Coordinator FAX	405-522-4275
Internet Address	http://www.oktax.state.ok.us
E-Filing Requirement	Yes
E-Filing Requirement Threshold	50 returns
ERO Application Requirements	Automatic acceptance into state program if accepted by the IRS.
Taxpayer Opt-out	yes
Application Deadline	http://www.oktax.state.ok.us
State E-File Deadline	15-Oct
Retain or Mail 8453	Retained by ERO
On-Line Filing Availability	Yes
On-Line Filing Retention Requirement	Retained by Taxpayer
On-Line Filing Separate 8453-OL Required	No
Paperless Filing Options	None
Acknowledgment/Acceptance	Acknowledge
Conditional Acceptance	No
Credit Card Payment Allowed	Yes
Direct Refund Deposit Timeframe	10 days
Balance Due Returns Allowed	Yes
ACH Debit of Balance Due Allowed	Yes
Forms Allowed	Resident Only
Federal and State/State Only	State-Only not allowed
Corporate Income Tax Electronic Filing Options/ Requirements	Federal/State 1120 E-File Program Optional

Oregon

ELF Coordinator	Stacey Weeks
ELF Coordinator e-mail	Stacey.H.Weeks@state.or.us
ELF Coordinator Phone	503-945-8642
ELF Coordinator FAX	503-945-8649
Internet Address	https://oregon.gov/DOR https://secure.dor.state.or.us/taxforms/
E-Filing Requirement	No
ERO Application Requirements	Automatic acceptance into state program if accepted by the IRS and your business address is in Oregon. If your business address is outside of Oregon or you are new to Oregon electronic filing, send a copy of your IRS form 8633 and your most recent IRS Austin Campus acceptance letter to: Oregon Electronic Filing, Revenue Building, Policy and Systems Unit, 955 Center Street NE, Room 401, Salem OR 907301-2555, or fax to 503-945-8649.
State E-File Deadline	15-Oct
Retain or Mail 8453	Retained by ERO
On-Line Filing Availability	Yes
On-Line Filing Retention Requirement	Retained by Taxpayer
On-Line Filing Separate 8453-OL Required	No
Paperless Filing Options	If the taxpayer elects to use the IRS self-select PIN for the e-file Program, and the IRS accepts it, the ODRS will now accept this PIN as the electronic signature for the Oregon tax return. By adopting this PIN alternative, the ODRS has effectively removed the need for Form OR-EF.
Acknowledgment/Acceptance	Acknowledge
Conditional Acceptance	No
Credit Card Payment Allowed	Yes
Direct Refund Deposit Timeframe	?
Balance Due Returns Allowed	Yes
ACH Debit of Balance Due Allowed	No
Forms Allowed	Resident, Non-Resident, Part-Year
Federal and State/State Only	State-Only allowed
Corporate Income Tax Electronic Filing Options/Requirements	None

Pennsylvania

ELF Coordinator	Richard Santo
ELF Coordinator e-mail	<mswisher@state.pa.us>
ELF Coordinator Phone	717-787-4017
ELF Coordinator FAX	717-772-4193
PATS Name	Meggan Swisher
Internet Address	http://www.revenue.state.pa.us
E-Filing Requirement	No
ERO Application Requirements	Automatic acceptance in state program if accepted by the IRS
State E-File Deadline	15-Oct
Retain or Mail 8453	Retained by ERO
On-Line Filing Availability	Yes
Self-Prepared Returns Permitted	Yes

Paperless Filing Options . . . . PA-8879 for returns with Federal PIN numbers. State Only returns will produce a PA-8453 instead of a PA-8879.

Acknowledgment/Acceptance . . . . Acknowledge

Conditional Acceptance . . . . Yes

Credit Card Payment Allowed . . . . Yes

Balance Due Returns Allowed . . . . Yes

ACH Debit of Balance Due Allowed . . . . Yes

Forms Allowed . . . . Resident, Non-Resident, Part-Year

Federal and State/State Only . . . . State-Only allowed

Corporate Income Tax Electronic Filing Options/
Requirements . . . . Federal/State 1120 E-File Program Optional

Rhode Island

ELF Coordinator . . . . Susan Galvin

ELF Coordinator e-mail . . . . galvins@tax.state.ri.us

ELF Coordinator Phone 401-222-2263

ELF Coordinator FAX 401-222-6288

Internet Address . . . . http://www.tax.state.ri.us

E-Filing Requirement . . . . No

ERO Application Requirements . . . . Automatic acceptance into state program if accepted by the IRS if located in Rhode Island. If located outside RI, the ERO must provide the RI state coordinator a copy of the IRS Form 8633 and IRS acceptance letter.

State E-File Deadline 15-Oct

Retain or Mail 8453 . . . . Retained by Taxpayer

On-Line Filing Availability . . . . Yes

On-Line Filing Retention Requirement . . . . Retained by Taxpayer

On-Line Filing Separate 8453-OL Required . . . . Yes

Paperless Filing Options . . . . No

Acknowledgment/Acceptance . . . . Accept

Credit Card Payment Allowed . . . . Yes

Balance Due Returns Allowed . . . . Yes

ACH Debit of Balance Due Allowed . . . . No

Forms Allowed . . . . Resident, Non-Resident, Part-Year

Federal and State/State Only . . . . State-Only allowed

Corporate Income Tax Electronic Filing Options/
Requirements . . . . None

South Carolina

ELF Coordinator . . . . Ruperto Manankil

ELF Coordinator e-mail . . . . manankr@sctax.org

ELF Coordinator Phone 803-898-5553

ELF Coordinator FAX 803-898-5339

Internet Address . . . . http://www.dor.state.sc.us/dor

E-Filing Requirement . . . . No

ERO Application Requirements . . . . Automatic acceptance into state program if accepted by the IRS.

Application Deadline . . . . http://www.dor.state.sc.us/dor

State E-File Deadline 15-Oct

Retain or Mail 8453 . . . . Retained by ERO

On-Line Filing Availability . . . . Yes

On-Line Filing Retention Requirement . . . .   Retained by Taxpayer
On-Line Filing Separate 8453-OL Required . . . .   No
Acknowledgment/Acceptance . . . .   Acknowledge
Credit Card Payment Allowed . . . .   Yes
Balance Due Returns Allowed . . . .   Yes
ACH Debit of Balance Due Allowed . . . .   Yes
Federal and State/State Only . . . .   State-Only allowed
Corporate Income Tax Electronic Filing Options/
Requirements . . . .   Federal/State 1120 E-File Program Optional

South Dakota

ELF Coordinator . . . .   Does not impose a personal income tax
Corporate Income Tax Electronic Filing Options/
Requirements . . . .   Does not impose a corporate income tax

Tennessee

ELF Coordinator . . . .   E-filing allowed for stocks and bonds tax
Corporate Income Tax Electronic Filing Options/
Requirements . . . .   None

Texas

ELF Coordinator . . . .   Does not impose a personal income tax
Corporate Income Tax Electronic Filing Options/
Requirements . . . .   None

Utah

ELF Coordinator . . . .   Douglas Hansen
ELF Coordinator e-mail . . . .   ddhanse@utah.gov
ELF Coordinator Phone . . . .   801-297-7575 or
       800-662-4335
       Ext 7575
ELF Coordinator FAX   801-297-7698
Internet Address . . . .   http://tax.utah.gov/forms/current.html
E-Filing Requirement . . . .   Yes - in conjunction with 2-D
E-Filing Requirement Threshold . . . .   100 returns
ERO Application Requirements . . . .   Upon receipt of federal acceptance, the ERO must notify the USTC, in writing, with the following: a copy of the IRS Form 8633, name of firm, complete address of firm including telephone number, FAX, EFIN, software vendor and transmitter used. ERO may fax this information to 801-297-7698 or mail to:
       Utah State Tax Commission
       Electronic Filing Section
       210 North 1950 West
       Salt Lake City, UT 84134-0210
Taxpayer Opt-out . . . .   yes
Application Deadline http://txdtm01.tax.ex.state.ut.us
State E-File Deadline 15-Oct
Retain or Mail 8453 . . . .   Retained by ERO
On-Line Filing Availability . . . .   Yes
On-Line Filing Retention Requirement . . . .   Retained by Taxpayer
On-Line Filing Separate 8453-OL Required . . . .   No

Paperless Filing Options . . . . Federal PIN
Acknowledgment/Acceptance . . . . Acknowledge
Credit Card Payment Allowed . . . . No
Balance Due Returns Allowed . . . . Yes
ACH Debit of Balance Due Allowed . . . . No
Forms Allowed . . . . Resident, Non-Resident, Part-Year
Federal and State/State Only . . . . State-Only allowed
Corporate Income Tax Electronic Filing Options/
Requirements . . . . Federal/State 1120 E-File Program Optional

Vermont

ELF Coordinator . . . . Trilene Roach
ELF Coordinator e-mail . . . . trilene.roach@state.vt.us
PATS Name . . . . Trilene Roach
Internet Address . . . . http://www.vermont.gov
E-Filing Requirement . . . . No
ERO Application Requirements . . . . Automatic acceptance into state program if accepted by the IRS.
Application Deadline . . . . http://www.state.vt.us/tax
State E-File Deadline 16-Oct
Retain or Mail 8453 . . . . Retained by ERO
On-Line Filing Availability . . . . Yes
On-Line Filing Retention Requirement . . . . Retained by Taxpayer
On-Line Filing Separate 8453-OL Required . . . . No
Paperless Filing Options . . . . None
Acknowledgment/Acceptance . . . . Acknowledge
Credit Card Payment Allowed . . . . Yes
Direct Refund Deposit Timeframe . . . . 10 days
Balance Due Returns Allowed . . . . Yes
ACH Debit of Balance Due Allowed . . . . Yes
Forms Allowed . . . . Resident, Non-Resident, Part-Year
Federal and State/State Only . . . . State-Only allowed
Corporate Income Tax Electronic Filing Options/
Requirements . . . . None

Virginia

ELF Coordinator . . . . Kerry Williams
ELF Coordinator e-mail . . . . kerry.williams@tax.virginia.gov
ELF Coordinator Phone 804-367-0240
ELF Coordinator FAX 804-367-0224
Internet Address . . . . www.tax.virginia.gov

E-Filing Requirement . . . . Yes - in conjunction with 2-D
E-Filing Requirement Threshold . . . . 100 Partners or more
ERO Application Requirements . . . . Automatic acceptance into state program if accepted by the IRS.
Taxpayer Opt-out . . . . yes
Application Deadline . . . . www.tax.virginia.gov
State E-File Deadline 15-Oct
Retain or Mail 8453 . . . . Retained by ERO
On-Line Filing Availability . . . . Yes
On-Line Filing Retention Requirement . . . . Retained by Taxpayer

On-Line Filing Separate 8453-OL Required	No
Paperless Filing Options	No - VA always uses the 8453 but does not mail it in
Acknowledgment/Acceptance	Acknowledge
Conditional Acceptance	No
Credit Card Payment Allowed	Yes
Direct Refund Deposit Timeframe	3-5 days
Balance Due Returns Allowed	Yes
ACH Debit of Balance Due Allowed	Yes
Forms Allowed	Resident, Non-Resident, Part-Year
Federal and State/State Only	State-Only allowed
Corporate Income Tax Electronic Filing Options/ Requirements	None

Washington

ELF Coordinator	Does not impose a personal income tax
Corporate Income Tax Electronic Filing Options/ Requirements	Does not impose a corporate income tax

West Virginia

ELF Coordinator	Jeff Anderson
ELF Coordinator e-mail	JAnderson@tax.state.wv.us
ELF Coordinator Phone	304-558-5370 ext 417
	304-558-5893 ext 417
ELF Coordinator FAX	304-558-1991
PATS Name	Jeff Anderson
Internet Address	http://www.state.wv.us/taxdiv
E-Filing Requirement	Yes
E-Filing Requirement Threshold	100 returns
ERO Application Requirements	ERO must send a copy of the federal acceptance letter and the federal Form 8633 to WVDTR.
Taxpayer Opt-out	yes
State E-File Deadline	15-Oct
Retain or Mail 8453	Retained by ERO
On-Line Filing Availability	Yes
On-Line Filing Retention Requirement	Mail
On-Line Filing Separate 8453-OL Required	Yes
Self-Prepared Returns Permitted	Yes, in Preparer & ERO box for form & EFile
Paperless Filing Options	WV-8453 will not print if using FD-8879
Acknowledgment/Acceptance	Acknowledge
Credit Card Payment Allowed	Yes
Direct Refund Deposit Timeframe	11 wkdays
Balance Due Returns Allowed	Yes
ACH Debit of Balance Due Allowed	Yes
Forms Allowed	Resident, Non-Resident, Part-Year
Federal and State/State Only	State-Only allowed
Corporate Income Tax Electronic Filing Options/ Requirements	None

Wisconsin

ELF Coordinator	Joy Walker or Marsha Gray
ELF Coordinator e-mail	efiling@dor.state.wi.us
ELF Coordinator Phone	608-267-9711
ELF Coordinator FAX	608-264-6884
Internet Address	http://www.dor.state.wi.us
E-Filing Requirement	Yes
E-Filing Requirement Threshold	100 returns
ERO Application Requirements	Automatic acceptance into state program if accepted by the IRS but ERO is required to mail federal Form 8633 to: Wisconsin Department of Revenue Tax Processing Bureau PO Box 8967 Madison, Wisconsin 53708-8967
State E-File Deadline	15-Oct
Signature Documents	None Required
On-Line Filing Availability	Yes
On-Line Filing Separate 8453-OL Required	No
Acknowledgment/Acceptance	Acknowledge
Conditional Acceptance	No
Credit Card Payment Allowed	Yes
Balance Due Returns Allowed	Yes
ACH Debit of Balance Due Allowed	Yes
Forms Allowed	Resident Only
Federal and State/State Only	State-Only allowed
Corporate Income Tax Electronic Filing Options/ Requirements	Federal/State 1120 E-File Program Optional

Wyoming

ELF Coordinator	Does not impose a personal income tax
Corporate Income Tax Electronic Filing Options/ Requirements	Does not impose a corporate income tax

Electronic Payment of Tax

The following states either have mandatory electronic funds transfer (EFT) programs or accept voluntary EFT payments for sales and use, corporate income, and personal income withholding taxes. States may have EFT requirements for payment of other taxes not listed below, such as motor fuel, tobacco, and alcohol taxes. Payment can be required by one or more method of electronic funds transfer. The most common means of EFT are Automated Clearing House (ACH) credit (the taxpayer calls the state with payment information and authorizes the electronic transfer; taxpayer incurs no cost) or ACH debit (the taxpayer initiates the transfer from its bank; taxpayer may incur an organization fee) and Fedwire. The chart set forth threshold requirements for each state; unless otherwise indicated, the threshold is identical for all three tax types. For purposes of determining if the threshold is met, the threshold amount applies separately for each tax type.

Some states require EFT payments, or reports covering such EFT payments, to be made on dates other than the prescribed due date for other taxpayers. Required dates for EFT payments are not discussed below.

State	EFT Requirements
Alabama	EFT required for taxpayers making individual payments of $25,000 or more.
Alaska*	EFT required for monthly or quarterly returns of $100,000 or more, and for annual returns of $150,000 or more.

*Alaska does not impose a personal income tax or sales and use tax

Arizona	
Corporate Income & Withholding taxes:	EFT required where tax liability for the preceding taxable year was $20,000 or greater.
Sales and Use:	EFT required if total sales tax liability in the preceding tax year was $1 million or more.

Arkansas	
Withholding & Sales and Use taxes:	EFT required where tax liability is $20,000 or more for withholding, in a calendar year.
	Retailers registered to collect Arkansas gross receipts (sales) tax that have average net sales of more than $200,000 per month for the preceding calendar year must prepay their sales tax by EFT.
Corporate Income:	EFT required for corporations with quarterly liability equal to or greater than $20,000.

California	
Corporate Income:	EFT required where (1) any estimated tax installment payment exceeds $20,000 or (2) total tax liability exceeds $80,000 in any taxable year. Corporation franchise (income) and personal income taxpayers not required to remit payments by EFT may elect, with Franchise Tax Board permission, to do so voluntarily.

State	EFT Requirements
Withholding:	EFT required where taxpayer's cumulative average payment for deposit periods in the 12-month period ending June 30 of the prior year was $20,000 or more. Taxpayers not required to pay by EFT may elect to do so with the approval of the EDD.
Sales and Use:	EFT required for taxpayers with an average monthly liability of $20,000 or more. Taxpayers whose liability is less than the threshold amount, and those who voluntarily collect use tax, may elect to remit the tax due by EFT for a minimum of one year with the approval of the State Board of Equalization.
Colorado	
Withholding:	EFT required for taxpayers with an annual estimated withholding tax liability of more than $50,000. Employers with estimated liability of $50,000 or less may voluntarily make deposits using EFT.
Sales and Use:	EFT required where sales tax liability for the previous calendar year exceeded $75,000.
Corporate Income:	No EFT requirements. Tax payments may be made by EFT voluntarily.
Connecticut	EFT required for individual taxpayers whose liability is greater than $10,000.
Delaware*	
Withholding:	EFT mandatory for employers required to deposit federal employment taxes by EFT.
Corporate Income:	No EFT requirements.
*Delaware does not impose a sales and use tax	
District of Columbia	For corporate franchise (income) and personal income taxes, the following taxpayers must remit payments electronically: Third party bulk filers; resident and nonresident taxpayers who are required to file a District tax return where the payment will exceed $25,000; and any other taxpayers as required or permitted under the D.C. Code. All business taxpayers filing monthly employer withholding tax returns must file and pay their withholding taxes electronically if the amount due for a period exceeds $25,000.
Florida*	EFT required where prior fiscal year tax equalled $30,000 or more. Taxpayers required to make estimated tax payments must remit both estimated tax and actual tax payments through EFT.
Sales and Use:	Any taxpayer who pays sales and use tax in an aggregate amount of $50,000 must pay communications services tax electronically for the following year.
*Florida does not impose a personal income tax	
Georgia	EFT required for payments exceeding $10,000. EFT required for every employer whose Georgia personal income tax withheld or required to be withheld exceeds $50,000 for the 12-month period that ended the preceding June 30.

State	EFT Requirements
Hawaii	EFT required where tax liability exceeds $100,000 for any taxable year. Taxpayers who have less than $100,000 in tax liability may request to pay taxes by EFT.
Idaho	All taxes due the state must be paid by EFT whenever the amount due is $100,000 or greater.
Illinois	EFT required for taxpayers whose tax liability for the preceding calendar year was $200,000 or more. Taxpayers may voluntarily apply to participate in the electronic funds transfer program.
Indiana	EFT required where taxpayer's estimated quarterly tax liability for the current year or the average estimated quarterly tax liability for the preceding year exceeds $10,000.
Iowa	
Corporate Income:	EFT required for estimated tax installments when tax liability for the preceding year exceeds $80,000.
Withholding:	EFT required for taxpayers who remit over $10,000 a month in withholding tax.
Sales and Use:	EFT required for (1) taxpayers with direct pay permits, and (2) taxpayers who remit over $5,000 a month in sales tax.
Kansas	EFT required for withholding taxes if total tax liability exceeds $100,000 in any calendar year.
Kentucky	EFT required where (1) the average payment per reporting period is more than $10,000, (2) the payment for each tax or fee required to be collected or remitted is made on behalf of 100 or more taxpayers, or (3) the aggregate of the funds to be remitted on behalf of others is $10,000 or more for each tax or fee required to be collected or remitted. Any taxpayer whose average payment of sales tax per reporting period exceeds $25,000 during the look back period must pay the tax by EFT.
Louisiana	EFT required if (1) payments made in connection with filing of business tax return averaged $10,000 or more per reporting period during the prior 12-month period; (2) a business tax return is filed more frequently than monthly and the average total payments during the prior 12-month period exceeds $10,000 per month; or (3) a withholding tax return and payment during the preceding 12-month period exceeds $10,000. Effective January 1, 2008, the applicable amounts above will all decreaase to $5,000.

State	EFT Requirements
Maine	Employers with withholding liability of $200,000 or more during the look-back period, and taxpayers with $400,000 or more of tax liability (other than for individual income tax, property tax, and estate tax) during the look-back period must remit payments by EFT. Maine Revenue Services determines look-back periods on a tax-specific basis. Taxpayers who are not required to remit tax payments electronically may do so voluntarily by contacting the Bureau of Revenue Services.
Maryland	EFT required if tax liability equals $10,000 or more. Taxpayers that do not meet the threshold may voluntarily remit payments by EFT.
Massachusetts	
Corporate income:	All corporations subject to the corporate excise tax, with more than $100,000 in gross receipts, sales, revenue, or income must pay taxes by electronic means.
Withholding & Sales and Use:	EFT required for wage withholding , sales and use tax, and room occupancy tax if the filer's combined liability for the three categories of taxes for the preceding calendar year was $10,000 or more.
Michigan	EFT required for sales and use taxes when total sales and use tax liability for preceding calendar year was at least $720,000. EFT required for personal income when the taxpayer has a tax liability for the preceding year of $480,000 or more. Payments of other taxes may be made voluntarily by EFT.
Minnesota	Voluntary EFT payments accepted for all tax types. EFT required for each tax type as follows:
Corporate income:	EFT required for all estimated payments where aggregate amount of estimated corporate franchise (income) tax payments made during previous fiscal year was at least $10,000.
Withholding:	Taxpayers who are required to deposit federal withholding taxes by EFT are also required to deposit Minnesota withholding taxes by EFT.
Sales and Use:	A taxpayer with a sales and use tax liability of $120,000 or more during a fiscal year ending June 30 must remit all liabilities in the subsequent calendar year by EFT.
Mississippi	The State Tax Commission may require any taxpayer owing more than $20,000 in connection with any return, report or other document filed with the commission to remit any such tax liability by EFT.
Missouri	EFT required for companies subject to quarter-monthly sales tax payment requirement and employers subject to quarter-monthly withholding payment requirement.
Montana*	EFT required where tax liability equals or exceeds $500,000. Taxpayers with a tax liability of less than $500,000 may voluntarily make payments by EFT.

*Montana does not impose a sales and use tax

State	EFT Requirements
Nebraska	EFT may be required for payments over $100,000. Three months notice is given to any taxpayer that is required to pay by this method. All taxpayers may voluntarily make EFT payments.
Nevada*	No EFT provisions.
*Nevada does not impose a corporate or personal income tax	
New Hampshire*	EFT required for taxpayers subject to the business profits and business enterprise taxes that have tax liabilities of $100,000 or more. Taxpayers that do not meet the threshold amount may register to make payments by EFT.
*New Hampshire does not impose a sales and use tax or personal income tax	
New Jersey	EFT required where prior year liability was $10,000 or more. Payers of gross (personal) income tax, transfer inheritance tax, and estate tax are exempt from the EFT requirement.
New Mexico	"Special payment method" (including ACH deposit, Fedwire transfer, or qualified check payment) is required if average tax liability was $25,000 or more per month during the previous calendar year.
New York:	
Withholding:	EFT required for taxpayers required to withhold an aggregate of $35,000 or more of New York state personal income tax, New York City personal income tax, New York City income tax surcharge, City of Yonkers income tax. Taxpayers are exempt from participation in the EFT Program if the aggregate tax withheld, pursuant to their most recent annual reconciliation of withholding, is less than $100,000. Taxpayers may apply to the Commissioner of Taxation and Finance for permission to participate in the EFT Program on a voluntary basis.
Sales and use:	Payment by EFT or certified check is required if, on or after June 1, the taxpayer's liability for the June 1 through May 31 period immediately preceding was more than $500,000 for state and local sales and use taxes or more than $5 million for prepaid state and local sales and use taxes on motor fuel and diesel motor fuel.
Corporate Income:	No EFT requirements.
North Carolina	EFT required where taxpayer liability averages at least $20,000 a month ($240,000 during the 12-month period). The $20,000 threshold applies separately for each tax.
North Dakota	No EFT requirements. Voluntary EFT program available.
Ohio	
Withholding:	EFT required where actual or required payments exceeded $84,000 during the 12-month period ending on the thirtieth day of June of the preceding calendar year.

State	EFT Requirements
Corporate Income:	EFT required where taxpayer's total liability exceeds $50,000 for the second preceding tax year. If two or more taxpayers have elected or are required to file a combined report, the tax liability of those taxpayers for purposes of the $50,000 level is the aggregate tax liability of those taxpayers after reduction for nonrefundable credits allowed the taxpayers. EFT required for pass-through entity personal income tax payments where tax liability is at least $180,000 for the second preceding qualifying taxable year.
Sales and Use:	EFT required where the total amount of tax equals or exceeds $75,000 a calendar year.
Oklahoma	EFT required for taxpayers with sales tax liability of $2,500 per month. No EFT requirements for corporate income tax or withholding.
Oregon* . . . . *Oregon does not impose a sales and use tax	EFT required for estimated corporate excise taxes and withholding if the corporation is required to make federal estimated tax payments electronically.
Pennsylvania	Payment by EFT (or alternatively by certified or cashier's check delivered in person or by courier) required if any individual payment due is $20,000 or more. Taxpayers not required to pay by EFT may do so voluntarily with the approval of the Secretary of Revenue.
Rhode Island	EFT required when tax to be paid exceeds $10,000.
South Carolina	Payment by EFT required if the amount owed for a filing period during the previous 12 months exceeds $15,000.
South Dakota* . . . . *South Dakota does not impose a corporate income or personal income tax	Taxpayers must apply to the Dept. of Revenue for permission to make electronic payments for sales and use taxes.
Tennessee	Taxpayers owing $10,000 or more in connection with any return may be required to make payment by EFT.
Texas* . . . . *Texas does not impose a personal income tax	EFT required for taxpayers that paid $100,000 or more during the preceding fiscal year in a single category of tax payments, if the comptroller reasonably anticipates that the taxpayer will pay at least that amount during the current fiscal year.
Utah	No EFT requirements for corporate income or withholding. Taxpayers with state and local sales and use tax liability of $96,000 or more for the previous year must transmit monthly payments by EFT. Voluntary EFT available by agreement with Tax Commission.

State	EFT Requirements
Vermont	EFT payments are allowed only for personal income tax withholding by employers. EFT payments are required if the employer expects their withhodling tax to be $9,000 or more quarterly.
Virginia	EFT required if average monthly tax liability exceeds $20,000. Taxpayers may also participate voluntarily in the EFT program.
Washington*	EFT required for taxpayers who have taxes due of $240,000 or more. The requirement applies only to taxes that are reported on the Combined Excise Tax Return.

*Washington does not impose a corporate income or personal income tax.

State	EFT Requirements
West Virginia	EFT required for taxpayers with tax liability of $100,000 or more. Taxpayer may also participate voluntarily in the EFT Program
Wisconsin	
Sales and Use, Withholding:	EFT required if the aggregate amount due in the prior calendar year was $10,000 or more.
Corporate income:	Corporate franchise (income) tax estimated tax payments and tax due must be paid using EFT if the net tax less refundable credits on the prior year's return was $40,000 or more.
	Voluntary EFT allowed for all these tax types.
Wyoming*	Taxpayers may voluntarily pay sales and use taxes electronically by using the Wyoming Internet Filing Service (WIFS).

*Wyoming does not impose a corporate income or personal income tax

Estimated Tax—LLCs

The following chart indicates whether estimated tax payments are required on behalf of nonresident members. Many states require the payment of estimated tax for nonresident members only when an election is made to file a composite return and unwitheld income tax liability of members included in the return is expected to exceed a threshold amount. State specific conditions or limitations placed on the requirement are noted in the Comments column. The chart does not reflect whether LLCs are required to pay estimated taxes on entity-level income or to withhold taxes on behalf of nonresidents.

State	Answer
Alabama	No
Alaska	N/A[1]
Arizona	No[2]
Arkansas	No[3]
California	No[4]
Colorado	No[3]
Connecticut	No[5]
Delaware	No[6]
District of Columbia	No
Florida	N/A[1]
Georgia	No[7]
Hawaii	No
Idaho	No[8]
Illinois	No[9]
Indiana	No
Iowa	No[10]
Kansas	No[11]
Kentucky	No[12]
Louisiana	No
Maine	No[13]
Maryland	Yes[14]
Massachusetts	No[15]
Michigan	No
Minnesota	No[16]

State	Answer
Mississippi	No[17]
Missouri	No[18]
Montana	No[19]
Nebraska	No
New Hampshire	No
New Jersey	No[20]
New Mexico	No
New York	Yes[21]
North Carolina	No
North Dakota	No[22]
Ohio	No[23]
Oklahoma	Yes[24]
Oregon	No[25]
Pennsylvania	No
Rhode Island	Yes[26]
South Carolina	No[18]
Tennessee	No
Texas	N/A[1]
Utah	No[8]
Vermont	Yes[27]
Virginia	No[28]
West Virginia	No
Wisconsin	No[29]

---

[1] No personal income tax.
[2] Voluntary estimated payments on a composite basis allowed.
[3] Unless a composite return is filed and unwithheld liability of nonresident member is $1000 or more.
[4] Unless a group return is filed and unwithheld liability of nonresident member is $200 or more.
[5] On or after June 6, 2006, LLCs no longer required to make estimated personal income tax installment payments on behalf of nonresident individual members.
[6] Unless a composite return is filed and unwithheld liability of nonresident member is $400 or more.
[7] Voluntary payments on composite basis may be paid on Form CR-ES.
[8] Estimated tax is voluntary.
[9] Unless a composite return is filed and unwithheld income of resident or nonresident member is $500 or more.
[10] Payment on a composite basis is voluntary.
[11] Unless a composite return is filed and unwithheld tax liability of nonresident is $500 or more.
[12] Effective January 1, 2005, LLCs are subject to the corporate income tax and the same estimated tax requirements that are applicable to C corporations.
[13] Unless a composite return is filed for nonresident members and aggregate unwithheld liability is $1000 or more.

[14] If tax liability exceeds $1000. The tax is the sum of the highest marginal individual tax rate (4.75%) and the lowest county tax rate (1.25%) applied to each nonresident individual member's distributive share or pro rata share of pass-through income plus the corporation income tax rate (7%) applied to each nonresident entity member's distributive share or pro rata share of pass-through income.

[15] Unless a composite return is filed and unwithheld income of nonresident member is $200 or more.

[16] Unless a composite return is filed and unwithheld tax liability of nonresident is $500 or more. For tax years beginning after 2005, quarterly estimated tax requirements apply to income subject to nonresident withholding.

[17] Unless a composite return is filed and unwithheld tax liability of nonresident shareholders exceeds $200.

[18] Unless a composite return is filed and unwithheld tax liability of nonresident member is $100 or more.

[19] Unless a composite return is filed and unwithheld tax liability of nonresident member exceeds $500.

[20] Unless a composite return is filed and unwithheld tax liability of nonresident member exceeds $400.

[21] If tax liability of corporate or nonresident member exceeds $300.

[22] Unless a composite return is filed and unwithheld liability of nonresident member is $500 or more.

[23] Unless a composite return is filed and unwithheld liability of nonresident individual shareholders exceeds $500.

[24] If tax liability of nonresident member exceeds $500.

[25] Unless a composite return is filed and unwithheld tax liability of nonresident member is $1000 or more.

[26] If withholding is required and aggregate tax liability derived from or connected with state sources is expected to be $250 or more.

[27] If unwithheld tax liability of nonresident member exceeds $100. After 2005, tax is equal to next-to-lowest marginal tax rate multiplied by member's pro rata share of income attributable to state sources.

[28] Unless a unified return is allowed and unwithheld liability of nonresident member exceeds $150.

[29] Unless a combined return is filed and unwithheld tax liability of nonresident member is $200 or more.

Estimated Tax—LLPs

The following chart indicates whether estimated tax payments are required on behalf of nonresident partners. Many states require the payment of estimated tax for nonresident partners only when an election is made to file a composite return and unwitheld income tax liability of partners included in the return is expected to exceed a threshold amount. State specific conditions or limitations placed on the requirement are noted in the Comments column. The chart does not reflect whether limited liability partnerships (LLPs) are required to pay estimated taxes on partnership-level income or to withhold taxes on behalf of nonresidents.

State	Answer
Alabama	No
Alaska	N/A[1]
Arizona	No[2]
Arkansas	No[3]
California	No[4]
Colorado	No[3]
Connecticut	No[5]
Delaware	No[6]
District of Columbia	No
Florida	N/A[1]
Georgia	No[7]
Hawaii	No
Idaho	No[8]
Illinois	No[9]
Indiana	No
Iowa	No[10]
Kansas	No[11]
Kentucky	No[12]
Louisiana	No
Maine	No[13]
Maryland	Yes[14]
Massachusetts	No[15]
Michigan	No
Minnesota	No[16]
Mississippi	No[17]
Missouri	No[18]

State	Answer
Montana	No[19]
Nebraska	No
New Hampshire	No
New Jersey	No[20]
New Mexico	No
New York	Yes[21]
North Carolina	No
North Dakota	No[22]
Ohio	No[23]
Oklahoma	Yes[24]
Oregon	No[25]
Pennsylvania	No
Rhode Island	Yes[26]
South Carolina	No[18]
Tennessee	No
Texas	N/A[1]
Utah	No[8]
Vermont	Yes[27]
Virginia	No[28]
West Virginia	No
Wisconsin	No[29]

---

[1] No personal income tax.
[2] Voluntary estimated payments on a composite basis allowed.
[3] Unless a composite return is filed and unwithheld liability of nonresident partner is $1000 or more.
[4] Unless a group return is filed and unwithheld liability of nonresident partner is $200 or more.
[5] On or after June 6, 2006, LLPs no longer required to make estimated personal income tax installment payments on behalf of nonresident individual partners.
[6] Unless a composite return is filed and unwithheld liability of nonresident partner is $400 or more.
[7] Voluntary payments on composite basis may be paid on Form CR-ES.
[8] Estimated tax is voluntary.
[9] Unless a composite return is filed and unwithheld income of resident or nonresident partner is $500 or more.
[10] Payment on a composite basis is voluntary.
[11] Unless a composite return is filed and unwithheld tax liability of nonresident partner is $500 or more.
[12] Effective January 1, 2005, LLPs are subject to the corporate income tax and the same estimated tax requirements that are applicable to C corporations.
[13] Unless a composite return is filed for nonresident partners and aggregate unwithheld liability is $1000 or more.
[14] If tax liability exceeds $1000. The tax is the sum of the highest marginal individual tax rate (4.75%) and the lowest county tax rate (1.25%) applied to each nonresident individual partner's distributive share or pro rata share of pass-through income plus the corporation income tax rate (7%) applied to each nonresident entity partner's distributive share or pro rata share of pass-through income.
[15] Unless a composite return is filed and unwithheld income of nonresident partner is $200 or more.

[16] Unless a composite return is filed and unwithheld tax liability of nonresident members is $500 or more. For tax years beginning after 2005, quarterly estimated tax requirements apply to income subject to nonresident withholding.

[17] Unless a composite return is filed and unwithheld tax liability of nonresident shareholders exceeds $200.

[18] Unless a composite return is filed and unwithheld tax liability of nonresident partner is $100 or more.

[19] Unless a composite return is filed and unwithheld tax liability of nonresident partner exceeds $500.

[20] Unless a composite return is filed and unwithheld tax liability of nonresident partner exceeds $400.

[21] If tax liability of corporate or nonresident partner exceeds $300.

[22] Unless a composite return is filed and unwithheld liability of nonresident partner is $500 or more.

[23] Unless a composite return is filed and unwithheld liability of nonresident partner exceeds $500.

[24] If tax liability of nonresident partner exceeds $500.

[25] Unless a composite return is filed and unwithheld tax liability of nonresident partner is $1000 or more.

[26] If withholding is required and aggregate tax liability derived from or connected with state sources is expected to be $250 or more.

[27] If unwithheld tax liability of nonresident partner exceeds $100. After 2005, tax is equal to next-to-lowest marginal tax rate multiplied by partner's pro rata share of income attributable to state sources.

[28] Unless a unified return is allowed and unwithheld liability of nonresident partner exceeds $150.

[29] Unless a combined return is filed and unwithheld tax liability of nonresident partner is $200 or more.

Estimated Tax—Partnerships

The following chart indicates whether estimated tax payments are required on behalf of nonresident partners. Many states require the payment of estimated tax for nonresident partners only when an election is made to file a composite return and unwitheld income tax liability of partners included in the return is expected to exceed a threshold amount. State specific conditions or limitations placed on the requirement are noted in the Comments column. The chart does not reflect whether partnerships are required to pay estimated taxes on partnership-level income or to withhold taxes on behalf of nonresidents.

State	Answer
Alabama	No
Alaska	N/A[1]
Arizona	No[2]
Arkansas	No[3]
California	No[4]
Colorado	No[3]
Connecticut	No[5]
Delaware	No[6]
District of Columbia	No
Florida	N/A[1]
Georgia	No[7]
Hawaii	No
Idaho	No[8]
Illinois	No[9]
Indiana	No
Iowa	No[10]
Kansas	No[11]
Kentucky	No[12]
Louisiana	No
Maine	No[13]
Maryland	Yes[14]
Massachusetts	No[15]
Michigan	No
Minnesota	No[16]
Mississippi	No[17]

State	Answer
Missouri	No[18]
Montana	No[19]
Nebraska	No
New Hampshire	No
New Jersey	No[20]
New Mexico	No
New York	Yes[21]
North Carolina	No
North Dakota	No[22]
Ohio	No[23]
Oklahoma	Yes[24]
Oregon	No[25]
Pennsylvania	No
Rhode Island	Yes[26]
South Carolina	No[18]
Tennessee	No
Texas	N/A[1]
Utah	No[8]
Vermont	Yes[27]
Virginia	No[28]
West Virginia	No
Wisconsin	No[29]

---

[1] No personal income tax.
[2] Voluntary estimated payments on a composite basis.
[3] Unless a composite return is filed and unwithheld liability of nonresident partner is $1000 or more.
[4] Unless a group return is filed and unwithheld liability of nonresident partner is $200 or more.
[5] On or after June 6, 2006, partnerships no longer required to make estimated personal income tax installment payments on behalf of nonresident individual partners.
[6] Unless a composite return is filed and unwithheld liability of nonresident partner is $400 or more.
[7] Voluntary payments on composite basis may be paid on Form CR-ES.
[8] Estimated tax is voluntary.
[9] Unless a composite return is filed and unwithheld income of resident or nonresident partner is $500 or more.
[10] Payment on a composite basis is voluntary.
[11] Unless a composite return is filed and unwithheld tax liability of nonresident partner is $500 or more.
[12] General partnerships are subject to withholding requirements. Effective January 1, 2005, limited partnerships are subject to the corporate income tax and must pay estimated tax if income tax liability for taxable year is expected to exceed $5,000.
[13] Unless a composite return is filed for nonresident partners and aggregate unwithheld liability is $1000 or more.

[14] If tax liability exceeds $1000. The tax is the sum of the highest marginal individual tax rate (4.75%) and the lowest county tax rate (1.25%) applied to each nonresident individual partner's distributive share or pro rata share of pass-through income plus the corporation income tax rate (7%) applied to each nonresident entity partner's distributive share or pro rata share of pass-through income.

[15] Unless a composite return is filed and unwithheld tax liability of nonresident partners is $200 or more.

[16] Unless a composite return is filed and unwithheld income of nonresident is $500 or more. For tax years beginning after 2005, quarterly estimated tax requirements apply to income subject to nonresident withholding.

[17] Unless a composite return is filed and unwithheld tax liability of nonresident partner exceeds $200.

[18] Unless a composite return is filed and unwithheld tax liability of nonresident partner is $100 or more.

[19] Unless a composite return is filed and unwithheld tax liability of nonresident partner exceeds $500.

[20] Unless a composite return is filed and unwithheld tax liability of nonresident partner exceeds $400.

[21] If tax liability of corporate or nonresident partner exceeds $300.

[22] Unless a composite return is filed and unwithheld liability of nonresident partner is $500 or more.

[23] Unless a composite return is filed and unwithheld liability of nonresident partner exceeds $500.

[24] If tax liability of nonresident partner exceeds $500.

[25] Unless a composite return is filed and unwithheld tax liability of nonresident partner is $1000 or more.

[26] If withholding is required and aggregate tax liability derived from or connected with state sources is expected to be $250 or more.

[27] If unwithheld tax liability of nonresident partner exceeds $100. After 2005, tax is equal to next-to-lowest marginal tax rate multiplied by partner's pro rata share of income attributable to state sources.

[28] Unless a unified return is allowed and unwithheld liability of nonresident partner exceeds $150.

[29] Unless a combined return is filed and unwithheld tax liability of nonresident partner is $200 or more.

Estimated Tax—S Corporations

The following chart indicates whether estimated tax payments are required on behalf of nonresident S corporation shareholders. Many states require the payment of estimated tax for nonresident shareholders only when an election is made to file a composite return and unwitheld income tax liability of shareholders included in the return is expected to exceed a threshold amount. State specific conditions or limitations placed on the requirement are noted in the Comments column. The chart does not reflect whether S corporations are required to pay estimated taxes on corporate-level income or to withhold taxes on behalf of nonresidents.

State	Answer
Alabama	No
Alaska	N/A[1]
Arizona	No[2]
Arkansas	No
California	No[3]
Colorado	No[4]
Connecticut	No[5]
Delaware	Yes[6]
District of Columbia	N/A[7]
Florida	N/A[1]
Georgia	No[8]
Hawaii	No[9]
Idaho	No[10]
Illinois	No[11]
Indiana	No
Iowa	No[12]
Kansas	No[9]
Kentucky	No[13]
Louisiana	No
Maine	No[14]
Maryland	Yes[15]
Massachusetts	No[16]
Michigan	No
Minnesota	No[17]
Mississippi	No[18]

State	Answer
Missouri	No[19]
Montana	No[20]
Nebraska	No
New Hampshire	N/A[7]
New Jersey	No[21]
New Mexico	No
New York	Yes[22]
North Carolina	No
North Dakota	No[23]
Ohio	No[24]
Oklahoma	Yes[25]
Oregon	No[26]
Pennsylvania	No
Rhode Island	Yes[27]
South Carolina	No[28]
Tennessee	No
Texas	N/A[1]
Utah	No
Vermont	Yes[29]
Virginia	No[30]
West Virginia	No
Wisconsin	No[31]

---

[1] No personal income tax.
[2] Voluntary estimated payments on a composite basis.
[3] Unless a group return is filed and unwithheld liability of nonresident shareholder is $200 or more.
[4] Unless a composite return is filed and unwithheld liability nonresident shareholder is $1000 or more.
[5] On or after June 6, 2006, S corporations no longer required to make estimated personal income tax installment payments on behalf of nonresident individual shareholders.
[6] Nonresident's estimated distributive share of income multiplied by 5.95%.
[7] Taxed same as C corporations.
[8] Voluntary payments on composite basis may be paid on Form CR-ES.
[9] Unless a composite return is filed and unwithheld tax liability of nonresident shareholder is $500 or more.
[10] Estimated tax is voluntary.
[11] Unless a composite return is filed and unwithheld income of resident or nonresident shareholder is $500 or more.
[12] Payment on a composite basis is voluntary.
[13] Effective January 1, 2005, S corporations are subject to the corporate income tax and the same estimated tax requirements that are applicable to C corporations.
[14] Unless a composite return is filed for nonresident shareholders and aggregate unwithheld liability is $1000 or more.

[15] If tax liability exceeds $1000. The tax is the sum of the highest marginal individual tax rate (4.75%) and the lowest county tax rate (1.25%) applied to each nonresident individual shareholder's distributive share or pro rata share of pass-through income plus the corporation income tax rate (7%) applied to each nonresident entity shareholder's distributive share or pro rata share of pass-through income.

[16] Unless a composite return is filed and unwithheld tax liability of nonresident shareholder is $200 or more.

[17] Unless a composite return is filed and unwithheld tax liability of nonresident is $500 or more. For tax years beginning after 2005, quarterly estimated tax requirements apply to income subject to nonresident withholding.

[18] Unless a composite return is filed and unwithheld tax liability of nonresident shareholder exceeds $200.

[19] Unless a composite return is filed and unwithheld tax liability of nonresident shareholder is $100 or more.

[20] Unless a composite return is filed and unwithheld tax liability of nonresident shareholder exceeds $500.

[21] Unless a composite return is filed and unwithheld tax liability of nonresident shareholder exceeds $400.

[22] If tax liability of corporate or nonresident shareholder exceeds $300.

[23] Unless a composite return is filed and unwithheld liability of nonresident shareholder is $500 or more.

[24] Unless a composite return is filed and unwithheld liability of nonresident individual shareholders exceeds $500.

[25] If tax liability of nonresident shareholder exceeds $500.

[26] Unless a composite return is filed and unwithheld tax liability of nonresident shareholder is $1000 or more.

[27] If withholding is required and aggregate tax liability derived from or connected with state sources is expected to be $250 or more.

[28] Unless a composite return is filed and unwithheld tax liability of nonresident shareholder is $100.

[29] If unwithheld tax liability of nonresident shareholder exceeds $100. After 2005, tax is equal to next-to-lowest marginal tax rate multiplied by shareholder's pro rata share of income attributable to state sources.

[30] Unless a unified return is allowed and unwithheld liability of nonresident shareholder exceeds $150.

[31] Unless a combined return is filed and unwithheld tax liability of nonresident shareholder is $200 or more.

Installment Payments

Many states allow taxpayers to pay past due taxes in installments, rather than in a lump sum payment. Some states require a showing of financial hardship or have other requirements that must be met before entering into an installment agreement. Other states merely give the taxing body the authority to enter agreements at its own discretion.

For states that allow installment payments, a written installment agreement is usually required. The agreement generally may be terminated by the state if the taxpayer fails to comply with the terms of the agreement, or fails to comply with other tax laws of the state. Some states may also terminate based on other factors, such as an improvement in the taxpayer's financial condition.

Although some states allow installment payments under the state's taxpayers' bill of rights, this chart identifies those states that have formal, statutory or regulatory, provisions regarding installment payments and, where applicable, identifies the provisions. This chart does not address estimated tax payments or property tax payments.

State	Installment Payment Provisions
Alabama	Installments allowed only after final assessment and termination of appeals; maximum length of 12 months; may be terminated for change in financial condition.
Alaska	No formal provisions.
Arizona	Installments allowed; financial report must be filed and taxpayer must be current in all filings.
Arkansas	Installments allowed only if liability is less than $1,000.
California	FTB-Installments allowed for personal income tax if liability, excluding interest, penalties, and additions, is $10,000 or less and taxpayer has complied with other installment agreements in preceding 5 years; maximum length of 3 years SBE-Installments allowed. SBE-Installments allowed.
Colorado	No formal provisions.
Connecticut	No formal provisions.
Delaware	No formal provisions.
District of Columbia	No formal provisions.
Florida	Installments allowed only if liability greater than $1,000.
Georgia	No formal provisions.
Hawaii	Installments allowed.
Idaho	Installments allowed.
Illinois	Installments allowed.
Indiana	No formal provisions.
Iowa	Installments allowed; extreme financial hardship; penalties and interest must be included.

State	Installment Payment Provisions
Kansas	Installments allowed; length and condition determined by taxpayer's financial condition of payment plan determined.
Kentucky	Installments allowed; 20% collection fee may be imposed; may be terminated for change in financial condition.
Louisiana	Installments allowed.
Maine	No formal provisions.
Maryland	Installments allowed only if taxpayer is current with all filings.
Massachusetts	Installments allowed; may be terminated if significant change in financial condition.
Michigan	No formal provision, however taxpayers who meet certain requirement are allowed to make installment payments.
Minnesota	Installments allowed; security may be required; maximum length of 2 years; may terminate agreement if substantial change in financial condition.
Mississippi	No formal provisions.
Missouri	No formal provisions; however, an agreement in compromise may allow for installment payments.
Montana	No formal provisions.
Nebraska	Installments allowed.
Nevada	Installments allowed; maximum length of 12 months.
New Hampshire	Installments allowed if liens recorded to secure debt; maximum length of 6 months; may be terminated if financial condition has sufficiently changed.
New Jersey	Installments allowed.
New Mexico	Installments allowed; security may be required; maximum length of 5 years.
New York	Installments allowed; may be terminated for change in financial condition.
North Carolina	Installments allowed; penalties may be waived in agreement; may be terminated for change in financial condition.
North Dakota	No formal provisions.
Ohio	Installments allowed for delinquent real and personal property taxes, otherwise no formal provisions.
Oklahoma	Installments allowed only when continued business operations are enjoined.
Oregon	Installments allowed; may be terminated if significant change in financial condition.
Pennsylvania	Installments allowed with approval of state treasurer; may be terminated if significant change in financial condition; maximum length of 7 years.
Rhode Island	A taxpayer who is unable to pay the tax liability in full may request an installment agreement specifying the amount of payments possible (Instructions to Form RI 9465, Installment Agreement Request). Within 30 days, the Division of Taxation will notify the taxpayer whether the request is approved or denied, or if more information is needed.
South Carolina	Installments allowed; maximum length of 1 year.
South Dakota	No formal provisions.

State	Installment Payment Provisions
Tennessee	Installments allowed.
Texas	Installments allowed; maximum length 3 years.
Utah	Installments allowed; may be terminated if substantial change in financial condition.
Vermont	No formal provisions.
Virginia	Installments allowed; may be terminated if collection is in jeopardy or significant change in financial condition.
Washington	No formal provisions.
West Virginia	Installments allowed.
Wisconsin	Installments allowed; application must include reasons for installments and proposed payment plan.
Wyoming	Installments allowed if payment would result in severe inconvenience.

Interest Rates on Underpayments and Overpayments 2006

Interest rates on underpayments and overpayments are set either by statute or by regulation pursuant to a statutory formula. Interest rates keyed to the prevailing prime rate at leading commercial banks or the prevailing discount rate generally are rounded to the nearest whole number. State rates keyed to the prevailing federal short-term rate (STR), as determined by Internal Revenue Code Sec. 6621(b), are rounded by all states to the nearest whole number. Most state rates are not adjusted if the relevant commercial or federal interest rate is less than 1% more or less than the state rate then in effect.

Chart reflecting rates for 2006: The following chart provides interest rates for 2006 listed in descending order, ending in the final quarter. The statutory formula used by each state to determine rates is also listed. NA denotes that interest rates for a given period are not yet available.

ALABAMA
Adjusted quarterly
Underpayments and overpayments
(fed. underpayment rate)

1-2006—3-2006	7%
4-2006—6-2006	7%
7-2006—9-2006	8%
10-2006—12-2006	8%

ALASKA*
Adjusted quarterly
Underpayments and overpayments (greater of 11% or fed. STR plus 5%)

1-2006—3-2006	11%
4-2006—6-2006	11%
7-2006—9-2006	11%
10-2006—12-2006	11%

* Alaska does not impose a personal income tax or a sales and use tax.

ARIZONA
Adjusted quarterly
Underpayments and overpayments (fed. underpayment rate)

1-2006—3-2006	7%
4-2006—6-2006	7%
7-2006—9-2006	8%
10-2006—12-2006	8%

ARKANSAS
Rate contained in statute
Underpayments and overpayments ... 10%

CALIFORNIA
Adjusted semiannually
Personal income tax rates
Underpayments and overpayments (fed. rate)

1-2006—6-2006	6%*
7-2006—12-2006	7%

Corporation franchise (income) tax rates
Underpayments

1-2006—6-2006		6%*
7-2006—12-2006		7%

Overpayments

1-2006—6-2006		3%
7-2006—12-2006		4%

* Additional 2% rate for large corporate underpayments, as defined by IRC 6621(c).

Sales and use tax rates
Underpayments (3% plus fed.
underpayment rate for previous
January or July)

1-2006—6-2006		9%
7-2006—12-2006		10%

Overpayments (13-week Treasury bill rates)

1-2006—6-2006		3%
7-2006—12-2006		4%

COLORADO
Adjusted annually
Underpayments and overpayments (previous 7-1 prime plus 3%) 9%*

*6% interest rate applies if payment of tax, or agreement to pay, is made within 30 days of notice of underpayment or nonpayment, and when a tax underpayment or nonpayment is cured voluntarily without notification from the Department of Revenue.

CONNECTICUT
Rate contained in statute
Underpayments 12%
Overpayments . . . .

Corporate income		8%
Personal income		9%
Sales and use:		12% *

* If the Commissioner, in his discretion, offsets any overpaid taxes against underpayments, the interest allowed on the overpayment and charged to the underpayment is also computed at 1% per month.

DELAWARE*
Rate contained in statute
Underpayments and overpayments 12%
* Delaware does not impose a sales and use tax.

DISTRICT OF COLUMBIA
Rate contained in statute
Underpayments 10%
Overpayments 6%

FLORIDA *
Adjusted semiannually
Underpayments and overpayments
(adjusted prime rate plus 4%)

1-2006—6-2006		10%
7-2006—12-2006		11%

* Florida does not impose a personal income tax.

GEORGIA
Rate contained in statute
Underpayments and overpayments 12%

HAWAII
Rate contained in statute
Underpayments and overpayments 8%

IDAHO
Adjusted annually
Underpayments and overpayments (2% plus fed. mid-term rate as applied on
Oct. 15 of prior year) 6%

ILLINOIS
Adjusted semiannually
Underpayments and overpayments*

1-2006—6-2006	4%
7-2006—12-2006	5%

For periods after 2003, the interest rate charged on tax underpayments and
paid on tax overpayments is (1) for the one-year period beginning with the date
of underpayment or overpayment, the short-term federal rate under IRC Sec.
6621 (currently 4%), and (2) for any period after the one-year period, the
underpayment rate under IRC Sec. 6621 (currently 7%).

INDIANA
Adjusted annually
Underpayments (prior-year average investment yield on state money, plus 2%)
. . . .   4%
Overpayments (prior-year average investment yield on state money) 2%

IOWA
Rate set annually by Director
Underpayments and overpayments 8%

KANSAS
Adjusted annually
Underpayments and overpayments (1% plus fed. underpayment rate on 7-1 of
prior year) 7%

KENTUCKY
Adjusted annually
Underpayments and overpayments (prior Oct. adjusted prime rate) 7%

LOUISIANA
Underpayment rate contained in statute
Underpayments 14%
Overpayments (2% above average 52-week Treasury bill rate on 9-30 of prior
year) 8%

MAINE
Adjusted annually
Underpayments and overpayments (Effective on July 1, 2006, the interest rate
imposed on overpayments and underpayments is increased to the prime rate
plus 3% (previously, 2%).) 10%

MARYLAND
Adjusted annually
Underpayments (greater of 13% or 3% plus prime) 13%
Overpayments (2% plus average investment yield on state funds for prior fiscal
year) 4%

MASSACHUSETTS
Adjusted quarterly
Underpayments (4% plus fed. STR)

1-2006—3-2006	8%
4-2006—6-2006	8%
7-2006—9-2006	9%
10-2006—12-2006	9%

Overpayments (2% plus fed. STR)

1-2006—3-2006	6%
4-2006—6-2006	6%
7-2006—9-2006	7%
10-2006—12-2006	7%

MICHIGAN
Adjusted semiannually
Underpayments and overpayments (1% above adjusted prime rate)

1-2006—6-2006	7.2%
7-2006—12-2006	8.2%

MINNESOTA
Adjusted annually
Underpayments and overpayments (prime rate) 6%

MISSISSIPPI
Rate contained in statute
Underpayments and overpayments 12%

MISSOURI
Underpayments (prime rate) 7%
Overpayments (previous 12-month
annualized average rate of return on all
funds invested by the Treasurer)

1-2006—3-2006	2.7%
4-2006—6-2006	3%
7-2006—9-2006	3.4%
10-2006—12-2006	3.8%

MONTANA *
Rate contained in statute
Underpayments and overpayments 12%
* Montana does not impose a sales and use tax.

NEBRASKA
Adjusted biannually
Underpayments and overpayments (3% plus fed. STR from previous July) .. 6%

NEVADA *
Rate contained in statute
Underpayments... 12%
Overpayments.. 6%
* Nevada does not impose a corporate income tax or a personal income tax.

NEW HAMPSHIRE *
Adjusted annually
Underpayments (Sept fed. underpayment rate)...................... 8%
Overpayments (underpayment rate minus 3%) 5%
* New Hampshire does not impose a sales and use tax.

NEW JERSEY
Adjusted quarterly if prime rate varies by more than 1% from previously determined rate.
Underpayments (3% plus Dec. fed. prime rate)

                                                              10%

Overpayments (prime rate)

      7%

NEW MEXICO
Rate contained in statute
Underpayments and overpayments 15%

NEW YORK
Adjusted quarterly
Corporation franchise (income) tax
Underpayments (fed. STR plus 5%)

1-2006—3-2006	9%
4-2006—6-2006	9%
7-2006—9-2006	10%
10-2006—12-2006	10%

Overpayments (fed. STR plus 2%)

1-2006—3-2006	6%
4-2006—6-2006	6%
7-2006—9-2006	7%
10-2006—12-2006	7%

Personal income tax
Underpayments (fed. STR plus 2%, 6% min.)

1-2006—3-2006	8%
4-2006—6-2006	8%
7-2006—9-2006	9%
10-2006—12-2006	9%

Overpayments (fed. STR plus 2%)

1-2006—3-2006	6%
4-2006—6-2006	6%
7-2006—9-2006	7%
10-2006—12-2006	7%

Sales and use tax
Underpayments (greater of 12% or the underpayment rate set by the Commissioner)

1-2006—3-2006	14%
4-2006—6-2006	14%
7-2006—9-2006	14%
10-2006—12-2006	14%

Overpayments (fed. STR plus 2%)

1-2006—3-2006	6%
4-2006—6-2006	6%
7-2006—9-2006	7%
10-2006—12-2006	7%

NORTH CAROLINA
Rate established semiannually by the
Secretary of Revenue
Underpayments and overpayments

1-2006—6-2006	7%
7-2006—12-2006	7%

NORTH DAKOTA
Rate contained in statute
Underpayments 12%
Overpayments . . . .

Corporate and personal income . . .	12%
Sales and use	10%

OHIO
Adjusted annually
Underpayments and overpayments (3% plus fed. STR) 6%

OKLAHOMA
Rate contained in statute
Underpayments . . . .   15% *
Overpayments . . . .   15% **
* Underpayments of corporate or personal income estimated taxes accrue interest at
annual rate of 20% for the period of the underpayment, unless annual tax liability is less
than $1,000 or if the taxpayer was an Oklahoma resident throughout the preceding taxable
year of 12 months and did not have any tax liability for the preceding taxable year.
** For corporate and personal income estimated tax or withholding overpayment only.

OREGON *
Rate contained in statute
Underpayments and Overpayments 5%
* Oregon does not impose a sales and use tax.

PENNSYLVANIA
Adjusted annually
Underpayments (Jan. 1 fed. rate) 7%
Overpayments (Jan. 1 fed. rate minus 2%)* 5%*
*For personal income tax overpayments (Jan. 1 fed. rate), 7%

RHODE ISLAND
Adjusted annually
Underpayments and overpayments (2% plus Oct. prime rate; min. 12%; max.
21%) 12%
  (18%
  effective
  October
  1, 2006)

SOUTH CAROLINA
Underpayments and overpayments
(fed. underpayment rate)*

1-2006—3-2006	7%
4-2006—6-2006	7%
7-2006—9-2006	8%
10-2006—12-2006	8%

* Additional 2% rate for large corporate underpayments, as defined by IRC 6621(c).
*The interest rate on refunds paid from July 1, 2004, through June 30, 2006, is 2% below
the established rates listed above.

SOUTH DAKOTA*
Rate contained in statute
Underpayments . . . .

(unintentional)	15%
(intentional)	18%

Overpayments 6%
* South Dakota does not impose a corporate income tax or a personal income tax.

TENNESSEE
Rate set annually by Commissioner
Underpayments and overpayments

7-2005—6-2006	10%
7-2006—6-2007	12%

TEXAS *
Adjusted annually
Underpayments 8.25%
Overpayments 4.06825%
* Texas does not impose a personal income tax.

UTAH
Adjusted annually
Underpayments and overpayments (fed. STR plus 2%) 6%

VERMONT
Adjusted annually
Underpayments and overpayments (average prime rate during prior 12 mos.) 6%

VIRGINIA
Adjusted quarterly
Underpayments and overpayments (2% plus fed. underpayment rate)*

1-2006—3-2006	9%
4-2006—6-2006	9%
7-2006—9-2006	10%
10-2006—12-2006	10%

* Additional 2% rate for large corporate underpayments, as defined by IRC 6621(c).

WASHINGTON *
Adjusted annually
Underpayments and overpayments (average fed. STR for preceding calendar
year plus 2%) 5%
* Washington does not impose a corporate income tax or a personal income tax.

WEST VIRGINIA
Adjusted semiannually
Underpayments

1-2006—6-2006	9.5%
7-2006—12-2006	9.5%

Overpayments

1-2006—6-2006	8%
7-2006—12-2006	8%

WISCONSIN
Rate contained in statute
Underpayments . . . .

Delinquent taxes	18%
Nondelinquent	12%

Overpayments 9%

WYOMING *
Adjusted annually
Underpayments (4% plus prime rate during preceding fiscal year) 9.1791%
Overpayments . . . . None
* Wyoming does not impose a corporate income tax or a personal income tax.

Interest Rates on Underpayments and Overpayments 2005

Interest rates on underpayments and overpayments are set either by statute or by regulation pursuant to a statutory formula. Interest rates keyed to the prevailing prime rate at leading commercial banks or the prevailing discount rate generally are rounded to the nearest whole number. State rates keyed to the prevailing federal short-term rate (STR), as determined by Internal Revenue Code Sec. 6621(b), are rounded by all states to the nearest whole number. Most state rates are not adjusted if the relevant commercial or federal interest rate is less than 1% more or less than the state rate then in effect.

Chart reflecting rates for 2005: The following chart provides interest rates for 2005 listed in descending order, ending in the final quarter. The statutory formula used by each state to determine rates is also listed. NA denotes that interest rates for a given period are not yet available.

ALABAMA
Adjusted quarterly
Underpayments and overpayments (fed.
underpayment rate)

1-2005—3-2005	5%
4-2005—6-2005	6%
7-2005—9-2005	6%
10-2005—12-2005	7%

ALASKA*
Adjusted quarterly
Underpayments and overpayments (greater of 11% or fed. STR plus 5%)

1-2005—3-2005	11%
4-2005—6-2005	11%
7-2005—9-2005	11%
10-2005—12-2005	11%

* Alaska does not impose a personal income tax or a sales and use tax.

ARIZONA
Adjusted quarterly
Underpayments and overpayments (fed. underpayment rate)

1-2005—3-2005	5%
4-2005—6-2005	6%
7-2005—9-2005	6%
10-2005—12-2005	7%

ARKANSAS
Rate contained in statute
Underpayments and overpayments 10%

CALIFORNIA
Adjusted semiannually
Personal income tax rates
Underpayments and overpayments (fed. rate)

1-2005—6-2005	4%
7-2005—12-2005	5%

Corporation franchise (income) tax rates

Underpayments

1-2005—6-2005	4%*
7-2005—12-2005	5%

Overpayments

1-2005—6-2005	1%
7-2005—12-2005	2%

* Additional 2% rate for large corporate underpayments, as defined by IRC 6621(c).

Sales and use tax rates

Underpayments (3% plus fed. underpayment
rate for previous January or July)

1-2005—6-2005	7%
7-2005—12-2005	8%

Overpayments (13-week Treasury bill rates)

1-2005—6-2005	1%
7-2005—12-2005	2%

COLORADO

Adjusted annually

Underpayments and overpayments (previous 7-1 prime plus 3%) 7%

CONNECTICUT

Rate contained in statute

Underpayments 12%

Overpayments . . . .

Corporate income	8%
Personal income	9%
Sales and use:	12% *

* If the Commissioner, in his discretion, offsets any overpaid taxes against underpayments, the interest allowed on the overpayment and charged to the underpayment is also computed at 1% per month.

DELAWARE*

Rate contained in statute

Underpayments and overpayments 12%

* Delaware does not impose a sales and use tax.

DISTRICT OF COLUMBIA

Rate contained in statute

Underpayments 10%

Overpayments 6%

FLORIDA*

Adjusted semiannually

Underpayments and overpayments
(adjusted prime rate plus 4%)

1-2005—6-2005	8%
7-2005—12-2005	9%

* Florida does not impose a personal income tax.

GEORGIA

Rate contained in statute

Underpayments and overpayments 12%

HAWAII

Rate contained in statute

Underpayments and overpayments 8%

IDAHO
Adjusted annually

Underpayments and overpayments (2% plus fed. mid-term rate as applied on Oct. 15 of prior year) 6%

ILLINOIS
Adjusted semiannually

Underpayments and overpayments*

1-2005—6-2005	2%
7-2005—12-2005	3%

For periods after 2003, the interest rate charged on tax underpayments and paid on tax overpayments is (1) for the one-year period beginning with the date of underpayment or overpayment, the short-term federal rate under IRC Sec. 6621, and (2) for any period after the one-year period, the underpayment rate under IRC Sec. 6621.

INDIANA
Adjusted annually

Underpayments (prior-year average investment yield on state money, plus 2%) 3%

Overpayments (prior-year average investment yield on state money) 1%

IOWA
Rate set annually by Director

Underpayments and overpayments 6%

KANSAS
Adjusted annually

Underpayments and overpayments (1% plus fed. underpayment rate on 7-1 of prior year) 5%

KENTUCKY
Adjusted annually

Underpayments and overpayments (prior Oct. adjusted prime rate) 5%

LOUISIANA
Underpayment rate contained in statute

Underpayments 15%

Overpayments (2% above average 52-week Treasury bill rate on 9-30 of prior year) . . 6%

MAINE
Adjusted annually

Underpayments and overpayments (Effective on July 1, 2005, the interest rate imposed on overpayments and underpayments is increased to the prime rate plus 3% (previously, 2%).) 8%

MARYLAND
Adjusted annually

Underpayments (greater of 13% or 3% plus prime) 13%

Overpayments (2% plus average investment yield on state funds for prior fiscal year) . 3%

MASSACHUSETTS
Adjusted quarterly

Underpayments (4% plus fed. STR)

1-2005—3-2005	6%
4-2005—6-2005	7%
7-2005—9-2005	7%
10-2005—12-2005	8%

Overpayments (2% plus fed. STR)

1-2005—3-2005	....	4%
4-2005—6-2005	....	5%
7-2005—9-2005	....	5%
10-2005—12-2005	....	6%

MICHIGAN
Adjusted semiannually
Underpayments and overpayments (1% above adjusted prime rate)

1-2005—6-2005	....	5.2%
7-2005—12-2005	....	6.2%

MINNESOTA
Adjusted annually
Underpayments and overpayments (prime rate) 4%

MISSISSIPPI
Rate contained in statute
Underpayments and overpayments 12%

MISSOURI
Underpayments (prime rate) 5%
Overpayments (previous 12-month
annualized average rate of return on all
funds invested by the Treasurer)

1-2005—3-2005	....	1.7%
4-2005—6-2005	....	1.7%
7-2005—9-2005	....	2.0%
10-2005—12-2005	....	2.3%

MONTANA *
Rate contained in statute
Underpayments and overpayments 12%
* Montana does not impose a sales and use tax.

NEBRASKA
Adjusted biannually
Underpayments and overpayments (3% plus fed. STR from previous July) 6%

NEVADA *
Rate contained in statute
Underpayments 12%
Overpayments 6%
* Nevada does not impose a corporate income tax or a personal income tax.

NEW HAMPSHIRE *
Adjusted annually
Underpayments (Sept fed. underpayment rate) 6%
Overpayments (underpayment rate minus 3%) 3%
* New Hampshire does not impose a sales and use tax.

NEW JERSEY
Adjusted quarterly
Underpayments (3% plus Dec. fed. prime rate)

1-2005—3-2005	....	8%
4-2005—6-2005	....	8%
7-2005—9-2005	....	8%
10-2005—12-2005	....	9.5%

Overpayments (prime rate)

1-2005—3-2005	5%
4-2005—6-2005	5%
7-2005—9-2005	5%
10-2005—12-2005	5%

NEW MEXICO
Rate contained in statute

Underpayments and overpayments	15%

NEW YORK
Adjusted quarterly
Corporation franchise (income) tax
Underpayments (fed. STR plus 5%)

1-2005—3-2005	7%
4-2005—6-2005	8%
7-2005—9-2005	8%
10-2005—12-2005	9%

Overpayments (fed. STR plus 2%)

1-2005—3-2005	4%
4-2005—6-2005	5%
7-2005—9-2005	5%
10-2005—12-2005	6%

Personal Income tax
Underpayments (fed. STR plus 2%, 6% min.)

1-2005—3-2005	6%
4-2005—6-2005	7%
7-2005—9-2005	7%
10-2005—12-2005	8%

Overpayments (fed. STR plus 2%)

1-2005—3-2005	4%
4-2005—6-2005	5%
7-2005—9-2005	5%
10-2005—12-2005	6%

Sales and use tax
Underpayments (greater of 12% or the underpayment rate set by the Commissioner)

1-2005—3-2005	14%
4-2005—6-2005	14%
7-2005—9-2005	14%
10-2005—12-2005	14%

Overpayments (fed. STR plus 2%)

1-2005—3-2005	4%
4-2005—6-2005	5%
7-2005—9-2005	5%
10-2005—12-2005	6%

NORTH CAROLINA
Rate established semiannually by the
Secretary of Revenue
Underpayments and overpayments

1-2005—6-2005	5%
7-2005—12-2005	5%

NORTH DAKOTA
Rate contained in statute

Underpayments		12%
Overpayments		
	Corporate and personal income	12%
	Sales and use	10%

OHIO
Adjusted annually

Underpayments and overpayments (3% plus fed. STR)	5%

OKLAHOMA
Rate contained in statute

Underpayments	15% *
Overpayments	15% **

* Underpayments of corporate or personal income estimated taxes accrue interest at annual rate of 20% for the period of the underpayment, unless annual tax liability is less than $1,000 or if the taxpayer was an Oklahoma resident throughout the preceding taxable year of 12 months and did not have any tax liability for the preceding taxable year.

** For corporate and personal income estimated tax or withholding overpayment only.

OREGON *
Rate contained in statute

Underpayments	6%
Overpayments	6%

* Oregon does not impose a sales and use tax.

PENNSYLVANIA
Adjusted annually

Underpayments (Jan. 1 fed. rate)	5%
Overpayments (Jan. 1 fed. rate minus 2%)*	3%*

*For personal income tax overpayments (Jan. 1 fed. rate), 5%

RHODE ISLAND
Adjusted annually

Underpayments and overpayments (2% plus Oct. prime rate; min. 12%; max. 21%) . . .	12%

SOUTH CAROLINA
Adjusted quarterly

Underpayments and overpayments (fed. underpayment rate)*

	1-2005—3-2005	5%
	4-2005—6-2005	6%
	7-2005—9-2005	6%
	10-2005—12-2005	7%

* Additional 2% rate for large corporate underpayments, as defined by IRC 6621(c).

*The interest rate on refunds paid from July 1, 2004, through June 30, 2006, is 2% below the established rates listed above.

SOUTH DAKOTA*
Rate contained in statute

Underpayments		
	(unintentional)	15%
	(intentional)	18%
Overpayments	6%

* South Dakota does not impose a corporate income tax or a personal income tax.

TENNESSEE
Rate set annually by Commissioner
Underpayments and overpayments

7-2004—6-2005	8%
7-2005—6-2006	10%

TEXAS *
Adjusted annually
Underpayments and overpayments (Jan. prime plus 1%) 6.25%
* Texas does not impose a personal income tax.

UTAH
Adjusted annually
Underpayments and overpayments (fed. STR plus 2%) 4%

VERMONT
Adjusted annually
Underpayments and overpayments (average prime rate during prior 12 mos.) 6%

VIRGINIA
Adjusted quarterly
Underpayments and overpayments (2% plus fed. underpayment rate)*

1-2005—3-2005	7%
4-2005—6-2005	8%
7-2005—9-2005	8%
10-2005—12-2005	9%

* Additional 2% rate for large corporate underpayments, as defined by IRC 6621(c).

WASHINGTON *
Adjusted annually
Underpayments and overpayments (average fed. STR for preceding calendar year plus 2%) 4%
* Washington does not impose a corporate income tax or a personal income tax.

WEST VIRGINIA
Adjusted semiannually
Underpayments

1-2005—6-2005	9.5%
7-2005—12-2005	9.5%

Overpayments

1-2005—6-2005	8%
7-2005—12-2005	8%

WISCONSIN
Rate contained in statute
Underpayments . . . .

Delinquent taxes	18%
Nondelinquent	12%

Overpayments 9%

WYOMING *
Adjusted annually
Underpayments (4% plus prime rate during preceding fiscal year) 8.001%
Overpayments . . . . None
* Wyoming does not impose a corporate income tax or a personal income tax.

Interest Rates on Underpayments and Overpayments 2004

Interest rates on underpayments and overpayments are set either by statute or by regulation pursuant to a statutory formula. Interest rates keyed to the prevailing prime rate at leading commercial banks or the prevailing discount rate generally are rounded to the nearest whole number. State rates keyed to the prevailing federal short-term rate (STR), as determined by Internal Revenue Code Sec. 6621(b), are rounded by all states to the nearest whole number. Most state rates are not adjusted if the relevant commercial or federal interest rate is less than 1% more or less than the state rate then in effect.

Chart reflecting rates for 2004: The following chart provides interest rates for 2004 listed in descending order, ending in the final quarter. The statutory formula used by each state to determine rates is also listed. NA denotes that interest rates for a given period are not yet available.

ALABAMA
Adjusted quarterly
Underpayments and overpayments (fed. underpayment rate)

1-2004—3-2004	4%
4-2004—6-2004	5%
7-2004—9-2004	4%
10-2004—12-2004	5%

ALASKA*
Adjusted quarterly
Underpayments and overpayments (greater of 11% or fed. STR plus 5%)

1-2004—3-2004	11%
4-2004—6-2004	11%
7-2004—9-2004	11%
10-2004—12-2004	11%

* Alaska does not impose a personal income tax or a sales and use tax.

ARIZONA
Adjusted quarterly
Underpayments and overpayments (fed. underpayment rate)

1-2004—3-2004	4%
4-2004—6-2004	5%
7-2004—9-2004	4%
10-2004—12-2004	5%

ARKANSAS
Rate contained in statute

Underpayments and overpayments	10%

CALIFORNIA
Adjusted semiannually
Corporation franchise (income) and personal income tax rates
Underpayments and overpayments (fed. rate)

1-2004—6-2004	5%*
7-2004—12-2004	4%*

* Additional 2% rate for large corporate underpayments, as defined by IRC 6621(c).

Sales and use tax rates

Underpayments (3% plus fed. underpayment
rate for previous January or July)

1-2004—6-2004	8%
7-2004—12-2004	7%

Overpayments (13-week Treasury bill rates)

1-2004—6-2004	1%
7-2004—12-2004	1%

COLORADO

Adjusted annually

Underpayments and overpayments (previous 7-1 prime plus 3%) 7%

CONNECTICUT

Rate contained in statute

Underpayments 12%

Overpayments ....

Corporate income	8%
Personal income	9%
Sales and use:	12% *

* If the Commissioner, in his discretion, offsets any overpaid taxes against underpayments, the interest allowed on the overpayment and charged to the underpayment is also computed at 1% per month.

DELAWARE*

Rate contained in statute

Underpayments and overpayments 12%

* Delaware does not impose a sales and use tax.

DISTRICT OF COLUMBIA

Rate contained in statute

Underpayments 10%

Overpayments 6%

FLORIDA *

Adjusted semiannually

Underpayments and overpayments
(adjusted prime rate plus 4%)

1-2004—6-2004	8%
7-2004—12-2004	8%

* Florida does not impose a personal income tax.

GEORGIA

Rate contained in statute

Underpayments and overpayments 12%

HAWAII

Rate contained in statute

Underpayments and overpayments 8%

IDAHO

Adjusted annually

Underpayments and overpayments (2% plus fed. mid-term rate as applied on Oct. 15 of prior year) 6%

ILLINOIS
Adjusted semiannually
Underpayments and overpayments*

1-2004—6-2004	1%
7-2004—12-2004	1%

For periods after 2003, the interest rate charged on tax underpayments and paid on tax overpayments is (1) for the one-year period beginning with the date of underpayment or overpayment, the short-term federal rate under IRC Sec. 6621, and (2) for any period after the one-year period, the underpayment rate under IRC Sec. 6621.

INDIANA
Adjusted annually

Underpayments (prior-year average investment yield on state money, plus 2%)	4%
Overpayments (prior-year average investment yield on state money)	2%

IOWA
Rate set annually by Director

Underpayments and overpayments	6%

KANSAS
Adjusted annually

Underpayments and overpayments (1% plus fed. underpayment rate on 7-1 of prior year)	6%

KENTUCKY
Adjusted annually

Underpayments and overpayments (prior Oct. adjusted prime rate)	4%

LOUISIANA
Underpayment rate contained in statute

Underpayments	15%
Overpayments (2% above average 52-week Treasury bill rate on 9-30 of prior year) . .	5.25%

MAINE
Adjusted annually

Underpayments and overpayments (conventional rate for unsecured commercial loans on 1st business day of preceding October) (Effective on July 1, 2004, the interest rate imposed on overpayments and underpayments is increased to the prime rate plus 3% (previously, 2%).)	6%

MARYLAND
Adjusted annually

Underpayments (greater of 13% or 3% plus prime)	13%
Overpayments (2% plus average investment yield on state funds for prior fiscal year) .	4%

MASSACHUSETTS
Adjusted quarterly
Underpayments (4% plus fed. STR)

1-2004—3-2004	5%
4-2004—6-2004	6%
7-2004—9-2004	5%
10-2004—12-2004	6%

Overpayments (effective 7/1/03, 2% plus fed. STR)

1-2004—3-2004	3%
4-2004—6-2004	4%
7-2004—9-2004	3%
10-2004—12-2004	4%

MICHIGAN
Adjusted semiannually
Underpayments and overpayments (1% above adjusted prime rate)

1-2004—6-2004	5%
7-2004—12-2004	5%

MINNESOTA
Adjusted annually
Underpayments and overpayments (prime rate) 4%

MISSISSIPPI
Rate contained in statute
Underpayments and overpayments 12%

MISSOURI
Underpayments (prime rate) 4%
Overpayments (previous 12-month annualized average rate of return on all funds invested by the Treasurer)

1-2004—3-2004	2.1%
4-2004—6-2004	2.1%
7-2004—9-2004	1.8%
10-2004—12-2004	1.7%

MONTANA *
Rate contained in statute
Underpayments and overpayments 12%
* Montana does not impose a sales and use tax.

NEBRASKA
Adjusted biannually
Underpayments and overpayments (3% plus fed. STR from previous July) 6%

NEVADA *
Rate contained in statute
Underpayments 12%
Overpayments 6%
* Nevada does not impose a corporate income tax or a personal income tax.

NEW HAMPSHIRE *
Adjusted annually
Underpayments (Sept fed. underpayment rate) 7%
Overpayments (underpayment rate minus 3%) 4%
* New Hampshire does not impose a sales and use tax.

NEW JERSEY
Adjusted quarterly
Underpayments (3% plus Dec. fed. prime rate)

1-2004—3-2004	7%
4-2004—6-2004	7%
7-2004—9-2004	7%
10-2004—12-2004	7%

Overpayments (prime rate)

1-2004—3-2004	4%
4-2004—6-2004	4%
7-2004—9-2004	4%
10-2004—12-2004	4%

NEW MEXICO
Rate contained in statute
Underpayments and overpayments 15%

NEW YORK
Adjusted quarterly
Corporation franchise (income) tax
Underpayments (fed. STR plus 3%) (5% eff. 4/1/03)

1-2004—3-2004	6%
4-2004—6-2004	7%
7-2004—9-2004	14%
10-2004—12-2004	14%

Overpayments (fed. STR plus 2%)

1-2004—3-2004	3%
4-2004—6-2004	4%
7-2004—9-2004	3%
10-2004—12-2004	4%

Personal income tax
Underpayments (fed. STR plus 2%, 6% min.)

1-2004—3-2004	6%
4-2004—6-2004	6%
7-2004—9-2004	6%
10-2004—12-2004	6%

Overpayments (fed. STR plus 2%)

1-2004—3-2004	3%
4-2004—6-2004	4%
7-2004—9-2004	3%
10-2004—12-2004	4%

Sales and use tax
Underpayments (greater of 12% or the underpayment rate set by the Commissioner)

1-2004—3-2004	14%
4-2004—6-2004	14%
7-2004—9-2004	14%
10-2004—12-2004	14%

Overpayments (fed. STR plus 2%)

1-2004—3-2004	3%
4-2004—6-2004	4%
7-2004—9-2004	3%
10-2004—12-2004	4%

NORTH CAROLINA
Rate established semiannually by the
Secretary of Revenue
Underpayments and overpayments

1-2004—6-2004	5%
7-2004—12-2004	5%

NORTH DAKOTA
Rate contained in statute
Underpayments 12%
Overpayments ....

Corporate and personal income	12%
Sales and use	10%

OHIO
Adjusted annually
Underpayments and overpayments (3% plus fed. STR) 4%

OKLAHOMA
Rate contained in statute
Underpayments .... 15% *
Overpayments .... 15% **
* Underpayments of corporate or personal income estimated taxes accrue interest at annual rate of 20% for the period of the underpayment, unless annual tax liability is less than $1,000 or if the taxpayer was an Oklahoma resident throughout the preceding taxable year of 12 months and did not have any tax liability for the preceding taxable year.
** For corporate and personal income estimated tax or withholding overpayment only.

OREGON *
Rate contained in statute
Underpayments 6%
Overpayments 6%
* Oregon does not impose a sales and use tax.

PENNSYLVANIA
Adjusted annually
Underpayments (Jan. 1 fed. rate) 4%
Overpayments (Jan. 1 fed. rate minus 2%)* 2%*
*For personal income tax overpayments (Jan. 1 fed. rate), 4%

RHODE ISLAND
Adjusted annually
Underpayments and overpayments (2% plus Oct. prime rate; min. 12%; max. 21%) . . . 12%

SOUTH CAROLINA
Adjusted quarterly
Underpayments and overpayments (fed. underpayment rate)*

1-2004—3-2004	4%
4-2004—6-2004	5%
7-2004—9-2004	4%
10-2004—12-2004	5%

* Additional 2% rate for large corporate underpayments, as defined by IRC 6621(c).
*The interest rate on refunds paid from July 1, 2004, through June 30, 2005, is 2% below the established rates listed above

SOUTH DAKOTA*
Rate contained in statute
Underpayments ....

(unintentional)	15%
(intentional)	18%

Overpayments 6%
* South Dakota does not impose a corporate income tax or a personal income tax.

TENNESSEE
Rate set annually by Commissioner
Underpayments and overpayments

7-2003—6-2004	8.25%
7-2004—6-2005	8%

TEXAS *
Adjusted annually
Underpayments and overpayments (prime plus 1%) 5%
* Texas does not impose a personal income tax.

UTAH
Adjusted annually
Underpayments and overpayments (fed. STR plus 2%) 3%

VERMONT
Adjusted annually
Underpayments and overpayments (average prime rate during prior 12 mos.) 6%

VIRGINIA
Adjusted quarterly
Underpayments and overpayments (fed. underpayment rate plus 2%)*

1-2004—3-2004	6%
4-2004—6-2004	7%
7-2004—9-2004	6%
10-2004—12-2004	7%

* Additional 2% rate for large corporate underpayments, as defined by IRC 6621(c).

WASHINGTON *
Adjusted annually
Underpayments and overpayments (average fed. STR for preceding calendar year plus 2%) 4%
* Washington does not impose a corporate income tax or a personal income tax.

WEST VIRGINIA
Adjusted semiannually
Underpayments

1-2004—6-2004	9.5%
7-2004—12-2004	9.5%

Overpayments

1-2004—6-2004	8%
7-2004—12-2004	8%

WISCONSIN
Rate contained in statute
Underpayments ....

Delinquent taxes	18%
Nondelinquent.................	12%

Overpayments 9%

WYOMING *
Adjusted annually
Underpayments (4% plus prime rate during preceding fiscal year) 8.427%
Overpayments ....   None
* Wyoming does not impose a corporate income tax or a personal income tax.

Mailing Rules

Most states provide that a return or payment is considered timely filed if the return or payment is placed in a properly addressed envelope and postmarked not later than the due date of the return or payment, regardless of when the return or payment is actually received by the tax authority. Additionally, some states extend this policy to include not only the U.S. Postal Service, but also private delivery services (such as those authorized under Sec. 7502(f) of the Internal Revenue Code).

The chart below indicates those states that follow the postmark rule, as well as those that extend the rule to private delivery services.

Weekends and holidays: All states provide that when a return or payment is due on a Saturday, Sunday, or legal holiday, the due date is extended to the first business day following the Saturday, Sunday, or legal holiday.

State	Postmark	Delivery Services	State	Postmark	Delivery Services
Alabama	Y	Y	Montana	Y	N
Alaska	Y	N	Nebraska	Y	N
Arizona	Y	Y	Nevada	Y	N
Arkansas	Y	N	New Hampshire	Y	N
California	Y	Y	New Jersey	Y	Y
Colorado	Y	Y	New Mexico	Y	Y
Connecticut	Y	Y	New York	Y	N
Delaware	Y	Y	North Carolina	Y	N
District of Columbia	Y	Y	North Dakota	Y	Y
Florida	Y	N	Ohio	Y	Y
Georgia	Y	Y	Oklahoma	Y	Y
Hawaii	Y	Y	Oregon	Y	Y
Idaho	Y	N	Pennsylvania	Y	N
Illinois	Y	N	Rhode Island	Y	Y
Indiana	Y	N	South Carolina	Y	Y
Iowa	Y	N	South Dakota	Y	N
Kansas	Y	Y	Tennessee	Y	Y
Kentucky	Y	N	Texas	Y	Y
Louisiana	Y	Y	Utah	Y	N
Maine	Y	N	Vermont	Y	N
Maryland	Y	Y	Virginia	Y	N
Massachusetts	Y	Y	Washington	Y	N
Michigan	Y	N	West Virginia	Y	N
Minnesota	Y	Y	Wisconsin	Y	N
Mississippi	Y	N	Wyoming	Y	N
Missouri	Y	N			

Managed Audits

A growing number of states are utilizing taxpayer-initiated or managed audits to reduce costs and improve tax compliance. Under a managed audit, the state sets up specific audit procedures and guidelines and the taxpayer or a third party hired by the taxpayer performs the audit. The state then reviews the taxpayer's results and issues an assessment for any unpaid taxes. All states with managed audit programs require a written agreement between the state and the taxpayer prior to the commencement of the audit to set forth the audit period, procedures, and scope of the audit.

As an incentive for taxpayers to utilize the program, many states offer a reduction or waiver of penalties and interest due for tax liabilities revealed during the audit period. Other advantages include reduced time spent at the business location by the auditor, time saved through the use of employees already familiar with the records and returns, and a limitation on the inclusion of "gray areas" in the audit.

Many states have eligibility requirements for participation in a managed audit program. Such requirements typically include a history of tax compliance, adequate resources available to dedicate to the audit, and an acceptable system of business recordkeeping.

The chart below sets forth the states that currently have managed audit programs or similar programs.

State	Managed Audit Provisions
Arizona	Managed audit applications may be submitted beginning in 2006 (2007 for corporate income tax).
California	Limited to sales and use tax.
Connecticut	Limited to sales and use tax.
Florida	State offers Certified Audit Program. Certified audits must be performed by qualified third parties.
Georgia	Managed audit agreement is unique for each taxpayer.
Idaho	Taxpayers seeking information on managed audits should contact Idaho State Tax Commission.
Illinois	State does not allow managed audits but does allow use tax managed compliance agreements.
Kansas	Limited to sales and use tax.
Maine	State has no formal provisions allowing managed audits, but Maine Revenue Services may make informal arrangements with a taxpayer to permit the taxpayer to perform some audit procedures.
Maryland	Limited to sales and use tax and unclaimed property.
Michigan	Taxpayers seeking information on managed audits should contact Department of Treasury Audit Discovery Division.
Minnesota	Field auditors may allow taxpayers to examine their own records during the course of a field audit if the auditor believes the taxpayer understands the issue to be examined.

State	Managed Audit Provisions
Nebraska	State offers Partnered Audit Program for all tax types except motor fuels, gaming, and property taxes. Allowed generally for small- to medium-sized businesses.
New Jersey	State does not offer a managed audit program but does allow use tax managed compliance agreements.
New Mexico	Applicable to all taxes administered pursuant to the Tax Administration Act.
North Carolina	Limited to sales and use tax and generally limited to businesses that do not make a large number of retail sales.
Ohio	Limited to sales and use tax. Preferred for businesses with few statutory exemptions and less complex audit issues.
Pennsylvania	State offers use tax compliance program that allows businesses to perform self-audits to determine use tax liability.
South Carolina	Informal program, generally limited to use tax compliance issues for small taxpayers.
Texas	Limited to sales and use tax.
Utah	Specific industries are selected for the self-review program.
Virginia	State does not allow managed audits but does allow use tax managed compliance agreements.
Washington	Under the Department of Revenue's managed audit program, the auditor assigned to the business determines whether the business has the ability to perform specific audit procedures.
Wisconsin	Limited to sales and use tax.

Record Retention

All states require taxpayers to maintain records to indicate the amount due for each tax administered by the state. Most states specify the period for which these records must be retained, while some states merely require that the records be kept without identifying a retention period.

The chart below indicates the specified record retention period (in years) for each state and tax. Entries marked with an asterisk (*) indicate that the state does not specify the retention period, while entries marked with an "N" indicate that the state does not impose that particular tax. The retention period may be extended due to audit, appeal, or agreement.

The following abbreviations are used for tax types: CI=Corporate Income; PI=Personal Income; SU=Sales and Use; MF=Motor Fuels or Gasoline; C/T=Cigarette; or Tobacco; and WH=Personal Income Withholding.

State	CI	PI	SU	MF	C/T	WH
Alabama	3	3	3	3	3	3
Alaska	*	N	N	*	*	N
Arizona	4	4	6	3	2	*
Arkansas	6	6	6	6	6	6
California	*[1]	*	4	4	4	*
Colorado	4	4	3	3	3	4
Connecticut	*	*	3	3	*	4
Delaware	3	*	3[2]	3	*	*
District of Columbia	*	*	*	*	*	*
Florida	3	N	5	3	3	N
Georgia	3	4	3	3	*	4
Hawaii	3	3	3	3	3	3
Idaho	*	*	4	*	*	4
Illinois	3	3	3	3	*	3
Indiana	3	3	3	3	3	5
Iowa	3	3	5	3	2	3
Kansas	3	3	3	4	3	3
Kentucky	4	4	4	4	4	4
Louisiana	3	3	3	2	3	3
Maine	3	3	6	4	6	6
Maryland	10[3]	10[3]	4	4	6	10
Massachusetts	3	3	3	3	3	3
Michigan	*	6	4	4	*	*
Minnesota	4	4	*	3.5	3.5	*
Mississippi	*	*	3	3	*	3
Missouri	4	4	3	*	3	*
Montana	*	*	N	3	*	5
Nebraska	*	*	3	3	*	*

State	CI	PI	SU	MF	C/T	WH
Nevada	N[4]	N[4]	4	3	*	N
New Hampshire	3/5[5]	*	N[6]	4	3	*
New Jersey	*	*	4	4	3	*
New Mexico	3	3	3	3	3	3
New York	*	4	3	*	*	*
North Carolina	*	*	3	3	*	*
North Dakota	3	3	3.25	3	*	3
Ohio	4	4	4	4	3	*
Oklahoma	*	*	3	*	*	*
Oregon	*[7]	*[7]	N	*[7]	*[7]	*[7]
Pennsylvania	3	4	3	2	*	*
Rhode Island	*	*	3	*	3	*
South Carolina	4	4	4	4	4	4
South Dakota	6[8]	N	3	3	*	N
Tennessee	3[9]	*	3	3	3	*
Texas	*	N	4	*	*	N
Utah	*	*	3	3	3	*
Vermont	*	*	*	3	3	*
Virginia	3	3	3	3	3	3
Washington	N[10]	N[10]	5	5	5	N
West Virginia	3[3]	3	3	3	3	5
Wisconsin	4	4	4	*	*	*
Wyoming	N	N	3	3	3	*

---

[1] Records must be kept for the period of time in which the taxpayer's franchise or income tax liability is subject to adjustment, but not to exceed eight years from the due date; the period of time during which a protest is pending before the FTB; the period of time during which an appeal is pending before the State Board of Equalization; or the period of time during which a refund lawsuit is pending in a state or federal court.

[2] Although Delaware does not impose a sales and use tax, records must be kept for use tax on leases of tangible personal property.

[3] Record retention period recommended by the Department.

[4] Business tax—4 yrs.

[5] Business and profits tax—3 yrs.; Business enterprise tax—5 yrs.

[6] Meals and Rooms tax 3 yrs.

[7] Record retention based on variable limitations periods.

[8] Banks and financial corporations only.

[9] Business and occupation tax.

[10] Business and occupation tax—5 yrs.

State Contacts

The following chart provides information that may be used to contact appropriate state sales and use tax agencies (for states with sales and use taxes). The listed mailing addresses and phone numbers (and email addresses, where available), are based upon information gathered from the state agencies and are subject to change. The names of individual state tax officials are also listed, where provided. The website addresses listed, which provide access to further information about a state's sales and use tax agency, should be checked prior to contact for verification.

States that do not impose sales and use tax are not included.

ALABAMA

Agency/Contact	Alabama Department of Revenue
Mailing Address	50 N. Ripley St. Montgomery, AL 36132
Telephone	(334) 242-1170
Website: http//	www.ador.state.al.us

ARIZONA

Agency/Contact	Arizona Department of Revenue
Mailing Address	Taxpayer Information and Assistance, P.O. Box 29086, Phoenix, AZ 85038-9086
Telephone	(800) 843-7196 (from 520 or 928 area code), (602) 255-2060
Website: http//	www.revenue.state.az.us

ARKANSAS

Agency/Contact	Arkansas Department of Finance and Administration, Roberta Overman, Manager, Sales and Use Tax Section,
Mailing Address	Office of Excise Tax Administration, 1816 W. 7th St. Rm. 1330, Little Rock, AR 72201
Telephone	(501) 682-1895
Email	sales.tax@rev.state.ar.us
Website: http//	www.state.ar.us/dfa/excise_tax_v2/st_index.html

CALIFORNIA

Agency/Contact	California State Board of Equalization (5 members)
Mailing Address	P.O. Box 942879, Sacramento, CA 94279-0001
Telephone	(800) 400-7115
Email	www.boe.ca.gov/info/email.html
Website: http//	www.boe.ca.gov

COLORADO

Agency/Contact	Colorado Department of Revenue, Taxpayer Service Division
Mailing Address	1375 Sherman Street, Denver, CO 80261-0013
Telephone	(303) 238-7378
Website: http//	www.revenue.state.co.us

CONNECTICUT

Agency/Contact	Connecticut Department of Revenue, Taxpayer Services Division
Mailing Address	25 Sigourney Street, Hartford, CT 06106-5032
Telephone	800-382-9463 (CT only), 860-297-5962
Email	drs@po.state.ct.us
Website: http//	www.ct.gov/drs

DELAWARE

Agency/Contact . . . . Delaware Department of Finance, Division of Revenue, Office of Business Taxes, John J. Maciejeski, Jr., Asst. Director

Mailing Address . . . . Carvel State Office Bldg., 820 N. French St., Wilmington, DE 19899

Telephone . . . . Business taxes: 302-577-8205

Website: http// . . . . www.state.de.us/revenue/default.shtml

DISTRICT OF COLUMBIA

Agency/Contact . . . . Office of the Chief Financial Officer, Office of Tax and Revenue

Mailing Address . . . . 941 N. Capital St., NE, 1st Floor, Washington, DC 20002

Telephone 202-727-4TAX

Website: http// . . . . cfo.dc.gov

FLORIDA

Agency/Contact . . . . Florida Department of Revenue

Mailing Address . . . . Tax Information Services, 1379 Blountstown Hwy., Tallahassee, FL 32304-2716

Telephone . . . . 800-352-3671 (FL only), 850-488-6800

Website: http// sun6.dms.state.fl.us/dor

GEORGIA

Agency/Contact . . . . Georgia Department of Revenue, Taxpayer Services Division

Mailing Address . . . . 1800 Century Blvd., N.E., Atlanta, GA 30345

Telephone . . . . (404) 417-6601

Email . . . . taxpayer.services@dor.ga.gov

Website: http// . . . . www.etax.dor.ga.gov/

HAWAII

Agency/Contact . . . . Hawaii Department of Taxation, Taxpayer Services

Mailing Address . . . . P.O. Box 259, Honolulu, HI 96809-0259

Telephone . . . . (800) 222-3229, (808) 587-4242;

Email . . . . Taxpayer.Services@hawaii.gov

Website: http// . . . . www.state.hi.us/tax/tax.html

IDAHO

Agency/Contact . . . . Idaho State Tax Commission

Mailing Address . . . . P.O. Box 36, Boise, ID 83722-0410

Telephone . . . . (800) 972-7660

Email . . . . taxrep@tax.idaho.gov

Website: http// . . . . tax.idaho.gov/

ILLINOIS

Agency/Contact . . . . Illinois Department of Revenue

Mailing Address . . . . James R. Thompson Center, 100 W. Randolph St., Chicago, IL 60601-3274

Telephone . . . . (800) 732-8866, (217) 782-3336

Website: http// . . . . www.revenue.state.il.us/

INDIANA

Agency/Contact . . . . Indiana Department of Revenue

Mailing Address . . . . 100 N. Senate Ave., Indianapolis, IN 46204

Telephone . . . . (317) 233-4015

Email . . . . www.in.gov/dor/contact/email.html

Website: http// . . . . www.in.gov/dor/

IOWA

Agency/Contact	Iowa Department of Revenue
Mailing Address	Taxpayer Services, P.O. Box 10457, Des Moines, IA 50306-0457
Telephone	(800) 367-3388 (IA only), (515) 281-3114
Email	idrf@idrf.state.ia.us
Website: http//	www.state.ia.us/tax/

KANSAS

Agency/Contact	Kansas Department of Revenue, Topeka Assistance Center
Mailing Address	Docking State Office Building, 915 SW Harrison St., Topeka, KS 66625
Telephone	(785) 368-8222
Email	tac@kdor.state.ks.us
Website: http//	www.ksrevenue.org

KENTUCKY

Agency/Contact	Kentucky Department of Revenue
Mailing Address	200 Fair Oaks Lane, Frankfort, KY 40620
Telephone	(502) 564-4581, (502) 564-3875 (fax)
Email	KRCWEBResponseSalesTax@ky.gov
Website: http//	revenue.ky.gov/

LOUISANA

Agency/Contact	Louisiana Department of Revenue
Mailing Address	P.O. Box 201, Baton Rouge, LA 70821
Telephone	(225) 219-7356
Email	SalesTaxInquiries@rev.state.la.us
Website: http//	www.rev.state.la.us/

MAINE

Agency/Contact	Maine Revenue Services
Mailing Address	Sales Tax, P.O. Box 1065, Augusta, ME 04332-1065
Telephone	(207) 624-9693, (207) 287-6628 (fax)
Email	sales.tax@maine.gov
Website: http//	www.state.me.us/revenue/homepage.html

MARYLAND

Agency/Contact	Comptroller of Maryland
Mailing Address	Revenue Administration Division Taxpayer Service Section 301 W. Preston St. Room 206, Baltimore, MD 21201
Telephone	(800) 492-1751 (MD only), (410) 767-1300 (Baltimore area)
Email	sut@comp.state.md.us
Website: http//	www.comp.state.md.us

MASSACHUSETTS

Agency/Contact	Massachusetts Department of Revenue
Mailing Address	P.O. Box 7010, Boston, MA 02204
Telephone	(800) 392-6089 (MA only), (617) 887-MDOR
Email	www.dor.state.ma.us/Feedback/feedback.htm
Website: http//	www.dor.state.ma.us/

MICHIGAN

Agency/Contact	Michigan Department of Treasury
Mailing Address	Lansing, MI 48922
Telephone	(517) 373-3200
Email	treasSUW@michigan.gov
Website: http//	www.michigan.gov/treasury

MINNESOTA

Agency/Contact	Minnesota Department of Revenue
Mailing Address	Mail Station 6330, St. Paul, MN 55146-6330
Telephone	(651) 296-6181
Email	salesuse.tax@state.mn.us
Website: http//	www.taxes.state.mn.us

MISSISSIPPI

Agency/Contact	Mississippi State Tax Commission
Mailing Address	Physical Address: 1577 Springridge Road, Raymond, MS 39154; Mailing Address: P.O. Box 1033, Jackson, MS 39215-1033
Telephone	(601) 923-7015, (601) 923-7034 (fax)
Email	www.mstc.state.ms.us/perl/ContactUs.pl#email
Website: http//	www.mstc.state.ms.us

MISSOURI

Agency/Contact	Missouri Department of Revenue
Mailing Address	Sales/Use Tax, P.O. Box 840, Jefferson City, MO 65105-0840
Telephone	(573) 751-2836
Email	salesuse@dor.mo.gov
Website: http//	dor.mo.gov/tax/business

NEBRASKA

Agency/Contact	Nebraska Department of Revenue
Mailing Address	301 Centennial Mall South, PO Box 94818 Lincoln, NE 68509-4818
Telephone	800-742-7474 (NE and IA only), (402) 471-5729
Email	www.revenue.state.ne.us/mail/ndrmail.phtml
Website: http//	www.revenue.state.ne.us

NEVADA

Agency/Contact	Department of Taxation
Mailing Address	1550 E. College Pkwy., Ste. 115, Carson City, NV 89706
Telephone	Carson City: (775) 684-2000, (775) 684-2020 (fax); Las Vegas: (702) 486-2300, (702) 486-2372 (fax)
Website: http//	tax.state.nv.us

NEW JERSEY

Agency/Contact	New Jersey Division of Taxation
Mailing Address	Taxation Building, 50 Barrack Street, Trenton, NJ 08695
Telephone	609-292-6400
Email	www.state.nj.us/treasury/taxation/ contactus_tyttaxa.html
Website: http//	www.state.nj.us/treasury/taxation

NEW MEXICO

Agency/Contact	New Mexico Tax and Revenue Department
Mailing Address	Tax Information/Policy Office, P.O. Box 630, Santa Fe, NM 87504-0630
Telephone	(505) 827-0700
Email	poffice@state.nm.us
Website: http//	www.state.nm.us/tax/

NEW YORK

Agency/Contact	New York State Department of Taxation and Finance
Mailing Address	NYS Tax Department Taxpayer Assistance Bureau, W. A. Harriman Campus, Albany, NY 12227
Telephone	800-972-1233
Website: http//	www.tax.state.ny.us

NORTH CAROLINA

Agency/Contact	North Carolina Department of Revenue
Mailing Address	P.O. Box 25000, Raleigh, NC 27640-0640
Telephone	(877) 252-3052
Website: http//	www.dor.state.nc.us

NORTH DAKOTA

Agency/Contact	North Dakota State Tax Commissioner
Mailing Address	Office of State Tax Commissioner, State Capitol, 600 East Boulevard Avenue, Bismarck, ND 58505-0599
Telephone	(701) 328-3470
Email	salestax@state.nd.us
Website: http//	www.state.nd.us/taxdpt

OHIO

Agency/Contact	Ohio Department of Taxation
Mailing Address	Sales & Use Tax Division 30 E. Board St. 20th Floor Columbus, OH 43215
Telephone	(614) 466-7351
Email	www-01.tax.state.oh.us/PROD/TaxMailWeb/global_emailus.html
Website: http//	tax.ohio.gov

OKLAHOMA

Agency/Contact	Oklahoma Tax Commission
Mailing Address	P.O. Box 26850, Oklahoma City, OK 73126-0850
Telephone	(405) 521-3160
Email	otcmaster@oktax.state.ok.us
Website: http//	www.oktax.state.ok.us

PENNSYLVANIA

Agency/Contact	Pennsylvania Department of Revenue
Mailing Address	Bureau of Business Trust Fund Taxes, Dept. 280905, Harrisburg, PA 17128-0905
Telephone	1-888-PATAXES, (717) 787-1064
Email	Online Customer Service Center via website
Website: http//	www.revenue.state.pa.us

RHODE ISLAND

Agency/Contact	Rhode Island Division of Taxation
Mailing Address	One Capitol Hill, Providence, RI 02908
Telephone	(401) 222-2950
Email	pmcvay@tax.state.ri.us
Website: http//	www.tax.state.ri.us

SOUTH CAROLINA

Agency/Contact	South Carolina Department of Revenue
Mailing Address	301 Gervais St.; P.O. Box 125, Columbia, SC 29214
Telephone	(803) 898-5788
Email	www.sctax.org/help/scenote.html
Website: http//	www.sctax.org

SOUTH DAKOTA

Agency/Contact	South Dakota Department of Revenue
Mailing Address	Business Tax Division, 445 East Capitol Avenue, Pierre, SD 57501-3185
Telephone	(800) 829-9188
Email	bustax@state.sd.us
Website: http//	www.state.sd.us/drr2/revenue.html

TENNESSEE

Agency/Contact	Tennessee Department of Revenue
Mailing Address	500 Deaderick St., Nashville, TN 37242
Telephone	(800) 342-1003; (615) 253-0600
Email	TN.Revenue@state.tn.us
Website: http//	www.state.tn.us/revenue

TEXAS

Agency/Contact	Texas Comptroller of Public Accounts
Mailing Address	P.O. Box 13528, Capitol Station, Austin, TX 78711-3528
Telephone	(800) 252-5555
Email	tax.help@cpa.state.tx.us
Website: http//	www.cpa.state.tx.us

UTAH

Agency/Contact	Utah State Tax Commission
Mailing Address	210 North 1950 West, Salt Lake City, UT 84134
Telephone	(800) 662-4335; (801) 297-2200
Email	taxmaster@utah.gov
Website: http//	www.tax.utah.gov

VERMONT

Agency/Contact	Vermont Department of Taxes Business Trust Taxes
Mailing Address	P.O. Box 547, Montpelier, VT 05601-0547
Telephone	(802) 828-2551; (802) 828-5787 (fax)
Email	www.state.vt.us/tax/contactemail.shtml
Website: http//	www.state.vt.us/tax/index.htm

VIRGINIA

Agency/Contact	Virginia Department of Taxation
Mailing Address	P.O. Box 1115, Richmond, VA 23218-1115
Telephone	(804) 367-8037
Email	TaxBusQuestions@tax.virginia.gov
Website: http//	www.tax.virginia.gov

WASHINGTON

Agency/Contact	Washington Department of Revenue
Mailing Address	P.O. Box 47478, Olympia, WA 98504-7478
Telephone	(800) 647-7706
Email	https://dor.wa.gov/content/contactus/Email/TaxQuestions.aspx
Website: http//	dor.wa.gov

WEST VIRGINIA

Agency/Contact	West Virginia State Tax Department
Mailing Address	West Virginia Tax Commission, Taxpayer Services Division, P.O. Box 3784, Charleston, WV 25337-3784
Telephone	(800) 982-8297; (304) 558-3333
Website: http//	www.state.wv.us/taxdiv

WISCONSIN

Agency/Contact	Wisconsin Department of Revenue
Mailing Address	2135 Rimrock Road, Madison, WI 53713
Telephone	(608) 266-2776
Email	sales10@dor.state.wi.us
Website: http//	www.dor.state.wi.us

WYOMING

Agency/Contact	Wyoming Department of Revenue, Daniel W. Noble, Administrator, Excise Division
Mailing Address	Herschler Bldg, 2nd Floor West, 122 West 25th Street, Cheyenne, WY 82002-0110
Telephone	(307) 777-5200
Email	DirectorOfRevenue@wy.gov
Website: http//	revenue.state.wy.us

Taxpayer Representation

State policies vary as to who is allowed to represent a taxpayer before the tax authority in administrative proceedings and receive confidential taxpayer information. Some states limit taxpayer representation to licensed attorneys, while others allow representation by CPAs or other accountants.

Some states also allow representation by persons other than attorneys or accountants, such as enrolled agents (before the IRS) or state recognized agents. Some states allow representation by any person with a valid power of attorney.

Most states require a specific form to be filed for authorization of a representative. Others do not specify a particular form that must be filed, but provide for information that must be included in an authorization. Finally, some states are silent on the issue of a form or required information.

Note: The chart below only reflects taxpayer representation before the taxing authority and administrative proceedings. Representation in judicial proceedings is governed by the laws and rules regulating the practice of law.

State	Attorney	Accountant	Other	Form
Alabama	X	X	X	2848A
Alaska	X	X	X	07-775
Arizona	X	X	X[1]	285/285 I
Arkansas	X	X	X	IRS 2848
California	X[2]	X[2]	X[2]	FTB 3520/BOE-392
Colorado	X	X	X	DR 0145
Connecticut	X	X	X	LGL-001
Delaware	X	X	X	IRS 2848/IRS 8821
District of Columbia	X	-	-	None specified
Florida	X	X	X	DR-835
Georgia	X	X	X	RD-1061
Hawaii	X	X	X	N-848
Idaho	X	X	X	Form 111
Illinois	X	X[3]	X[3]	IL-2848
Indiana	X[4]	X[4]	X[4]	POA-1
Iowa	X[4]	X[4]	X[4]	IA14-101/IA2848
Kansas	X[3]	X[3]	X[3]	None specified
Kentucky	X	X	X	None specified
Louisiana	X	X	-	R-7015[5]
Maine	X[3]	X[3]	X[3]	2848ME
Maryland	X	X[6]	X[6]	None specified
Massachusetts	X	X	X	M-2848
Michigan	X	X	X	Form 151
Minnesota	X	X	X	REV-184
Mississippi	X	-	-	None specified
Missouri	X	X	X	Form 2827
Montana	X	X	X	None specified
Nebraska	X	X	X	Form 33
Nevada	X	X	X	None specified
New Hampshire	X	X	X	DP-2848

State	Attorney	Accountant	Other	Form
New Jersey	X	X	-	M-5008
New Mexico	X	X	X	None specified
New York	X	X	X[7]	DTF-14/DTF-14.1
North Carolina	X	X[6]	X[6]	Form 58
North Dakota	X	X	X	Form 500
Ohio	X	X	X	TBOR-1
Oklahoma	X	X	X	BT-129
Oregon	X	X	X	150-800-005
Pennsylvania	X	X	X	REV-467
Rhode Island	X	X	X[8]	RI-2848
South Carolina	X	X	X	SC 2848
South Dakota	X	-	-	None specified
Tennessee	X[3]	X[3]	X[3]	RV-2052
Texas	X	X	X	01-137
Utah	X	X	X	None specified
Vermont	X	X	X	PA-1
Virginia	X	X	X	PAR 101
Washington	X	X	X	None specified
West Virginia	X	X	X	WV-2848
Wisconsin	X	X	X	A-222
Wyoming	X	X	X	None specified

[1] If amount at issue is less than $25,000.
[2] Representative authorized but not defined.
[3] Informal proceedings only.
[4] Anyone with a power of attorney may represent.
[5] Form only used after audit assessments.
[6] Enrolled agents only.
[7] Authorized for certain proceedings only.
[8] Any person approved by the IRS.

Whole Dollar Reporting

For purposes of corporate and personal income (or franchise) taxes, some states allow (while others require) dollar amounts be rounded to the nearest dollar for reporting of income and computation of tax. Rounding rules require that an amount less than 50 cents be rounded down to the nearest dollar, while amounts greater than or equal to 50 cents be rounded up to the nearest dollar.

The chart below indicates the states that require whole dollar reporting for corporate and/or personal income taxes, as well as the states that allow the taxpayer the option to use whole dollar reporting. For states in which whole dollar reporting is optional, if the option is chosen, it must be used for all applicable amounts.

State	Whole Dollar Reporting	State	Whole Dollar Reporting
Alabama	Required	Missouri	Optional
Alaska[1]	N/A	Montana	Optional
Arizona	Required	Nebraska	Required
Arkansas	Required	Nevada[2]	N/A
California	Required	New Hampshire	Optional
Colorado	Required	New Jersey	Optional
Connecticut	Required	New Mexico	Optional
Delaware	Required	New York	Optional
District of Columbia	Optional	North Carolina	Required
Florida[1]	Required	North Dakota	Required
Georgia	Required	Ohio	Optional[3]
Hawaii	Required	Oklahoma	Optional
Idaho	Required	Oregon	Required
Illinois	Required	Pennsylvania	Required
Indiana	Optional	Rhode Island	Optional
Iowa	Required	South Carolina	Optional
Kansas	Required[4]	South Dakota[2]	N/A
Kentucky	Optional	Tennessee	Required
Louisiana	Required	Texas[1]	Optional
Maine	Required	Utah	Required
Maryland	Optional	Vermont	Optional
Massachusetts	Optional	Virginia	Optional
Michigan	Required	Washington[2]	N/A
Minnesota	Required	West Virginia	Required
Mississippi	Required	Wisconsin	Optional
Wyoming[2]	N/A		

[1] Corporate income only; no personal income tax.
[2] State imposes neither a corporate nor a personal income tax.
[3] Tax Commissioner authorized to require.
[4] Required for personal income (silent as to corporate income).

Index

TEN